DATE DUE

3-9-14			
			PRINTED IN U.S.A.

CHRISTIANS IN CHINA

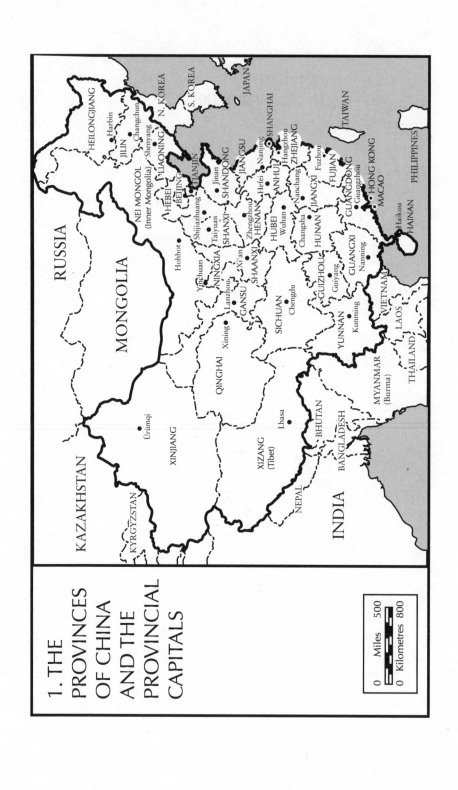

1. THE PROVINCES OF CHINA AND THE PROVINCIAL CAPITALS

JEAN-PIERRE CHARBONNIER

Christians in China:
A.D. 600 to 2000

Translated by
M. N. L. Couve de Murville
Archbishop Emeritus of Birmingham, England

Maps by David Notley

IGNATIUS PRESS   SAN FRANCISCO

Original French edition
Histoire des Chrétiens de Chine
© 2002 by Les Indes Savantes, Paris

Cover design by Roxanne Mei Lum

Cover photograph by Jean-Pierre Charbonnier

Cathedral of Guiyang, provincial capital of Guizhou
Province. The façade was damaged during the Cultural Revolution, leaving the building in a bad state of
repair. The church was fully renovated in 2005.

© 2007 Ignatius Press, San Francisco
All rights reserved
ISBN 978-0-89870-916-2
Library of Congress Control Number: 2004114950
Printed in the United States of America ∞

CONTENTS

I

RELICS FROM CHINA'S PAST

Traces of Christianity from the Seventh to the Fourteenth Century.

II

THE FRIENDSHIP OF WISE MEN

*The Meeting of Catholicism and Confucianism
in the Sixteenth and Seventeenth Centuries.*

III

WITNESSES ON THE RUN

The Gospel is Preached to Poor Peasants in the Eighteenth and Nineteenth Centuries.

AUTHOR'S PREFACE

During my priestly ministry, I came to know Chinese Christians in Singapore, where I worked from 1959 to 1993. I did not know Christians from China itself, although in 1982 I had visited the mainland and met bishops and priests from some of the major cities, and I even celebrated a Mass in Latin at Xi'an. I had not, however, had contact at the grassroots level. One day in 1983 a visitor from China turned up at the Singapore Information Centre, where we were trying to establish contacts with Catholics in China. He was a sailor, twenty-three years old, who came from Fuzhou in Fujian Province. His ship had put in at Singapore, and he wanted to see a priest because his parents had said to him, "You are going to Singapore. Try to find a priest and go to confession."

It was Sunday, and I asked whether he had been to Mass. He said that he did not know what Mass was, nor confession, and he had never been to either. I asked him whether there was a priest in his hometown, and he said that there was, but that he had gotten married so that no one went to church anymore. I wondered whether the sailor really was a Catholic and asked him to say the Our Father, which he did at once in his Fujian dialect, followed by the Hail Mary. He told me that they were six brothers and sisters at home and that they said the Rosary together every night. His name was Xinqiang, which means "Strong Faith".

A few months later, the sailor came to see me again. It was raining heavily, and he took a damp piece of paper out of his pocket. He said, "Our *guniang* (sister) wants me to buy the books on this list." The ink had run, but I could make out the characters which listed a missal, the Bible, *The Imitation of Christ*, and St. Thérèse of Lisieux' *Histoire d'une Âme* (*The Story of a Soul*). The nun had scribbled on the side, "If you can't find these, buy any books from our Church". I felt that the crumpled piece of paper was bringing a powerful message from a community, which had been buried for a long time in the shadows and was now struggling to reappear in the light of day.

Translation of the preface to the second edition of *Histoire des Chrétiens de Chine* (Paris: Les Indes Savantes, 2002).

During the Cultural Revolution, it seemed as if Christians in China had been completely annihilated, and yet their faith survived. In fact, the trials that they had suffered during the previous forty years were but a recent phase of the sufferings they had had to endure more than once, over the previous three centuries and more. The communities that are the most vigorous have roots that lie deep in the soil of China's past. The Christian faith is the faith of their ancestors. To begin with, during the first and second generations of Christianity's presence in China, that faith was fragile and vulnerable, but later it became part of family tradition, which meant that it benefited from the tenacity of the basic Chinese principle of filial piety. If one wants to understand Catholics in the China of today, one has to know something about their past.

This is not easy, in spite of the impressive number of books on the history of Christianity in China, because most of them are about the history of the missions. In such studies, foreign missionaries dominate the scene, and Chinese Christians seem to provide the background to the story. Of course, one cannot study Chinese Christians without knowing something about those who brought the Gospel to them, but the story must center on the Chinese. Fortunately a recent study does just that. The first volume of the *Handbook of Christianity in China*, edited by Nicolas Standaert, S.J.,[1] covers the period from A.D. 635 to 1800 and includes several sections on Chinese Christians (pp. 380–455).

The history of Christianity in China records the meeting of two very different civilizations. The West had been deeply influenced by the Judeo-Christian tradition and China by the Confucian tradition. Two recent studies have underlined the difficulties inherent in such a meeting. Jacques Gernet's *China and the Christian Impact: A Conflict of Cultures*[2] gives the impression that there were two cultures in watertight compartments that just could not communicate. René Laurentin centers his study[3] more directly on Christian history in China, but the subtitle, *After Missed Opportunities*, with its negative implication about the past, does imply that a new era has dawned.

---

[1] Leiden: Brill, 2001.

[2] Cambridge, U.K.: Cambridge University Press, 1985; translation of *Chine et Christianisme: Action et Réaction* (Paris: Gallimard, 1982).

[3] *Chine et Christianisme: Après les occasions manquées* (Paris: Desclée de Brouwer, 1977).

There is, however, a drawback in equating "China" and "Christianity" as if the two were on the same level. China is a country; Christianity is a religion. Moreover, Christianity cannot be identified with the West, although some Christians still seem to find the idea attractive. It would be better to compare Chinese Christianity and European Christianity, or else Western Christianity and Chinese Confucianism.

One also needs to ask why so many studies start from the assumption that Christianity is a foreign religion where China is concerned. It is worth noting that today the Communist government in Beijing recognizes Christianity as one of the religions of China, together with Buddhism, Taoism, and Islam.

The Christians of today's China are aware that they belong to a modern and independent country and that they are a local Church, free from the control of foreigners that she had known in the past. It is true that for Catholics the idea of an autonomous Church needs to be refined so that her relation to the Universal Catholic Church and to the Holy Father is maintained. Nevertheless, the present development of the Church in China remains a significant fact of the twentieth century. If the Chinese are to develop the characteristic features of their Church, they must become more aware of her historic roots. This happens when anniversaries are commemorated for outstanding Christians of the past who have played a key role in the development of their Church. Thus the review *Catholic Church in China*, published in Beijing, always has articles on Church history.

In 1989 the Shanghai Academy of Sciences published a small book *Catholicism in China Yesterday and Today*, that tells the whole history of Chinese Catholicism. In view of the present political context, the book naturally emphasizes the achievements of the Church, independent since the "Liberation" of 1949, and it also contrasts this with the shackles that hindered the Church in the past, when she was subjected to the colonial powers of the West. This black-and-white presentation of the past is, of course, useful in a propaganda war, but it cannot stand up to a more careful examination of history. Even a Communist author such as Gu Yulu recognizes positive elements in the past, such as evangelization in the spirit of Matteo Ricci and the contribution made by Christians to education and social welfare. It is more difficult for Gu Yulu to face up to the sufferings that have been inflicted on the Church by the present regime, but he is positive about the relations between Christian morality and Communist morality, showing that the two can coexist profitably, although they derive from very different points of view.

Gu Yulu's book is about Chinese Catholicism only and does not consider other Christian churches. This is a common approach in China, where Catholicism and Protestantism are considered as two different religions. Today's ecumenical attitude calls for a reassessment of this approach. Kenneth Scott Latourette's foundational work *A History of Christian Missions in China*, first published in 1929, treats equally of the development of the Catholic and the Protestant Churches. The same is true of the work of the Benedictine Columba Cary-Elwes, *China and the Cross: A Survey of Missionary History*.[4] Ralph Covell's book *Confucius, the Buddha, and Christ*[5] clearly shows how the proclamation of the Gospel in China caused similar problems for both Catholics and Protestants, problems that were solved by developing a similar approach.

I consider that one needs to go further and to examine more closely the history of Islam in China. Islam is a monotheistic religion, based on the adherence of believers to a message. It was brought to China by Arabs and had to face many problems in penetrating the cultural world of China. Christians would find it useful to compare the way Muslims have integrated their community into the Chinese way of life with the path that Christians have followed.

During the past forty years the Church in Taiwan has produced a large number of historical studies. The work of the late Fang Hao has been particularly useful in making known a whole range of outstanding Chinese Christians. Archbishop Lokuang has put together a detailed history of the religious orders and congregations who have worked in China. Fr. Joseph Motte, S.J., though not Chinese himself, has written two books that give its proper place in the history of China to native Christians. These books were published in Taipei by Kuangchi in the Chinese language with the titles *History of the Catholic Church in China* (1970) and *Lay Chinese Apostles* (1978). The contemporary scene is less well known, but a certain number of studies and personal accounts have been published, mainly in Hong Kong. Since contacts between Taiwan and mainland China have been resumed,

---

[4] New York: 1957.
[5] Maryknoll, N.Y.: Orbis Books, 1986.

university professors and historians in Taiwan have concentrated on studying the evolution that has occurred within the People's Republic of China.

I have written this book with such an approach in mind. I wanted to describe the main lines of the history of Christianity in China but to tell the stories of actual Chinese Christians at every period, so as to emphasize the unfolding of a constant cultural interaction. The questions I tried to answer were these: How did the Church develop over many centuries in a civilization different from ours? How do Christians in China give witness to their faith? How do they contribute to the life of the Church Universal?

The Christians of China belong to a people who have been molded over the centuries by rich cultural and religious traditions. It would be impossible adequately to describe within the compass of this book the numerous currents of these great traditions, their development and interaction. However, Confucianism, Buddhism, and Taoism must always be taken into consideration as the cultural stock onto which Christianity has been grafted in China. Christians may have rejected the practices of these religions, but they have been deeply influenced by them as regards their view of morality, their spirituality, and also their way of living the Christian life. There is no need to trot out the term *inculturation* at this point. The Christians of China belong to a Chinese culture, as we will try to show. If they are sometimes labeled as "foreigners", that is because they belong, like Christians in every country, to a kingdom that is not of this world, which does not prevent them from fulfilling their task conscientiously and working actively for the renewal of the society they live in.

—Jean-Pierre Charbonnier, M.E.P.

TRANSLATOR'S PREFACE

Fr. Jean-Pierre Charbonnier and I were students of the Seminary at Versailles over fifty years ago. It was a pleasure therefore to meet again to prepare the English edition of his book *Histoire des Chrétiens de Chine* (published by Desclée, Tournai, and Bégédis, Paris, 1992; second edition by Les Indes Savantes, Paris, 2002.) In translating this text I have been conscious of the need to interpret the complexities of the material covered, for readers who may be neither Chinese, nor French, nor Catholic. Indications at the end of each chapter show where I have thought it necessary, with the approval of the author, to include new material, for the better understanding of the narrative and of the cultures treated. I have also tried to include references to material published in English since 1992.

We would like to express our sincere appreciation of those who have helped us in many ways to bring this project to a conclusion. My thanks are due firstly to the Very Reverend Fr. Jean-Michel Cuny, Superior of the *Missions Étrangères de Paris*, his colleagues and the community at the Rue du Bac. I have enjoyed their hospitality and friendship on the numerous occasions when I have stayed at the *Missions Étrangères* during the preparation of this book.

Our special gratitude goes to the following who have read the translation in its entirety and have made many valuable suggestions for its improvement: Professor Hugh Baker, Professor Emeritus of Chinese at the School of Oriental and African Studies, University of London; Dr. Anne Birrell, Clare Hall, University of Cambridge; the Rev. Andrew Beer, Priest of the Diocese of Arundel and Brighton; Miss Jane Elliott, and Mr. David Kingston, formerly member of the scientific staff of the Medical Research Council.

We have also been greatly helped by those who have made comments on particular chapters: Dr. Sebastian Brock, of the Oriental Institute, University of Oxford; Dr. Frances Wood, Head of the Section of Chinese, Manchu and Mongolian at the British Library, London; the Rev. Father Robert Murray, S.J., Fellow of Heythrop College, University of London; Professor David Morgan, Professor of Humanities at the University of Madison, Wisconsin; and the Rev Father Edmund Ryden, S.J., of the Socio-Cultural Research Centre,

Fujen University, Taiwan. We are very grateful to all those mentioned but remain entirely responsible for the views expressed and for any inaccuracies contained in the book.

We wish to thank especially Don Raffaele Farina, S.D.B., Prefect of the Vatican Library, for permission to consult the collections in the *Biblioteca Apostolica Vaticana* and in the *Archivio Segreto Vaticano*. Dr. Clara Yu Dong, of the Department of Manuscripts at the Vatican Library, has been particularly helpful in our search for material. We are grateful to Mlle. Annie Salavert, Bibliothèque Orientale, Missions Étrangères de Paris, and the librarians of the following collections who have invariably been helpful: Library of the School of Oriental and African Studies, University of London; Cambridge University Library; Library of Heythrop College, University of London; St Michael's College Library, University of Toronto; Biblioteca Universita Urbaniana, Rome. Mr. Mark S. Mir, Research Fellow of the Ricci Institute for Chinese-Western Cultural History at the University of San Francisco, helped us in finding illustrations to supplement those in the second edition of the French volume.

Unless otherwise stated, all translations of quotations from the French are ours. As regards geographical names, we have usually followed *The Times Atlas of the World*, tenth edition (London: Times Books, 2000). Other names follow, wherever possible, Dorothy Perkins, *Encyclopedia of China*, (Chicago and London: Fitzroy Dearborn, 1999).

April 2006
+ M. N. L. Couve de Murville
Archbishop Emeritus of Birmingham, U.K.

ABBREVIATIONS

A.A.S. *Acta Apostolicae Sedis*, Libreria Editrice Vaticana, Vatican City

A.M.E. Archives des Missions Étrangères de Paris, 128 Rue du Bac, Paris 75007

B.S.O.A.S. *Bulletin of the School of Oriental and African Studies*, Thornhaugh Street, Russell Square, London WC1H OXG

C.S.C.O. *Corpus Scriptorum Christianorum Orientalium*, Catholic University of America and Université Catholique de Louvain, Secrétariat au C.S.C.O., Waversebaan 49, Louvain

D.T.C. *Dictionnaire de Théologie Catholique*, Librairie Letouzey & Ané, 87 Boulevard Raspail, Paris 75006

E.C. *Encyclopedia of China*, Dorothy Perkins (Chicago and London: Fitzroy Dearborn, 1999)

J.A.O.S. *Journal of the American Oriental Society*. Distributor: University of Michigan, Ann Arbor.

J.O.S. *Journal of Oriental Studies*, Centre of Asian Studies, University of Hong Kong

J.R.A.S. *Journal of the Royal Asiatic Society*, Journal of the Royal Asiatic Society of Great Britain and Ireland, 60 Queen's Gardens, London W2 3AF

N.C.E. *New Catholic Encyclopedia*, Catholic University of America, Washington, D.C.

S.F. *Sinica Franciscana*, Collegium S. Bonaventurae ad Claras Aquas, Grottaferrata, Rome

S.P.C.K. Society for Promoting Christian Knowledge, Holy Trinity Church, Marylebone Road, London NW1

Standaert *Handbook of Christianity in China, vol. 1: 635–1800*, edited Nicolas Standaert (Leiden: Brill, 2001)

Z.D.M.G. *Zeitschrift der Deutschen Morgenländischen Gesellschaft*

The Four Municipalities, Twenty-two Provinces, and Five Autonomous Regions of China

Municipalities under Central Government

BJ	Beijing	SH	Shanghai
CQ	Chongqing	TJ	Tianjin

Provinces

AH	Anhui	JS	Jiangsu
FJ	Fujian	JX	Jiangxi
GS	Gansu	JL	Jilin
GD	Guangdong	LN	Liaoning
GZ	Guizhou	QH	Qinghai
Hai	Hainan	SC	Sichuan
Heb	Hebei	SN	Shaanxi
HL	Heilongjiang	SD	Shandong
Hen	Henan	SX	Shanxi
HB	Hubei	YN	Yunnan
HN	Hunan	ZJ	Zhejiang

Autonomous Regions

GX	Guangxi-Zhuang	NX	Ningxia-Hui
NM	Nei-Menggu	XJ	Xinjiang-Uighur
	(Inner Mongolia)	XZ	Xizang (Tibet)

I

RELICS FROM CHINA'S PAST

Is Christianity a foreign religion as far as China is concerned? One could say yes, because of the very nature of the Gospel message, which is a revelation of the transcendent God who saves sinful humanity. A history of salvation seems in many ways alien to the Chinese religious tradition, both Taoist and Confucian, which is a search for the ritual harmony between heaven and earth.

But one can also say no, because Christianity has been rooted in Chinese soil since the Tang dynasty, more than thirteen centuries ago. The monks of the Syrian Church who came from Persia in the seventh century, although they were few in number, brought with them the message of God's kingdom.

These first Christians to reach China came by way of the Silk Road, along which were many Buddhist temples. Christianity was rejected by Confucian China, however, together with Buddhist institutions in the ninth century, but it survived in the northern steppes, where it became associated with the Mongols. When a Mongol dynasty, the Yuan, came to power in China in the thirteenth and fourteenth centuries, Christian churches were opened in various parts of the country, and it was then that Christian missionaries from the Latin West first reached China.

These first Christian foundations should not be considered as being of purely archeological interest. They belong to the living tradition of Christianity in China, a country that is especially relevant today as a privileged place of meeting for the great religions of the world.

Xi'an Stele

The earliest existing evidence of Christianity in China is provided by the Xi'an Stele, erected in 781 in Shaanxi Province. It records the coming of the first Christian missionaries in 636 and attests that their writings were examined and approved by the Taizong Emperor (r. 626–649, Tang Dynasty), so that they could be propagated in the Empire. The inscription is in Chinese with 1,756 characters, arranged in vertical lines. At the bottom of the inscription is a seventy-word Syriac inscription (in Estrangela script), recording the names of bishops and monks of the East Syrian Church.

THE XI'AN STELE

The city walls of Xi'an, in northwest China's Shaanxi Province, evoke a prestigious past. Today many visitors go to Xi'an. They visit the tomb of China's first emperor, some thirty-seven miles (sixty kilometers) to the east of the city, at the foot of Mount Lishan. There they can see a surprising sight: a buried army made of clay figures, infantry and cavalry whose motionless ranks emerge from the thick layers of yellow earth where they have been buried for twenty-two centuries. This silent army is witness to a political reality that is unique to China, the unity and the continuity of an empire founded in the third century before the Christian era by Emperor Qin Shi Huangdi, who is buried in a tumulus-shaped mound, as yet unexcavated.

On the other side of the city of Xi'an, about fifty-five miles (ninety kilometers) to the west, there is another famous site, which does not, however, attract the attention of visitors from abroad. It is the Taoist shrine of Luguantai, which is visited only by a few Chinese pilgrims. They drive to this place along roads that the local inhabitants use as threshing floors during harvest time. A shady track leads to a small hill in front of higher slopes covered by thick woods of bamboo. On this hill is a temple dedicated to Laozi. There are galleries on either side of the temple that have been recently restored and contain exhibits of the most authentic religious traditions of China. Next to the newly painted statues of the great masters of the Tao, one notices two black stelae engraved with delicate characters in white. The text comprises the 5,000 characters of a very ancient version of the *Daode jing* (translated by A. Waley as *The Book of the Way and Its Power*), the classic text of Taoism, which describes its fundamental intuition concerning the ultimate power animating everything that exists. This book has had an enormous influence on Chinese culture and remains the most widely translated Chinese book. Historians today accept that it is a composite work, but legendary accounts related that Laozi wrote it at Luguantai, before departing forever to the mountains of the west, the dwelling place of the immortal ones.

The Unearthing of a Christian Monument

Near this Taoist sanctuary, the oldest Christian monument in China was discovered in 1623 or 1625.[1] In 1663, Fr. Danielle Bartoli, S.J., gave the following enthusiastic account of the find:

> The Fathers were getting ready to bring the light of the Gospel to the province of Shaanxi and its majestic capital of Xi'an when, a few months before they were due to arrive, . . . workers were digging the foundations of some building or other near Zhouzhi, about thirty miles to the west of the capital, and came upon traces of buildings. When these were cleared, they found a large marble slab, which was removed and cleaned with care. It was discovered to be covered with writing, some of it Chinese, some of strange shape, belonging to another language that nobody knew, but both texts carved with rare perfection.[2]

After the period of Fr. Matteo Ricci's residence in Beijing, from 1601 to 1610, the Jesuits were actually preparing the evangelization of the province of Shaanxi, and criticism was leveled at them for introducing a new religion into China. At that very time the discovery of a Christian stele almost a thousand years old brought to light the preexistence of a considerable Christian past in China. The discovery was so timely, and it provided such a good basis for the missionary projects of the Jesuits, that their detractors in Europe accused them of faking the whole episode.

The foreign priests were not the only ones, however, who rejoiced at what had happened. Zhang Gengyu, a Chinese Christian and a disciple of Matteo Ricci, realized at once how important the inscription was. He copied it and sent it to Hangzhou to a famous scholar recently baptized, Dr. Leo Li, who published the text shortly afterward. Soon after its discovery the great black stone, weighing two

---

[1] Western seventeenth-century sources give 1625 as the date of discovery, but several contemporary Chinese Christian sources indicate 1623. Peter C. H. Hiu, "An Historical Study of Nestorian Christianity in the T'ang Dynasty between A.D. 635–845" (unpublished Ph.D. dissertation, School of Theology, Southwestern Baptist Theological Seminary, Ft. Worth, Tex., 1987), pp. 15–16, accepts 1625 as the date of discovery. However, Nicolas Standaert, S.J., *Handbook of Christianity in China*, vol. 1: *635–1800* (Leiden: Brill, 2001), p. 15, considers that it is impossible on the known evidence to decide either way.

[2] Danielle Bartoli, *Dell' Historia della Compania de Giesu: La Cina. Terza parte dell' Asia* (Rome, 1663). Quoted in French translation in H. Havret, "La stèle chrétienne de Si-Ngan-Fou", *Variétés sinologiques*, pt. 2, no. 12 (Shanghai, 1897), pp. 34–35, from which this translation is made.

tons, was transported to Xi'an and placed in the Buddhist temple of the Cult of Benevolence, *Chongren si*, to the west of the city. This temple had in fact been built on the grounds of the former Syrian Christian monastery of the Yining quarter of Xi'an. Certain historians inferred from this that it was in the Yining temple that the stone had been discovered in the first place, but P. Y. Saeki established by his research that the Tang Emperor, Taizong (r. 626–649) had built two Nestorian monasteries, one in the Yining quarter of Xi'an, and the other near the village of Wuqun, ten miles (sixteen kilometers) or so to the southeast of Zhouzhi and not far from the Taoist shrine of Luguantai. It was near Luguantai that the stone was found.[3]

At the beginning of the twentieth century, the famous stele was finally transferred from the Buddhist *Chongren si* temple to the Provincial Museum of Shaanxi, where it is protected from vandalism and from the weather. There one can see the tall, black stone, placed on a massive carved tortoise in the maze of monuments that constitutes the Forest of Stelae. This unique Christian monument is next to hundreds of similar stones, inscribed with the Confucian classics and the canonical writings of Buddhism. The limestone block is 9 feet high, 3 feet 6 inches wide, and 1 foot thick (2.79 meters high, 1.02 meters wide, and 0.29 meters thick); 1,756 Chinese characters are carved on the stone in vertical lines, and have seventy words in Syriac Estrangela script at the lower end of the inscription. The stone forms a long rectangle, surmounted by a rounded pediment, which carries the title of the monument, nine characters disposed in a square. Above it is the cross, delicately etched under a triangle whose curved sides evoke the gables of Chinese dwellings. At the top of the composition a circular object, which looks like a large pearl, is held in the claws of two mythical creatures, dragons resembling lizards with wolfish heads, whose scaly bodies are intertwined. The nine large Chinese characters of the title can be rendered thus:

> Monument of the propagation in China
> of the Luminous Religion from Daqin.

The term *luminous religion* translates the Chinese *Jingjiao*. The mention of Christ the light of the world in the inscription itself clearly

---

[3] P. Y. Saeki, *The Nestorian Documents and Relics in China* (Tokyo: Maruzen, 1951), pp. 29–33.

indicates that it is about Christianity and not about a cult of light, derived from Persian traditions. The word Daqin is a place name, the traditional name given by the Chinese to the eastern part of the Roman Empire, and primarily to Syria, the point of arrival of the Silk Road. The first harbingers of the Gospel in China seem to have come from Persia, but their Church had been established in Syria much earlier, at the very beginning of the Christian era.

Detail of inscribed panel, Xi'an Stele

A cross of East Syrian design is shown, emerging from a lotus flower. Inscription in cap large Chinese characters, to be read from top to bottom and from right to left: *da qin* (the West); *jing jiao* (religion of light); *liu xing zhong guo* (introduced to China); *bei* (stele), which can be translated "Memorial of the introduction into China of the luminous religion from Syria."

The Luminous Religion

The Christian stele was erected in the year 781. Its author was the priest Jingjing, whose name means "the pure one of the luminous religion". The Syriac part of the inscription gives his name as Adam and calls him Chorbishop and Papash of Chinastan. He belonged to one of the four great Christian monasteries founded in China at that period. His text begins by summarizing the essentials of the Christian message:[4]

Certainly, eternal in its truth and serenity, earlier than all origin and without beginning, infinite in its spirituality and its impassibility, later than all endings, transcendent being; he who, concentrating his mysterious power, made creation, who inspired the saints with his supreme majesty; who can this be but the transcendent person of our Triune Unity, the true Lord, without beginning, A-lo-ho.

He marked out the cross to fix the four cardinal points; he stirred the primal Breath so as to produce the two principles. Darkness and emptiness were transformed, and heaven and earth opened; sun and moon moved, and days and nights existed. He opened and perfected ten thousand beings; he made and raised the first man. He endowed him especially with excellent harmony; he gave him rule over the immense number of creatures. The nature [of man] in his primitive state was without pain and not puffed up; his heart, with serene candor, was without desire at the beginning.

But he allowed So-tan to practice deceit and deck out with ornaments the pure essence. He interposed the equality of greatness in the midst of [what was] good; he inserted mysterious identity in the midst of what was evil. Thus 365 sects, shoulder to shoulder and confusing their tracks, wove in disharmony the net of the law. Some pointed to created objects and invoked them as their lords; others created a vacuum with being and thus abolished both; others addressed prayers to ask for happiness; others displayed virtue so as to mislead. Their thoughts were restless; their passions suffered. Worn out by exhaustion, they obtained nothing; burned and tormented, they were consumed one by one; in the heaping up of darkness they had lost the way, and for a long time they were moving away from the excellent return.

Then the distinct person of our Triune Unity, the venerable Radiant Mi-she-ho, entering and veiling his true Majesty, came to the world, similar to men. An angel made the good news known, and a Virgin brought forth the Holy One in Daqin; a brilliant star announced the happy event, and Persia, having seen its brilliance, came to bring gifts. [The Messiah] accomplished the old law, which had been formulated by

---

[4] Nicolas Standaert comments in *Handbook of Christianity in China*, p. 3 on how easy it is to misinterpret the text of the Xi'an Stele; we have therefore given an English translation of Paul Pelliot's French version, which Standaert considers "extremely precise"; Oeuvres Posthumes de Paul Pelliot, *Recherches sur les Chrétiens d'Asie Centrale et d'Extrême-Orient II,1: La Stèle de Si-Ngan-Fou* (Paris: Éditions de la Fondation Singer-Polignac, 1984), pp. 43–49.

the twenty-four holy ones to govern families and empires according to the great plan; he established the new doctrine of the Holy Spirit of the Triune Trinity, which is not expressed in words, so as to give formation in the practice of virtue according to the correct faith. He instituted the rule of the eight stations, purifying the stains and perfecting the truth; he opened the door of the three constants, giving access to life and destroying death. He hung up his radiant sun to break the empire of darkness, and then the impostures of the devil were all overthrown; with the oar he propelled the ship of mercy so as to give access to the luminous palace, and beings with souls were then really saved. And when all the possible work was achieved, at full noon he ascended to the truth.

He left behind the twenty-seven holy books, in which he expounded the Great Reform, so as to remove the barrier which closed the spiritual [life]. The law [of his disciples] is to baptize by water and by the Spirit, who washing away vain ornaments purifies in simplicity and candor; as a seal they hold the cross that joins the four luminous dimensions and unites without distinction. By the wood that they strike,[5] they make the sounds of charity and right doing to ring out; by the rite facing toward the east, they reach the road of life and glory. They let their beard grow because their action is open; they shave the crown of their head because they do not have interior passion. They do not have slaves because they do not distinguish among others noble or common classes; they do not amass wealth, giving their own example of complete abnegation. Their fasting is perfected by retreat and meditation; their defenses grow strong through tranquility and vigilance. Seven times a day, they have ritual hymns, greatly helping the living and the dead; every seven days, they celebrate a service, purifying the heart and renewing its candor. This true and eternal doctrine is transcendent and also difficult to describe; since its meritorious practice is dazzling, we are compelled to call it the Luminous Religion.

This text includes expressions deriving from both the theological vocabulary of the Syrian Church and from the popular religious language common at the time in eastern Asia. Its opening sentences derives from Taoist thought: God is "the origin of origins", the Tao of the universe, pure and undivided. He put in motion the primeval breath, *qi*, and produced the double principle, *yin-yang*. But this teach-

---

[5] A wooden gong, hung in church towers, was characteristic of Syrian churches. It was called *semantron*, "a thing for giving a signal", from the Greek word for mark or sign. *Semantron* does not occur in Syriac texts, which use the Syriac word *naqosha*, from *nqash*, to strike.

ing is given precision by reference to biblical tradition and to the theology of the Councils of the Western Church: God is "Trinity, one mysterious Person, not begotten". The theme of separation between light and darkness is emphasized, probably under the influence of Persian religious tradition. Persia, that is, the Magi (Mt 2:1–12), came to do homage by their gifts to the incarnate God when they saw the light of the star. Buddhist terminology also appears in several passages of the text concerning the Messiah: "shining Lord of the universe", "establishing the rule of eight commandments, freeing the world from sensuality and making it pure"; the "ship of mercy, carrying its passengers toward the dwelling place of light". These are so many images, which recall the beliefs of Mahayana Buddhism concerning the Pure Earth. According to this school, souls cross the ocean of suffering to reach the paradise of the west, the Pure Land, where Amithaba reigns, the Buddha of infinite light.

There is no mention in the text of the bloody sacrifice of the Cross as the act of redemption. The only sacrifice mentioned is the unbloody sacrifice, which the ministers of this religion celebrate every seventh day, an allusion to the Sunday Eucharist. Christ is presented primarily as the master of wisdom, who destroyed death and glorified life. The Cross, "carried like a sign by his ministers" is presented rather as indicating his "influence in the four quarters of the world" and thus the universality of salvation without distinction of race or social status. The homage paid by the Byzantine churches of the West to the glorious *Pantokrator* is thus combined with the spiritual search for inner purity, characteristic of the Buddhist traditions prevalent at the time. The expressions used in this text would have been common during the eighth century in the religious centers along the Silk Road, all the way from Daqin to distant Chang'an, capital of the Tang Dynasty in China. The expression *Da Qin*, Great Qin, must have been coined in China itself at the time of its Qin Dynasty, i.e., 221 to 206 B.C., "apparently thinking of it as a kind of counter-China at the other end of the world".[6]

---

[6] Edwin G. Pulleybank, "The Roman Empire as Known to Han China", *J.A.O.S.* 119, 1 (1999): 71.

Following the doctrinal introduction to the text, there is a second part that is equally interesting. It records the main stages of the establishment of the Luminous Religion in China, underlining its official approval by imperial authority. At the time when the Xi'an Stele was erected, in A.D. 781, there had been organized state structures in China since the Shang Dynasty (1750–1040 B.C.). The Xia Dynasty (traditionally dated 2200–1750 B.C.), often referred to in later Chinese literature, is now generally considered to be legendary, since no physical remains from this period have so far been found. In China the first evidence for writing dates from the Shang Dynasty. Dr. W. G. Bolz writes, "As far as anyone knows, writing was invented *ex nihilo* four times, and only four times, in human history: in Egypt, in Mesopotamia, in Mesoamerica, and in China. The earliest known writing that can be recognized unambiguously as Chinese dates from the time of the late Shang state. This is the period from about 1200 B.C. to about 1050 B.C. and is fully two millennia later than the first appearance of writing in Mesopotamia and nearly as long after the emergence of writing in Egypt."[7] The creation of a unified empire for the whole of China dates from 221 B.C. and was the work of the first emperor, Qin Shi Huangdi, who is buried in the pyramid-shaped burial mound at the foot of Mount Lishan, east of Xi'an, where the terracotta army watches over him. Certainly long before the emergence of the Tang Dynasty, in A.D. 618, the Chinese empire was founded upon institutions with both a moral and a political aspect. Every religion within the Empire was expected to integrate itself harmoniously into the established order; the Christian stele thus constitutes an official act, witnessing to the integration of the Luminous Religion into it.

At the time of the arrival of the first Christians in the seventh century after Christ, the emperors of China were not great scholars, nor were they steeped in Confucian tradition. The Li royal family, founders of the Tang Dynasty, were military leaders of nomadic origin, who had grown up in the steppes of north China. They had a passionate love of horses and are depicted in the princely tombs of the Xi'an region, riding wildly or playing polo. The first Tang em-

---

[7] William G. Bolz, "The Invention of Writing in China", *Oriens Extremus* 42 (2000/01): 1.

perors were successful in their military expeditions westward, against
the various ethnic groups, who dominated central Asia, so that, between A.D. 630 and 635, Chinese military posts were built ever further to the west at strategic points controlling the Silk Road. In 640
Chinese settlers founded the kingdom of Gaochang, whose extensive
ruins can still be seen near the great oasis of Turfan in Xinjiang-
Uighur Autonomous Region. Merchants and monks then plied their
way, skirting the edge of deserts and finding shelter in the famous
monasteries, which were under the protection of the Chinese administration. It was during the reign of the first Tang emperor, in A.D.
635, that a Christian named Alopen reached Xi'an, the capital (which
partly overlaps with the site of the ancient capital known in antiquity
and in the Middle Ages as Chang'an). "Alopen" might be a Chinese
transcription for "Abraham", the name of a bishop who precisely at
that time was sent to China by the patriarch Ichoyahb, Catholicos of
Seleucia-Ctesiphon. The story of that mission has been described in
narrative form by Nahal Tajadod in the last chapter of her book *Les
Porteurs de lumière*.[8] The event is thus described in the stele inscription:

> When Learned Emperor Taizong inaugurated the [imperial] fortune
> with splendor and magnificence and let his gaze fall upon men with
> discernment and holiness, there was in the kingdom of Daqin [a man]
> of superior virtue, called A-lo-pen. Having consulted the omens of the
> blue heavens, he took with him the true scriptures; having examined
> the musical tones of the winds, he faced difficulties and dangers. In the
> ninth year of the Zhenguan era [i.e., 635] he reached Chang'an. The
> emperor ordered the minister of state, the Honorable Fang Xuanling,
> to proceed with the imperial guard to the suburb of the west and, af-
> ter having welcomed A-lo-pen as guest, to welcome him to the palace.
> The emperor had the holy books translated. In the library; within the
> forbidden doors, he inquired about the doctrine. He learned perfectly
> that [the doctrine] was correct and true and prescribed by special order
> that it be propagated.
>
> In the twelfth year of the Zhenguan era [i.e., 638] in the seventh
> month, in the autumn, an imperial edict stated, "The Tao does not have

---

[8] Nahal Tajadod, *Les Porteurs de lumière*, Église chrétienne de Perse IIIe–VIIe siècles
(Paris: Plon, 1993), p. 330. The author is an Iranian, doctor in Chinese, who depicts in the
style of a contemporary narrative the story of Christianity in the Persian Empire at the time
of the sending of the first Christian missionaries.

an eternal name; the holy one does not have an eternal mode. They institute doctrine according to different regions and save the living in a mysterious way. The greatly virtuous A-lo-pen of the kingdom of Daqin, bringing from afar his holy books and his images, has come to offer them to the supreme capital. If one examines the doctrinal tendency of these [holy books], it is a mysterious and transcendent nonaction; if one considers their fundamental principle, it establishes the essential about the production [of beings] and their fulfillment. In its statements [this doctrine] does not have redundant words; in its concepts, it is free from entanglements [literally, "fish nets"]. It saves creatures and is of profit to men. It is fitting that it should be diffused in the empire. Let the competent authorities establish forthwith, in the Yi-ning quarter of the capital, a Daqin monastery and recognize the vows of twenty-one religious."

Jingjing the priest attached great importance to this official recognition. The fact that in the text Christian teaching was assimilated to one of the forms of the Tao did not constitute a theological problem for him. The pluralism was political, and this suited Jingjing. He used it to Christianity's advantage, trying to show obliquely that the Luminous Religion was called to take over from the Confucian and Taoist traditions. The passage, which follows the text of the imperial edict in the inscription, indicates the author's apologetic intention:

The virtue of the house of Zhou had been lost, and the gray-blue chariot had gone up towards the west; the wisdom of the great Tangs shone, and the radiant breeze blew towards the east.

The mention of the house of Zhou indirectly introduces Confucius (551–479 B.C.) who exalted the period of domination of the duke of Zhou (1042–1036 B.C.) as the golden age of China's past. In fact, the Zhou Dynasty had made Xi'an their capital, had created in their kingdom a feudal system based on land, and had established their overlordship over several other kingdoms in China. But for Confucius they had represented much more. He believed that their era represented a state of perfect harmony between heaven and earth, when human behavior was regulated by the law of heaven and the state enjoyed perpetual peace. When Confucianism developed into an intellectual school, it tried in vain to restore the idealized conditions of the Zhou period by means of the observance of ritual and the establishment of moral behavior, based on well-ordered human relations. In Jingjing's inscription, however, it is the eclipse of the house of

Zhou that is evoked, an allusion to the Warring States Period (403–221 B.C.), when many cities were sacked and the various kingdoms in China fought against each other. By association, it is Confucianism that is being diminished.

The "gray-blue chariot" refers to the another great school of wisdom, that of Laozi. According to legend, Laozi lived in the sixth century B.C. and left the decadent court of Luoyang at the age of 160, traveling on a chariot drawn by a black bull and crossing the Hangu Pass to the west. The guardian of the pass, Yinxi, asked him for his spiritual testament, whereupon Laozi wrote the *Daode jing*, (*The Book of the Way and Its Power*), whose 5,000 characters are engraved on two stelae at the shrine of Luguantai, near Xi'an, as previously mentioned. Laozi then continued his journey to the mountains of the west and was never seen again. In fact, *Daode jing* was written down in the third century B.C.; it drew its lesson from the shortcomings of Confucian morality to advocate a return in all simplicity to the life-giving source of the universe, thus avoiding hidebound divisions. Whereas Confucianism was concerned with regulating the behavior of rulers and their subjects, *Tao*, the Way, recommended a government that governs least as the best sort of government. It taught that being in touch with the *Tao*, the source of everything that exists, means reaching the fundamental unity in which all contradictions are resolved. During the first centuries of the Christian era, Taoism was to develop into an organized religion with its own priesthood and temples. The Tang rulers of Chang'an (Xi'an) considered themselves as descended from Laozi, so that Jingjing the priest was well advised in his text to mention Laozi's chariot, since this alluded to the west from which the Luminous Religion had come like a breeze blowing toward the east, at the very time when the Tang Dynasty was being established. Was this not implying that Christianity was the new incarnation of the *Tao*?

The text continues with a description of the development of the Luminous Religion, thanks to the support of Emperor Gaozong (649–683). It states that monasteries were founded in all the provinces and notes that, at the end of the seventh century and the beginning of the eighth, the Luminous Religion suffered from powerful Buddhist monks and was held up to ridicule by low-class Taoists. This refers to the time when Empress Wu Zetian, who was effective ruler from 660 to 705, seized power and eventually proclaimed herself emperor, the

Laozi, riding to the west on a bull, holding the Daode jing

According to legend, Laozi lived in the sixth century B.C.; however his most important text, *Daode jing* (the Book of the Way and its Power), was not written down until the third century B.C. Daoism, with Confucianism and Buddhism, became one of the great religions of China. Daoism developed its own cultic and temple tradition and encourages its worshippers to seek the *Dao*, the source of everything that exists, so as to reach the unity in which all contradictions are resolved. Engraving by Ding Yunpeng (Nanyu).

only woman who ruled China in her own right; such a development was against the tradition of Confucianism, but justification for it was found in the Buddhist scriptures.

The inscription records that these dark years were followed by a return to favor, which allowed priests and high officials from the West to renew contacts with China. Diplomatic and commercial interests also came into play, and the Xuanzong emperor who ruled from 712 to 755, gave tangible proof of his favorable attitude toward Christians. Princes were sent officially to visit the monasteries, and portraits of "the five emperors" were displayed in them.[9] The emperor Xuanzong chose the names of the monasteries and wrote them out with his own hand, thus imparting a fundamental element of Chinese culture, for which the writing of each character is not only an art form but also an expression of the inner nature of the writer. No wonder that Jingjing the priest uses lyrical language to describe this integration of the Luminous Religion into the political and cultural order of the time:

> The precious tablets made their jewels to shine, and their beams shone forth as purple clouds; the wise maxims filled the air and, springing forth, made the bright sun go pale. The gracious gifts were higher than the mountains of the south; the overflowing benefits were as deep as the eastern ocean.

There follows a list of all the favors bestowed by the successors of the Xuanzong emperor until the year 780.

The final section of the text on the stele contains a prayer that virtue may reign among men, that there may be peace in the empire and that heaven may multiply its blessings. There follows a surprising eulogy of the donor of the stele, a priest of the Church of the East called Yi-si, who lived nearly 150 years after the coming of Alopen in A.D. 635. He occupied an exalted position in the civil and military administration, although he was not of Chinese origin. This important civil servant gave considerable endowments to different monasteries and paid for the extension and the repairs of their buildings. He thus

---

[9] The five emperors or sage kings were legendary figures of the prehistoric period in China who were reputed to have taught the arts of civilization to the Chinese people. They were considered as heavenly figures who continued to guarantee moral order and prosperity in the land.

promoted the spiritual influence of the monasteries and their works of practical charity:

> He has made new efforts on behalf of the Radiant Religion; persevering in perfect virtue, he is helpful through his generosity. Each year he brings together the monks of the four monasteries; he serves them with respect and makes for them carefully prepared offerings during fifty days. Those who are hungry come and are fed; those who are cold come, and he clothes them; he looks after the sick and makes them get up again; he places the dead in the coffin and buries them in peace.

The text on the monument ends with a poetic passage in which the main lines of the inscription are summarized: glory to God, honor to the emperors and to the high dignitaries who have made the development of the Luminous Religion possible.

The Syrian Church of the East

The monks whose arrival in A.D. 635 is recorded on the Xi'an Stele were from the Syrian Church in Persia. The term *Daqin* in the phrase "the Luminous Religion from Daqin" refers to the West in a general way, and more particularly to Syria, which was the place of origin for what is called, from the European point of view, the Church of the East. Christianity came to Antioch, the principal city of Syria, during the time of the apostles. At Antioch the followers of Christ were first called Christians (Acts 11:26). From there Christianity spread eastward very early, to the northern part of present-day Iraq (Nisibis, Arbil) and to the south (Baghdad) by the beginning of the second century. Fr. Jean-Maurice Fiey, O.P., by a careful examination and dating of the sources, has established evidence supporting the tradition that St. Mari brought the Gospel to Ctesiphon on the Tigris before the year 116.[10] It is probable that Christianity reached Persia soon afterward, by the second half of the second century.

During the early centuries of the Christian Church, Antioch had an ecclesiastical predominance that extended beyond the Greek-speaking areas of the Mediterranean basin and beyond the frontiers of the Roman Empire, to areas that are part of present-day Syria and Iraq. At

---

[10] J. M. Fiey, *Jalons pour une histoire de l'Église en Iraq* (Louvain: C.S.C.O., 1970), Subsidia 36, pp. 39–44.

that time they belonged to the Persian Empire and were predominantly Semitic speaking, so that the liturgy of Antioch was celebrated there in Syriac, a later form of Aramaic. Many of the specifically biblical terms in the Christian literature of the seventh-century Syrian mission to China are thus in Syriac, not in the Greek forms that were more familiar to Christians in the West: e.g., *Allaha*, God; *Isho'*, Jesus; *Meshiha*, Christ (Messiah); and *Ruha-de-Kudsha*, the Holy Spirit.

The frontier between two warring states, the Roman Empire and the Persian Empire, divided the area of Antioch's influence eastward. When the Iranian dynasty of Sasanian kings began to rule Persia in 226, Zoroastrianism became the official religion. A caste of priests tended the altars on which the cult of fire was celebrated, and the high priest crowned the shah, consecrating him as the representative on earth of Ormuz, the god of light. When the Roman Empire adopted Christianity as the religion of the state in the fourth century, the small Christian groups within the Persian Empire became suspect as representatives of a hostile power. They were harshly persecuted in Persia from 340 to 378. However, in 410 a council was held in Seleucia, near Baghdad, that normalized relations with the state.

Christology

A further estrangement between the Church of the Mediterranean world and the regions of the East occurred in the fifth century because of christological controversies. By that time theologians from Alexandria in Egypt had become well known for their pervasive use of allegory in their interpretation of the Old Testament; they also tended to emphasize the divine nature of Jesus in a way that overshadowed his humanity. Antioch's school of theology, however, preferred a more literal approach to the words of Scripture; Cardinal Newman was to say of this school, "Its comments on Scripture seem to have been clear, natural, methodical, apposite and logically exact."[11] The Antiochene theologians produced writings that emphasized the fully human nature of Jesus Christ, with a human soul and free moral activity, exercised in his redemptive work.

---

[11] J. H. Newman, *The Arians of the Fourth Century* (London, 1876), p. 407.

Controversy arose on the question how far this stress on the distinction of the two natures in Christ was compatible with Catholic belief in the oneness of the Person of Christ, the Divine Person of the Word of God, the Second Person of the Trinity. Nestorius (c. 381–451), a Syrian priest who became bishop of Constantinople, fueled theological controversy by preaching against the popular title *Mother of God* given to Mary, the mother of Jesus; he preferred the title *Mother of Christ*. A council of bishops, summoned by the Roman emperor, was held at Ephesus in 431, which was recognized as the Third General Council; it deposed Nestorius and a certain number of other bishops, and after the council was over, a text was produced, the *Edict of Union*, which was gradually accepted by the bishops within the Roman Empire as a true expression of the Christian faith. However, these decisions were never accepted beyond the limits of the Roman Empire, so that Mesopotamia and Persia were effectively separated from the Churches of both Antioch and Constantinople.

Doctrinal conflict took place over the theological attempt to formulate the union of the two natures of Christ in the Divine Person of the Word of God, without any diminution of the humanity of the Savior. In the Mediterranean world and the medieval European culture that followed it, theological speculation continued for many centuries and refined a notion of person that safeguarded the Catholic faith in the Incarnation, while respecting it as an unfathomable mystery. It is relevant to quote the comment at a recent theological dialogue (1998) of Mar Bawai Soro, a bishop of the Assyrian Church of the East who works in the United States:

> Criterion for orthodoxy should not be confined to certain terminological formulae, but should be subject to confessing the Apostolic Kerygma, the true faith that is biblically based and that points to the transcendance of God's mystery in Jesus Christ, the Savior of the world. Nestorius was orthodox in that he confessed the oneness of Christ, yet his theological theses and, more so, his articulation of them, could not sufficiently express his faith, at least in terms that were acceptable to Cyril of Alexandria, and, in due course, to the ancient Christian Church in the Roman-Byzantine Empire.[12]

---

[12] *Third Non-official Consultation on Dialogue within the Syriac Tradition*, edited on behalf of Pro Oriente by Alfred Stirnemann and Gerhard Wilflinger (Vienna: Pro Oriente, 1998), p. 90.

To a considerable extent, the difficulties between the Church of the East and the great Churches of Rome, Constantinople, and Alexandria came from the fact that Christians outside the Roman Empire were not part of Mediterranean culture, the *oikoumene*. The difficulties were often linguistic, since Greek-speaking bishops and Syriac-speaking ones used crucial terms, with important philosophical implications, in different ways. Thus the Greeks translated the Syriac word *qnoma* as "person", and when they read statements from the Church of the East about "the two Natures of Christ and their *qnome*" they understood them as affirming two Persons of Christ. This became for Greeks characteristic of Nestorianism, but in fact *qnoma* in Syriac means "individual characteristics". Syrians mentioned them because they wanted to emphasize the individual properties of Jesus as a fully human being, since human nature only exists as individuated.

There was also on the part of the Syrians a reluctance to indulge in philosophical speculation. Dr. Sebastian Brock writes, "The combination of geographical and political separation of the Church of the East from Christianity in the Roman Empire had a further important consequence from the point of view of Christology: since the Church of the East was not directly involved in the fierce christological controversies taking place in the Roman Empire from the 430s onward, its theological language and its understanding of certain technical terms remained comparatively 'old fashioned'."[13] As a result, the Church of the East was cut off from the theological advances in Christology that took place in the West, although it never denied the one Person of Christ, active for our salvation in the harmonious unity of two distinct natures.

One also needs to bear in mind, when trying to assess the causes of division, that there was a constant and underlying tension between the native Semitic populations of the Near East and the dominant Hellenistic civilization of the Mediterranean world. This tension often found an outlet through open opposition in specific areas, such as theology, which became the carriers of what was really a wider cultural clash. Christopher Dawson assessed it thus: "Syrian Christianity

---

[13] S. P. Brock, "The Christology of the Church of the East in the Synods of the Fifth to Early Seventh Centuries: Preliminary Considerations and Materials", in *Aksum-Thyateira: A Festschrift for Archbishop Methodios* (London, 1985), ed. G. Dragas; reproduced in Sebastian Brock, *Studies in Syriac Christianity* (Aldershot: Ashgate Variorum, 1992), XII, p. 130.

was the religion of a subject people who found in it their justification against the pride of the dominant culture".[14]

The Xi'an Stele inscription tells us a certain amount about the practices of the missionaries of the seventh-century Syrian Church of the East. They were conscious of the differences of culture, so that they explained exterior aspects that would have been strange to the Chinese: the wooden gong or *semantron* that hung in their church towers, the custom of facing east to pray, the shaven crowns of the monks, their luxuriant beards. They referred to the cross as the sign of Christians, to the week of seven days as the basis of their principal act of worship, and to the seven daily hymns as the rhythm of their daily prayer. At the same time they adopted the obsequious style of the Chinese court and the repeated expressions of gratitude for the favor and benevolence of the emperor. The end of the inscription also reflects the hierarchy of Chinese society: glory to heaven, honor to the emperor, respect for the high dignitaries and scholarly mandarins who administer the empire.

---

[14] Christopher Dawson, *The Making of Europe: An Introduction to the History of European Unity* (London: Sheed and Ward, 1946), p. 99.

[In this chapter, additions to the French text have been made by the translator to the following sections:

"The Luminous Religion": The penultimate paragraph has been added.

"Imperial Permission": The first paragraph of this section has been considerably expanded. The paragraph beginning "The mention of the House of Zhou" has been expanded.

"The Syrian Church of the East" and "Christology": The whole of these two sections is an addition to the French text—TRANS.]

2

THE SCRIPTURE TRANSLATIONS OF CHANG'AN

The Xi'an Stele, by expressing the doctrines of Christianity in a language accessible to the religious traditions of eighth-century China, shows a high degree of cultural adaptation. The inscription also indicates that the personnel of the Luminous Religion were integrated into the imperial administration of the Tang Dynasty. Such achievements, however, were only possible because Persian monks, disseminating Christian teaching, were able to reach China. The Persian missionaries who arrived in Chang'an in A.D. 635 had traveled over 4,000 miles (c. 6,500 kilometers) through some of the most difficult terrain in the world. That they were able to do this depended on the existence of trade routes, which also gave evidence of an impressive degree of organization.

The Silk Road

In the 1870s a German geographer, Baron Ferdinand von Richthofen, gave the name *Seidenstrasse* (Silk Road) to these routes, from the most precious commodity that was transported along them. It needs to be remembered that there was not one road but often several parallel routes and that most of them did not resemble the image conjured up by the word "road".[1] The Chinese were the first people to produce silk from the cocoons of silkworms, a technique that they discovered in prehistoric times. They were writing documents on silk before they had invented paper in 200 B.C. Silk reached the West as a commercial commodity in the first century after Christ and was highly prized by the Romans, although its origin remained mysterious; the Romans

---

[1] References in J. M. Fiey, *Pour un Oriens Christianus Novus: Répertoire des Diocèses Syriaques Orientaux et Occidentaux* (Beirut: In Kommission bei Franz Steiner Verlag Stuttgart, 1993), no. 49, Beiruter Texte und Studien, p. 101, *sub* Kashghar. For the best recent description of the Silk Road and its history see Frances Wood, *The Silk Road* (London: Folio Society, 2002).

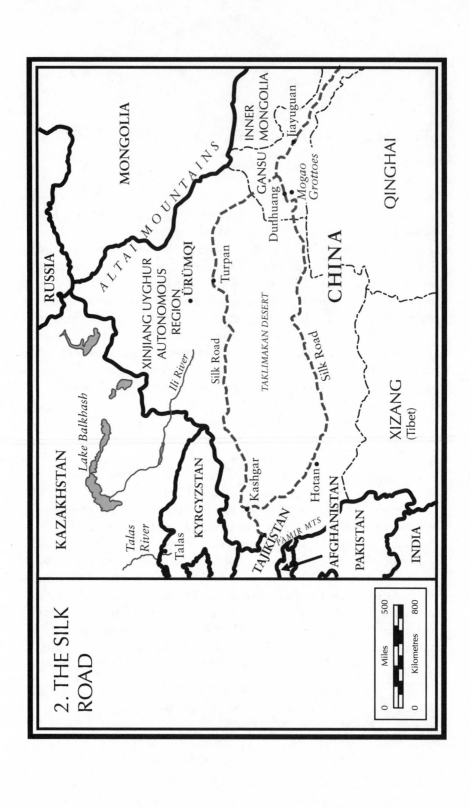

2. THE SILK ROAD

RUSSIA

MONGOLIA

KAZAKHSTAN

Lake Balkhash

Ili River

XINJIANG UYGHUR
AUTONOMOUS
REGION

• ÜRÜMQI

A L T A I M O U N T A I N S

INNER MONGOLIA

Jiayuguan

GANSU

*Mogao
Grottoes*

Dunhuang

Turpan

Silk Road

TAKLIMAKAN DESERT

CHINA

QINGHAI

*Talas
River*

Talas

KYRGYZSTAN

Silk Road

Kashgar

Hotan •

PAMIR MTS

TAJIKISTAN

AFGHANISTAN

PAKISTAN

INDIA

XIZANG
(Tibet)

0   500
Miles

0   800
Kilometres

thought that it grew on trees, and their Oriental suppliers did nothing to dispel this belief.

At the time of the first Christian missionaries, the trade routes from the West started in the region that the Chinese called *Daqin*, centering on Syria, and crossed upper Iraq and northern Persia (modern Iran), along the edge of the Caspian Sea. They then meandered through parts of present-day Afghanistan and Tajikistan, reaching a formidable range of mountains, the High Pamir, known as the "roof of the world". The summits of these mountains were covered with perpetual snows, and the more accessible passes were 17,000 feet (5,200 meters) high. Men and beasts who had not been incapacitated by altitude sickness then faced the dangers of avalanches and rock falls along the tracks that the caravans followed; bandits also lay in wait to plunder the caravans, which needed an escort of armed men. Once all these difficulties had been overcome, travelers from the West descended to the desert of the Tarim Basin, as it is called today. Its name, in the tongue of the Uighur people who inhabit the region, is *Taklimakan*, "go in, and you won't come out", which adequately expresses its reputation, as does its other name, "the sea of death". The Taklimakan, which is immediately north of Tibet, stretches for 620 miles (1,000 kilometers) from west to east and is the largest desert in the world after the Sahara. Its immense sand dunes are raked by fierce winds from the north, and it suffers from sand storms of unparalleled intensity and from extreme variations in temperature. However, in recent times huge deposits of oil, natural gas, and minerals have been discovered under the Taklimakan, so perhaps its isolation will not last much longer.

Travelers from the west reach the edges of the Taklimakan at the modern city of Kashgar, in the present-day Xinjiang-Uighur Autonomous Region. At the beginning of our era, Kashgar was at the parting of the two routes that skirted the desert to the north and to the south. There were a few oases on these routes, but caravans could not have traversed this arid region without the two-humped Bactrian camel. This remarkable animal could cross the sand dunes of the Taklimakan, travel without water for two weeks at a time, and survive extremes of temperature while carrying loads of nearly 500 pounds (230 kilograms). Until the advent of the twentieth century, camels were the only effective pack animals for this part of the journey. However, neither man nor beast was required to travel the whole

of the Silk Road in either direction; caravans would cover only certain stages of the Road. At the end of each stage the sale of goods,
involving an appropriate increase in price, would be negotiated with
the next company of merchants, to take the merchandise further toward its destination. Caravans could number hundreds of men and
up to 1,000 camels The production of silk was a Chinese monopoly
until the sixth century, when peoples farther west, Parthians and then
the Byzantines, discovered how to make it. Two Persian monks from
Hotan, south of Kashgar, are reputed to have smuggled silkworm
eggs out of China in a hollow bamboo stick and to have presented
them to Emperor Justinian at Constantinople in 552. However, silk
was not the only commodity transported along the Silk Road. From
China also came porcelain, gemstones, incense, tea, and spices; from
the West arrived such quantities of gold that the Roman Empire was
at times alarmed by the drain on its bullion; also jade, glass, furs,
wine, and magnificent Ferghana horses from present-day Uzbekistan.

Caravans traveling eastward converged on the now-famous region
of Dunhuang, where the northern and southern routes round the Taklimakan Desert met. Nearby was Jiayuguan Pass, known as the Gate
of Jade, which marked the entry into the Celestial Empire and was
at the western end of the complex of defenses known as the Great
Wall of China. There were still 800 miles (c. 1,300 kilometers) to
go before reaching Chang'an (Xi'an), capital of the Tang emperors,
whose rule coincided with a period of peace and prosperity for China
that historians describe as a golden age. When the first Christian missionaries arrived in 635, the population of Chang'an was approaching
two million, which would have made it the largest city in the world
at that time. It was a cosmopolitan city, deriving immense profit from
its position as the point of departure and arrival for travelers on the
Silk Road. The cultural "transfusion" of religious belief was facilitated
through this mercantile route, which marked the way that Buddhism
had followed into China from India in the first century after Christ.

A Missionary Church

The arrival of Christian missionaries in China in the seventh century
was made possible by the existence of a vigorous missionary Church
in Persia that was able to make use of the possibilities for evange-

lization offered by the Silk Road. One of the effects of the doctrinal controversies and divisions of fifth-century Christianity was the recognition in the East that the head of the Church in the Persian Empire was the metropolitan of Seleucia-Ctesiphon, on the Tigris, some twenty miles (thirty-two kilometers) south of Baghdad. During the course of the sixth century he assumed the titles of Catholicos and Patriarch.[2] A remarkable missionary effort then took place, following the Silk Road and also the trade routes on both shores of the Persian Gulf to Arabia and India.

The arrival of the Persian monks in Chang'an can be seen as part of that movement, which led at its apogee to the creation of twenty-seven metropolitan sees and 230 bishoprics.[3] Dennis Hickley has pointed out how important for the success of the first Christian missions in China was the fact that the Syrian Church in Persia had adapted to a situation where it was not the dominant religion.[4] The state religion of the Persian Empire was Mazdeism (Zoroastrianism). Christians were merchants, to some extent financiers and physicians, but they did not provide the aristocracy or the rulers of the empire. Once Persian Christians had dissociated themselves from the Byzantine West and after the end of the fourth-century persecutions of Christians in Persia, they were given a status roughly equivalent to the later Ottoman *Melet*, i.e., a people with their own religion and customs, like the Jewish community. Such recognition gave them a certain autonomy in return for their support for the government of the shah; this status continued after the conquest of the Persian Empire by Arab Muslims in 641.

What exactly was the teaching that the Persian Christian monk Alopen brought to Chang'an, the capital of the Tang Dynasty, in A.D. 635 and which was submitted to the examination of the emperor? Modern research has identified some thirty Syrian Christian documents from China, of which nine are original manuscripts. The Japanese scholar P. Y. Saeki studied these documents exhaustively, comparing them to the Syrian originals of the Chinese translations.[5]

---

[2] See Fiey, *Pour un Oriens Christianus Novus*, pp. 43–145, for a list of the dioceses of the Syrian Church of the East and references to their history.

[3] Fiey, ibid.

[4] Dennis Hickley, *An Outline History and Some Considerations Concerning the Nestorians in China during the Tang Dynasty* (London: China Study Project, 1980), pp. 31–33.

[5] P. Y. Saeki, *The Nestorian Documents and Relics in China* (Tokyo: Maruzen, 1951).

He identified two documents that he considered to have been translated at Xi'an in 635 and 641. The Sinologist Fr. Yves Raguin, S.J., has also given a special place to these two texts.[6] The two manuscripts are of major importance, both for their contents and literary form, because they constitute the first statement of the Christian faith by writers of Chinese whose previous religious vocabulary was Buddhist. Their catechesis, however, was comprehensive and included a faithful account of the Passion of Christ. The Xi'an Stele, whose text was composed almost 150 years later as the official account of a religion that has been integrated into society, does not have the same Gospel flavor. It is important, therefore, to examine the older documents in order to appreciate the first proclamation of the Christian faith in China.

The Sutra of Jesus the Messiah

According to P. Y. Saeki, the oldest of these Syrian Christian texts is the *Sutra of Jesus the Messiah*.[7] Its primitive character is indicated by its language and by the way Chinese characters are used to render foreign words. The Chinese expressions used will be perfected in the course of time as Christianity becomes indigenized. In these first texts many foreign words are not translated but are merely transcribed by a series of Chinese characters, used as syllables; the Chinese characters thus used to render Syriac or Sanskrit syllables often have unfortunate meanings if they are read as ideograms. Thus the word Messiah is rendered *Mi-shi-suo*, using three Chinese characters that mean literally "the place where the poem was lost". In later texts Messiah was written *Mi-shi-ho*, with different characters that can be read "the accomplished master". More confusing was the translation of God as *Fo*, which is the term used for the Buddha, or else as *Tianzun*, which is another Buddhist term for the godhead. The Holy Spirit is written *Liang feng*, "cool breeze", whereas the term that prevailed later was *Jing feng*, "pure breeze". Particularly unfortunate was the choice of the characters to write the name of Jesus; the two signs used

---

[6] Yves Raguin, S.J., "Le Jésus-Messie de Xi'an" in *Le Christ Chinois: Héritages et Espérance* (Paris: Desclée de Brouwer, 1998), Collection Christus no. 87, pp. 35–55. English translation by Betty Ann Maheu, "Jesus-Messiah of Xi'an" in *Tripod* 124 (2002): 39–54.

[7] *Sutra*: a set of aphorisms in Sanskrit literature, from a root meaning "string".

mean literally "displaced rat". Later texts avoided such blunders by selecting characters that are better adapted. These primitive mistakes can be explained in different ways. They could be due to foreigners who did not know Chinese well, or they could be the work of scribes who were making fun of Christianity.[8] Saints and angels are given names borrowed from the Buddhist pantheon. The predominance of Buddhist terms is doubtless due to the fact that the imperial office of translations employed mostly Buddhist experts.

The *Sutra of Jesus the Messiah* is composed of 206 verses. The first twenty verses are an invocation to the invisible God and to the heavenly spirits who serve him. There follows a description of humankind as capable of knowing God, but distant from him because of sin and the condition of mortality. The text goes on to say that human beings have to make a choice between "the way of heaven" and "the way of evil". Sin has come into the world because of the disobedience of our first ancestor in the orchard (v. 54). The transmission of original sin is explained according to the Buddhist understanding of retribution: "All living beings must consider the consequences of acts committed in a previous existence" (v. 55). This is followed by the first mention of salvation: "The Most High (*Tianzun*) by accepting suffering has lifted up all beings".

The *Sutra* continues with the statement that unfortunately human beings have lost their way by worshipping idols that can neither move nor speak. Those who do good fear God and welcome the teaching of the Most High. Those who do evil are handed over to *Yan-luo wang*, the king of the underworld (v. 76). All living beings should repent of the sins they have committed (v. 78). Those who fear the Lord of Heaven should also fear their sovereign on earth (v. 80). The sovereign has received his power from the Most High. He is holy. All should obey him. The first four commandments are summed up as follows:

---

[8] For the practice of using pejorative associations in transcription, see Dr. Anne Birrell's comment: "many of the ancient Chinese names for other lands and peoples are probably based on the transliteration of foreign names. Nevertheless, it is evident from the transliterations in the *Classic* that the tendency was to choose offensive and demeaning graphs to reproduce foreign sounds, rather than those that enhanced the local pride and self-esteem of other peoples." *The Classic of Mountains and Seas*, translated with an introduction by Anne Birrell (Harmondsworth: Penguin Classics, 1998), introduction pp. xxx–xxxi.

Three things are important; the first is to obey the Lord of heaven, the second is to obey the holy sovereign, the third is to obey one's father and mother (vv. 90–92).

The other commandments of God, from the fifth to the tenth, are then enumerated. They are called "vows", following Buddhist terminology. The precepts of charity follow, according to the description of the judgment in Matthew 25: to feed the hungry, to give a cup of milk to the thirsty workman, to clothe those who are naked. Other precepts are taken from the books of Leviticus and Deuteronomy. Certain norms of the way of Christian living are taken from the *Didache*: fair judgment, humility, respect for servants, etc.[9] The long list of moral counsels ends with verse 148, in which the author, after stating that all human beings have turned away from God and have sinned, introduces the history of the Incarnation and of the sacrifice of redemption.

The text relates that the Virgin Mary, whose name is rendered *Moyan*, conceived her child through the intervention of the Holy Spirit (*Liang feng*: literally cool wind or cool breeze). She gave birth to a son named *Isho'*. A star shone on the place where the Lord could be found; "the star was as big as a cart wheel" (v. 162). The Messiah started preaching to the people when he was only twelve years old and urged them to do good. He was baptized in the Jordan by John the Baptist, and the Holy Spirit came down from heaven in the form of a dove, while a voice said, "The Messiah is my son; everyone must listen to him and obey his commandment to do good." "Those who had all sorts of diseases came to the Messiah and wished to touch or get hold of his *Ka-sha-ya*[10] and they were all cured" (v. 180). He cured the sick and drove out demons. The Messiah created twelve disciples and in the end suffered the Passion. Evil men plotted against him and tried to get rid of him by lawful judgment. As they could not find a valid accusation, they "came into the presence of the Great King *P'i-lo-tu-ssu* [Pilate]" (v. 190), who washed his hands of the blood of this innocent man.

---

[9] The *Didache tôn Apostolôn, Instructions of the Apostles*, an early Christian text, probably from the late first or early second century and from the Church of Antioch in Syria.

[10] *Kashaya*: the Sanskrit name for a plant giving a yellow-red dye, and secondarily for yellow-red dyed cloth, worn as a cloak by holy men in India who were mendicants. It is transcribed by characters used as syllables in the Chinese text. Note by Yves Raguin, S.J., "Le Jésus-Messie de Xi'an" in *Le Christ Chinois: Héritages et Espérance*, p. 40, n. 6.

The Messiah gave up his body to these wicked men to be sacrificed for the sake of all humankind and made the whole world know that human life is as precarious as a candle light (v. 198). Thus out of charity he gave up his life for the sake of all humankind, suffering death for them (v. 199).

The manuscript ends abruptly with the death of Christ. The last lines have been cut off, perhaps shorn by the local warden of a library who wanted to ensure that the roll had a neat appearance. The last development, on the Passion of Christ, shows that the Syrian Church had no objection to speaking of redemptive sacrifice. The text follows St. John's Gospel in emphasizing the innocence of Jesus and his sovereign freedom in accepting death out of love for all humankind. It is a pity that the manuscript has been cut short, as one is left wondering how the Resurrection of Jesus would have been presented.

The Discourse of the Master of the World on Almsgiving

The second Syrian document in Chinese does refer to the Resurrection and Ascension of Jesus. The manuscript, which identifies itself as dating from 641, is entitled *Discourse of the Master of the World on Almsgiving, Part 3*. The phrase "master of the world", rendered in Chinese as *Shizun*, is a Buddhist term for *Guanyin*, the goddess of mercy (rendered as *Kannon* in Japanese). In India this was a male deity known as *Avalokitesvara*, but the deity had been given a female aspect in China by the time of the twelfth century. *Shizun*, Master of the world, was a helpful deity, full of mercy toward suffering humanity. The Syrian missionaries borrowed the title *Shizun*, "Master of the World", to describe Jesus the Savior, in contrast to *Tianzun*, God who is "Master of heaven".

The text of the *Discourse* is composed of 262 verses; it speaks of the death and Resurrection of Jesus as follows:

Without the sin of Adam and Eve, one could not have hoped for the announcement of the joyful news. Like the sheep led to the slaughterhouse, he opened not his mouth and made no complaint. . . . He thus suffered punishment for love of you, so that the seed of Adam in you was won and transformed by him. It seems clear that, if the Messiah suffered death in his body composed of the five elements, his life did not end there (vv. 96–100).

The earthquake and the tearing of the veil of the temple in Jerusalem, when Jesus gave forth his last breath, are attributed to the
"sanctifying transformation" operated in Jesus; similarly the resurrection of the virtuous men who came out of their tombs and were
seen in Jerusalem. The appearances of the risen Jesus are described
thus:

> And he stayed with them during fourteen days and a month. Not a day
> passed without his appearing to them in obscure places (v. 109).

There follows a long account of Jesus' burial by Joseph of Ari-
mathea, the posting of guards before the tomb, the stone rolled in
front of it, and the appearances to the holy women.

> But the guards say that the One, according to the prophecies, is the
> Messiah and that his Resurrection from the dead is also written down
> in the prophecy; behold the Messiah is risen; he is gone (v. 135).

The text continues with the appearances to the disciples, the promise of the Holy Spirit, the sending on their mission. The Ascension
of Christ is described in apocalyptic terms:

> Behold the heavens opened, and the Messiah, entering into the heavenly
> light, appeared in the sky. In heaven there was the heavenly figure of a
> man seated in the midst of the breath of the great mercy. Thus was the
> great transformation, sanctifying humanity, accomplished (vv. 149–50).

All human beings are summoned to rise from the dead:

> Those who believe in the Messiah know without a shadow of doubt
> that they will rise from "the yellow springs"[11] and that all human beings
> without exception will rise from the dead (v. 164).

The events of Pentecost are narrated in these terms:

> Ten days after his Ascension, the Messiah again strengthened the faith
> of his disciples. He introduced them to the secret of the Way and gave
> them the Holy Breath (v. 165). Having received the Holy Breath, they
> had the power to teach about the Messiah to all nations and races of
> humanity and to reveal to the whole of humanity the judgment of the
> master of heaven (v. 168).

---

[11] "Yellow Springs": the traditional Chinese term for the underworld, where the mortal
soul sinks and perishes.

There follows the story of the spreading of the Gospel into all countries, in spite of persecution. The disciples were often subjected to hatred and repression, although their only desire was to fulfill their task to the best of their ability, and they were bringing peace and reconciliation. Christian believers were martyred in Syria and Persia under the Sasanian Dynasty during the first half of the fifth century. The anonymous author of this text, however, explains that it is for that very reason that the people of these regions have now accepted the cult of the Master of heaven.[12]

> Although only 641 years have elapsed since the birth of the Messiah in his five elements, nevertheless he is known in all parts of the world (v. 223). Every wise person can see what his manifestation is, as well as the mysterious art of transformation into sanctity (v. 224).

The anonymous author issues a warning against the temptations of idolatry, which may be due to the proximity of Zoroastrian cults that came from Persia to Chang'an, where they had their temples.

> Those who go astray are those who fear men or who worship the sun, the moon, the stars, and even the gods of fire (v. 244).

He warns those who are led astray by the demons *Yakshas* and *Rakshasas* that they will go into the burning fire of hell. These devils, who devour men and women, were figures well known to Buddhists. Here again the author makes use of popular demonizing imagery to instill fear into ordinary mortals.

It can be seen therefore that the *Discourse of the Master of the World on Almsgiving*, like the *Sutra of Jesus the Messiah*, presented a comprehensive and honest account of the Christian doctrine of salvation. The emphasis laid on the Messiah as light of the world reflected the

---

[12] Dennis Hickley, *The First Christians in China: An Outline History and Some Considerations Concerning the Nestorians in China during the Tang Dynasty* (London: China Study Project, 1980), pp. 15–16, discusses how it was possible to claim in 641 that Syria and Persia had adopted Christianity. He suggests that in 641 the latest news of Persian affairs to have reached Chang'an would have been the successful campaigns of the Byzantine Emperor Heraclius and the collapse of Sasanian Persia, interpreted as a Christian victory. The conquest of Persia by Islamic forces from Arabia was determined in 641 by the Muslim victory over the last Shah Yezdegard III at the battle of Nihavend, but news of this would not necessarily have reached Chang'an when the text was written. Firsthand accounts would, however, have reached the Tang capital eventually, since the son of Yezdegard III and other members of the royal family took refuge in Chang'an after having fled from Persia.

background of a Persian culture that was steeped in Mazdeism. Numerous concepts and expressions, familiar to Buddhists, witness to common credal parallels. Some scholars have emphasized Christian and Mazdean influences on Buddhists of the Pure Land, so that the small Christian community could well have appeared as one branch of the great Buddhist tradition.

Nestorian?

Finally, it can be seen from such expressions of the faith that the theology of the eastern Syrian Church presents the two natures and the one Person of Jesus Christ in a way that does not noticeably alter the general presentation of the doctrines of the Incarnation and salvation. To describe such a church as Nestorian is to give it a name that eastern Christians never gave themselves. Their Church did not derive from Nestorius in the way in which, for instance, Lutherans can be said to derive from Luther. Recently Dr. Sebastian Brock has argued cogently for the abandonment of the term *Nestorian* when referring to the Syrian Church of the East.[13] In the ecumenical climate of today, it is easier to see that the starting point for understanding can be the common affirmation of the faith as expressed in the Council of Nicea and the acceptance of the one Person of the Divine Word, active for our salvation in the harmonious unity of two distinct natures. Such an approach is beginning to bear fruit, as for instance in the rapprochement between the Catholic Church and the Assyrian Church of the East. On November 11, 1994, Pope John Paul II and Mar Dinkha, Catholicos of the Assyrian Church of the East, signed

---

[13] S. P. Brock, "The 'Nestorian' Church: A Lamentable Misnomer", *Bulletin of the John Rylands University Library of Manchester*, 3, no. 78 (1996):23–35. Nowadays the Syrian Church in Iraq, which is not in communion with Rome, uses the name Assyrian Church of the East. Dr. Brock comments on this usage: "Only when European concepts of nationalism reached the Middle East in the late nineteenth century did members of the Church of the East begin to feel the need to discover a national identity that was not solely based on the idea of membership of a religious community. For them a suitable focus was found in the term 'Assyrian', and the resultant Assyrian nationalist movement has today even been extended to include members of other churches of Syrian liturgical tradition such as the Syrian orthodox." S. P. Brock, "Christians in the Sasanian Empire: A Case of Divided Loyalties" in *Studies in Church History* 18 (Oxford, 1982), reproduced in S. P. Brock, *Syriac Perspectives in Late Antiquity* (London: Variorum Reprints, 1984), VI, p. 19.

a christological declaration in Rome: "As heirs and guardians of the faith received from the apostles as formulated by our common Fathers in the Nicene Creed." Its formulation of that faith is as follows:

> Christ . . . is not an "ordinary man" whom God adopted in order to reside in him and inspire him, as in the righteous ones and the prophets. But the same God the Word, begotten of his Father before all worlds without beginning according to his divinity, was born of a mother without a father in the last times according to his humanity. The humanity to which the Blessed Virgin Mary gave birth always was that of the Son of God himself. That is the reason why the Assyrian Church of the East is praying to the Virgin Mary as "the Mother of Christ our God and Savior". In the light of this same faith the Catholic tradition addresses the Virgin Mary as "the Mother of God" and also as "the Mother of Christ". We both recognize the legitimacy and rightness of these expressions of the same faith and we both respect the preference of each Church in her liturgical life and piety.[14]

---

[14] "Common Christological Declaration between the Catholic Church and the Assyrian Church of the East (November 11, 1994)", *A.A.S.* 87, no. 8 (August 7, 1995):685–86. Text in English.

[The introductory paragraph of this chapter and the section on "The Silk Road" are additions to the French text.

The first two paragraphs of the section "A Missionary Church" are an addition to the French text. The third paragraph is an expanded version of the introduction to this chapter in the French text.

The section "Nestorian?" is an addition to the French text.—TRANS.]

3

THE DUNHUANG GLORIA

A history of printing, published by the National Library of Beijing in 1961, mentions in the following terms the discovery of the Dunhuang manuscripts by Aurel Stein in 1908:

> The Diamond Sutra, printed in the year 868 . . . is the world's earliest printed book. . . . This famous scroll was stolen over fifty years ago by the Englishman Ssu-t'an yin [Stein], which causes [Chinese] people to gnash their teeth in bitter hatred."[1]

The discovery of ancient manuscripts and works of art in the area of the Taklimakan Desert began toward the end of the nineteenth century.[2] From ruined cities buried in the sand along the routes of the old Silk Road, precious sculptures and manuscripts were unearthed and sent to Europe, few to begin with but increasing in number as interest grew. An exploring land surveyor from India and a Russian vice consul in Kashgar began the trend. In 1890 a French expedition to the Taklimakan area and Tibet brought back to Paris antiquities, including a manuscript. Sven Hedin, a Swedish geographer, explored the Taklimakan between 1895 and 1899. A German explorer, Von Le Coq, brought many manuscripts and wall paintings back to Berlin in 1907. These discoveries were of immediate interest to scholars from the West, because in India itself the oldest Buddhist liter-

---

[1] Quoted in Peter Hopkirk, *Foreign Devils on the Silk Road: The Search for the Lost Cities and Treasures of Chinese Central Asia* (Oxford: Oxford University Press, 1984), p. 174.

[2] In addition to Peter Hopkirk's highly readable account, there is an abundance of material on Dunhuang. See especially Aurel Stein, *Serindia: Detailed Report of Explorations in Central Asia and Westernmost China* (Delhi: Motilal Banansidas, 1980), 5 vols., a reprint of the first ed. (Oxford, 1921). Sir Aurel Stein, *Ruins of Desert Cathay: Personal Narrative of the Three Expeditions in Central Asia and Westernmost China* (London: Macmillan, 1912), 2 vols. Lionel Giles, *Six Centuries at Tunhuang: A Short Account of the Chinese Manuscripts in the British Museum* (London: The China Society, 1944). For fine reproductions of the works of art with descriptions, see Roderick Whitfield, *The Art of Central Asia: The Stein Collection in the British Museum* (Tokyo: Kodansha International, 1982–1985), 3 vols. Jacques Gies, *La collection Paul Pelliot du musée national des arts asiatiques — Guimet* (Tokyo: Kodansha International, 1994), 2 vols.

ature had largely disappeared through the later prevalence of Hinduism and Islam. Orientalists were alerted to the possibility of discovering hitherto unknown Buddhist texts in central Asia, and this is exactly what happened when Chinese, Tibetan, and other translations of lost Sanskrit originals saw the light of day in the sensational finds at Dunhuang.

Shrines and a Library

Around 1899 a Chinese Taoist monk, Wang Yuan-lu, while restoring a shrine in the Mogao caves, fifteen miles (twenty-four kilometers) southeast of Dunhuang, accidentally discovered a door camouflaged by crumbling painted plaster. A chamber was revealed whose floor was entirely covered to a height of ten feet (three meters) with rolls of manuscripts, many of them grouped in canvas casings.

Dunhuang had been known as a Buddhist center since the introduction of Buddhism from India in the first century. Many monks from India and central Asia settled there, and it became renowned for Buddhist studies. Monks and nuns constituted a considerable proportion of its population, and also laymen who wanted to work in the administration. In the ninth and tenth centuries there were seventeen monasteries in Dunhuang.

Dunhuang, on the edge of Gansu Province in the far northwest of China, was the last Chinese city for travelers going westward on the Silk Road. It became customary for those setting out on the perilous journey to visit the grottoes of *Mogao*, a name that means *Unequaled Heights*; they were also known as *Qian fodong, Thousand Buddha Grottoes*. At Mogao a limestone cliff dominates for the length of one mile (1.6 kilometers) the barren valley of the Dachuan River. Over the centuries the natural caves in the cliff had been supplemented by hundreds more, carved out of the limestone to form chapels and shrines, richly decorated with frescoes and painted sculptures. Not only is this the oldest surviving Buddhist site in China, it also contains some of the most important Buddhist art in the world. In fact, an academy of painting had been established to train artists to work in the shrines, which were being added to from the fourth to the fourteenth centuries. Many of the chapels were created through the benefactions of private individuals, who dedicated *ex votos*, either praying for success before setting out on the dangerous journey west or giving thanks for a safe return. Eventually there were more than a thousand chapels at Mogao, of which 492 survive.

After his discovery of the hidden library, the monk Wang was in the habit of giving ancient manuscripts from the Dunhuang cache as occasional presents to local mandarins, so that word went round the area that texts of outstanding quality were to be found nearby. The first European to see the hidden grotto with the manuscripts was Aurel Stein, who arrived in May 1907. He was by birth a Hungarian Jew who was brought up a Christian by his parents and later acquired British nationality. He had done extensive Oriental and archeological studies at Vienna, Leipzig, Oxford, and the British Museum, but he never learned Chinese, which he later much regretted. In 1888, at the age of twenty-six, he began work in the Indian education service, where he became a friend of Rudyard Kipling's father and also obtained the support of Lord Curzon, the British viceroy, who made it possible for him to mount a series of expeditions in the region of the Taklimakan Desert.

When Stein, who was later knighted by King Edward VII, thus becoming Sir Aurel Stein, arrived at Dunhuang in 1907, he did not know about the existence of the hidden library. He was told about it by a trader from Ürümqi and at once made it his business to win the confidence of Wang Yuan-lu, providing substantial donations for the restoration of his chapels and shrines. Stein was thus authorized to remove 7,000 manuscripts and paintings on silk, as well as one fresco, cut out of the wall of a shrine. These finds from Dunhuang filled twenty-nine crates, which arrived at the British Museum in London in January 1909, together with other antiquities that Stein had collected at different sites. Unfortunately, since Stein could not read Chinese, and his Chinese interpreter, Chiang Ssu-yeh, was not an expert in deciphering ancient texts, manuscripts were chosen for their appearance rather than their contents, with the result that the British Library now houses among its treasures from Dunhuang 1,000 copies of the *Lotus Sutra* and 500 copies of the *Diamond Sutra*, when so much of far greater interest might have been taken. Fortunately a French scholar was at hand who was able to make a more discriminating selection.

Paul Pelliot (1878–1945) was a brilliant young sinologist, a product of the Oriental languages section of the École du Louvre in Paris. He was only thirty when he arrived at Dunhuang but had experience of the Far East, having been in Beijing during the Boxer Rebellion of 1900, after which he was appointed to the staff of the École Française d'Extrême Orient in Hanoi. Pelliot knew twelve languages, in addition to Chinese, and was experienced at deciphering ancient texts. This was to prove invaluable because of the range of different languages represented in the Dunhuang hidden library—Chinese, Sanskrit, Tibetan, Sogdian, Khotanese, Kutchean, Uighur, Turkic, and even a fragment in Hebrew. Pelliot arrived at Dunhuang in February 1908 and was able to stay until May, much longer than Stein had done; he describes his conditions of work in a letter to a colleague:

> On March 3, it being Shrove Tuesday, I was able to enter the Holy of Holies. I was dumbfounded. Since items had been removed from this library during the last eight years, I thought it would have been seriously depleted. Imagine my surprise at finding myself in a recess some 2.50 meters [8 feet, 2-1/2 inches] square and stacked up higher than a man's height on three sides with two and sometimes three rows of rolled up manuscripts. . . . Most of the manuscripts were incomplete, having been shorn at the beginning or the end. . . . But the few dates that I read were all earlier than the eleventh century. . . . I had soon made up my mind. I was determined to examine the whole library, briefly at least, whatever efforts it might cost me. It was impossible to unroll to their full length the 15,000 to 20,000 rolls that were there; I could not have done that in six months. But I needed to open each roll, identify the nature of each text, and assess the chance that it might be a new text, unknown to us. Then I had to make two piles: one would be the cream of the collection, the rare texts that I had to have at any price; the other would have the texts that one would like to obtain, while accepting that it might not be possible to do so. Although I worked hard, this preliminary stage took me more than three weeks. I got through nearly 1,000 rolls a day, which must be a record. I was working at full speed, crouched in the recess, positioned like a race driver rather than a philologist. Later I went at a slower pace. . . . However I don't think I missed anything important. Every single roll and every scrap of paper—God knows there were many of those in tatters—went through my hands. I did not put aside anything that looked as if it belonged to the class of material I was looking for. . . . So, in spite of the manuscripts that had been given away as presents, in spite of the passage of our colleague Stein, I found

the great majority of bundles were still sewn in their casings, in other words, they were just as they had been when they were put in the grotto, more than eight centuries ago.[3]

Glory to the Trinity: The Dunhuang Gloria

Among the precious texts identified by Pelliot was a small roll of Christian origin, now in Paris at the Bibliothèque Nationale, which contains a hymn to the Holy Trinity, known as the Dunhuang Gloria. It is a Chinese translation of the *Gloria in excelsis Deo* as used in the liturgy of the Syrian Church of the East. A. C. Moule, whose translation from the Chinese is given here, considered that this manuscript is second in importance only to the Xi'an Stele itself. A radiant faith in the Trinity emanates from this prayer, filled as it is with Buddhist expressions. In spite of the difficulties of language, it expresses the essence of the *Gloria*.

The highest heavens with deep reverence adore,
The great earth earnestly ponders general peace and harmony,
Man's first nature receives confidence and rest,
Aloho, the merciful Father of the universe.

All the congregation of the good worship with complete sincerity,
All enlightened nature praise and sing,
All who have souls trust and look up to the utmost,
Receiving holy merciful light to save from the devil.

Hard to find, impossible to reach, upright, true, eternal,
Merciful Father, shining Son, Holy Spirit, King,
Among all rulers you are Master Ruler,
Among all saints (*bodhisattva*), you are Emperor of the Law (*dharma*).

You eternally dwell in mysterious light without shore or boundary,
Bright majesty thoroughly searches out the finite.
From the beginning no man has been able to see [you],
Nor may [you] be imagined by the eye of flesh.

---

[3] Letter from Paul Pelliot to Émile Sénart, March 26, 1908: published in Paul Pelliot, "Une bibliothèque médiévale retrouvée au Kan-sou", *Bulletin de l'École Française d'Extrême Orient* 8 (1908):505–29; quoted by Marie-Roberte Guignard in her preface to *Catalogue des Manuscrits Chinois de Touen-Houang (Fonds Pelliot Chinois)* (Paris: Bibliothèque Nationale, 1970), vol. 1; nos. 2,000–2,500, p. xi.

Alone completely perfect in clear holy virtue,
Alone divinely majestic in unmeasured strength,
Alone unchanging and grandly existing,
The root and source of all goodness and also without summit.

We now recite [your] mercy and kindness,
Sighing for your mysterious joy to enlighten our realm,
Honored Mi-shih-he most holy Son,
You who have crossed victoriously this world of suffering,
Save beings who are without help.
Glorious King who lives eternally,
Blessed lamb of mercy,
Who take upon yourself the pain of the world and do not refuse
    suffering,
Have pity on all the living; take away the burden of accumulated sins,
Restore nature in its purity, give rest.

Glorious Son seated at the right of the Father,
Your throne is elevated in the sublime heights; listen to our prayers.
Send down the raft that will save us from the stream of fire.
Lord, merciful Father,
Lord, our Master,
Lord, King of the Law,
Lord, universal deliverer,
All-powerful Lord, come and help those who are weary.
All eyes are turned toward you.
Send down the dew upon the parched earth,
Make those you refresh grow in the root of goodness.
Most holy, universally honored Mi-shih-he,
We adore you with the merciful Father, ocean-treasure of mercy,
And the most Holy Spirit, humble and pure,
Law clear and without shadow.[4]

Another Chinese text discovered by Pelliot in 1908 provides some
historical evidence for the expansion of the Syrian Church from
the seventh to the tenth centuries. *Zun jing*, which is on the same
manuscript roll as the Dunhuang Gloria, can be translated *Book of
Praises*; it is a kind of litany, commemorating holy persons and their

---

[4] A. C. Moule, *Christians in China before the Year 1550* (London: Society for Promoting
Christian Knowledge, 1930); reprinted by Ch'eng Wen Publishing Company, Taipei, 1972,
pp. 52–57.

writings.[5] A note added at the end of this text gives an idea of the spread of the Syrian Church into eastern Asia:

> The list of all the religious books of this Church of Daqin includes 530 works in all. They are all written in "sanskrit" on pages [of paper]. The priest Jingjing translated some thirty of these books into Chinese. Most of the sutras on patra leaves or on bound parchments have not yet been translated.

In fact, the thirty sutras in Chinese are not all Christian. Pelliot and his colleague in Paris, Édouard Chavannes (1865–1917), professor of Chinese language and literature at the Collège de France,[6] identified three of these books as Manichean. Most of the books brought from Persia and Syria had not been translated into Chinese. Although they are described as being written in "sanskrit", this turns out to be a generic term, covering Syriac, Persian, Turkic, Uighur, and a few other languages.

Dunhuang had been under Tibetan rule since about 780, which was fortunate for this type of religious literature, since all foreign religions were to be banned in China from the middle of the ninth century, and many religious texts were then destroyed. It is probable that the note at the end of *Zun jing* was written between 995, which is the

---

[5] *Catalogue des Manuscrits Chinois de Touen-Houang*. Fonds Pelliot Chinois de la Bibliothèque Nationale, vol. 4; nos. 3,501–4,000. Publications hors serie de l'École Française d'Extrême Orient; 1991, pp. 332–33. Catalogue no. 3,847, textes nestoriens: a. Éloge de la Ste. Trinite, ff. 2 and 3; b. Tsouen King, ff. 4 and 5.

[6] The Collège de France is the successor of the Collège des Trois Langues, founded by King Francis I of France in 1529, to circumvent the hold of late medieval scholasticism on the University of Paris by offering courses on biblical languages independently of the faculty of theology. In that respect (though not in its institutional structure) it paralleled the creation of Regius professorships at Oxford and Cambridge during the same period. The college was renamed Collège Royal de France as subsequent royal endowments augmented the number of professorial fellows (who constituted the entire membership of the college) by creating additional chairs, independent of the faculties of the university, as the need was perceived: surgery, Arabic, anatomy, botany, canon law, Syriac. After the revolutionary turmoil of the 1790s, the College was reestablished on different lines to enable chairs to be provided for outstanding personalities and scholars, but without creating permanent chairs in specific subjects. It now consists of fifty-two professorial chairs whose holders are appointed by the minister of education. They are chosen for their personal qualities, the title of each chair being personal to the holder, who determines the subject of the courses of lectures. The lectures do not lead to any qualifications; they are free and open to the public. The buildings of the college, in the Latin Quarter of Paris, go back to the seventeenth and eighteenth centuries and have been augmented by a large number of laboratories since the 1930s.

date of the latest manuscript found in the Dunhuang cache, and the early eleventh century, when it is thought that the manuscripts were brought together in the hidden chamber. "It is generally believed that the manuscripts in this cave were sealed up no later than the Xixia occupation of Dunhuang in 1035."[7] There is disagreement among historians as to why these texts were thus collected and hidden. One theory is that it was due to the threat of the invasion of Gansu and Ningxia by the Tangut people around 1030. Another possible cause is the creation of a Muslim kingdom in the area of the western Taklimakan about the same period; the iconoclastic tenets of the Koran would have posed a threat to richly illustrated Buddhist texts, as it had done to statues and wall paintings. It has also been maintained that the collection is a Geniza, i.e., a repository of texts no longer in use but too sacred to be destroyed. Whatever the reasons, we can be grateful that the Buddhist monks of Dunhuang gathered the contents of the libraries of their several monasteries to secrete them in the chamber at Mogao caves.

Another piece of evidence for a later Christian presence at Dunhuang was published in 1994.[8] It is a small fragment in Syriac with a few lines from St. Paul's Letter to the Galatians (7:7–10), probably from a lectionary for liturgical use. This first text in Syriac so far identified from Dunhuang was not from the library cache and is dated between 1250 and 1368. The editors consider that it is probably evidence of a Syrian parish or monastery at Dunhuang, but nothing else is known about it.

As for the small Christian communities in China, they seem to have been linked more and more to the nomadic communities of central Asia, whence they were to emerge with the Mongols in the thirteenth century.

Mazdeans and Manicheans

At the beginning of the seventh century, Chinese soldiers made incursions as far as Sogdia, a region south of Lake Balkhash, near Samarqand, which was then occupied by a Turkic population, which pro-

---

[7] *China Archaeology and Art Digest*, Hong Kong, 1 (1996), p. 146.

[8] Wassilios Klein and Jurgen Tubach, "Ein syrisch-christliches Fragment aus Dunhuang/China", *Z.D.M.G.* 144 (1994):1–13.

vided the Chinese with the renowned Ferghana horses in exchange
for silk. Their religion was strongly influenced by Mazdeism (Zoroastrianism).

Manicheans from Persia had also settled in Sogdia; their founder,
Mani, a Persian noble who lived in Mesopotamia in the third century,
preached a religion combining Christian, Buddhist, and Mazdean elements. Mani was rejected both by Christians and by the Persian
authorities and died a martyr for his beliefs. His religion spread
eastward, and there are at least two Manichean manuscripts from
Dunhuang. Empress Wu Zetian supported Manicheanism and authorized its cult in 694. Manichean priests, who were expert in astrology
and astronomy, introduced the seven-day week in China, associating it
with the seven planets. In the ninth century, however, Manicheans, as
well as other foreign religions, were banned in China; they could only
survive as secret societies, opposed to the government. Manichean influence was still felt in the fourteenth century in China and influenced
the ideology of the new dynasty, the Ming (which reigned from 1368–
1644), whose name means "light".[9]

The Golden Age of Buddhism in China

To the east of the Pamir Mountains, in the present-day Xinjiang-
Uighur Autonomous Region, there are Buddhist sanctuaries at regular intervals along the northern and the southern routes skirting
the Taklimakan Desert. In the first century, monks came from northern India and established flourishing communities there. Some of the
treasures of Buddhist art from this region have reached the West,
often in a sorry state after having suffered repeated damage over the
centuries. Thus the statues of Buddha in the caves of Bezeklik, near
Turpan, have had their eyes pierced or their heads cut off by Muslims, who would not tolerate human representations of the godhead.
Later the wall paintings, which Albert von Le Coq had cut from the
rock and deposited at the Ethnological Museum in Berlin, were destroyed by Allied bombing during the Second World War. However,
near Dunhuang one can still see wall paintings, wonderful for their

---

[9] For Manichaeism see S. N. C. Lieu, *Manichaeism in Central Asia and China* (Leiden:
Brill, 1998), Nag Hammadi and Manichaean Studies 45.

color and delicacy, which cover 480,000 square feet (45,000 square meters) in the 492 caves of the cliffs of Mogao.

In A.D. 629 a Chinese pilgrim, Xuanzang (596–664), had left the capital, Xi'an (Chang'an), six years before the Christian Alopen reached it. Xuanzang traveled westward, along the extensive routes of central Asia, and reached Kashmir and the holy places in north India where the Buddha had lived. There he learned Sanskrit and, after having been away for sixteen years, returned to Xi'an in 645, bringing into China a precious collection of Buddhist scriptures. He then oversaw the translation of these texts. The great Pagoda of the Wild Goose, which is still to be seen in Xi'an, was built in 652 by order of the Gaozong emperor (649–683) to house the *sutras* that Xuanzang had brought back. The odyssey of this monk is well known in the Chinese world and is celebrated in the long sixteenth-century novel attributed to Wu Cheng'en, *Xiyou ji, Pilgrimage to the West*, also known as *The Monkey Pilgrim* from its chief character. Jacques Gernet says that Xuanzang "directed until his death the most prolific translating teams in the whole history of Chinese Buddhism".[10] In the course of these last eighteen years of his life, he and his teams were responsible for about a quarter of all the translations of Indian Buddhist texts into Chinese. (They translated 1,338 chapters out of the total of the 5,084 chapters that were translated by 185 teams of translators over six centuries.) The few texts of the Syrian Church of the East that have been translated into Chinese are like a drop in the ocean compared to the number of the Buddhist *sutras*.

Buddhist scriptures were carefully preserved in all the libraries that are situated at the back of rock temples; in addition, Buddhists literally dug themselves into China by carving out of cliffs thousands of grottoes, filled with statues and covered with paintings. From the fifth to the eighth centuries, majestic statues of the Buddha in his various manifestations were carved into cliff faces, and also *bodhisattvas*, watching over the salvation of suffering humanity before retiring to the perfect repose of nirvana. These statues, many of them gigantic, were originally made in the darkness of vast caves; today they often appear in the light of day as the result of earthquakes and rock falls. The best known groups of sculptures are on the edge of the steppes,

---

[10] Jacques Gernet, *A History of Chinese Civilization* (Cambridge, U.K.: Cambridge University Press, 2nd ed., 1996), p. 279. Original ed. *Le Monde Chinois* (Paris: Armand Colin, 1972).

just as the romanesque churches of Europe line the pilgrim ways to St. James of Compostella. The caves of Yungang near Datong in northern Shanxi Province were carved from 489 onward. The caves of Longmen are near Luoyang in Henan Province; most of them were carved during the Tang Dynasty. Empress Wu Zetian enriched them with prestigious statuary; there are more than 1,300 caves at Longmen, containing over 2,100 grottoes and about 100,000 sculptures. There are also Buddhist caves at Maiji Shan, near Tianshui (Gansu Province). Buddhist cave art derives from architectural traditions first developed on the confines of India and Persia, which were later taken up on the main stages of the Silk Road.

The Expansion of Islam

The flourishing of Buddhism and of the small dependent Syrian Christian community in China was made possible to a large extent by Chinese control of the routes to the West. However, in the middle of the eighth century, Arab cavalry appeared on the western limits of the Tang Empire. The Arabs, having destroyed the Sasanian Dynasty and occupied Persia by 652, had reached Kashgar at the beginning of the eighth century. Chinese forces attacked them in 751 south of Lake Balkhash, on the Talas River, in modern Kazakhstan, but were disastrously defeated. This meant that the Chinese lost control of the Silk Road in the western Tarim Basin area, around the city of Kashgar, which became, and has remained, an Islamic city. However, the battle of Talas did mark the end of Arab expansion eastward.

Arabs were not unknown at the court of Xi'an (Chang'an), where they were called *Dashi*. In 651 an embassy from the third caliph, Uthman (644–656), had arrived there, but the Muslim envoys refused to kowtow to the emperor. This deep prostration was performed by kneeling on the ground and touching it three times with the forehead. In Chinese society it was an expression of respect; government ministers kowtowed to the emperor; commoners kowtowed to government officials; children kowtowed before their parents; members of a family kowtowed to their ancestors. However, the Arabs were not attracted by this practice and flatly refused to observe it, so that, after much discussion, they were granted an exemption to the rule by reason of "the different custom" of their barbarous country.

At that time, the power of the Chinese Empire was also being challenged in its heartland by the rebellion of a military leader, An Lushan. This general, who had a Sogdian father and a Turkish mother, was in command of three military regions in north China. In 756 he repudiated the authority of the emperor and occupied Luoyang and Xi'an. The Tang emperor, Xuanzong, fled to Chengdu and, in order to regain power, appealed for help from Tibetans and Uighurs, who made themselves masters of northwest China as a result. The emperor also obtained help from Muslim troops, many of whom subsequently settled in the country and married Chinese wives. They remained faithful to the worship of the one God, while adopting the exterior forms of Chinese life. Since they did not proselytize openly, they were on the whole left alone and increased in numbers. Not only did they have many children, but they also bought children from poor Chinese families. This was at a time when Islamic civilization was respected abroad because of the prestige of the Abbasid Dynasty in Baghdad. Islam thus assumed the role that the Sasanian Empire of Persia had enjoyed before the Arab conquest. It became the intermediary between China and the West, which had the unfortunate effect of cutting off Chinese Buddhism and Christianity from their countries of origin.

The Banning of Foreign Religions

From the ninth century onward, Buddhism and Christianity were in fact under increasing pressure in China. Estates owned by Buddhists were growing in number, whereas the revenues of the imperial treasury were decreasing. Wealthy merchants from abroad settled in the cities of the interior, but the local population began to resent their presence. At the same time the highly trained civil service attributed the failure of government to the abandonment of authentic traditions and began to adopt a xenophobic attitude as a result.

The civil service of the Chinese Empire constituted one of its most remarkable institutions. Its members were called *shenshi*, literally, "scholars wearing belts with hanging ends". The Portuguese gave them the name Mandarin, from *mandar*, to govern. In Western texts they are referred to as *literati* or gentry. The term "scholar-gentry" is preferable because it was not a class entered by birth, in the European sense of "gentry" or *petite noblesse*. Entry into this elite corps, with its enormous influence, was by means of examinations, requiring years of study. The path to success was available to those who passed the examinations, whatever their family, birth, or religion. Candidates were recruited by quota from every province, and a series of examinations determined the status of candidates. Some failed; some were confined to lower grades, while others proceeded to higher ones, the highest rank of all being allocated to those whose examinations were presided over by the emperor in person.

The matters examined were literary and philosophical, and they required a thorough knowledge of the Confucian classics. Style counted for a great deal, and so did literary skill, calligraphy, and poetical expression. Only a relatively small percentage were taken into the imperial administration on the results, but all successful candidates became members of the local scholar-gentry, with legal and financial privileges that guaranteed their maintenance and their influence in society. They wore special uniforms and could decorate the saddles and reins of their horses with fur, brocade, and embroidery; no commoner, however wealthy, could lay claim to such splendor. They had a role to play through their influence in a wide range of local concerns. Only scholar-gentry could attend official ceremonies in Confucian temples. They functioned as local arbiters, preferring to resolve local disputes by settlement out of court. In times of war, they would raise a local militia. The raising of funds to repair city walls, canals, and bridges was their responsibility, as well as the defense in a general way of the cultural heritage of the country. The formal imperial magistrates, who usually came from a different province, worked closely with the local scholar-gentry. Although the latter were not part of the administration, the magistrates needed them to act as intermediaries with the local population. Since the scholar-gentry shared the same highly prized education, they were the social equals of imperial civil servants and had access to them. The magistrates represented the formal power of the state, and the scholar-gentry, through their local influence, supported that power and facilitated its exercise for the good of society.

The Chinese examination system for the recruitment of the imperial civil service and the creation of a scholar-gentry class had been put in place under the Han Dynasty (206 B.C. to A.D. 220) and lasted until almost the end of the Qing Dynasty (1644–1912), the examinations for the imperial bureaucracy being abolished in 1905. Compared with the attempts of royal governments in Europe to rule through hereditary aristocracies, the Chinese system was remarkably enlightened and long lasting.[11]

It is clear that once the imperial administration and the scholar-gentry turned, toward the end of the Tang Dynasty, against foreigners and foreign religions, these could not long survive in China. The movement against foreigners that began in 826 rapidly spread and led to the imperial decree of 845 that banned foreign religions:

> The fifth year of the Huichang era, Emperor Tang Wuzong published the following decree:
>
> Under our three illustrious dynasties, *Fo* was never heard of. Since the Han and Wei Dynasties, this sect, which introduced statues, began to spread in China. Since then these foreign customs have gradually spread in the country, without being sufficiently noticed. They are increasing every day. The people are unfortunately influenced by them, and the state suffers. In the two courts, in all the cities, in the mountains, one sees only bonzes, male or female. The number of monasteries and their splendor increase every day. Many workmen are occupied in making statues of varied materials. Much gold is used in decorating them. There are many who forget their prince and their parents and turn to a monk as their master. There are even rogues who abandon their wife and children and seek refuge among the monks so as to avoid the law. Could anything be more pernicious? Our ancestors had a saying that if there was a man who was not ploughing, or a woman who was not working at silk making, someone in the state was suffering from hunger or cold as a result. What can the effect be today of the infinite number of bonzes, men and women, who live and are clothed by the sweat of others and who keep an infinite number of workmen busy, building on every side and decorating splendid buildings at great expense? Does one need to look elsewhere for the cause of the empire's exhaustion under

---

[11] I. C. Y. Hsü assesses the advantages of the Chinese scholar-gentry system as follows: "the system selected men of superior intelligence and common sense for public service. It set up objective and impartial standards for social advancement and reduced the chances for nepotism and other forms of favoritism. It made the society more egalitarian by permitting nearly all its members to rise to the top through individual merit rather than through birth and wealth. It encouraged social flexibility and tended to blur class distinctions. The convergence in government of educated men from all walks of life and all parts of the country created a force of unity. The intellectuals of the country formed an educated bureaucracy that assisted the government rather than criticized it, as opposed to intellectual habits in the West. Put on the scales, the advantages of the examination system probably outweighed the disadvantages." *The Rise of Modern China* (Oxford and New York: Oxford University Press, 2000), 6th ed., p. 79.

the four dynasties Jin, Song, Qi, Liang [265–556] and for the dishonesty that then prevailed?

As for our Tang dynasty, the princes who founded it, having had successful recourse to the force of arms so as to restore its former tranquility to the state, made it their concern to regulate it by wise laws. Far from deriving anything from this vile foreign sect to achieve this, from the beginning of the Zhenguan era, Taizong declared himself opposed to it; but he proceeded too gently, and the ill only increased. As for me, having read and weighed everything that was submitted to me on this question, and after mature deliberation with wise counselors, I have made up my mind. Since something is wrong, it must be put right. All my enlightened and zealous officials in the provinces are pressing me to put this matter in hand. They consider that it would stop at the source the errors that are flooding the empire. It is the way to reestablish the government of our ancestors; it is for the common good; it is the life of the people. How could I ignore such a situation?

I therefore command as follows: firstly, that the more than 4,600 large monasteries that are spread throughout the whole empire shall be completely destroyed. In consequence the men and women who lived in these monasteries and whose number has been counted as twenty-six wan (260,000) shall return to the world and pay their contribution in taxes. Secondly, that the more than four wan (40,000) of lesser monasteries that are spread throughout the countryside shall also be destroyed. Consequently, all the land that was attached to them, amounting to some 1,000 wan of qing,[12] shall be annexed to our domain, and some fifteen wan (150,000) of slaves that belonged to the monks shall be entered onto the rolls of the magistrates and be counted as part of the population.

As for the foreign monks who came here so as to make known the law that obtains in their kingdoms, they number about 3,000, both from *Daqin* (Syria) and *Muhuba* (Persia). I order that they too return to the world, so that there may be no diversity in the customs of the empire. Alas, there has been too long a delay in restoring things to their former state; why delay longer? The matter has been decided and is now closed. In view of the present decree, let its execution proceed. Such is our good pleasure.[13]

This text reveals the extent to which Buddhism had put down roots in China, in contrast with the monks from *Daqin* (Syria) and *Muhuba*

---

[12] 1,000 wan of qing equals 10 million qing. Since the qing measures 100 mu, or 15.13 acres, this would be the equivalent of 236,000 square miles (612,000 square kilometers).

[13] Henri Havret, *Variétés sinologiques*, no. 12, "La stèle chrétienne de Si-Ngan Fou", 2e partie. Histoire du monument (Shanghai, 1897), pp. 250–52.

(Persia), who are considered as foreigners. The text only mentions 3,000 monks of the Syrian Church of the East, compared with 260,000 Buddhist monks and nuns. The decree orders that they should all be secularized.

The first Christians in China thus shared the great trials that Buddhists underwent. They had been accepted in China under the same conditions as the Buddhists, and they were close to Buddhism by their religious language and by their monastic form of life. They were now cut off from the Churches they had come from, and, since they had made few converts among the Chinese population, they disappeared almost entirely for the next three hundred years. However, Christians, scattered among the tribes of the north, the northeast and the northwest, were to find their way into China again at the time of the Mongol invasions.

[The introductory paragraphs to this chapter and the section "Shrines and a Library" are additions to the French text.

In the section "The Banning of Foreign Religions", the three paragraphs on the civil service of the Chinese Empire are an addition to the French text.—TRANS.]

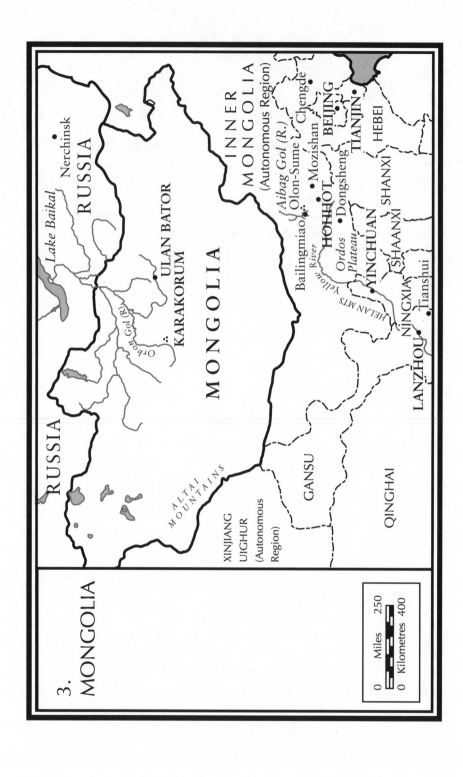

3. MONGOLIA

4

THE CROSS AMONG THE MONGOLS

Marco Polo is famous as the European whose description of China was the first account to become well known in the West. He spent some twenty years in Asia in the thirteenth century, and his *Description of the World* was written down once he had returned to Europe.[1] In it he relates a story that he had heard about a Mongol prince, Nayan, descended from the brother of Genghis Khan, who had rebelled in 1287 against his cousin Kublai Khan, the ruler of China. There was a battle between the armies of the two princes, at the end of which Nayan's army was defeated and Nayan was executed.

> You must know that Nayan was a baptized Christian, and in this battle he had the Cross of Christ on his standard. . . . After the Great Khan had won this victory, the various races of men who were there—Saracens, idolaters and Jews, and many others who do not believe in God—made mock of the Cross that Nayan had borne on his banner. They jeered at the Christians who were there: "See how the Cross of your God has helped Nayan, who was a Christian!" So unrestrained was their mockery and their jeering that it came to the ears of the great khan. Thereupon

---

[1] The literary composition of *The Description of the World* presents many problems; see Peter Jackson, "Marco Polo and His Travels", *B.S.O.A.S.* 61 (1998):82–101. Some 120 manuscripts survive, and, since many of them contain material that is not found in the others, five groups of manuscripts can be discerned. The literary genre of the collection is not the record of the travels of one man, but a description of the world from different sources. The origin of many of the descriptions and events is often unclear, and some of the events narrated have been shown to be incompatible with the known chronology of Marco Polo. He was in the service of Great Khan Kublai, emperor of China, for part of his time in East Asia, but seems not to have known Chinese, since the names that he gives to places and things are almost entirely Persian or Turkish. This has led Dr. Frances Wood to surmise that perhaps Marco never went to China at all but relied on the accounts of others; see Frances Wood, *Did Marco Polo Go to China?* (London: Secker and Warburg, 1995) and *The Silk Road* (London: Folio Society, 2002), pp. 121–24. Scholars on the whole have not accepted Dr. Wood's thesis and have pointed out that Marco Polo's use of Persian is to be expected since it was the lingua franca throughout the Mongol Empire, including China. See D. O. Morgan, "Marco Polo in China—or Not", *J.R.A.S.* 6 (1996), pp. 221–25; Igor de Rachelwiltz, "Marco Polo Went to China", *Zentralasiatische Studien* 27 (1997):34–92.

he rebuked those who mocked at the Cross in his presence. Then he summoned many Christians who were there and began to comfort them. "If the Cross of your God has not helped Nayan," he said, "it was for a very good reason. Because it is good, it ought not to lend its aid except in a good and righteous cause. Nayan was a traitor who broke faith with his liege lord. Hence the fate that has befallen him was a vindication of the right." The Christians answered: "Most mighty lord, what you say is quite true. The Cross would not lend itself to wrong-doing and disloyalty like that of Nayan, who was a traitor to his liege lord. He has received what he well deserved.[2]

This incident illustrates many characteristics of the period when the Mongols dominated China and large parts of Asia. Christians, Jews, and Muslims, as well as other believers and nonbelievers, were present in the entourage of the Mongol chieftains; the Cross had prestige as the emblem of the Christians and could be used in a quasi-magical way on occasion. The religious policy of the great khan was a kind of pragmatic pluralism, which made use of all religions as positive elements for the well-being of his empire. As a result, the period of Mongol rulers provided an opportunity for Christian missionaries, who were able freely to make the Gospel known in their dominions for some 150 years.

The Mongol War Machine

The great khan mentioned in Marco Polo's account was Kublai Khan. He was the grandson of Genghis Khan, a Mongol chieftain whose original name was Temujin (c. 1167–1227). Temujin had united the tribes of the Mongolian steppes, a vast area equivalent to modern Outer Mongolia and the Inner Mongolian Autonomous Region. The steppe, between impenetrable forests to the north and deserts to the south, stretches far to the west, beyond Mongolia into Europe. It is a predominantly treeless region of rough grassland, which for the

---

[2] R. E. Latham (trans.), *The Travels of Marco Polo* (London: Penguin Books, 1958), pp. 117, 118. For Nayan's 1287 campaign against Kublai Khan, which was supported by the Jurchens, see Morris Rossabi, *The Jurchens in the Yuan and the Ming* (Ithaca, N.Y.: Cornell University China-Japan Project, 1982), p. 8. Rossabi sees the aim of the khan's opponents as the preservation of a nomadic lifestyle, whereas Kublai Khan was creating a sedentary and increasingly sinicized society.

most part cannot sustain agriculture but is suitable for the pasturing of flocks and herds. For many centuries, intertribal warfare had been a characteristic of the nomadic clans that inhabited the Mongolian steppe. Temujin's genius outwitted his rivals, crushed his enemies, and incorporated their population into a single group, united by fealty to him. Temujin was proclaimed khan of the Mongols at the *quriltai* (i.e., assembly of notables) of 1206. His achievement was proclaimed as uniting all the "dwellers in felt tents", and he was raised up on the felt carpet in the ceremony which inaugurated his rule. It was probably then that he took the name Genghis Khan, the Mongolian word *chinggis* meaning firm or strong.

The main "raw material" produced by Mongolia was the horse, and Genghis Khan organized the Mongol cavalry into an instrument of war that changed the history of the sedentary peoples of Asia, the Middle East, and eastern Europe during the following centuries. In Mongol society, the army was coterminous with the tribe; "the Mongol army was a cavalry force, and the training that was needed for leading the nomadic life of the steppe was not very different from that required by the Mongols' kind of cavalry warfare. The conversion from peaceful nomad activity to warlike preparedness could be speedy and total."[3] All Mongols learned to ride when they were three or four years old, girls as well as boys. Every tribesman between sixteen and sixty was a warrior. Genghis Khan divided his troops into decimal units, the major fighting force being the *tuman* of 10,000 horsemen, subdivided into smaller multiples of ten. It was an army composed mainly of cavalry, archers, swordsmen, and lancers mounted on rapid ponies. The horses were trained so that, when they were at a gallop, the riders could shoot a bow in any direction. The power of their heavy bows was such that they could kill at 600 feet (183 meters). Mongol soldiers traveled with a string of horses, riding them in turn or providing mounts for foot soldiers, so that Mongol cavalry might have had as many as three, four, or five horses per man, allowing it to operate over a distance of 100 miles (160 kilometers) a day.

Genghis Khan imposed strict discipline on his troops, so that his armies proved to be a force of extraordinary rapidity, maneuverability, and cohesion, able to defeat any army that could be put in the field at

---

[3] David O. Morgan, "Aspects of Mongol Rule in Persia" (unpublished doctoral dissertation, School of Oriental and African Studies, University of London, 1977), p. 133.

the time. The other element of his success was terror. He proclaimed the right of the Mongols to universal overlordship, so that any resistance was considered as rebellion, meriting the extermination of a city's entire population. In extenuation David Morgan writes, "Unlike many other Asiatic conquerors, the Mongols did not generally indulge in wanton cruelty as such. Countless thousands of innocent people were killed, but normally this was done as quickly and efficiently as possible, without the use of torture."[4] Once the knowledge of the quick and efficient Mongol way spread, it proved a powerful deterrent against resistance.

Genghis Khan's war machine was so successful that, when he died in 1227, Mongol armies had ranged from the Pacific Ocean to the Adriatic Sea and had conquered the north of China, central Asia, Persia, and eastern Europe, as well as establishing their suzerainty over Korea. It has been argued by David Morgan that it was the very effectiveness of the Mongol army machine that propelled it into ever-widening circles of conquest:

> The tribes of the Mongolian steppelands, not for the first time, had a supreme ruler. . . . But unless something decisive was done with the newly formed military machine, it would soon dissolve into quarreling factions again, and Mongolia would revert to its earlier state. This, to my mind, is at least one explanation for the beginnings of the Mongols' astonishing career of conquest. A superb army, potentially invincible in the field in thirteenth-century conditions, had been successfully created. But if it was not used against external enemies, it would not remain in being for long.[5]

A Christian Presence among the Nomads

Before the Mongols invaded China, they first imposed their power on the areas of Chinese influence among the nomads to the north and northwest of China itself, an area known as "the Sinicized Empire". Among the tribes that Genghis Khan thus subjected to his rule, some were partly Christian: the Keraits, Önguts, Uighurs, Merkits, and Naimans. Missionaries of the Syrian Church of the East had been

---

[4] David Morgan, *The Mongols* (Oxford: Blackwell, 1990), p. 93.

[5] Ibid., p. 63.

at work among these tribes, though unfortunately we do not, in most cases, know the time or circumstances of their coming.

The Keraits were a Turkic group and lived on the Orhon River, near Lake Baikal. Many of them were Christians,[6] and this was to have potentially important results, since Genghis Khan's youngest son, Tolui, married a Christian Kerait princess; Sorqaqtani was his chief wife, who was to become very influential, the mother of Hulagu and Kublai. The Uighurs lived where seven million of them live today in the Xinjiang-Uighur Autonomous Region; they speak a Turkic language belonging to the Altaic family of languages. Their writing was derived from the Syriac script and became the basis for the Mongol alphabet when, in 1204, Genghis Khan decided that it was time that the Mongols learned to read and commissioned a Uighur captive, Tatatunga, to adapt Uighuric script to the Mongolian language.[7] The Uighurs were more civilized than most of the fierce tribes of the steppes, and they provided the Mongols with many scribes, doctors, and civil servants. There is no record of Christian missionaries among the Uighurs, but in the twelfth century the largest religious group among them was composed of Syrian Christians, followed in numbers by Buddhists. Today the Uighurs are mostly Sunni Muslims.

The Khitai, who were called *Liao* by the Chinese, had occupied the areas of the steppes in the tenth century. They levied an annual tribute of silver and silk on the Chinese Song Dynasty, which had established itself at Kaifeng, Henan Province, in 960. In the twelfth century, however, the power of the Khitai was shaken by attacks from Jurchens, coming from the northeast. Some of the Khitai leaders took refuge in Xinjiang and set up the kingdom of the Black Khitai (*Karakhitan*) in the valley of the Ili River, between Ürümqi and Samarqand. The Khitai were steeped in Chinese civilization and played an active part in

---

[6] The Syriac writer Bar Hebraeus (1226–1286) attributes the conversion of 200,000 Keraits in 1007 to a mission sent by the metropolitan of Merv, in present-day Turkmenistan. Dr. Erica Hunter has shown that the ethnic term Kerait is probably interpolated in the narrative and comments, "The integral role that Bar Hebraeus allocates to the metropolitan of Merv suggests that the conversion took place in Transoxania, probably among the Öghuz, rather than in the distant realms of the Kerait in Mongolia, where the incumbent at Kashgar might have been more conveniently located to perform such duties." Erica C. D. Hunter, "The Church of the East in Central Asia", *Bulletin of the John Rylands University Library of Manchester* 78 (1996):139.

[7] Bold Bat-Ochir, *Mongolian Nomadic Society: A Reconstruction of the "Medieval" History of Mongolia* (New York: St. Martin's Press, 2001), p. 9.

commercial exchanges; the Mongols considered them as Chinese, as did the Persians. In fact, the Persians called China *Kitai* from the name Khitai, and this was the origin of Marco Polo's name for China— *Cathay*. Buddhists and Syrian Christians lived side by side in the kingdom of Karakhitan, which corresponds roughly to a large part of Chinese Xinjiang and modern Uzbekistan. A bishop of the Syrian Church of the East was archbishop of Samarqand and metropolitan[8] under the authority of the catholicos patriarch of Seleucia-Ctesiphon, who from the eighth century lived in Baghdad. Although not all Karakhitai became Syrian Christians, a good many of them did.

In north China and covering the area from Gansu Province to the north of Shaanxi Province, another political entity had been created in the eleventh century by the Tangut, a people of stock rearers who had become rich through their control of a stretch of the Silk Road. They had founded an empire to which they gave the name of the most ancient Chinese dynasty, the Xia. Their capital, Yinchuan, was built in the well-watered plain between the Yellow River and the Helan mountain range, which shelters it from desert winds, atrocious carriers of sand. Today the ruins of the Tangut imperial palace cover twenty-five acres (ten hectares). Mausoleums, shaped like pagodas nine stories high, and seventy tombs, now badly eroded, are scattered over an area of fifteen square miles (forty square kilometers). This is all that remains of a once prosperous civilization, because the Mongols descended on Xixia (western Xia) in 1209 as a kind of "practice run" for invading China itself in 1211. The army of Genghis Khan later came back to obliterate the Tanguts and to execute their ruler in 1227. The memory of their destruction is preserved to this day by the name given to the region, Ningxia, which means "the repose of Xia". The Tangut language was Tibeto-Burmese and they had invented their own writing, using Chinese characters. The texts that survive indicate that their beliefs were Buddhist and Taoist.

Christians were also to be found in the region of the Ordos Plateau,

---

[8] Pelliot considers that Samarqand was probably a metropolitan see from the fifth or sixth century, Oeuvres Posthumes de Paul Pelliot, *Recherches sur les Chrétiens d'Asie Centrale et d'Extrême Orient* (Paris: Imprimerie Nationale, 1973), p. 6; but J. M. Fiey, *Pour un Oriens Christianus Novus: Répertoire des Diocèses Syriaques Orientaux et Occidentaux* (Beirut: Franz Steiner Verlag Stuttgart, 1993), Beiruter Texte 49, p. 128, considers that it is not known when various Turkish tribes, whose conversion is reported in the eighth and eleventh centuries, first had bishops. The existence of a see at Qand is attested about 900.

an area of sparse grassland that lies north of Ningxia and in the great bend of the Yellow River, in present-day Inner Mongolia. The Ordos region is known to have been the homeland of the Christian Öngut tribe, although, once again, it is not known when it converted to Christianity. This tribe is described as being of Turco-Mongol origin, and its members often bore the names of Christian apostles or patriarchs. Since the beginning of the twentieth century, several hundred small crosslike bronze objects have been found in this area. Their quantity supports the idea that they are tokens of popular devotion, and a Christian origin is implied by their resemblance to the "Maltese cross", which is also found on other east Syrian objects.[9] Fr. Antoon Mostaert (1881–1971), a Belgian missionary who worked in the area inhabited by the Mongols of today, described how these crosses were found: "The Mongols constantly dig them up, from old graves and elsewhere: they know nothing of their history, but wear them on their girdles, especially the women, and use them with a lump of mud to seal up their doors."[10] Several of these little crosses are engraved with cross motifs and bird motifs. Some have at the center the fylfot or swastika, the symbol of streaming light customarily found on statues of the Buddha, which is an emblem of good fortune in popular Buddhism.

To the east of the Khitai, a third empire had emerged in the eleventh century. They were the Jurchen, ancestors of the Manchu; they spoke a Tungusic language. The Jurchen established their Dynasty, the Jin (1115–1234), and cooperated with the Song Dynasty in expelling the Khitai from the northeast of China, as mentioned earlier. The Jurchen then turned against their Chinese allies and captured their capital, Kaifeng, in 1126. The Song emperors were forced to move their capital southward to the sea, at Hangzhou in Zhejiang Province, the starting point of the great canal that controlled the internal trade of China all the way to Beijing. However, it was not long before the Jurchen themselves began to feel the onslaught of the Mongol cavalry. In 1213 the Mongols crossed the Great Wall, and two years later they captured Beijing, in spite of fierce resistance, by

---

[9] Standaert, pp. 52–53.

[10] Quoted by P. Y. Saeki, *The Nestorian Documents and Relics in China* (Tokyo: Maruzen, 1937), p. 423 from an article by Fr. Mostaert. For his biography, see *Monumenta Serica*, 1945. Fr. Antoon Mostaert, a member of the Congregation of the Immaculate Heart of Mary (the Scheut Fathers), worked in the region of the Ordos from 1906 to 1926.

tunneling under the walls of the city. During the following decades, under the leadership of Genghis Khan, the Mongols succeeded in controlling the whole of northern China. In 1235 his son Ogodei (d. 1241) established the Mongol capital at Karakorum on the Orhon River, 200 miles (320 kilometers) west of Ulan Bator. Genghis Khan's grandson, Kublai Khan (1214–1294), conquered southern China and in 1267 brought his winter capital to Beijing, which he called by the Turkish name Khanbalik (the town of the khan).

The Mongols in China were faced with the problem of ruling vast agricultural territories with only limited knowledge of administration. They therefore turned to intermediaries who had experience of the country and knew how to extract profit from its trade network; these were mainly former Khitai or Jurchen, both Muslims and Christians. Toward the end of the thirteenth century, the story of Marco Polo shows that a European could be in the employ of the khans. It also mentions other Europeans who had settled in China. In fact, the Mongols gave preference to non-Chinese personnel in their administration, so as not to become completely dependent on a Chinese bureaucracy. However, they also took over many Chinese institutions, and in 1271 they adopted the dynastic title the Yuan. Khanbalik became known to the Chinese as *Dadu* (great capital).

There are also a few archeological indications of the presence of Syrian Christians in the Beijing region before the arrival of the Mongols. At Fangshan, thirty miles (fifty kilometers) southwest of Beijing, Sir Reginald Johnston[11] discovered in 1919 two blocks of marble on which Syrian-type crosses had been carved. These crosses emerge from a lotus flower, and one of them is surrounded by clouds and a Syriac inscription in the angles of the cross that reads: "Look upon it and hope in it."[12] An inscription on stone dated 960, i.e., at the time of Khitai (*Liao*) domination, commemorates the rebuilding of a temple in 952. The incised text indicates that the blocks of marble with the crosses were in the former temple, called *Chong sheng si: Temple of the cult of the Saint*. The name is the same as the temple

---

[11] Sir Reginald Johnston (1874–1938) had been the tutor of Puyi, the last emperor of China.

[12] Arthur C. Moule, *Christians in China before the Year 1550* (London, S.P.C.K., 1930), p. 88.

in Xi'an where the Christian stele was kept for a long time, but this may be coincidence.

It was in the same region that a young man called Sauma came to find shelter in a cave and to live the life of a hermit. He was a fervent Syrian Christian who was destined to take part in an adventure that gives him a special place in the history of Christians in Asia.

Two Pilgrims from China

Sauma's story is known thanks to a Syriac text, written by a contemporary.[13] He was born around 1225, the son of Christian Uighurs who lived at Beijing, and was given the name *Sauma*, which means "fasting" in Syriac. The full name would have been Bar Sauma, "son of the fast", implying that he was born in Lent or else that he had been given the name of a relative who was a "Lenten child". His parents had destined him to become a married priest, but at twenty he decided that he wanted to become a monk. For three years he begged his parents to let him try his vocation, and when they eventually let him go, he donned the robe of a monk and was tonsured by Mar George, metropolitan of Khanbalik.[14] Since the time of Catholicos Timothy I (780–823), China had been considered by the Syrian Church of the East as an ecclesiastical province.

Sauma now became known as Rabban Sauma, *Rabban*, "our master", being the title given to monks of the Syrian Church. For seven years, Rabban Sauma followed the eremitical life, fasting and doing penance, after which a young man called Mark came to join him and to share his life of solitude. He was twenty years younger than Sauma, an Öngut born in 1245, the son of an east Syrian archdeacon from

---

[13] It was first edited by Fr. Paul Bedjan in 1888. Sir Ernest Budge's English translation is from the second, complete, edition: *Histoire de Mar-Jab Alaha Patriarch* [sic] *et de Raban Sauma* (Paris and Leipzig, 1895). See Standaert, p. 52. This important text has been reedited with a translation into Italian and copious notes by Pier Giorgio Borbone, *Storia di Mar Yahballaha e di Rabban Sauma* (Turin: Silvio Zamorani, 2000). For a very readable account in English see Morris Rossabi, *Voyager from Xanadu* (Tokyo and New York: Kodansha, 1992).

[14] See Borbone, *Storia di Mar Yahballaha e di Rabban Sauma*, p. 57, n. 3, for the identification of Mar Giorgio as metropolitan of Khanbalik and of north China. Mar, the Aramaic word for "lord", is the title given to bishops of the Syrian Church of the East.

Koshang in Inner Mongolia, the capital of the Önguts, known by them as Olon-Sume (see chapter 5, note 15).

> One day they meditated saying, "It would be exceedingly helpful to us if we were to leave this region and set out for the West, for we could then [visit] the tombs of the holy martyrs and Catholic Fathers and be blessed [by them]. And if Christ, the Lord of the Universe, prolonged our lives and sustained us by his grace, we could go to Jerusalem, so that we might receive complete pardon for our offenses, and absolution for our sins of foolishness."[15]

It was especially young Mark's idea. Sauma tried to talk him out of it to begin with, then yielded to his pleading. They both went into town to prepare their venture and to find some companions for the journey. Many objections were made to their plan but nothing could make them change it. They set out and made a first stop at Koshang (Olon-Sume), the capital of the Önguts, Mark's birthplace in Inner Mongolia. The governors of the city, who were sons-in-law of two great khans, gave them a warm welcome but tried to persuade them to stay.

> "Why are you leaving this country of ours and going to the West? For we have taken very great trouble to draw hither monks and fathers from the West. How can we allow you to go away?" Rabban Sauma said to them, "We have cast away the world. And as long as we live in the society of men there will be no peace for us. Therefore it is right that we should flee because of the love of Christ, who gave himself unto death for our redemption. . . . Although your love moves us not to depart . . . we earnestly desire the separation, but wherever we shall be we shall always remember, according to our feebleness, both by night and day, your kingdom in [our] prayers." And when the lords of the city saw that their words had no effect upon them and that they would not yield to their persuasion, they selected for them gifts, namely, beasts on which to ride and gold, and silver, and wearing apparel.[16]

The two monks said that they did not know what to do with all these gifts, but the governors, who were aware of the difficulties of the road, said to them:

---

[15] This and the following quotations are from the translations from the Syriac in Ernest Budge, *The Monks of Kublai Khan Emperor of China or The History and the Life and Travels of Rabban Sawma, Envoy and Plenipotentiary of the Mongol Khans to the Kings of Europe, and Markos Who as Mar Yahballaha III Became Patriarch of the Nestorian Church in Asia* (London: Religious Tract Society, 1928), p. 133.

[16] Ibid., p. 136.

Accept these gifts from us as a loan, and if some occasion of necessity should befall you, spend what you need from them; if, on the other hand, the necessity does not arise, and you arrive safe and sound, distribute them among the monasteries and habitations of the monks which are there, and among the Fathers, so that we may enjoy association with our western Fathers.[17]

They did leave in the end and traveled to their first stop, "the city of Tangut" (probably in Ningxia). Local Christians overwhelmed them with presents and blessings. Afterward they had to go through desolate lands, waterless and ravaged by war. Six months later they reached Kashgar, at the foot of the Pamir Mountains. With countless difficulties, they managed to cross the mountain passes and came at last to the monasteries of Khorasan Province in Persia, which depended on the metropolitan of Merv. The two pilgrims from China then skirted the southern end of the Caspian Sea, intending to travel to Baghdad so as to greet the catholicos, the leader of their church.

Mongols in Persia

By the mid 1270s, when Rabban Sauma and Rabban Mark reached Persia, the Mongol Empire had evolved considerably since the death of Genghis Khan in 1227. The vast areas conquered by the Mongols had been divided among his sons so as to constitute independent khanates, or kingdoms. There were eventually four of these. The Great Khanate was composed of Mongolia and China, with its capital at Beijing. To the west was the Chagatai Khanate, centered on Samarqand and Bukhara in central Asia and ruled by the descendants of Genghis Khan's second son, Chagatai. The Khanate of the Golden Horde (named perhaps from the color of the khan's tent)[18] covered the area of the Pontic Steppe in present-day Russia, north of the Black Sea. Its khans were descended from Genghis Khan's eldest son, Jochi.

The fourth area of Mongol power was created in Persia, Iraq, and eastern Anatolia by one of Genghis Khan's grandsons, Hulagu, son of

---

[17] Ibid., p. 137.

[18] "Gold was the imperial color, and everything associated with the Chinggisid line was characterized as 'golden'." Thomas T. Allsen, *Culture and Conquest in Mongol Eurasia* (Cambridge, U.K.: Cambridge University Press, 2001), p. 88.

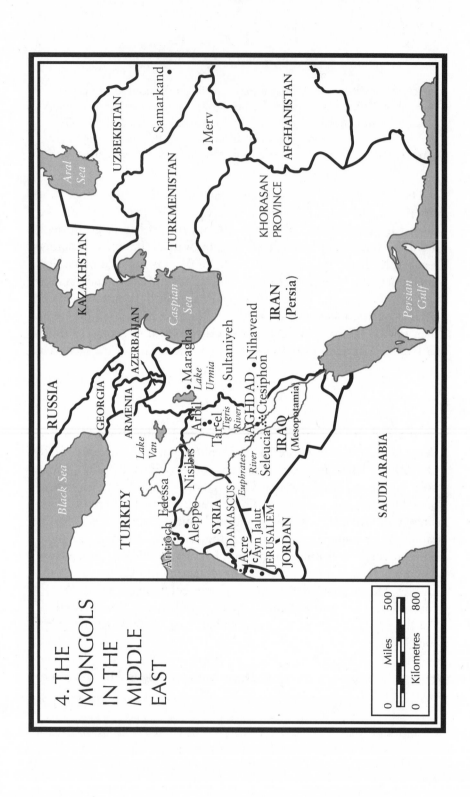

4. THE
MONGOLS
IN THE
MIDDLE
EAST

Miles
0 — 500

Kilometres
0 — 800

RUSSIA

KAZAKHSTAN

UZBEKISTAN

Samarkand

Aral
Sea

TURKMENISTAN

Merv

AFGHANISTAN

KHORASAN
PROVINCE

Caspian
Sea

IRAN
(Persia)

Persian
Gulf

GEORGIA

AZERBAIJAN

ARMENIA

Maragha
Lake
Urmia

Sultaniyeh

Nihavend

Lake
Van

Arbil

Tel

Ta'el

BAGHDAD
Ctesiphon
Seleucia

Tigris
River

IRAQ
(Mesopotamia)

Black Sea

TURKEY

Nisibis

Edessa

Euphrates
River

Antioch

Aleppo

SYRIA

DAMASCUS

Acre
c.Ayn Jalut

JERUSALEM

JORDAN

SAUDI ARABIA

Genghis Khan's youngest son, Tolui. This kingdom had a different status from the others, because it had not been allocated by Genghis Khan before his death, as had the other khanates. Hulagu was known as the il-khan, which probably meant "subordinate khan".[19] In theory Hulagu was subject to the great khan in China, but in fact he and his successors acted as independent rulers. Hulagu invaded Iraq in 1258 with a large army and besieged Baghdad. When the city surrendered, several hundred thousand inhabitants were put to the sword, and the caliph was executed, thus bringing to an end five hundred years of Muslim rule by the Abbasid caliphs, the titular heads of Sunni Muslims.

As had happened in China, the new Mongol ruler relied to a considerable extent on minority groups for his administration, in this case Jews and Syrian Christians. An entirely new situation thus occurred for Christians, especially as there was a strong Christian element in the new il-khan's family. Hulagu's mother was the Christian Kerait princess Sorqaqtani, and most Keraits were Christians. Hulagu himself practiced Shamanism, the traditional practice of the Mongols, with its quest for cures, knowledge of the future, and control of the powers of nature through magic. His chief wife, Doquz, however, was a Christian, and it was due to her intercession that the Christians of Baghdad were spared when the population was put to the sword in 1258. Hulagu's successor, Il-Khan Abaqa, also had Christian wives, both Syrian and Orthodox; one of them was Maria, the illegitimate daughter of the Byzantine emperor, Michael Paleologus.[20] When the two pilgrims from China were making their way south toward Baghdad in the mid-1270s, there was thus a real possibility that Persia would one day be ruled by a Christian dynasty.

In fact, Rabban Sauma and Rabban Mark met the catholicos while they were crossing the province of Azerbaijan in northern Persia. He was on visitation at Maragha, and they were overjoyed to see him:

> They fell down on the ground before him, and they wept as they did homage to him, and they behaved as if they saw our Lord Jesus Christ in the person of Mar Denha the Catholicos. . . . And when he asked them, "Whence do you come?" they replied, "From the countries of

---

[19] For the derivation of this title, see ibid., pp. 21–22.

[20] See James D. Ryan, "Christian Wives of Mongol Khans: Tartar Queens and Missionary Expectations in Asia", *J.R.A.S.* 8 (1998):411–28.

the East from Khanbaliq, the city of the king of kings, the khan. We have come to be blessed by you, and by the Fathers and the monks, and the holy men of this quarter of the world. And if a road [opens] to us, and God has mercy upon us, we shall go to Jerusalem."[21]

They visited all the holy places of Armenia, but the road to Jerusalem was too dangerous, so they went to Mar Denha at Baghdad and visited the shrines there, especially the shrine of Mar Mari, "the apostle, the teacher of the East"; after which they were allowed to live as monks again for about two years in the monastery of St. Michael, at Tar'el near Arbil. Mar Denha, however, saw the role that these exceptional men could play in the Church of the East. He proposed to send them back to China, making the younger one, Mark, metropolitan and making Sauma visitor general. Mark was only thirty-five when he was consecrated bishop and made metropolitan for the cities of Cathay and Ong, Ong designating the land of the Öngut, north of Shanxi Province. He was given a new name, Yaballaha. However, because of the wars that were raging in Asia at the time, travel was impossible in that direction as well, so the two companions returned for the time being to their cells in the Monastery of St. Michael, Tar'el.

The following year, in February 1281, the Catholicos, Mar Denha, died, and the metropolitan archbishops gathered to elect a new patriarch. To make a choice among the prestigious metropolitan sees of Syria and Persia was difficult, and so they turned to the new arrivals. Mar Yaballaha was elected in spite of protesting that he was too young, that he was inexperienced, and that he did not know Syriac. The reasons for this choice are given in the biography of the new patriarch:

> The kings who held the steering poles of the government of the whole world were Mongols, and there was no man except Mar Yaballaha who was acquainted with their manners and customs, and their policy of government, and their language.[22]

The Fathers then submitted the election for approval to Il-Khan Abaqa, the son and successor of Hulagu, who had died in 1265. Mar Yaballaha was duly consecrated in November 1281, the third catholicos of that name.

---

[21] Budge, *Monks of Kublai Khan*, p. 140.
[22] Ibid., pp. 152–53.

Hulagu's reign as il-khan of Persia had not been altogether successful, after his dramatic entry into the Middle Eastern world with the annihilation of the caliphate of Baghdad. He had then invaded Syria with the intention of conquering Egypt, having sent an ultimatum to the Islamic rulers of Egypt, the Mamluks. This was couched in the usual Mongol terms, claiming the overlordship of the whole world and threatening the Mamluks with dire consequences if they showed the slightest inclination to resist. It was then that the unexpected happened. At Ayn Jalut in Galilee, Hulagu's army suffered a crushing defeat at the hand of the Mamluks in 1260. The Mongols, who had seemed invincible, were compelled to evacuate Syria. This was the first major Mongol defeat anywhere, and it marked the high water mark of Mongol expansion in the West. It also produced an immediate change of attitude on the part of Il-Khan Hulagu, who began to look for allies among European rulers. Between 1263 and 1292, there were no fewer than eight embassies between a succession of il-khans who dropped any reference to world domination and proposed alliances to the sovereigns of the West. The Mamluks employed similar tactics and actually made an alliance against the il-khans with the Mongol ruler of the Golden Horde in Russia.

Hulagu's grandson, Arghun, became il-khan in 1284 and sent a letter to Pope Honorius IV the following year, outlining plans for joint action in the Levant. In 1286 a second embassy was sent, about which we know a great deal, since Rabban Sauma was chosen to be the il-khan's envoy, although there were many Europeans in Persia who might have been suitable. Letters and gifts for the kings of the Greeks, the Franks, and the Pope were entrusted to Sauma, as well as thirty horses and 2,000 gold pieces for his personal use.

Rabban Sauma's Mission to Europe

Rabban Sauma reached Constantinople by the Black Sea in 1287. From there he set sail for Naples and traveled on to Rome, but, when he arrived there in April, Pope Honorius IV had just died. The cardinals submitted Rabban Sauma to lengthy interrogations, and his replies throw light on the way Christians in China regarded their tradition. The cardinals asked him, "Which of the apostles taught the Gospel in your quarter of the world?" He said:

Mar Thomas, Mar Addai, and Mar Mari taught the Gospel in our quarter of the world, and we hold at the present time the canons that they delivered unto us.[23]

Rabban Sauma was clearly convinced of the apostolic origin of the Syrian Church of the East, an important point when seeking communion with the Apostolic See of Rome. There is, however, no authentic evidence for the presence of Mar Thomas, the apostle St. Thomas, in Iraq, even if only on his way to India. He is never referred to as the founder of the Church of Seleucia-Ctesiphon or mentioned in any of the ancient calendars of the East Syrian Church,[24] though obviously by the thirteenth century he had been "annexed" retrospectively by that church. As regards St. Addai, the earliest evidence presents him as bringing the Gospel in subapostolic times to Edessa (modern Urfa or Sanhurfa in Turkey) and Nisibis (modern Nuseybin in Turkey). This tradition is generally accepted as authentic, but there is no early evidence for his presence any further south.[25] According to Fr. J. M. Fiey, however, St. Mari has a better claim to the evangelization of southern Iraq by the end of the first or the beginning of the second century A.D., and in particular to the foundation of a place of worship on the hill of Kohé, near Ctesiphon.[26] The coming of Christianity at an early period from the Apostolic See of Antioch to Edessa, and then further east into the Sasanian Empire, is generally accepted today as historical, and this, basically, is what Rabban Sauma was claiming. He goes on to extol the missions of his church in far eastern Asia and to claim that there were many Mongol converts, and important ones too:

> Know that many of our Fathers have gone into the countries of the Mongols, and Turks, and China and have taught them the Gospel, and at the present time there are many Mongols who are Christians. For many of the sons of Mongol kings and queens have been baptized and confess Christ. And they have established churches with them in their military camps. . . . No man has come to us Orientals from the Pope. The holy apostles whose names I have mentioned taught us the Gospel,

---

[23] Ibid., p. 173.

[24] Cf. J. M. Fiey, *Histoire de l'Église en Iraq* (Louvain: C.S.C.O., 1970), Subsidia 36, p. 35.

[25] Ibid., p. 39.

[26] Ibid., pp. 41–42.

and to what they have delivered unto us we have clung to the present day.[27]

When the cardinals questioned Rabban Sauma on the content of his faith, he replied:

I am come from remote countries neither to discuss nor to instruct in matters of the faith, but I came that I might receive a blessing from Mar Papa, and from the shrines of the saints, and to make known the words of the king and of the catholicos. If it be pleasing in your eyes, let us set aside discussion and, if you will, direct someone to show us the churches here and the shrines of the saints.[28]

This was a revealing confrontation between two different mentalities; on one side an Asian Christian whose first concern was prayer in sacred places, and on the other theologians representing the Roman Magisterium, with its concern for doctrinal accuracy. They probably considered the envoy from the catholicos patriarch as not very orthodox and were trying to assess whether, in view of his Nestorian connections, they could consider him as belonging to "the True Church".

As regards what Rabban Sauma reported about the great khan of the Mongols, he was no doubt saying what he considered could be understood by his interlocutors when he spoke of the numerous Mongol princes who were Christians. Would he also have explained to these theological experts of Western Christendom the liberal attitude of his sovereign toward all religions, as long as his subjects behaved as good citizens? In any case, splitting hairs did not interest Rabban Sauma. What he really wanted was to say his prayers at the tombs of the apostles, where he probably felt closer to Christ, his Savior, and to procure some relics of the saints that he could bring back with him.

From Rome, Rabban Sauma continued his tour of the West and reached Paris. He had an audience with King Philip IV, "Philip the Fair", who made fine promises of military contribution to a Crusade, none of which came to anything, but Sauma was more impressed by the University of Paris:

---

[27] Budge, *Monks of Kublai Khan*, p. 174.
[28] Ibid., p. 177.

There were in it 30,000 scholars who were engaged in the study of ecclesiastical books, that is to say of commentaries and exegesis of all Holy
Scripture, and also of profane learning. . . . And they engaged constantly
in writing, and all these pupils received money for subsistence from the
king.[29]

Rabban Sauma and his companions also admired the tombs of the
kings of France in the Benedictine Abbey Church of St. Denis, near
Paris. They saw the royal effigies, covered with gold and silver, and
the crowns of these princes, their arms and their robes placed upon
their tombs. He noted:

500 monks were engaged in performing commemoration services in the
burial place of the kings, and they all ate and drank at the expense of
the king.[30]

King Philip showed them personally the crown of thorns and a
fragment of the true Cross, which he told them had been brought
back from Jerusalem by his ancestors (in fact by his grandfather, St.
Louis).

From Paris they traveled to Bordeaux and were received by the king
of England, Bordeaux being part of the Duchy of Aquitaine and, as
such, under English rule since the time of the Plantagenets. They
presented Edward I with the letters and gifts from Il-Khan Arghun,
and, when the king heard mention of Jerusalem, he was very pleased
and said to them:

We, the kings of these cities, bear upon our bodies the sign of the Cross
and we have no other thought except this matter.[31]

The king of England invited Rabban Sauma to celebrate Mass and
received Holy Communion from his hand. He also declared:

Thus shall you say to King Arghun and to all Orientals: we have seen
a thing than which there is nothing more wonderful, that is to say, that
in the countries of the Franks there are not two Confessions of Faith, but

---

[29] Ibid., p. 183.
[30] Ibid., p. 184.
[31] Ibid., p. 186.

only one Confession of Faith, namely, that which Jesus Christ confesses; and all the Christians confess it.[32]

Rabban Sauma and his companions spent the winter at Genoa, becoming more and more disillusioned about the prospect of any effective intervention in the Holy Land on the part of Westerners. They were waiting impatiently for the election of a new pope, and in February 1288, Cardinal Jerome Masci was elected, taking the name Nicholas IV. He was the first Franciscan pope. He had been one of the cardinals who interviewed the Syrian monk, and, as a Franciscan, he had a missionary outlook and wasted no time in welcoming the embassy from Persia. The letters from Il-Khan Arghun were presented to the Pope, who invited the embassy to stay in Rome for the Easter celebrations. They were so pleased to celebrate the Eucharist in the Eternal City according to the Eastern Syriac rite:

> Rabban Sauma said to Mar Papa, "I wish to celebrate the Eucharist so that you may see our use." And the Pope commanded him to do as he had asked. And on that day a very large number of people were gathered together in order to see how the ambassador of the Mongols celebrated the Eucharist. And when they had, they rejoiced and said, "The language is different, but the [liturgical] use is the same."[33]

Rabban Sauma went further and asked to receive Communion at the hands of the Pope, who agreed that this should be done on the following Sunday, which was Palm Sunday.

> [The Pope] consecrated the mysteries and gave the eucharistic mystery to Rabban Sauma first of all—he having confessed his sins—and the Pope pardoned his transgressions and his sins and those of his fathers. And Rabban Sauma rejoiced greatly in receiving the eucharistic mystery from the hand of Mar Papa. And he received it with tears and sobs, giving thanks to God and meditating on the mysteries that had been poured out upon him.[34]

Before the Pope would allow them to depart, he entrusted to Rabban Sauma precious gifts for Arghun and for the Catholicos Yaballaha III.

---

[32] Ibid.

[33] Ibid., p. 190.

[34] Ibid., p. 191.

He sent to Mar Yaballaha a crown for his head that was of fine gold and was inlaid with precious stones; and sacred vestments made of red cloth through which ran threads of gold; and socks and sandals on which rich pearls were sewn, and the ring from his finger; and a *Ptiho* or signed statement that authorized him to exercise patriarchal authority over all the children of the East.[35]

The letter from the Pope to the patriarch was dated April 7, 1288 and was accompanied by a precise statement of the Catholic and Roman faith and by an exhortation to instruct the clergy and the Christian people accordingly. It did not in fact recognize the supremacy of the patriarch over the East. The statement on the Catholic faith ends with an unambiguous affirmation of the universal supremacy of the Roman Pontiff.

The End of a Dream

Rabban Sauma then began his return journey and doubtless conveyed to his former traveling companion Mark, now catholicos in Baghdad, the message of the Pope about the unity of all Christians and the primacy of the Holy See. A letter to Pope Benedict XI written from the catholicos some years later, in 1304, seems to bear witness to the reality of that union.

> We believe in the holy Roman chief Pontiff and universal father of all believers in Christ, and confess that he is the Successor of Blessed Peter, universal vicar of Jesus Christ over all the sons of the Church from the East to the West; love and affection for whom is fixed in our hearts; and we owe obedience to him, and ask and implore his blessing, and are ready for all his commands.[36]

Rabban Sauma's mission had hardly any political results, but there were spiritual benefits to be gained from the ecumenical exchanges between East and West. Arghun loaded Sauma with honors on his return and built a church for him near the palace, so as to keep him at his side and benefit from his prayers. One of the king's sons, Khar-

---

[35] Ibid., p. 196. *Ptiho'* indicates an open (letter), i.e., a letter patent.

[36] Moule, *Christians in China*, pp. 123–24. From the Latin text quoted by Budge in *Monks of Kublai Khan*, pp. 99–100.

banda, was baptized by the patriarch and given the name Nicholas in honor of the Pope. His religious affiliation was, however, eclectic, and he was also at various times a Shamanist, a Buddhist, and both a Sunni and a Shi'i Muslim. Arghun's other son, Ghazan, became a Muslim; Arghun himself remained a Buddhist.

The princes in Europe had agreed to a vague plan of campaign and to a *rendez-vous* at Damascus in 1291, but in fact nothing happened. Arghun had sent another embassy to Europe in 1290, but this time Rabban Sauma was not one of the king's envoys. Arghun himself died in 1291, and the plan for a military campaign in Syria and Palestine died with him. In the same year the Crusaders' fortified city and port of Acre, the last Crusader foothold in Palestine, was taken by Mamluk forces from Egypt and its defenders slaughtered. The unexpected opportunity for an alliance between the Mongol rulers of Persia and the Christian kings of Europe was thus lost. If it had been realized, it might have established Mongol power in Syria as the necessary guarantee for the survival of a Christian kingdom of Palestine.

Rabban Sauma died in Baghdad in 1294, around his eightieth year. His friend the Catholicos, Yaballaha, presided over his funeral rites "with lamentations that reached to the skies".[37] The following year, Ghazan succeeded as il-khan and, having become a Muslim, was followed by most of the Mongols in Persia. The wholesale destruction of Christian, Jewish, and Buddhist places of worship then began. Yaballaha, who had been the young Öngut Mark, lived on until seventy-two, dying in 1317. He was left to face old age alone and far from his native land. The bright promise of his consecration, thirty-six years previously, had not been fulfilled. He had been chosen as catholicos because he spoke the Mongol tongue, and it had been thought that he would understand Mongol ways. In fact, he had difficult relations with the il-khans and was imprisoned for a time and even tortured. His last recorded words were a *cri de coeur*: "I am tired of serving the Mongols."[38] He lived to see Islam dominate Persia during the last years of the Mongol kings. The dynasty died out in 1335, after which local potentates seized power in various parts of the ilkhanate—Turks, Mongols, Persians. As monasteries and churches were destroyed in

---

[37] J. M. Fiey, *Chrétiens Syriaques sous les Mongols*, p. 60.
[38] Ibid., p. 79.

Persia and Iraq, the Christians, who had had such high hopes at the coming of the Mongols, were reduced to being a despised and insecure minority. In China the Yuan Dynasty was to survive for another generation before it too disappeared in 1368.

[The following paragraphs have been added by the translator.

"The Cross among the Mongols", the first paragraph introducing the text by Marco Polo and the third, fourth, fifth, and sixth paragraph are added.

"A Christian Presence among the Nomads", The nine paragraphs of the section have been substantially added to.

The first three paragraphs of the section "Mongols in Persia" have been added and also the seventh paragraph on Il-Khan Hulagu.

The last two paragraphs of the section "The End of a Dream" have been added.—Trans.]

5

A BELL TOWER AT KHANBALIK

When Rabban Sauma visited Rome, Paris, Bordeaux, and Genoa, he discovered a new world; he discovered Christendom. The Europe of the thirteenth century that he saw had received its inheritance from Rome and Greece, from the Semitic world of the Bible and from the Germanic tribes that had settled within the limits of the Roman Empire. From this amalgam, the Fathers of the Church and Benedictine monks had laid the foundation of a Christian culture. The thousands of scholars that Sauma heard about in Paris came from the four quarters of Latin Christianity and represented one of the greatest contributions of medieval Europe to civilization—universities. When Sauma was in Paris, similar corporations of masters and students were to be found at Bologna, Oxford, Cambridge, Montpellier, Padua, Naples, Salamanca, and Toulouse.

The Christian civilization of the Europe of that time can be compared to the neo-Confucian civilization of Song Dynasty China. In Europe St. Thomas Aquinas (1225–1274) had created a theological and philosophical synthesis, combining the Greek and Latin inheritance (which had come via the Arabs and Jews of the Islamic world) with the teaching of the Judeo-Christian tradition. One century earlier the Chinese philosopher Zhu Xi (1130–1200) had created a rational synthesis that incorporated Buddhist and Taoist elements within the great Confucian tradition inherited from the ancients.

There were, however, marked differences between these two civilizations. The political order of China at the time of the Song emperors derived from moral and ritual principles that regulated relations between subjects and sovereign on the model of family relations. There was indeed a religious aspect to this harmonization of heaven and earth, but man was at the center, and "heaven" was more or less equivalent to nature, whereas the polity of medieval Christianity rested on a much stronger sense of the claims of a God who must be "first served".[1] Spiritual power dominated temporal power, since the Church could compel the obedience of civil society. The Pope crowned the Holy Roman Emperor and conferred on him an authority that was divine. The confrontation of these two powers caused conflicts that troubled medieval society but also imparted a certain dynamism to political and intellectual life. Thus, at the end of the thirteenth century, the lawyers of Philip the Fair (King Philip IV of France, r. 1285–1314) put in place institutions that strengthened royal power. The king, while claiming to be "a true son of the Church", declared that he was sole master in the temporal domain. He lost patience at the interference of papal power within his kingdom, and in 1303 French troops burst into the little town of Anagni near Rome and took Pope Boniface VIII prisoner. Their commander was said to have slapped the Pope across the face. "*Il sciaffo di Anagni*" sent a frisson of horror throughout Christian Europe, but the Pope's inability to respond made the limitation of papal power evident. It marked the beginning of the breakup of Western Christendom, as the kings of Europe took over the notion of divine right and used it to their own benefit. Such conflicts could not have happened in China, where there was no distinction between religion and political power.

One of the reasons for the political tensions that arose within Western society was the emergence of an economy based on trade. Large towns obtained special franchises and became extremely wealthy. The emergence of these centers of prosperity was marked by the building of magnificent cathedrals and town halls; foremost among them was Venice. At the beginning of the thirteenth century, Pope Innocent III had launched the Fourth Crusade, and the merchants of Venice rented their fleet to the Crusaders for a large sum. However, once the fleet was under sail, the Venetians persuaded the Crusaders to turn aside from their destination and launched them against Constantinople (Byzantium, Istanbul), the capital of the eastern Roman Empire, which was captured and sacked. For the Venetians it was a convenient way of eliminating their main rival in the trade of the eastern Mediterranean, but the sack of Byzantium in 1204 contributed to the fatal weakening of the forces of Christendom. For the Ortho-

---

[1] The phrase *Dieu premier servi*, "God must be first served", was a favorite saying of St. Joan of Arc (c. 1411–1431).

dox Churches, struggling against the constant pressure of Islam, the destruction of their capital city by fellow Christians was an appalling betrayal that they would never forget.

This barbaric act also augured ill for the future of western Europe because it showed that economic interests would prevail over religious principle. Powers desirous of profit began to use religion for their own ends. In due course the journey of the Venetian Polo family to China and the fascinating *Description of the World* composed from Marco Polo's account aroused the desire of Europeans for gain. After they had done with the plunder of gold from the Americas, they would turn to new conquests in the spice islands of the East and in the land of silk.

The Mongol Threat in the West

A few years after the sack of Byzantium, Christendom, weakened as it was by internal divisions, was faced by an unexpected threat, as mentioned in the previous chapter. In 1224 fierce Mongols on their rapid steeds appeared in Russia and crushed the cavalry of the princes of Kiev. In 1236 Batu, grandson of Genghis Khan, came back to Kiev and settled with his army in the Russian steppe, founding the Empire of the Golden Horde, which extended from the Urals to the Danube. Four years later, the Mongols attacked Poland and Hungary, annihilated the army of the Teutonic knights, and reached the Adriatic Sea. Rumors about the cruelty of the Mongols circulating in Europe caused a panic, in the same way as Attila and the Huns had done nine centuries before. Someone who had survived the Mongol attack on Hungary wrote:

> The days of perdition are close; the end of the world is imminent; I can tell you in all conscience that those who fall into the hands of the barbarians will wish that they had never been born, for they will be the prisoners, not of the Tartars but of Tartarus (hell) itself.[2]

However, the Mongol onslaught was threatening Muslim lands even more than Christian ones. The question arose whether it would be

---

[2] Clement Schmitt, O.F.M., *Histoire des Mongols* (Paris: Éditions Franciscaines, 1961), p. 11.

possible for Europeans to get in touch with Christian Mongol chieftains and to establish an alliance with them.

The barons of Germany, faced with the immediate threat from the
East, prepared for a crusade against the enemy. At the meeting of the
First Council of Lyons in 1245, the question of how to finance such
an undertaking was discussed, but it was not clear how one could deal
with an enemy when it was not known what its intentions were or
its real strength or sometimes even its whereabouts. Mongol armies
could disappear as quickly as they had come, and nobody in the West
knew why.

Pope Innocent IV, who had been elected in 1243, decided to send
an envoy to find out more about the Mongols. He chose an Italian
Franciscan, Giovanni di Plano Carpino, an observant and courageous
man, who had diplomatic experience and had proved his worth in
Egypt during the Fifth Crusade in 1219, when he had gone to meet
the sultan to negotiate the return of Jerusalem (which did not in
fact take place). Plano Carpino was in his sixties and managed his
brief well. He left Lyons on April 16, 1245 and reached Mongolia
by July 1246, having covered about 7,000 miles (11,000 kilometers).
The great khan, Ogatai, third son of Genghis Khan, had died in 1241,
and the *kuraltai* to elect his successor had only just accomplished its
work, so that the Italian Franciscan witnessed the enthronement of
Kuyuk, Ogatai's son, near the Mongolian capital of Karakorum. The
new khan received the letters from the Pope and had them translated.
Unfortunately Pope Innocent, who had just attempted to depose the
Holy Roman Emperor, Frederic II, adopted a lordly tone when ad-
dressing monarchs, and his letter had not sufficiently expressed respect for the great khan's authority. The Mongol monarch gave his
reply to the friar at a public audience, and it was couched in forceful
terms:

> Your petition says that we should be baptized and become Christian.
> We reply briefly that we do not understand how we are obliged to do
> this.
>
> Another thing: in your letter you say that you are surprised at the
> number of men, Christians especially, who have been massacred, par-
> ticularly in Poland, Moravia, and Hungary. That also we do not un-
> derstand. However, so as not to appear to ignore this matter, we tell
> you to reply thus: because they did not obey the letter of God and the
> order of Genghis Khan and of the khan (Ogatai) and, after having held

a great council, killed our ambassadors; therefore, God has ordered us to exterminate them and delivered them into our hands. Had God not done this, what could man have done to man?

You men of the West, you think you are the only Christians, and you despise others. How do you know on whom God deigns to bestow his favor?[3]

The great khan ended by saying that if the Pope and Christian kings really wanted peace, they and their armies should surrender to him. From the diplomatic point of view Giovanni di Plano Carpino's embassy was a failure, but once he got back to Europe in 1247 he wrote his *Ystoria Mongalorum*, which is full of precious observations on a people hitherto unknown in the West and on the conditions of the journey to such distant lands.

Missions Diplomatic and Religious

In the years that followed, other delegations were sent to the East, with greater or lesser measures of success. While St. Louis (Louis IX of France) was in Cyprus (1250–1254) after his release from captivity in Egypt, some Mongol chieftains contacted him with a view to testing the ground for an alliance against Islam. This was a unique opportunity for the West, but one that, as has been indicated in the previous chapter, was completely mismanaged. The king sent a Dominican friar, André de Longjumeau, who returned in 1251 with information about the presence of Nestorians among the Mongol chieftains and their wives. St. Louis took an interest in the religious aspect of these exchanges and decided to send a Franciscan missionary, Willem van Rubroek from Saint-Omer in Flanders, with simple letters of introduction.

Willem van Rubroek left Constantinople in May 1253 and reached the camp of Great Khan Mangu in January 1254. He sent a long letter to King Louis, written in his own hand and full of precise and fascinating observations. What he says about the religious practices at the court of the Mongol king is revealing, both of the pluralism of the Mongols in religious matters and of the theological assurance

---

[3] *S.F.*, vol. 1, Fr. Benedictus Polonus, p. 143. Quotations from *S.F.* are our translation from the Latin.

of the Franciscan. He counted twelve temples at Karakorum for the idol worshippers of various nations, plus two mosques and a church. Among the idolaters he numbers the Buddhists and the *Tuins*, a word that, according to René Grousset, derives from the Chinese *Dao ren*, man "of the Dao" or "of the Way", and referred to the Taoists.[4]

On the eve of Pentecost (May 30, 1254), the khan decided to hold a theological discussion with the representatives of three different religions. He appointed three secretaries as arbitrators: one Christian, one Muslim, and one Tuin. The khan saw to the good order of the debate by ruling as follows:

> This is the command of Mangu, and let no one dare to say that God's command is any different. He orders that no one should dare to utter words that are aggressive or insulting to another, nor should anyone cause a disturbance which would bring this meeting to an end, and this under pain of death.[5]

As opponent to Rubroek the Tuins chose "one of their own number who came from Cathay". He put forward as subject of discussion "how the world was made or what happens to souls after death". Rubroek suspected that behind these questions there lay a whiff of Manichean heresy, to which he attributed the Buddhist belief in the transmigration of souls:

> They all belong in fact to this Manichean heresy, according to which half of the things that exist are bad and the other half good, and there are at least two principles of existence. As for souls, they all think that these pass from one body to another.[6]

Rubroek avoided getting entangled in this question and drew his opponent on to his own terrain:

> We believe firmly in our hearts and we confess with our mouth that God exists, that there is only one God who is one with a perfect unity. What do you believe about that?
> He replied: fools say that there is only one God, but the wise say that there are several. Are there not many lords in your country, and

---

[4] René Grousset, *The Empire of the Steppes: A History of Central Asia* (New Brunswick, N.J.: Rutgers University Press, 1970), p. 597, n. 78: "The name of *Tuinan* or *Tuin*, by which Rubruck and other western missionaries designated Buddhist monks, must come from the Chjinese *tao-jen*, 'men of the road', or 'of the way', referring to the *sramana*."

[5] *S.F.*, vol. 1, Fr. Gulielmus de Rubruc, *Itinerarium*, p. 294.

[6] Ibid., p. 295.

is there not here a much greater lord, Mangu? It is the same with the gods. They are different according to different regions.

I said to him: you are taking a bad example if you compare men to God. That way, any powerful lord on his lands could be compared to God. And when I wanted to contest the resemblance he prevented me, asking: What is your God like, since you say that there is only one? I replied: our God, apart from whom there is no other, is all powerful, and therefore he does not need the help of anybody; on the contrary, everyone needs his help. But it is not like that with human beings. No man can do everything, which is why there are many lords on the earth, because no one can carry the burden of everything. He also knows everything, and therefore he does not need advisers; on the contrary, all wisdom comes from him. He is also the supreme good and does not need the good things that we have; on the contrary, "it is in him that we live and move and have our being" (Acts 17:28).[7]

Since Rubroek emphasized the all-powerful nature of God, the Tuin objected with the problem of evil:

If your God is what you say he is, why did he make half the things that exist bad? Rubroek replied: that's not true. He who created evil is not God, who is good.[8]

The affirmation of one all-powerful God delighted the Muslims who were present. The discussion ended with limited agreement on the part of monotheist believers and with the discomfiture of the Buddhists.

There was an old priest present from the Uighur sect, who say that there is only one God and who nevertheless make idols. The Nestorians spoke with him for a long time, giving him a complete account as far as the coming of Christ on Judgment Day and using examples to explain to him, as well as to the Muslims, the Trinity. They all listened without making any objection, but no one said: I believe, I want to become a Christian. When it was all over, the Nestorians and also the Muslims sang out loud, but the Tuins were silent. Afterward, everyone had plenty to drink.[9]

Heavy drinking was common under the Mongol tents of black felt (*gers*, often called *yurts* in the West) made from yak hair. It was effec-

---

[7] Ibid.
[8] Ibid.
[9] Ibid., p. 297

tive remedy against the icy winds of the steppe. The Franciscan was a large, strong man, who seems to have become accustomed to *kumis*, the fermented mare's milk that was the staple drink of the Mongols. On the occasion of this theological contest, the Syrians and the Catholics had worked together at trying to get the idea of the transcendence of the one God across to pagans; in addition, the Syrians had given an outline of the history of salvation and had even broached the difficult doctrine of the Trinity. Rubroek, however, did not like the Syrian Christians. He accused them of being drunkards and criticized their singing, saying that he "refrained from braying with them", but he had his own stock of Latin hymns and particularly liked the triumphal hymn for Passion Sunday, *Vexilla Regis Prodeunt*:

Vexilla Regis prodeunt	The standards of the king go forth.
Fulget crucis mysterium	The mystery of the Cross shines like lightning.
Arbor decora et fulgida	O tree both beautiful and dazzling
Quae tulit praedam Tartari	Who snatched the prey from the Tartar.

Rubroek innocently admits his indiscretion in this respect: "In fact we did carry the cross through the camp, held aloft as we sang the *Vexilla Regis prodeunt*, which struck the Muslims with amazement."

An Italian Archbishop of Beijing

It was not until the last decade of the thirteenth century that the first elements of Latin Christianity implanted themselves in China proper. Pope Nicholas IV responded to Rabban Sauma's visit by sending his own legate to China, chosen among those pilgrim Franciscans who devoted their lives to traveling for the sake of Christ. Giovanni da Montecorvino was designated, an Italian from south of Naples, born in 1247, a man of outstanding caliber. He had already been to Constantinople, Armenia, and Persia. Montecorvino put together a team of Franciscan brothers and instructed them about the beliefs of the various religions and heresies they would meet. The Pope wanted them to be positioned in the different Catholic communities along the road to China.

Giovanni da Montecorvino set out in July 1289. Since the way through central Asia was blocked by Muslims, he and his group sailed along the coast of India and stayed for thirteen months with the com-

Bishop Giovanni da Montecorvino, O.F.M.

Giovanni da Montecorvino from Salerno, an Italian Franciscan, came to China as emissary from the Pope to its Mongol rulers and worked as a missionary from 1294 until his death. He was consecrated first Archbishop of Beijing in 1313. Aided by communities of Franciscans, he established groups of Latin Catholics in Mongolia and on the coast. After the end of the Yuan dynasty in 1368, both Syrian and Latin Catholic Christians disappeared from China, through circumstances that are unknown. Painting by J.-B. Jacobs for a missionary exhibition held in Rome in 1924.

munity known as the Church of St. Thomas. From there they were able to sail to China, since Mongol rule extended by then to the south and southeast of the country. In 1294 Montecorvino arrived at Beijing, soon after the death of Kublai Khan, so that the Pope's letter, which had been signed at Rieti on July 13, 1289, was given to the new emperor, Timur Khan. The Pope recommended his envoy in diplomatic terms:

> Shortly after the beginning of our promotion we received in audience trustworthy messengers who had been sent by the magnificent Prince Arghun, famous prince of the Tartars, who told us plainly that your Magnificence bears a feeling of great love toward our person and the Roman Church and also toward the nation or people of the Latins. And the said messengers earnestly begged on behalf of the king that we should send some Latin monks to your court.[10]

The Pope calls down divine blessings on the Mongol sovereign and recommends the group of Franciscans to him. Another letter from the Pope, dated July 15, 1289, was sent to "the venerable patriarch of the Nestorians", Yaballaha, asking him to protect the Franciscans and to facilitate their apostolic work.

Something is known of Montecorvino's work in China through two letters that he sent from Beijing to his religious superiors. Here are the more significant passages from his first letter, dated January 8, 1305:

> With the letter of the Lord Pope, I invited the emperor himself to the Catholic faith of our Lord Jesus Christ. But he has grown too old in idolatry. But he bestows many kindnesses on the Christians, and it is now the twelfth year that I am with him.[11]

Montecorvino goes on to complain about the monopoly exercised by the Syrian Christians. They do not allow him to build even a small chapel outside their church. He says that for five years he has been the victim of their calumnies. He also suffers from isolation:

> I indeed was alone in this pilgrimage without confession for eleven years, until Brother Arnold, a German of the province of Cologne, came to me, it is now the second year. I have built a church in the city of Khanbalik

---

[10] Translation by A. C. Moule, *Christians in China before 1550* (London: S.P.C.K., 1930), p. 168. From a manuscript chronicle of c. 1377 in the Bibliothèque Nationale, Paris.

[11] Ibid., p. 172, letter of Jan. 8, 1305.

[Beijing], where the chief residence of the king is, and I finished it six years ago; where also I made a bell tower and put three bells there. I have also baptized there, as I reckon, up to today about six thousand persons. And if there had not been the above-named slanders I should have baptized more than thirty thousand. . . . Also I have bought one after another forty boys, the sons of pagans, of an age between seven and eleven years, who were as yet learning no religion. And I have baptized them and taught them Latin letters and our rite; I have written for them thirty psalters with hymnaries and two breviaries, with which twelve boys now know our office. . . . And the lord emperor is greatly delighted with their chanting. I strike the bells at all the hours, and perform the divine office with a congregation of "babes and sucklings".[12]

These few details are sufficient to give an idea of this new community at Beijing. It was a sapling of Latin Christianity that the Franciscans were trying to plant on its own, separately from the Syrian Church of the East. The hostility of the local Christians is understandable; they were totally isolated, and their ecclesiastical province was virtually independent, having only the remotest connection with the catholicos in Baghdad. His connection with the Pope would have meant little to them, supposing that they had even heard about it. The Franciscans, for their part, were conscious of belonging to the one true Church. Pitilessly they retailed the errors of the Syrians and converted some of them. Montecorvino tells the story of an outstanding convert, "good King George", the head of the Öngut people.

A certain king of that region from the Nestorian school, who was a relation of the great khan called Priest John of India, became a friend of mine the first year that I arrived here and was converted by me to the truth of the Catholic faith. He received minor orders and would wear sacred vestments to serve me when I was celebrating [Mass][13] so that the other Nestorians accused him of apostasy. However, he led a great part of his people to the true Catholic faith; and he built a beautiful church with royal splendor in honor of our God, the Holy Trinity, and our Lord the Pope and in my name, calling it the Roman Church.[14]

---

[12] Ibid., p. 173.

[13] At that time, there were four minor orders in the Latin Church (acolytes, readers, exorcists, and doorkeepers), which, with the tonsure, admitted to the clerical state but did not have the sacramental character of the major orders (bishops, priests, and deacons). After the Second Vatican Council (1962–1965) the minor orders were reduced to two in the Latin Church and the tonsure was abolished.

[14] *S.F.*, vol. 1, Fr. Joannes de Montecorvino, *Epistolae*, Jan. 8, 1305, p. 348.

The "King George" mentioned by Montecorvino was Kuolijisi, ruler of the Önguts, whose Christian name was Korgiz (George). His capital city, on the Aibag Gol River, was identified by excavation in 1929 as present-day Olon-Sume[15] the Koshang, which was the birthplace of Mar Yaballaha III (see chapter 4). It is in Inner Mongolia, 12-1/2 miles (twenty kilometers) northeast of Bailingmiao. Montecorvino tells us that it was a twenty-day journey from Beijing. The site is surrounded by walls and includes the ruins of the prince's palace, some tombs with carvings of east Syrian crosses, a stone tablet with an inscription in Chinese, and the ruins of a number of buildings, including the foundations of what is probably the church built by Prince George for Montecorvino. On the site of the church were found stones carved with leaves in the Gothic style and a statue, headless unfortunately, whose rendering of the folds of garments resembles contemporary European work.[16]

Montecorvino emphasizes the role of the prince in liturgical celebrations, and this illustrates the usage of the Syrian Churches. Their custom has been, and often remains, the bestowal of the minor orders of reader and subdeacon on large numbers of young men and even teenagers, who are in the sanctuary during the liturgy.[17] Montecorvino obviously wanted to emphasize that Prince George's conversion to the Latin rite had not deprived him of this privilege. Forty years previously Rubroek, in his rather unfavorable description of the Syrian Church in China, had gone so far as to write that "the bishop comes rarely and, when he comes, ordains all the boys, so that nearly all men are priests".[18] There is, however, no corroboration for such practice, and it is possible that Rubroek mistook the bestowal of minor orders for ordination to the priesthood.

Prince George was killed in battle in 1298, and his tomb is at Olon-Sume, less than a mile (1 kilometer) from the palace enclosure. The stone tablet bears an inscription dating from 1347 with a genealogy of the Öngut princely line which records that, because John the son of George was still a child, the Chinese emperor had decreed that

---

[15] Cf. Namio Egami, "Olon-Sume et la découverte de l'Église Catholique Romaine de Jean de Montecorvino", *Journal Asiatique* 240 (1952):155–67. See also Standaert, pp. 53–55, 58, 60, 65.

[16] Egami, *Journal Asiatique*, p. 164.

[17] We are grateful to Dr. Sebastian Brock for this information.

[18] *S.F.*, vol. 1, Fr. Gulielmus de Rubruc, *Itinerarium*, p. 238.

Juxahan, brother of his mother, should become king of Gaotang. At the time when Montecorvino wrote this letter, Prince George had been dead six years, and most of the Öngut entourage that had been converted to Catholicism had returned to the Syrian Church. The prince had been a powerful patron of Syrian Christians, and one can understand how upset they had been to lose him.

In the same letter Montecorvino asked that liturgical books and stories of saints should be sent to him. He also gives information about his use of the Mongol language:

> I have learned competently the Tartar language and writing, which is the common language of the Tartars, and I have translated into that tongue and writing the whole of the New Testament and the psalter, which I have had written out beautifully in their writing. . . . I had arranged with King George, had he lived, to translate the whole of the Latin office so that it would be sung everywhere in his dominions. And when he was alive, the Mass was celebrated in his church according to the Latin rite using that text and tongue, including the words of the canon and the preface.[19]

Montecorvino wrote a second letter in February 1306, in which he informs his superior of the rapid development of the Catholic community. He had built a second church, which was near to the khan's palace. The land had been bought by a merchant, Pietro de Lucalongo, who had accompanied the friar as far as China, which he entered at Quanzhou, although he did not reach Khanbalik until 1293.[20] The new buildings included a residence with a chapel capable of holding 200. After the Feast of All Saints, 400 people had been baptized. Montecorvino also had six copies of the Old Testament made, in three different languages: Latin, Persian and "Turcic".

It is interesting to note that the transition in the liturgy from Latin to Mongolian was not a problem for Montecorvino. Much later, in the seventeenth century, endless efforts were made by missionaries in China to obtain from the Roman authorities authorization for a liturgy in Chinese. For a short time permission was given to the Jesuits for the celebration of Mass in Chinese, but this was soon withdrawn, and Latin continued to be obligatory in the Roman rite until the Second Vatican Council (1962–1965). When the use of vernac-

---

[19] *S.F.*, vol. 1, Fr. Joannes de Montecorvino, *Epistolae*, Jan. 8, 1305, p. 350.
[20] Cf. Standaert, p. 69.

ular languages in the liturgy was authorized by the Council, Taiwan and Hong Kong rapidly put it into practice, whereas Catholics on the mainland, cut off as they were by then from the Holy See, were much slower in applying the liturgical reforms (see chapters 28 and 29).

In his earlier letter (January 8, 1305) Montecorvino was already complaining about being fifty-eight years old and asking for pastoral help. In 1307 Pope Clement V sent seven Franciscans, whom he ordained bishops before their departure. The Pope told them to ordain Giovanni da Montecorvino a bishop (he had only been a priest up till then) and to become his auxiliary bishops. Montecorvino was to become archbishop of Beijing and metropolitan of Cathay. Three of the Franciscans reached China in 1313: Andrea da Perugia, Peregrine da Castello, and Gerardo Albuini, from Cremona. We know this thanks to a letter written by Andrea da Perugia from Guangzhou in January 1336.

Zaitun, the city of the olive tree, is the Arabic name for Quanzhou, a port in Fujian Province that was already of importance in the fourteenth century. After Montecorvino had been created archbishop of Beijing, Andrea da Perugia remained with him for five years. He then went to Zaitun, where Gerardo Albuini had been made bishop. Andrea's letter tells us what followed:

> There is a large city near the sea that is called Zayton in Persian, in which a rich Armenian lady has built a large and beautiful church, which by her wish was erected by the archbishop into a cathedral and adequately endowed. She gave the church to Brother Gerard the bishop and to our brethren who were with him while she was still alive and left it [to them] after her death.[21]

Gerardo Albuini having died, Peregrine da Castello succeeded him as bishop, and, on his death, Andrea da Perugia became bishop. In a wood near the city, he built a chapel with a residence, where there was room for twenty Franciscans. The cost of the building was provided thanks to a pension, called *alafa*, drawn from the imperial treasury.

Quanzhou was a large cosmopolitan city, the crossroads of the southeast coast of China. Numerous Muslims and Syrian Christians had settled there. Many Christian archeological finds were made in Quanzhou, some of them at the time of the Jesuit missions in

---

[21] *S.F.*, vol. 1, Fr. Andrea da Perugia, *Epistola*, Jan. 1336, pp. 374.

景教教徒的须弥座祭坛式石墓上的碑石，雕刻一对
捧圣物的天使，富有波斯、希腊与中国文化艺术相互影响的色彩。

East Syrian Tombstone

Carving on an East Syrian tombstone at Quanzhou, Fujian Province. A Syrian cross is supported by two angelic beings with Buddhist stylistic features. Foreign merchants established themselves in trading posts along the east coast of China during the Yuan dynasty. Many were East Syrian Christians and Roman Catholics, living among Buddhist and Muslim communities.

---

the seventeenth century, when they were the object of passionate study by the missionaries and their Chinese converts. Many more Christian monuments have been discovered since the 1940s, when the old city walls of Quanzhou were demolished at the time of the Japanese invasion.[22] One of them is the tombstone of Andrea da Perugia, who probably died in 1332.[23] Of particular interest is the combination of styles on some of these artifacts: "The decoration on the stones, such as cloud motifs, flowers, and angels, were in all probability carved by Chinese artisans according to the instructions of foreign Christians, and the influence of the artisan's traditional training is clear from the strong resemblance of the angels to the *apsarara* (goddesses, female *devas*) that are found on Buddhist relics in Quanzhou."[24] At about the time when Andrea da Perugia was writing his letter, the Franciscan community in Quanzhou received a visit from the Italian friar Odoric da Pordenone, who had left Italy about 1314 and arrived in

---

[22] See Standaert, pp. 55–57.
[23] Cf. John Foster, "Crosses from the Walls of Zaitun", *J.R.A.S.* (1954):17–20, pl. XVII.
[24] Standaert, p. 55.

China in 1323. Everything interested him, and he had a descriptive talent that can be described as journalistic. He brought to Quanzhou relics of some Franciscans who had recently been martyred in India. Arriving in Guangzhou (Canton), he marveled at the cathedral of the Franciscans and then went up to Beijing, where for three years he assisted Archbishop da Montecorvino, who was by then in his eighties. Pordenone has left us this interesting description of the court of the Mongol ruler[25] and of the place that Christians held within it:

> I will tell one thing about the great khan which I saw. The custom in those parts is that, when the said lord goes through that region, people light a fire in front of the door of their house, and they put perfumes on it so that the smoke arises and gives out a sweet odor to their lord as he passes by, for great crowds go to meet him.
>
> Once when he came to Khanbalik and it was confirmed that he was coming, our bishop and our other Franciscan brethren and I went to meet him, traveling for two days. And when we drew near to him, we placed the cross on a wooden pole so that it could clearly be seen. I held the thurible, which I had brought with me, and we began to chant loudly the antiphon *Veni Sancte Spiritus*, etc. And as we sang, he heard us and had us called and ordered that we be brought to him.
>
> As mentioned above no one, apart from his guards, dares to approach the distance of a stone's throw from his chariot unless called, and when we had approached him with the cross held high, he immediately took off his helmet or head covering, which was of inestimable value, and reverenced the cross. I immediately put incense in the thurible I was carrying, and the bishop took the thurible from my hands and incensed him.
>
> Those who thus approach their lord always bring something with them . . . so that we had carried with us some apples, which we offered to him on a dish. He took two of the apples and ate a little of one of them. Then our bishop gave him his blessing. After that he told us to stand back, so that the horses that were coming behind him and the great crowd should not cause us any inconvenience.[26]

It appears that the cross of the Franciscans did not have to make way before that of the Syrian Christians. Shortly afterward Archbishop Giovanni da Montecorvino came to the end of his earthly course and

---

[25] Yesun Temur, great grandson of Kublai Khan, was emperor of China, 1323–1328.

[26] *S.F.*, vol. 1, Fr. Odoricus de Portu Naonis, *Relatio* (written at Padua at Odoric's dictation in 1330), pp. 492–94.

went to rest in the Lord, whom he had served so well during this life. He died about 1330 and had been for thirty years in China, where he had done exceptional work, keeping up excellent relations with the Mongol sovereigns, training Christians to read the Bible and to take part in the prayer of the liturgy, and setting up bishoprics in the commercial centers of south and central China. He had a magnificent funeral, which was attended by a large crowd, both Christian and non-Christian, pieces of his clothing being eagerly sought after as precious relics.

The Franciscan Missions Fade Away

After the death of their archbishop, the Catholics of Beijing were for several years without a leader. The emperor understood their concern and agreed to send an embassy to the Pope, asking for a new envoy and for the pontifical blessing. The Chinese delegation reached Benedict XII at Avignon in 1338. He gave a favorable reply to its requests and dispatched a new mission, led by John of Florence, better known as Giovanni Marignolli. This group was one of the largest sent to China. Although a certain number dropped out on the way, thirty-two friars and laymen reached Beijing in 1342. The khan received them with great solemnity and was delighted with the horses that the Pope had sent him. Marignolli wrote in his *Relatio*:

> We went into the khan's presence, I wearing the sacred vestments, preceded by a very beautiful cross and accompanied by candles and incense, chanting the *Credo in unum Deum* in the presence of the khan, dwelling in his glorious palace. When the chant was ended, I gave the solemn blessing, which he humbly received.[27]

This glorious entry was to be the prelude to four years of pastoral visits and religious debates, which the legate seemed thoroughly to enjoy:

> There were several successful disputations with the Jews and other sects, and a great harvest of souls was made in the empire.[28]

Unfortunately Marignolli's mission was a temporary one. He had not been appointed archbishop, and after four years he made it clear

---

[27] S.F., vol. 1, *Relatio Fr. Johannis de Marignolli*, p. 529.
[28] Ibid.

Tombstone of Catherine de Viglione

At the top, the Virgin Mary with the infant Jesus. Below, scenes from the martyrdom of St. Catherine. Below right, a kneeling figure, carrying an infant, probably representing a friar interceding for the soul of the deceased. The Latin inscription reads: IN NOMINE DOMINI AMEN HIC JACET KATERINA FILIA QUONDAM DOMINI DOMINICI DE VILIONIS QUAE OBIIT IN ANNO DOMINI MILLESIMO CCC XXXX II DE MENSE JUNII. Yangzhou, Jiangsu Province: 1342.

to the great khan that he did not want to stay any longer and departed for Avignon, promising that a Franciscan cardinal would replace him with full jurisdiction. In fact this did not happen, and the Catholic Church in China was again left without direction. Other bishops were later appointed to the see of Beijing, but they seem never to have reached it. The absence of any documentation means that the history of the Latin Church in fourteenth century China ends in complete obscurity.

The Virgin of Yangzhou

The towns of Yangzhou and Zhenjiang, sixty-two miles (100 kilometers) to the northeast of Nanjing, also had considerable communities of Christians, both Latins and Syrians. Marco Polo had stayed at Yangzhou, which was a prosperous city on the Grand Canal.[29] When the ramparts of the city were pulled down in 1951, workmen found a carved stone, dated 1342, that had been built into the base of the wall near the south gate. A second stone, dated 1344, was discovered in the same area a few days later. Both stones carry a Latin inscription, carved in elongated Lombardic capital letters:

> In the name of the Lord Amen Here lies Catherine daughter of the late Lord Dominic de Viglione who died in the year of the Lord 1342 in the month of June.[30]

> In the name of the Lord Amen Here lies Antony son of the late Lord Dominic de Viglione who departed in the year of the Lord 1344 in the month of November.[31]

---

[29] The early French manuscripts of Marco Polo's *Description of the World* say that he had been governor of Yangzhou (*gouverna*), an impossible claim since the names and nationalities of the governors of Yangzhou are on record. It has been suggested that this is a copyist's error for *sejourna*, meaning that he had stayed there; cf. Frances Wood, *The Silk Road* (London: Folio Society, 2002), p. 125.

[30] Francis A. Rouleau, S.J. "The Yangchow Latin Tombstone as a Landmark of Medieval Christianity in China", *Harvard Journal of Asiatic Studies* 17 (1954):346–65. IN NOMINE DNI AMEN HIC IACET KATERINA FILIA QDAM DOMINI DNICI DE VILIONIS QUE OBIIT IN ANNO DOMINI MILLEXIMO CCCXXXXII DE MENSE IUNII +.

[31] Richard C. Rudolph, "A Second Fourteenth-Century Italian Tombstone in Yangchou", *J.O.S.* 13 (1975):133–36; Hong Kong University Press. IN NOMINE DNI AMEN HIC IACET ANTONIUS FILIUS QDAM DNI DOMINICI DE VILIONIS QUI MIGRAVIT ANNO DNI MCCCXXXXIIII DE MENSE NOVEMBRIS +.

The name de Viglione is known as that of a Venetian family that had been involved with trade in the East since the twelfth century. Both inscriptions are surmounted with delicately etched figures. The ones above Catherine's inscription show Mary carrying the child and scenes from the martyrdom of St. Catherine of Alexandria. Below these is a kneeling friar, carrying the figure of a child, probably representing the soul of the deceased. In the context, it may indicate the Catherine de Viglione had been a benefactress of the friary. The scenes above Antony's inscription show Christ at the top, sitting with outstretched arms, displaying his wounds, indicating that this is a representation of the Last Judgment. On either side are two saints, John the Baptist and Michael. Angels blow trumpets, figures rise from the tombs or kneel naked in supplication, but lower down is St. Anthony Abbot, the patron saint of the Viglione, and a robed figure kneels holding an infant, interceding for the departed.

These monuments are all that remain of the great medieval adventure of the Franciscans in China. They brought to it the bright flame of western Christianity, hoping to submit the Mongol empire to the supreme spiritual authority of the Pope. The Great Khan for his part only wanted a blessing so as to strengthen his power, even though he might have to receive it "in all humility". In 1368, however, the foreign Mongol dynasty in China collapsed and the rebel, Zhu Yuanzhang, a Han Chinese, founded the Ming dynasty in Nanjing.

6

ARABESQUES IN CHINESE INK

Muslims and Jews had taken part in some of the religious debates organized by the Mongol authorities, and Marignolli congratulated himself on the success that his side had won, but perhaps he was declared the winner out of politeness toward a guest who had come a long way. The Mongols had no special regard for Christians, but they knew, from having lived in China a long time, that a guest of honor must not be made to lose face, especially if the powers that be approve of him. Muslims and Jews formed a foreign enclave in China, as did Christians, both Syrian and Latin. They had all grown rich under the Mongols, and their prosperity had often been the cause of hatred on the part of the local population. However, when Mongol power collapsed, Muslims continued to reside in China and to increase in numbers, whereas Syrian Christians and Franciscan missions gradually disappeared toward the end of the fourteenth century. Jews, who were closely associated with Muslims, formed a smaller community, which was well established, at least in the city of Kaifeng in Henan Province. The Jews, however, were eventually absorbed into Chinese society and disappeared, whereas Muslims survived. But estimates of the number of Muslims in today's China vary greatly.

Chinese Muslims remained faithful to Islam and to their religious customs, although in the course of time many of them gradually merged with ethnic Chinese. Others continued to form an ethnic minority, as in the steppes of the northwest of China. This raises questions for Christians who ask themselves how it was that Muslims managed to remain in China, to integrate into the life of the country, and to obtain toleration for their monotheistic and exclusive religion.

Ethnic Implantation

Islam came to China under the first Tang emperors at the same time as the Syrian Christians, and there were official embassies to the court

古蘭经

中阿文对照详注译本

闪目氏·仝道章译注

译林出版社

Qur'an

Bilingual edition of the Qur'an in Chinese and Arabic, published in Nanjing by the Yilin Press in 1989. The Arab missionary Abu Waggas built a mosque in Guangzhou (Canton) in the seventh century; Islam developed in China mostly through immigration. Trade with India and Persia led to the settlement of Muslim communities, especially in the ports of Quanzhou and Guangzhou. At the time of the Mongol emperors, an Islamic academy translated Arabic texts into Chinese. Cultural exchanges followed through the influence of Arab mathematics and astronomy. It is estimated that there are over thirty-five million Muslims in the People's Republic of China (1990 census).

of Chang'an. The first Muslims to settle in China were soldiers; then came merchants and monks, who often arrived by sea. Abu Waggas landed at Guangzhou in the seventh century and built a mosque there "in memory of the saint" (*Huai Sheng si*), i.e., in honor of Muhammad, the messenger of Allah. The tall cylindrical minaret, which was then constructed on the bank of the Pearl River, was used as a lighthouse. The mosque is still in use, some way to the north of the river now, and witnesses to 1,300 years of Muslim history in China. One can also visit the tomb of the apostle Abu Waggas in the gardens near the Foreign Trade Centre, where the Guangzhou Fair takes place.

There are also vestiges of the first Islamic missionaries in the old city of Quanzhou in Fujian Province. According to *Minshu*, the Book of Fujian Province, which was written in 1629 by the historian He Qiaoyuan, four Muslim missionaries arrived in China between 618 and 626. One of them preached at Guangzhou, and one at Yangzhou, and the other two came to Quanzhou, where they were buried. According to local legend, their tomb glowed with light at night. These "holy tombs" are still venerated at a leafy site on the eastern edge of the city.

Chinese historians distinguish several phases of Muslim implantation in China, each with a different name, which indicates progressive integration. They were called *Dashi fa*, "the Arab law", at the time of the Tang and Song Dynasties, from the seventh to the twelfth centuries; they were then called *Hui fa*, "the Hui law", under the Yuan Dynasty; finally they were referred to as *Hui jiao*, "the Hui religion", or *qingzhen jiao*, "the religion of pure truth", under the Ming Dynasty (1368–1644) and the Qing Dynasty (1644–1912).[1] The use of the word *Fa*, "law", during the medieval period reflects the influence of the Buddhist Way of the Dharma, which is rendered by *Fa*.

Under the Tang Dynasty, the use of the word *Dashi* (pronounced *Dayi*), "Arabs", identified Muslims by their ethnic and political origins. They were to be found in some ten ethnic minorities, often of Turkish origins, and were also referred to by these minority names: Uighurs, Kazakhs, Kirghiz, Sala, Uzbeks, Tajiks, etc. Families of sol-

---

[1] These distinctions are analyzed by Ma Qicheng in his chapter "*Lueshu yisilanjiao zai zhongguo de zaoqi quanbo*", "A Brief Account of the Early Spread of Islam in China", p. 176, in the book *Yisilanjiao zai Zhongguo* (*Islam in China*), Ningxia Popular Press, 1982.

diers and merchants settled among the Han Chinese and married Chinese women, so that, after several generations, they became practically indistinguishable from the Chinese. They were then called Hui, which is why Islam was eventually called *Huijiao*, "religion of the Hui", a name that also carries an ethnic connotation, since the use of the word *Hui* derives from the first syllable of Uighur.[2] There exists a Ningxia-Hui Autonomous Region in northwest China, whose capital is Yinchuan on the Yellow River, a center for horse trading since the time of the Tang Dynasty (618–907 A.D.).

The development of Islam in China owes more to the incidence of migration than to a missionary drive for converts. The growth of the Muslim community can also be attributed partially to interracial marriages and to the buying of children. Marriages with Chinese women always profited Islam, for a Chinese bride entered her husband's family and naturally adopted its religion. Filial piety demanded it, if not conviction, whereas a Muslim father would not allow his daughters to marry Chinese "idolaters".

Additional factors favorable to Islamic implantation were the commercial, scientific, and technical relations between Islamic countries and the Chinese Empire. Muslim merchants from the ports of the Persian Gulf would sail along the coast of India, put in at the Strait of Malacca, then use the monsoon winds to reach the coast of south China. They brought luxury goods, such as ivory, incense, copper, and rhinoceros horn, which was much used in Chinese medicine. These would be exchanged for silk, porcelain, and the spices of the south islands. Paper making had been introduced from China to Muslim Persia at the time of the Tang Dynasty, and there was a paper mill in Baghdad by the end of the eighth century.[3]

Muslims also offered China many scientific and technical services. A Muslim architect worked at the construction of the palace of the great khan at Khanbalik. An Islamic academy, instituted during the reign of Kublai Khan, oversaw the translation of Arabic texts. The Persian mathematician, astronomer, and geographer Jamal al-Din arrived in China during the reign of Great Khan Mongke (1251–1259). In 1267

[2] According to Bai Shouyi's book in Chinese, *Zhongguo Yisilanshi cungao: Essays on the History of Islam in China* (Ningxia Popular Press, 1983), p. 21.

[3] Cf. Thomas T. Allsen, *Culture and Conquest in Mongol Eurasia* (Cambridge, U.K.: Cambridge University Press, 2001), p. 176.

he presented the court with a globe representing the earth and was then commissioned to produce a massive descriptive geography with maps, which was completed in 1291.[4] In 1271 a Muslim Astronomical Observatory was created by Kublai Khan at Beijing with Jamal al-Din as director.[5] The first emperor of the Ming Dynasty, as soon as he came to power in 1368, transferred this institution (it had become the Institute of Muslim Astronomy by then) to his new capital, Nanjing.[6] Arabic influence is also evident in Chinese mathematics. The use of algebraic calculations spread in China under the Mongols, and this had an influence on the mathematician and astronomer Guo Shoujing.

Cultural exchanges between the two civilizations, Chinese and Islamic, were promoted by the observations of great Muslim travelers. They noted especially the vitality of the communities of believers. In the mid ninth century, at the very time when Buddhists and Syrian Christians were being persecuted in northwest China under the Tang Dynasty, an Arab called Suleiman wrote this description of the Muslim community in Guangzhou:

> There are an imam and a mosque there. Muslim merchants from everywhere flock to Guangzhou. A judge, appointed by the emperor of China, deals with lawsuits between believers according to Muslim custom. . . . A few days each week must be set aside for the common prayer of the faithful and for the reading of the sacred texts. Worship ends with blessings on the sultan of Islam. The judge is an honest man who listens to complaints in all fairness. Everything is based on the Koran, the Hadiths, and Muslim custom.[7]

The judge mentioned in this text was responsible for the *fanfang*, the Muslim quarter, which was a territorial concession where the faithful were concentrated. Such an administrative arrangement had been more clearly codified at the time of the Song Dynasty (960–1279). The head of the Muslim quarter, who was called *fanzhang*, was a respectable Arab, chosen by the Chinese authorities. He had an office for Muslim affairs, and it was his responsibility to collect taxes from the Muslim merchants and to be the arbitrator in their disputes.

---

[4] Ibid., pp. 107–9.

[5] Ibid., p. 167.

[6] Ibid., pp. 168, 173.

[7] Ma Qicheng, ibid., p. 183. Translation from the French translation of the Chinese text.

Within the Muslim community he was called the *kadi*, and, as well as being judge, he looked after the religious activities of the community. The *fanzhang*'s administrative duties thus combined religious and political aspects, in accord with Muslim tradition. Muslims in China were not assimilated by the Chinese population, but they were surrounded by it, like islands separately administered, authorized by the government and tolerated by the population.

At the time of the Song emperors, famous mosques were built in China. The ruins of the mosque at Zaitun (Quanzhou) can still be visited today. It was built in 1009 and restored in 1310. The walls and the monumental gate, which is still standing, are in Arab style. On the stone lintel of the entrance arch are carved verses 18–19 of sura 3 of the Koran, in Arabic script:

> Allah bears witness that there is no God but him, and so do the angels and the sages. He is the Executor of Justice, the Only God, the Mighty, the Wise One. The only true faith in God's sight is Islam.

The great traveler Ibn Battuta left Tangier in 1325 for a voyage that lasted twenty-nine years and took him to Islamic centers in Africa, the Middle East, and Asia. When he landed at Quanzhou he was impressed by the port facilities, calling it the greatest port in the world. According to various stone inscriptions, there were at that time six or seven mosques in Quanzhou.

Ibn Battuta then went up to Beijing, where he was able to visit the mosque in Ox Street, which was built in 996, at the time of the Song Dynasty. The name of the street alludes to the former Muslim monopoly of the beef trade. The original mosque was rebuilt under the Ming Dynasty in the style of a Buddhist temple. From the outside only the minaret indicates that the building is a mosque. Inside Arabic inscriptions from the Koran in letters of gold blend with the Chinese style of the coffered ceiling. The various parts of the building date from three dynasties—the Song (960–1279), the Ming (1368–1644), and the Qing (1644–1912)—which is in itself a sign of the continuity of Islam in China and also evidence of its aesthetic integration into Chinese culture.

At the time of the Song Dynasty, Christians in China only constituted a small remnant. Under the Ming they disappeared altogether, whereas the Muslims were building mosques and taking an active part in the economic and cultural life of the country. Outstanding Muslim personalities marked those periods.

At the time of the Song, Mi Fei (1051–1107) took up again the style of the Tang landscape painters, introducing his own stipple technique. He painted pine trees, crowned with delicately rendered needles, against a background of mist from which emerge the tops of mountains. Mi Fei and the great poet Su Dongpo worked together and covered acres of paper, while happily drinking jugs of wine, but Mi Fei's Buddhist and Confucian friends could not understand his Islamic faith. It was the same some centuries later; the Jesuit lay brother Giuseppe Castiglione (1688–1766) became a painter at the court of the Qianlong emperor, where his portraits and pictures of horses and banquets were much appreciated, whereas his Christian faith was ignored, though tolerated for the sake of his art.

At the beginning of the fifteenth century under the Ming Dynasty, a Muslim eunuch distinguished himself in the south China seas as commander of the imperial fleet. Zheng He (1371–1434) came from Yunnan Province and was the son of a *haji* (someone who had been to Mecca on pilgrimage). He had originally been called Ma, as were many Muslims, because it is the first syllable of Mahomet (Muhammad). The Chinese character for Ma means horse, which could also be understood as an allusion to Arab horses. Zheng had been castrated to enter the Beijing harem of the future Yongle emperor and was later put in charge of important naval expeditions under Yongle and his successor, the Xuande emperor. Between 1405 and 1433 Zheng commanded no less than seven naval expeditions along the coasts of southeast Asia, India, the Persian Gulf, and the east coast of Africa. His Muslim religion was a great asset in the regions he explored, which had varying degrees of Muslim presence —Champa in Vietnam, Java, Palembang, Atcheh in north Sumatra, Ormuz at the mouth of the Persian Gulf, and Jeddah, not far from Mecca.

For each expedition, about 20,000 men were taken on board the large junks of the Chinese fleet. Zheng He saw to it that his men were disciplined, thus establishing friendly relations, especially with the countries of southeast Asia. He had such a good reputation with the Chinese who had emigrated there that they made him into a god called San Bao (the Threefold Treasure) and consecrated a temple to him in Melaka, which became very popular. Today's Malay Muslims obviously do not go to the Chinese temple to worship him, but they have created a museum where Zheng He's exploits are well presented.

Thanks to the number of Chinese who had settled in the Malay peninsula and in Indonesia, trade developed in the southern seas, and, a hundred years later, the Portuguese were to benefit from this commercial network. They found trade between spice islands and south China ports profitable and often settled in the area rather than returning to distant Europe.

Mosques and Chinese Temples

Muslims had come a long way since their arrival in China in the seventh century. They were hardly affected by the expulsion of foreign religions in the ninth century because they benefited from the support of the powerful Abbasid caliphs of Baghdad and from the cultural influence of Persian Islam. Nor did the destruction of Islamic Baghdad by the Mongols in 1258 weaken their influence. They found a place in the administration of the Mongols, who respected their Muslim faith, as they did other religions. The rebellions in China that sapped Mongol power in the fourteenth century did not derive from a purist antiforeigner movement, as the Confucian reformist movement had done at the time of the Tang in the ninth century. Trouble came from secret societies, like the Red Turbans, who inspired peasant uprisings. Their inspiration came from a popular syncretism that combined Buddhist, Taoist, and Manichean beliefs. After Zhu Yuanzhang had seized power at Nanjing in 1368, he made use of the services of qualified Muslims.

The integration of Muslims into Chinese society took place under the aegis of ethnic pluralism, as authorized by the Chinese state. In the case of the Hui, such a policy was crowned with success. The exterior forms of their public life became Chinese, but the faith of Islam remained intact at the level of private life. By means of religious services at the mosque and the customs regulating diet and marriage laws, the Islamic communities of China remained members of the worldwide Muslim *Umma*. Religious observances remained internal to the Muslim communities, which knew how to avoid the kind of outward signs that would have provoked the anger of the Chinese. Muslims generally avoided any aggressive proselytism.

The mosques built at the time of the Ming Dynasty (1368–1644) looked from the outside like Buddhist temples with curved roofs and a series of monumental gates. The inner sanctuary was the great hall of prayer, whose floor was covered with carpets and where the *minbar*, with its recess in the direction of Mecca, was richly decorated. In sharp contrast to the Buddhist temples, there were no statues. Large inscriptions of Koranic texts in Arabic script reminded the faithful of the Prophet's message and invited them to prayer.

It was only toward the end of the seventeenth century that Muslim writings in Chinese began to be produced, at a time when the three monotheistic religions were required to justify their existence within a Confucian society. The society of the Han, which was purely Chinese in its tradition, was not at all inclined to welcome the teachings of the Koran. Economic interests or family ties seem to have been the motive of the few conversions to Islam that occurred. Muslims were given a place in society in virtue of the principle "each one according to his custom", but custom was not expected to disturb unduly the ritual unity of the Confucian Empire.

Among the ethnic minorities of northwest and southwest China, however, many Muslims were not integrated into the Han minority. They often belonged to groups of Turkish origin, which were restive under a Chinese administration. There was always the possibility that the situation would lead to open conflict, in which case Islam became a factor that unified race, language, and movements for political independence. At later periods in Chinese history, there were violent Muslim uprisings and this is a possibility that still needs to be reckoned with today.[8]

Cases of subversive activity should not obscure the fact that Muslims on the whole have been successful in winning acceptance in Chi-

---

[8] See Peter Mullarky, "An Analytical Account of the Muslim Rebellions in North-West China (1862–1878): The Causes, Course, Suppression and Subsequent Pacification, with an Examination of the Significance of this Period for Contemporaneous and Subsequent Developments in China" (unpublished M.A. dissertation, School of Oriental and African Studies, University of London, 1998).

nese society, but this was not to happen to the new wave of Christians who appeared on the coasts of China in the middle of the sixteenth century. These "Foulangkis"[9] came as would-be conquerors and missionaries, and their intention was not only to trade with the Chinese but also to convert them.

---

[9] *Foulangki* is the Chinese rendering of the word *Frank*, the name given by Arabs to the Portuguese and the Spaniards.

II

THE FRIENDSHIP OF WISE MEN

Can the Christian message be accepted by a Confucian society? In the late Ming Dynasty, at the end of the sixteenth century, a number of great Confucian scholars gave a favorable welcome to the message of the first Jesuit missionaries. These Chinese scholars were upright and generous men, anxious to reform the decadent and corrupt administration of their country. They also tried to create wealth for its peoples and to bring them prosperity.

The missionaries came into conflict with conservative Confucians, who were fearful of the threat posed by foreign powers and hostile to any change in the ritual order, as inherited from the ancients.

There was opposition at a deeper level too. The ritual order of China was being challenged by a prophetic message. The wise men of this world were disconcerted by the Cross of Christ.

7

THE DISCOMFITURE OF
THE CONQUISTADORS

In recent years, small groups of pilgrims from Hong Kong, Taiwan, or Japan have taken to visiting the little island of Shangchuan (San-cian), some twelve and a half miles (twenty kilometers) from the Province of Guangdong on the south coast of China. Steps lead from the shore to a small white church with gothic windows. Inside, a large gray tombstone bears the dates: "Born 7 April 1506. Died 3 December 1552". Behind the church, steps lead through the scrub and up a rocky slope to a semicircular platform cut out of the rock, where a tall plinth supports the statue of St. Francis Xavier. An ancient memorial tablet, dated 1639, is fixed to the base of the monument and has the following inscription in Chinese and Portuguese:

> Here was buried
> Saint Francis Xavier
> of the Company of Jesus
> Apostle of the East

This is where St. Francis Xavier died, gazing at the sea and the Chinese mainland, which he would never reach. He was looked after by his faithful Chinese servant, Anthony, whom he had brought from Goa to be his interpreter. Two and a half months after Francis Xavier's burial, his body was exhumed, on February 17, 1553, and brought on the *Santa Fe*, first to Melaka and then to Goa. The mortal remains of this great missionary thus traveled back on the way he had come, along the Portuguese trading posts.

At the time of St. Francis Xavier's death, almost two centuries had elapsed since there had been any sign of Christianity in China. When Marignolli had been there from 1342 to 1346, the Franciscan communities were still flourishing. They died out later because of lack of recruits and material support. No more personnel came from the West, and the financial support, which the Mongol administration had provided, ceased when the Yuan Dynasty was overturned. After Marignolli's departure from Beijing in 1346, ten clerics were appointed to the see of Beijing at various periods, but nothing more is known about them. It is doubtful whether any of them ever reached the Chinese capital. In 1371 an apostolic delegate, Francesco de Polio, was sent to China with twelve companions, but they were never heard of again. There is only information about the last cleric sent to China by Rome in the Middle Ages, who was taken prisoner by the Turks in 1475. After seven years, he was released and died in Italy, never having gotten anywhere near Beijing.

At the time the sea routes to the East were under Muslim control and were dangerous for Christians, nor could travelers reach China overland, although there was a Latin Christian base in Persia, where Pope John XXII had made the new town of Sultaniyeh into an archbishopric with six suffragan sees in 1318.[1] Nearly a century later, the Dominican archbishop of Sultaniyeh was entrusted with responsibility for the Church in China, but by then no contact could be established as the routes through central Asia were blocked.

The east Syrian Christians probably survived in China a little longer than the Franciscans, but they were so involved with the Mongols that they must, in many cases, have disappeared with them. There is hardly any information to go on, although some of the Jesuits working in China in the seventeenth century picked up residual information about Christian practices a hundred years previously.[2]

Christendom Divided

The main factor that brought the European missions to east Asia to an end was, however, the division of Western Christianity rather than difficulties in China itself. At the end of the fourteenth century, the

---

[1] The bull *Redemptor Noster* of Pope John XXII (April 1, 1318) altered the pastoral provisions for Latin Christians in Asia, dividing responsibility between Dominicans and Franciscans. Sultaniyeh became the metropolitan see for western Asia, which was entrusted to the Dominicans. Khanbalik became the metropolitan see for eastern Asia, entrusted to the Franciscans. Armand Olichon, *Les Missions* (Paris: Bloud et Gay, 1936), p. 163.

[2] Kenneth Scott Latourette, *A History of Christian Missions in China* (S.P.C.K., 1929), p. 75: "In the early part of the seventeenth century some Jesuits then in China were told by a Jew that as late as the first half of the sixteenth century there had been those in north China who used the sign of the cross, but they had been persecuted and had been absorbed either into the pagan community or into the Muslim or Jewish bodies."

countries of Europe grouped themselves round two claimants to the papacy, one in Rome and one in Avignon. The "Great Schism of the West" lasted for forty years. At the same time, the eastern part of Christianity was under the attack of the Ottoman Turks.

These Turks were themselves under pressure from a fearsome leader who had emerged in the region of Samarqand, Timur Leng, meaning "Timur the lame", known in the West as Tamerlane (1336–1405). He was Mongol by birth, a Muslim in religion, and Turkish in language and culture. Professor David Morgan gives a summary of this unsavory character:

> His career, from bandit to conqueror, bears some resemblance to that of Chingiz Khan. . . . His army was organized in much the same way . . . and he was undeniably a highly gifted and successful general. But he indulged in destruction and wanton cruelty to an extent that Chingiz would have considered pointless; and it may be felt that, as a man who had been brought up as a Muslim and in a highly "civilized" society, he had less excuse.[3]

Timur carved out for himself an empire that stretched from Asia Minor to India, and the crushing defeats that he inflicted on the Turks seriously weakened the Ottoman Empire. Christian nations, however, were in no position to profit from the situation. Greeks and Latins were fighting each other, and the Latin Churches were divided by the Great Schism. In 1453 Sultan Muhammad II besieged and captured Constantinople, and the eastern Roman Empire, Byzantium, ceased to exist. Constantinople became Istanbul, the capital of the Ottoman Empire, and for the next 300 years Europe lay open to Turkish invasions.

It was a time when the traditional institutions of Christendom were shaken by a series of events: political upheaval, armed conflict, natural disaster, and intellectual crisis. Faithful believers sought peace of soul in mystical and affective union with the suffering Christ. This troubled period produced a little book that became a spiritual classic, *The Imitation of Christ*. It is attributed to Thomas à Kempis (c. 1379–1471), from Kempen by Düsseldorf, who became a canon regular at the monastery of Mt. St. Agnes, near Zwolle in the Netherlands. The emphasis on salvation by inner conversion was soon to inspire saints for a new age, such as St. Ignatius Loyola and his disciples in

---

[3] David Morgan, *The Mongols* (Oxford: Blackwell Publishing, 1986), p. 201.

the Society of Jesus. Much later *The Imitation of Christ* was translated into Chinese and is today the most widespread book of spirituality in China, having been one of the first to be reprinted after the Cultural Revolution.

Spaniards and Portuguese Share Out the World

The image of a humble and suffering Redeemer was not the one projected by Spanish and Portuguese seamen as they sailed round the world. The peoples of the Iberian Peninsula had had the experience of protracted struggles against the Moors, the *Reconquista*, which had begun in the small Christian kingdoms of the Pyrenees in the early Middle Ages and ended with the conquest of the emirate of Granada in 1492. The faith of such Catholics had the quality of tempered steel and inspired the conquerors who planted the cross in America, Africa, and Asia. They baptized wholesale populations, which had scarcely been catechized, and they did it in a way that was an act of annexation, if not a reduction to slavery, rather than a call to the freedom of the children of God.

The momentum that drove the men of the Renaissance to break the mold of their ancient world witnesses to their extraordinary energy. The Italians of the fifteenth century had created the new humanism of arts and letters. Their cities had become wealthy through Mediterranean trade, and their politicians followed rules for political action derived from Machiavelli (1469–1527). Meanwhile the Spaniards and the Portuguese had received from the Arabs the scientific knowledge that made the progress of astronomy, geography, and navigation possible, so that they were ready to turn toward the ocean. An Italian, Flavia Gioia, had been inspired by a Chinese original to perfect the *bossola*, a small box containing a magnetic needle that revolved so as to indicate the north. The astrolabe, also inherited from the Arabs, made it possible to measure the height of the polar star above the horizon.

It was Henry "the Navigator" (1394–1460) who took the initiative in what became the discovery of the world by Europeans when he began to explore the coasts of Africa. He was the son of John I, king of Portugal. Thanks to Prince Henry, the Azores and the Cape Verde

Islands were discovered, and his ships reached as far as Lagos. Further exploration was made possible by the maritime expertise that he built up in Portugal, and this bore fruit at the end of the century when another Portuguese navigator, Bartholomeu Dias (d. 1500), rounded the southern tip of Africa and gave its name to the Cape of Good Hope in 1488. Vasco da Gama (1469–1524) set sail from Portugal in 1497 and went up the east coast of Africa as far as Kenya, where he was fortunate to engage the services of an Arab pilot who guided the flotilla to Calicut on the southwest coast of India. Vasco da Gama was back in Lisbon by 1499, having discovered a new way of reaching the spice islands and the famous Cathay, which had fired European imaginations since Marco Polo's *Description of the World*. An era of Portuguese control of the Indian Ocean thus began, which made Lisbon the center for the distribution of spices in Europe. Seven years previously the Genoese sailor Christopher Columbus, with the support of the Spanish sovereigns, had set sail westward with three caravels, looking for a way to reach India. On October 12, 1492, he had landed in America.

The newly discovered lands were considered as conquests for Christ, according to the outlook of the time, which saw Christendom as a temporal power, legitimated by a spiritual authority. The rights of the previous inhabitants were not considered. When they were baptized, they became the subjects of Catholic monarchs, thousands of miles away. However, a way had to be found for sharing these new dominions between Catholic nations, and here the Pope was considered as arbitrator. The Portuguese had received papal privileges, granting them sovereignty over lands yet to be discovered. Once the Spaniards had begun to sail to the New World, they appealed to the Pope, challenging the Portuguese monopoly. Alexander VI, the Borgia Pope, tried to settle the matter by dividing the spheres of influence of the two countries in America by the Treaty of Tordesillas in 1494. This arrangement has sometimes been presented as an attempt to divide the whole globe between the two nations, but this was not really the case, and, as a result of the treaty, the colonial expansion of Spain and Portugal proceeded with a greater measure of agreement than would otherwise have been the case. The last testament of Queen Isabella of Castile makes the link between conquest and missionary activity explicit:

Our absolute desire, in petitioning Pope Alexander VI to bestow upon us half the islands and the continents of the ocean, was to make every effort to lead the peoples of these new countries to convert to our holy religion, to send them priests, religious, prelates, and others, instructed and fearing God, so as to educate them in the truths of the faith and to give them a taste for Christian life and a knowledge of its customs.[4]

The Portuguese were also extending their influence in Asia and had established a string of forts on the coast of India and in the direction of China. The question then arose as to how far they should go. The 1494 Treaty of Tordesillas had only considered the Atlantic and had agreed a line running from north to south 1,680 miles (2,700 kilometers) west of the Cape Verde Islands (46 degrees, 30 minutes west of Greenwich). East of that line was Portuguese territory, i.e., Brazil, and to the west was Spanish South America. It was more difficult to establish a practical line of demarcation in Asia, amid the archipelagos of the spice islands. The calculations of sixteenth-century cartographers differed and tended to justify those already in possession. However, in 1529 Portugal and Spain agreed by the Treaty of Saragossa on a line 12 degrees west of the Moluccas (Maluku) (116 degrees east of Greenwich), which, if projected northward, reached the south coast of China between Guangzhou and Fujian. West of the line was to be a Portuguese sphere of influence, and east of it was to be Spanish.

During the sixteenth century, the Spaniards duly expanded into Asia, but, unlike the Portuguese, they came to it from the east, as Fernando Magellan (c. 1480–1521) had done. He reached Cebu in the Philippines in 1521, having sailed across the Atlantic, through the straits that now bear his name, at the southern tip of America, and then crossed the Pacific in ninety-eight days. In 1542, Ruy Lopez de Villalobos came to the Philippines, naming them in honor of Prince Philip, the son of Emperor Charles V. Miguel Lopez de Legazpi established Spanish military control over them from 1564 to 1570 and became the first governor, making Manila the capital. The Philippines marked the limit of Spanish expansion westward.

When missionaries from Spain and Portugal arrived in Asia, they experienced the tensions between their home governments, so that the first attempts at evangelization were undermined by sordid con-

---

[4] Text quoted in French translation by Daniel-Rops, *L'Église de la Renaissance et de la Réforme* (Paris: Arthème Fayard), p. 314.

flicts between the two powers. The Portuguese made great play of the mission that they had received from the Church by documents dated 1452 and 1454, Pope Nicholas V having conferred upon King Affonso and his successors the right of patronage over the ecclesiastical administration of lands "already acquired or to be acquired". In return the kings of Portugal undertook to build churches and to send and support priests, both secular and religious, and they were careful to benefit from the control that the *Padroado* gave them and to carry out their duty as patrons of the missions.[5] They also acted as heirs of the Crusaders and attempted to destroy Muslim settlements along the seaways. Once they had secured access to the Indian Ocean by way of the Cape of Good Hope, the Portuguese were in a position to attack the Ottoman Empire from the rear and, by dominating the sea lanes of the Indian Ocean, to wrest from it the substantial revenues to be made from the trade in spices. The viceroy, Affonso de Albuquerque, founder of the Portuguese empire in the East, captured Goa in 1510 and, in the following year Melaka, which was appreciably nearer to the spice islands. Malacca, or Malaca, now appears on maps as Melaka. It is a city on the west side of peninsular Malaysia (formerly Malaya), on the channel that separates it from Sumatera and is still called the Strait of Malacca. Albuquerque built a fortress on the hill of St. Paul at Melaka and made it a Christian center. Jesuits, Dominicans, Franciscans, and Augustinians established monasteries there, and in 1557 a diocese of Malacca was established by the *Padroado*. St. Francis Xavier visited Melaka five times. As far as peninsular Malaysia was concerned, Melaka was a fortified enclave on the coast, and Christianity remained limited to the city itself, which became a starting point for missionaries sailing further east.

Muslims were strongly implanted in the region, especially in the northern areas of the islands of Sumatera and Java. The Portuguese tried to convert the peoples who had not yet been won over by Islam, but their greed did not attract many converts. Their real aim was to establish as direct a contact as possible with the spice-producing islands, first among which were the Moluccas Islands between Celebes and New Guinea. The name appears on modern maps as Maluku, the sea to the west of it still being known as the Moluccas Sea. The area

---

[5] For the Portuguese *Padroado* see N.C.E., vol. 10, pp. 1114–15, article by A. Da Silva Rego, *sub nomen* Patronato Real.

was conquered by the Netherlands East India Company in the seventeenth century and is now part of Indonesia. However, the Portuguese did not want to occupy territory or undertake cultivation; what interested them was trading the finished products—nutmeg, cloves, cinnamon, ginger, and pepper, which were the source of considerable wealth on the European market.

The First Folangjis in Canton

The first Portuguese expedition from Melaka to China took place in 1521, and its arrival in Guangzhou was the subject of a report by Gu Yingxiang, a Chinese civil servant:

> Fo-lang-ji is the name of a country and not of a cannon.[6] In the year Ding-chou of the Zhengde reign (1517) I was acting overseer in the Guangdong, and I was interim commissioner for coastal affairs. Two large sea vessels arrived unexpectedly and made directly for the postal station of the town of Guangzhou, saying that they had brought tribute from the land of Fo-lang-ji. The commander of the ships was called Ka-pi-tan. The ships' company had protruding noses and deep-set eyes; they were wearing turbans of white linen on their head, according to the custom of the Muslims. News was immediately carried to the viceroy, His Excellency Chen Xixian, who was then gracing Guangzhou with his presence. He gave orders, since these people knew nothing of etiquette, that they should be instructed for three days, in the appropriate ceremonies in the Guang Xiao Si, after which they were introduced. Since it was noted that Da Ming Hui Dian [the collection of laws of the Ming Dynasty] contained no report of tribute received from the said nation, a complete report of the incident was transmitted to His Majesty, who authorized the sending [of persons and presents] to the ministry [of rites]. His Majesty was at the time on visitation in the southern provinces, and [the foreigners] were left for nearly a year in the same dwelling place as myself. When his present Majesty ascended the throne, the interpreter [Pires] was condemned to death because of the disrespectful behavior [of the foreigners] and his men were sent back as prisoners to Guangzhou and expelled from the province. During the long stay that these people

---

[6] In Chinese *Folangji chong*, meaning "Frankish cannon", was a current expression at the time. It was therefore necessary to specify that the report was about the Portuguese and not their firearms.

made in Guangzhou, they showed their predilection for the Buddhist scriptures.[7]

The Portuguese had been treated as vassals, as were all foreign delegations to China, and their behavior had been considered disrespectful because they had not conformed to the Chinese ritual. As for the reference to their predilection for the Buddhist scriptures, this could be an allusion to their zeal for making the Gospel known, since the term *Buddhist* was a generic one for foreign religions. Matteo Ricci was also identified at first as a Buddhist monk.

The wearing of a white turban in the Muslim manner might have been adopted as a way of misleading the enemy during the crossing, or it might have been in order to get a better reception in Guangzhou. However, the Muslims who had been in Guangzhou for a long time lost no time in warning the Chinese authorities about the Folangjis. After protracted negotiations, the Portuguese obtained permission to anchor off a small uninhabited island, a few miles from the estuary of the Guangzhou River, and this was only authorized for three months in the year. They could sail to Guangzhou from the island, but they were not allowed to stay in Guangzhou.

St. Francis Xavier had worked in India from 1541 to 1545 and then spent two years in Japan (1549–1551), where he had discovered a civilization that had been greatly influenced by China. Confucianism and Buddhism had come to Japan from China, and so had ideographic writing. In early 1552, St. Francis was back in Goa, where, on April 9, he wrote to St. Ignatius Loyola in Rome.[8] This letter is of particular significance as it shows St. Francis planning his visit to China as a result of his experience in Japan. Whereas in India he had worked among the poor and the lower castes, in Japan he had donned better clothing and sought to dispute with the Buddhist priests. In writing to St. Ignatius, he describes the qualities that are required for missionaries in Japan and emphasizes the need for intellectual formation. Although St. Francis himself never reached China, his approach,

---

[7] Text quoted from Cordier by Henri-Bernard Maître, *Aux portes de la Chine: Les Missions du XVIe siècle: 1514–1588* (Tientsin, 1933), pp. 26–27. Translation ours from the French translation.

[8] *Lettres de Saint François Xavier*, trans. by Léon Pagès (Paris: Poussielgue-Rusand, 1855), vol. 2; livre vii, lettre xv; pp. 296–99.

gained from the experience of Japan, was the one later followed by the Jesuits in China.

> In six days, if God allows, we shall leave for the empire of China,[9] three of our party being members of the Company [of Jesus], two of them priests. The said empire is situated opposite Japan, but is far greater in extent and has a great number of eminent minds and doctors of profound learning. As far as I have been able to discover, education and study are held in great honor there, and those who are the greater scholars hold most eminent places in rank and authority. It is well known that the religions that flourish in Japan have come there from China.[10] . . . Our brothers who are to be chosen for the universities in Japan will require great virtue and great strength of soul, since they will face so much suffering and so many trials.[11] Moreover they will require outstanding intelligence and learning in dealing, in a way that is both nimble and accurate, with the innumerable questions that the Japanese ask. They need to be especially competent in philosophy, especially in logic, so that they can refute and convince the hardheaded Japanese, making them see clearly that they are not consistent in their arguments and are always contradicting themselves. I would also recommend that the brethren should be competent in astronomy.[12]

Francis was determined to bring the Gospel to the Chinese mainland, but the Portuguese merchants, whose relations with the Chinese were proving very difficult, did not want to be burdened with this additional problem. However, they did agree to transport him to the island of Shangchuan, where, as mentioned above, he remained quite alone with his Chinese servant, waiting in vain for a ship to bring him to Guangzhou. He died on December 3, 1552, exhausted with fever and under the gray sky of a winter's morning.

The question arises as to who was the first Christian missionary to enter China during the sixteenth century. Was it a Jesuit or a Dominican? In 1555, the Jesuit provincial Melchior Nuñez Barreto spent two months in Guangzhou in an attempt to obtain the release

---

[9] In fact St. Francis Xavier did not reach Shangchuan until the last week of August 1552.

[10] Ibid., p. 297. Translation ours, from Léon Pagès' French translation of the Latin originals.

[11] St. Francis Xavier lists among the trials the fact that the brethren will not be able to celebrate Mass and so will be deprived of Holy Communion, the hatred of the Japanese for foreigners, the hostility of the Buddhist priests, the diet, and the cold.

[12] Ibid., p. 299.

of six Christian prisoners, of whom three were Portuguese. In that same year, a Portuguese Dominican, Gaspard de la Cruz, preached the Gospel in Guangzhou for several months with an audacity that is to the credit of the friars preachers. Portuguese Dominicans had in 1545 created a Congregation of the Holy Cross for the East Indies. Three years later they sent a dozen friars to Goa and then to Melaka. Gaspard de la Cruz was one of them and sailed from Melaka to Cambodia, where he founded a first mission. However, he came up against the hostility of Buddhist monks and persuaded the friendly captain of a Chinese junk to take him and a few companions to China. They went by Macao, where the Portuguese authorities approved his undertaking, and reached Guangzhou in 1555. He gave a self-assured account of the success that attended his preaching:

> I preached frequently. My strange physical appearance and my dress drew the attention of a large crowd, who blocked the streets. They always listened to my words attentively and asked me some questions. . . . They said that my teaching was excellent and that they had never heard so much.[13]

The crowd was expressing, in a polite Chinese way, that they had not understood a thing, but the Dominican was elated by what he imagined to be his success and gave his zeal free rein:

> His preaching had such great effect that one day he went as far as to knock a statue off its pedestal, telling the people that it was only stone and that they were worth more than stone. Some of them replied, "You are right."[14]

The local mandarins felt that there would be no point in contradicting such a man, but they were concerned by the effect that his ill-considered actions might have on the people. They had him arrested with the intention of putting him to death, but limited themselves finally to expelling him from the country. In doing so, they were following a regulation of which Gaspard was aware, since he wrote:

> In this kingdom there are two obstacles to spreading the faith; the first is that any innovation is forbidden; the second is that foreigners are only

---

[13] Gaspard de la Cruz' account is quoted in José Maria Gonzalez, O.P., *Historia de las Misiones Dominicanas de China 1632–1700*, vol. 1, (Madrid, 1964), p. 14, n. 11.

[14] Ibid.

entitled to stay at Canton with the permission of the mandarins and that they only allow this for a limited period, after which one must leave China.[15]

After his expulsion, Gaspard continued his apostolic work in India and later in Portugal, where he died nursing victims of the plague. He wrote a *History of China* dedicated to King Sebastian of Portugal, in which he denounced the "deplorable and monstrous" excesses of the Portuguese elders in Macao and blamed them for his expulsion. He alleged that they had brought upon themselves the hatred of the Chinese, who called them "men of the devil". The expression "foreign devils" obviously goes back a long way.

Macao as a Base

In 1557 the Chinese government gave official approval to a Portuguese settlement in Macao. Near the mouth of the Pearl River, there is a small peninsula, *Aomen*, which means "the door of the creek" or "the gully". At the entrance of the creek sheltered by the peninsula is a small temple, much visited by Chinese sailors and dedicated to *Ah Ma*, "the holy mother", hence the name "Mak ao", the creek of the Holy Mother.

Under the shelter of Macao's fort, the Christian population slowly increased. They were 400 in 1557 and 1,000 in 1582,[16] mostly Portuguese merchants and their families. A Jesuit bishop, Andrea Oviedo, who had the title of patriarch of Ethiopia, came in 1566. He administered the Catholic community until a diocese of Macao was created in 1576, which was taken in charge by Bishop Leonardo de Sa in 1581. From 1586 a number of religious orders followed the Jesuits in building monasteries in Macao: Franciscans, Augustinians, and Dominicans. Macao thus became the religious center for missionaries going to China and Japan, although this small cluster of Church buildings remained cut off from the local Chinese population. In 1573 the Chinese authorities built a wall across the narrow neck of land that

---

[15] Quoted in A. Marie, O.P., *Missions dominicaines dans l'Extrême-Orient* (1865), p. 103.

[16] Lin Jiajun, *Studies on the History of the Diocese of Macao* (Macao: Administrative Services of Catholic Affairs of Macao, 1989); in Chinese.

links the peninsula to the mainland. In this wall was a gate that was only opened every five days for market. On other days five strips of paper were stretched across the gate to seal it. On the lintel of the archway was an inscription: *Fear our greatness and respect our virtue.*[17] Although this small Portuguese colony was despised by the Chinese, it did receive a visit from the great Portuguese poet Luis Vaz de Camões (1524/5–1580), who stayed there in the early days of the colony, from 1556 to 1558. In his epic poem *Os Lusíadas* he celebrated the heroic deeds of his fellow countrymen:

> You, whom no form of danger
> Prevented from conquering the infidel . . .
>
> You, Portuguese, as few as you are valiant,
> Make light of your slender forces;
> Through martyrdom, in its manifold forms,
> You spread the message of eternal life:
> Heaven has made it your destiny
> To do many and mighty deeds
> For Christendom, despite being few and weak,
> For thus, O Christ, do you exalt the meek!
>
> There will be no lack of Christian daring
> In this little house of Portugal.[18]

Unfortunately the pride of the Lusitanians in the achievements of their nation sometimes eclipsed elementary feelings of Christian fraternity. The Portuguese in Macao did not only try to overcome pagans, according to the expression used by Camões. They claimed an exclusive right to do so and sometimes went as far as opposing the Spanish missionaries who were trying to bring the Gospel to China. A little group of Franciscans had an unfortunate experience in this respect.

Before a Closed Door

The Franciscans, the Augustinians, and the Dominicans had done successful work in Mexico with the support of the conquistador Fer-

---

[17] Quoted from Montalto by Henri-Bernard Maître, *Aux portes de la Chine: Les Missions du XVIe siècle: 1514–1588* (Tientsin, 1933), p. 88.

[18] Luis Vaz de Camões, *The Lusíads*, canto 7; stanzas 2, 3, 14. (Oxford: Oxford University Press, 1997), translated by Landeg White, Oxford World Classics, pp. 139, 141.

nando Cortés. Having handed these missions over to the diocesan clergy on the completion of their task, they decided to go to China to undertake new missions. Setting their sights westward from Mexico on another Spanish colony, they established contact with some Chinese in the Philippines and dreamed of evangelizing from there the mysterious land of Cathay.

On May 21, 1579, six Franciscans set off from the Philippines, led by Pedro Alfaro. They were three Spanish priests, one Italian priest, and two members of the Franciscan third order. After an unusually rough crossing that lasted a month, they landed in Guangzhou and celebrated a first Mass in secret on June 24, the feast of St. John the Baptist. A Chinese who had been baptized in Manila put them up and managed to conceal their presence from the authorities for several months. Unfortunately one of the missionaries fell ill as a result of the hardships he had endured and died on the boat that had brought them over.

According to Columba Cary-Elwes, some Portuguese merchants in Guangzhou secretly informed the Chinese authorities of the presence of the newcomers. They were concerned to defend their exclusive privileges and suspected the Spaniards of trying to infiltrate Guangzhou. They therefore denounced them as spies, sent to facilitate a Spanish conquest, on the line of the conquest of the Philippines, and they advised the Chinese to expel them. The Franciscans were thrown into prison and expelled after two months of ill treatment.[19] However the missionaries did not return to Manila but stayed on in Macao, in spite of the hostile attitude of the Portuguese authorities. The general history of Franciscan missions gives a much more serene account of what happened: "The Spaniards were well received [in Macao] and even obtained permission to build a small friary dedicated to our Lady of the Angels."[20] It was recorded that a Chinese Buddhist monk had been baptized after having received instruction in the Christian faith. Five young Portuguese noblemen joined the Franciscans as novices. Unfortunately these happy beginnings did not last. The history of the Franciscan missions continues:

---

[19] Columba Cary-Elwes, *China and the Cross* (London: Longmans, 1957), p. 83.

[20] Marcellino de Civezza, *Histoire universelle des Missions franciscaines* (Paris: Tolra, 1899), vol. 2, translated from the Italian by Victor Bernardin de Rouen, O.F.M.; p. 216. Translation ours from the French.

The devil, to foil the undertakings against his kingdom, encouraged the rivalry that the spirit of nationalism had created between the Spaniards and the Portuguese. All of a sudden a rumor spread that the fathers were spies acting for Spain. This rumor caused so much turmoil that Fr. Alfaro, who did not want to be the cause of any unrest, handed over the administration of the friary to Fr. Gianbattista Pesaro, who was Italian, and himself took a ship for Goa, together with Brother Rodriguez.[21]

The boat that Fr. Alfaro had taken for Goa was shipwrecked off the coast of Vietnam. Fr. Pesaro, the new superior in Macao, was threatened by the Portuguese authorities and forcibly embarked on a ship bound for Melaka, but, once he got there, he saw the new *capitan general*, who sent him back to Macao with letters of recommendation. Pesaro did not waste his time and opened a seminary and a college for local catechists, recruiting twenty young men, Japanese, Chinese and Vietnamese, but Portuguese hostility brought this whole enterprise to an end.

A Scientific Inquiry

In order to reach China without running foul of the Portuguese, Spanish missionaries were obliged to respect the hypothetical line traced by the papacy and running north and south from the Maluku Islands. Guangzhou lay to the west of this line, in the zone of Portuguese interest; the Chinese coast to the east lay in the Spanish zone. The Spaniards were therefore entitled to travel north from Manila and to attempt to establish themselves in Taiwan and in the province of Fujian, which faces it on the mainland.

A group of Spanish Augustinian friars thus managed to visit China in 1575, four years before the unfortunate experience of the Franciscans in Macao. The Chinese corsair, *Lim Ah Hong*, had attacked Manila in November 1574, and the governor of the Philippines cooperated with a Chinese naval squadron in a military expedition against the corsair. Guido de Lavezares had succeeded Legazpi, the effective founder of Spanish rule in the Philippines, as governor. Lavezares wanted to establish a base on the Chinese coast, as the Portuguese had done at Macao, and he therefore persuaded the Chinese admiral

---

[21] Ibid., p. 217.

to arrange for a party from the Philippines to visit the mainland. The Chinese authorities were well aware of what the Spaniards wanted and were equally determined to prevent it. Fr. Martín de Rada, who had been in the Philippines since 1565 and had just finished his term of office as Augustinian provincial, was put in charge of the small group, which was graced with the title of embassy. He had used his time in the Philippines to learn Chinese and was obviously suitable. The embassy consisted of two friars, two Spanish officers and some Indian and Chinese personnel. They sailed to Xiamen (Amoy) in the south of Fujian Province and were received in audience by the governor of Quanzhou with all the honors due to vassals. Following the ritual proper to such an occasion, the Spaniards had to address the governor on their knees, which can hardly have pleased these proud Castilians.

Fr. Martín de Rada (1533–1578) was a remarkable man, the first person to protest against the abusive treatment that the native Filipinos were receiving from some of the Spaniard colonists. He had studied as a layman at the Universities of Paris and Salamanca, before becoming a friar at the age of twenty at Salamanca, where he joined the Hermits of St. Augustine (known in England as the Austin friars). He had a reputation as mathematician, cartographer, and astronomer, his technical knowledge in these fields helping to ward off Portuguese claims that the Philippines were within the Portuguese sphere of influence. Fr. Martín was also a linguist, to whom were attributed a work on the language of Cebu and one on the Chinese language, *Arte y Vocabulario de la lengua china*. The embassy is said to have taken some 100 Chinese books back to the Philippines, which would make it a pioneer of Western sinology.[22]

The governor of Quanzhou sent the Spanish party on to the viceroy at Fuzhou, which gave them the opportunity of making many interesting observations on life in China. Since the Viceroy was required

---

[22] There exist two extensive notices on Fr. Martín de Rada, with descriptions of all publications and letters that can be attributed to him. Gregorio de Santiago Vela, O.S.A., *Ensayo de una Biblioteca Ibero-Americana de la Orden de San Agustín*, (Madrid: Provincia de Filipinas, 1922), vol. 6, *ad nomen*, pp. 444–60. Isacio Rodriguez Rodriguez, O.S.A., and Jesús Alvarez Fernandez, O.S.A., *Diccionario Biografico Agustiniano: Provincia de Filipinas* (Valladolid: Estudio Agustiniano, 1992), vol. 1, *ad nomen*, pp. 93–117. We are grateful for these references to Fr. Jesús Alvarez, O.S.A., lecturer in Church history at the Estudio Teológico Agustiniano de Valladolid.

to submit a report to the emperor, the Spaniards had time to visit the city of Fuzhou. Unfortunately they went as far as the city gates, which they examined with care, and this aroused suspicion. They were placed under house arrest, although they continued to be plied with banquets, and were then compelled to leave China after only three months, having been there from July to early October 1575.

China thus remained closed to both Portuguese and Spaniards. Their behavior in the Philippines and in the other countries of southeast Asia was all too well known to the Chinese authorities, who were doubtless well informed by Muslim administrators and merchants, so that foreign visitors were sent away, more or less politely. The approach of these conquistadors was not the right one for penetrating the "bamboo curtain". Men were needed who were prepared to be scrupulously respectful of Chinese rites of social behavior, and who were cognizant of the official principles of the Chinese Empire. It was also necessary to know how one could get round official principles while saving appearances, so that no one would lose face. Men who were both scholars and diplomats were needed, and such were actually present in Macao in 1582 in the form of the Italian Jesuits.

8

MATTEO RICCI'S JOURNEY

Catholics in today's China affirm their autonomy but are glad to emphasize the contribution made to the history of their country by the
Italian Jesuit Matteo Ricci. In 1983 they celebrated the fourth centenary of his arrival in China, and in October 2001 three international
colloquia were held (one in Beijing, one in Hong Kong, and one in
Rome), marking the fourth centenary of Ricci's arrival in Beijing. This
coincided with the publication of his complete works in Chinese. The
Shanghai historian Gu Yulu emphasized that Ricci's method of evangelization was a success because it respected the laws and customs of
China:

> During that period Matteo Ricci and the foreign missionaries were able
> to live and evangelize in China for three reasons. They followed local
> custom and adapted Catholicism to the context of the China of that
> time; secondly, they entered into relation with the elite; thirdly some of
> the Jesuits were scholars at the service of the imperial court.
>
> The Chinese who were baptized at the time became Christian mainly
> because of their intellectual acceptance of Catholic teaching.[1]

In order to assess this judgment, one has to follow Matteo Ricci
as he traveled from Macao to Zhaoqing and Shaoguan in Guangdong Province, then to Nanjing, Nanchang, and finally Beijing. At
the same time as this journey from the south to the north of China
was taking place, a spiritual journey occurred within Ricci himself. As
he went, Ricci learned from China and revised his concept of what
mission should be. In fact, he absorbed the language and culture of
China to such an extent that he was making mistakes in Italian when
he decided to keep a diary in 1608, two years before his death.

Fr. Nicolas Trigault, a Belgian Jesuit, arrived in Beijing a month

---

[1] Gu Yulu, *Zhongguo tianzhujiaoshi guoqu he xianzai* (*History of Catholicism in China, Past and Present*), (Shanghai: Academy of Social Sciences, 1989), p. 179.

before Ricci's death on May 11, 1610. He carefully preserved Ricci's notes which he published in Latin in 1615, with some additions and alterations of his own. The result was translated into French and published in Lille by a relative of Trigault in 1618 with the title *Histoire de l'expédition chrétienne au Royaume de la Chine, 1582–1610*. This lively narrative was reedited in 1978 and provides many of the concrete details for Fr. Ricci's story.[2]

Scientific and Humanist Education

When Matteo Ricci arrived in Macao in August 1582, he found a Jesuit center already in existence with the specific purpose of undertaking missions adapted to China and Japan. Fr. Alexander Valignano, S.J., who was in charge of the missions in East Asia with the title of visitor general, had just returned from Japan with four Japanese princes whom he was accompanying on an embassy to Rome. Fr. Valignano was in favor of the approach adopted by another remarkable Italian Jesuit, Fr. Michele Ruggieri, who had been in Macao for three years when Ricci arrived. Ruggieri's approach was to adopt the Chinese language and culture when teaching, rather than trying to turn the Chinese into Europeans by converting them to Christianity in a way that made them alien to their own tradition. Fr. Ruggieri was still learning thousands of Chinese characters in 1582, and he had translated into Latin an anonymous manual of good behavior for children. This was no doubt *San zi jing, Three Character Classic*, which young Chinese children used to chant in three-syllable meter.[3] The opening lines of *San zi jing* are:

[2] Matteo Ricci and Nicolas Trigault, *Histoire de l'expédition chrétienne au royaume de la Chine, 1582–1610* (Paris: Desclée de Brouwer, 1978), introduction by Joseph Shih, S.J.; Collection Christus, no. 45. Published with a grant from the Ricci Foundation; 740 pages.

[3] From the Yuan to the Qing Dynasties, the single most popular primer was *San zi jing*. It had 356 alternating rhyming lines of three characters each and employed 514 characters in all. It is interesting to note that Ruggieri's example was followed centuries later by the first professor of Chinese at Cambridge, U.K., Herbert Allen Giles (1845–1935), who wrote in the preface to his English translation of *San zi jing* that "to foreigners who wish to study the book-language of China, and to be able to follow out Chinese trains of thought, [its importance] can hardly be overestimated. Serious students would do well to imitate the schoolboy and commit the whole to memory". See Endymion Wilkinson, *Chinese History: A Manual* (Cambridge, Mass.: Harvard University Asia Center, 2000), pp. 49–50.

> Ren zhi chu,   xing ben shan
> Xing xiang jin   xi xiang yuan
> Gou bu jiao   xing nai qian
> Jiao zhi Dao   gui yi zhuan

> Humans at birth   are by nature good.
> Their natures are alike; habit makes them different.
> If they are not taught,   their nature will go wrong.
> The Way to teach them is by valuing special rules.[4]

Ruggieri translated the Ten Commandments into Chinese during his first year in China. He had soon understood that moral teaching was of first importance to the Chinese. His disciples called him *Shifu*, "Master". On February 7, 1583, he wrote to the general of the Jesuits:

> During the first three years of my stay in China, I spent my time learning the characters, and I wrote some books on doctrine, a flos sanctorum, a method for confession, and a Doctrine.[5]

The last mentioned text, a "doctrine", was in fact a catechism in question-and-answer form, composed in Latin and translated into Chinese with the help of a Chinese copyist. Ruggieri had completed the first draft in 1581, and it was published in 1584. Its Chinese title was *Tianzhu shilu* (*True Record of the Lord of Heaven*).

The Jesuits had been well prepared for the task that awaited them through the education that they had received in the colleges and universities of Europe. Michele Ruggieri, born in 1543 at Spinazzola in Apulia, had studied law at Naples, then philosophy at the Collegio Romano, founded by St. Ignatius in 1551, the most outstanding of

---

[4] Ibid., p. 50, n. 43. The first two lines are based on *Lunyu*, xvii, 2. *Lunyu*, meaning "conversations", is usually called the *Analects* in English, from the Greek word for "selection". On this work, see Irene Bloom's chapter "Confucius and the Analects" in William Theodore de Bary and Irene Bloom, *Sources of Chinese Tradition* (New York: Columbia University Press, 1999), vol. 1, p. 42: "The Analects is the single most important source for understanding the thought of Confucius." Its twenty short chapters or books contain "recollections of conversations that transpired among Confucius and his disciples or between Confucius and rulers of several of the feudal states that he visited. . . . There are also descriptions of the man, brief but telling vignettes of the way he appeared to those most intimately acquainted with him."

[5] Joseph Shih, S.J., *Le père Ruggieri et le problème de l'Évangélisation en Chine* (Rome: Pontificia Universitas Gregoriana, 1964), p. 14.

Jesuit educational institutions, which was later to develop into the Gregorian University. He then entered the novitiate at St. Andrea in Rome and left for India in 1577. Matteo Ricci, born at Macerata on the Adriatic in 1552, had begun his classical studies at the Jesuit college in the town before going to the Sapienza University in Rome. He then joined the Jesuits and also did his novitiate at St. Andrea. From 1573 to 1575 he studied at the Collegio Romano. Lectures there covered the logic and physics of Aristotle, as well as mathematics, geometry, astronomy, and cartography. He was taught by a German Jesuit from Bamberg, Christopher Clavius (c. 1527–1612), a friend of Kepler and Galileo, who became well known through his work for the reform of the Gregorian calendar. Ricci's spiritual director at the Collegio Romano was the rector, Vincent Bruno, from Rimini, author of a manual for meditation that St. Francis de Sales was later to recommend.[6] Ricci was also skilled in making astrolabes, clocks, and other machines, and this was to prove very useful in China.

When Ricci was studying theology in Rome, it is possible that he attended the lectures of Robert Bellarmine (1542–1621), later proclaimed a saint and doctor of the Church. Bellarmine developed his talent as an apologist at the service of the Catholic Reformation. Ricci, too, was to make use of apologetics—though not against Protestants (who had not as yet reached China), but against Buddhists. In 1577 Ricci completed his theological studies by spending one year at the University of Coimbra in Portugal; he then sailed from Lisbon on a Portuguese galleon bound for India. Ricci, who had delicate health, stayed for four years in India, where he taught at the College of St. Paul at Goa and was ordained priest in 1580. At the request of his former fellow student at Rome, Michele Ruggieri, Fr. Valignano then called Ricci to Macao, where he arrived on August 7, 1582.

Zhaoqing 1583–1588: The Temple of the Flower of the Saints

While Ricci was looking after catechumens at Macao's College of St. Martin, Ruggieri had his first opportunity of visiting imperial China. At that time, the viceroy of Guangdong Province resided at Zhao-

---

[6] According to Fernando Bortone, S.J., *P. Matteo Ricci S.I.: Il Saggio d'Occidente* (Rome: Desclée, 1965), p. 40.

qing, sixty miles (100 kilometers) from Guangzhou on the West River.
He found it convenient to do so because he was safe from Japanese
pirates at Zhaoqing and closer to Guangxi Province, for which he
was also responsible. The viceroy summoned to his court the bishop
and the governor of Macao, hoping to extort from them the presents
that were customary on such an occasion. The Portuguese, however,
evaded the viceroy's invitation by charitably suggesting to the Jesuits
that they might wish to profit from the opportunity. So Fr. Michele
Ruggieri and Fr. Francesco Pasio presented themselves before the
viceroy and gave him a bronze clock, which Ricci had just brought
from Europe, and a prism, which refracted white light.

Ruggieri asked the viceroy whether he could remain in Zhaoqing to
study Chinese and was assigned a residence in *Tianning*, the Temple
of Celestial Peace, which is still the name of the main street of the
city. The two Jesuits stayed there for five or six months, mandarins
and other officials coming to visit them. From the Chinese viceroy's
point of view, the Jesuits were a special sort of Buddhist monk, which
is why they were authorized to live in a temple, where they had to
wear monks' robes and shave their heads. Unfortunately, the helpful viceroy was sent somewhere else, and the two Jesuits returned to
Macao, much to their disappointment. Fr. Pasio was sent to Japan.

An unexpected stroke of luck followed. Letters arrived from the
new Chinese governor, Wang Pan, inviting the Jesuits to return to
Zhaoqing and authorizing them to build a residence and a chapel. In
September 1583 Ruggieri set out again, with Ricci this time. They
were offered land next to a large pagoda that was being built. The
"Flowered Pagoda" is known today as *Chong xi ta*, the Pagoda of
Happiness, and it still dominates the quays of the West River.

As soon as Ruggieri was back in Zhaoqing, he wasted no time in
contacting a young catechumen whose instruction he had undertaken
a few months previously and to whom he had entrusted the altar on
which he had said Mass. Ricci noted that they found the altar in a
place where everything was spotless and added, "Above the altar (because there was no image) the name of God was written on a tablet
with two large characters: *Tianzhu*, 'To the God of heaven'. On the
altar there were seven or eight incense burners full of fragrant per-
fumes."[7]

---

[7] Shih, *Histoire*, p. 221.

By disposing things in this way, the young Chinese catechumen had resolved the thorny question of how to translate the name of God. *Tian*, "heaven", the term in current use in China, was too impersonal and too close to the idea of "nature". *Tianzhu*, "Master of heaven", was the name for God later adopted by Catholics.

The Jesuit fathers behaved with great courtesy. They informed the governor that they had come to the kingdom of China from very far away, having been drawn by its great renown. They thanked him for the ground they had been given, and they did so in the kowtow position, after having touched the ground with their forehead. They also began to instruct a certain number of Chinese, although they noted that these had perhaps been attracted by the desire for novelty. They usually relied on an interpreter, although sometimes they spoke Chinese, in spite of their rudimentary knowledge of the language. It seems that they already ventured to criticize the cult of idols, although they were in a Buddhist environment. They did this starting from the ethical position of the Chinese classics themselves, toward which they seem to have had the attitude of Jesus Christ toward the Mosaic law.

At Zhaoqing, Ricci and Ruggieri were still at an early stage of their search for a catechetical method. They also had somewhat strained relations with the Buddhists, but this was for practical reasons. The monks found it difficult to accept a foreign presence near their monastery, and the Jesuits had to explain to the governor that they were not qualified to preside over Buddhist ceremonies. Governor Wang Pan, however, was very positive and presented the Jesuits with two large tablets, bearing typically Buddhist inscriptions. The first one had three characters: *Xian Hua Si*, "Temple of the Flower of the Immortals"; this was hung above the door. The second, with four characters, *Xi lai Jing tu*, "Pure Land come from the West", was placed in the reception room. "Pure Land come from the West" was a common expression of the Pure Earth School, which believed that the paradise of Amithaba, the Buddha of infinite light, was situated faraway in the sacred mountains of the west. The two missionaries interpreted the first inscription as praise of Mary, the Mother of Jesus, "Flower of the Saints". They saw in the second a recognition of Christianity's origins, "the Holy People of the West".

The Zhaoqing populace, however, did not like "foreign devils", and unfortunately the monks encouraged this deeply rooted hostility. The rumor went around that the missionaries were behind the building of

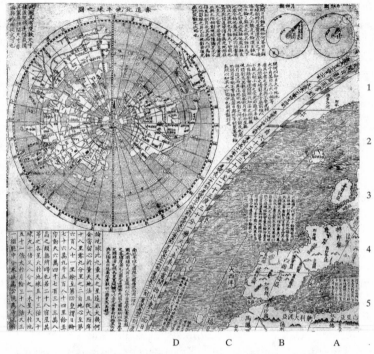

Fr. Matteo Ricci's map of the world

Ricci used his knowledge of mathematics and cartography to produce maps of the world with China in the center. The third one, made in Beijing in 1602, was composed of six sections, each seven feet high, on paper mounted on silk scrolls. The inscriptions on the map are in Chinese characters, giving place names, countries, and scientific and astronomical information. The central position on the globe thus given to China by the map produced a favorable response from the learned men of the East. It has been described as "one of the most celebrated maps in the history of cartography" (Standaert). The 1602 Map is in the Vatican Library; reproduction from the photograph in P. M. d'Elia, S.J., *Fonti Ricciane*, (Rome, 1949), vol. 2, plate II.

the big pagoda, and the prospect of being overshadowed by such a large Christian building was intolerable to the Buddhist community. Matteo Ricci, however, was adept at getting the authorities on his side. For instance, he used his skill in cartography to change the map of the world that was on the wall of the residence, so that the Latin names were translated into Chinese and the layout of the continents was altered, China, the middle kingdom and not Europe, being in the center.[8] Nicolas Trigault was so pleased to show how Ricci did it:

> I remember what he invented to win the approval of the Chinese. The Chinese believe that heaven is round but they think that the earth is square, and they are convinced that in the middle of it their Empire is situated, which is why they cannot tolerate the way in which our geographers depict China as being tucked away in a corner of the far east. However, since they could not follow the mathematical demonstration by which it is easy to prove that the earth and sea constitute a single globe, and furthermore that this sphere, from the nature of the circle, has no beginning or end, he changed our depiction somewhat, shifting the first meridian of the *Îles Fortunées* [the Canary Islands] to the edges of the map, to the right and to the left, so that the Kingdom of China appeared in the center of the map, which gave them the greatest pleasure and satisfaction.

Ruggieri's 1586 Journey

Although it was necessary to win the approval of the Chinese, the cause of evangelization was not necessarily furthered thereby. After Michele Ruggieri had been for two years in Zhaoqing, something happened that showed how uncertain he was about ensuring a future for the mission. Thanks to the favorable attitude of Governor Wang Pan and his successor, Zheng Yilin, Ruggieri had the opportunity of traveling into Zhejiang Province, to the northeast of Guangdong and Fujian Provinces. He was hoping in this way to profit from Governor Zheng Yilin's regular visits to Beijing so as to accompany him there. Ruggieri well understood the pyramidal structure of the Chinese state, which meant that nothing could be done without first obtaining permission from the emperor himself:

> The greatest difficulty in converting this kingdom of China lies not in any will to resist on their part—for they have no difficulty in under-

---

[8] Ibid., p. 240.

standing matters to do with God, and they understand that our law is holy and good—but in the great subordination that they observe in the obedience of some to others, depending on their rank, all the way up to the king. That is why everything depends on the king's eventual desire and wish to summon the fathers to his presence, for I do not doubt that he would immediately grant them leave to preach and teach their doctrine to all those who wished to receive it.[9]

In fact Ruggieri was not able to fulfill his plan of going up to Beijing, since he was only authorized to go as far as Shaoxing in Zhejiang Province. In January 1586 he set out, accompanied by a young Jesuit, Almeida. The two fathers found that the inhabitants of Zhejiang were different from those of Guangdong and less hostile to foreigners. They also formed a better impression of Buddhist monks, as appears from Almeida's account of their stay in the town of Gaoling.[10]

Fr. Joseph Shih underlines the importance for Ruggieri of his experience in Zhejiang Province:

Although the condition of monk was a humble one, it did give to the missionaries a precise advantage. It made them more accessible to the general population, and it entitled them to enter directly into conversation on questions to do with religion.[11]

Ruggieri noticed that there were various forms of popular religion in China, and he began to be aware of their importance. He then planned an expedition to Wudang Shan (Mount Wudang), in northwest Hubei Province, one of the sacred mountains of the Taoists. It is dedicated to the cult of Zhen Wu, the "true master of arms", who won immortality by practicing the control of breathing on a little terrace slung between heaven and earth. Many Taoist temples have been built on Wudang Shan, and it is unfortunate that Ruggieri was not in fact able to go there either. Personal contact with the masters of the Tao would have given to the Christian missionaries of the sixteenth century new insights into Chinese religiosity, especially as

---

[9] Letter of Ruggieri written from Macao (Nov. 12, 1581). Translation in Jacques Gernet, *China and the Christian Impact: A Conflict of Cultures* (Cambridge, U.K.: Cambridge University Press, 1985), p. 16. Originally published in French: Jacques Gernet, *Chine et Christianisme: Action et Réaction* (Paris: Gallimard, 1982).

[10] Shih, introduction to *Histoire*, p. 32

[11] Ibid., p. 34

the Chinese have a saying that they are Confucianists in public but Taoists in private.

Although Ruggieri's intention continued to be the penetration of the Chinese popular milieu, he was never in a position to carry out his mission in this way. In Hubei he came up against a political problem once again because he needed an official authorization to remain. The friendly governor, Zheng Yilin, found, once he had reached Zhejiang Province, that he was caught in a network of intrigue and began to withdraw his support from the two missionaries. The latter understood that it would be impossible for them to work effectively as long as they depended on the goodwill of local mandarins; only imperial authorization could give them security. In 1588, therefore, Fr. Valignano sent Ruggieri to Rome to request from the Pope that he send an official embassy to the emperor of China. Ruggieri never came back to China and died in Italy at Salerno in 1607.

Shaoguan 1589–1595: A Disciple among the Scholar-Gentry

Meanwhile Matteo Ricci continued his attempts to contact the class of the scholar-gentry. Since he could not stay in Zhaoqing without the governor's protection, he did obtain permission to settle some 150 miles (250 kilometers) to the north, in the town of Shaoguan. With Fr. de Almeida as his companion, he traveled up the Bei Jiang to Shaoguan, which is built at the meeting of two rivers. On August 24, 1589, their boat stopped on the east bank, some seven and a half miles (twelve kilometers) before the town. The two Jesuits were invited as "bonzes from the west" to take up residence at the *Nanhua si*, the famous monastery of the Flower of the South. This sanctuary is situated on the wooded slope above a fertile valley and is famous because of Hui Neng (638–713), the sixth patriarch of the Chan sect of Buddhism (*dhyana*). The introduction of Chan Buddhism to China is attributed to Bodhidharma, who supposedly traveled from India in A.D. 520, but Hui Neng is regarded by many as the actual founder of Chan Buddhism in China. He taught that enlightenment is not a gradual process but the direct awakening of the True Self, as experienced suddenly by a student who has been grappling with the problem of suffering.

The Jesuits were surrounded by swarms of Buddhist monks, who welcomed them with great pomp, although secretly they wanted the Westerners to go away as soon as possible. The monks suspected that the civil authorities had foisted the Jesuits on them to reform their way of life, which was distinctly lax. As for the fathers, they refused to bow to any of the statues, which was noted as unusual. They did not want to stay in the monastery, and they let the authorities know this. Eventually the Jesuits were given what they wanted: a piece of land at the edge of the town, which was quiet and easy of access and where they could build a residence for themselves. However, this piece of land also belonged to a Buddhist temple, and as a result the fathers had many problems, as had happened at Zhaoqing. Their small community was sorely tried by the death of Fr. de Almeida, then by that of Fr. de Petris, who had replaced him. Eventually in 1594 Fr. Lazarus Cattaneo joined them, and this made it possible for Ricci to concentrate on his studies.

His priority was to perfect his knowledge of Chinese, and, to do this, he asked for help from Qu Taisu, a member of the scholar-gentry class who was the son of an influential mandarin. This young man came from Jiangsu Province, and, after studying Buddhism, he had turned to alchemy. Having heard rumors about the secret techniques of foreigners, he was hoping to learn from them how to transform cinnabar into silver.[12]

Gradually Ricci introduced Qu Taisu to a more scientific approach, teaching him *The Treatise on the Sphere* by Clavius and the first book of the *Elements* of Euclid. Qu Taisu was proud to have acquired this new learning and also took an interest in the religious teaching of the fathers, asking questions about obscure points of doctrine. He became a Christian and put the Jesuits in touch with his friends among the official class. It was on Qu Taisu's advice that Ricci gave up wearing the robe of a Buddhist monk and adopted the garb and the style of a learned Confucian. He changed his appearance in this way in 1595, twelve years after his arrival in China, having first obtained permission from his superior, Fr. Valignano. Before he left for Nanjing, he let his beard grow and wore the high headdress, rather like a

---

[12] Cinnabar: mercury sulphide (HgS), the principal ore of mercury, which has a bright red color.

bishop's mitre, which gave him status in the hierarchy of the scholar-gentry.

Ricci tells us that, in his relations with mandarins, he "followed the polite usage of the *Xiucai* and the scholars, which is markedly more dignified than the behavior of Buddhist monks". The *Xiucai* (*Hsiu-ts'ai*) were those who had passed the first examination for entry into the imperial civil service, the preliminary district examination. This gave the successful candidates entry into the scholar-gentry class, but they were only lower gentry, and they were relatively young, their average age being twenty-four.[13] By this time Ricci was forty-three. He then left Shaoguan, where his memory seems to have been totally forgotten. In 1984 the Shaoguan municipality published a little book in Chinese that lists all the famous people who have come to the town during the course of history. Fr. Ricci is not mentioned.

Nanjing and Nanchang 1595–1599: Worldly Friends

Since 1591, Ricci had been working away at a Latin translation of the Four Books of Confucianism, which had become part of the Confucian canon since the time of the philosopher Zhu Xi in the twelfth century. They are *The Analects* (*Lunyu*, *Sayings of Confucius*), *The Book of Mencius* (*Mengzi*), *The Great Learning* (*Daxue*), and *The Doctrine of the Mean* (*Zhongyong*). Ricci did not only translate. He learned them by heart, as Chinese candidates for the civil service examinations had to do, so that he could produce apposite quotations in support of his arguments during the course of literary contests. Although Ricci had not taken the official Chinese examinations, he was in fact worthy of the Xiucai title.

Ricci's knowledge of the Confucian classics entitled him to take part in the debates organized by the Shuyuan, the meetings of regional academies where scholar-gentry discussed their interpretations of the great Confucian tradition within the context of solemn ceremonial. Following the example of these academies, Ricci conceived of the Jesuit residence not as a cloister or church, but as a literary club where

---

[13] For a detailed description of the examinations and classes of the civil service in imperial China, see Immanuel C. Y. Hsü, *The Rise of Modern China* (Oxford: Oxford University Press, 2000), 6th ed., pp. 75–79. Also W. F. Mayers, *The Chinese Government* (Shanghai, 1897), pp. 76–83.

it was possible to hold discourse on science, ethics, and religion. A more directly doctrinal teaching was reserved for those who really wanted initiation into the Christian faith.

At Nanchang he was the object of considerable curiosity and patiently accepted being importuned by the indiscreet. He made astronomical instruments and wrote a treatise in Chinese on mnemotechnics. More significantly, he composed in Chinese a *Treatise on Friendship*, to which Qu Taisu wrote a preface.[14] By weaving such bonds of friendship, Ricci was hoping to do two things: further the proclamation of the Gospel and find a way for reaching Beijing by means of these new contacts.

Ricci was well aware that some of his friends and disciples were motivated by worldly considerations. He moved very slowly toward the path that would lead to a fuller proclamation of salvation in Jesus Christ. Writing to the general of the Jesuits in 1596, he explained his method thus:

> We only venture to move forward very slowly . . . it is true that up till now we have not explained the mysteries of our holy faith, but we are nonetheless making progress by laying the principal foundations: God Creator of heaven and earth, the immortal soul, the judgment given to the good and the bad; all these things were unknown to them up till now, and they did not believe in them.[15]

Such was the approach that Ricci used in writing *Tianzhu shiyi* (*The True Meaning of the Lord of Heaven*), a treatise that had a considerable influence upon the educated class of China.[16] The first draft of this book was completed in 1596, and it was published in 1603. It was different in approach from Ruggieri's catechism, which had run into difficulties as an instrument of teaching because the notion of receiving a message from God as the result of revelation seemed totally

---

[14] The Chinese text of Ricci's *Treatise on Friendship* and an Italian translation have been published by Pasquale M. D'Elia, "Il trattato sull'Amicitia", *Studia Missionalia* 7 (1952):425–515.

[15] Quoted by Shih, introduction to *Histoire*, p. 38.

[16] The Chinese text of this treatise, with an English translation, has been published with introduction and notes by Douglas Lancashire and Peter Hu Kuo-chen, S.J., under the title *The True Meaning of the Lord of Heaven* (*T'ien-chu Shih-i*), A Chinese-English Edition, ed. Edward J. Malatesta, S.J. (Taipei, Paris, and Hong Kong: Ricci Institute, 1985), Variétés Sinologiques: New Series 72. The publication was a joint one by The Institute of Jesuit Sources, St. Louis, U.S.A., and The Ricci Institute for Chinese Studies, Taipei, Taiwan.

alien to the Chinese tradition. The content of that revelation made matters worse because of the shock that was produced on educated Chinese minds by the scandalous notion of the Incarnation of God and his death on a Cross. In fact, Ruggieri's catechism was destroyed by the Jesuits in 1596, once Ricci had completed his first draft of *The True Meaning of the Lord of Heaven*, although it was later revised and reedited (in 1637).

The editors of the 1985 edition of the text and translation of *Tianzhu shiyi*, (*The True Meaning of the Lord of Heaven*), explain the author's intention thus: "Ricci was striving to expound Catholic thought with the aid of China's cultural heritage. To proceed in such a fashion meant that it was manifestly impossible to give an account of those elements of the faith classed as pure revelation, and also impossible to compile a 'catechism'. For these reasons *The True Meaning of the Lord of Heaven* can appropriately be called a 'preevangelical dialogue'."[17] Ricci used to some extent the style of the dialogues of Socrates and Plato, and much of his book incorporates actual conversations on ethical and religious topics that Ricci had had with his learned friends. They were referred to in the book as *The Chinese Scholar* and *The Western Scholar*. The chapters of his book have titles such as "A Discussion on the Creation of Heaven, Earth, and All Things", "A Discussion on Spiritual Beings and the Soul of Man", "Refutation of False Teachings Concerning Reincarnation", and "A Discussion on the [Confucian] Teaching That Human Nature is Fundamentally Good". Only in the final chapter does the discussion reach topics concerning Christianity, which the Chinese found puzzling, such as "The Meaning and History of Celibacy among the Clergy" and "An Explanation of the Reason Why the Lord of Heaven was Born in the West". Salvation is mentioned in a general way: "[The Lord of Heaven] . . . acted with great compassion and descended to this world himself to save it and experienced everything [experienced by man]",[18] but there is no specific mention of the death and Resurrection of the Savior.

In *Tianzhu shiyi*, (*The True Meaning of the Lord of Heaven*), Ricci used a dialectic method, which was influenced by medieval European Scholasticism, proceeding in argument by means of fine distinctions and the close examination of contradictions. This too was unfamil-

---

[17] Ibid., p. 15.
[18] Ibid., p. 449; VIII, 580.

iar to the Chinese mind, which preferred the intellectual pursuit of convergent harmony. However, Confucian scholars did appreciate the way in which Ricci refuted Buddhist and Taoist beliefs. While Ricci was at Nanjing, he had acquired a certain reputation during a debate at a banquet where he held his own against the famous monk Huang Hong'en, better known to his contemporaries as San Huai.

Ricci was trying to provide an introduction to the Gospel by pointing out the similarities between Confucian ethics and the natural law as understood in Western philosophy. Once this had been done, it would be possible, in the case of those who wanted to learn more about Christian teaching, to disclose the astonishing mysteries of the Christian religion, and this could lead to the act of faith, which changed seekers into believers. The following chapter describes the spiritual progress of some of these converts.

Beijing 1600–1610: Dialogue with Great Scholars

After many disappointments, Ricci did manage at last to establish a residence in Beijing in 1601 and stayed there until his death in 1610. However, his longstanding plan of having an interview with the emperor ran into many obstacles and was never realized. First of all, Ricci was held up in Tianjin, where the eunuch Matang put him into prison for six months. This grasping civil servant went through the baggage of the missionaries and found a crucifix, which he considered to be a dangerous instrument of black magic. He confiscated all the presents that were to be offered to the emperor, even a chalice. However, on January 4, 1601, the fathers did reach the capital, where they were subjected to an investigation by the office of rites, whose officials had to take into consideration the intrigues of the powerful palace eunuchs. The eunuchs agreed to present the clock, which Ricci had brought, to the emperor, and, since it had to be given and maintained in working order, this meant that the fathers were allowed to reside in Beijing.

The Wanli emperor (r. 1563–1620) was pleased to receive the gifts brought by the missionaries and was particularly impressed by a painting of Jesus and his Mother, Mary, whose three-dimensional effect he found quite surprising. However, he did not grant an audience to the Jesuits, nor did he authorize the diffusion of Christianity within the

Tomb of Fr. Matteo Ricci, S.J. (1552–1610)

Tomb of Matteo Ricci in the Zhalan (Chala) Cemetery to the northwest of Beijing, on land given by the emperor. This was within the enclosure of a Catholic institution which became after 1949 a school for Communist Party managers.

empire. Ricci's mandarin friends used their influence in high places to promote Ricci, and this was not without results, since the Jesuits obtained land near the Xuanwu Gate, to the southwest of the city, where Nantang, the South Church, now stands.

If Ricci had dreamed of converting the Chinese emperor, as formerly Constantine, the emperor of Rome, had been converted to Christianity, then his dream proved illusory. Perhaps it was better that it should have been so, because the kingdom of God is not of this world. The identification of Imperium and Church in Europe had led to great ambiguity.[19] For Matteo Ricci the disappearance of such an illusion made it impossible to envisage the mass conversion of the people of China, but he did succeed in bringing to Christianity a certain number of high-ranking scholars, although they were not the intermediaries who could transmit the Christian message to the sovereign. On the contrary, their concern for righteousness tended to put them among the opposition, because they belonged to a group of civil servants who were critical of the corruption that flourished in government circles. Their concern was to have a reforming action based on a purer form of Confucianism that would be closer to its origins and better founded intellectually.

The small residence of the Jesuits in Beijing became a meeting place for many friends, among them catechumens and neophytes. Some of them were great scholars who worked with Ricci in translating scientific books. The little Christian community in Beijing increased steadily in spite of many difficulties. Ricci, writing to the general of the Jesuits, Aquaviva, in a letter of August 22, 1608, mentions more than 300 believers.[20] In other parts of the country Christian communities went through various hardships. In Shaozhou the church was attacked by the local population. In Guangzhou, a laybrother, Huang Mingsha, was executed, thus becoming the first Jesuit martyr

---

[19] Cf. Nicolas Standaert's analysis: "With the wisdom of hindsight, it is clear that this classical European model simply was not applicable to the position of the emperor of China as the embodiment of Confucian values. In his cultic role as the son of heaven, the emperor had to fulfill a whole range of sacerdotal duties; as a 'prince of the *literati*' he was supposed to represent Confucian orthodoxy, and as a universal ruler he symbolized China as the civilized center of the world. In this configuration it would be unthinkable that the imperial *persona* would come to play the role of a pious Christian monarch." Standaert, p. 492.

[20] Cf. Columba Cary-Elwes, O.S.B., *China and the Cross* (London: Longmans Green, 1957), p. 93.

in China. In 1607 there was a wave of anti-Christian feeling in Nanchang, but in Nanjing there were reported to be a hundred Christians.

Matteo Ricci's approach suited those Chinese who were prepared to be well disposed toward the new Western religion. However, he did not attract only the learned; his reputation also spread among the people. Future generations, forgetting his polemic against the idolatry of the Buddhists, actually consecrated altars to *Li Madou pusa*, "Bodhisattva Ricci", seeing him as a deity to whose painted or sculptured image in the temple offering would be made. As for the Communist intellectuals of today, who reject all superstition, they record with approval Ricci's contribution to science, his respect for the Chinese moral tradition, and his submission to the authority of the state. It is true that some Communist historians, like Hou Wailu, criticized Ricci's science as inadequate and backward in comparison with contemporary scientific progress in Europe, but Hou Wailu was writing at a time when the Chinese Communist Party avoided any contacts abroad and would not have tolerated anything that seemed to favor foreigners.

From the Christian point of view, Matteo Ricci was successful in responding to the needs of a chosen group within Chinese society. Scholars with a real concern for truth and justice welcomed his presentation of the Gospel. Their interpretation of doctrine and their apologetics laid the foundations of Chinese Christianity.

9

CHRISTIAN SCHOLARS

According to a Confucian proverb, "A gentleman works with his brain; he is not active with his hands." Does this adequately represent the status of scholars in Chinese society? After the time of the Song Dynasty (960–1279), scholars tended to become refined intellectuals, producing literary and moral formulas, skilled at composing poetry and sensitive to all kinds of artistic expression. Their ideal was to sit at a table, furnished with brushes for writing and painting, with a large stone on which ink was ground, and facing a landscaped garden where rocks surrounded a lake. The whole system of state examinations, based on a knowledge of the classics of Confucianism, produced a class of men who were formed by moral principles and trained in the art of human relations. The Four Books of Confucianism had been established as the basis of Confucian orthodoxy by the neo-Confucian scholar Zhu Xi (1130–1200). A series of examinations gave entry to the civil service and to the benefits that it conferred, such as an imperial pension and access to the many ways of making money while exercising the office of administrator. If ever a member of the scholar-gentry class fell into disgrace, his retirement would be bittersweet. He could still devote himself to reading, composing treatises, practicing calligraphy, and the meticulous cultivation of the plants in his garden.

Because of the system by which the scholar-gentry were recruited through success in examinations, they occupied an important part in the administration. However, they did not actually control the power of the state, since this was in the hands of the imperial family and the eunuchs who dwelt in the imperial palace. When the imperial dynasty declined, it sometimes happened that the eunuchs gained control of power, and their intrigues and corruption undermined the whole administrative system. This was the situation that obtained when Matteo Ricci came to live in Beijing, during the last period of the Ming Dynasty.

Confucian orthodoxy was established by the state in imperial China, but it was a double-edged sword. Corrupt civil servants could hide their misdemeanor under the hypocritical cover of fine principles, but honest civil servants could also invoke just principles to denounce corruption. They would refer to the principles of Mencius (c. 372–289 B.C.), the second most important thinker of Confucianism, who had laid down how the will of heaven was to be known. The respect of moral virtue was to be preferred to wealth, social rank, and even life itself. Mencius wrote, "For that reason, he who understands the will of heaven does not stand by a wall that threatens collapse."[1] At the beginning of the seventeenth century, a group of scholar gentry, who had mostly been dismissed from the imperial service, refounded the Donglin Academy, an institution of Confucian learning that had originally been created in the twelfth century and had later died out. The leaders of the new academy had openly criticized the immoral behavior of high-ranking officials, and in 1603 they began to rebuild a place for their meetings at Wuxi, on the shores of Taihu, the Great Lake, in Jiangsu Province. There they discussed the possibilities of political reform and began to create, in effect, an opposition party. Among the scholar-gentry another movement was also gaining ground, encouraging the study of science and technology so as to work more effectively for the prosperity of the country. These movements were the work not of dilettanti in ivory towers, but of educated men who were well aware of their political and practical obligations.

The scholars with whom the Jesuits had managed to establish contact belonged to such minority groups, which combined moral integrity with a desire for political reform and scientific progress. They were also looking for a source from which to derive personal spiritual renewal. Unfortunately their association with foreigners made them particularly vulnerable to the hostile maneuvers of corrupt civil servants.

A Man Persecuted in the Cause of Right

The Jesuits, in their Beijing residence, came to know an honest magistrate called Feng Yingjing (1555–1606) who had dared to denounce the corruption of the palace eunuchs. As a result he was falsely accused and dismissed from office. In 1601, just before he was sent to

---

[1] *Discourses of Mencius*, bk. VII, chap. 1, v. 2.

prison, he established contact with the Jesuits, who already knew him by reputation and gave him their moral support. During the three years that he spent in prison, the fathers regularly kept in touch with him and continued to support him morally. They gave him a copy of their latest Chinese publication, *Ershiwu yan* (*Book of Twenty-Five Words*), inspired by the *Manual of Epictetus*, translated and commented by Matteo Ricci. They chose it because this book of ethics does not encourage stoical resignation. In fact, it reacted against an evolution of Confucian thought that could have led to a fatalistic understanding of the law of heaven. Ricci, however, was a "worshipper of God", so that what he put forward was basically an understanding of what is proposed by faith. He gave Feng Yingjing the understanding that God is our heavenly Father who invites human beings to accept his plan for them.

Once Feng Yingjing had come out of prison, he wrote a preface to *Ershiwu yan* in 1604 that discreetly expressed his own faith: "I do not wish to hide the gift of a holy man from the West. I desire that all men on earth who dwell under the same law of heaven may see where they should go."[2]

A way had been opened, and men of outstanding quality were beginning to follow it. Three of them have been given a special place in history with the title "the three great pillars of Chinese Catholicism". They were Paul Xu Guangqi, Leo Li Zhicao, and Michael Yang Tingyun.

Xu Guangqi: Scholar and Patriot

Xu Guangqi was born in Shanghai in 1562. He entered the competition for the state examinations but failed to get through several times until, at age thirty-six, he obtained the title of *Juren*, and then the title of *Jinshi*. Finally he won the highest distinction of the em-

---

[2] Quoted in Shih, *Histoire*, introduction, p. 58. See however the reservations in Standaert, p. 478: "A close look at these prefaces and at the writings composed by Feng in the years just before his death shows that his ideas fundamentally differed from those of Ricci." Standaert, ibid., n. 18, refers to Paul Demiéville, p. 98, concerning another preface contributed to a book by Ricci, as "wondering whether Ricci had been the principal author of Feng's preface to *Tianzhu shiyi*". Paul Demiéville, "Les premiers contacts philosophiques entre la Chine et l'Europe", *Diogène* 58 (1967):81–110; reproduced in Gisèle de Jong (ed.), *Choix d'études sinologiques 1921–1970 par Paul Demiéville* (Leiden: Brill, 1973), pp. 488–517.

pire by qualifying for the prestigious Hanlin Academy, a government body of scholars that provided the grand secretariat of the administration. *Hanlin* means literally "forest of writing brushes": the academy composed diplomatic letters and poetry, which was highly prized in China, and it also had historiographical duties for all state papers. For instance, it prepared the official chronicle of each emperor's reign, which, sensibly, was not made public until after the death of the sovereign. The Hanlin Academy has been described as "a haven for the bright young talents and . . . an excellent training center for their political careers".[3]

Xu Guangqi met Fr. Lazzaro Cattaneo, S.J., (1560–1640), at Shaoguan, in northwest Guangdong Province, and in 1600, when he was passing through Nanjing, he came to know Fr. Matteo Ricci, who gave him Mark's Gospel and a copy of *Tianzhu shiyi* (*The True Meaning of the Lord of Heaven*). Xu Guangqi was impressed by the scholarship of the Jesuits and by the solidity of their doctrine, and he began to learn about the Christian faith. Three years later he suddenly asked Fr. João da Rocha, S.J. (1565–1623), for baptism. The Jesuit required that he should spend eight days on catechesis and made him read *The Book of the Ten Commandments* as well as *The True Meaning of the Lord of Heaven*. He was then baptized, taking the name Paul.

In the spirit of filial piety so dear to Confucian scholars, Xu Guangqi converted his father and then his whole family. From 1604 to 1607 he followed the teaching of Matteo Ricci in Beijing and worked with him on the translation of works of mathematics, astronomy, geography, and hydraulics.

Xu Guangqi was back in Shanghai in 1608, having been forced to retire by the intrigues of corrupt officials. He spent his time in study and writing and also welcomed Fr. Cattaneo and other Jesuits to his house, helping them to make Christianity known. He wrote a few books on Christianity and many scientific treatises.

In 1609 Xu Guangqi created a house-church in the place where he lived in Shanghai. More then 200 recent converts came to this *Xujiahui*, "estate of the Xu family", which was pronounced *Zikawei* in Shanghai dialect. It is in the southwest part of the city and has continued to this day to be one of the most dynamic centers of the Catholic

---

[3] Emmanuel C. Y. Hsü, *The Rise of Modern China* (Oxford: Oxford University Press, 2000), 6th ed., p. 54.

Church in China. *The Xu Family Annals* list the many activities of Paul Xu Guangqi on behalf of the Church. He saw to it that his parents and their friends, who had become Catholics, regularly received the sacraments. He made it his business to find replacements for priests when they were in short supply. When foreign priests were in danger, he gave them shelter, and sometimes he would act in their defense. Following on the persecution that broke out in Nanjing in 1616, he composed a work of apologetics; *Bianxue zhangshu* ("A Dialectical").[4] This was widely diffused and was even engraved in stone. He also wrote poetry expressing his devotion to Jesus and Mary, as well as his attachment to the Ten Commandments and the Beatitudes. In other words, he fulfilled his duty as a Christian in a typically Confucian way, with due concern for a conscientious observance of the Commandments and of the ritual and with attentive care for the spiritual welfare of those around him.

In addition, Xu Guangqi was a scientist whose work aimed at practical results and who was concerned for the welfare of the state. In Beijing he was able to compare his own conclusions with those of Fathers Ricci, Pantoja, and de Ursis and thus to assess the learning of the West. His special interests were in those areas for which dynastic rulers were responsible, areas linked to ritual and government in China: the establishment of the calendar, cartography, and the making of instruments for astronomical observations. In 1612, a year after Ricci's death, Xu Guangqi published a translation of the first six parts of Euclid's *Elements* and a treatise on trigonometry. He thus familiarized himself with logical methods deriving from Greek thought and was able to improve the precision of Chinese mathematics by paying greater attention to its systematic processes. The requirements of accurate translation also caused him to create new technical terms that enriched the vocabulary of Chinese mathematics.

Xu Guangqi's scientific spirit was even more effective in its application to agriculture. He reacted strongly against the more or less fatalistic attitude that led people to say, "The climate is not good for such a crop." He would answer, "Perhaps so, up to a point, but we must experiment." Against objections that northwest China was an arid region, he would propose the new methods of irrigation that

---

[4] Fang Hao, *Biographies of the History of Catholicism in China* (Hong Kong: Catholic Truth Society, 1967), vol. 1, p. 105. In Chinese.

he had talked about with Fr. Sabatino de Ursis, S.J. (1575–1620).
He was convinced that the prosperity of the country depended on its
agricultural productivity. His ideal was to work for the development
of China according to the motto *Fu guo qiang bing*, "Rich country,
strong army". Xu Guangqi's open attitude led him to proclaim that
the enrichment of the country depended on improved agricultural
productivity, trade with Japan, and the adoption of technology from
abroad.

In 1619, toward the end of the Wanli emperor's reign (1563–1620),
Xu Guangqi was summoned urgently to Beijing because of a military
situation, which had become critical. The Manchus, descendants of
the Jurchen, controlled most of the area north of the Great Wall and
were increasing their pressure on the Ming Dynasty, which they were
to overthrow in 1644. Some 45,000 Chinese soldiers had been killed
on the Liaodong Peninsula, and there was a danger that the imperial forces would disintegrate. Xu Guangqi was ordered to take over
the training of the army and immediately created corps for military
formation and saw to their supplies. He was particularly concerned
with their defective armament and appealed for help to his friend Li
Zhicao and to the Jesuits in Macao, hoping that the latter would help
him to buy cannons from the Portuguese. He was also considering
the manufacture of armaments, when it transpired that the imperial
treasury was empty. The emperor drew back before the prospect of
raising the necessary finance, and Xu Guangqi, deeply disappointed,
handed in his resignation.

In the second year of the new Chongzhen emperor (1629), Xu
Guangqi found himself in the capital once more. He had been appointed to a high post in the office of rites. There was chaos in
the Beijing observatory that year because the methods inherited from
Guo Shoujing and the Muslim astronomers had proved defective in
calculating the exact time of an eclipse. The emperor appointed Xu
Guangqi to revise the calendar, which had been drawn up 300 years
previously at the time of the Mongols. He called his friend Li Zhicao from Nanjing and invited the Jesuits Niccolò Longobardo (1565–
1655) and Terrenz (1576–1630), a Swiss Jesuit friend of Galileo, to
translate into Chinese the theory on which Western astronomy was
based. Xu Guangqi also had new measuring instruments made, so
as to improve the observatory's equipment. His efforts in this area
were entirely successful, and it is thanks to him that Fr. Adam Schall,

S.J. (1591–1666), and the Jesuit astronomers were entrusted with the drawing up of the calendar, a task of great importance because of its political implications. It was considered that the destinies of an empire governed by the "Son of Heaven" depended on close harmony with the movement of the cosmos.

During the last years of his life, Xu Guangqi received the highest honors. In 1632 he was made minister with extensive powers, but the Chongzhen emperor behaved as an absolute monarch, ignoring bad news and listening to a clique of flatterers, who excluded honest counselors. Xu Guangqi was powerless to prevent the inevitable decline of the Ming Dynasty, as the Manchu armies prepared to invade and the peasants of Shaanxi and Henan Provinces rose in revolt under the exactions of landowners.

Xu Guangqi was an old man by now, but he never became disillusioned, remaining faithful to his duties as a civil servant and a Christian. His life was marked by the regular rhythm of his religious duties: prayer, meditation, and Mass in the morning; examination of conscience in the evening. He would welcome the Jesuits to the palace as if they were members of his own family; Fr. Longobardo had free access to it, accompanied by the lay brother Qiu Yong.

Without giving up, Xu Guangqi continued to work throughout his last illness. As he lay dying, he was still worrying about a memorandum on agriculture and, with his latest breath, said to those round him, "That memo? . . . Is the copy ready? . . . Present it to the emperor . . . that's my last wish." His body was taken to Shanghai and buried in the family property. One can still see the grassy tumulus over the tomb, at the bottom of a little garden called Nandan, near the present Zikawei Church. In 1983 the civil and religious authorities in Shanghai celebrated the 350th anniversary of his death. In front of the tomb there is an impressive stone statue of his head and shoulders on a massive plinth. His name is carved on the monument in letters of gold, the calligraphy being that of Zhou Gucheng, vice-president of the permanent Committee of the People's National Assembly. The Nandan garden has been renamed Guangqi Garden. The face of the great man's statue bears a slight smile, redolent of wisdom and peace. His tall civil servant's headdress has two horizontal earpieces, which give the impression of a cross behind the head—the halo of a Confucian sage.

Li Zhicao: Filial Disciple

Li Zhicao was a great friend and colleague of Xu Guangqi, whom he resembled in many ways. They shared a love of science and its practical applications, they were both friends of Matteo Ricci, and they had both converted to Christianity.

Li Zhicao was born in Hangzhou in 1565 and successfully passed the governmental examinations. In 1594 he became *Juren* and in 1598 *Jinshi*, being appointed to an official post in Nanjing. He went up to Beijing in 1599 to a higher post, and two years later he visited for the first time the residence of the Jesuits, gazing with amazement at their map of the world. He then began to absorb the science of the West and worked closely with Matteo Ricci, writing the prefaces to some fifty books written by the fathers.

Li Zhicao began to acquire a Christian vision of the world by reading *The True Meaning of the Lord of Heaven*. He wrote a preface for it and in 1607 actually had the text of the preface engraved on stone at Hangzhou. He also wrote a preface for *Ji ren shi bian* (*Ten Essays on Remarkable Men*), in which he expressed his admiration for the men of God.[5] As he had a sufficient knowledge of the Christian faith, he asked to be baptized, but the Fathers required that he should separate from his concubine, which he was not prepared to do. When he fell gravely ill, he made a vow to put away his concubine if he recovered. In doing this, he thought no doubt of his eternal salvation, but he had also been profoundly touched by the care shown him by Matteo Ricci, who was by now old and ill. Ricci baptized him at last, and he was given the name Leo. While Li Zhicao recovered fully, Ricci began seriously to decline, and his condition was not improved by the number of visitors who had come to Beijing for the state examinations and who wanted to see him while they were there. Li Zhicao considered Ricci as a father who had given him new life of soul and body; he felt it his duty to arrange a solemn funeral for him in Beijing and to find a massive coffin. Thanks to these arrangements, the emperor finally granted to the Jesuits a piece of land at Zhalan (Chala), to the north-west of the city, which became a cemetery for Ricci and his colleagues. Burial in Chinese soil was a privilege that seemed to consecrate all that the sage from the West had achieved.

---

[5] Fang Hao, ibid., p. 115.

In 1625 Li Zhicao received a copy of the Syrian Christian inscription on the Xi'an Stele, which had just been discovered. He immediately grasped the historical importance of this discovery and wrote a note that attracted the attention of both the Jesuits and Chinese scholars. Most of the latter, deeply attached as they were to their centuries-old tradition, had found it very difficult, in spite of their admiration for the fathers, to accept a new teaching, which had been in China barely thirty years. The Xi'an Stele completely altered this perspective, because its inscription, recording the arrival of Syrian monks in 635, proved that Christianity had been in China for nearly a thousand years.

When the project for obtaining cannon from the Portuguese was under discussion, it was to Fathers Longobardo and Manuel Dias that Li Zhicao turned for help, and, when they objected that they were men of peace and not of war, Li explained that the cannon were a pretext and that his real aim was to facilitate their stay in China. He said, "It is like a needle; once the clothes have been sewn, it is not needed any more."

Once Li Zhicao began to feel his age, he withdrew to Hangzhou and edited *Tianxue chuhan* (*First Letters in the Science of Heaven*), the first collection of Christian Chinese literature. It brought together nineteen pieces by missionaries and scholars, which combined religious teaching and scientific writing. This combination was not accidental, because for Li Zhicao, as for his friend Paul Xu, science leads to God, and God is the foundation of all science.

In 1629 Li Zhicao was sixty-five and not in good health. Nevertheless he responded to Xu Guangqi's request and came to Beijing to work on the calendar. He died there a few months later, Paul Xu holding his hand and the missionaries praying all around him. They owed Li Zhicao a great deal. He had protected and encouraged them in so many ways, watching over their health, their well-being, and their security, and doing all he could to help them in their study of the Chinese language. He often regretted that there were so few of them and tried to arrange for more missionaries to come. His own contribution to Christianity in China was a major one, so that he can truly be said to be the first apostle of the Church in Hangzhou.

Through Li Zhicao's influence, another outstanding scholar from Hangzhou decided to break with Buddhism and to ask for baptism. This happened in 1611, when Yang Tingyun came to offer his condolences to Li Zhicao upon the death of his father. Yang Tingyun had no children by his first wife and had married a concubine, of whom he was very fond and who had given him two sons. He wanted to keep her and complained of the uncompromising attitude of the fathers:

"The Western fathers are really strange. I, with [my power] as censor, am serving them, so why is it not possible? Can they not just allow me to have one concubine? I do a lot for them in my capacity as censor. Why is it that they will not allow me to have one concubine? It would not have been the case with Buddhist followers." Li Zhicao sighed and said, "By this you know the Western fathers really cannot be compared to Buddhist followers. The commandments of the West were promulgated by God and observed by the saints of former times. To observe them is virtue; go against them, and you will be punished. The difference between virtue and punishment is very clear. If you [only] pander to [your] whims, what then of the commandments? The fathers think of saving men; they do not want to be praised themselves. They want to abolish worldly customs, but do not dare to transgress religious laws: that's the position of the fathers. Their virtue is complete and full. You know that you have failed, but you do not change. What's the benefit then in following it?"[6]

These strong words overcame Yang Tingyun's hesitations. He separated from his concubine, making sure that she had a house to live in and proper subsistence. Then he was baptized on Easter Day at the age of forty-five, taking the name Michael.

Yang Tingyun was close to his friend Li Zhicao through his career as scholar and high civil servant, but he differed from him considerably in terms of his Buddhist contacts and his spiritual requirements. His father was a member of *fangshenghui*, Society for Releasing Life, a lay-Buddhist association encouraged by the famous monk Zhu Hong (1535–1615). This monk promoted "compassion for all sentient be-

---

[6] N. Standaert, *Yang Tingyun, Confucian and Christian in Late Ming China: His Life and Thought* (Leiden: Brill, 1988), p. 54.

ings as manifested in the observance of nonkilling and the release of animals" and "the promotion of popular morality through the system of merits and demerits outlined in his book *Zizhilu* (*The Record of Self-Knowledge*)".[7] He also aimed at harmonizing the three great religious traditions of China: Confucianism inducing moral perfection, Taoism renewing vital energy through its rituals, and Buddhism seeking for interior peace. Zhu Hong lived in the Yunqi Monastery, which clings to the flank of the Mount of Clouds, some twelve and a half miles (twenty kilometers) south of the town of Hangzhou, on the heights dominating the Qiantang River. This vast flow of water is regularly swept by a tidal bore, and the dwellers on its banks relied on the prayers of the monks for safety. Today one can see on the north bank of the river the majestic Six Harmonies Pagoda, which proclaims interior harmony through the six precepts of Buddhist law, with its cosmic harmony between heaven, earth, and the four cardinal points. The Buddhism of Zhu Hong gave a privileged place to monastic life, but also encouraged welfare societies with lay participation. "This lay-Buddhist movement and the combination of the three teachings [of China's religions] laid a theoretical foundation for the absorption of Buddhism into the personal lives of members of the literati-official class."[8]

Once Yang Tingyun had become a Christian, he continued to follow the Buddhist tradition of charitable societies and founded *Renhui*, Benevolent Society, with the help of his wife. This project, involving the whole family, his wife, her two daughters, and the two sons born of the concubine, is described by Yang Tingyun's Christian biographer, who had the details from Fr. Aleni:

> There was a Fangshenghui Society for Releasing Life in Wulin [= Hangzhou]. Every year it wasted a large amount of money on buying birds and fish only to release them. Since Yang Tingyun was a Christian, he knew that the love of animals should be inferior to the love of man. Therefore, he gathered some good gentry comrades together and established a *Renhui* "Benevolent Society". The regulations were easy and appropriate. The purpose was extensive and refined. Every month they came together in the church and put donations into a box. A loyal gentleman was asked to control the use of the donations: the hungry should

---

[7] Ibid., p. 38.
[8] Ibid.

be fed, the cold should be clothed, the thirsty should be refreshed, the sick should be cured, travelers should be helped materially, prisoners should be ransomed, the dead should be buried. Innumerable were the poor and helpless, from all places, who benefited from the society.[9]

Long before Yang Tingyun became a Christian, he was already outstanding for his honesty and justice in the exercise of his official duties. Having been successful in the official examinations, he was appointed magistrate at Anfu in the prefecture of Ji'an, Jiangxi Province, where he remained from 1592 to 1599. He showed his concern for the people by reducing taxes, building granaries, and opening schools for children. Many of the scholar-gentry in the area were imbued with the thought of the neo-Confucian philosopher Wang Yangming (1472–1529) from Zhejiang Province. He reacted against the neo-Confucianism of Zhu Xi (1130–1200), which taught that moral perfection can only be acquired after a laborious enquiry into the nature of things and required vast learning. Wang Yangming's thought was different. It was inspired by the Buddhist *Chan* tradition and located perfection in the interior demands of a pure conscience. In the neighborhood of Anfu, some twenty *shuyuan* (local academies) sought inspiration from Wang Yangming's quest for moral integrity. Thus *Fuli shuyuan*, the Academy for the Return to the Rites, militated against the lust for gain and for power and encouraged a return to the norms of *xiao* (filial piety), friendship and kindness. Yang Tingyun was no doubt guided by such principles and conscientiously fulfilled the requirements of his station, thus deserving from local people the name *ren hou*, "benevolent marquess".

Yang Tingyun, with his concern for interior rectitude rather than learning, was following a way that was different from that of Li Zhicao and Xu Guangqi. He was appointed censor in Beijing on March 13, 1602, and no doubt joined his two friends, who took him to see "the wise man from the west", but Yang Tingyun admitted that he could not understand Matteo Ricci's learned expositions. He was later to write in the preface to a book on applied mathematics:

> In the past I met M. Ricci in his residence in the capital and for several days we discussed the "names and principles" [of things]. We became intimate friends. However, I could not understand theories about geometry, circles, and hypotenuses. Ricci sighed, "Since I came to the capital,

[9] Ibid., p. 62.

Li Zhicao and Xu Guangqi are the only two intelligent persons I have met."[10]

It is possible that Yang Tingyun had been upset by the way these scholars attacked his Buddhist friends. They had criticized them in these terms: "Since the Buddhists desire and venerate their own nature and reject the omnipotence of God, they disavow the grace of God. Alone and arrogantly they oppose him. Therefore, we say: if it is not stupid, it is perverse!"[11]

This dismissive judgment did not do justice to the Buddhist way of salvation. In fact, Buddhist meditation and asceticism aim at the exact opposite of what is superficially rejected here, since they seek to kill selfish desire and to dissolve the human ego. Buddhists do not set themselves up against a personal God, since they do not know about his existence. In fact, Buddhist popular devotion seeks certain forms of grace and pardon by having recourse to the intercession of bodhisattvas like Guanyin, the mother of mercy. What the Jesuits were doing was emphasizing Confucian teaching on salvation through moral behavior, and this ran the risk of conveying to their converts an incomplete notion of the grace of God.

It is interesting to note what Yang Tingyun's understanding of Christian doctrine was. He expressed his views on this more profoundly than either Li Zhicao or Xu Guangqi. He grasped that the essential character of the new law was to love God and to love human beings. To begin with, he attempted to express his notion of God by using the neo-Confucian philosophic tradition. He started from Zhang Zai's conception of the origin of all beings as being "father and mother". He wrote that "father and mother" cannot be the same as *qian kun*, "heaven and earth", which are material and without consciousness. God, Master of heaven, is the great "Father and Mother". Children have the duty of showing filial piety toward their parents, but even more so does the Master of heaven, the supreme Lord, deserve to be honored. Our love for God is shown to be real by a love for human beings that expresses itself through the works of mercy, accompanied by detachment from self. Yang lists seven works of mercy, taken from the parable of the Last Judgment in the Gospel

---

[10] Ibid., p. 53. From Yang Tingyun's preface to Ricci's *Tongwen suanzhi* (*Tongwen suanzhi bianxu*) 23 V, pp. 2904, 6 through 2905, 4.

[11] Ibid., p. 53.

of Matthew (25:31–46). He lists seven acts of self control, *qi ke*, "*The Seven Disciplines*", taken from a short treatise written by Matteo Ricci in collaboration with Fr. Diego de Pantoja and Xu Guangqi and entitled *Practical Counsels for Fighting Against the Seven Capital Sins*. Its spiritual program is described in Confucian terms:

> By overcoming the bad basis of one's mind, one can plant the seeds of virtue in one's mind. And whatever supplies love is purely the mind of the way (*Daoxin*), and the mind of the way is purely the mind of heaven (*Tianxin*).[12]

By expressing thus the history of salvation, Yang Tingyun remained faithful to Chinese tradition. He identified humanity's original state of happiness with the golden age of early Chinese myth, when the holy emperors ordered the world.[13] It was the wise kings of the three dynasties of antiquity who knew how to transmit *Tao*, the Way. After the duke of Zhou, however, the way deteriorated progressively, in spite of the intervention of Confucius, the Taoists, and the Buddhists. In his *Dai yi pian* (*Treatise for Dissipating Doubts*), published in 1621, Yang Tingyun wrote:

> In ancient times, the "natural teaching" (religion) was in man's heart. . . . After the three dynasties, saints and sages were remote, wickedness and falsehood increased more and more, the "natural teaching" in man's heart dripped away day after day. . . . And then the utmost benevolence happened; with his unlimited pity, which nobody can estimate, he descended from heaven and adopted a human body. He was called *Yesu*, which means "Savior of the World". He was born in a real place, it occurred in the country of Judea, he really had a mother, she was Mary, and it really happened at a certain moment, it was at the end of the Western Han Dynasty, the year *gengshen* (1 B.C.).[14]

Yang Tingyun explained that the Savior, born among men, reestablished the straight Way, of which the fathers from the West are the messengers. Only their teaching can restore the true Tao, which has been obscured in China since the time of the first Qin emperor.

---

[12] Ibid., p. 121. Quoting the preface of *Qi ke* (*The Seven Disciplines*).

[13] See especially Anne M. Birrell, *Chinese Mythology: An Introduction* (Baltimore: Johns Hopkins University Press, 1993).

[14] N. Standaert, *Yang Tingyun, Confucian and Christian in Late Ming China: His Life and Thought*, pp. 129–30.

After the Qin Dynasty, the reverence for heaven began to decrease, and from the Han Dynasty onward, reverence for Heaven declined. During 1,600 years the teaching of heaven was dark and unclear, and there was nobody to explain faults. M. Ricci came from overseas and was the only one to understand thoroughly the basis of the Way. He really could cultivate it and prove it.[15]

Yang Tingyun explained original sin as "the root of an evil nature", "a seed that creates sins". Baptism purifies all the faults of the past. By this he meant mainly personal faults. The revelation of the way in all its purity makes it possible to cultivate virtue. Yang Tingyun does not omit to mention the work of grace. He says that the Lord of heaven has doubtless given to man *ming wu*, a clear conscience, but has also given him *ai yu*, love, to guide him on the path to goodness. He sees the "holy favor" of grace mainly as a support given to virtuous men to increase their capacity to do good. Yang Tingyun faithfully practiced a daily examination of conscience, noting the number of sins committed during the day. He derived this practice from Fr. Alani's book *Rules for Confession*, for which he had written the preface. However, such a practice was also customary in neo-Confucian circles, where it was called "examination of self". It also had similarities with the counting of meritorious and faulty actions, which was enjoined by the Buddhists of Hangzhou.

These similarities should not be considered as syncretistic compromises. Yang Tingyun had systematically broken all links with Buddhists since his baptism. The Buddhist monks had left his house, and their altar had been transformed into a chapel of the Holy Redeemer. Yang Tingyun had prayed and fasted to obtain the conversion of his father, then of his mother, and finally, though not without difficulty, of his wife. Once the latter had become a Christian, she saw to it that the entire household was catechized. Her daughter, Agnes, became an example to the faithful of Hangzhou. As Yang Tingyun's life was drawing to a close, he felt it his duty to build a residence and a church for the fathers, a project that had always been close to his heart. He bought some land to the north of the city and actively supervised the work, transporting material with his own hands. He died suddenly during the winter of 1627, and his son completed the work.

---

[15] Ibid., pp. 130–31.

Yang Tingyun has sometimes been called "an apostle in mandarin's clothing", a term that certainly expresses his zeal in spreading the faith, but one must not forget that it was as a neo-Confucian scholar that he used all his skill in the reflection and presentation of the Christian message. In the same way as the apologists and fathers of the Church had done in the Mediterranean culture of the early Christian centuries, he operated a fusion of the Chinese cultural heritage and the Gospel. He did this in all honesty, according to his understanding of the theology that the Jesuits transmitted to him.

Michael Yang Tingyun may have gone further than Paul Xu Guangqi and Leo Li Zhicao in his interpretation of Christian doctrine, but in many respects he remained very close to them. These three anticipated what were to be seen later as the characteristics of Chinese Catholics. They combined a moral attraction for the Christian way of salvation with a practical approach toward good works, discipline in observing the commandments of the Church, devotion to the sacraments, faithfulness in prayer, and a constant concern for the conversion of their families.

CANDIDA XU:
A MOTHER OF THE CHURCH

How much is known about the women of the first Christians in China
—wives, concubines, devoted daughters? They were often kept hidden in the living quarters reserved for them, and yet they were capable of courageous initiatives. Their mysterious presence deserves to
be investigated, for, in the shadow of the great scholar converts, fervent Christian women flourished. How did they live their faith, and
what role did they play in the Church of China at her beginning?

The Condition of Women

A brief overview of Chinese society is needed to answer these questions, but unfortunately not a great deal is known about the conditions of women in the early periods. Sinological studies of women in
Chinese history and culture are at the exploratory stage of investigation, with much research still needed on this topic. Since the beginning of Chinese civilization, the masculine and the feminine have
been considered not as unequal, but as two opposed but complementary principles, one, the *yang*, being luminous and strong, the other,
the *yin*, being mysterious and weaker, but both necessary for the harmony of nature. At the practical level, mothers were very highly considered if they gave birth to a son who could perform the cult of
the ancestors and thus ensure the continuity of the family. Confucian
tradition endowed these ideas with a ritual and moral aura. Confucius
himself went into mourning in an exemplary way after his mother's
death.

In Chinese peasant society, women participated actively in the work
of the fields. This was particularly so in the case of the women of the
Hakka, a distinct group in Jiangxi and Guangdong Provinces who belong to the Han ethnic majority but whose dialect, closer to Mandarin
than to the Cantonese of southern China, indicates their immigrant

origin.[1] The Hakka have their own customs and cuisine as well as their own dialect, and, until recently, their preference was to choose a wife who was tall so that she could carry the yoke with its heavy pails of water without their touching the ground. Hakka women had more freedom than other Chinese women, and they never had their feet bound.

Among mandarins, however, at the time of the Song and the Ming Dynasties, women were confined to their own part of the house, at the back of the master's dwelling. The birth of a daughter was not always welcome, because of the necessity of providing for her education and dowry to the profit of the future husband's family. Marriage contracts were arranged between families, often because of financial considerations or political interests. A substantial sum of money was given to the bride's family in compensation for the cost of her education. Sometimes the husband subject to such a contract might be a child and, if he came to die young, his wife would be obliged to remain a widow all her life out of filial piety. Arches were built to honor such heroic widows who consecrated their whole lives to the service of their in-laws.

Although girls could not attend school, educated families often gave them instruction at home, sometimes providing a tutor. Some women became famous for poetry, music, and even the martial arts. Chinese theater had plays about the "women generals" of the Yang family. The young female warrior Hua Mulan is as well known in China as Joan of Arc in France. A radiant beauty like Xi Shi, who lived in the fifth century B.C., was sent by the king of Yue to seduce the king of Wu so that he neglected his duties of state and was killed in bat-

---

[1] For the condition of the women in Hakka society, see Ono Kazuko, ed. Joshua A. Fogel, *Chinese Women in a Century of Revolution 1850–1950* (Stanford, Calif.: Stanford University Press, 1989), p. 2: "Although the Hakka people are Han Chinese, they originally were not native to this region of south China, but immigrants who arrived there from distant Henan, Shandong, and Anhui over the course of several centuries. These newcomers settled on remote hill land of such low productivity that they could not possibly support their families through agriculture alone. The men therefore found employment outside the villages, and the women shouldered the burden of cultivating the land as well as of managing the household. In these virtually propertyless families, the men had no cause to dominate the women, and the women in turn had no reason to be dependent on the men. Hakka women did not practice footbinding, the symbol of the 'cultured woman'. With their bare, natural feet, they spent their days in demanding physical labor, sometimes in the company of men and sometimes in place of men who worked away from the villages."

tle by the Yue. There is a Chinese saying: "every girl's lover thinks she is as beautiful as Xi Shi." Wang Zhaojun, a beautiful concubine, gave proof of her patriotism when she was ordered to marry a wild Mongol, prince of the Xiongnu tribe, so as to promote his alliance with the Han emperor in the first century A.D. Women too were able to gain access to the imperial family as concubines and then attain supreme power, as did Empress Wu Zetian at the time of the Tang Dynasty in the seventh century A.D. Yang Guifei so besotted a later emperor of the same dynasty that she brought about his utter ruin and that of the nation.

Young ladies of mandarin families, with little to do, could dream of these exceptional heroines, but the classical texts of Confucianism put before them the duty of filial piety, which was to show total devotion to their husband's family, to be attentive and obedient to their mother-in-law, and to produce a son. Should they fail in this mission, they had to be prepared to see their husband take a concubine who would be more successful. Women had their own social circles, which were separate from those of men. Only singers and actresses were present at banquets, at which they served the men with drink, thus earning contempt for their promiscuous behavior. Sometimes students from good families would forget their overriding duty of preparing for the official examinations and spend their allowance in the flowered boudoirs of courtesans.

Grand-daughter of a Convert Scholar

Anne Birrell has drawn attention to the small number of notable female authors for the main periods of Chinese history: "a total of nineteen noteworthy female authors for the two millennia from the first century C.E. through the nineteenth century".[2] This can be explained in part by the choice of literary genres available to both genders, since plays and novels were not an option for women. In the

---

[2] "An index of the numerical representation of notable female authors may be gleaned from the following figures for the main historical periods: two in the Han Dynasty; three in the early medieval era (plus five song makers); three in the T'ang Dynasty; two in the Sung Dynasty; one in the Ming Dynasty; and eight in the Ch'ing Dynasty." Anne Birrell, "Women in Literature", in *The Colombia History of Chinese Literature*, ed. Victor H. Mair (New York: Columbia University Press, 2001), p. 218.

late sixteenth century, however, an important development occurred that Dorothy Ko summarizes thus: "For the first time in Chinese history, a considerable number of women managed to publish their writings within their lifetime; at the same time, printed books became so accessible that reading ceased to be the prerogative of the upper echelon of the traditional elite. A booming publishing industry was instrumental both in the birth of the woman reader-writer and in the emergence of a reading public."[3] This was to have an important influence on the kind of life that Candida Xu was able to live in the following century, because of the new areas of activity that became open to some women: "Even a cursory look at descriptions of seventeenth-century urban life in local histories, private writings, and fiction suggests a contrasting picture of the vitality of women's domestic and social lives, as well as the degree of informal power and social freedom they apparently enjoyed."[4]

At all levels of the social scale, the mixing of men and women continued to be frowned upon, however. Only Buddhist monks were allowed to converse with women and to counsel them. Since the Jesuit fathers had opted for the status of Confucian scholars, it was practically impossible for them to see women. Fr. Philippe Couplet had criticized these restrictions, but it is due to him that we know about a remarkable woman from Shanghai, Candida Xu (1607–1680), who was the granddaughter of Paul Xu Guangqi, the scholar convert described in the previous chapter.[5] We are relatively well informed about her because her life was written in Latin by her spiritual director, Fr. Philippe Couplet, S.J., (1623–1693), a Belgian Jesuit, with the title *Historia Nobilis Feminae Hsiu Christianae Sinensis*. It was translated into French by P. d'Orléans and published in Paris in 1688 with the title *Histoire d'une Dame Chrétienne de la Chine, Candida Hiu, où, par occasion, les usages de ces peuples, l'établissement de la religion, les maximes des missionaires et les exercices de piété des nouveaux Chrétiens sout expliqués.*[6]

---

[3] Dorothy Ko, *Teachers of the Inner Chamber: Women and Culture in Seventeenth-Century China* (Stanford, Calif.: Stanford University Press, 1994), p. 29.

[4] Ibid., p. 9.

[5] See chapter 9, pp. 161–65.

[6] The short Latin title of Fr. Couplet's book (*Story of the Noble Christian Lady Hsiu*) was replaced by a longer title in the French translation (*Story of a Christian Lady from China Candida Hiu in which, as the opportunity occurs, are described the custom of the people, the institutions of religion, the teaching of the missionaries and the pious practices of the new Christians.*)

Candida Xu (1607–1680)

The granddaughter of a notable convert to the Catholic Faith, Candida was brought up in Shanghai. She was the mother of eight children and regularly distributed food for beggars at her house in Shanghai, where she also created a home for abandoned children. Her eldest son was a member of the scholar-gentry and Candida used his position in the imperial inspectorate to help priests and to build churches in some of the provinces to which he was sent and which she sometimes visited with him. Candida's life was written in Latin by Fr. Philippe Couplet, S.J., and published in Paris in 1688 in a French translation which includes this illustration.

The book was also translated into Spanish, Dutch, and Italian, but not Chinese. "The author hoped that learning about such a fine Chinese Christian would inspire European women, especially wealthy widows, to work, as she did, for the conversion of the Chinese, and he proposed her as a model for imitation, spiritual as well as financial".[7]

Candida Xu was born in 1607, four years after her grandfather had been baptized, and she was brought up as a Christian. She received the name Candida at baptism in honor of the saint, celebrated on that day. Her mother was very pious and taught her how to pray. When she was ten, she used to say the Rosary every day, though apparently in rather a haphazard way. Once when she fell ill, she attributed her malady to the lack of assiduity in prayer.

She must have been rather a mischievous child. She was spoiled by her grandfather and would play with his clocks, his globe of the world, his crystals, and other strange knick-knacks that the Jesuits had given him. After Xu Guangqi's death she gave all these curios back to the fathers, advising them to use them to win the favors of the rich and powerful.

Candida's childish amusements did not last long, as her mother died when she was fourteen, and two years later her father married her to a rich young man who was not a Christian. Permission was readily given for mixed marriages at a time when there were so few Christians in China. She bore him eight children, three sons and five girls. Her husband was deeply touched by her attentiveness, her goodness, and her patient prayer, and eventually he was baptized too, though only two years before his death at the age of forty-six.

Candida took the greatest care in supervising her children's education in the faith. She had heard the Jesuit fathers say that European families came together for evening prayers, and she introduced this custom to her family. Every day the children and the personnel of the house were invited to prayer in common, which included some spiritual reading. Knowing how difficult it was for Chinese girls to go to confession, she made sure that her daughters came to greet the priests so that they became used to talking to them. She would also have meetings of pious women in her house and train them to

---

[7] Standaert, p. 394. For the part played by women in the spread of Christianity in China, with bibliography, see Standaert, pp. 393–98.

visit the sick, to instruct them in the faith, and to bring the priests to them when they needed the anointing of the sick.

A Strong Woman of Many Good Works

Candida had become a widow relatively early. Her widowhood brought her greater freedom, and she used it for forty years to fill her life with many activities. In order to help the fathers financially, she turned her house into a workshop for embroidery on silk; her daughters, servants, and friends were all put to the task. She thus managed to raise funds that were sent to twenty-five or so priests, scattered in the different provinces. With the help of her father, James Xu, she contributed to the building of several churches in the Songjiang region, south of Shanghai, where the Marian Basilica of Sheshan now stands.

Three Christian associations were founded in the region at that time: the Congregation of Mary, the Society of the Holy Angels for the care of children, and Confraternity of the Passion. Candida had a special devotion to the Passion of the Savior and practiced numerous mortifications. There were also a Society of St. Ignatius for literary and doctrinal study and a Society of St. Francis Xavier for catechesis. Candida actively supported all these groups, providing crucifixes, holy pictures, rosaries, and candles, and seeing to the printing of booklets. In the biggest church of Shanghai, she would preside each year at a distribution of prizes.

As it was not easy for girls to go out, Candida asked the fathers to translate books for them. This made the Jesuits come down from the heights of astronomy and philosophy to compose simple little treatises on spirituality. Candida gave hundreds of them away to her acquaintances so that the Christian message spread among all levels of society.

Apostolic Journeys

Candida's eldest son, Xu Zuanzeng (c. 1627–1696), whose baptismal name was Basil, entered the imperial inspectorate and was obliged to travel in different provinces.[8] His mother took the opportunity of going with him, thus escaping from the secluded life of most

---

[8] For the details of Basil Xu Zuanzeng's life, see Standaert, p. 429.

women. When she arrived at Nanchang in Jiangxi Province, she was indignant when she saw the miserable appearance of the little church and immediately bought more land and had a large church built. When she reached Hubei Province, she learned that there was only one priest in the whole province and that no one knew where he was. She wrote at once to the superior of the Jesuits, asking him to send a priest to Wuhan, the capital of Hubei. This was in 1657, when eight French Jesuits had just arrived in China, three of whom were brothers called Motel. Fr. Jacques Motel, S.J., was sent to Wuhan, and in due course two churches were built, one on either side of the Yangzi River. It has been estimated that Candida helped to establish in all one hundred churches, chapels, and oratories.[9]

When Basil was sent to Sichuan Province in 1661, Candida would have liked to travel with him, but the journey was dangerous and might have endangered her health. She made her son promise to continue with the good work, and in fact he had a church built at Chengdu, the capital of Sichuan, and another at Chongqing, the largest city in the province. His mother intervened once again with the Jesuit superior, thanks to which Fr. Claude Motel (1618–1671) was sent to Sichuan Province and lived in an apartment in Basil's residence at Chongqing.

Once Candida was back in Shanghai, she followed her son's journeys from afar. When he was transferred to Henan Province in 1664, she informed Fr. Christian Wolfgang Herdtricht, S.J. (1625–1684), in the neighboring province of Shanxi. The priest came to see Basil at Kaifeng, a large city on the Yellow River, hoping to build a church there. There had been a Catholic church at Kaifeng previously, served by the Portuguese Fr. Rui de Figueredo (1594–1642), but it had been destroyed in 1642 by a disastrous flood of the Yellow River in which Fr. de Figueredo himself was drowned. To make things worse, the Ming Dynasty was coming to an end, and many parts of the country were in anarchy. A rebel force under Li Zicheng threatened Kaifeng, and the city authorities tried to defend the city by opening the dikes of the river, with the unfortunate result that 300,000 of the inhabitants were drowned.

The Catholic church at Kaifeng was rebuilt by 1666, but a violent persecution then broke out against Christians at the instigation of the

---

[9] Ibid., p. 428.

eunuch Yang Guangxian. Foreign priests were arrested and taken to Beijing and then Macao. Candida sent them financial help and intervened with the authorities so that the prisoners should be decently treated. Her son Basil supported her in all this, but was dismissed from his post soon afterward.

After six years, things went back to normal. Basil was exonerated and received a new posting in Yunnan Province in 1671. However, he was not very firm in his Catholic faith and wrote a book of moral counsels, following the Buddhist doctrine of retribution through the transmigration of souls and containing also astrological speculations. His mother was very upset about this and did penance with tears and many prayers. She told him to hand over his writings and the printing blocks of the book and had them destroyed in the presence of a missionary. Basil complied with all this, obedient son that he was. He made a general confession and did penance, his main concern being to appease his mother's sorrow.

A Lady of Charity

As well as being concerned with the welfare of the Church throughout the country, Candida responded to the needs of the poorest in an intelligent way. Beggars came to her house in such numbers that the staff were put out by their insistence. She therefore had a door made at the back of the house, giving access to a yard for the beggars, where she would serve them herself. Many babies, sick or abandoned, died after a few weeks. Candida taught the midwives to baptize those who were in danger of death. Parents often rejected girl babies. Candida obtained funds from the rich families of Suzhou and opened a house where abandoned babies could be brought, cared for, and baptized. This service was organized in other parts of China and continued to develop until, much later, it became the concern of the Work of the Holy Childhood.

Candida's zeal was amazing in its ingenuity. When she came across some blind people who lived by telling fortunes, she provided for their material needs, instructed them in the faith, and sent them out on a mission. Their instructions were to stop misleading people by their divinatory practices and instead to tell them the story of salvation through Jesus Christ. The converted blind thus brought light to the poor. Crowds used to form around these storytellers, who soon became professional in their delivery and used rhythm to tell their Gospel stories, beating time with the help of wooden clappers.

Magnificat

When Candida reached her sixtieth birthday, all her family gathered round her, according to the ritual of the empire, since the kingdom of China is "a great family under heaven". The mother of a high-ranking civil servant had to be honored in a solemn manner. For eight days receptions, banquets, and festivities followed one another. Candida sat on a throne in the middle of her children, grandchildren, and servants, and everyone did obeisance before her with the greatest respect. After the ceremony, Candida took off her silver headdress, decorated with pearls. One by one, she took the pearls off and gave them to the poor. Then a troupe of actors came in, and the sound of musical instruments filled the house. Later Candida retired to her chapel, which was dedicated to Mary, the Mother of Jesus, and gave thanks to God for all that he had given to her family.

Candida died on July 24, 1680, having received the sacraments and surrounded by her family at prayer. A large cross was placed on her tomb, inscribed with texts from the creed. Under the inscription I.N.R.I. (*Iesus Nazarenus Rex Iudeorum*), the three Chinese characters for faith, hope, and charity had been inscribed. Fr. Couplet added a final word to this edifying story:

> One should add that Madame, at the moment when she closed her eyes, gave the impression of great peace, without any shadow of suffering. On her face was an expression of joy, as if she could see heaven and the Savior, accompanied by angels, coming to welcome her to his heaven.[10]

Shortly before her death, Candida heard that her spiritual director was due to go to Rome and hastily gathered some presents, including a chalice for the Church of St. Ignatius. She wanted to express her gratitude to the Pope, the head of the Church, and to the messengers who had brought the Gospel to China. She also donated some money for the collection of Chinese books that Fr. Couplet took to Rome

---

[10] Couplet, *Historia Nobilis Feminae*.

and presented to Innocent XI in 1685.[11] Some of these books are in the Vatican Library still, including Fr. Buglio's 1670 translation of the Roman missal.[12] Many years later Pope Pius XI quoted her as an example for Catholic Action in China. She was so faithful to the teaching that she had received and at the same time so inventive in all sorts of good works, a real "mother of the Church in China". "A great lady and a holy widow, she rivaled those holy matrons who, in the early centuries of the Church, supported the pontiffs and the priests of Rome."[13] One can still see her spiritual legacy at work among the Catholics of the Shanghai of today. There is a dynamism about them that derives from roots that go back more than three hundred years. The great Catholic families of Shanghai have remained faithful in spite of everything, and their faith expresses itself today in devotions, publications, and a great variety of good works, just as it had done in the seventeenth century.

---

[11] Standaert, p. 428.

[12] Ibid., p. 627.

[13] Noël Gubbels, *Trois siècles d'apostolat: Histoire du Catholicisme au Hu-Kwang depuis les origines 1587 jusqu'à 1870* (Paris: Éditeurs 36 avenue Reille, 1934), Collection Missionarius, p. 19.

[Illustrations on following pages: Title Page of the Buglio Missal in Latin. (Vatican Library, Borg. Cinese 352 (1) 2).

Title of the Chinese text: *Misa jingdian*, (MISA Official Prayer). (Vatican Library, Borg. Cinese 352 (1) 1).

Authorization: *Translated by the Western Jesuit Ludovico Buglio, corrected by Gabriel de Magalhaes, Christian Herdtrich, Philippe Couplet, François de Rougemont, Adrianus Greslon, of the same Congregation, authorized by the Prefect Ferdinand Verbiest.* (Vatican Library, Borg. Cinese 352 (1) 1 v). © Vatican Library.

New material has been added to the French text of sections "The Condition of Women" and "Grand-daughter of a Convert Scholar" in Chapter 10.—Trans.]

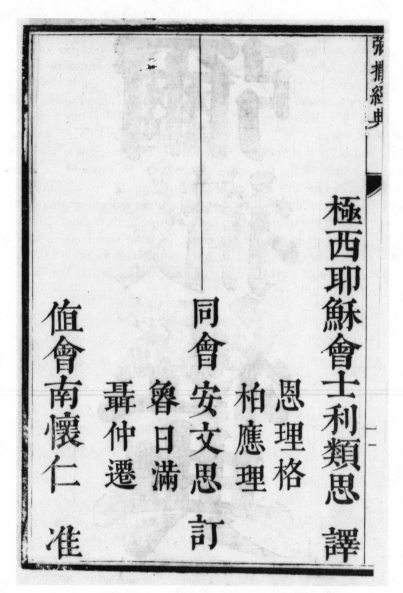

The Roman Missal in Chinese (1670)

Fr. Ludovico Buglio, S.J. (1606–1682) translated into Chinese the 1570 Missal of Pope Paul V. It was printed in Beijing in 1670 from wood blocks, to be read by the faithful and in the expectation that Rome would grant permission for the celebration of Mass in Chinese, but this did not happen. We are grateful to Dr. Clara Yu Dong, of the Department of Manuscripts at the Vatican Library, for the translations.

Misa Jingdian

Literally "Scripture Missal" or "Classic Missal". Jingdian is a term used to describe classic Confucian, Taoist, Buddhist, and Christian texts.

MISSALE
ROMANVM
auctoritate
PAVLI V. PONT. M
Sinicè redditum
A
P LVDOVICOBVGLIO
SOC. IESV

PEKIM
In Collegio eiusd. Soc.
AN. M. DC. LXX.

Latin title page of Fr. Buglio's Chinese Missal.
Printed in Beijing 1670.

EUNUCHS AND THE KINGDOM

The Acts of the Apostles relate how the deacon Philip baptized the eunuch, who was treasurer of the queen of the Ethiopians (Acts 8:27). Eunuchs were also found in China from ancient times. War prisoners and criminals were castrated and made to work in the harems of rulers and important officials. Some eunuchs came from humble origins and were recruited to serve the court. They accepted voluntary castration when they came into its service, following the appropriate ritual, during which the candidate signed a declaration that he was accepting of his own free will such an operation and would henceforth be "wedded" to the interests of the court only.[1] Since the eunuchs were in charge of the imperial harem, they knew how to win the patronage of the most influential concubines.

The Power of the Eunuchs

The most dramatic example of the role of eunuchs in Chinese politics occurs in the third century B.C. When Emperor Qin Shi Huangdi (r. 221–210 B.C.) died away from the court, the eunuch Zhao Gao brought the body back in a covered chariot and managed to keep his death a secret, ensuring the usual delivery of food to the imperial apartments and using the emperor's seals to produced faked documents, including a letter to the heir apparent, ordering him to commit suicide, which the unfortunate prince heroically but ill-advisedly did. At the time of the Han Dynasty (206 B.C.–220 A.D.), the number of eunuchs grew greatly under the protection of emperors who relied on them as on a "spiritual divan". They interfered to such an extent in matters of state that they attracted the hatred of the great landed

---

[1] See the study by Chen Cunren in *Lianhe zaobao, The United Morning Press*; Taiwan, Apr. 1987.

families and the scholarly civil servants. In A.D. 189, 2,000 eunuchs were massacred when the capital city Luoyang was captured.

At the time of the Ming Dynasty (1368–1644), key posts at court were entrusted to eunuchs, in spite of the decrees that sought to keep them away from politics by forbidding them from taking degrees. But in fact many of them acceded to vital and lucrative posts at court. Some eunuchs also successfully carried out military assignments, like the Muslim Admiral Zheng He, at the beginning of the fifteenth century. Others were corrupt and cruel, such as Liu Jin a century later, who tortured honest civil servants, built up his personal fortune by manipulating taxes and exacting commissions, and had temples built in his honor. Finally he amassed a stock of weapons, which made him suspect of sedition. He was arrested in 1510; all his clique of friends were dismissed from their posts, and he was cut up into small pieces, the Chinese punishment for traitors.

At the beginning of the seventeenth century, when the Ming Dynasty was nearing its fall, the eunuchs at court played a particularly important role in politics. Both Christian mandarins and foreign missionaries found themselves involved in their intrigues. At the time when Fathers Ricci and Pantoja were sailing up the Grand Canal with suitcases full of presents for the emperor, the eunuch Matang, a powerful and grasping man, was in charge of the administration of taxes in the Tianjin region. He confiscated some of the presents and held up the travelers on their journey. When the fathers reached Beijing, members of Matang's clique intrigued to prevent the Jesuits from seeing important civil servants. This scheming aroused the indignation of the director of the board at the ministry of rites, which was responsible for welcoming foreign delegations. After Ricci's death, the Jesuits received a sort of compensation for all the troubles to which they had been subjected at the hands of the eunuchs, when they were given for their cemetery the villa of a eunuch who had been condemned to death.

Eunuchs and Persecution

In 1616 the scholar Shen Que, who had just been appointed vice-minister of rites in Nanjing, unleashed a violent persecution against the fathers from abroad. Shen Que was a highly educated man, who had passed the palace examination for the civil service in 1592, the same year as Yang Tingyun.[2] The small Christian community at Nanjing was then being looked after by Fr. Alvaro de Semedo, S.J., (1585–1658) and Fr. Alphonso Vagnone, S.J. (1566–1658), a church having been opened with great ceremony in 1611. Such ostentation was a departure from the discreet style adopted by the Catholic community at its beginnings, and it proved to be a mistake. Shen Que composed three memoranda, petitioning the Wanli emperor to ban the foreign religion and to banish the missionaries. Complaints against them were listed: the foreign fathers used offensive terms like "Lord of heaven"; their calendar was not orthodox; they preached against the cult of the ancestors; they had acquired land next to the mausoleum of Zhu Yuanzhang, the founder of the dynasty; they were buying converts, offering them three taels of silver each; they had built a temple whose architecture was abnormal; they were making converts among the people and also some civil servants; the influence of the fathers on the people was unwholesome; their followers met in darkened rooms, washed themselves in holy water, and wore amulets. The fathers even drew near to women in order to rub them with oil and sprinkle them with water. All this pointed to an unorthodox and subversive religion.

Shen Que also noted that the place of burial granted to Matteo Ricci was being used to bury other fathers as well, whereas it had been granted originally specially for a personality "come from afar". In addition Shen Que warned that the foreign fathers were only invoking the name of the Lord of heaven as a way of extending their dominion. He quoted as evidence what happened at Luzon in the Philippines, where the Folangjis pretended that they had come to preach the doctrine of the Master of heaven and had then deceived the king of the island so that they could take over his country.

Shen Que's three memoranda contained a number of accusations that were to be used time and again against Christians. It was essentially a defense reaction against the cultural shock caused by the presence of foreigners, whose new religion subverted traditional rites. There were, however, more personal reasons behind Shen Que's at-

---

[2] N. Standaert, *Yang Tingyun, Confucian and Christian in Late Ming China: His Life and Thought* (Leiden: Brill, 1988), p. 6, n. 9.

tack, and one must ask why he was so aggressive in contrast to the indifference shown by so many other Chinese.

A personal incident may have started things off by causing a loss of face. Sheng Que had once invited his former fellow student, Yang Tingyun, to a celebration that included a play. Halfway through the performance, "Yang Tingyun took exception to the lewd quality of one of the acts on the ground that it violated the sixth commandment of Christianity. Shen Que became extremely angry and berated Yang Tingyun for his Christian beliefs,"[3] whereupon Yang Tingyun got up and left. Shen Que was put out by this incident and, as a result, doubtless listened more attentively to the complaints of the Buddhists from Hangzhou who were indignant at the Christian claim that their cult was idolatrous. According to certain sources, Buddhists offered Shen Que a substantial donation of 10,000 silver taels.[4] Shen Que could not hope to receive such sums from Christians, so that his criticism of their wealth may derive from the fact that he had not received anything.

The fact that Shen Que belonged to a group with a particular political influence may also have had a role to play. Rivalry was constant between the eunuchs and the scholarly mandarins. Since Christians were being supported by a group of Christian scholar-gentry, Shen Que may have been trying to discredit that particular group of mandarins by attacking their friends. It may also have been a case of an ambitious civil servant, seeking to gain a reputation by putting through an imperial measure likely to have general support. Whatever the reasons, Shen Que obtained what he wanted. The decree of August 20, 1616, ordered the arrest and expulsion of the fathers and the confiscation of their property. Their enemy would have liked to condemn them to death, but he had to observe the terms of the decree. As a result, some of the fathers were badly treated, manhandled, shut up in narrow cages, and conducted to Guangzhou, whence they were shipped to Macao. However the application of the decree in China was not universal.

Three years after the decree of expulsion, Shen Que had retired to Hangzhou, and persecution died down. It is characteristic of Yang

---

[3] Ibid., pp. 91–92.

[4] Goodrich L. Carrington and Fang Chao-ying, ed., *Dictionary of Ming Biography: 1368–1644* (New York and London: Columbia University Press, 1976), vol. 2. p. 1157.

Tingyun's benevolent and optimistic attitude that he tried to make contact with the persecutor of Christians. He visited Shen Que, his former fellow student, to tell him that he was sheltering some Jesuits in his house and that he wanted Shen Que to come to visit them and to have a discussion with them, because Yang Tingyun was sure that he "would find them totally different from what he thought".[5] Unfortunately, the offer was not taken up.

The reign of the Wanli emperor was, however, drawing to a close. In 1619 he died, and his son followed him to the grave a month later, poisoned perhaps by the eunuchs. His grandson, Tianqi, aged sixteen, acceded to the throne. The young emperor had been since childhood under the sinister influence of the eunuch Wei Zhongxian (1568–1627), who was said to have had himself castrated so as to pay his gaming debts by finding employment at court. Wei Zhongxian profited from the favors of the nurse of the new emperor and was appointed to the office of rites. He used his power to have the eunuchs and mandarins hostile to his clique assassinated and concentrated his attacks on the Donglin Academy, a center of political opposition influenced by the great scholar Gu Xiancheng. The buildings of the academy at Wuxi in Jiangsu Province were destroyed in 1625, and a year later many of its members were arrested, tortured, and put to death.

The Tianqi emperor died unexpectedly in 1627, which meant an unlooked-for turn of fortune for the mandarins and Christians. The new emperor, Chong Zhen, Tianqi's brother, a conscientious man, banished the eunuch Wei Zhongxian, who hanged himself rather than face trial, and the learned members of the Donglin Academy came back into favor. The situation of the empire, however, did not improve, as the pressure of the Manchu armies on its northern frontiers increased and groups of rebel soldiers rampaged throughout the interior. The Ming Dynasty was approaching its end.

In spite of these precarious circumstances, Christianity began to make progress again in the provinces and at court. Beginning in 1628 a new center of Christian life began in Shaanxi Province. The scholar Wang Zheng (1571–1644), who came from that region, had a church and a residence built for Fr. Adam Schall, whom he had known in Beijing, and he took its name title from the first commandment, *Chong*

---

[5] Standaert, *Yang Tingyun*, p. 92.

yi tang, Sanctuary of the One. Wang Zheng had a lively mind, interested in everything, especially machines. He had read his way into the Christian faith through *Qi ke* (*The Seven Disciplines*). He also knew Nicolas Trigault and helped him to finalize his lexicon on the pronunciation of Chinese characters *Xi ru er mu zi* (*The Ears and the Eyes of the Western Scholar*), published in 1626 at Hangzhou. Wang Zheng was baptized in 1616 at the age of forty-five and wrote a treatise entitled *Wei tian ai ren jilun* (*The Fear of God and the Love of Men*), in which he described his own spiritual journey, first Buddhist, then Taoist, then Christian. He was enthusiastic about the discovery of the Xi'an Stele and proud of this relic of the Christian past, which had been discovered in his own province. With Fr. Schall, he translated the lives of famous Christian saints and published these notes with the title *Chong yi riji suibi* (*The Little Journal of the Sanctuary of the One*).

Eunuchs and the Gospel

In the spring of 1630, Fr. Johann Adam Schall von Bell, S.J. (1592–1666), the German astronomer who had been in China since 1619, was urgently recalled to Beijing, where the brilliant Fr. Johann Terrenz Scheck, S.J. (1576–1630), was dying. Fr. Schall took over from him at the Office of the Calendar and continued his work on the reform of the Chinese calendar and also made astronomical instruments. His knowledge of mathematics and the exactness of his calculation won the favor of the Chongzhen emperor. Through having access to the palace, Fr. Schall became a friend of a number of eunuchs and introduced them to the Gospel. Did he intend to use this as a way of gaining access to the emperor himself? The Jesuits still dreamed of a new Constantine for China, as the sequel to this story indicates.

Strangers at that time could never see the emperor. Those who could influence him were the ladies of the palace, but only eunuchs had access to their apartments, and the eunuchs were on the whole unhelpful. However, a Chinese Jesuit lay brother, Qiu Lianghou, set to work and instructed some of the better-disposed eunuchs in Christian teaching. Ten of them were baptized in 1631. One of them, the commander of the guard, took the name Protasius, but he became the victim of slander and was expelled from the palace. He went to

join Fr. Longobardo to help in his ministry. Two of the other converts were brothers and took as their patrons Nereus and Achilleus.
Achilleus, whose Chinese name was Pang Tianshou, was to distinguish himself by his unshakable loyalty to the last representatives of
the Ming Dynasty.

In due course the influence of these new converts began to make itself felt among the highest ranks of the court. A eunuch called Wang,
who had been attached to the service of the previous emperor's nurse,
was the best placed, although he had been downgraded for some misdemeanor. However, he had not taken umbrage and humbly accepted
the good advice he had received. He was also obsessed by a great
number of superstitions present in native beliefs, and it took a long
time, during his course of instruction in the Christian faith, to free
him from them. When he was finally baptized, he took the name
Joseph and made a good Christian, always pleasant and kind. He was
referred to as "a grain of gold in a bath of mud", which says a lot
about how the personnel at court were considered.

Conversions among the Ladies at Court

The "grain of gold" became the precious seed of Christianity in
the secret apartments of the Forbidden City. Joseph Wang made the
Gospel known to several ladies of the palace and baptized them. His
influence soon spread to a privileged group, the twelve or so favorites
who tended to the emperor every day. They talked about the Gospel
message to the emperor himself, who appreciated their testimony.
In 1637, eighteen high-ranking ladies were baptized. Those closest
to the emperor were called Agatha, Helen, and Isabel. Agatha was
outstanding for her intelligence and other qualities, and the emperor
held her in high esteem. Conversions continued to occur, and by 1642
there were about fifty new Christians in the imperial apartments, encouraging each other in the practice of the faith, although there were
occasional tensions. One of the ladies flew into a violent temper once
with a colleague and was then struck by remorse. She ran to the door
of her victim, humbly acknowledged her fault, and begged for forgiveness. The story of the incident reached the ears of the empress,
who was greatly impressed.

Joseph Wang, the eunuch who had baptized these ladies, also looked after their spiritual progress. He would bring them together regularly in a chapel dedicated to Mary and give them instruction. He also distributed objects of piety that the Jesuit Fathers had given him: rosaries, relics, and holy pictures. Agatha made a vow of chastity and seemed to have scruples about being required to accompany the emperor to the Buddhist temple when he went there to make his devotions. Joseph Wang had said that the fathers strictly forbade the cult of idols. When Agatha attended such ceremonies, she sidled to a corner, running the risk of being disgraced.

These converts were not only assiduous in prayer. They were practical and wanted to sponsor good works. They collected money for the fathers, made vestments for the liturgy, and helped Joseph Wang in his apostolate. Young Secunda, aged fifteen, converted seven of her colleagues. In 1640 the Jesuits tried to organize these ladies on the model of a religious institute and named one of them as superior. The drawback was that these women were never able to attend Mass or receive any of the sacraments, since no priest was ever allowed into the area of the palace where they lived. Fr. Adam Schall occasionally said Mass in the palace, but only Christian eunuchs could attend.

Did any of this influence the emperor himself? The Chongzhen emperor was an impulsive and inconsistent man. Some of the things that he did gave the Christians hope, but then he would do something entirely different to discourage them. One day the palace Christians were surprised to see that the emperor was avoiding Buddhist monks and had removed the statues of Buddha from his rooms. A few days later, the statues were back again. Any thoughts that might have been entertained about the conversion of the emperor to Christianity were in fact illusory. His end was a tragic one. In April 1644 the rebel chief Li Zicheng and his army appeared at the gates of Beijing, and the eunuchs admitted them to the Forbidden City. The emperor fled by the north gate of the palace and hanged himself in a pavilion of the Hill of Contemplation. The dreams, which Christians had entertained, had proved to be illusory, and had passed the Forbidden City by.

A Constantine without a Throne

Even though the Ming Dynasty was tottering to its end, the hope of conversion seemed to persist. At Beijing events were following on each other with speed. General Wu Sangui wanted to avenge the Chongzhen emperor, and also his own father, who had been tortured to death by the rebels. But, in order to clear the city of rebel forces, he had no alternative but to ally himself with the Manchu armies and opened the pass in the Great Wall to them. Manchu cavalry poured in and routed Li Zicheng's rebel forces, after which the Manchus turned against General Wu Sangui, occupied Beijing, and refused to leave. They then proclaimed the end of the Ming Dynasty and installed a Manchu dynasty, the Qing, who were to remain in power until 1912. Once again China was ruled by foreign emperors.

The principal duty of the Jesuits being to announce the kingdom of God, they were not bound to be loyal to the former dynasty. Fr. Adam Schall remained in Beijing at the service of the first Qing ruler, the young Shunzhi emperor (r. 1644–1661). In fact he was soon on very good terms with him, the emperor calling him *Ma-fa*, "grandfather". Later Fr. Schall took a part in the education of his successor, the Kangxi emperor (r. 1661–1722), who is generally considered as one of the greatest rulers of China.

However, some of the Jesuit fathers accompanied the ousted imperial family as it fled from the advancing Manchus to the southern provinces of Guangdong and Guangxi. Pang Tianshou, the eunuch who had taken the name Achilleus at baptism, continued to serve his former master faithfully and followed him on his headlong flight to the south. Even he began to weaken and to think of resigning when he saw the civil servants of Guangdong Province abandoning the Ming and rallying to the new dynasty in 1647. However, the Austrian Jesuit, Fr. Andreas Xavier Koffler (1612–1652), who was with the refugees, gave Pang Tianshou new courage, reminding him of the filial piety he owed to his sovereign.

Two other Christians did their best to protect the flight of the Ming. They were Thomas Qu Shisi, governor of Guangxi Province, and Luke Jiaolian, who actually inflicted a severe defeat on Manchu forces at the battle of Guilin. This gave a respite to the Ming emperor, whose court settled at Guilin for a time, and, while there, Pang Tianshou actually built a Catholic church, to which he welcomed catechumens. He also asked Fr. Koffler to join them from Zhaoqing, since his deepest desire was to convert the whole imperial family. The three ladies closest to the emperor were baptized; the empress dowager, who took the baptismal name Helen; the emperor's mother, who was baptized Mary; and the wife of the emperor, the empress, who was baptized Anne. These developments provoked murmurs of dissent at the court-in-exile, but the Yongli emperor did not intervene, preoccupied as he was by the worsening situation. He sent two Christian mandarins to Macao with presents for the church, hoping to obtain military aid.

Soon after her baptism, Empress Anne gave birth to a son, and the question arose whether the heir to the throne would be baptized. At first the emperor refused the conditions laid down by Fr. Koffler, that the child should be brought up a Christian, that later he should have only one wife, and that he should not have concubines. As the baby became very ill and was in danger of death, the emperor eventually gave way to the pleading of the Christian women of his entourage, and the child was baptized Constantine, a name that was a program in itself.

At the end of 1648, the last Ming emperor dispatched Fr. Koffler to Macao to urge his need for military help, and in January 1649 the Portuguese sent 400 men and two cannons to Zhaoqing, where the emperor had taken refuge near Guangzhou, 100 miles (160 kilometers) from Macao. About the same time the Jesuit superior, Fr. Sambiasi, died at Guangzhou and was replaced by Fr. Alvaro Semedo, who briefly visited Zhaoqing and was back in Macao by April 1649. He sent a Polish Jesuit, Fr. Michael Boym (1612–1659) to be with Fr. Koffler and the imperial family at Zhaoqing. They did not stay there long. The approach of Manchu troops compelled the emperor to go up the West River to Wuzhou and then retreat westward as far as Nanning, the capital of Guangxi Province, on the borders of Vietnam. There the pathetic remnant of the once illustrious house of Ming was trapped in a desperate situation.

It was then that the empress dowager, Helen, together with the eunuch Pang Tianshou, wrote letters to Pope Innocent X and to the general of the Jesuits, which were entrusted to Fr. Michael Boym and two Chinese mandarins to be taken to Rome. In her letter to the Pope (dated November 4, 1650), the empress testified that she and the heir to the throne had been baptized. She asked the Holy Father to pardon her sins and to grant her a plenary indulgence. She prayed for the reestablishment of peace and unity within the empire of the Ming. It was a final cry for help. The empress dowager died in 1651, and Fr. Koffler was captured by a troop of Manchu soldiers the following year and executed.

Meanwhile Fr. Michael Boym was wending his way to Rome with only one Chinese companion, Andrew Xu, the other having died at Macao. He encountered many difficulties, being tracked by Manchu forces and finding the Portuguese unhelpful, since they were afraid of alienating China's new rulers. Fr. Boym reached Venice in 1652 and was received by the doge, but when he got to Rome he had the humiliation of being considered a fraud. Neither the Pope nor the cardinals of *de Propaganda Fide* were willing to receive him. The fortune of the two envoys changed after Pope Innocent X's death in 1655. Andrew Xu was admitted to the Society of Jesus in 1656, and Pope Alexander VII then sent the two envoys back, replying to the letters that had arrived from China four years previously and expressing his desire for the return of peace to the war-torn Chinese Empire.

The attempted journey back to China proved as difficult for Fr. Michael Boym and Andrew Xu as the outward one had been. They were nearly captured off India by Dutch ships blockading Goa, and, when they neared the coast of China, the Portuguese forbade them from landing at Macao. By then it was eight years since they had set out on their journey. They tried to reach China by way of Vietnam and landed in the kingdom of Tonkin, hoping to reach Guangxi Province over the mountains, but all the passes were guarded by Manchu soldiers, whereupon the Tonkin authorities refused to allow them to stay in the country. Fr. Michael Boym was thus completely cornered and unable to complete his unbelievable journey. Release came to him from a higher authority; he fell ill and died on April 22, 1659, at the age of forty-seven.[6] Andrew Xu buried him by the side of the road and planted a cross upon his grave. He then turned his face toward China and, going up into the mountains, disappeared from history.

Two years previously, the eunuch Pang Tianshou, Achilleus by baptism, had ended his earthly course in Yunnan Province, surrounded by members of the Christian community there. Before dying he said

---

[6] For Fr. Michael Boym and Andrew Xu, see Standaert, pp. 449, note 2. The dates and some details of Fr. Boym's life are given in Joseph Dehergne, S.J., *Répertoire des Jésuites de Chine de 1552 à 1800* (1973), pp. 34–35.

to them, "Today I am happy to die in peace. It is the greatest grace I have received from my conversion and my baptism. It will be the same for you. Always remember it. Always be faithful."

It must be admitted that the Yongli emperor did not deserve such devoted service. He was irresponsible and, even in desperate circumstances, only seemed interested in snatching at pleasure, with the result that he was devoid of all authority. Nevertheless, a small faithful group followed him to the end, as he fled into Burma (present-day Myanmar), pursued by the Manchu soldiers of the same General Wu Sangui who had tried to defend Beijing for his dynasty. The Burmese handed him over to the Chinese, and he was brought back to Yunnan Province, where, in spite of his protestations and invectives, he was strangled with a bowstring in 1661. It seems that the young Constantine suffered the same fate, though some sources say that he died two years later at the age of fifteen.

Thus came to an end the illusions of many Westerners who had dreamed of a Christian Chinese Empire. It was a dream both tragic and pathetic: pathetic for the Christians of the West, who thought that they could reproduce their own history in another part of the world; tragic because it contradicted the Christian message itself, which proclaims a kingdom not of this world.

12

CONFUCIANS AS ARBITRATORS

The Gospel had reached an imperial court that was falling apart. Some of the women and some of the eunuchs had responded, but those who wielded power were contacted at a time of crisis when their concerns were elsewhere. However, a few high-ranking civil servants did accept Christian teaching, and this gave hope that others might also be converted.

The question must be asked, however, whether the members of the scholar-gentry class who had been converted were representative of Confucian society. To what extent were these converts understood and accepted in the cultural world of China?

A more difficult question follows: Could the Confucian tradition absorb the new religion from the West? This question was debated throughout the seventeenth century by Muslims and Jews as well as Christians. It was particularly important for Christians because their proselytism was more proactive. The debate marked an important new stage in the growth of Christianity in China, because it made it possible to see how a Chinese could be a Christian and which Chinese were more likely to accept Christian teaching.

Confucius for the Gospel

Nicholas Trigault recorded the verdict of Xu Guangqi on the matter:

> Dr. Paul was questioned about what the Christian faith really consisted of, and he replied, defining the whole thing neatly in four words: *Cuie Fu Pu Giu (qu fo bu ru);* that is: it eliminates idols and fulfills the law of scholars.[1]

---

[1] Translated from Shih's French translation in *Histoire de l'expédition chrétienne au royaume de la Chine, 1582–1610*, Matthieu Ricci, Nicolas Trigault (Brussels: Desclée de Brouwer, 1978), p. 21.

Fr. Trigault's translation is really an interpretation. The two characters *Qu Fo* that he translates "it eliminates idols" actually mean "rejection of Buddhism". Xu Guangqi belonged to the group of scholars that was reacting against Wang Yangming's brand of neo-Confucianism, which they considered as too much marked by Buddhist influences (see above chapter 9, p. 170). They, on the contrary, thought that to seek only interior purity, on the Buddhist model, was too individualistic. They considered that the most urgent task was to work for the moral reform of a "corrupt" society. They also wanted to contribute to the prosperity of the state through the progress that science and technology would bring about.

Christian foreigners who came to China, having been influenced by the Bible, were also critical of Buddhism when they saw so many statues of Buddhas and bodhisattvas, which they took to represent false gods. They therefore called Buddhism an "idolatrous sect". The main Chinese objection to Buddhism, however, was different. Those with a Confucian education criticized it for causing moral deviation by abandoning the way of traditional orthodoxy, whereas the doctrine of the Lord of heaven, with its Ten Commandments and its seven victories against the cardinal sins, seemed to provide a more solid basis for the orthodox way. Many non-Christian scholars agreed with them. Thus a certain Zhang Ruitu (1576–1641) wrote:

> Mencius spoke of "serving heaven" and our saintly Confucius of "mastering oneself". Who could believe that you are from a foreign country when your principles are so exactly in agreement with ours? What can the difference of places matter compared with the identity of minds and the universality of reason?[2]

Jacques Gernet quotes additional evidence and comments, rightly, that Chinese scholars only saw a difference of degree between their understanding of "heaven" and that of learned men from the West. For the Chinese, heaven meant nature and the principle of its organization or cosmology. Westerners made things clearer by putting greater emphasis on the Lord of heaven. In his preface to a book by Fr. Aleni, Chen Yi admitted that certain things "depend on the Governor of heaven". The positive attitude of certain of the Chinese

---

[2] Jacques Gernet, *China and the Christian Impact: A Conflict of Cultures* (Cambridge, U.K.: Cambridge University Press, 1985), p. 35. Quoting Ch'en Shou-I (1936).

scholars toward the doctrine of the Lord of heaven is expressed in the prefaces that they contributed to books written or translated by Western scholars. Their positive attitude depended on the fact that the doctrine of the Lord of heaven seemed to them to agree with their great Confucian tradition and also because it confirmed and emphasized the moral demands of self-perfection.

Confucius against the Gospel

Points of contact between the civilizations of East and West were really to be found at the level of natural religion. Things became more difficult when Westerners attempted to explain further the mysteries of revealed religion. The idea that the Son of God had become man and had then been put to death in a vile manner on a Cross seemed utterly unreasonable to the Chinese mind. The same applied to the request for the conversion of one's lifestyle as the result of the imparting of such information and to the demand that worship should be given to the crucified Savior.

A writer called Chen Honguang from Fuzhou was outraged by such newfangled teaching and appealed to the words of Confucius in order to defend the authentic worship of heaven:

> Confucius used to say: . . . "to study the realities of the most humble kind in order to raise oneself to the comprehension of the highest matters, what is that if not 'serving heaven'." To abandon all this in order to rally to this Yesu who died nailed to a Cross, of whom Ricci speaks and whom he identifies as the Sovereign on high, to prostrate oneself before him and pray with zeal, imploring his supernatural aid, that would be madness.[3]

In fact Christian worship was a source of scandal for a Confucian like Chen Honguang, who was concerned to maintain the prescribed rites and hierarchy. He wrote:

> The fact that they serve one single Master of heaven means that they place on the same level son and father, subject and sovereign.[4]

---

[3] Ibid., p. 120. *Bianxue Chuyan*: referring to *Po xie ji* (smash heresy) PXJ, V, 8b–9b.
[4] Ibid., p. 118; referring to *Bianxue Chuyan*, PXJ, V, 4a.

To Confucians, the commandment that requires human beings to love God above all things seems to disrupt the right order required by filial piety. The idea that all must be treated as equals threatens the solidarity of the family. The sacrifice of the Mass, which is offered by the faithful to the Lord of heaven, ignores Chinese cultic order, for only the emperor was qualified to offer sacrifice to heaven. As for the sacraments for the forgiveness of sins and for the anointing of the sick, they seemed to uninitiated observers to be magical practices, since they ensure, according to Catholic moral theology, a forgiveness of sins *ex opere operato*, by means of the action that is performed.

As for the liturgical gatherings of Christians, they are identified with *Xie jiao*, the practices of illegal religious sects. Christian converts organized themselves in fact into communities that observed the rules of sacramental practice and Christian morality, and the Jesuits took seriously the observance of the discipline of the post-Tridentine Church. From the Chinese point of view, their credit was high as long as they limited themselves to the exchange of considerations about science and ethics, but from the Jesuit point of view these were only preliminary to announcing the Gospel. Among the fathers themselves, there might be disagreement as to how long this preliminary stage might last, but all were agreed that their aim was to win souls for Jesus Christ. Once those under instruction had been sufficiently instructed in the faith and introduced to the practice of prayer, they were asked to give up all practices incompatible with the commandments of God and of the Church. This meant the destruction of "idols" on family altars, the sending away of concubines by men who had several wives, and the giving up of ceremonies and customs associated with false belief. The application of these requirements could vary, according to the personality of the fathers and their degree of diplomacy, but the end result was the same. Reactions could be brusque on the part of scholars and Buddhists who were not part of the circle of friends of those who had become Christians. One of them expressed his indignation in a text from the period of the late Ming, dated 1638:

> The most upsetting thing of all is that they destroy [the statues of] our saints, cut off the heads of our deities, break the tablets of our ancestors, and put a stop to [the continuance of] cults, endeavoring by all this to topple our sages and masters and sever our connections with our fathers

and ancestors, so as to sweep away all our moral principles and school traditions.[5]

The Jesuits between Two Fires

The Jesuits realized what shock waves they were causing, and, not wishing to alienate their scholar friends, they asked themselves how they should proceed. Fr. Matteo Ricci had emphasized the need for forming a small number of well-instructed Christians, able to give witness to their faith. He had written to his superior:

> At this early stage especially, it is necessary to concentrate on a few rather than a large number and to have among them some graduate scholars and mandarins whose standing can give confidence to those who are frightened by this novelty.[6]

This policy led to the creation of small groups of Christians, based on families. These communities of scholar-gentry remained completely Chinese, since they were convinced, as Ricci had been, that Christian teaching agreed with the purest form of Confucianism, as it had been at the beginning. However, their rejection of Buddhism and of various forms of neo-Confucian philosophy, theology, and metaphysics cut them off from Chinese society. Although remaining Confucian, they had in fact made a choice without perhaps realizing all its implications. Ricci, however, knew very well that he had put them into a new orbit, by having introduced subtle changes to the "Confucian program". He wrote:

> It has been a great advantage to attract to our way of thinking the principal part of the group of scholar-gentry, who adhere to Confucius, while interpreting in our favor certain things that he left uncertain in his writings. In this way our [converts] won the esteem of those scholars who do not worship idols.[7]

In fact the esteem that Ricci mentions was limited to a few friends who sought the company of the wise men from the West for different reasons. Many of them questioned the way in which Ricci claimed to

---

[5] Ibid., p. 175; quoting *Xiedu shiju* (1638), PXJ, III, 33b.
[6] Shih, *L'Histoire de l'expédition*, p. 40.
[7] Ibid., p. 22.

represent a purer form of Confucianism. *Ru jia*, the school of scholars, constituted a living tradition, and, over the centuries, many commentaries had been produced that could hardly be separated from
supposedly primitive texts. In Western Christianity, too, one has to
ask whether it is a good method to accept the Gospels only and to
reject the writings of the Fathers of the Church and the decisions of
the Magisterium. Sixteenth-century European Reformers were condemned as heretics precisely because they wanted to interpret biblical
texts without any reference to the later developments of tradition, and
yet this was the method that Ricci wanted to apply to the corpus of
Confucian writings.

There was no Church in Confucianism, but only a collection of
rituals, endorsed by the state. If Christians rejected these rites, they
could be condemned as heretics. Priests from the West could be imprisoned and deported, because they had introduced a foreign religion that disturbed the ritual of the empire. Some of the fathers from
abroad realized the danger of the situation and took up a more tolerant position toward some of the traditional rites. They realized that
the cult of the ancestors was essential to Chinese family life, and they
tried to justify it morally by seeing it simply as an act of filial piety.
Such an attitude, however, was not always understood.

> Only the barbarians never reflect that every tree has its root, every river
> its source. That is why, right at the beginning, they truly did forbid peo-
> ple to make sacrifices to their ancestors. Later on, having been criticized
> for doing so, they changed their tune. And now, among the populace,
> people are allowed to honor their father and grandfather in the same
> sanctuary as the Master of heaven.[8]

Xu Dashou saw this as showing a total lack of any sense of hierarchy on the part of the Western barbarians. It seemed to him that
they dared to place on the same footing the Lord of heaven, to whom
they gave privileged status, and the ancestors of private individuals.

Some of the Jesuit fathers had foreseen that this was precisely the
sort of confusion that would occur and the kind of criticism that would
be made. They therefore undertook a thorough study of the question. Fr. Niccolò Longobardo (1565–1655), who came from Sicily,
concentrated on the question. He was encouraged by Fr. Pasio, the

---

[8] Gernet, *China and the Christian Impact*, p. 186; quoting Zuopi by Xu Dashou, 19b–20a.
10 chap. in *Poxie ji*, vol. 4.

visitor of the province of Japan, to study carefully the texts of the Confucian tradition, and he also consulted members of the scholar-gentry. Having discreetly gone back to Beijing after the persecutions of 1621–1622, Fr. Longobardo spent about two years writing a small treatise on the Chinese notion of God, the soul, and immortality. This *Brief Reply Concerning the Controversies . . .* was sent round to all the Jesuit residences in China. In 1625 Longobardo became superior of the missions in China, a position that he retained until his death in 1654.

As the result of Fr. Longobardo's research, it became clear that seventeenth century Confucians recognized no divinity but heaven, whose natural virtue is diffused among the "Ten Thousand Beings" of the universe. This belief is characteristic of neo-Confucianism, an amalgam of Confucianism, neo-Taoism, and Buddhism. Fr. Longobardo concluded that it is therefore not suitable to use the word *Tian*, heaven, for God. He also said that the Chinese did not have a clear, univocal idea of the immortality of the soul, which was true enough as there were several belief systems. He therefore concluded that Christians should be forbidden from practicing the traditional Chinese rites in order to preserve the integrity of their Christian faith.

It is possible that the results of Fr. Longobardo's inquiry were in part influenced by his first experience of evangelization, which had occurred in the region of Guangzhou. He had worked actively for conversions, both among the people and among the scholar-gentry, and he had soon built a church, but his apostolic zeal provoked a fierce reaction from Buddhists and others. It was then that the Jesuit lay-brother, Huang Mingsha, had been arrested and beaten so severely that he died of his wounds.

Fr. Longobardo had been sent to Beijing in 1609 and so had had time to reflect on Fr. Ricci's method of a temporary and partial compromise as the starting point of evangelization. His personal inclination, however, was to make clear decisions so as to avoid all confusion. This clear-cut attitude was the one adopted by the majority of the Jesuits in Japan, but it was not that of the Jesuits in China, who had to be more prudent because of the official posts that they held in the imperial administration. Such public appointments made it possible for them in fact to protect their fellow Jesuits discreetly when they were subjected to penal action in the courts. The more accommodating policy was the one adopted by the Jesuits in China and, toward the middle of the century, Fr. Francisco Furtado, S.J. (1587–1653), in fact had Fr. Longobardo's text destroyed.

A Muslim Spirituality

Fr. Ricci's method of "temporary and partial compromise" could be seen as being merely a strategy for obtaining conversions, but in fact it demanded an intercultural dialogue that had far wider implications. By emphasizing within the Confucian tradition those elements that were compatible with Christian teaching, Ricci had drawn attention to a common area of natural religion and morality. Such a meeting ground could apply to relations with other religions. Muslims and Jews in China certainly recognized its importance.

Muslims had also been persecuted under the Ming Dynasty. In the region of Quanzhou they had, as a result, adopted the names of the Han majority of the population, and many of them had taken refuge in remote villages along the coast. Some Muslim intellectuals had sought to demonstrate that the teachings of the Koran were not incompatible with the Confucian tradition. Some had also been inspired by Ricci's *The True Meaning of the Lord of Heaven*, an unexpected use of this book to which Ricci himself alluded: "Many people from the sect of the Saracens purchase *Tianzhu shiyi*, because it seems to conform with their doctrine."[9]

Toward the end of the Ming Dynasty, Muslim texts, written in Chinese, began to make their appearance. The first concern of their authors seems to have been to prevent the Muslim faithful from becoming too Chinese. Unlike Christian apologists of the same period, they did not aim at converting Confucians. Rather they presented the content of Islamic belief in Chinese terms so that Muslim believers could understand. At the same period, Muslim schools were created and also some institutes of Islamic studies. In one of the mosques of Shaanxi Province, a Chinese inscription had been preserved that expresses the atmosphere of the period.

> Muhammad, the great sage of the West, lived in Arabia long after Confucius, the sage of China. Though separated by ages and by countries,

---

[9] Reference in D'Elia, *Fonti Ricciane*, vol. 2, p. 179; quoted in Gernet, *China and the Christian Impact*, p. 257, n. 123.

they had the same mind and truth. The great Western sage (Muhammad) passed away ages ago. . . . His teachings were to purify oneself by bathing, to nourish one's mind by diminishing the wants, to restrict one's passions by fasting, to eliminate one's faults as the essential element in self-cultivation, to be true and honest as the basis for convincing others, to assist at marriages, and to be present at funerals.[10]

Muslim practices were thus explained in terms that were acceptable to neo-Confucians and Buddhists, the practices listed being acts of filial piety and a practice of virtues expressing fidelity to the ancestors, according to the ritual of the Hui ethnic group. According to Islamic belief, the purpose of these practices is to "honor God, Creator of the world"; the inscription comments thus:

> Emperor Yao said, "Reverence heaven." Emperor T'ang said, "By reverence one improves himself daily." Emperor Wen said, "Worship Shang-ti." Confucius said, "For him who sins against heaven, prayer is useless." All these sayings are practically the same. Apparently they possessed the same conviction and belief.[11]

This ancient text anticipated certain developments in apologetics that were not far from the views of Matteo Ricci and Xu Guangqi, according to whom Confucianism at its beginnings was the same as Islam. They thought that in the course of time it had deteriorated, which explained their present differences and the attacks made against Islam. However, Muslim writers did not launch into diatribes against neo-Confucianism and Buddhism. On the contrary, their first writings in Chinese were inspired by Sufi mysticism and developed in a very positive way a method of spiritual perfection that was the equal of neo-Confucian methods. Wang Daiyu (c. 1570–1660), who taught at Nanjing, wrote a treatise, *Qingzhen Daxue* (*The Great Muslim Study*), a title taken from one of the Four Books of Confucianism, *Daxue* (*The Great Learning*). In it, he describes how knowledge of self can lead to knowledge of God and to the highest degree of mystical union. Ma Zhu (1640–1711), a Muslim from Yunnan Province, had been a witness to the death throes of the deposed Ming emperor. He wrote

---

[10] Translation by Marshall Broomhall, *Islam in China: A Neglected Problem* (London: Morgan Scott, 1910), pp. 84–85. Quoted in Raphael Israeli, *Muslims in China: A Study in Cultural Confrontation* (London and Malmö: Curzon Press; Atlantic Highlands, U.S.A.: Humanities Press, 1980), Scandinavian Institute of Asian Studies, Monograph Series no. 29; p. 34.

[11] Translation by Broomhall, p. 85; quoted in Israeli, pp. 34–35.

Qingzhen Zhinan (*Guide to Islam*), in which he distinguished three degrees on the way to perfection. The Chinese word *cheng*, "degree", was borrowed from the Buddhist vocabulary and can also be translated as "vehicle". The Three Vehicles were firstly *chang dao*, the usual way; *zhong dao*, the middle way: and lastly *zhi dao*, the perfect way. Ma Zhu comments on them:

> The usual way is like the body of man; the middle way is like the heart of man; the perfect way is like the destiny of man.[12]

The French sinologist Françoise Aubin explains these grades as follows:

> At the level of ordinary people, the usual way, also called "the vehicle of the rites", or "the vehicle of the religion", is the way of the Shariat, of the observance of the fundamental Koranic commandments, as they are taught in the mosques . . .
> At the level of disciples, the middle way or "the vehicle of the way", that is the way of the Tari-kat, is the mystical fulfillment experienced in the framework of a Sufi order or confraternity.
> At the level of the highest initiation, the perfect way or "the vehicle of [transcendental] truth", *zhen cheng*, is the way of Haqiqat, or the hidden reality.[13]

A Chinese Form of Judaism

Interpretations of Islam in Confucian terms flourished at the end of the seventeenth century and in the eighteenth century. The small Jewish minority had acquired an Islamic culture on its way to China and was also associated with this trend. A large number of Jews had emigrated to China from the Middle East in the seventh century, and in the twelfth century many Jews moved from Hangzhou to Kaifeng, in Henan Province, so that there were more than 1,000 Jewish bankers and traders in the city during the fourteenth and fifteenth centuries. Toward the end of the Ming Dynasty, 200 to 300 Jewish families lived there.

---

[12] Jin Yijiu, *Sufeipai yu hanwen yisilanjiao zhushu* (*The Sufi Sect and Muslim Books in Chinese*), in Studies on Chinese Islam, Qinghai Popular Presses (1987), p. 122.

[13] Françoise Aubin, "En Islam chinois: quels Naqshbandis?" *Varia Turcica* 18 (1985); Naqshbandis, Actes de la table-ronde de Sèvres, May 2–4, 1985, p. 499.

In 1605, Ai Tian, a member of the Jewish community in China, went to Beijing, where he met Matteo Ricci. He saw in Ricci's room a painting of the Virgin Mary with Jesus and John the Baptist and thought that it represented Rebecca with her sons, Esau and Jacob. Once Ai Tian felt that he could trust Ricci, he told him about the Jewish community at Kaifeng and also about the presence of some "adorers of the Cross" in the city. Ai Tian seems to have heard about the teaching of the Jesuits on the Ten Commandments, and he thought that the learned men of the West observed the Mosaic law. The Jesuit lay brother Anthony Leitao was then sent to Kaifeng, but he did not find any descendants of Christians from the Syrian Church of the East; it seemed that they had died out shortly beforehand. There had been a synagogue at Kaifeng since 1163. When Brother Leitao was there the head of the synagogue had just died, and a request was sent to Fr. Matteo Ricci, suggesting that he might come to replace him.[14]

The ancestors of the Jews in Kaifeng had suffered under Muslim domination, but they had kept the deposit of their Jewish faith, with the observance of their festivals, their dietary laws, their Hebrew Bible, and their books of prayers. Their spoken language had been Persian, which was replaced by Chinese. The Jewish community had been in Kaifeng for many centuries and had become very Chinese in character. Some of its members had risen to high posts in the administration, as had happened in the case of Muslims. For example, Zhao Yingcheng (1619–1657), who was Jewish, passed the scholar-gentry examinations in 1646 with the grade of *Jinshi* and became inspector in Fujian and Hukuang (Hunan) Provinces. The Kaifeng synagogue had inherited a precious collection of scrolls and books, but unfortunately these were lost in the flood of 1642, which had been intended to drown the rebel forces besieging the city. In 1663 a stele was put up, describing the Hebrew religion in the same terms as the lost inscriptions:

> The composition of the Scriptures, although written in an ancient script and of different pronunciation, is in harmony with the principles (*li*) of the Six Classics, and in no case is there anything not in harmony with them.[15]

---

[14] Joseph Dehergne and Donald Daniel Leslie, *Juifs de Chine, à travers la correspondance inédite des jésuites du XVIII* [e] *siècle* (Rome, 1980), published by Les Belles Lettres, Paris, p. 129.

[15] The stone inscription of 1663, obverse. Text and translation in William Charles White,

These copies of the Hebrew Scriptures in Chinese were studied with great care by the Jesuits, who were concerned to verify the translations of the names of God and other biblical expressions. The Jesuits wanted to know how the Jews had remained faithful to their biblical tradition while being integrated into a Chinese Confucian milieu—questions that were to be raised especially in the seventeenth century, at a time when Westerners were bitterly divided over the question of Chinese rites. As for the Jewish community in China, it decreased in numbers and became increasingly isolated, until it was assimilated by its Chinese environment and disappeared altogether.

Chinese Jews: A Compilation of Matters Relating to the Jews of K'ai-feng Fu (New York: Paragon Books Reprint, 1966), 2nd ed., p. 62. The first edition was published in 1942 by the University of Toronto Press and the Department of Chinese Studies, Royal Ontario Museum, Toronto. Dr. William Charles White (1873–1960) was the first Anglican bishop of Hunan. Quoted in Israeli, *Muslims in China*, p. 84.

III

WITNESSES ON THE RUN

Gradually Catholic communities were organized, and churches were built. Jesuits were no longer on their own, since Dominicans and Franciscans had arrived in China, but without the same humanist and scientific training as the Jesuits. The friars preached in the provinces with a crucifix held aloft. They prepared their converts for martyrdom in an empire that was increasingly ruled according to Confucian principles.

The controversy about ancestor worship reflected the struggle between two civilizations, each strongly attached to its own tradition. When Catholics were forbidden by the Roman authorities from practicing Confucian rites, conversions among mandarins and scholars became more difficult. Foreign missionaries could only remain in China secretly and without any security.

This development favored the evangelizing methods of Chinese priests, Chinese catechists, and Chinese consecrated virgins, who preached the Gospel directly to the poor.

Would this mean that the Church was condemned to a marginal existence in a great civilization like that of China, where mandarins and scholars had a prevailing influence?

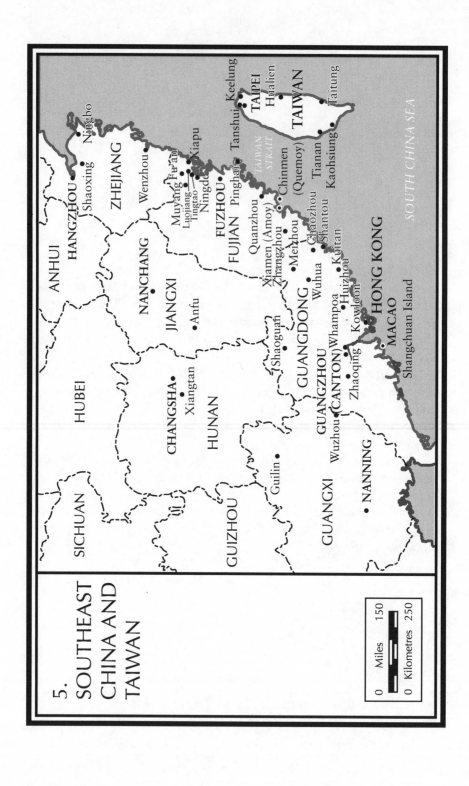

5.
SOUTHEAST
CHINA AND
TAIWAN

Miles   150
Kilometres   250

ANHUI

HANGZHOU
Shaoxing
Ningbo

ZHEJIANG

Wenzhou

NANCHANG

JIANGXI
Anfu

Muyang Fu'an
Luojiang
Tingtao
Ningde
FUZHOU
FUJIAN
Quanzhou
Xiamen (Amoy)
Zhangzhou
Meizhou
Wuhua
GUANGDONG
GUANGZHOU
(CANTON) Whampoa
Wuzhou
Zhaoqing

Xiapu
Pinghai
Chinmen
(Quemoy)
Chaozhou
Shantou
Kuitan
Huizhou
Kowloon
HONG KONG
MACAO

Tanshui
Keelung
TAIPEI
Hualien
TAIWAN
Taitung

TAIWAN
STRAIT

Tianan
Kaohsiung

SOUTH CHINA SEA

Shangchuan Island

HUBEI

CHANGSHA
Xiangtan

HUNAN

Guilin

GUIZHOU

GUANGXI
NANNING

Shaoguan

SICHUAN

13

THE GOSPEL IN THE PROVINCES

At the end of 1631, two Spanish Dominicans and five companions set sail from Formosa (Taiwan) for the Chinese mainland. The governor of the Philippines had sent this embassy to the viceroy of Fujian Province with a view to establishing commercial relations. The Dominicans dreamed of establishing a mission in China. They had made two unsuccessful attempts since their first coming to Taiwan, five or six years previously. They then hoped to do better, as a captain had advised them to abandon their frail craft and to come on his solid sampan. Suddenly disaster struck. The missionaries had been betrayed and were attacked, first of all by the ship's crew and then by pirates. Five of their party were killed, including Fr. Sierra. Somehow Fr. Angelo Cocchi escaped and managed to reach the shore. Angelo Cocchi, O.P. (1597–1633), was born in Florence and had joined the Dominicans in his native land, but had been sent to Spain to study theology at Salamanca. He traveled to East Asia via Mexico and had been since 1522 in the Philippines and Taiwan. He knew the Chinese language and Chinese ways and had the pleasant manner of an Italian, which stood him in good stead when he arrived on the mainland in such desperate circumstances. Some Christians in Fu'an heard about his plight. They were converts of the Jesuits who had left the area because they did not have enough priests. The Christians from Fu'an sought out Fr. Cocchi and arranged for him to be transported to their town "in a closed sedan chair that maintained only the faintest pretense of secrecy, as crowds gathered and looked inside when the bearers put the chair down".[1] Once he reached Fu'an, he found some ten Christians who were converts of the Jesuits and was befriended by local scholar-gentry and students. Fr. Giulio Aleni, S.J., also gave him support, so that the Spanish mission to China was able

---

[1] For the details of Fr. Angelo Cocchi's arrival in Fu'an, see John E. Wills, "From Manila to Fuan: Asian Contexts of Dominican Mission Policy", in D. E. Mungello, ed., *The Rites Controversy: Its History and Meaning* (Nettetal: Steyler Verlag, 1994), pp. 119–20.

to make a small beginning, although it subsequently had to face many trials.[2]

During the first decades of the seventeenth century, conditions were not too unfavorable for the missions. There were a few highly placed Christian civil servants who were able to exert a favorable influence on local magistrates. Moreover, the Catholic Church had not yet imposed severe restrictions on the observance of Confucian family rites. Rome was in fact aware of the need to adapt pastoral methods to local conditions. In 1615 a decree of the Roman Curia had permitted the use of Chinese in the liturgy, and in 1633 the Chinese missions were opened to the various missionary congregations, so that Dominicans and Franciscans were able to share the work hitherto undertaken by the Jesuits. Many converts received from the missionaries a solid training in Christian devotion and discipline. This first evangelization established deep roots and its beneficial results can still be felt in China today.

Christian communities increased in Fujian, as in other provinces. According to the estimates of a contemporary Jesuit, Fr. Martino Martini (1614–1661), the total number of Christians in China in 1627 was 13,000.[3] He noted that they were present in the following provinces: Jiangxi, Zhejiang, Jiangnan, Shandong, Shanxi, Shaanxi, and Zhili. Ten years later E. R. Huc estimated that they numbered 40,000.[4] Fr. Servière indicated that at the end of the Ming period there were missions in all the provinces except Yunnan and Guizhou and calculated that there were 109,000 Christians in the Celestial Empire in 1663.[5]

The Dominicans in Fujian Province

Fr. Angelo Cocchi worked hard after the favorable welcome that he had received in Fujian, instructing and baptizing whole families. Af-

---

[2] José Maria Gonzalez, O.P., *Historia de las Misiones Dominicanas de China 1632–1700* (Madrid, 1964), vol. 1, pp. 48–55, 71–79.

[3] Martino Martini, *De statu et qualitate Christianorum in Sina*, p. 16, quoted in Évariste Régis Huc, *Christianity in China Tartary and Thibet* (London: Longmans Brown, 1857–1858), vol. 2, p. 290.

[4] Ibid.

[5] Joseph de la Servière, *Les anciennes missions de la Compagnie de Jésus en Chine (1552–1814)* (Shanghai, 1923), pp. 31, 35. Also quoted by Huc and Latourette.

ter three years he had built a church at Fu'an and one at Tingtao
(Dingtou), twenty-five miles (forty kilometers) further south. Because
he could not cope with the numbers, he appealed to the Philippines
for help. The Dominican Province of the Rosary sent him Fr. Juan
Bautista de Morales (1597–1664), a Spaniard, born at Ecija in the
province of Seville, who had been in East Asia since 1522. He had
learned Tagalog while in the Philippines and had also looked after the
Chinese community there, so that he could read Chinese and speak
the Fukien dialect. With him came Antonio de Santa Maria Caballero
(1602–1669), a Spanish Franciscan. The two priests arrived in Taiwan
in April 1643 and waited at Tanshui for the sampan that Fr. Angelo
Cocchi was to send them. They saw a ship sailing inshore, with a
cross instead of a flag at the masthead. The captain was a catechist,
and the sailors were all Christians, but when they reached Fujian they
were just in time to assist Fr. Cocchi on his deathbed. Fr. Morales
and Fr. Caballero, however, were destined to work in China for some
thirty years.

The Spanish missionaries were impressed by the fervor of the first
Christians of Fujian. Fr. José Maria Gonzales, who wrote a history of
the Dominican missions, recorded some impressive accounts of conversions. Andrew Hong was one of Fr. Cocchi's first converts, and he
went on to found the Christian community at Tingtao.[6] He belonged
to an important local family, the Hong. One day a catechism came
into his hand, and he read it through. He was profoundly moved and
could not sleep afterward. As he belonged to a local literary society,
he shared his discovery with them. Surely, he said to them, one ought
to be concerned to save one's soul, as this book teaches. The group
was negative in its reactions and warned him about this new way,
maintaining with learned argument that the way indicated by Confucius was the safer one. He had, however, a young friend, also called
Hong, who agreed to accompany him in a further quest for truth.

The two earnest seekers heard that there was a foreigner in Fu'an
who taught a sublime doctrine and so they went there and were kindly
received by Fr. Cocchi, who arranged for them to be instructed by a
certain Joachim. They were baptized shortly afterward and took the
names Andrew and Thomas. It was thanks to them that a Christian

---

[6] José Maria Gonzales, O.P., *Historia de las Misiones Dominicanas de China* (Madrid, 1964),
vol. 1, pp. 226–28.

community was created at Tingtao and that Fr. Cocchi was able to
build a church there. Thomas died three years later "in the peace of
the Lord". Andrew contributed to the building up of the new community by his tireless activity on its behalf. He led a life of prayer
and was extremely generous to those in need, giving away his clothes
and even, on one occasion, offering to give away his bed.

Andrew Hong's wife, however, did not approve of this sort of behavior. Already, before he was baptized, there had been tensions between them because of his intolerance and his lack of understanding. He had forbidden her to welcome to their home any woman
of doubtful reputation, a reference no doubt to numerous mah-jong
players of the area, who enjoy a good gossip. If Andrew Hong learned
that one of the women he disapproved of had come to a session in
his house, he would break the chair she had sat on and smash the
cup she had used for her tea. It is not surprising that his wife came
to hate her husband and to give him a hard time.

When he was baptized, things became worse to begin with, but
then Andrew changed his attitude. He patiently accepted his wife's
harassment and, in the intervals between storms, began gently to instruct her in the Christian faith. Finally, she too asked to be baptized, receiving the name Teresa, and she proved to be an active catechist among her friends, the mah-jong players. Their home became
a peaceful one, and this was noticed locally, in contrast no doubt to
what had been observed before.

Andrew and Teresa were on good terms with the Spanish Dominicans. When the fathers had to go to Fuzhou to defend themselves
against an anti-Christian decree, Andrew and his wife pleaded to go
with them, but Fr. Morales persuaded them not to come, as they
would almost certainly have been thrown into prison.

Andrew and Teresa made progress together in the spiritual life and
decided to adopt a life of sexual continence, while continuing to live
together. Andrew became a member of the Third Order of Saint Dominic, an association of lay people who shared some of the prayers of
the Dominicans and had regular meetings. Fr. Gonzalez noted that
in 1648 there were only sixteen women who were tertiaries of St.
Dominic, so there would probably have been fewer men. That same
year, Andrew Hong became very ill and, after seven months, died a
holy death in the arms of Fr. Garcia.

The story of Andrew Hong reveals certain characteristics that later

François Pallu (1626–1684)

Vicar Apostolic in Asia. The principal founder of the *Missions Étrangeres de Paris*. Consecrated Bishop in 1658, he was sent to East Asia as Vicar Apostolic in 1662 and reached Thailand, returning to Europe to work for the recruitment and funding of missionaries. In 1681 he was sent to Asia with the grandiloquent title of *Administrator Apostolicus Sinarum* and actually reached China in 1684, but died at Muyang, Fujian Province, on October 29, 1684. Engraving.

became typical of the Catholic communities in north Fujian. People in that area have a brusque manner, tending to extremes. From the spirituality of the Spanish missionaries, they derived a singleminded and uncompromising faith. Local fervor and Spanish faith thus produced an explosive mixture, which continued to produce sparks during the history of the province. For instance, in 1990 thirteen members of the underground Church, including one bishop, were arrested near Fu'an.

Soon after the coming of Christianity to the area, ardent converts came into conflict with Confucian civil servants, who were suspicious of the foreign presence and influence in the area and wanted to defend the Chinese moral tradition. Anti-Christian writings multiplied from 1633 onward. These texts were collected and published in several editions with different prefaces. The complete edition was given a preface in 1639 by Huang Zhen and was made up of eight volumes under the title *Collection for the Destruction of Vicious Doctrines (Poxie ji)*. Several of these writings were composed in south Fujian and were aimed at the Jesuit Fr. Giulio Aleni, who had settled in Zhangzhou in 1635. The magistrates in the north of the province adopted the same hostile attitude toward the Dominican friars, who preached, holding the crucifix aloft.

The fiery Fr. Morales was not afraid to attack head on a pagan scholar from Fu'an who had written two anti-Christian books that he intended to send to the emperor. The first book concerned good government. The second attacked Christian teaching. Naturally it criticized the missionaries for forbidding the rites in honor of Confucius and the ancestors, but many other accusations were made against the law of the Christian God, his clergy, baptism, and confession. As regards the latter, they argued that the forgiveness of sins was so simple that it made life too easy for criminals. The Virginity of Mary was also turned to ridicule, which infuriated the Dominicans, who were zealous promoters of devotion to Mary and the Rosary. The mandarin who had published these arguments against Christianity happened to be passing through Tingtao when Fr. Morales was there. The Dominican hurried to the residence of the magistrate and asked for certain clarifications, reprimanding him energetically. A lively argument followed, so much so that the mandarin took fright and rushed out into the street, calling for help and shouting that the father was trying to kill him.

This made the mandarin even more determined to take the matter to Beijing, to the extent that he had the books printed and sold some of his land to pay for the journey. Meanwhile certain mishaps occurred to his family, which the Dominicans interpreted as a warning from heaven and which did make him worried, so that he consulted a fortune teller (*tangki, tongji*), asking whether he was doing the right thing. The fortune teller took up his brush and wrote the enigmatic oracle:

> As thou hast done, so wilt thou receive.
> Confucius and Mencius are there. [*Kong Meng zai nali.*]

When the Dominicans heard about it, they chose to read the final words as a question: "Where are Confucius and Mencius?" The outcome of the story is not told.

Neither the Dominican Morales nor the Franciscan Caballero were prepared to compromise about the ban on Confucian rites. They considered these as superstitious and were surprised that, before they arrived on the scene, the rites had been tolerated. Morales drew up a list of twelve questions concerning the practices that the Jesuits had authorized, and he wrote a report that underlined the religious nature of Chinese rites. He decided that the only thing to do was to carry the case to Rome personally, thus firing the first shot in what was to become the painful controversy among Catholics over the question of Chinese rites. In 1640 he left Manila with the Franciscan Fr. Antonio de Santa Maria Caballero, but Fr. Caballero did not go further than Macao, leaving Fr. Morales to travel through India and Persia. He found that the danger was not only sunstroke but also heat stroke, the heat being so extreme that the only way to survive was to cover one's face with a cloth soaked in water.[7] When he reached Basrah, he abandoned the Dominican habit to dress as a Turk while traveling in the Ottoman Empire through Iraq. At Alexandretta in Turkey (modern Iskanderun), he boarded a ship for Venice and was glad to put on the black-and-white habit of the Dominicans again. He reached Rome in February 1643, having spent three years on the journey.[8]

Pope Innocent X accepted Morales' argument, and in 1645 the

---

[7] Ibid., p. 244.
[8] Ibid., p. 249.

Congregation *de Propaganda Fide*, "for the propagation of the faith", issued the first condemnation of the rites in honor of Confucius (proposition 8) and those in honor of the dead (proposition 9) and ordered that the tablets of the ancestors should be removed from the homes of Christians (proposition 11).[9] When the news of this reached China, Fr. Martino Martini, S.J., who was a friend of the scholars of Hangzhou in Zhejiang Province, reacted immediately and wrote, demonstrating that the rites were purely civil in character and did not constitute a danger to the faith. The Jesuit's case was submitted to a different Roman Congregation, the Holy Office, also known as the Roman Inquisition, and renamed today the Congregation for the Doctrine of the Faith. A decree of the Holy Office, approved by Pope Alexander VII on March 23, 1656, accepted Fr. Martini's view of Chinese rites, whereupon the Congregation for the Propagation of the Faith seemed to modify its position by producing some general instructions in 1659, which emphasized the need for respecting local customs. These instructions were interpreted by Fr. Martini's supporters as supporting his position. Contradictory directives, coming from afar, poured oil on the fire, since both parties were now able to claim authoritative Roman documents in their favor.

The Chinese were dumbfounded by such a controversy about their own customs, which was raging between foreigners. On the whole, they took up positions according to the views of whichever group of missionaries had brought them the faith. The principle of filial piety led them to accept the directives of their spiritual leaders. They were willing to accept the Christian practice of prayer for the dead as an adequate replacement for the Chinese rites, but they suffered from lack of understanding on the part of their relatives and friends when they were seen to give up traditional family ritual. The dilemma was worse for Christian members of the scholar-gentry class, since by their status they were required to celebrate the rites in honor of Confucius. To refuse them brought their patriotism into question. It can be said that in general the forbidding of Chinese rites provided ammunition for the enemies of the Church and seemed to justify the persecution of Christians. It must be remembered, however, that the

---

[9] The propositions listed by Morales are mentioned by Minamiki, S.J., *The Chinese Rites Controversy, from Its Beginning to Modern Times* (Chicago: Loyola University Press, 1985), 353 pp.

refusal to sacrifice to the gods had also brought persecution upon Christians at the time of the Roman Empire.

Fr. Morales was the first to suffer from the backlash provoked by his controversy with Confucian civil servants. In 1645, shortly after he had returned from Rome, it was made clear to him that he could no longer continue his ministry in Fujian Province. He moved north to Zhejiang Province, persecution in one place thus becoming the occasion for the greater spread of the Gospel, as had happened in the early days of Christianity, when Christian Jews in Jerusalem were forced to disperse throughout the Diaspora. Strangely enough, the region of south Zhejiang, to which the Dominicans now moved, became a trouble spot where fervent Christians indulged in internecine quarrels. Even today, the 20,000 or so Catholics living south of Wenzhou are divided into two camps. Some are *Tang nei*, "within the Church", and accept the control of the government over the churches, which are officially open. Others are *Tang wai*, "outside the Church", and claim to be completely faithful to Roman directives, refusing any compromise with "patriotic" Catholics. Such divisions have much deeper origins than the recent constraints of Communist policy.

Franciscans in Shandong Province

Fr. Antonio de Santa Maria Caballero, the Franciscan who had arrived in Fujian Province at the same time as Fr. Morales, was as fervent as he was in preaching the Gospel. A Spaniard from Valencia, he was full of zeal but somehow prone to mishap. He had studied at the University of Salamanca and became a Franciscan at sixteen. Sent first to the Philippines, he learned Japanese from the lepers whom he looked after and was hoping to go to Japan, but instead he was sent to help Fr. Cocchi in Fujian. The Jesuits in China, knowing about his brash approach, tried to prevent him from preaching and sent him to Nanjing to obtain permission from their superior. When he reached Nanjing, he was locked up for several months, after which the Jesuits had him bound hand and foot and thrown into a boat bound for Fujian. He had an active ministry there until 1649, but when persecution broke out he decided to go to Korea. He got as far as the Great Wall in Manchuria, but was arrested and arrived, rather crestfallen, in Beijing. This time, however, the Jesuits were more helpful. Fr. Adam

Schall no doubt gave him a lecture on the drawbacks of adopting such a cavalier attitude toward the laws of the empire, but he did find a place for Fr. Caballero in Shandong Province, giving him a letter of recommendation and some presents for the mandarin at Jinan, the capital of the province. This well-mannered approach had the desired effect. Fr. Caballero went on to found the Christian community at Jinan and built a church dedicated to Our Lady of the Angels, a favorite devotion of the Franciscans. Fr. Buonaventura Ibañez, O.F.M. (1610–1691), joined Fr. Caballero, and over the next three years the two priests baptized over 1,500 people. This new Catholic community soon had its golden legend, which is chronicled by Fr. Domingo Martinez:

> A little girl, whose baptismal name was Angela, died. Three months after her death, she appeared in a dream to her father, surrounded by such brilliant light that he was overwhelmed and asked if she was really seeing God. She said, "Yes, I see him face to face. So that you may be convinced, look tomorrow in such and such a hiding place. You will find in it an idolatrous prayer formula. Burn it." He went to the place mentioned and found the formula there.[10]

It sounds as though this story were part of the stock of stories used by the Franciscans to discourage local superstitions. The idolatrous formula was no doubt a talisman on yellow paper, inscribed with esoteric characters, such as Taoist priests use for their exorcisms. Appearances in dreams are common in popular stories. Stories about miracles, visions, and cures are told in connection with conversions in both Shandong and Fujian Provinces and elsewhere. Accounts of supernatural happenings were already a part of the Chinese religious tradition and did not cease after conversion to Christianity. On the contrary, they flourished with renewed vigor once they were grafted onto the stock of Christian teaching. It was not only Franciscans and Dominicans who collected such stories, sprung from local tradition. The Jesuits too had colleagues who had the reputation of miracle workers.

---

[10] P. Domingo Martinez, *Compendio Histórico de la Santa Provincia de Philipinas*, etc. c. XIX and XX, quoted by Marcellin de Civezza, O.F.M., *Histoire universelle des Missions Franciscaines*, translated from Italian into French by Fr. Bernardin de Rouen, O.F.M., (Paris: Tobra, 1898), vol. 2, Chine, p. 241.

Fr. Louis Le Comte (1665–1728), who wrote the history of the Society of Jesus in the seventeenth century, was glad to quote the miraculous exploits of Fr. Étienne Faber, although he did introduce a certain reserve into the story:

> Those who witnessed his actions used to tell their children about the wonders that he worked, so as to confirm them in the faith. Although one does not have to believe everything that they said, one cannot deny that on many occasions God contributed in an extraordinary way to the great work that he [Fr. Faber] undertook for his glory.[11]

The foundation of the flourishing Christian community in Hanzhong in south Shaanxi, for instance, is linked to a story about locusts. A plague of locusts descended on the land and was devouring the crops. The peasants went to Fr. Faber and begged him to free them from this catastrophe, whereupon the father took the opportunity of telling them about God and the necessity of salvation through faith. They seemed responsive, and so he put on his surplice and stole and issued forth in great ceremony to say prayers and sprinkle the fields with holy water. The next morning, all the locusts had disappeared, and the peasants, feeling safe once more, forgot all about God and salvation through faith, whereupon dense clouds of locusts reappeared. The peasants rushed to the father, fell at his feet, and begged forgiveness for being so fickle, making an act of faith on the spot. The story goes on to tell that

> the father, to test their faith, kept them asking for a long time. Eventually he felt inspired, as he had been before, said the prayers, and sprinkled the fields with holy water. The next morning there were no locusts. The whole village was convinced and followed the spirit of God. They were all instructed in the faith, and a church was founded that was long considered as the most fervent of all the missions in China, although it has been abandoned for some years.[12]

Pagans also admired Fr. Faber and claimed that he confronted tigers in the steep mountain passes of the Qingling Mountains. He ordered

---

[11] Louis Le Comte, *Un Jésuite à Pékin. Nouveaux mémoires sur l'état présent de la Chine: 1687–1692* (Paris: Phébus, 1990), p. 402.

[12] Ibid., p. 403.

them not to attack travelers any more, and they duly obeyed. That is why nonbelievers considered Fr. Faber as a god and called him Fang Tudi. The statue of Fang Tudi wore a chasuble and had on his head a *jijin*, the biretta that priests wore in China for saying Mass.[13] When Fr. Le Comte was writing the passage quoted above, Hanzhong Church had been abandoned, but it flourished unexpectedly at the beginning of the eighteenth century: the young Andrew Li, who came from a village of the region, became the great apostle of the neighboring Sichuan Province.

Nowadays the Catholic community of Hanzhong is full of vitality and has produced two bishops and some ten young priests. Fr. Faber's tomb is much frequented by the peasants of the area, whether they are Catholics or not. They burn propitiatory papers there and attribute curative powers to the leaves of the nearby trees and water from the pond. During the Cultural Revolution the church was destroyed, but in 2000 the site was given back to the Catholics, and the official "patriotic" bishop is planning to build a place of prayer upon it.

Doctrine Through Prayer

Evidence shows that in the sixteenth century the Gospel was being taught in all the provinces of China. This was an extraordinary achievement, and the question arises how a handful of missionaries and catechists were able to ensure that catechumens and catechists received an adequate formation in the faith. The answer is perhaps to be found in the Chinese love of prayer, their aptitude for learning prayers by heart and for repeating them tirelessly. Right from the beginning of evangelization in China, Michele Ruggieri and Matteo Ricci profited from this aptitude and included the essential elements of doctrine in the formulas recited in prayer. In doing so they were utilizing a method that was widely used at the time by nonbelievers and that St. Francis Xavier had also employed, explaining the truths of the faith by means of the Creed, the Our Father, and the Hail Mary. Once Ricci and Ruggieri were settled in their Beijing residence, they produced a definitive text of these prayers with the help

---

[13] Louis Pfister, *Notes biographiques et bibliographiques sur les Jésuites de l'ancienne mission de Chine 1583–1773* (Shanghai, 1932), p. 205. No. 65, Étienne Faber or Le Fèvre.

of Xu Guangqi and Li Zhicao. One of the gems of this first series of prayers was by Fr. Pantoja, the author of *Qi ke*, (*The Seven Disciplines*). The excellent style of this text is probably due to Pantoja's close collaboration with Li Zhicao. The small book called *Sheng jiao ri ke*, (*Daily Prayers of the Holy Religion*), which was reprinted in the People's Republic around 1980, thus contains the text of prayers that are over 300 years old.

In September 1990 *Catholic Documentation*, published by the Guangqi Society in Shanghai, listed the prayers most often recited by Chinese Catholics according to their authors. Thus Fr. Niccolò Longobardo is the author of morning and evening prayers, the prayers of the Mass, the litany of the Sacred Heart, the litany of Our Lady and the litany of the saints. Fr. Emmanuel Diaz (1574–1659) is the author of the litany of St. Joseph. Fr. Giulio Aleni (1582–1649) composed the litany of the Blessed Sacrament. These three Jesuits were helped in their work of translation by Yang Tingyun. When persecution broke out in Nanjing in 1616, they had sought refuge in Yang Tingyun's house in Hangzhou, which became a center of prayer for the convert scholars of that town. According to A. M. Colombel, the house of the Jesuits at Hangzhou was then "like the heart of the mission". Yang Tingyun set up in his nearby house "two printers to multiply the books of religion. . . . In 1621, the residence entered 1,300 adult baptisms on its registers."[14] Fr. Emmanuel Diaz in 1628 praised the Hangzhou Christians, "who apply themselves daily to the devotions of the Rosary and to other devotions, which are found in a book called in that tongue *Ge co* (*ri ke*), (*The Daily Exercises*), which the fathers are in the habit of distributing to everybody."[15]

Fr. Gaston Fereira (1571–1649) composed *The Fifteen Decades of the Rosary*. In 1628 *Tianzhu shengjiao nianjing congshu* (*The General Collection of Prayers of the Holy Religion of the Lord of Heaven*) was published at Wulin in Guangxi Province and contained sixty-one prayers. It was frequently republished with additions from various sources. In 1665 the Beijing Jesuits, Fr. Ferdinand Verbiest and Fr. Ludovico Buglio, prepared a revised and corrected edition of *Sheng jiao ri ke* (*Daily*

---

[14] Auguste M. Colombel, S.J., *Histoire de la Mission du Kiang-nan* (Shanghai, 1895–1905), vol. 1, chap. 6, pp. 247–48.

[15] Paul Brunner, S.J., *L'Eucologe de la Mission de Chine: Editio Princeps 1628 et développements jusqu'à nos jours* (Münster: Aschendorff, 1964), Etudes et documents Missionaires 28, pp. 27–28.

Prayers of the Holy Religion). This they qualified as *ne varietur*, as if they wanted to establish a quasi-canonical collection of prayers. In fact, during the second half of the seventeenth century, the Dominicans, the Franciscans, and the Augustinians reprinted this collection with many additions of their own.

The Franciscan Manual of Jinan contains new prayers composed by Jesuits as well as Franciscans. The oldest known example of this manual dates from 1701. It also includes prayers introduced by the Franciscan Fr. San Juan Bautista, who came to Shandong Province in 1685. These were *The Prayer of the Seven Sorrows of the Holy Mother*, *The Prayer of the Seven Sorrows and Seven Joys of St. Joseph*, *The Litanies of St. Francis of Assisi*, and a *Prayer of St. Peter of Alcantara*.

To this day, elderly Catholics in the villages of China cherish like heirlooms prayer books that have been transmitted from generation to generation. Most of them were destroyed in the frenzy of the Cultural Revolution, which began in 1966, but Christians were able to hide a few in the cavities of walls. Anyway, they knew these prayers more or less by heart. In 1983 the young Catholic sailor from Fujian, passing through Singapore (see our introduction, p. 9), was in the Zhonglian Documentation Center, examining the large number of religious books published in Hong Kong and Taiwan since the Second Vatican Council (1962–1965). It was not easy to make a choice. Then his eye fell on an old book with a black cover and red edges that had been overlooked during the periodical updating of stock. His face suddenly lit up, and he just said, "That's my book!"

14

THE FIRST CHINESE BISHOP

The Spanish Dominicans had the honor of giving his religious education to the first Chinese priest, who became later, in spite of them, the first Chinese bishop. His name was Gregory Luo Wenzao (1616–1691). He was baptized in 1634 by a Franciscan and was consecrated bishop by another Franciscan in 1685.

The First Chinese Priest

Fr. Antonio Caballero, O.F.M., had hardly been in Fu'an, Fujian Province, a year when a young Chinese of eighteen came to hear his sermons and asked to be enrolled as a catechumen. After a few months' instruction, Fr. Antonio baptized him, giving him the name Gregory. The Luo family were Buddhist peasant farmers from Luojiang (i.e., the village of the Luo family), near Fu'an. After his baptism, Gregory stayed with his spiritual father and helped as a catechist. The other members of his family also later became Christians. Gregory accompanied Fr. Caballero on his numerous journeys—to Nanjing, Beijing, and Manila. Frequent travel was necessary because of the pressure of anti-Christian persecution. Gregory was arrested in 1637, at Ningde between Fu'an and Fuzhou. He spent twenty-three days in prison, where he was singled out for particularly cruel treatment. Afterward, Fr. Antonio and Gregory were pursued from town to town, ending up at Macao in 1644. They took ship for Manila in October, but a storm cast them on the coast of Vietnam, where they were interned for several months, before finally reaching Manila in May 1645.

Gregory decided to give his life to God and entered St. Thomas' College at Manila, where the Dominicans employed him as a servant, while allowing him to study part time. He learned Spanish and Latin and studied the rudiments of philosophy. According to the custom of the time, his name was changed from Luo to Lopez, "because it sounds more Catholic". After two and a half years, Gregory was sent back to Fujian, where the fathers were in considerable difficulties. From 1647 to 1662, he traveled all over the province, preaching the Gospel "in season and out of season", without fear of danger. The arrival of the Manchu authorities in Fujian in 1646 gave the enemies of Christians the opportunity for showing their loyalty to the new dynasty. On January 15, 1628, the Dominican Francisco de Capillas was beheaded, after having bravely given witness to the faith during many months in prison. He was the first Spanish Dominican martyr in China, and his death, far from intimidating Christians, strengthened their faith. Gregory Luo continued his task of building Christian communities. He also gave proof of technical skill by working at the building of a church. He kept the project going by working as laborer and architect by turns; the church was finished in just over a year.

On January 1, 1660, Gregory was clothed in the Dominican habit by Fr. Morales, thus becoming a member of the Order of Friars Preachers. His Franciscan spiritual father was far away by then, in the icy lands of north China. Gregory had doubtless been drawn to the Dominican ideal by his studies at St. Thomas' College, Manila. He made his simple vows on the feast of St. Thomas the Apostle, July 3, 1651, and the following year he returned to Manila, staying at the Dominican friary and studying philosophy and theology at St. Thomas' University. He was ordained a priest on July 4, 1654 by Archbishop Miguel Poblet of Manila. His first Mass gave enormous satisfaction to all the Christian Chinese of Manila, who felt that they had a priest of their own race at last.

The Only One in the Empire

By the next year, Gregory Luo was back in Fujian Province, where anti-Christian repression was intensifying. In 1655, however, foreign missionaries were still able to work in China, and the Dominicans built a church at Fuzhou. Local mandarins were not required to ban Christians when no such instructions were coming from Beijing. Fr. Adam Schall, S.J., was on good terms with the first emperor of the Manchu Dynasty, the Shunzhi emperor (r. 1644–61), as mentioned in chapter 11. Fr. Schall was appointed president of the Board of the

Calendar, a position that gave him the opportunity of helping foreigners through the friendly relations that he built up with civil servants who were appointed to the provinces. In 1650 he undertook the construction of the Nantang church, "the South Church" in Beijing, which was finished two years later.

The Shunzhi emperor died unexpectedly of smallpox in 1661, at the early age of twenty-two, and the situation worsened as far as Christians were concerned. The future Kangxi emperor was only seven. Old Manchu regents, such as General Aobai, treated the Chinese like slaves and eliminated experienced counselors from court. Chinese scholars, who had been put to one side under the Shunzhi emperor, plotted together to recover their situation. Both Muslims and conservative scholars had never forgiven the Jesuit astronomers who had replaced them at court. Yang Guangxian (1597–1669), a Chinese converted to Islam, was particularly virulent and began to plot Fr. Adam Schall's downfall. Yang had a deep-seated conviction that Chinese culture was superior to all others and denounced the introduction into China of Western science and Western morals. He saw them as signs of a conspiracy against the empire. From 1659 to 1664, he produced violent diatribes against everything coming from the West. These texts were collected under the title *Bu de yi* (*It Is Too Much*). Among them was a tract, *Pi xie lun* (*Refutation of Depraved Doctrines*), in which he defended the Confucian tradition against Christian teaching, which he considered a tissue of absurdities:

> When he came to be born on earth to save mankind, the Master of heaven ought to have promoted rituals and music, distributed the virtue of humanity and righteousness, in order to usher in an era of good fortune for men everywhere on earth. Instead of that, he only performed minor beneficent acts, such as healing the sick, raising the dead, walking on the water, and producing food by magic means, and he only concerned himself with matters of paradise and hell.[1]

When Yang Guangxian came to consider the way in which Christians had been forbidden to practice Confucian rites, his indignation knew no bounds:

---

[1] Jacques Gernet, *China and the Christian Impact: A Conflict of Cultures* (Cambridge, U.K.: Cambridge University Press, 1985), p. 159. Quoting *Pi xie lun*, p. 1116.

Given that the barbarians vilify heaven [by saying that it is brute matter organized by the Master of heaven], there is nothing surprising about the fact that they order their followers to destroy the sacred tablets of heaven and earth and of relatives and masters. They have respect neither for heaven nor for the earth nor for the son of heaven. They have no respect for parents since Yesu had no father.[2]

Yang Guangxian took up and developed a whole series of accusations against Christians which had been formulated in Fujian more than twenty years previously—for instance, that they held absurd beliefs, like the idea that there could be a Lord of heaven; that he could have died an ignominious death on a Cross; that his mother, Mary, could have been a virgin.

Yang Guangxian determined to destroy Fr. Adam Schall. He profited from the weak government of the regency period to file an accusation against him with the Office of Rites. He claimed that Schall was guilty of plotting against the security of the state, since his intention and that of the other Jesuits was to open a way for foreign powers. Yang won his case. Fr. Schall, who was seventy-four years old, was condemned to death by strangulation. But the Lord of heaven, it seems, did intervene to protect his aged astronomer: just when everything was ready for the execution, an earthquake occurred, which was interpreted as meaning that Fr. Schall's enemies were in the wrong. The empress dowager granted him a pardon.

It was, however, too late to go back on a decree proscribing foreign priests, which had been promulgated in January 1665. They were arrested and brought together at Beijing, some thirty of them, mostly Jesuits. Most of them were taken to Guangzhou, where they were subjected to a five-year house arrest (March 1666 to September 1671). This brought together members of different religious orders under the same roof: nineteen Jesuits, three Dominicans, and one Franciscan.[3] It turned out to be a blessing in disguise, since these men of different nationalities and different religious traditions were at last able to share their experiences from different parts of China and from different *milieux*. They put their time of internment to good use by thinking about the advantages and disadvantages of their different apostolic methods. The Jesuits among them worked on translations

---

[2] Ibid., p. 184. Quoting *Pi xie lun*, p. 1125.
[3] For the details of the priests' stay in Guangzhou, see Standaert, p. 313.

of the main Confucian writings. The priests also tried to reach a common mind on the difficult question of Confucian rites. After some fifty sessions for discussion, spread over the years 1667 and 1668, they agreed on forty-two articles that were, on the whole, favorable to a tolerant attitude. One of the priests, however, Fr. Domingo Fernandez Navarette, O.P. (1618–1689), who was not the least influential among them, soon drew back from assenting to the articles and defended a more rigorist position when he returned to Rome.

While all the missionaries were under house arrest or in the process of being expelled, the 175 or so Catholic churches throughout the country were without any priests. Fr. Gregory Luo was the only exception, and, since he was Chinese, he found it easier to move between the different communities without being discovered. Thus, practically overnight, he found himself faced with enormous responsibilities. In May 1665, he took the risk of traveling to Manila to ask for help. He came back with ample funds to help the internees at Guangzhou and the refugees in Macao. Religious congregations delegated him to visit their parishes, now without priests. He therefore set about visiting some ten different provinces. From Guangzhou he went to Fujian, then to Shandong, to Hebei, and as far as Jilin Province in Manchuria. In the center of the country, he crossed Jiangxi and Hunan to reach distant Sichuan Province. It was an amazing achievement, which took him two years. Not only did he bring strength and courage to communities that had been weakened by persecution. He also baptized a large number of catechumens, 556 in the islands off the coast of Fujian and more than 2,000 in the rest of the country.

The First Chinese Bishop

All these trials had given the European missionary orders time to think things over. Since repeated persecutions had made the presence of foreigners precarious, it was becoming clearer that only priests from China itself could be relied on to continue the evangelization of the country. What Fr. Gregory had achieved on his own was an evident demonstration that a Chinese priest had all that was needed to exercise the pastoral oversight of a bishop. Fr. Navarette wrote to the Congregation *de Propaganda Fide* in Rome and put this point of view forward.

In Rome itself the idea of providing native priests for the mission churches had been gaining ground over the previous twenty years. Numerous calls in this direction had come from Alexandre de Rhodes (1593–1660), a French Jesuit, born in Avignon and descended from Spanish Jews. He had been in various parts of present-day Vietnam from 1624 to 1646. Expelled from Tonkin in 1630 after having made many converts, he had done equally fruitful work in the Cochin region, whence he had also been banished more than once.[4] As soon as Fr. de Rhodes returned to Rome in 1649, Pope Innocent X gave him an audience, at which Fr. de Rhodes asked for bishops for the missions in Asia. The Pope referred the matter to the Congregation *de Propaganda Fide*, which had been founded in 1622.

The Holy See had for some time been trying to ensure a better system for directing and coordinating the work of the missions. Up till then, different religious orders had taken on assignments without any overall plan being possible, but members of such orders were often transferred by their superiors, so that they could not guarantee the permanence that was necessary for the growth of the local Church. The *Padroado* also created difficulties, as Portuguese authorities tended to use it as a way of preventing other nationals from working in what they regarded as their sphere of influence. According to the arrangements of the *Padroado*, which had been granted to the Portuguese crown by the papacy in the fifteenth century (see chapter 7), all missionaries working in a Portuguese area had to swear allegiance to the king of Portugal, and all Church appointments were made by the civil authorities. The Jesuits always respected this arrangement, which is why they usually embarked for East Asia at Lisbon and many of them studied at Coimbra as part of their missionary training. But Portugal is a small country and by the seventeenth century it was clear that many opportunities were opening up for missionary activity in Asia to which Portugal was not responding. To ensure the development of local churches in Asia, there was need for qualified volunteers who

---

[4] Fr. de Rhodes also deserves to be remembered for his achievements in the linguistic field. He had devised a system for writing Vietnamese, using the letters of the Latin alphabet, augmented by accents, cedillas, and diacritical points. This method avoided the use of ideograms, and, although Vietnamese is in some ways more complex than Mandarin, since it has a greater number of tones, Fr. de Rhodes' system, used in his *Catechismus* published in Rome in 1651, makes it possible to read Vietnamese without having to memorize the thousands of characters needed for reading Chinese. It is still in use today.

could supplement the work done up till then by the Portuguese, the Spaniards, and the Jesuits and who might be more free to take pastoral initiatives. Since it was a time when French power was beginning to dominate Europe and French culture was approaching its zenith, it would obviously be advantageous to the missions if the energy and intelligence of such a nation could be harnessed to the missionary endeavor. Thanks to Fr. Alexandre de Rhodes, S.J., and to the Paris Jesuits, such volunteers were soon to be recruited in France for this very purpose through the Company of the Blessed Sacrament. For all these reasons, the Congregation *de Propaganda Fide* had been created in Rome in 1622 as one of the departments of papal administration, and its role was to provide the central direction and to guide the combined operations that the missionary situation in Asia and elsewhere required.

The Company of the Blessed Sacrament was an association of priests and lay men and women who were trying to renew the spiritual life in the French Church and to increase its influence on society. It had begun its work in 1629 and organized it through weekly meetings, at which each member reported on the activity and achievement of the past week. The Company of the Blessed Sacrament soon became influential, some of its members belonging to the highest *noblesse* and to the class of "parliamentarians" who administered the law courts of France. Someone like St. Vincent de Paul, for example, became a member. It had considerable financial support and, as well as promoting prayer, especially devotion to the Blessed Sacrament, it undertook relief work in hospitals and prisons, as well as working for the poor and destitute in general. It also undertook various social campaigns, and, since its deliberations were secret and members did not reveal their membership of the company, it soon aroused suspicion. For instance, it started campaigns to stop dueling, to exclude Protestants from certain occupations, and to repress immorality and vice. It even tried to ban Molière's play *Tartuffe*, which made fun of religious bigots and hypocrites. Eventually, in the 1660s, the meetings of the company were officially banned by the French authorities.

The Company of the Blessed Sacrament took an early interest in the work of the foreign missions, and this was welcomed by the new Congregation *de Propaganda Fide* in Rome, which wanted less politics and more spirituality in the management of the missions. The Company of the Blessed Sacrament had started a Committee for Mis-

sions among its members. An active member of this committee, M.
du Plessis, acquired in 1663 a property in the Rue du Bac in Paris.
This house belonged to the Carmelite Jean Duval, also called Bernard
of St. Theresa, bishop of Babylon, who had bought it in 1644 with
a view to prepare missionaries for his diocese in the Middle East. It
became the nucleus of the present *Missions Étrangères de Paris*.[5] Louis
XIV incorporated the association of secular priests for the missions by
letters patent of 1663, and since then thousands of French missionaries have gone to East Asia as members of an institution of which
the French Church can be rightly proud. An endearing aspect of the
Missions Étrangères is that their buildings and gardens occupy the site
on which they were founded, unlike so many ecclesiastical institutions
in France, which have been expelled from their original buildings by
a succession of anticlerical government measures from the eighteenth
to the twentieth centuries. French influence in Asia was too well sustained by missionaries for such treatment to be inflicted on the interesting group of buildings that occupy the corner of the Rue du
Bac and the Rue de Babylone and have served the *Missions Étrangères*
for nearly 350 years. The missionaries, many of them martyrs, who
trained there for the priesthood would have known the chapel (where
Gounod was to be organist), the seminary, built in the classical French
style which combines simplicity and magnificence, the crypt which is
both museum and shrine, the parterres, the trees and the lawns of
one of the finest gardens of the 7e *arrondissement*, near the *Hôtel de
Matignon*, the official residence of French prime ministers.

French Influence in East Asia

It was not long before the *Société des Missions Étrangères* (henceforth
referred to as the Paris Foreign Missions) made its influence felt in
East Asia. Two French priests, who had played a large part in its
foundation and who were members of the association, which was its
directive body, were François Pallu, canon of St. Martin of Tours,
and Pierre Lambert de la Motte, from the diocese of Évreux. Pope
Alexander VII ordained Pallu as bishop in St. Peter's, Rome, in 1658.
Lambert was ordained on June 11, 1660, in Paris. The Pope sent

---

[5] Jean Guennou, *Missions Étrangères de Paris* (Paris: Fayard, 1986), pp. 103–13.

them to China as vicars apostolic, with the titles of titular sees from antiquity and jurisdiction over areas not yet constituted as dioceses. Vast areas of China were thus entrusted to the new bishops, but the Holy See acted secretly, without involving the Portuguese in any way, or informing them of this new arrangement, which ignored their privileges. The new Congregation *de Propaganda Fide* was so afraid of the Portuguese reaction to these new arrangements that Pallu and Lambert were instructed not to reveal the purpose of their journey, their itinerary, or their destination.[6] They therefore tried to avoid any contact with the Portuguese as they sailed to East Asia, so that the Portuguese bishops of Macao and Melaka were surprised to learn about the arrival of French bishops in what they had considered as their sphere of influence. Naturally, the Portuguese were not pleased, and tensions arose.[7] Rome did not at first inform the religious orders either, and this also proved to be a fruitful source of misunderstanding, since many of the orders were exempt from episcopal jurisdiction and did not take kindly to receiving directives from the new vicars apostolic.[8] It also bode ill for the future that the Paris Foreign Missions became what Mungello describes with undue generalization as "an intensely anti-Jesuit society",[9] so that yet another division was introduced among the missionaries working in China. Not only were the Portuguese hostile to the priests from Paris. The French priests who had just arrived, despite the friendly relations that they maintained with the Jesuits in France, were led to work independently of the Jesuits in East Asia. They were upset by the commercial practices of the Jesuits in the East and their claim to have a monopoly on mission work.

The Congregation *de Propaganda Fide*, meanwhile, did give to the new vicars apostolic excellent and clear directives, signed by the secretary in Rome on November 10, 1659. They can be summarized as follows:

---

[6] Ibid., p. 73.

[7] Ibid., p. 70.

[8] Ibid., pp. 70–71.

[9] D. E. Mungello, *The Forgotten Christians of Hangzhou* (Honolulu: University of Hawaii Press, 1994), p. 155. The so-called conflict between the Paris Foreign Missions and the Jesuits actually did not involve the two Societies as such, but was limited to divergence among individual missionaries at certain periods.

1. They were to create a native clergy.

2. They were to adapt themselves to the habits and customs of the country, without meddling in politics.

3. They were to take no important decisions without referring to Rome, and especially they were not to consecrate any bishops without a mandate from the Congregation.[10]

Bishop Lambert de la Motte set out for East Asia in 1660, Bishop Pallu in 1662. They met in January 1664 at Ayutthaya, the old capital of Thailand, some fifty miles (eighty kilometers) north of Bangkok, which is now an archeological site much visited by tourists. The two bishops responded to the instructions of *Propaganda* by founding a seminary there. Bishop Lambert made Ayutthaya his headquarters and undertook his missionary journeys from there to Tonkin and the Cochin region of present-day Vietnam, ordaining the first native priests of the area. He never went as far as China, dying at Ayutthaya in 1679, with a reputation for holiness.

As for the Congregation's third directive, concerning the ordination of bishops, Bishop François Pallu referred to it ten years later, when he recommended the nomination of Gregory Luo for bishop in China. When Bishop Pallu was on his second journey to East Asia in 1670, after having sailed round the Cape of Good Hope, he met the Dominican Fr. Navarette, who had been expelled from China. Navarette told him about Fr. Gregory Luo and his qualities, so that Bishop Pallu promoted his candidature in Rome.

In August 1673, a meeting of the superiors of the missions in Thailand, Cochin, and Tonkin had taken place, and Fr. Navarette was there. Everyone spoke of Gregory Luo's exceptional qualities, and his candidature was recommended. On January 4, 1674, he was appointed vicar apostolic of Nanjing, with responsibility for administering the Church in Zhili, Shandong, Shanxi, Henan, Shaanxi, and also Korea. Pope Clement X sent him a magnificent pectoral cross and a ring. Because of the delays in travel, it was only in 1677 that Fr. Luo heard of his appointment. At first he tried to avoid having to take on such a responsibility. There were several reasons for this. His personal humility was no doubt one of them, but there was also a realistic assessment of the difficulties that had beset the French vicars apostolic. The religious superiors of the missions were solidly

---

[10] Guennou, *Missions Étrangères de Paris*, p. 74.

entrenched and invoked the standing given to them by long experience. The new vicars apostolic had come to China under the aegis of the Congregation *de Propaganda Fide*, which was a new entity in the mission field, and they had been too ready to criticize the pastoral adaptations that the local situation required. They had also tried to introduce a rigorous spirituality, which had not been welcomed and brought upon them the accusation of Jansenism. Gregory Luo might well have thought that there was no chance of a poor Chinese priest being able to impose his authority in a situation where these highly qualified Europeans had failed to do so.

Fr. Luo sized up the difficulties realistically. Fr. Navarette's Dominican colleagues did not share his broadmindedness. They made Luo feel his inferiority, so that psychological fears and real obstacles held up the ordination for ten years. Gregory wrote to the Pope, begging to be relieved of this burden. The reply came from Innocent XI, elected in 1676, who interpreted Gregory's refusal as an act of humility and instructed the master general of the Dominicans to order the Chinese priest to accept under obedience. The master general's letter arrived at its destination in 1681, whereupon the superior of the Dominican Province of the Philippines, to which Gregory belonged, stepped in and threatened Gregory with expulsion from the order if he accepted. He also said that the Dominicans would cease all funding and that the Spanish missionaries would be recalled from the mainland. The superior gave as reason for such drastic threats Gregory's insufficient theological formation and his overly tolerant, Jesuit attitude on the question of Chinese rites. Fr. Luo was even put under restraint in the Philippines and was only able to return to China by appealing from this sanction to the highest civil magistrate of the king of Spain in the colony. He also received practical help from the superior of the Augustinians, with whom he took refuge in Manila for one year and eight months. During that time he lived in the beautiful buildings of the Augustinian monastery, which have recently (1995) been restored, with their church and gardens, an example of the way the first settlers in the Philippines were able to create a Spanish environment in a tropical and colonial setting.

In 1681 Bishop François Pallu was appointed *Administrator Apostolicus Sinarum* (general administrator of the missions in China) in what was yet another attempt by the Congregation *de Propaganda Fide* in Rome to exert a more effective control over the situation. This ad-

ditional title was given to strengthen his authority, and, for the third
and last time, Pallu traveled from Europe to East Asia. He was helped
on his journey by the king of Thailand and again avoided Portuguese
ports, entering China by way of Taiwan. He reached Xiamen (Amoy)
in January 1684, the religious superiors in Fujian Province reluctantly
giving him residence at Muyang, not far from Fu'an and Tingtao,
where the first Dominican parishes had been established. By then
Pallu was worn. out and seriously ill, preparing, as the deeply spiritual man that he was, for his last great journey. When Gregory Luo
arrived at Muyang at the beginning of November 1684, hoping to
be consecrated bishop, he found that Pallu had died on October 29.
Gregory, whose episcopal appointment went back to 1674, did manage to be ordained bishop at last on April 5, 1685, by Bernardino
della Chiesa, the Franciscan bishop of Guangzhou.

The Apostolate of the Possible

Gregory Luo was in his seventies by the time he bravely took on his
responsibilities. He went to live at Nanjing, where he had to build
a residence for himself, separate from the residence of the Jesuits.
The new bishop obtained help from Giovanni Francesco Nicolai da
Leonissa (1656–1737), an Italian friar minor of the Reformed Observance, who became his vicar apostolic for Hunan and Guangdong.
Leonissa was a good theologian and could make up for Gregory's
shortcomings. Each year Bishop Luo faithfully wrote a report of his
activities and what difficulties he had encountered. He wanted to visit
all the provinces for which he was responsible, but in 1687 he noted
that he could only make his pastoral visits in the Jiangnan region
of Jiangsu Province (the area round Nanjing) because he could not
afford to travel further.

One of the big problems that Bishop Luo had to face was the question of Chinese rites. Bishop Pallu had, before his death, divided his
responsibilities as vicar apostolic and general administrator of China
between the Franciscan Bishop della Chiesa in Guangzhou and another new arrival from France, Charles Maigrot de Crissey (1652–
1730), who was not ordained a bishop until 1700 but who wielded
a delegated episcopal jurisdiction as vicar apostolic. Maigrot, a priest

Gregory Luo Wenzao (1616–1691)
First Chinese Bishop of the Latin Rite

Luo Wenzao was born in a Buddhist family near Fu'an, Fujian Province and became a Christian at eighteen. He joined the Dominican Order in the Philippines and was ordained priest in 1654. From 1655, Luo Wenzao worked in China and was appointed Bishop by Pope Clement X in 1677, although he was not consecrated until 1685 because of opposition from some of the European missionaries. He then worked mainly in Jiangsu Province and became the first Bishop of Nanjing.

of the Paris Foreign Missions who had been in China since 1684, strictly applied the ban on the Confucian rites, whereas Bishop Luo, while trying to abide by it, pointed out that the Church in China would lose half her members if the prohibition were too strictly applied. Although an oath of obedience to the directives on Chinese rites was required of all missionaries, Bishop Luo took it upon himself to grant dispensations in certain cases, especially where the French Jesuits working in Beijing were concerned. He explained why he did this in a characteristic appeal to Chinese tradition:

> In each region of China there are grain stores for emergencies. Anyone who opens such a store without a formal directive from the emperor is liable to the death penalty. But it has happened that, during a terrible famine in a distant province, many people would have died of hunger if one had had to wait for directives from the emperor. The local mandarin took it upon himself to open the grain stores, while sending a report on what he had done to the imperial court. He was congratulated for his initiative and his name is forever remembered.[11]

Bishop Luo was probably not looking for congratulations, but he gave evidence in the whole matter of common sense, combined with an overriding loyalty, a combination that was to be characteristic of many Chinese priests.

Bishop Luo was equally wise in dealing with the ordination of native clergy. He chose candidates from among catechists or Christian members of the scholar-gentry class of mature years, considering that they were more likely to be faithful than younger men. It was difficult for them to learn Latin, and so Bishop Luo applied a privilege that Pope Alexander VII had granted to native priests in 1659: native-born priests who did not know Latin could be ordained as long as they could read out loud the Latin words of the canon of the Mass and of the sacramental formulas, the meaning of these texts having been duly explained to them. In one of his reports, Bishop Luo went through the list of seventeen priests at work in his vicariate. There were thirteen Jesuits and four Franciscans. Seven were in the Jiangnan region of Jiangsu Province, five were in Shandong Province and five were in Zhili (Hebei).[12] Such small numbers were inadequate for the needs of

---

[11] Fang Hao, *Biographies of the History of Catholicism in China* (Hong Kong: Catholic Truth Society, 1967), vol. 2, p. 154. Our translation is from the French translation of the Chinese original.

[12] Ibid., p. 156.

numerous Christians. Bishop Luo was determined to ordain Chinese priests, but he was very careful about choosing them. On August 1, 1688, he ordained five candidates at Macao, who had been Jesuit lay brothers and who were all over fifty. They were not actually the first Chinese Jesuit priests, as Fr. Emmanuel Zheng Weixin (1633–1673), a native of Macao (who had been given the name Manuel de Sequeira), had accompanied Fr. de Rhodes to Europe, joined the Company of Jesus in Rome, and was ordained priest at Coimbra in 1664.[13]

In 1690, the Portuguese gained a victory over the growing French influence in East Asia, which had shown itself by the number of vicars apostolic appointed by the Congregation *de Propaganda Fide*, without any regard for the rights of the Portuguese *Padroado*. Pope Alexander VIII was locked in conflict with Louis XIV at the time over several issues concerning the Church in France. The French king had reached the summit of his power and influence in Europe, and in 1682 he imposed the *Gallican Articles* on the Church of France, one of the articles asserting the superiority of general councils over the Pope. As a result Alexander VIII refused to ratify the appointments of French bishops who had accepted the *Articles*, so that a considerable number of French sees were vacant. The Curia was therefore glad to snub the overweening ambition of Louis XIV, when an opportunity for doing so presented itself. Pedro II, king of Portugal, petitioned that the vicariates of Nanjing and Beijing should be promoted to territorial dioceses as part of the *Padroado*. This involved a considerable financial commitment on the part of the Portuguese crown, which would be responsible for all the expenses of the clergy, including their travel and their upkeep, and would also be required to contribute to the cost of building churches and cathedrals, but in return the Portuguese would have the right of appointment to all ecclesiastical posts. Vicars apostolic only exercise a derivative jurisdiction, as delegates of the Pope, whereas territorial bishops enjoy the full status of the episcopal office within the territory of their dioceses. In the face of the new dioceses, vicariates apostolic faded away, so that Charles Maigrot suddenly found himself without a territory to administer, at least until the boundaries of the new dioceses should be declared.

Gregory Luo became the first bishop of Nanjing, and Bernardino

---

[13] For Fr. Zheng Weixin, see Standaert, p. 449.

della Chiesa the first bishop of Beijing. Soon afterward, on February 27, 1691, Bishop Luo died. Toward the end of his life, he had had a stele inscribed to the memory of his Franciscan spiritual father, Antonio de Caballero, who had given him the grace of new life through baptism. Fr. Caballero had died over twenty years previously, and his tomb had been sadly neglected. Bishop Luo saw to its repair, and perhaps the fine epitaph, which he placed upon it, was by way of reparation for the way Fr. Caballero had been treated at times during his twenty-six years spent as a missionary in China.[14]

The most famous of the priests whom Bishop Luo had ordained in Macao was Wu Yushan, a scholar and well-known painter who came from Changshou in Jiangsu Province. He had been introduced to the Christian faith by the Jesuit fathers François de Rougemont and Philippe Couplet, and was baptized when he was forty. His wife having died, he entered the Jesuit novitiate at Macao at the age of fifty-one. After his ordination in 1688, he had an active apostolate for thirty years in Shanghai and Jiading. He was an active man, traveling everywhere in all weathers, but he was also capable of sleeping peacefully in a small boat, buffeted by storms. Like Bishop Luo, whom he accompanied in his latter years, Wu Yushan had the gift of explaining Catholic teaching simply and profoundly. He gave up painting but wrote a great deal of poetry, which can still provide inspiration for Chinese priests. In his poetry, he expressed the soul of his ministry and gave much place to the poor and their struggle for existence. He shared the joys and sorrows of fisherfolk and peasants and gave expression to them through his poetry, exhorting them to continue the struggle and to grow in faith and charity. He was the only one of the three priests ordained in 1688 who stayed at the side

---

[14] Text of the epitaph that Bishop Luo placed on the tomb of Fr. Antonio de Santa Maria Caballero, O.F.M. *SF* II, p. 329:

A. R. P. F. ANTONIO A S. MARIA
ORDINIS MINORUM, MINISTRO ET PRAEFECTO VERE APOSTOLICO
AB EXILIO CANTONENSI AD COELESTEM PATRIAM EVOCATO
ANNO M. D.C. LXIX
DECIMO TERTIO KALENDAS IUNII
FR. GREGORIUS LOPES, EPISCOPUS BASILITANUS
ET VICARIUS APOSTOLICUS NANKIM,
PATRI SUO SPIRITUALI, RESTAURATO SEPULCRO,
LAPIDEM HUNC
GRATITUDINIS MONUMENTUM EREXIT

of Bishop Luo, whose death grieved him deeply, and left him with
anxieties for the future. Wu Yushan wrote this elegy for his friend:

> The venerable bishop, glorious by his merit,
> Transmitted to only three the gift of priesthood,
> Under distant skies they proclaim the true Way.
> Faithfully I followed him, and now I am alone.
>
> The cold has taken us unawares. The friend has left us.
> Suddenly death took him, as into lasting sleep.
> I gaze toward the north, on the sky of Jinling.
> I weep a thousand tears, meanwhile the clouds above
> Drift toward the south. The rain is turned to blood
> And the great dream I knew reaches out to the Lord.
>
> Those who follow the Way are already so few . . .
> The Way is close to us, but who will be committed to it?[15]

---

[15] Chinese text in the review *Zhongguo Tianzhujiao* (*The Catholic Church in China*) 8 (Beijing, 1988):44–45.

[In the section "The First Chinese Bishop", the third paragraph has been substantially added
to; the fourth and fifth paragraphs have been added.
  A new section "French Influence in East Asia" has been created, and its first paragraph
has been substantially added to. The third and sixth paragraphs of this section have been
added to. In the section "The Apostolate of the Possible," paragraph four has been added.
—TRANS.]

15

CATHOLIC FAITH AND CONFUCIAN RITES

Five French Jesuits, dispatched to China by Louis XIV, arrived at Beijing on February 8, 1688. This delegation had been invited to China by the Kangxi emperor, who needed the services of Western mathematicians, largely because of the need for accurate calendrical calculations. Thanks to the negotiations of the Flemish Jesuit Ferdinand Verbiest (1623–1688), director of the Imperial Office of Astronomy, this mission had been entrusted to the Jesuits. It was also thanks to him that the party, which landed at Ningbo, was saved from prosecution by the viceroy of Zhejiang. Hardly had they arrived when they were saddened to learn of Fr. Verbiest's death. One of them wrote this appreciation of him:

> There was hardly anyone in China who was not impoverished by his death. It was due to his care, his zeal, and his prudence that the Christian religion, which had been decimated and nearly destroyed by the last persecution, was reorganized. He maintained the fervor of older converts and supported the weakness of new ones by showing constant interest in all their activities. By his letters of recommendation he gave a certain standing to missionaries in the provinces. He had saved Macao when it became suspect to the Manchus. The state, whose interests he had served on several important occasions, owed him a great deal, so that Europeans, Chinese, and even the emperor all considered him as their father.[1]

When Fr. Adam Schall died in 1666, his personal enemy Yang Guangxian was at the head of the Office of Astronomy. In 1669 the young emperor, Xuanyue, aged fifteen, assumed power after a long period of regency, since he had been only six when he inherited the throne. Xuanyue is known in history by the regnal name, which was given to Chinese emperors after their death. His was Kangxi, which means "lasting peace" and describes the characteristic of his long

---

[1] Louis Le Comte, *Un Jésuite à Pékin: Nouveaux mémoires sur l'état présent de la Chine 1687–1692* (Paris: Phébus, 1990), pp. 60–61.

reign, which lasted until 1722. He soon gave proof of his political skill by getting rid of the Manchu regents, who had governed in his name, and then ordered a careful inquiry into the functioning of the Office of Astronomy. Since the inquiry revealed contradictory reports from the Office, the Kangxi emperor ordered Fr. Verbiest to check the figures, and when the calculations of the Westerners were found to be more accurate, Yang Guangxian was dismissed. Verbiest was appointed in his place and took the opportunity to have the late Fr. Adam Schall rehabilitated, as well as five other Christian Chinese astronomers who had been unjustly executed. The Imperial Office of Astronomy was to remain under European astronomers until the beginning of the nineteenth century.

The Edict of Toleration: March 22, 1692

Fr. Ferdinand Verbiest soon won the emperor's favor. He improved the equipment of the Beijing Observatory by having new measuring equipment and a new heavenly sphere cast in metal. The sphere became famous; in 1988, a copy was unveiled at the University of Louvain for the three hundredth anniversary of Verbiest's death. The emperor needed light cannon to put down the rebellion of General Wu Sangui and turned to Verbiest, on the principle that if one could make a sphere of the heavens, one could make cannon. The Jesuit hesitated at first, considering such a task incompatible with his status as a priest, but he eventually agreed, for fear that the civil servants hostile to Christians would use his refusal as evidence of a foreign plot against the empire. In other ways, too, the emperor had a good impression of Christians, when, for instance, the Jesuits Fr. Jean-François Gerbillon and Fr. Tomé Pereira played a useful part as interpreters and negotiators in preparing the Treaty of Nerchinsk, which was signed with Russia on September 7, 1689.

From the point of view of the Jesuits, all the services that they were providing for China had as their aim to obtain from the emperor official protection for Christians. Before Fr. Verbiest's death in 1688, he expressed himself clearly on the subject:

> Sire, I die a happy man because nearly every moment of my life has been employed in the service of Your Majesty; but I ask you, most humbly,

to remember after my death that all I have done has had no other aim
but to obtain a protector for the most holy religion in the world from
you, the greatest king of the East.[2]

All the services provided by the Jesuits, however, never succeeded
in obtaining from the emperor what they most desired, an imperial
decree authorizing the existence of Christianity in China. From the
emperor's point of view, the favors bestowed on individuals were dictated by self-interest only and were limited to those few who were
useful: Fr. Claudio Filippo Grimaldi, to whom he had entrusted a
special mission in the West; Fr. Antoine Thomas at the Bureau of
Mathematics; and Fathers Jean-François Gerbillon and Joachim Bouvet, who could provide information on geometry and philosophy.

However, two events did bring about the promulgation of an imperial edict guaranteeing a certain toleration for Christians. One was
an excessive persecution of Christians in Zhejiang Province, and the
other the intervention of a member of the imperial family, who was
provoked to intervene by the persecution.

In Hangzhou, Zhejiang Province, the viceroy had destroyed all the
churches and ill-treated the Jesuit superior, Fr. Prospero Intorcetta.
The repressive policy continued in spite of a warning from Song-
gotu (d. 1703),[3] a man close to the emperor, who had served in the
Imperial Guard and had thus helped the young Kangxi to get rid of
the regent Aobai in 1669. Song-gotu was also uncle by marriage to
the empress, and thus great-uncle to the heir apparent. He occupied
an influential position in the civil service, having received an education that was both Manchu and Chinese. His influence had also been
strengthened by the resolution of the border dispute between China
and Russia; it was Song-gotu who had led an army to the north and
negotiated the favorable treaty of 1689 with the delegation sent by
the Tzar of Russia, Peter the Great. The Treaty of Nerchinsk was
the first treaty made by China with a European power, and Song-
gotu had been greatly helped by the presence of the Jesuit fathers,
who acted not only as interpreters but also as advisers. The Treaty

---

[2] Ibid., p. 73.

[3] In Jesuit sources Song-gotu is referred to as Prince Sosan, a name composed of *So*, the
first syllable of his Father's name *Soni*, and *san*, "three", because he was the third son. Soni
had been one of the four regents after the death of the Shunzhi emperor.

of Nerchinsk was drawn up in five different languages, Latin being the one that was signed by the contracting parties.[4]

The Jesuits in Beijing had tried to persuade the Kangxi emperor to stop the persecution of Christians in Zhejiang Province, but he was loath to go against the unfavorable advice of the Office of Rites. It was then that Song-gotu intervened, though he was not a Christian, and forcefully drew the attention both of the emperor and the Office of Rites, to the services rendered by the Jesuits and to the good behavior of Christians.

The emperor adroitly prompted the Office of Rites to submit a petition to the throne, which was the basis for the promulgation of an edict of toleration. The petition ran as follows:

> Heoupatai, subject of Your Majesty, president of the Supreme Tribunal of Rites, . . . presents his most humble request with all the submission and respect which he and his assessors owe to all His Majesty's commands, especially when he bestows on us the honor of requesting our advice on important matters of state.
>
> We have seriously considered the matter of Europeans, who, having been drawn from the end of the world by the renown of Your Majesty's exceptional prudence and by your other great qualities, have crossed the vast expanse of the oceans that separate us from Europe. Since these Europeans have lived among us, they have deserved our esteem and gratitude by the outstanding services that they have rendered to us in wars, both civil and foreign, by their unremitting hard work in writing useful and curious books, and by their integrity and their sincere affection for the public good.
>
> In addition, the Europeans lead quiet lives; they cause no trouble in the provinces; they harm no one; they commit no crimes. Moreover, their doctrine has nothing in common with the false and dangerous sects existing within the Empire, so that their teaching does not lead to sedition.
>
> Since therefore we do not prevent either the lamas of Tartary or the bonzes of China from having temples or from offering therein incense to their pagodas, much less could we forbid Europeans, who do not teach anything against good laws, from having their own churches or from preaching their religion publicly therein. . . .
>
> We therefore decide that the temples dedicated to the Lord of heaven,

---

[4] Cf. Arthur H. Hummel, *Eminent Chinese of the Ch'ing Period* (Washington, 1943), pp. 663–66. See also Standaert, p. 445.

in whatsoever place they may be found, should be preserved, and that those who wish to honor this God should be allowed to enter such temples, to offer him incense, and to practice the cult practiced heretofore by Christians, according to their ancient custom. Therefore let no one henceforth furnish any opposition whatsoever thereunto.[5]

According to Fr. Le Comte's account, "The emperor received this decree with irrepressible joy," an overoptimistic assessment, since the Kangxi emperor was well aware of the true feelings of his civil service. His authority was sufficiently well established by this time to allow him to follow a more tolerant attitude, and the decree contributed to internal peace, but it is impossible to draw the conclusion that he had any personal sympathy for Christian teaching. Nevertheless this declaration of official approval was doubtless encouraging for the Catholics of Beijing and also for the Orthodox, who had been present in the capital for some years. The first Orthodox had been Russian soldiers, taken prisoner when the fortress of Albazin was captured by the Chinese in 1685. Some of these were recruited into the Chinese Imperial Guard and married Chinese women, who became Christians. It was recorded that in 1692 a Chinese businessman and a mandarin and his whole family were baptized into the Orthodox Church.[6]

The Chinese Rites Issue and Its European Context

The imperial decree of toleration rested on a fragile base. In that respect, it could be compared to the directives from the Holy See, authorizing a certain toleration of Chinese rites. In both cases, the bitter controversies that arose among missionaries were to make things worse and to provoke harsher regulations on the part of the sovereign authorities involved.

Many different elements came into play during the famous rites controversy. For instance, missionaries had different experiences according to their *milieux*; some worked among peasants, as in Fujian, while others shared the outlook of the scholar-gentry immersed in politics. Another source of conflict arose because the authority wielded

---

[5] Le Comte, *Un Jésuite à Pékin*, pp. 499–500.

[6] Mark K. Chang, S.J. *A Historical Sketch of Christianity in China* (Taiwan: Window Press, 1985), p. 60.

by religious superiors over their members (Jesuits, Dominicans, Franciscans) was independent of the episcopal jurisdiction claimed by the vicars apostolic, who had been sent by the Congregation *de Propaganda Fide* in Rome. Tensions were also caused by the presence of different nationalities—Portuguese, Spanish, French, Italians—each exhibiting different attitudes and, to some extent, the interests of the countries from which they came. It also sometimes happened that personal conflicts occurred between members of the same religious order, as seems to have been the case of the Jesuit from Brittany, Claude de Visdelou (1656–1737), whose position on Chinese rites differed from that of the Society of Jesus in China.

However, the conflict did not remain at the level of priests committed to promoting the Gospel. It went much further and became a great theological debate between two different conceptions of mission and Catholic doctrine. The Jesuits, with their humanist education, responded to the moral and political values that they saw in Chinese civilization, and they were ready to accept these values as Christian, as long as they contributed to "the greater glory of God". On the other side were the Dominicans, Franciscans, Vincentians, and the Paris Foreign Missions, who were struggling with popular superstition in the countryside and who had fewer contacts with the scholar-gentry. They tended to preach first the Cross of Jesus Christ and salvation through grace, even though this might scandalize those who were wise in the eyes of the world.

In China, the debate had immediate practical consequences. Would ecclesiastical authorities grant or withhold certain permissions? Would the Confucian authorities intervene by the use of force?

In France itself, the Chinese rites controversy fanned the embers of longstanding quarrels between the party of the *dévots*, "the prigs", and the more liberal Jesuits. The *dévots*, who had been lampooned in Molière's play *Tartuffe* (1664), were regularly denounced as Jansenists, while the Jesuits, whose moral theology had been caricatured in Pascal's *Lettres Provinciales* (1657), were stigmatized as laxists.

The quarrel reached a crisis in China during the last decade of the seventeenth century, when the spark that lit a conflagration was ignited by Msgr. Maigrot, vicar apostolic of Fujian. Charles Maigrot was a Parisian who is described as having been "a very pious teenager".[7]

---

[7] See especially "Charles Maigrot's role in the Chinese Rites Controversy" by Claudia

He had studied theology at the Sorbonne[8] and had obtained his doctorate. He then entered the Paris Foreign Missions and left for East
Asia in 1682. As mentioned in the previous chapter, he had received
part of Pallu's vicarial powers before the latter's death in 1684. As
befits a doctor of the Sorbonne, Maigrot spent a great deal of time
and energy in studying the religion of China. He was more assiduous
than any other missionary in trying to learn to read Chinese, collecting manuscripts and books on Chinese philosophy and religion, and
he wrote on them at length, though many of his works still remain
unpublished in various archives.[9] His overall judgment was negative.
Collani writes, "Maigrot did not have a high opinion of the Chinese
and their culture. His view stood in sharp contrast to that of the
Jesuits in China. Maigrot thought the Chinese incapable of deriving
metaphysical truth, and moreover their books appeared to him rather
poor."[10]

Maigrot's position was actually precarious when he launched his
mandate against Christian participation in Chinese rites to the ancestors. The status of his vicariate was still uncertain after the creation of the new dioceses under the Portuguese in 1690, and he had
run into trouble with the clergy of Fujian, who refused to take the
vow of obedience to him as vicar apostolic, which Pope Innocent XI

---

von Collani in *The Chinese Rites Controversy: Its History and Meaning*, ed. D. E. Mungello
(Nettetal: Steyler Verlag, 1994). Monumenta Serica Monograph Series 33, p. 149.

[8] *La Sorbonne* was the name given to a college of the University of Paris, founded in
the thirteenth century by Robert de Sorbon, chaplain to Louis IX. Its members taught and
studied theology, and it became the faculty of theology of the University of Paris (apart
from the theology schools of the friars). In the Middle Ages the standing of the Sorbonne
was such that it often acted a part of the *Magisterium* of the Church, giving its corporate
approval or condemnation of many doctrinal issues. The French Revolution destroyed all the
ancient universities in France so that Napoleon created in 1808 a new centralized university
system without any organic continuity with what had gone before. The name *Sorbonne* or
Nouvelle Sorbonne continued, however, in current usage to describe the faculties that occupied
the buildings of the old Sorbonne College, that is, the faculty of letters and the faculty of
science of the University of Paris, together with some other institutes such as the *École des
Hautes Études* and the *École des Chartes*. The upheavals of 1968 in France led to the creation of
several universities in Paris, numbered from I to XIII. Some of these have retained the word
Sorbonne in their title, such as *Paris I — Panthéon Sorbonne: Paris III — Nouvelle Sorbonne: Paris
IV — Sorbonne*, though with even less justification than the use of the name in the nineteenth
century. See the article in *Catholicisme* 14, cc. 310–17; *sub nomen* Sorbonne.

[9] Von Collani, "Charles Maigrot's Role", pp. 174–79 for an analysis of Maigrot's published works.

[10] Ibid., p. 179.

had authorized in 1678. His colleague, the Franciscan Bernardino della Chiesa, had had the same difficulty and, with Italian realism, soon ceased to require the vow. Maigrot liked to have things cut and dried, and nowhere did he make this clearer than in the mandate that he promulgated on March 26, 1693, by which missionaries were forbidden to allow Christians to take part in "the solemn sacrifices or oblations that are offered twice a year to Confucius and their ancestors".[11] Maigrot specified that missionaries were "never and for no reason whatsoever" to allow Christians to perform, take part in, or attend such rites. Moreover, he seemed to contradict the edict of March 23, 1656 (see chapter 13), by which Alexander VII had recognized the civil character of the rites, and he impugned the Pope's judgment on the grounds that, since the facts submitted to the Pope had been inaccurate, the answers, "though given in the right and wise way by the Holy See", could not be taken as a valid basis for allowing the Chinese to venerate Confucius and their ancestors.

If Maigrot expected his mandate to produce order and orthodoxy among the Christians of Fujian, he must have had a rude awakening. The Jesuits questioned the validity of the mandate because of the current uncertainty of Maigrot's status in canon law. Chinese Christians refused to obey, fearing proceedings against them by the imperial office of rites. However, it was impossible to leave the matter at a local level because Maigrot had used his rather shaky authority to make a negative ruling on the efficacy of a papal edict. The only thing to do was to bring the situation to the notice of the Holy See and to seek a definitive judgment from Rome, which is exactly what Maigrot wanted. He dispatched Nicolas Charmot, a priest of the Paris Foreign Missions, to Paris and Rome at the end of 1693 with an abundant documentation against the Chinese rites and the accommodating way in which the Jesuits had interpreted them. Charmot reached Rome in 1697 as procurator of the Paris Foreign Missions, and was to remain there until his death in 1714. Charmot wasted no time in submitting Maigrot's case to the Holy Office and to the Pope, Innocent XII, and he continued to be Maigrot's indefatigable agent in the Eternal City.

Meanwhile, Maigrot and Charmot were active in promoting their case in Paris too and prevailed on the archbishop of Paris, Louis-Antoine de Noailles, who was no friend of the Jesuits, to submit the

---

[11] Ibid., pp. 152–54, for the translation of the Latin text of the prohibitions in the mandate.

question of the Chinese rites to the theological faculty of the University of Paris, the Sorbonne. On October 18, 1700, six propositions taken from the writings of the Jesuits Le Comte and Le Gobien were condemned by the Sorbonne. These quotations had been carefully selected and were brought together without their context. They gave the impression that the two authors affirmed that China had been for a long time naturally Christian, so that the truths that the Church had always proclaimed as revealed by God appeared as unnecessary. In the eighteenth century, the authors of the *Encyclopédie* were delighted to take note of this view, since it seemed to offer evidence that a society could be well ordered without having recourse to the superstitious beliefs of revealed religion.

Directives from Rome

Because of these controversies, Rome was forced to produce general directives for distant China, whose civilization was little known or understood in Europe, and whose vast territory entailed much local diversity. The case of the Chinese rites was under examination in Rome from 1699 until judgment was given in 1704. The Jesuits challenged Bishop Maigrot's edict and produced a document of major importance for the debate. They had obtained from the Kangxi emperor himself a declaration that the rites in honor of Confucius and the ancestors were a purely civil and ethical ceremony, without religious content.

At this time, the standing of Jesuits at the French mission in Beijing was high. They had obtained land to the northwest of the city for building a new residence and a church, dedicated to the Holy Redeemer, which was called *Beitang*, the North Church. The emperor himself honored them by donating tablets with suitable inscriptions to be placed in the church. Louis XIV also gave precious gifts to the mission, and the solemn blessing of the church took place on December 9, 1703. Non-French Jesuits were also building in Beijing, a church dedicated to St. Joseph, *Dongtang*, the East Church.

Meanwhile, the case was proceeding in Rome, and the declaration by the emperor concerning the nonsuperstitious character of the Chinese rites was hardly given proper consideration. In fact, the imperial rescript was interpreted in a negative way, as being an unwarranted interference by the civil authority in a purely theological and ecclesiastical question. On November 20, 1704, Pope Clement XI signed the decree *Cum Deus Optimus*, which was not, however, immediately made public. It rehearsed the whole history of the controversy and proclaimed that the Confucian rites were idolatrous and superstitious, concluding with a negative judgment that forbade Catholics from taking part in them. Only Christian civil servants who could not absent themselves from official ceremonies would be allowed a passive and inactive presence. When Pius XI examined the question again many centuries later, in 1935, a different decision was reached, and Catholics were allowed to celebrate them as purely civil rituals with a political and social significance. (See chapter 24.)

A Papal Legate in China

While Rome was still preparing the long-awaited decision, Charles Maillard de Tournon (1668–1710) was dispatched to East Asia by Pope Clement XI with a view to resolving certain difficulties concerning the Malabar rites in India and applying the Roman decision, when it came, to the Chinese rites. Tournon was born in Savoy, which was then an independent dukedom, French speaking for the most part, and had spent his whole career at Rome in the papal administration. At thirty-three, in preparation for his mission to the East, he was consecrated bishop and given a titular see as patriarch of Antioch. He was also made legate *a latere* with extensive powers to take decisions on the spot without referring back to Rome. Tournon sailed to India without calling at Lisbon, thus ignoring the administrative center of the extensive Portuguese establishment in Asia, the *Padroado*. He left Europe in February 1703 and arrived in Indian waters in November, avoiding Goa to mark his independence as legate, and sailing directly to Pondicherry, on the coast of Coromandel, a port that was under French rule since 1674. Tournon then became ill so that he could not personally investigate the problem he was sent to solve. Relying on information from others, he condemned sixteen aspects of the Malabar rites by a decree of June 1704, which plunged Indian Christians into forty years of inextricable difficulties. The archbishop of Goa, who had received no official notification of the presence of a papal legate in his territory, forbade the application of the decree through-

Cardinal Charles Maillard de Tournon (1668–1710)
Papal Legate in China

Cardinal Tournon was sent to China in 1703 by Pope Clement XI as Legate, Apostolic Visitor and Titular Patriarch of Antioch; his instructions were to resolve disagreement among missionaries about whether Christians were entitled to take part in Confucian prayers and rites for the ancestors. Although the Kangxi Emperor had declared that these were civil ceremonies, the Legate applied a papal ruling that Catholics could not take part in them. As a result, about half the missionaries in China were expelled. In 1707 the emperor sent Tournon to Macao, ordering the Portuguese to put him under house arrest, although he had been made a cardinal in 1707. Tournon died on June 8, 1710, without being released, and the Pope had his remains brought back to Europe and interred in the chapel of the College of Propaganda in Rome. (Vatican Library, St. Chigi II, 1453). Engraving by Girolamo Rossi, il Giovane, (1682–1762). © Vatican Library.

out the whole of his extensive patriarchate. Things did not bode well for China.

Meanwhile the legate had sailed to Macao, where he refused to enter the port, the governor and the bishop being obliged to wait on him on an islet, where Tournon informed them of his legatine powers. Before these could come into force, the Portuguese authorities required Tournon to submit his brief of appointment for examination so that its stipulations could receive the royal *bene placitum*, according to the terms of the *Padroado*.[12] This the legate refused to do and set sail for Guangzhou the next day, leaving the Portuguese incensed at the way he had ignored their rights.

Tournon had no firsthand knowledge of East Asia and knew no Oriental languages. He has been described as "very much aware of his authority, convinced of the rights of Propaganda Fide, not inclined to treat considerately the rights of local patronage. He could not show the infinite patience which the situation required, nor did he have the skill to obtain real submission under the cover of granting superficial satisfaction. He had bad health . . . and was prevented from garnering needed information from sources that were sufficiently numerous and sufficiently varied."[13]

On December 4, 1705, the papal legate arrived in Beijing and, before the end of the month, was received by the Kangxi emperor with much ceremony. The audience was cordial and seemed full of promise for the establishment of permanent diplomatic relations between China and the Holy See, a proposal by Tournon to which the emperor seemed to accede. Unfortunately, mishaps then began to accumulate. Tournon became ill, probably from a duodenal ulcer, so that he could not undertake a general visitation of the missions and was thus prevented from acquiring firsthand knowledge of Chinese Christians. He seems to have been in pain for much of the time, and this led him to ignore some of the conventions required by Chinese good manners. He was often irritable and lost the poise required of diplomats. He had shown his hand as soon as he arrived in Beijing by talking about the differences between Confucianism and Christian-

---

[12] Jno Godinho, *The Padroado of Portugal in the Orient: 1454–1860* (Bombay, 1924), pp. 4–5.

[13] S. Delacroix, ed., *Histoire universelle des missions catholiques* (Paris, 1957), vol. 2, pp. 345–48. Quoted in *Catholicisme* 15, c. 140; *sub nomen* Tournon. For a summary of the events of Tournon's legation, see Standaert, pp. 358–60.

ity and expressing his reservations concerning the position taken up by the Jesuits on the question of the Chinese rites. Worst of all, he failed to consult the Chinese themselves on the point at issue, and he listened to the enemies of the Society of Jesus without seeking to arrive at a balanced view of a complex question.

Opposition to the Jesuits was clearly a moving force among many of those who at the time considered Confucian rites as unacceptable. Maigrot, Charmot, Noailles, Tournon—it is probably not unfair to say that some of them harbored ill feelings against the Jesuits and were hoping to use a condemnation of the rites by Rome as a means of discrediting the Society. The reasons for this unpopularity are to be found in the power conflict that developed in the last decades of the seventeenth century between the Jesuits and the first vicars apostolic sent to the Far East by the Congregation *de Propaganda Fide*. First of them all, Bishop Pierre Lambert de la Motte confronted the Jesuits in Siam and Cochin, condemning their commercial practices, their worldly concerns, and their claim to monopolize mission work. In return he was victim of their calumnies. A more general opposition to the Jesuits developed in the following century for numerous reasons that have been described by John McManners in "The Fall of the Jesuits", a chapter of his book *Church and Society in Eighteenth-Century France*.[14] Suffice it to say here that an anti-Jesuit movement was to gather such strength in Catholic Europe during the eighteenth century that it led to the expulsion of all members of the Society from Portugal (1759), Spain (1767), and their overseas territories, often in conditions of vindictive cruelty, unworthy of civilized nations. The kingdom of the two Sicilies (1767) and the grand duchy of Parma (1768) followed suit. In France the Society was declared illegal in 1764 and its property confiscated, although its members were not expelled from the country and were given small pensions. Finally, the Society was suppressed universally by the Franciscan Pope Clement XIV in 1773, which led to the withdrawal of the Jesuits from Beijing and their replacement by the Vincentians.

On June 29, 1706, the papal legate had his second audience with the Kangxi emperor. By then the emperor knew that Tournon's presence was not only concerned with establishing diplomatic relations, but

---

[14] John McManners, *Church and Society in Eighteenth-Century France* (Oxford: Oxford University Press, 1998), vol. 2, pp. 530–61.

with decisions being taken in Europe by the papacy concerning Chinese Christians. The emperor laid down his ground rule that Christianity had to be compatible with Confucianism; otherwise Europeans would not be allowed to remain in China.[15] The legate then talked about the differences between Christianity and Confucianism and said that he was advised by Bishop Charles Maigrot, a great expert on Chinese texts who had just arrived in Beijing. The emperor was due to depart for Manchuria the next day and therefore summoned Maigrot to meet him there, at Chengde, old Jehol, 124 miles (200 kilometers) to the northeast of Beijing. It was there in 1703 that the Kangxi emperor had begun to build the summer palace of the Manchus, to which he gave the enticing name *Bishu Shanzhuang*, "Fleeing-the-Heat Mountain Villa".[16] Meanwhile Maigrot was questioned by two mandarins, who soon ascertained the limits of his knowledge of Chinese.

The interview between the emperor and Maigrot took place on August 2, 1706.[17] Tournon was not present, but all Europeans in Manchuria were summoned and several Jesuits from China, including the procurator. The court too was present as the emperor examined Maigrot on his knowledge of Chinese. Speaking in Chinese, he asked, "Do you understand Chinese books?" Maigrot replied, "Very little." The emperor then explained that he had summoned Maigrot because the legate had said that he was well versed in Chinese books. He asked Maigrot whether he had read the Four Books of Confucius. Maigrot replied that he had. The emperor asked, "Do you remember what you have read?" Maigrot said that he did not. The emperor said, "You have read and not learned by heart?" Maigrot replied, "In Europe it is not the custom to learn by heart." At this point it became apparent that Maigrot did not understand the emperor very well, and so Fr. Dominique Parrenin, S.J., was made to interpret. The emperor asked, "Am I right that you cannot quote two words of the Confucian Four Books?" Maigrot confirmed that he could not. He was then asked to translate the four characters above the imperial throne, but could only manage some of them.

---

[15] Von Collani, "Charles Maigrot's Role", p. 162.

[16] For a description of a visit to the site of Chengde in the 1980s, see William Dalrymple, *In Xanadu: A Quest* (London: Harper Collins, 1990), pp. 289–93.

[17] For the account of the interview, see von Collani, "Charles Maigrot's Role", pp. 164–67.

The interview had begun badly. Maigrot was in the presence of one of the greatest and most cultured of China's rulers, who had studied the classical texts of Confucianism, as well as a wide range of writings on Chinese literature, geography, mathematics, and music. The emperor had commissioned many collections of Chinese texts and various encyclopedias and dictionaries, including the *Kangxi Dictionary*, which became for more than 200 years the standard dictionary of the Chinese language. In 1700 he had ordered the production of *Gujin tushu jicheng* (*A Collection of Books and Illustrations of Ancient and Modern Times*), which when completed was the largest work ever printed in the world.[18] This was the sovereign to whom Maigrot had been recommended by the legate as "a great expert on Chinese". It was obviously a rather rapid assessment on the part of the man who had been sent by the Pope to be the leader of Christians in China. Far from being an expert, Maigrot was publicly exposed as a brash and ignorant European. There was worse to come.

During his second audience with Tournon, the emperor had already found it difficult to get the European envoy to accept the importance of the document that he, the emperor, had sent to Rome affirming the civil character of the Confucian rites. It seemed as though the legate had "presumed to correct the Chinese emperor's personal definition of his own country's religious ceremonies".[19] Maigrot's interview took a similar turn. The Kangxi emperor wanted to know why Maigrot objected to *Tian*, "heaven", as the name for God. Maigrot replied that *Tian* did not mean "Lord of heaven". The emperor lectured him like a slow learner: "I am very surprised at you. Did I not already state that *Tian* is a much better expression for the Lord of Heaven than *Tianzhu* . . . ? Tell me, why do the people call me *wansui* (ten thousand years)?" Maigrot replied, "This is to indicate that they wish Your Majesty innumerable years." "Well, learn from that," replied the emperor. "The true meaning of Chinese words does not always coincide with their literal meaning." Fr. Antoine de Beauvollier, the procurator of the Jesuits, tried to come to the rescue of the hapless Maigrot. He explained that the character *Tian* was composed of two others, "one" and "great", and therefore meant first great or first being, existing before heaven, earth, and universe. But Maigrot

---

[18] E.C., *sub nomen* Kangxi, p. 252.

[19] John McManners, *Church and Society in Eighteenth-Century France*, vol. 2, p. 539.

was adamant. He did not accept that *Tian* and *Tianzhu* could mean the same thing.

One must ask why there seemed to be total lack of understanding on both sides about what was at issue. Bishop Maigrot was acting as the product of centuries of biblical thought and Christian theology in stating that the term *Tian*, "heaven", was inadequate in referring to God and that Christians could only use a phrase like *Tianzhu*, "the Lord of heaven". Maigrot's notion of God indicated a being who is not part of the visible world, but is its transcendent cause, outside space and time; a being, moreover, who is creator of all that exists and, as such, closer to human beings than any creature can be. The Kangxi emperor, in contrast, was imbued with the thought of Confucius, according to which *Tian*, "heaven", is a comprehensive reality, including the visible "dome of heaven", as well as nature, divine providence, and the great unknown who has called all this into existence. To change the name of this reality would have displaced a central element of Confucianism.

From the point of view of the Chinese, disagreeing publicly with the emperor was the ultimate loss of face, but, once the interview was over, the Kangxi emperor pursued the matter further. He seemed to be trying, not to catch Maigrot out, but to elucidate. The next day, August 3, 1706, the oldest son of the emperor, Prince Yinti, summoned Maigrot to an interview and questioned him again about his views. Had they changed in any way? Maigrot said that they had not. The emperor's decision was swift. He issued a decree, given to Maigrot on August 4, informing him that he would be exiled. He was then placed under house arrest. The emperor gave him another chance in October, when he was again interviewed to find out whether he would change his mind, but he continued to be adamant, so that a final decree on December 17, 1706, ordered his deportation to Macao. He arrived there in February 1707 and boarded an English ship, bound for Galway in the west of Ireland. Once in Europe, Maigrot wrote to the Pope, asking to be allowed to retire to the seminary of the Paris Foreign Missions. Clement XI was, however, magnanimous. He invited Maigrot to come to Rome and made him a canon of St. Mary Majors, where he collected material on Chinese rites until his death in 1730.

A worse fate awaited the legate, Charles Maillard de Tournon. The emperor had also sent him a mandate on August 3, the day after

Maigrot's memorable audience, which contained the not unmerited comment: "When you were standing in front of me, I already told you that Europeans cannot understand the meaning of our books correctly, but want to discuss them. They are similar to people standing in front of a door and wanting to discuss the things inside the house".[20]

Missionaries Expelled

On December 17, 1706, the emperor issued an edict requiring all missionaries to obtain a certificate (*piao*) to be granted only to those who agreed "with the method of Matteo Ricci" and who declared their readiness to stay forever in China.[21] "Agreeing with the method of Matteo Ricci" meant accepting Chinese rites. It was around this time that Tournon learned at last of the 1704 decree of the Holy Office, *Cum Deus Optimus*, which had not been made public at the time of its promulgation. It forbade Christians from taking part in the Confucian rites in honor of the ancestors and forbade the use of *Tian*, "heaven", as the object of worship, authorizing only *Tianzhu*, "the Lord of heaven". Tournon chose this moment to make the Roman decisions public, although the Jesuits begged him not to. He also published instructions at Nanjing on February 7, 1707, laying down how the missionaries were to reply to the questions of the Chinese authorities when they made application for their residence certificate. They were to say that they could only observe customs in accordance with Christian law, that the ceremonies in honor of Confucius and the ancestors were unacceptable, as was the cult of tablets representing the soul of deceased parents. Tournon, as legate, declared that such was the decision of the Holy See and ordered that his instructions be obeyed by all Christian religious personnel in China, under pain of excommunication. It has been estimated that the number of missionaries in China was reduced by about one-half, as a result of the expulsions resulting from these various administrative requirements and to the natural loss of personnel.[22]

The Kangxi emperor was infuriated by what he considered as the

---

[20] Von Collani, "Charles Maigrot's Role," p. 168.
[21] Standaert, p. 359.
[22] Ibid., p. 360.

arrogance of the papal legate and by the interference of an exterior power in the affairs of China. Tournon was arrested on June 13, 1707, and deported to Macao, with the order of the emperor that he should be kept in custody until the Chinese delegation, which had been dispatched to Rome to elucidate the matter, should return. The Portuguese could hardly believe the good fortune that delivered into their hands the prelate, who had consistently ignored their *Padroado*, plunged their Indian missions into confusion by his ill-advised decrees, and represented the growing influence of the French vicars apostolic in China. The emperor had only enjoined that Tournon remain in Macao until the return of the Chinese delegation, which had been dispatched to Rome. Unfortunately it was lost at sea and never reached its destination.

The Portuguese authorities in Macao posted around the residence of the legate what appeared to be a guard of honor, but soon showed that he was under house arrest by preventing him from going out and restricting access to him. Tournon had attempted to exercise his legatine authority by issuing an edict that had been publicly displayed throughout the city. The governor ordered its removal and warned the inhabitants that the legate had no authority whatsoever in Macao. A herald, accompanied with trumpet and drum, went through the city, proclaiming that anyone who obeyed any of Tournon's orders would be remanded in custody.[23] Tournon was ill and, not surprisingly, depressed. The Portuguese authorities spared him no humiliations; not only was he confined to his residence but so also was his suite, and an attempt was made to take away the twenty Chinese servants who looked after them. There were difficulties too about supplies of fresh water, and the household complained that they had to drink salty water.

Tournon showed Christian resignation throughout all these vexations, and, as will be seen in the next chapter, those who did manage to elude Portuguese vigilance and visit him were impressed by his attitude. It was ironic that, when the news of Tournon's first interview with the emperor reached Rome, there had been jubilation at its apparent success. Clement XI made him a cardinal at the consistory of August 1, 1707, and six missionaries were dispatched to bring him

---

[23] José Maria Gonzales, O.P., *Historia de las Misiones Dominicanas de China 1700–1800*, vol. 2, p. 39.

the news of his elevation to the Sacred College and the cardinal's
red hat, the symbol of his exalted office.[24] The missionaries, who arrived on an English ship, received small thanks for their long journey,
as the governor put them in prison on their arrival and kept them
there for five months.[25] Some of the clergy in Macao, the Dominicans especially, were inclined to accept the authority of a cardinal in
their midst, whereupon they were reprimanded by the vicar general
of Macao. Tournon riposted by excommunicating the vicar general.[26]
Since neither recognized the jurisdiction of the other, the situation
was not substantially altered. The sacred roman purple made no difference as far as the Portuguese authorities were concerned. Tournon
remained a prisoner until the end. He died on June 9, 1710, at the
age of forty-one, six months after the arrival of his cardinal's hat.

Pope Clement XI approved of Tournon's decisions unreservedly
and rejected the appeals against them that came to him from China.
A further pontifical decree of September 25, 1710, from the Holy
Office confirmed all Tournon's prohibitions. Since there was a good
deal of variation in the way these decrees were applied in China, the
Pope promulgated on March 19, 1715, an apostolic constitution, *Ex
illa die*, requiring an oath of obedience from all missionaries, to be
taken on the Bible, according to a formula that was specified. It was
all too much, and the Jesuits, who were faced with the distress of
Christians who continued to practice the traditional rites, wondered
whether they were justified in refusing them the sacraments.

In 1720 a second legatine embassy set out from Rome to the Kangxi
emperor. It was led by an Italian, Mezzabarba, titular patriarch of
Alexandria, who tried to salvage something from the wreck by letting it be understood that some arrangement might be possible. On
November 4, 1721, he discreetly sent a letter from Macao to all the
bishops in China, declaring that, although he altered none of the
requirements of *Ex illa die*, he was able to draw attention to eight
permissions that offered the possibility of taking part, in a nonsuperstitious way, in Chinese ceremonies. However, all that this conciliatory move achieved was to relaunch the controversy and to increase

---

[24] Cf. Edward J. Malatesta, "A Fatal Clash of Wills", ed. D. E. Mungello, *The Chinese
Rites Controversy*, p. 233.

[25] Gonzales, *Historia de las Misiones Dominicanas de China*, vol. 2, p. 39.

[26] Godinho, *The Padroado of Portugal*, p. 8.

the confusion. Mezzabarba's eight permissions were definitively condemned by the decree *Ex quo singulari* of Benedict XIV (July 11, 1742), which rehearsed the whole history of the controversy and brought it to a close.

Imperial Absolutism

The great Kangxi emperor died in 1722, and with him went the hopes, nursed so patiently by the Jesuits, that there might be permanent protection for Christians in China. This emperor, the second of the Manchu Dynasty, was certainly an enlightened monarch who had brought peace and prosperity to China. In his palaces at Beijing he had a building called *Ruyiguan*[27] adapted to provide workshops for the painters, engravers, architects, and mechanics who were working for him. Some Jesuits were employed there, mending clocks and other machines that had been brought from Europe. There too, from 1715 onward, worked a Jesuit painter, the lay brother Giuseppe Castiglione (1688–1766), originally from Milan, who produced works of art that combined the European and the Chinese styles of painting.

It must, however, be said that the Kangxi emperor was not at all impressed by the teaching on Christianity that the Jesuits tried to convey to him. He liked its moral approach, but he advised the fathers to eliminate some of their doctrines if they wanted to make Christianity more acceptable. He himself was steeped in Confucian tradition, where he found a solid foundation for imperial power. In 1670 he wrote an exhortation in sixteen maxims, each of which was condensed into seven characters. He had assimilated the Confucian tradition, which based the authority of the sovereign on his moral and intellectual superiority. *Zhi tong*, political power, had to be in harmony with *Dao tong*, the moral power of the Tao. The emperor used to test the extent of the knowledge of his higher civil servants regularly, and he would do this with foreigners too. This reveals a tendency for imperial authority to become absolute and to try to control thought, whereas under the previous dynasty, the Ming, Confu-

---

[27] *Ruyiguan* means literally "office of the so-pleasing". *Ruyi* denotes an emblematic stick or wand, associated with Taoism, and means literally "as [it] pleases", thus suggesting that the arts and crafts carried out in this palace building were *ruyi*, "leisure", activities.

cian thinkers could still exercise a critical role in relation to the civil service. They now found themselves compelled to conform to the ideological orthodoxy, which was identified with the thinking of the emperor.

At the same period in the West, the "sun king", Louis XIV of France (r. 1643–1715), also assumed the character of an absolute monarch, whose power was based on a divine right. When the king attended Mass at the chateau of Versailles, the courtiers in the nave below turned and faced the king in the balcony at the west end of the chapel, while he alone faced the altar. However, there was always in Europe a clear distinction between spiritual authority and temporal authority, the former being represented by an institution in the form of the papacy. Bossuet, bishop of Meaux and a favorite court preacher, could exclaim "Gentlemen, consider the greatness of the powers that we contemplate from below!"[28] and go on to point out the precarious nature of kingship. Such a thing would not have been possible in China, where the spiritual was identified with the temporal and where the emperor was deemed to make the union of heaven and earth present in his person.

The idea, entertained by some of the missionaries, that the emperor could be brought to kneel before the Lord of heaven was completely illusory and would have been contradictory in Chinese terms. Even more unlikely was the prospect of ever bringing such an emperor to obey the directives of *Jiaohuang*, "the Emperor of religion", i.e., the Pope, directives that came from far away, from the barbarians of the West. To the Chinese emperor, claims that such commandments were binding on his subjects seemed utterly unsuitable, improper, and harmful. Such interference, moreover, threatened the very rules that ensured the cohesion of the empire's moral order.

Toward the end of his life, the Kangxi emperor became more impatient with the missionaries who were trying to circumvent his rules, and he was sometimes cruel. He thus repeatedly humiliated the Vin-

---

[28] Jacques Bénigne Bossuet (1627–1704), bishop of Meaux, in his funeral oration preached in the Abbey Church of Saint-Denis on August 21, 1670, for Princess Henrietta Anne Stuart, duchess of Orleans, the sister of Charles II, king of England, who had married Louis XIV's brother, Philippe, duke of Orleans. The passage quoted continues, "While we tremble under the hand [of kings], God strikes them as a warning to us. Their very elevation brings this about, for, far from sparing them, he is not afraid to sacrifice them as a means of instruction for the rest of mankind."

centian Fr. Teodorico Pedrini (1671–1746), a clavichord player he liked to listen to, for he was very fond of music. Generally, however, Kangxi was above doing more than interning or expelling the missionaries who disobeyed his laws too openly. His successors were to be much more rigorous in their treatment of Christians.

Toleration at Court: Concealment in the Provinces

The new emperor, Yingzhen (1678–1735), whose regnal name was to be Yongzheng, came to power at the end of 1722. His attitude toward missionaries was soon to cause them disappointment. He began by eliminating all his rivals to the throne. Some of them had received support from foreign missionaries, such as Fr. João Mourao, S.J., who was exiled to Xining in Qinghai Province and later executed in a case that involved the Sunu family. The Manchu prince, Sunu, was fourth cousin of the emperor. He never became a Christian, but several of his sons did, through the example of Suerjin, the third son, who happened to see a Christian tract among secondhand books in a stall in Beijing. He read other Christian books and was convinced that their doctrine conformed to that of ancient Chinese books. Other members of the family and their wives were baptized, whereupon the emperor summoned Sunu to explain how he had lost control of his family by allowing his sons to become Christians. Many members of the family were sent into exile. In 1727, nine Sunu princes were condemned to execution for following a seditious religion, although this was postponed.[29]

Yongzheng imposed restrictions on missionaries to support the repressive measures against them that had been imposed by a mandarin in Fujian. The Dominicans had always preached openly in the Fu'an region without regard for the consequences. The emperor therefore signed a decree of the office of rites in January 1724, which was couched in the following terms:

> The Europeans at court are useful because of the calendar and in other ways, but those who reside in the provinces are not at all useful. They attract to their religion ignorant people, both men and women; they build churches where men and women meet indiscriminately under the

---

[29] See Standaert, pp. 445–46, for the Sunu family converts.

pretext of praying together. This is of no profit to the empire. Following the proposals put forward by Chongto of Fujian, those at court are not to be ill treated. As for those who are dispersed throughout the empire, if they can be useful, let them be sent to court. As for the others, let them be sent to Macao.[30]

Among the Europeans in the capital who "could be useful", one must reckon the Orthodox mission, composed of four priests and six students. This was a scientific delegation, protected by the clauses of the Treaty of Kiakhta (1727). An orthodox church was therefore built in the courtyard of the Russian embassy. Relations with the Catholic missionaries were friendly. Some outstanding Russian sinologists worked at Beijing and introduced their compatriots to various aspects of Chinese culture.

The imperial decree of 1724 was disastrous for Catholics in the short term. All the missionaries in the provinces were rounded up and escorted to Guangzhou, and these draconian measures were repeated periodically until the colonial period of the nineteenth century. Henceforth, missionaries could only enter China secretly, but one result of imperial policy was that the Gospel was taken to the remoter regions of the country and to the poorest inhabitants.

Yongzheng wanted to rule over the minds of his subjects, even more than his father had done. He republished the *Sacred Edict* with its sixteen maxims and assumed the role of a religious leader. The palace where he had resided before becoming emperor was made into a lama temple, the famous *Yonghe gong* in Beijing, which has recently (1991) been restored. By inclination, he adhered to Chan Buddhism, but he did not reject Taoism and was thinking of imposing a new religion for China that would be composed of Confucianism, Buddhism, and Taoism. This kind of project revealed the religious aspect of Confucianism, but showed that it could also become a dangerous tool of political power, leading to a self-sufficient regime, rejecting all external influence.

The missionaries in Beijing attempted to mitigate the effects of the decree of 1724 and to persuade the Yongzheng emperor to adopt a less harsh approach, whereupon he gathered them together and delivered a harangue that contained these significant and perceptive words:

---

[30] Columba Cary-Elwes, *China and the Cross* (Longmans, 1957), p. 163, quoting *Lettres édifiantes et curieuses* (1780), new ed.; vol. 19, p. 327.

Matteo Ricci came to China in the first year of Wanli. I will not comment on what the Chinese did then. I am not responsible for it. But in those days you were very few in number, nearly nothing, and you did not have many people belonging to you, nor churches. But your law spread rapidly. We saw this and did not dare to say anything. But if you were able to deceive my father, do not think that you are going to deceive me.

You want all Chinese to become Christians, and your religion requires this of you. I know that very well. But if that were to take place, what would happen to us? We would become the subjects of your kings. Your Christian converts only acknowledge you. In a time of unrest they would only listen to you. I know that, at present, there is nothing to fear. But when ships come in their thousands and tens of thousands, then there could be trouble.[31]

The emperor was far sighted; there was indeed trouble in the nineteenth century, when the colonial powers, eager for trade, used force to open China to the outside world.

The repression of Christians that was launched in 1724 did not affect all parts of China equally. There exists an account by the Austrian Jesuit Gottfried Xaver von Laimbeckhoven (1707–1787), of the situation of the 8,000 or so Christians that he found in the Huguang region, north of Lake Dongting when he arrived in 1739. He explained how it was that they had not greatly suffered so far:

Firstly because Christians are made up mostly of poor and common folk, living from the work of their hands, so that anyone who wants to make money could not do so by persecuting them. Secondly because Prince Joseph, who is viceroy of this province and of imperial blood, is a Christian, but this is so secret that he has never asked my predecessor, Fr. Sequeira, to come to see him. In order to fulfill his religious duties, he only contacts the native Jesuit (first of all Fr. Stephen Siu, a Vincentian, and then Fr. Moraes, S.J.).[32]

Even so the mission's existence was precarious, and it had to operate in secret. The priest lived on a boat and only went out at night. He would meet the faithful who had gathered in a private house and

[31] Mailla, *Histoire générale de la Chine*, vol. 11, p. 400 and following; quoted by A. Thomas, *Histoire de la Mission de Pékin depuis les origines jusqu'à l'arrivée des lazaristes* (Paris: Louis Michard, 1923), pp. 320–21.

[32] Noël Gubbels, *Trois siècles d'apostolat. Histoire du catholicisme au Hu-Kwang depuis les origines, 1587 jusqu'à 1870* (Paris: 30 avenue Reille, 1934), Collecta Missionaria, p. 157.

would give them a class in doctrine, with the help of a catechist. Toward eleven o'clock at night he would begin to hear confessions, until about three in the morning. Then the catechumens who had completed their preparation would be baptized. About four in the morning, he would offer the Holy Sacrifice of the Mass, then return to his home on the water.[33] Fr. von Laimbeckhoven was resolutely optimistic and, relying on the power of God's grace, brought in a good harvest of souls. He was appointed bishop of Nanjing in 1752 and also administered the diocese of Beijing after 1757, returning to die in Jiangnan in 1787.

It was missionaries sent by the Congregation *de Propaganda Fide* who then took over from the Jesuits in Huguang (Hunan and Hubei), especially Chinese priests who had been trained in the College of the Holy Family in Naples. The founder of this "Chinese college" was a diocesan priest, Matteo Ripa (1682–1746), who had worked as painter and engraver at the court in Beijing for thirteen years. From its foundation in 1732 until it closed in 1888, the Naples college trained 106 Chinese priests, of whom twenty-three were natives of the Huguang region. The Chinese priests from Holy Family College were practically the only ones who ensured the pastoral care of Catholic communities in central China, from the time of the suppression of the Jesuits in 1773 until the creation of a new vicariate, which was entrusted to Italian Franciscans in 1838.[34]

---

[33] Ibid., p. 159.

[34] Ibid., pp. 199, 202.

[Considerable additional material has been added to the French text of the sections *A Papal Legate in China* and *Missionaries Expelled* of chapter 15.—Trans.]

16

ANDREW LI: CHINESE PRIEST

The Manchu Dynasty reached its zenith during the first years of the Qianlong emperor, who reigned from 1736 to 1795. Jacques Gernet calls him and his two predecessors "enlightened despots", especially because their power rested on a rigorous application of the Confucian moral order. From 1702 to 1776, the Jesuits in Beijing published a yearly account of life in China called *Lettres édifiantes et curieuses*, which contributed to making the sophistication of Chinese civilization known in Europe during the Age of Enlightenment. Thus the Jesuit lay brother Jean-Denis Attiret (1702–1768), who was a court painter, gives a striking picture of the splendors of the court at Beijing:

> The emperor's palace at Beijing is at least as large as the city of Dijon (I quote it as a term of reference because you know Dijon). It consists of a great number of buildings, separate from one another, disposed with wonderful symmetry and surrounded by vast courtyards, by gardens and flowerbeds. The façades of all these buildings shine with gilding, colors, and glaze. Their interiors are filled with the most beautiful and the most costly ornaments and furniture that China, India, and Europe can produce.[1]

Jesuit architects and artists contributed to the creation of these imperial buildings, since they worked on the famous palace of *Yuanmingyuan*, "garden of perfect brightness", also known as the "old summer palace", built for the Qianlong emperor. It was badly damaged by British and French troops in 1860, and again by the army of the eight powers during the Boxer Rebellion of 1900, although its ruins are still visible.

However, the Chinese empire's official façade, both artistic and moral, concealed much misery among the people. Such a splendid edifice was in fact threatened in several ways. As Jacques Gernet notes, the official teaching was accompanied by censorship and persecution:

---

[1] Quoted by Édouard Duperray, *Ambassadeurs de Dieu à la Chine* (Paris: Casterman, 1956), pp. 172–73.

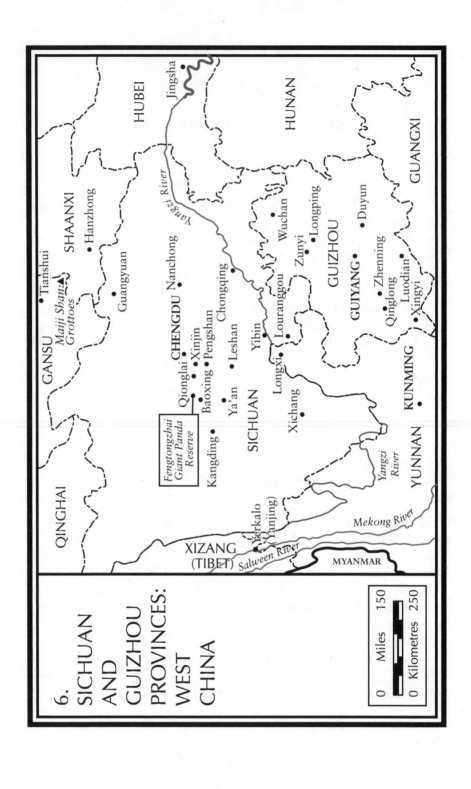

6.

SICHUAN
AND
GUIZHOU
PROVINCES:
WEST
CHINA

HUBEI

Jingsha

HUNAN

GUANGXI

SHAANXI

GANSU

Tianshui
Maiji Shan:▲
Grottoes

Hanzhong

Guangyuan

CHENGDU Nanchong

Yangzi River

Wuchan

GUIZHOU

Longping

Zunyi

GUIYANG

Duyun

Zhenming

Qinglong Luodian
Xingyi

Qionglai Xinjin
Baoxing Pengshan

Chongqing

Ya'an Leshan

Yibin

Longxi

Louranggou

SICHUAN

Xichang

Kangding

Fengtongzhai
Giant Panda
Reserve

KUNMING

QINGHAI

Yangzi
River

YUNNAN

Mekong River

Merkalo
(Yanjing)

XIZANG
(TIBET) Salween River

MYANMAR

0	Miles	150
0	Kilometres	250

On top of the new regime's [the Manchus] abundant efforts to develop an official educational system, and to increase the number of schools, came the censoring and persecution of writers convicted, or even only suspected, of hostility to the foreign dynasty or of lack of goodwill. This policy became harsher under Yongzheng [1723–1735] and ended in the great literary inquisition of 1774–1789 in the reign of Qianlong: 10,231 works in 171,000 chapters were put on the index of prohibited books, and over 2,320 of them were completely destroyed. At the same time brutal measures were taken against the authors and their relations— execution, exile, forced labor, confiscation of property, and so on.[2]

As this account shows, these "enlightened despots" were not known for their toleration. Already by the middle of the eighteenth century, signs of decay were beginning to appear. The rapid growth of the population caused new problems, while droughts, epidemics, and other natural disasters were aggravated by the corruption of venal officials. Underground movements, which were planning revolt against the foreign Manchus, found inspiration in the Taoist and Buddhist traditions, and some Christian converts too came from these patriotic movements. *Bai lian jiao*, the sect of the white lotus, brought things to a head by leading a peasant rebellion (1796–1804), which was eventually crushed by Qing troops, but conditions continued to worsen under the Jiaqing emperor (r. 1796–1821) and Daoguang emperor (r. 1821–1850), thus bringing the country to the tragic outcome of the Taiping Rebellion (1850–1864) and to the armed intervention of foreign colonial powers.

The persecutions inflicted on Christians in the eighteenth century must be seen against this background: imperial absolutism, the fear of foreigners, Confucian conservatism, and the repression of local anti-Manchu rebellions. Foreign priests were forbidden to reside in China, except for those in Beijing who were in the service of the emperor. Christianity was generally classified as belonging to the category *xie jiao*, "subversive sects", which meant that its adherents were permanently exposed to repressive action by the authorities. In remote provinces far from Beijing, however, mandarins varied in their degree of strictness, so that in the southwest of China Christian communities survived and even made progress, thanks to the zeal of Chi-

---

[2] Jacques Gernet, *A History of Chinese Civilization* (Cambridge, U.K.: Cambridge University Press, 1996), p. 508.

nese priests, and to the catechists and consecrated virgins who assisted them.

Chinese Priests and Their Training

At the beginning of the eighteenth century, Chinese priests were still few and far between. Pascal D'Elia, writing in 1723, mentions four or five elderly priests. In 1733 there were ten more, who had been trained by the Jesuits of Macao and Beijing. The Portuguese of Macao were very particular about which Chinese they would admit to the priesthood, demanding the same training as obtained in European seminaries. The French fathers in Beijing tended to go more quickly, cutting back on the study of Latin, as far as possible, and ordaining men of mature years. They had all the basic texts in Chinese, thanks to the work of Fr. Buglio. He had been a pioneer of the mission in Sichuan Province in 1640 and had been brought back to Beijing by Manchu troops after the crushing of the Zhang Xianzhong Rebellion. He used the time to translate into Chinese books that would be most useful to priests: the missal, the breviary, the ritual, manuals of moral theology, and the *Summa Theologica* of St. Thomas Aquinas (*Prima Pars; Tertia Pars*). However, the struggle to obtain permission for a liturgy in Chinese from the Roman authorities, which had lasted during the whole of the seventeenth century, was already a lost cause. In spite of the concern for adaptation, expressed in the instructions of 1659, the Congregation *de Propaganda Fide* came down firmly in favor of Latin. Even the vicars apostolic sent out by the Congregation realized the difficulties. Bishop Pallu beseeched the cardinals "to dispense local bishops from having to know Latin, while waiting for a few years to have a good number of priests who know Latin, among whom persons apt to replace the first bishops will not be lacking".[3] It was no use. The ambitious project for the creation of native bishops had to be abandoned, and only Gregory Luo was consecrated at this period.

In 1702, Fr. Jean Basset (1662–1707), a member of the Paris Foreign Missions who was originally from Lyons in France, wrote a long memorandum, entitled *Avis sur la Mission de Chine* (*Animadversions on the China Mission*). At the time, he was stationed at Chengdu, the

---

[3] Quoted in François Bontinck, *La lutte autour de la liturgie chinoise au XVIIe siècle et XVIIIe siècle* (Louvain-Paris: Nauwelhaerts, 1962), p. 149.

capital of Sichuan, and he described the sorry state of the Church in the province. He saw only one remedy, which was to translate the Bible into Chinese and authorize the liturgy in Chinese. He drew attention to the fact that the apostles had used the vernacular language of their time, and he wrote that it was the only way to make the Chinese familiar with the Christian message. While Fr. Basset was waiting for a reply to his memorandum, he recruited three young children during his travels in Shaanxi Province. He was hoping to train them for the priesthood and asked a colleague, Fr. Jean-François de la Baluère (1668–1715), to look after their education. La Baluère began by teaching them both Latin and Chinese. Basset pointed out that they would learn better if they learned Chinese only to begin with; he was still waiting for a favorable response to his project for a Chinese liturgy. It is ironic that one of these children became one of the best Latin scholars in China. During the ten years when Andrew Li was the only priest in Sichuan Province, he kept a very full diary, written entirely in Latin.

Wandering Seminarians

Fr. Jean Basset invited Andrew Li to follow him when the boy was only eight years old. He belonged to a deeply Catholic family from the Chenggu district in the Hanzhong region of south Shaanxi, which had been evangelized at the time of the Ming by Fr. Etienne Faber, S.J., the wonder worker (see chapter 13). Andrew had only just left his family when he became seriously ill, and his life seemed to be in danger. After a year, however, he recovered, although he always had bad health. Like St. Paul, whom he resembled in several ways, the strength of the Gospel seemed to shine through his weakness. Fr. Basset wrote to his superior, Bishop Artus de Lionne (1655–1713):

> Little Andrew, who seemed to be at death's door, is on the way to recovery. He seems always very willing, and so is the other Chinese boy, who cried until his mother let him come here. They are profiting to the full from the trouble that is being taken over their education. I do not think that, even in Europe, it would be possible to find children as well-disposed as these two. When they serve Mass, they look like little angels.[4]

---

[4] Quoted from Launay, *Histoire des Missions de Chine, Mission du Se-Tchoan* vol. 1, pp.

Bishop de Lionne was the son of one of Louis XIV's ministers of state, Hugues de Lionne. He had been appointed vicar apostolic in Sichuan Province in 1696. Having recruited four priests for his vicariate in 1700, he entrusted Chengdu and the western part of Sichuan to Fathers Basset and de la Baluère. Two Vincentians also came to help him, an Italian, Luigi Antonio Appiani, C.M. (1663–1732), and a German, Johannes Müllener, C.M. (1673–1742). The Congregation of the Mission had been founded by St. Vincent de Paul, and its members are usually called in English-speaking countries "Vincentians". In France, they are called "Lazarists" because they were first established in Paris in an old priory building dedicated to St. Lazare. Their official name, Priests of the Mission, popularized the name "missionary". The Congregation *de Propaganda Fide* had sent the first Vincentians to China with the view to opening a seminary, and they thought that there was a chance of doing this in a remote region. Bishop de Lionne asked them to look after the eastern part of Sichuan, including Chongqing, the largest city in the province. Since the priests of the Paris Foreign Missions were in the western part of Sichuan, there were thus two missionary congregations in the same province. Although they were so few in number and facing the same formidable difficulties, the priests of the two societies found nothing better to do than to quarrel over territory, and the Chinese priests who worked with them were drawn into the conflict.

The Kangxi emperor had, as mentioned in the previous chapter, decreed that all foreign missionaries should apply for a *piao*, an official certificate, if they wanted to remain in China (decree of December 17, 1706). It would only be granted to priests who accepted "the method of Matteo Ricci", i.e., allowed Christians to attend Confucian rites. This brought great trouble upon the priests in Sichuan. Fr. Appiani had accompanied Legate de Tournon to Beijing, and, when he returned to Chengdu, he was thrown into prison. The two French missionaries from the Paris Foreign Missions had to leave the province and went with their seminarians, Andrew Li, Stephen Su, and Anthony Tang, to Guangzhou. There Fr. Basset suddenly died in December 1707, after having only been ill a few days. Fr. de la Baluère was compelled to go on to Macao, like all the Europeans who

---

70–71, in Armand Olichon, *Aux origines du Clergé chinois. Le père André Ly Missionaire au Se-Tchouan 1692–1775* (Paris: Bloud & Gay, 1933), p. 82.

refused to apply for the *piao*. He arrived there in March 1708, with his three seminarians.

In spite of the Portuguese, the seminarians managed to get in touch with the legate, Cardinal de Tournon, who was under house arrest. They were touched by the kindness he showed them and by the warmth of his welcome. Many years later, Fr. Andrew Li wrote down his impressions of that meeting:

> When I was a boy, I met priests from some of the European countries whose arrogance was in complete contrast to the kindness of the missionaries who had devoted themselves to my education. Some of them went as far as adopting the proud and solemn style of the more important mandarins, and these priests would get the faithful to go down on their knees and bow down to the ground before them. We were really surprised when we saw a prince of the Church, the papal legate, stand up when we arrived and receive our humble greetings with such kindness.[5]

Cardinal de Tournon wanted to take part in the two-year preparation of the Chinese seminarians for ordination and to guide them personally during that time. He therefore decided to confer the tonsure on Andrew Li and Anthony Tang[6] and called a meeting of all the clergy to tell them of his intention. Although the news of his elevation to the Sacred College had reached Macao, the priests would not hear of such a thing. Andrew Li wrote:

> After His Eminence had told those present at the meeting of his plan, he asked for their approval. All of them energetically expressed disagreement. The reason given for this unanimous opposition was our unworthiness. The Chinese are proud, unreliable, and ungrateful.[7]

Fr. de la Baluère was the only one to point out that such faults were not unknown among Europeans. The legate was not to be put off, however. Andrew Li writes:

> The venerable legate, in spite of the opposition of those around him, generously conferred upon us the clerical tonsure, thus opening to the Chinese nation entry to the Catholic priesthood.[8]

---

[5] Ibid., pp. 120–21, quoting Andrew Li's diary, p. 339.

[6] Since the eighth century, the clerical tonsure in the Latin Church marked entry into the clerical state. It was abolished by Paul VI after the reforms of the Second Vatican Council (1962–1965).

[7] Olichon, *Aux origines du clergé chinois*, p. 124, quoting Andrew Li's diary, p. 221: "*Sinenses superbi, inconstantes atque ingrati, sacris ordinibus propterea sunt indigni.*"

[8] Ibid., p. 125, quoting Andrew Li's diary, p. 221.

Fr. de la Baluère was expelled from Macao in 1713 but went back in secret, with his pupils, to Sichuan Province. In February 1715 they found in Chengdu the catechist, Lin Chang, who had looked after the Christians in the area by himself during the eight years while they were away. A few months later La Baluère caught a chill while crossing a torrent on a sick call, and this developed into pneumonia. Andrew Li was with him when he died and recorded his last words:

> Andrew, I ask you to obey the catechist Lin Chang, whom I am giving you as superior. . . . My children, I ask you to remember the promises that you have made to God. I ask you to put all your heart and all your strength into your study and the practice of piety. . . . I am giving my copies of the work of Cicero to Anthony and Andrew.[9]

Philibert Le Blanc (1644–1720), appointed vicar apostolic of Yunnan in 1696, was responsible for the seminarians. In 1717 he sent seven Chinese seminarians to the General College in Thailand, which had been founded by Bishop Lambert de la Motte in 1665. The college had already been through many difficulties, but from 1717 to 1727 it was flourishing in Mahapram, a peaceful place in the suburbs of Ayutthaya. The rector was Fr. Andrew Roost, a graduate of the Sorbonne, the theology faculty of the University of Paris, who had been rector of the Collège du Trésorier, a medieval foundation (1268) of the same university. The arrival of the Chinese students at Mahapram boosted the numbers, so that in 1718 there were fifty seminarians, divided into six classes where philosophy, theology, classics, Latin, and Oriental languages were taught.[10] Unfortunately the success of the seminary seems to have provoked the jealous hostility of the Portuguese. Fr. Roost was accused of Jansenism and had to plead his cause with his bishop. Young Andrew Li, who was a student in theology by then, gave proof of his proficiency in Latin by boldly defending his rector. In 1725, Andrew Li, aged thirty-three, was ordained priest by Bishop Louis Champion de Cicé, (1648–1737), vicar apostolic in Siam.

---

[9] Ibid., p. 130, quoting Launay, *Histoire des Missions de Chine*, vol. 1, p. 92, who himself quotes the last will and testament of La Baluère, dictated in Latin to Andrew Li on Oct. 15, 1715; A.M.E., vol. 431, p. 13.

[10] According to Paul Destombes, M.E.P., *Le Collège général de la Société des Missions étrangères de Paris 1665–1932* (Hong Kong: Nazareth, 1934), p. 41.

Fr. Andrew Li, like his colleague Fr. Anthony Tang, now considered that he belonged to the Paris Foreign Missions, which had been responsible for his training and from which he received a small salary. For a year he worked at the college and then went to Guangzhou in September 1726 and put himself at the disposal of Fr. Antoine Guignes (d. 1741), the procurator of the Paris Foreign Missions in China, who made him take the anti-Jansenist oath that had recently (1713) been required by the bull *Unigenitus* of Pope Clement XI. Fr. Guignes then sent him to Fujian Province, where the district of Xinghua was still administered by the Paris Foreign Missions, although most of the province was entrusted to the Spanish Dominicans. Anthony Tang soon joined him there. Both these young priests found the first years of their ministry encouraging. Andrew had a great admiration for Fr. Pedro Sans I Jorda, O.P. (1680–1747), who was to become vicar apostolic of Fujian and to be martyred in 1747 (see Appendix D: *Saints and Blessed from China as Listed in the Roman Martyrology 2001*, under May 26).

Persecution broke out in Fujian in 1729 so that Andrew had to take refuge in the south of the province, in the Linding and Zhangzhou districts. He fell ill and went to Guangzhou in 1731 to recover. With Anthony Tang, he taught three students who were due to go to the General College.

In 1732, Fr. Andrew Li was sent by his Paris Foreign Missions superior to Sichuan, only to find that the Vincentian vicar apostolic, Bishop Johannes Müllener, was the only one in Sichuan Province (the M.E.P. vicar apostolic, Bishop de Lionne, having died in 1713) and that he intended to administer the Church with his Vincentian colleagues only. He, too, had worked hard at promoting Chinese vocations and had ordained Fr. Paul Su in 1722.

There was nothing for it but to go elsewhere, so Andrew Li accepted a mission in Huguang, the old name for the present-day provinces of Hunan and Hubei. For two years he lived at Hengdishi (Hubei), where he had to win the approval of a Portuguese Jesuit, Fr. Duarte, who had founded the Christian community there. In 1733 a priest from the province of Auvergne in France joined him, Fr. Joachim Enjobert de Martiliat, M.E.P. (1706–1755). Both of them were determined to find a way of entering Sichuan, on the grounds that the Paris Foreign Missions had been working in that province at the beginning of the century. They left Xiangtan in Hunan and reached the Yangzi River at Jingsha. There they met Fr. Luigi Maria Maggi, an Italian Dominican, who was gravely ill, with a high temperature and a pain in his leg. Fr. Li nursed him back to health, and Fr. Maggi, wanting to help the two M.E.P. priests, wrote to Bishop Müllener on their behalf, pointing out that the Congregation *de Propaganda Fide* gave a certain latitude to vicars apostolic as to whom they authorized to work in their area. Fr. Li and Fr. de Martiliat followed the course of the Yangzi River upstream and, although Bishop Müllener's attitude was hardly enthusiastic when Fr. Andrew Li arrived at Chengdu at the end of 1734, managed to find a base in Sichuan Province. The bishop sent a message through Fr. Su that Andrew Li was not authorized to live in Chengdu; he was only to visit Christians up to a distance of sixty to 120 miles (100 to 200 kilometers) to the southwest of Chengdu, from Qionglai to Pengshan, and as far as Yazhou in the direction of Tibet. Immediately, Fr. Li began to visit conscientiously the small Christian communities in the area. For three years he instructed, baptized, and strengthened in the faith converts who had been more or less faithful up till then. In spite of this evidence of Fr. Li's outstanding pastoral zeal, Bishop Müllener remained unforthcoming and obviously did not want him in Sichuan Province, referring repeatedly to the territorial directives of the Congregation *de Propaganda Fide*. Fr. Li always answered him point by point, indicating the imprecision of these directives, and continuing his work regardless. In March new directives came from Rome, authorizing Fr. de Martiliat and the Paris Foreign Missions to stay in Sichuan Province. Bishop Müllener then entrusted to Andrew Li those areas where he had already been at work, as well as the town of Leshan (Kiatin) further south, hoping that he would make an attempt at entering Yunnan Province.

Fr. Li did in fact move in that direction. He made Pengshan his base. With Fr. de Martiliat and the catechist Lin Chang, he prepared the foundation of Christian communities in Leshan and even further south at Yibin (Suifu), but he also made sure that he had a base in the capital city of Sichuan Province by buying a house in Chengdu for 120 dollars.

Afflicted in Every Way but Not Crushed
(2 Corinthians 4:8)

In 1740 Fr. Andrew Li had his first experience of being humiliated before a Chinese court of law. He was arrested at the beginning of July because there was a drought in the region of Pengshan, and, since the prayers of the Buddhist monks were ineffective, Christians were blamed for the spell causing the drought. Fr. de Martiliat noted this brief account of the cross-questioning:

> He [the judge] called Mr. Andrew with the Christian Simon Choay. He questioned him on what he did, on the pupils, and then he said, "The Christian religion is a bad religion and forbidden by our superiors, and yet you still dare to teach it to others?" He answered, "The religion is true, it is not bad; I have never heard that it has been prohibited, and my family has been Christian for more than three generations." "How dare you say that it is not bad? Slap him across the face." He was slapped ten times across the face with an instrument like the sole of a shoe. He then said to him, "You deserve to be condemned, but as I see that your limbs are disabled I grant you mercy."[11]

Fr. Andrew Li got away lightly on this occasion because the chief officer of the guards of the court came from the same village as he did. This is an example of *tongxiang*, "helping people who come from the same village". However, Fr. Li was to have further and much more painful dealings with the courts.

Persecution succeeded persecution for various minor reasons, and Fr. Li was involved, either directly or indirectly. Any Christian known to be harboring a European priest could be in serious trouble; sometimes foreign priests would give themselves up to the authorities in order to avoid the worst. Sometimes priests brought trouble on themselves, like Jean-Hyacinthe de Verthamon, M.E.P. (b. 1700), member of a noble family in the French province of Périgord, who threw caution to the winds and considered any prudent course of action as cowardice. He was arrested (in 1745 or 1747), and, when Fr. Li told him that the thing to do was to make a small offering to the magistrate, he flatly refused. Expelled from China in 1752, he wrote contemptuously, "It was the Christians who forced me to leave." Many

---

[11] Quoted from *Journal de Joachim Enjobert de Martiliat*, June 1740, A.M.E. 434, p. 593, by Launay, *Histoire des Missions de Chine*, vol. 1, p. 171.

Christians, no doubt, were not particularly brave either. A man from Sichuan, who had given up Christianity, said, "Europeans get away with being exiled; we are the ones who are beaten."

Fr. Andrew Li was arrested again in 1754, at the same time as Fr. Urbain Lefebvre, who had managed to gain entry into Sichuan Province, but was arrested as soon as he arrived. Fr. Li appeared before the judge four times and, on his fourth appearance, was given twenty strokes of the cane. Fr. Lefebvre was sent back to Macao and wrote an account of his adventures, in which he tells of Fr. Li's strength and calm:

> Andrew Li was questioned about other Christians and refused to give any names. When he was asked how long he had been a Christian, he said that his ancestors had been Christians. The most remarkable part of his interrogation went as follows; the mandarin said to him, "You are over seventy and you are a Christian, yet you are without honor or nobility. We, however, as you can see, are influential in the empire, and we have rank and degrees, from which you can deduce that everything that your religion promises is vain and unreasonable." The priest answered, "The Christian religion does not promise a passing or earthly happiness, but it promises eternal bliss to all, and to everyone who adores the true God, follows the commandments, and listens to the voice of conscience."[12]

In 1761 there was trouble again when ill-intentioned non-Christian neighbors denounced some Christians who had not observed the traditional rites during the funeral of one of their relatives. The police raided the house at Chengdu, confiscated books in Latin and Chinese and liturgical vestments, and arrested a few Christians and students who were in the house. Fr. Andrew Li was not far away and came back at once to the provincial capital. He gave a reasonable explanation of how the books and vestments came to be in his possession and obtained freedom for the prisoners, but he himself was put into the cangue, a heavy wooden board which was locked round the neck. The sentence was to wear it for seventy days and to receive forty strokes of the cane, but fortunately it was reduced because of his age and because of the celebration of the seventieth birthday of the dowager empress.

These frequent vexations from the judges were but a small part of the troubles that Andrew Li had to face all through his life. He often

---

[12] Ibid., p. 314.

had serious bouts of illness. In 1745, when he had had an ulcer on the foot for more than a year, he made a vow to St. Joseph and then applied a poultice of lard and fish, whereupon the ulcer was cured. Far worse for the priest was the mental suffering caused by the behavior of bad Catholics: lapsation, apostasy, denunciations, betrayals, quarrels, indiscretions, and calumnies. He bore it all with patience. The Cross of Jesus Christ was at the center of his spiritual life. The words of encouragement that he wrote to one of his Chinese colleagues reveal the secret of his perseverance:

> The heart of the priest should above all burn with ardent love for the honor of God and with great zeal for the salvation of souls. If he is totally devoted to these, he will consider as nothing the labors and the sorrows of his ministry, the sacrifice of his blood and even of his life. He will offer these up with a great and generous heart, like a holocaust offered in homage to the truth of the Gospel.
>
> Our Lord, when he offered himself up as a mediator between God and men, humiliated himself and became obedient unto death, even death on a Cross. . . .
>
> Which of the ministers of the Lord, serving such a master, would nourish in his heart any other ambition than to imitate, during his whole life, the humility and the patience of the Lord Jesus.[13]

I Believed and Therefore I Spoke (2 Corinthians 4:13)

Andrew Li carried the treasure that is the Gospel in a "vessel of clay", but the power of the Spirit manifested itself by his speech, his writings, and his constant concern for the Christian communities for which he was responsible. His pastoral ministry shows how preoccupied he was with instructing the faithful, introducing them to prayer and to the life of the sacraments, and correcting them with gentle patience when they fell away. He knew how to combine firmness, prudence, and understanding. He began, in 1740, to translate the Catechism of the Council of Trent into Chinese, and he also translated

---

[13] French translation in Jean-Marie Sédès, *Une grand âme sacerdotale: Le prêtre chinois André Ly 1692–1775* (Paris: Desclée de Brouwer, 1944), p. 117. Latin original in *Journal d'André Ly 1746–1763*, ed. Adrien Launay, (Hong Kong: Nazareth, 1924), 2nd ed., p. 262, under Nov. 3, 1753. "*Quidem et ante omnia, in corde ministri evangelici primas obtineat ardens divini honoris cultus amor, et ingens salutis animarum zelus.*"

lessons that Fr. Basset, M.E.P., had prepared for recent converts. He drew up an order of service for Christian funerals, integrating suitable local customs into the ceremony. Due to the circumstances, he was really taking on the full responsibilities of a head of mission.

Bishop Müllener died in 1742, whereupon Bishop Maggi, O.P., who had been his coadjutor for three years, succeeded. Andrew Li had nursed Fr. Luigi Maggi back to health eight years previously at Jingsha, but unfortunately in 1743 Fr. Maggi died also, whereupon Fr. de Martiliat, M.E.P., who was already vicar apostolic for Yunnan Province, took on responsibility for Sichuan as well. Persecution then ensued (1746–1747) so that Fr. de Martiliat was forced to leave China and died in Rome in 1755. Andrew Li was therefore left as the only priest in Sichuan. It was then that he decided to keep a diary so as to perform his ministry with due attention to the directives of the Church.

Fr. Li's diary is really an account of his pastoral work, which he could submit every year to his superiors in Macao. It contains the details of more than fifteen years of work, from June 15, 1747, to the end of 1763. He looked after all the Christian communities of the province, whatever their nationality or their origin. His one regret was that he could not give the sacrament of confirmation to recent converts. In 1751 Fr. Li drew up regulations for marriages, which were accommodating as regards the marriages between Christians and non-Christians. His overriding concern was the welfare of persons, and this led him to put forward proposals that were sometimes wide of canonical regulations. For instance, he was concerned about young women who had been abandoned by their husband. Sometimes the man had left years previously, and everything seemed to indicate that he had done so for good, leaving the wife without means of support and exposed to many dangers. Could such women not be granted permission to remarry? He wrote:

> Few are the women strong enough, by a special grace of God, to live chastely without their husband. Often when they lack the essentials to feed or to clothe themselves, they lose all modesty and turn to prostitution or, even worse, they hang themselves or take poison. . . . That being so, it would be better if the Church were to fix an exact lapse of time, after which a woman, who does not know whether her husband is alive or dead, could proceed to a second marriage, rather than remain in

a state where she is without any support and in grave danger of losing both body and soul.[14]

He also drew up regulations for reconciling to the Church after a public penance those who had publicly renounced the Catholic faith. He always radiated compassion and hope and did everything possible to help those Christians who were in difficulty, but at the same time he was firm on essentials and would not give the sacraments to Christians who were totally uninstructed in the faith.

Fr. Li was very happy when two Chinese priests joined him in 1749. They were Fr. Luke Li and Fr. Stephen Xu, who had been ordained at Macao two years previously. In 1753 came a decree from Rome, which officially entrusted Sichuan Province to the Paris Foreign Missions. Unfortunately no one at the time considered the possibility of appointing Fr. Andrew Li as vicar apostolic, although he had been exercising that ministry in fact for the previous seven years. Europeans considered themselves as the only ones capable of directing the life of the Church, even when there were no Europeans available.

Therefore a young French priest, François Pottier (1726–1792), who had been ordained at Tours in 1753, arrived in Sichuan three years later with the title of pro-vicar apostolic and responsibility for the five or six thousand Christians scattered throughout the province. Fortunately he had enough humility and common sense to realize that he had everything to learn from the Chinese priests who had toiled on their own for the previous ten years. The year of his arrival, Fr. Pottier wrote a letter for the directors of the seminary of the *Missions Étrangères* in Paris, which gave a detailed description of the pastoral methods of Fr. Andrew Li (whom he calls Monsieur André).

October 20, 1756

Monsieur André has the following principles:

1) In the evening he is present at communal prayer and, immediately afterward, a school child or someone else asks some questions from the catechism, everyone being present; each time six or seven questions with the same number of answers are gone through.

2) When he has to bring extreme unction [the sacrament of the sick] to the father or the mother of a family, he first brings together all the

---

[14] Launay, *Histoire des Missions de Chine*, vol. 1. p. 304.

children, large and small, in-laws and others less related, so that they can ask forgiveness from the father or mother for any offenses they may have committed against them. I have seen the ceremony once. The children were in tears, and so was the father, who was to receive the sacrament, and who gave them a little exhortation. It really was very moving.

3) Whenever he leaves a house where he has stayed while administering the community in a certain area, he blesses the house, and also the fields if that is possible. He also blesses other houses if he is called upon to do so. . . .

6) He admits no one to confession without instructing them on the Ten Commandments, the commandments of the Church, and on the sacrament of confession. After confession, he does not admit them to Communion without their having heard the instruction on Communion, the Mass, indulgences, etc. . . .

7) Since most of the Christians are ignorant and simple and do not know how to make their thanksgiving immediately after Mass when they have been to Communion, the missionary makes his thanksgiving out loud, and the Christians who have been to Communion make it with him, repeating it after him.[15]

Educating Christians in the beliefs of their faith was at the center of Fr. Li's concerns. He did not want ritual bereft of understanding and insisted on explaining sacramental practices as part of his doctrine classes. That is why he composed or translated a whole range of little books as guides for confession, Communion, the Mass, and the rites of marriage and funerals. He also produced collections of prayers, and every year he saw to the printing of a liturgical calendar. He also wrote a book of apologetics, giving a survey of the three traditional Chinese religions and contrasting them with the truth proclaimed by Christian teaching. He translated books of meditation and composed a treatise of moral theology, because of his concern for the education of Chinese seminarians and priests.

Concern for Vocations

As Fr. Andrew Li got older, he worried increasingly about vocations to the priesthood. In Chengdu he watched over a group of children

---

[15] Ibid., pp. 297, 298, from A.M.E. 445, p. 809: *Lettres aux Directeurs des Missions Étrangères*, October 20, 1756.

to whom he taught Latin. He was good at Latin himself and was in favor of a thorough priestly training so that Chinese priests would be as well educated as European ones. He considered that a knowledge of Latin was essential for Chinese priests to have access to the sources of doctrine: Scripture, the writings of the Fathers of the Church, the decrees of the Magisterium. He also thought that Chinese priests would only be respected by foreigners if they knew Latin. That is why he regretted that there were not more priests coming from the General College in Thailand; on the other hand, he welcomed the good results of the Chinese College of the Holy Family, founded in Naples by Fr. Matteo Ripa in 1732.

Fr. Li's last years were in fact devoted to the training of seminarians. Fr. Pottier having sold the house in Chengdu in 1764, Fr. Li moved with seven students to a cottage in Fenghuangshan, some four miles (seven kilometers) to the west of Chengdu. His poor little school reminded Fr. Li of the stable at Bethlehem, and he called it the Seminary of the Nativity. Although he was becoming very deaf, he was still able to teach; and then in 1770 the secret seminary was betrayed to the authorities; the cottage was destroyed; shepherd and flock were dispersed. The students were sent to the General Seminary in Thailand, where they did not persevere. Andrew Li, having completed his long course in the service of the Gospel, died in 1774.

Ten years previously, when Fr. Li was already unwell and handicapped, he had been considered for episcopal ordination. At the time, a member of staff at the Seminary of the Foreign Missions in Paris, Fr. Kerhervé, was invited to become vicar apostolic of Sichuan Province. His health was not good, and he pointed out that Fr. Andrew Li would be much better qualified to take on such a task. He wrote to Monsieur Christophe de Lalanne, superior of the Paris Seminary of the Foreign Missions, "Andrew Li would carry out this task much better. Everyone considers that this venerable priest is the heart and soul of the mission."[16]

---

[16] Olichon, *Aux origines du clergé chinois*, p. 394.

SYNODUS

VICARIATUS SUTCHUENSIS

HABITA

IN DISTRICTU CIVITATIS

TCONG KING TCHEOU

Anno 1803.

Diebus secunda, quinta, et nona
Septembris.

ROMAE MDCCCXXII.

TYPIS SACRAE CONGREGATIONIS
DE PROPAGANDA FIDE.

The Synod of Sichuan

Title page of the *Acta* of the Synod of Sichuan, printed in Rome in 1822
by the Congregation *de Propaganda Fide*. In the eighteenth century Christianity was able to develop in Sichuan Province, largely through the ef-

forts of a remarkable Chinese priest, Andrew Li, born in Shaanxi Province and trained at the Seminary of the *Missions Étrangères de Paris* in Thailand. From 1734 until his death in 1774 he built up small Catholic communities in Sichuan by visiting them regularly and producing practical instructions for many aspects of Church life, including the training of catechists. By 1802 there were sixteen Chinese priests and an estimated 40,000 Christians in Sichuan, which made it possible for Bishop Gabriel-Taurin Dufresse, Vicar Apostolic, to call a synod of priests, meeting near Chongqingzhou, west of Chengdu, in 1803. Bishop Dufresse was martyred in Chengdu in 1815 and canonized by Pope John Paul II in 2000. © Archives of Propaganda, Rome.

This tribute came rather late, but it was nonetheless significant. Fr. Li had in fact acted as head of the mission and had shown great faith, devotion, and pastoral sense. His humble work laid the foundation of the Church in Sichuan. In 1766 and 1767 three French priests and one Chinese priest came to the province. Fr. Li seems to have had a premonition of their arrival and had announced it with joy two months previously. When Fr. Martin Moye (1730–1793) came to Sichuan in 1773, he discovered with amazement the task that had been accomplished by Andrew Li. He considered that there was no equal to this Chinese priest, either for the excellence of his character or for the number of his writings or for his strength in adversity. He wrote, "Andrew Li did not know what it was to be afraid."

When Fr. Pottier became vicar apostolic for Sichuan in 1769 (as opposed to pro-vicar, which he had been before), he worked effectively for more than twenty years to develop the missions. He took up again the education of future priests in Sichuan itself and founded a seminary in 1780 at Longki (Longxi) near the border with Yunnan Province. Between 1780 and 1814, forty priests came from this seminary, which was transferred to Luoranggou shortly after its foundation.

By the end of the eighteenth century, the Church in Sichuan was relatively prosperous, in spite of many setbacks and the insecurity of the Catholic Church in China as a whole. It had been estimated in 1756 that there were in the province 4,000 Christians and two priests; by 1802 the numbers had risen to 40,000 Christians and sixteen Chinese priests. The pastoral experience that had been created made it possible to compose a directory, laying down the conditions of Christian life and the ministry of the sacraments. In 1803 the vicar apostolic was Bishop Jean-Gabriel Dufresse (1750–1815), who was later to die a martyr's death. He called the first synod to be held in China in modern times. It met near Chongqingzhou, a day's walk west of Chengdu, and brought together thirteen Chinese and two French priests. The decisions were mainly concerned with the sacraments. Chapter 10 of the directory considered the ministry of priests and recommended fervor in their spiritual life and discretion in temporal matters. The directives of the Synod of Sichuan were to guide the apostolate in the province until the Synod of Shanghai in 1924.

17

CATECHISTS WITNESS TO THE FAITH

When all the Catholic priests were expelled from Sichuan Province in 1707, only the catechist Lin Chang remained. He traveled from one end of the province to the other and looked after the Christians well. Six years later, Fr. de la Baluère returned and, as he lay dying in 1715, entrusted his seminarians, who had already been tonsured, to Lin Chang with these words:

> Don't be too soft on the students. Make sure that they are always busy in ways useful for their salvation. They should obey you in everything . . . if Monsieur Le Blanc[1] or anyone else in authority asks for these pupils, let him have them, but they should come back to you later; then you can go to preach the Gospel and to assist the Christians.[2]

In 1719, Bishop Müllener appointed Lin Chang as general catechist for the whole province. He was so outstanding that he received the clerical tonsure and was ordained acolyte. Two years later, a Muslim named Ma Hongji plotted with an official, also Muslim, to acquire the church in Chengdu and transform it into a mosque. Both addressed an accusation to the mandarin Yun Xianzhong, letting him hope for a substantial monetary benefit. They thus provoked a persecution against Christians, and Lin Chang was arrested and tortured. While in prison, he managed to convert one of his fellow prisoners. Bishop de Cicé considered the possibility of ordaining him priest, and Lin Chang was set to learning the canon of the Mass by heart, but, although he preached very well in Chinese, he was completely incapable of reading an alphabet or pronouncing Latin sounds. He continued his work of evangelization to the end and died on August 6, 1745.

In many ways, Sichuan was favorable ground for evangelization, as the largest migration of modern times in China took place in the

---

[1] Fr. Philibert Le Blanc, M.E.P. (1644–1720), was vicar apostolic of Yunnan Province.

[2] Armand Olichon, *Aux origines du clergé chinois. Le père André Ly Missionaire au Se-Tchouan 1692–1775* (Paris: Bloud & Gay, 1933), p. 131.

seventeenth and eighteenth centuries to this southwestern province, which had up till then been desolate and sparsely populated. The population went up from an estimated two million in 1680 to fifteen million in 1760, mainly by immigration from the provinces of Hubei, Guangdong, Fujian, and Jiangxi.[3] The imperial administration attempted to control immigration and to provide institutions for the protection and moral support of settlers. Some of these institutions had religious affiliations, such as the *huiguan*, which were mutual-assistance organizations based on the place of origin of a particular group of settlers. "Most *huiguan* were organized as temples dedicated to the deities or patron saints of the provinces that sent migrants to Sichuan."[4] Immigrants could receive from them not only a sense of security and belonging, but also spiritual comfort. They could also find a vision of the world that seemed more meaningful than orthodox Confucianism. Popular religions based on communities thus opened on to the prospect of a better life for individuals, both in this world and in the next. This could lead to joining one of the sects, especially the White Lotus Sect in the case of Sichuan,[5] and it could also lead to conversion to Christianity.[6] It is significant that women were especially active in the White Lotus Sect[7] and that, as indicated in the following chapter, some Catholic women also adopted an active apostolic role in Sichuan. Muslims were an important minority, engaged in commerce rather than farming, dwelling in cities and towns and forming close-knit communities.[8]

The Vocation of a Catechist

The influence of a man like Lin Chang clearly shows that catechists were not just interpreters for the foreign priest who could not speak

---

[3] See Jean Charbonnier, *Les 120 Martyrs de Chine canonisés le 1er Octobre 2000* (Paris: Églises d'Asie), p. 29. Robert Eric Entenmann, "Migration and Settlement in Sichuan 1644–1796" (unpublished doctoral dissertation, University of Harvard, Cambridge, Mass., 1982), pp. 157–79, 255.

[4] Entenmann, "Migration and Settlement in Sichuan 1644–1796", p. 188.

[5] Ibid., pp. 191–93.

[6] Ibid., pp. 194–96.

[7] Ibid., pp. 236–37.

[8] Ibid., p. 191. Muslims in Sichuan numbered "perhaps 400,000" at the beginning of the twentieth century.

Chinese. Fr. Andrew Li was convinced that theirs was a specific vocation, and he composed a special ceremony for the installation of a catechist. In his diary, he gives an account of such a ceremony in the Christian community at Taoba, near Chongqing:

December 9, 1755

Following the custom of Early Christians, after three days of fasting and public prayers, because we could not proceed to an election as we were so few in number, we drew lots for three catechists from the Lieou family.

After Mass had been celebrated for them and in front of the priests and the faithful, the three were invited to lay hands on the crucifix and to swear the following oath:

"I, the undersigned, _____, having been called in spite of my unworthiness to the office of catechist, and considering that I do not have the right to refuse the request of my superiors and the unanimous call of my fellow Christians; humbly prostrate before the altar of Our Lord Jesus Christ crucified and his representative; in the presence of my relatives and friends, I swear and promise, from the heart and by the words of my mouth, to fulfill my duties faithfully by the grace of God.

I will be fair, never yielding to a consideration of persons. I will scrupulously and obediently watch over the promulgation and execution of orders from religious leaders, which concern the interests of the Church. I will never take the liberty of concealing anything concerning them.

If ever I should break my vow and my oath, if by my bad example I should do harm to religion and thus deserve to be removed from my office, I shall spontaneously own up to my fault, and I submit in advance and willingly to the penances that will be imposed on me by my superiors."[9]

The phraseology of the oath suggests that some of the catechists were probably not of the same caliber as Lin Chang. It also happened that conversions to Christianity and submission to its discipline caused violent reactions from the family. Quarrels, denunciations, and calumnies could be provoked by the demands of Christian marriage, the ban on loans at high interest, the taking of vows of virginity, and the rejection of the traditional cult of the ancestors. Catechists, who had the duty of applying Church discipline, were the first victims of such tensions. Some of them just kept quiet about

---

[9] Olichon, *Aux origines du clergé chinois*, pp. 322–23.

the more awkward rules of Christian life. Others were involved in deals involving money and became victims of blackmail. Most of the catechists were fathers of families who worked voluntarily and who had to consider the welfare of their families. It was not they who attracted converts, but rather those who had just become Christians and were full of zeal for spreading the faith.

There were, however, other catechists who worked for the Church full time, announced the Gospel to nonbelievers, and visited Christian communities. From such catechists came vocations to the priesthood. The *Monita ad Missionarios*, "Directives for Missionaries", issued by Bishop François Pallu and Bishop Lambert de la Motte in 1664 when they were at Ayutthaya in Thailand, give some indications of this. Missionaries were requested by the *Monita* to appoint a catechist or someone at the head of each local community with a view to creating a local Church. They were also to select those most responsible as candidates for the priesthood. In fact, a time of service as catechist was the best testing for future priests. This is what happened in the case of Benedict Sun, John Baptist Jiang, and Augustine Zhao Rong, who accompanied Fr. Jean-Martin Moye, M.E.P., on his pastoral rounds. Benedict Sun was ordained priest in 1777 by Bishop Pottier after five years of service. He died in prison nine years later. John Baptist Jiang and Augustine Zhao Rong were ordained priests in 1781 after having spent barely one year in the new seminary at Longki.[10] Zhao Rong (1746–1815) had an unusual preparation for the priesthood. He was born in a family with no Christian connections and enrolled in the imperial army when he was twenty. In his hometown of Wuchuan, in Guizhou Province, Zhao witnessed the repression of Christians in 1774, and, among a group of prisoners, he met Fr. Jean-Martin Moye, who made a deep impression on him by his charity, the way he prayed, and the forcefulness of his catechesis. When Fr. Moye was released, Zhao went with him and was baptized at the age of thirty on St. Augustine's Day, taking Augustine as his Christian name. He spent the next five years helping priests and learning about the life of the Church on the ground. When the Chinese priest who was his guide told Bishop Pottier about him, and how fearless and effective he was, Zhao was ordained and sent, after

---

[10] François Gourdon, "Le clergé indigène au Setchoan", *Bulletin des Missions Étrangères* 22 (1923): 603.

a few years, to lay the foundation of a difficult mission among the Lolo ethnic minority in Yunnan Province.[11]

At the time of the violent persecution under the Jiaqing emperor (r. 1736–1820), Zhao Rong was taking the sacraments of the sick to someone's home when he was identified by a criminal and taken to the court of justice at Qionglai in Sichuan and from there in a sedan chair to the provincial capital at Chengdu. The judge treated him harshly, ridiculing his faith and having no regard for his seventy-three years. He was given seventy strokes on the shins with a bamboo stick and then eighty blows on the face with a leather sole. He died in prison a few days later on January 27, 1815.[12] St. Augustine Zhao Rong now heads the list of the 120 Chinese martyrs who were canonized by Pope John Paul II on October 1, 2000.[13] The feast of all the 120 Chinese martyrs canonized by Pope John Paul II on October 1, 2000, is celebrated on July 9, under the title *Sanctorum Augustini Zhao Rong, presbyteri, et sociorum, martyrum*. In addition, St. Augustine Zhao Rong is commemorated on March 21, though with the proviso that he died *die incerto*.

Bishop Gabriel Taurin Dufresse also died in the Sichuan persecution of 1815. He had been a bishop for fifteen years by then and had been in East Asia since 1776. Gabriel Dufresse was a native of the mountainous region of the Auvergne, in central France, and a priest of the Paris Foreign Missions. Once he arrived in Sichuan, he spent his first nine years learning Chinese and visiting isolated Christian homesteads in the north of the province. He was arrested and deported in 1785 to the Philippines but came back secretly four years later and took up his ministry again, this time in the province of Guizhou and west Sichuan. There was a lull in persecution at

---

[11] The Lolo, also known as the Yi, are a farming people who also had a reputation as warriors. They now number about 6.5 million, and inhabit mostly Yunnan and Sichuan Provinces. Most of them live in mountainous areas where they grow cash crops and gather wild plants for herbal medicine. They speak six different dialects, belonging to the Tibeto-Burman group of the Sino-Tibetan linguistic family. The history of the Lolo can be traced back at least 2,000 years. They seem to have developed their own culture in relative isolation. They produced their own system of writing (in which each sign represented a syllable), their own solar calendar, and until 1949 they practiced slavery in the remote area of (Mount) Liang Shan on the Yunnan-Myanmar border. There is a Lolo religion, which is animistic and based on the belief that all things have a good or bad spirit in them. See E.C., *sub nomen* Yi.

[12] Charbonnier, *Les 120 Martyrs de Chine*, pp. 32–33.

[13] See Appendix D.

the time, and Dufresse was consecrated bishop at Chengdu (July 25, 1800). As mentioned in the previous chapter, he was able to preside over the first synod in 1803. In 1815 persecutions broke out again with dire results. Some 800 Christians were brought to trial in Chengdu at various times, and, of these, 740 renounced the Christian faith on the spot. Bishop Dufresse had to go into hiding and move continually from place to place. He went to seek refuge with some Christians near Xinjin, some eighteen miles (thirty kilometers) south of Chengdu, but he had been seen. The local mandarin was informed that a European had been carried across the river by a young man called Dong Laojiu. The young man was apprehended and beaten so severely that he gave the bishop's hiding place away. That was on May 18, 1815. After that, Bishop Dufresse was interrogated several times and appeared before a series of courts of justice of increasing importance, until the final judgment on September 13, 1815 which took place toward midnight in the palace of the viceroy of Chengdu. The viceroy had followed the case closely and had decided to condemn the bishop to death, without referring to the emperor. After the act of accusation had been read, the viceroy asked the prisoner: "Does the matter stand thus?" "The matter stands thus", replied the bishop, and was condemned forthwith to decapitation.

The bishop was then taken just over a mile (two kilometers) beyond the north gate of the city to the place of execution. Thirty Christians accompanied him and were told by the mandarin that they would be hanged unless they renounced Jesus Christ. One of them immediately did so, but the others remained steadfast. They knelt before Bishop Dufresse, asking him to absolve their sins and to give them a last blessing. He gave them a short exhortation and then bowed to the executioner, who struck off his head with one blow of his saber. He was sixty-four years old and had been a priest for thirty-nine years. The prisoners who had been brought along with him were not executed but were condemned to exile.[14] St. Gabriel Taurin Dufresse is one of the 120 Chinese martyrs canonized by Pope John Paul II. He is commemorated in the Roman martyrology on September 14.

---

[14] See Charbonnier, *Les 120 Martyrs de Chine*, pp. 26–28, 33–35.

Two catechists of exceptional quality were also canonized in 2000, Peter Wu Guosheng (1768–1814) and Joseph Zhang Dapeng (1754–1815).[15] They were both from Guizhou Province, which had been evangelized from the east part of Sichuan. Christians in this area of southwest China were often the victims of local persecutions, but, because these attracted attention, this sometimes had the result of producing conversions. The majority of the population at that time were tired of the brutality of corrupt mandarins, so that a popular slogan was *fan Qing fu Ming*, "overthrow the Qing (Dynasty); restore the Ming (Dynasty)". The Sect of the White Lotus and other groups hostile to the government were becoming more active, and Christians, who were also classed officially as *xie jiao*, "subversive sect", sometimes profited from the effects of such antigovernment trends.

In times of government repression, however, Christians were victimized. The repression could be brutal, but it was not continuous. Many local mandarins wanted to maintain peace and ignored the illegal activities of religious groups, although some of them, with an eye to making money, profited from arrests, which entailed the confiscation of property, and from imprisonment, which led to bribery to secure release.

At the end of the eighteenth century the *Nouvelles Lettres Édifiantes* (vol. 1, p. xiii) noted an increase in the number of conversions to the Catholic Church in Sichuan, Yunnan, and Guizhou Provinces. The number of adult baptisms were as follows:

1786	469
1792	1,508
1795	1,401
1800	1,250
1804	2,143

In Guizhou Province, there were 600 Catholics in 1799.[16] Such was the background to the fruitful apostolate of Peter Wu and Joseph Zhang.

---

[15] Ibid., pp. 42–48. St. Joseph Zhang Dapeng is commemorated in the Roman martyrology on March 12, and St. Peter Wu Guosheng on November 7.

[16] Adrien Launay, *Histoire générale de la Société des Missions étrangères*, vol. 2, p. 393.

Wu Guosheng came from Longping, some eighteen miles (thirty kilometers) to the southeast of Zunyi. Today the beautiful church at Zunyi has been transformed into a memorial to the glory of Mao Zedong because it was there that the leaders of the Red Army met in January 1935 during the Long March. Wu Guosheng's parents were nonbelievers from a humble background. They were poor, but they were honest and, because people trusted them, they were able to open an inn. It happened that one day Guosheng welcomed a traveler from Sichuan who was a Christian and spoke to him about Jesus Christ. Guosheng was a man of good will and with an open mind. He accepted the message of the Gospel and was so happy with this discovery that he shared it with his parents and invited them to honor the true God as well. The inn soon became a meeting place for Christians. Guosheng was very direct in his methods. He would hail passersby, get them to sit down, and start to tell them about God. Fr. Matthias Luo from Sichuan, who had been ordained in 1783, heard about him and came personally to Longping. There he could see for himself how strong Guosheng's faith was, but he found his way of doing things rather excessive. He put him to the test and did not baptize him straightaway, sending him to Sichuan, where he stayed with Catholics of long standing. Guosheng spent some time at Chongqing and realized that his behavior did not really correspond to the teaching of Jesus. He changed his ways, and Fr. Luo baptized him finally in 1796, giving him the name Peter.

Thus strengthened in the faith, Guosheng proclaimed the Gospel more effectively and created Christian communities that soon numbered several hundred. He was arrested during one of the persecutions and did not try to escape, since he was wearing chains for the sake of Christ. Once in prison, he supported the new Christians who were with him, and they all prayed together out loud. The mandarin ordered him to trample on the crucifix and abjure his faith, but he preferred to face death, reciting the Rosary on the way to execution. As he passed his friends, they laid gifts on the way, and when he reached the place where he was to die, he knelt down, raised his eyes to heaven, and cried out with a loud voice, "O heaven, heaven, my dwelling place! I see the glory of heaven; I see Jesus the Savior." He was executed on November 7, 1814, at the age of forty-six. The Christians of that region claim that many miracles have taken place through his intercession, and even nonbelievers invoke his protection. His tomb was spared during the Cultural Revolution of 1966, and pilgrims go there regularly and plant lots of little crosses in the ground.

Zhang Dapeng: Martyr from Guiyang

Catholics in Guizhou also venerate the martyr Zhang Dapeng. He was fourteen years older than Wu Guosheng and came from Duyun, some sixty miles (one hundred kilometers) to the east of Guiyang, the provincial capital. He sought uprightness and inner purity, and he joined at first *Qingshuijiao* (The Religion of Pure Water), a group who fasted and were connected with the Sect of the White Lotus. Then he adopted the teaching of Taoist masters.

When he was forty, he settled in Guiyang as the business partner of a certain Wang, a silk merchant. Wang's son had gone to Beijing to obtain the *Juren* degree with a view to entering the civil service, and while he was there he met some Christians, who introduced him to the Gospel. Wang's son was glad to obtain his degree, but he was even more proud to be baptized and to be called Xavier. He brought back a whole stock of Christian books, which Zhang Dapeng began to read, especially the catechism. As he became more and more interested in the teachings of Christianity, he very much wanted to be baptized, but there were difficulties. His first wife having remained childless, Dapeng had married a concubine, who bore him a son. For a time he decided to give up the idea of baptism, whereupon Fr. Matthias Luo sent the catechist Laurence Hu Shilu and other Christians from Sichuan, intending to open a mission in Guiyang with some of the converts that Xavier Wang had made. They convinced Dapeng that he should change his lifestyle so as to receive the grace of baptism, and he therefore separated from the concubine, making provision for her future. She was given a dowry and was married to a Christian. In 1798 Dapeng went to Longping, where the catechist Peter Wu gave him a warm welcome and Fr. Matthias Luo admitted him to the catechumenate, so that he could start preparing for baptism.

There was, however, strong opposition from Zhang's family. Some of his relatives were mandarins, and his two younger brothers, who were adopted, occupied posts in the administration of justice. They thought that if Dapeng became a Christian, they would be dishonored and would even be in danger, and this was borne out by what had happened to Xavier Wang. He was reported to the authorities by his uncle, who was displeased by the number of conversions taking place round him. Wang's father had to pay a heavy fine, and Wang's family were distraught and forbade Christians from holding meetings in their house. Dapeng left and opened a small shop where he exchanged *sapeks*.[17] Dapeng and his friends managed to save enough to buy a house in a secluded place, outside Guiyang's Luguanmen Gate. There they could meet without attracting attention and welcome the priest when he came to visit. Dapeng was baptized in 1801 by Fr. Matthias Luo, on the spot where Guiyang Cathedral now stands. He chose Joseph as his baptismal name and proclaimed the Gospel with even greater enthusiasm.

Dapeng's adopted brothers, however, were furious at what had happened. One of them denounced Catholics as members of the Sect of the White Lotus, particularly the catechist Laurence Hu, who was arrested on May 5, 1801, with some other Christians. Joseph Dapeng was away at the time on a business trip, however, and thus avoided the raid by the authorities. He was always careful not to put himself unnecessarily at risk. Once danger was past, Dapeng returned to Guiyang, where according to Bishop Louis Faurie, who was vicar apostolic of Guiyang in the 1860s, he was remembered as having been "the heart and soul of the Mission".[18]

Dapeng converted his wife and Anthony, his son by the concubine, who had been retained by his father according to Chinese usage. Many people came to Dapeng's talks, including several women. He also visited an old people's home, where he gave alms and spoke about God. Unfortunately, the director of the home took offense at this. He was about to report Dapeng, who hastily disappeared and went to stay for several months at Xingyi, on the borders of Yunnan Province. When he returned, Fr. John Tang asked him to run a school, where he taught the catechism for three years.

There was another crisis in 1812, when the Sect of the White Lotus rose up in revolt. Christians were accused of being involved and suffered in consequence. Dapeng got out in time, but ten or so

---

[17] The *sapek* was the smallest coin in imperial China, worth a thousandth part of a tael. A tael was worth one ounce of silver.

[18] Quoted by Adrien Launay, *Les Trente cinq vénérables serviteurs de Dieu, français, annamites chinois, mis à mort pour la Foi en Extrême-Orient de 1815 à 1862* (Paris: Lethielleux, 1909), p. 308.

Christians were arrested, including Anthony, his son, who was only eighteen. The young man was threatened and then promised favors if he would reveal his father's hiding place, but he steadfastly refused. He was exiled to Longcun, to the east of Guizhou Province, where he died the following year. Dapeng was grief-stricken by the loss of his son, but he kept his heart free of all hatred and went on spreading the Gospel even more zealously. However, he did not feel safe at Xingyi and withdrew as far as Chongqing in Sichuan Province, where he met Bishop Jean-Gabriel Dufresse. The bishop saw the strength of his faith and advised him to return to Guiyang, where he could comfort the faithful and give them guidance. He said:

> My son, why do you flee when your brothers are in danger? You have a wonderful opportunity for serving God. By going away, have you not abandoned the duties of your office and thus harmed yourself? I beg you to return immediately to Guizhou. Go back to the faithful. Your office of catechumen requires that you watch over them.[19]

Dapeng received the sacrament of reconciliation and Holy Communion and then traveled back to Guiyang, where he was obliged to wander from one hiding place to another. He converted yet another nine people, when the governor of the city put a price on his head. It was his wife's younger brother who betrayed him in 1815 for the money, leading the officers of the court to his hiding place in person. When they saw his great height and his white hair, they treated him with respect as they brought him back to the city in chains. Once he was in prison, he met many Christian friends, who were harshly treated but remained firm in the faith. Dapeng appeared before four tribunals, and the governor, out of regard for his family, offered to release him if he would simply agree to apostatize. He flatly refused, in spite of the repeated pleas of his family and friends. He was finally sentenced to death and heard the news without showing any emotion, regretting only that he could not go to confession or receive Communion. This capital sentence was referred to Beijing, which at that time could be reached in forty days by the imperial mail. On January 22, 1815, the Jiaqing emperor confirmed execution by hanging.[20] It was on March 12 in Guiyang that Joseph Dapeng was led to the place of execution, and, as he approached, people noticed that there were

---

[19] Ibid., pp. 309–10.
[20] Charbonnier, *Les 120 Martyrs de Chine*, p. 48.

tears in his eyes. His friends asked him why, and he answered, "They are tears of joy. Pray to God for me." His parents threw themselves at his feet, begging him to change his mind. "Please don't cry", he said. "I am dying because of faith in God, not for having committed a crime." The executioners then put a rope round his neck and hanged him from a gibbet in the form of a **T**. He was beatified in 1909 by Pope Pius X and canonized by Pope John Paul II in 2000.

Catechists and Their Ministry

By the witness of their blood, the catechists of China contributed to the laying of the foundation of their Church. Gradually their ministry evolved in two ways. Some were responsible for the local community, and some were traveling evangelists. Those responsible locally had a permanent role as *huizhang*, "head of a community", or as the teacher of a small school where they taught the catechism. Traveling evangelists were more fully committed to the service of the Gospel, whether they accompanied a priest or were sent alone on a mission. Their task was the conversion of nonbelievers, which implied that they had sufficient training in apologetics and theology. They often gave instruction to converts also.

Whether looking after an area or traveling, catechists were required to be without reproach as regards their faith and their way of life. A bad catechist could ruin a community that had been built up at the cost of much sweat and blood.

Bishop de Martiliat, vicar apostolic of Yunnan, became administrator of Sichuan, Huguang (Hunan and Hubei), and Guizhou when Bishop Maggi died in 1744. He was the first one to compose a rule for catechists, which is summarized in sixteen paragraphs:

1. Daily meditation; Communion once a month.
2. Cultivate the virtues of humility, patience, love of one's neighbor; study doctrine thoroughly by doing some spiritual reading every day.
3. Welcome converts but with prudence; examine their intentions, their moral conduct, and their character.
4. Baptize the children of Christians, if they are in danger of death; baptize adults who are dying if they have the faith and are well disposed.
5. Teach Christians the laws of marriage and make sure they observe them.

6. Keep accounts of the offerings made by the faithful; be responsible for books and holy pictures.

7. Visit the sick, tell the priest about them, and visit the dying if the priest is away.

8. Make arrangement for funerals.

9. Look after widows and orphans.

10. Reconcile Christians when they quarrel.

11. Admonish those Christians who are drunkards, gamblers, quarrelsome, or lazy.

12. If a Christian has not come to church for a month, find out the reason for his absence.

13. In the absence of the priest, bring Christians together on Sundays and holy days of obligation; lead the prayers and announce the feasts and days of abstinence for the following week; read from a book chosen by the bishop; instruct catechumens.

14. Explain the catechism to children and encourage parents to watch over the education of their children.

15. If the priest in charge of the community is less than six miles (ten kilometers) away, go to see him every first Sunday of the month; if not, then go to see him at Easter and on the feast of the Assumption, bringing a report on any problems in the community.

16. Read over these regulations every first Sunday of the month.[21]

For a long time these regulations were to guide the later developments of the office of catechists. In several regions of China, schools for catechists were created, and eventually these offered more developed courses for catechetics. The main characteristics of the catechist's ministry, however, were established more permanently during the eighteenth century: it evolved among the poor population of the provinces; at a time when foreign priests were, more often than not, absent; and when Chinese priests also had to go into hiding.

Today one still meets catechists who are *huizhang*, leaders of the community, fully aware of their duties. In 1986 some young Christians from Singapore, who were visiting the churches of north China, were greatly impressed by one of the catechists. The visitors were active militants, trained by Catholic Action groups in Singapore. They thought that they would help the Christians of Xi'an by bringing them publications that were unobtainable on the mainland. On Sun-

---

[21] Following Jos. Jennes, C.I.C.M., *Four Centuries of Catechetics in China* (Taipei: Huaming, 1976), pp. 108–9. English translation of a Flemish original.

day morning they came across a *huizhang*, and it was the visitors who were strengthened in their faith. The local catechist was glad to welcome these young Christians who had come from so far away, and he invited them to his home and began to comment on a Gospel passage in a powerful and lively way. He said to them, "It is Sunday, and it is my duty as a catechist to instruct you today."

18

APOSTLES FOR WOMEN

The dedication shown by the consecrated virgins in the Catholic Church was equal to that of the catechists. Catechists were mostly involved with male Chinese. The virgins gave a service that complemented that of the catechists and was directed at women and children. These two ministries of male catechists and consecrated virgins had developed in the same historical and geographical circumstances. They were the product of a popular and provincial milieu during a time of persecution. The most fervent center of this sort was to be found in the southeastern province of Fujian during the seventeenth century under the influence of Spanish Dominicans. Later on French priests of the Paris Foreign Missions learned from the Fujian experience and transferred certain pastoral methods to the western provinces of Sichuan, Yunnan, and Guizhou. The Vincentians and Jesuits, who were facing the same problems, adopted a similar approach in central and northern China.

Consecrated Life

The Spanish historian José Maria Gonzalez, O.P., devoted one chapter of his study of the Dominicans in China to the heroic struggle of the consecrated virgin Petronilla Teing.[1] She came from a rich non-Christian family from Xiapu southeast of Fu'an and was brought up a Buddhist. Like the Buddhist monks, she would undertake long fasts. Her mother came from the Hong family in the village of Tingtao, where there were many Christians, and when Petronilla went to stay there, she would be warned against the Christians in case she became a Catholic. "Me a Catholic!" she would say "Never!"

---

[1] José Maria Gonzalez, O.P., *Historia de las Misiones Dominicanas in Sina*, vol. 1, 1632–1700 (Madrid, 1964), chap. 10, pp. 181–84: "Conversión y lucha heroica de la virgen cristiana Petronilla Teing".

However, Gonzalez says that, because she was a girl, her curiosity was aroused, and she made discreet inquiries of her maternal grandfather. "What is the religion of Christians?" she asked. The grandfather knew about Christians, since there were already so many of them in Tingtao. He explained to her, "Christians adore a supreme Lord of heaven and earth. He is infinite. All things, visible and invisible, have their origin in him. They say that those who follow his law obtain heaven as their reward, but that those who are evil are punished in hell for eternity." The child was profoundly troubled by these words and began to fear that she might be in error. She had another uncle called Peter, who was a Christian and a member of the scholar-gentry, and she received more information from him. She then decided to become a Christian, even if it were to cost her life. Her mother tried to put her off and told her that, when people are baptized, the priest opens them up with a great knife and pours water inside them to wash away the sins inside them. The little girl was not very happy with this information, but she did observe that the village was full of Christians who had not expired as a result of their baptism. Why should she be the only one to die of baptism? Anyway, if she did die, would she not enter at once into a blissful eternity? Finally, the mother herself decided to become a Christian and was baptized at the same time as her daughter, who was eleven years old.

When Petronilla reached the age of eighteen, she made a solemn promise to consecrate her virginity to the Lord, according to the rule of the third order of St. Dominic. A great change came over her life then. She had been the only daughter of a well-considered family who was beautiful and rather pretentious and wasted her time in futile pursuits. She now began to spend a long time in prayer, to fast, and to get up in the middle of the night to recite matins, as in a monastery. These penances prepared her, in fact, for much worse trials later on. When she was twelve, her father had promised her in marriage to a young man who was a Christian. When he and his family heard that she had made a vow of virginity, they were very disappointed at having lost the prospect of such a fine marriage, not to mention the bride-price that they had paid for her. When her parents offered to return the bride-price, the groom and his parents refused and demanded that the contract of marriage be maintained. Petronilla's parents decided to avoid a lawsuit by sending her to her fiancé's house. She spent the whole of Lent doing penance, planned to cut her hair short on Good

Friday and then to run away to Tingtao and seek refuge with some of her relations there. Christian friends then thought of a scheme to save face. She was to agree to go through all the exterior ceremonies of marriage, on condition that she would be freed eight days later by the family of her would-be husband. Petronilla was naive enough to accept such a charade, but she was determined to make her situation clear. She entered the wedding hall in all her wedding attire, then took off all her jewels and laid them on a table, saying, "Here are all my jewels. I give them back to him who gave them to me. He will be free to marry whom he will. I remain free for my Jesus." There was utter dismay. All the ladies present begged Petronilla to change her mind, but she remained firm and was left in her room with a serving maid, sent by the Christians of Muyang.

The would-be bridegroom then began to play up. Forgetting his promise, he made a scene in Petronilla's room, chased away the servant, and tried to seduce Petronilla. She maintained her composure and spent the whole night in prayer before a picture of the Savior. Next morning, Fr. de Capillas[2] arrived to comfort her and to reprimand the bridegroom, who had not kept his side of the bargain. By this time, he was eaten up with desire and began to put pressure on Petronilla, without however daring to go into her presence. Meanwhile, she was being pressured to such an extent by her relatives and friends that she decided to make a bold gesture. In front of everybody, she took a pair of scissors and cut off her long tresses.

Her mother was at her side and supported her during all these trials, but the groom's family was relentless, seized the mother, and put her on a boat to Tingtao. Petronilla was left all on her own, was not allowed to see the missionaries, and was told that, even if she were in danger of death, she would not be allowed to go to confession. She replied coolly that she would make an act of contrition and her sins would be forgiven.

The young man was so frustrated that he lost confidence in his Christian faith and listened to those who told him that a miracle would happen and Petronilla would be his if he sacrificed to the local

---

[2] The Spanish Dominican Francesco Fernandez de Capillas (1607–1648) was to be beheaded at Fu'an on Jan. 15, 1648, after a year in prison. He is the proto-martyr of China and was canonized with the other Chinese martyrs by Pope John Paul II in 2000. His commemoration in the Roman martyrology is on Jan. 15. See Jean Charbonnier, *Les 120 Martyrs de Chine*, pp. 17–18.

gods, which he did. This gave him confidence to try another onslaught on Patronilla's bedroom, but she was so exasperated that she seized a chamberpot and emptied the contents on his head. He roused the whole neighborhood by his screams, and, once he had washed and changed his clothes, he came back with a stick and thrashed her. Her father and brothers intervened in time to save her life and hid her in another room. Now it was the turn of her family to face reprisals. In the end she and her whole family left the district and went to live in Fu'an. Petronilla had won after an ordeal that had lasted seven months.

She was now able to lead a regular life of prayer and mortification and converted her father and her whole family to Christianity. In fact, she was to be revered in the whole region as the founder of the Catholic community of Xiapu and the first Dominican tertiary. In Fu'an she is considered a saint. To this day the Catholics of Xiapu have remained great fighters, who are ready to suffer all sorts of indignities for the faith. In 1988 there was a seminary of the underground Church in the area, training young priests for the service of such irrepressible Christians.

Petronilla's story illustrated the considerable cultural shock that was caused by the arrival of Christianity in rural China. Today certain aspects of the evangelization of those days would be presented differently—for instance, the stark choice between the threat of hell and the offer of heaven, the immediate introduction to the demanding spirituality of religious orders issuing from the Middle Ages, and the slight attention given to local traditions concerning marriage and the family. However, parallels can be found in the history of the early Church for a stark and demanding presentation of Christianity, which nevertheless laid solid foundations for the future.

The Dominicans themselves derived some important lessons from what might be called the somewhat crude evangelization of their first years in China. They soon put together sensible regulations for consecrated virgins in Fujian, and these were taken up later by Bishop de Martiliat, the vicar apostolic of Yunnan, when he also became responsible for Catholics in Sichuan, Huguang (covering present-day Hunan and Hubei), and Guizhou Provinces. He promulgated on November 1, 1744, a rule, which adapted the principles of religious life to the special circumstances of Christian virgins in China. He emphasized the essentials: a retired life in the family's home, prayer, obedience, manual labor, and a life of spiritual simplicity and detachment. No vows were to be taken before the age of twenty-five. This first form of consecrated life excluded any apostolic work outside the home. These virgins were only to be apostles within their family.

Catechetical Instruction for Women and Children

During the last decades of the eighteenth century, consecrated virgins in China were called to come out of their isolation and to take an active part in the Christian instruction of women and girls. This was due largely to Fr. Jean-Martin Moye (1730–1793), who was pro-vicar apostolic in east Sichuan and Guizhou Provinces from 1773. Moye was a priest of the Paris Foreign Missions who spent some ten years in China before being expelled during the persecution of 1784–1785. Before going to East Asia, he had founded the Sisters of Providence in Lorraine for the free education of village children but, once back in France, he had to flee because of the Revolution and died in Trier.[3]

Fr. Moye's first impression in China was that the women were more faithful and dedicated than the men, but that their education was very deficient. Most of them could not read and were obliged to learn prayers by heart. Fr. Moye realized how much consecrated virgins could contribute to the Church in China. He was the first to entrust them with missionary work and to use their help to start small schools for girls. Unfortunately, his first attempts were not successful and put the project in danger of being abandoned. One of the tasks that Fr. Moye entrusted to women was the baptism of babies in danger of death. He attached great importance to this work of salvation, having been influenced by the theological considerations of a French Vincentian, Fr. Pierre Lollet.[4] Infant mortality was high in Sichuan Province because of famines and epidemics, and Fr. Moye considered that the pastoral care of neonates was being neglected. He trained women called *baptiseuses* to baptize these babies, all of whom,

---

[3] For Jean-Martin Moye, M.E.P., see ibid., pp. 223–27. He was beatified by Pope Pius XII in 1954 and is commemorated in the Roman martyrology on May 4.

[4] In 1764 Fr. Jean-Martin Moye had had a leaflet printed, *Du soin extrême qu'on doit avoir du baptême des enfants*. This was a four-page resumé of the treatise *Embriologia sacra . . .* (Palermo, 1745) by Francesco Emmanuele Cangiamila, which was approved by Pope Benedict XIV in 1756. See Cangiamila in D.T.C. 2, c. 1507.

unfortunately, died after having received eternal life through baptism. Catherine Luo, near Chongqing, was reported to have baptized 2,000 babies; 30,000 were baptized between 1778 and 1779. Malicious rumors began to circulate among the population to the effect that "baptism kills babies".[5] It was necessary to be more discreet, and pastoral directives were soon sent out to that effect.

Fr. Moye's campaign and the overzealous activity of the *baptiseuses* probably hampered his wider plans for starting apostolic work that consecrated virgins could undertake. He wanted to make them voluntary catechists and teachers for girls. Here his experience as founder of the Sisters of Providence stood him in good stead, and he modified the rule composed by Bishop de Martiliat for consecrated virgins, to produce an institute that would be more structured and would have its own spirituality. Fr. Moye had a French colleague, Fr. Jean François Gleyo, M.E.P. (1734–1786), who was opposed to his project to begin with, but changed his mind after having conveniently seen a vision. His advice to Fr. Moye about the proposed institution was, "It should be founded on devotion and intimate consecration to the Blessed Virgin. If I had to choose, I would call them *Daughters of the Congregation of the Blessed Virgin*."[6]

The status of consecrated virgins already existed within the Catholic Church; Fr. Moye's great contribution was to make them into catechists. Fr. Jean Guennou writes, "The founder considered them as the Chinese branch of the Congregation of Providence, for he wrote to the sisters in Europe on May 29, 1781, 'I explained to them our four fundamental virtues, simplicity, abandonment to providence, poverty, and charity, and I said to them that these are the four columns on which we are building our edifice.' "[7]

Fr. Moye was very demanding where the spiritual life was concerned and tried to make prayer accessible to the uneducated and to the poorest. He simplified the texts of prayers written by the Jesuits and by Fr. Andrew Li, and he wrote his own. He composed meditations that could be said between each Hail Mary of the Rosary so as

---

[5] Georges Goyau, *Jean-Martin Moye, missionaire en Chine 1772–1783* (Paris: Alsatia, 1937), p. 97.

[6] Ibid., p. 141, quoting A.M.E. 501:275.

[7] Jean Guennou, M.E.P., *Une spiritualité missionaire Le bienheureux Jean Martin Moye 1730–1793* (Paris: Apostolat des éditions, 1970), p. 222.

to encourage the imitation of Mary. Some of his prayers were to be recited with one's arms stretched out in the form of a cross.

The vicar apostolic of Sichuan Province, Bishop Pottier, was rather worried about this exaggerated devotion. It seemed to him that, after too many baptisms, there were now too many prayers. He and Bishop Jean Didier de Saint-Martin, who became his coadjutor in 1783, were opposed at first to the creation of a new institute for active consecrated virgins. They pointed out the practical drawbacks of the project: the teachers are too young; they live too far from their families so as to be near their pupils; they are exposed to various dangers, not least calumnies from non-Christians; sometimes they lead the prayers of the assembly when men are present. The two bishops felt that, the local mentality being what it was, such practices were bound to cause scandal.

Bishop Pottier realized that it was an important issue and referred to Rome for guidance. By an instruction dated April 29, 1784, the Congregation *de Propaganda Fide* gave a decisive ruling. It approved the creation of girls' schools managed by consecrated virgins, as long as certain conditions were observed. The consecrated virgins were not to preach or to read publicly to congregations. They were not to take any vows before the age of twenty-five, and these were only for three years at a time; their parents were to be capable of providing for their upkeep; those who were in charge of educating girls had to be at least thirty years old; teaching could only be given in their own family home or in a house designated by the priest. Bishop de Saint-Martin added further details in a pastoral letter of September 1, 1793. Those consecrated virgins who were teaching women catechists had to be at least forty years old; they had to be well instructed doctrinally and to teach by way of conversation and not as if giving sermons; they were not to instruct men, unless the latter were in danger of death.

These regulations were to be maintained for more than a century. Later, there was an attempt to make the consecrated virgins live in community and to transform their institutes into a religious congregation. Bishop René Boisguérin, M.E.P., thought that this was a mistake. He had come to China in 1928 and worked in Sichuan Province for twenty-three years, first as a priest, then as Bishop of Yibin (Suifu). His comments on the ministry of consecrated virgins were made in 1983 in a private letter:

When I arrived in China as a missionary in 1928, they were still in existence and formed the core of our teachers of religion. For 150 years, living as they did in families, they taught generations of Christians. In 1932, there was an attempt to "institutionalize" them by turning them into nuns. This was probably a mistake from the point of view of the apostolate. Religious life imposed strict rules that limited their work. To my way of thinking, the two styles of life could have been maintained as distinct, and this would greatly have furthered their effectiveness. During the ten years when I was living in the countryside, I had Chinese consecrated virgins teaching doctrine in my schools. . . . They were solidly trained doctrinally, and their dedication to the Church was without bounds. . . . Since they did not live in community, they were always available. They played an outstanding role in the evangelization of Sichuan.[8]

Virgin and Martyr

The consecrated virgins in China were as heroic as their brother catechists and did not hesitate to shed their blood in the service of the Gospel. One of the first to be martyred was Agatha Lin (Lin Zhao), an apostle for the women of Guizhou Province, who was the first to evangelize the Miao people.[9]

Lin Zhao came from the village of Machang in the Qinglong district of Guizhou. Her father was a salt merchant, and he and his wife were fervent Christians who had been converted by Zhang Dapeng,

---

[8] Letter of Jan. 5, 1983, from Bishop Boisguérin to Fr. Pierre Jeanne. (Papers of the China Service of the *Missions Étrangères* in Paris.) Bishop Boisguérin's comments were contaned in a letter dated January 5, 1983, sent to Father Pierre Jeanne from Liverpool. Bishop René Boisguérin (1901–1998), of the Paris Foreign Missions, a native of Falaise in Normandy, came to China in 1928 and worked in Sichuan Province for twenty-three years, first as a priest then, from 1946, as vicar apostolic and Bishop of Yibin (Suifu). In 1951 the Communists put him in prison, where he was harshly treated; after having beem condemned for espionage at a public trial, he was expelled from China in 1952. Once he was back in Europe, Bishop Boisguérin was asked by the Congregation for the Propagation of the Faith to be responsible for the Chinese Catholic community in England and Wales, a task that he carried out for over thirty years. In 1986 he returned to France, dying in Provence in 1998.

[9] The Miao (also called the Hmong) are one of China's minority ethnic groups. There are c. 7.4 million Miao (1990 census) living in the southwestern provinces. They also inhabit neighboring Vietnam, Laos, and Thailand, mostly in mountainous areas, where they practice slash-and-burn agriculture. Their religion is a form of spirit worship to maintain contact with their ancestors. See E.C., *sub nomen* Miao, p. 323.

while he had taken refuge in their region. When Lin Zhao was born in 1817, her father was in prison for having refused to renounce the Catholic faith, and he only came back three years later. Agatha had been baptized by her mother when she was only three days old. The little girl was pretty and bright, and her parents loved her dearly. They taught her to read and write, and her mother made her an expert needlewoman. According to custom, her father agreed to a marriage contract for her when she was still a child. She knew nothing of this and decided later to consecrate her life to God. When she reached the age of eighteen, her father revealed to her that she was promised to a certain Liu. She explained that it was quite impossible as she had consecrated her life to God, and she backed this up with lengthy spiritual arguments. Her parents did not insist and annulled the contract.

That year, a priest called Fr. Matthew Liu passed through the village of Machang, and Agatha told him about her plan. He advised her father to send her to Guiyang, the capital of Guizhou Province, where the consecrated virgin, Annie Yuan from Sichuan, had opened a school for girls. Agatha eagerly started to study, but after two months the school had to close because of persecution. The pupils were sent home, but Agatha went with the head teacher to Longping, near Zunyi, where she continued her studies for two years. When she returned home, she found her mother on her own because her father had been arrested again. Agatha stayed at home with her aging mother and read a lot in her spare time.

Fr. Matthew had noticed how capable Agatha was and asked her to teach the girls in the area. When she was twenty-five, she duly made her vows, according to the rules put in place by Bishop de Martiliat a hundred years previously. After her father's death, Agatha and her mother went to stay with some relatives in the district of Zhenning. There she made several converts and managed to open premises for their meetings.

Bishop Étienne Albrand, consecrated in March 1849, was then administrator of the Catholics in Guizhou Province, and he soon noticed Agatha's exceptional qualities. He asked her to come to Guiyang and entrusted her with the direction of a house of formation for consecrated virgins. She had to do a lot of walking, up hill and down dale, to follow up her pupils in their families, and this was partic-

ularly painful because her feet had been deformed by being bound
when she was a child, according to the custom of Chinese well-to-do
families. With the help of a walking stick, she cheerfully kept going.
Her father having left her some money after his death, Agatha was
able to buy a house near Xingyi, which was both chapel and school,
and also some land, which provided income for the expenses of the
priest when he came to visit. She herself lived on very little and did
not even buy a coffin, as local custom required. She was much respected for the example that she gave and prevented many Christians
from falling away.

In 1854, a year after the death of Bishop Albrand, the new administrator of the diocese, Fr. Paul Perny, sent Agatha to Maokou, a
Miao village in Langdai district, where she was to see to the education of women. She found this new assignment difficult, as she was
dealing with people who could not read or write, but she accepted
the challenge with infinite patience. She went to live in the house of
the traveling catechist Jerome Lu Tingmei (1811–1856), an unusual
Miao who had studied the Chinese classics. When he was a young
man, he sought for the truth and became a fervent adept of *Qingshui
jiao*, "the religion of pure water", as Augustine Zhang Dapeng had
been before becoming a Christian. Lu Tingmei had been converted
by reading Christian books and became the apostle of the Miao, not
only in Guizhou Province but also in Guangxi.

After two long years, Agatha had the joy of seeing her Miao converts receiving baptism. Fr. Perny noted that without her it would
have been impossible to maintain the outpost at Maokou. Agatha was
perhaps worn out by the difficulties of her work, because she is reported as saying to her pupils that she would like to follow the example of her holy patron and shed her blood for Christ. St. Agatha
was a Christian martyr in Sicily who was cruelly tortured in the third
century. Agatha Lin Zhao's wish was soon to be granted.

At the beginning of 1858 a magistrate from Guiyang raided the village of Maokou. Agatha and the catechist Jerome Lu Tingmei were
arrested and brought to court together. The judge asked her why
she was not married; such immoral behavior would indicate that she
belonged to a subversive sect. Agatha replied coolly that triumphal
arches were erected in honor of young widows who had remained
virgins all their lives. He then asked what she, a Han Chinese, was
doing among the Miao. She replied, "I have come to teach them the

books. . . . In this region, the girls do not know the Chinese language and Chinese manners; that is what I teach them, so that they can make a good marriage and converse easily with their husband's relatives. I also teach them to be obedient. Finally these girls learn to give to everybody the honor that is their due."[10] It was difficult to fault such a program; nevertheless Agatha and Jerome Lu Tingmei were condemned to death. She and Jerome were dragged down to the riverside, where they knelt side by side. The executioner struck her several times with his cutlass before she collapsed and her head was severed from her body. Agatha and Jerome, the first Miao martyr, were put to death on January 28, 1858. They were beatified by Pope Pius X in 1909 and canonized with the 120 Chinese martyrs in 2000.[11]

Many other consecrated virgins have their place among the martyrs of China: Lucy Yi (Yi Zhenmei) from Sichuan, executed in Guizhou four years after Agatha; Rose Fan (Fan Hui) and Mary Fu (Fu Guilin), both from Hebei, massacred by the Boxers in 1900. Many more sacrificed their lives in the service of the Gospel, in conditions of poverty and insecurity, often perishing through beatings and subjected to insults. The Vincentians have recorded their passing in Hubei and Hebei, the Jesuits in Jiangsu, Henan, and Anhui. The legacy of such intrepid women is far from having died out. Fearless women like them continue to make their contribution to the Church in China. In January 1988, thirty bishops from Asia gathered in Hong Kong for a study week on the life of the Church in China. During the Eucharist, commemoration was made of the martyrs of today. On the altar were two relics from Inner Mongolia. One was a broken pectoral cross which had been picked up in the street; the other was the dress of a young girl who had been beaten to death for having professed her faith in Christ.

---

[10] Quoted in Adrien Launay, *Mission de Kouy-tcheou*, p. 500.

[11] For a fuller account of Agatha Lin Zhao, see Jean Charbonnier, *Les 120 Martyrs de Chine*, pp. 92–101. Agatha and Jerome Lu Tingmei are now celebrated together with the saint martyrs of China on July 9. They are also commemorated in the Roman Martyrology on January 28.

IV

THE COLONIAL PERIOD: AMBIVALENT EXPANSION

The countries of Europe, while they were going through their Industrial Revolution, were rivals in the search for markets throughout the world. The colonial powers compelled China to open up to outside trade, so that the Christians of China, now overshadowed by new missions from the West, found themselves under the protection of foreign interests. Such foreign interventions came as a shock to the Chinese, a people proud of their culture and independence, and they provoked antiforeign feelings. The first victims of this xenophobia were the Chinese Christians, who appeared as traitors to their country. Scattered as they were in the various provinces, they were exposed to the fury of the population and to the cruelty of local mandarins. The progress made by the Church in the nineteenth century was largely destroyed by the Boxer Rebellion of 1900.

The first half of the twentieth century was marked by the fall of the Manchu Empire and by an attempt at nationalistic modernization. This gave Christians, both Catholics and Protestants, greater opportunities for serving the country's progress. They were soon, however, overtaken by new revolutionary forces, which adopted popular antiforeigner feeling, so that little weight was attached to the social services provided by Christians or to their participation in the struggle against the Japanese invasion. China's new masters condemned them as being the "running dogs" of imperialism.

1. *Upper Part of the Xi'an Stele*
The stele, made in 781 A.D., records the coming of monks from the East Syrian Church to Xi'an in 635 A.D. Above the inscription and the cross, a sphere is held by two dragons, intertwined scaly creatures resembling lizards with large jaws, who symbolize the imperial authority of the stele. © JPC

2. Dunhuang Painting of a Saint of the East Syrian Church
Painting on silk from the Mogao Grottoes, near Dunhuang in Gansu province;
brought to the British Museum, London, in 1909 by Sir Aurel Stein. The painting has three crosses characteristic of East Syrian design, with arms of equal
length widening from the center. The moustache and slight beard, both in red,
confirm a Christian identification. © The Trustees of the British Museum

3. *Details of the Dunhuang Painting*

Top image: Attempted reconstruction of the painting by the Japanese artist, Furuyama; P.Y. Saeki, *The Nestorian Documents and Relics in China* (Tokyo, Maruzen, 1951); illustration 21, facing p.408.

Bottom left: East Syrian Cross on the center of the headdress of the saint.

Bottom right: Two East Syrian crosses, one on the collar, the other below.

© The Trustees of the British Museum

4. *The Great Buddha of Leshan*
The image, carved on a cliff in Sichuan province in the 9th century A.D., is 230 feet (70 metres) high. © M. Emmanuel François-Sappey

5. *A Bronze Ordos Cross*
Cross found on the banks of the Yellow River near the Ordos Plateau. Size
2 inches (52 mm.) square; presented to Campion Hall, Oxford, by R. Strauss.
Since the beginning of the 20th century, several hundreds of these small crosses
have been dug up, often from graves, in the Ordos Plateau, an area which lies
north of the Ningxia-Hui Autonomous Region and south of the great bend of
the Yellow River in present-day Inner Mongolia. They were probably made by
the Christian Ongut tribe, who lived on the Ordos Plateau (9th to 11th century).
The swastika or fylfot, a Buddhist symbol of illumination, was a popular sign of
good luck, often represented on these crosses. Collection Campion Hall, Oxford.
© Campion Hall

6. Miniature of a Mongol King and Queen of Persia
13th–century Gospel lectionary in Syriac estrangela script. The reading for
the Feast of the Exaltation of the Holy Cross is accompanied by a miniature
showing the Emperor Constantine and Empress Helen holding the cross. They
have marked Mongol features and are probably intended to depict the Mongol
rulers of Iraq and Iran in the second half of the 13th century, Hulagu, Ilkhan
of Persia, and his Queen, Doguz. (Vatican Sir. 559, f.223v.). ©Vatican Library

7. *The Gold Cruciform Seal of the Patriarch of the East Syrian Church*
The device in red is the stamp of the seal of Yahballaha III, Patriarch of
Seleucia-Ctesiphon (1281–1317). The seal impression produces a square of 6¾
inches (17.3 cm.), with a Greek key border. Within the square is a Syrian cross
with arms widening from the center, on which an inscription in Turkish (written in the Syriac estrangela alphabet) records the command of the Mongol
Ilkhan: that prayers are to be offered for him and his descendants, that the
Patriarch is to be the sole guardian of the seal, and that Christian notables
and ecclesiastics are only to approach the Ilkhan with the permission of the
Patriarch. The impression of the seal (red ink) is on a letter written in Arabic
(black ink). At the bottom of the stamp, a few words have been added in Syriac
serto script (black ink): "[May] our Lord [be] with us all, amen." The variety of
languages and writings on the document illustrate the multi-cultural character of the Mongol Empire. The letter was sent in 1302 to Pope Boniface VIII
by Patriarch Yahballaha III, the young Christian Ongut from Mongolia, who
had come to Iraq as a pilgrim and had been elected Patriarch in 1281. Archivio
Segreto Vaticano, A.A. I–XVIII, 1800 (1). © Archivio Segreto Vaticano

8. *Portuguese Caravel*
Contemporary painted illustration of one of three Portuguese caravels
which sailed to Africa and Asia in 1552 under the command of Fernao Soares
de Albergaria; reproduced in *Memoria das Armadas,* published in the series
Comenoracoes dos Descobrimentos Portugueses by Instituto Cultural de
Macau, 1995. © Ricci Institute

9. *St Francis Xavier's Chapel on Shangchuan Island*
Francis Xavier died on Shangchuan Island on December 3, 1552, within sight of mainland China. His body was exhumed on February 17, 1553 and taken first to Melaka and then to Goa, India. © JPC

10. *Portraits of Paul Xu Guangxi and his grand-daughter Candida Xu*
Modern paintings of Paul Xu Guangxi and Candida Xu, exhibited in 1990 at the Holy Spirit Study Centre, Aberdeen, Hong Kong, at a yearly session of the China Bridge Group. Xu Guangxi (1562–1633), a member of the scholar-gentry from Shanghai, met Fr. Matteo Ricci at Nanjing and was baptized in 1603. Xu Guangxi worked in several departments of the imperial administration and was instrumental in bringing the Jesuits to Beijing in 1629 to revise the Chinese calendar. He established a house-church in Shanghai and was thus one of the founders of the strong Catholic tradition that later developed in Shanghai and has survived all the vicissitudes of history.

Candida Xu (1607–1680), Xu Guangxi's grand-daughter, was brought up in the Shanghai Catholic community. Married at sixteen and the mother of eight children, she made her house a center for the Catholic apostolate. She became a widow relatively early and devoted much of her life to raising funds so as to support priests in the adjoining provinces. © JPC

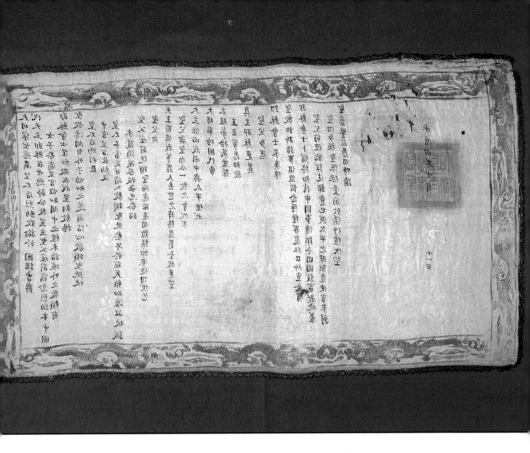

11. *Letter from the Chinese Empress Helen to Pope Innocent X 1650*
Letter of November 4, 1650 from the Dowager Empress Helen, mother of the
last emperor of the Ming dynasty, to Pope Innocent X. The letter, written on
silk, was taken by Fr Michael Boym, S.J., on the long and adventurous journey to Rome, which he reached in 1655, by which time Innocent X had died.
Alexander VII received the empress' letter, in which she informed the Pope that
she had been baptized and asked him to pray for her and to send more Jesuits
to China. She also prayed for the restoration of the Ming and said that she was
prepared, once peace had been restored to the vast Chinese empire, to send a
representative to Rome. (Vatican Library, Borg. Cin. 531). ©Vatican Library

12. *The Kangxi Emperor (1661-1722)*

Anonymous artist. The reign of the Kangxi emperor was the longest in the history of China and he is considered as one of the greatest and most cultured of its rulers. He had studied widely and commissioned many scholarly works, including the Kangxi Dictionary, which became for 200 years the standard dictionary of the Chinese language. During the Kangxi emperor's reign, the first treaty was concluded between China and a Western country, regulating the border between China and Russia. During the negotiations, two Jesuits acted as interpreters and counsellors for the Chinese delegation. (Treaty of Nerchinsk 1689). Unfortunately Cardinal de Tournon's ill-advised embassy to China (1705–10) altered the emperor's previously favorable attitude toward missionaries, half of whom were expelled from the country. © Ricci Institute

13. *Gold Medal of Pope Clement XI for the Year 1702*
The Holy See had the custom of illustrating various aspects of its policy by
striking gold medals every year. Clement XI (r. 1700–1721) had announced
in 1701 his intention of sending Charles de Tournon as legate to China to
resolve the controversy between missionaries over Confucian rites. The medal
for 1702 indicates in a general way the impulse that the Pope intended to
give to the missions. Enlarged. The reverse shows the Pope handing the book
of the Gospels to a missionary. Inscription: VADE ET PREDICA: GO AND
PREACH (Archivio Segreto Vaticano: A.A, Arm I-XVIII, 1790). © Archivio
Segreto Vaticano

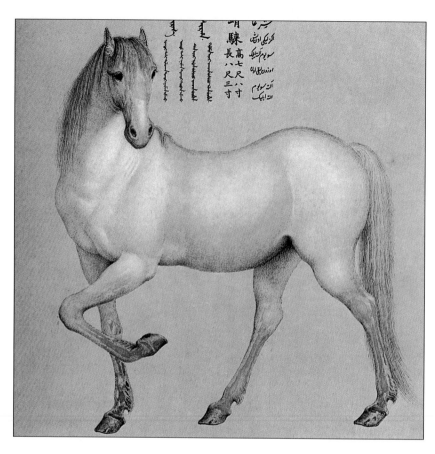

14. *One of the Four Steeds of Ferghana Painting by Castiglione*
One of four horses from Ferghana (Uzbekistan) presented to the Qianlong emperor c.1748 and painted by Giuseppe Castiglione. Castiglione (1688–1766), a Jesuit lay brother born in Milan, came to Beijing in 1715, where he worked as a painter for over fifty years. With other missionary painters, he became part of the ateliers of Chinese artists at court. Castiglione evolved a style of painting that combined Chinese medium with European practice, such as linear perspective, the use of shading to indicate volume and a more realistic representation through knowledge of anatomy, especially that of horses. He became the favorite European court painter of the Qianlong emperor. Portrait and description, in Manchu, Chinese and Arabic, of one of the most prized of imperial horses: measurements length 8 feet, 3 inches; height 7 feet, 8 inches.
© Ricci Institute

15. *Painting of the Qianlong Emperor on Horseback*
Painting by Giuseppe Castiglione, S.J. The Qianlong emperor (r. 1736–1795)
was himself a poet, painter and calligrapher; Castiglione was high in his favor
as an artist, which did not prevent the emperor from maintaining the policy of
excluding missionaries from China. Only those who were scientists, artists or
architects were officially tolerated and they were not allowed to receive converts.
© Ricci Institute

St. Joseph Zhang Dapeng, 1754–1815;
catechist.

St. Lucy Yi Zhenmei, 1815–1862;
consecrated virgin, catechist.

St. Anne Wang Cheng, 1886–1900;
consecrated virgin.

16. *Three Chinese Martyrs Canonized by Pope John Paul II on October 1, 2000*
Twentieth–century watercolors, from *Zhonghua xundao sheng ren zhuanlue*
(Brief Biographies of the Martyr Saints of China), published by the commission
of the Taiwan Bishops' Conference for the canonization of 120 Chinese martyrs.

17. *Cixi Empress Dowager of China*

Empress Dowager Cixi (b. 1835, d. 1908), wielded ruthless power through her
control of the imperial court during the final fifty years of the Qing dynasty and
was largely responsible for preventing the effective reform of the Chinese Empire.
Portrait of H.I.M. the Dowager Empress of China, Cixi (Tz'u Hsi), painted
in 1905–6 by Hubert Vos (1855–1935). Photograph by courtesy of the Fogg Art
Museum, Harvard University Art Museums, Cambridge, Massachusetts. Bequest
of Grenville L. Winthrop. © 2004 President and Fellows of Harvard College

18 A. *The Temple of Heaven, Tientan Park, Beijing* © JPC

18 B. *Schoolchildren at Beijing examine the sphere of heaven, devised by the Jesuit astronomer, Fr. Ferdinand Verbiest, in the 17th century* © JPC

19 A. *A Taoist priest in the Temple of the Eight Immortals (Ba xian an) at Xi'an, Shaanxi Province* © JPC

19 B. *The Taoist Temple of the Green Goat (Qingyang gong), Chengdu, Sichuan Province* © JPC

20 A. *The wheel of Dharma on the roof of the Jokhang Temple, at Lhasa, Tibet, flanked by the statue of two does, an allusion to the first sermon of the Buddha in the deer park at Sarnath, India* © iStockphoto.com/Alan Tobey

20 B. *A Tibetan Catholic Family in Yerkalo* © J.A. Rollin, M.E.P.

21 A. *Young lamas on the Jokhang Temple roof, Lhasa, Tibet* © JPC

21 B. *Mosque at Hohhot, Inner Mongolia, built at the time of the Ming dynasty* © JPC

22 A. *Confucian dance in the Confucian temple at Deyang, Sichuan Province, in 1992* © JPC

22 B. *The statue of Confucius in the Confucius Temple in Beijing, surrounded by students from Hong Kong* © JPC

23 A. *The Church of the Holy Redeemer, Beijing; called Beitang, "the North Church"; formerly the church of the French Mission in Beijing* © JPC

23 B. *Graves on land in Beijing granted by the emperor for the burial of Jesuits, and later Vincentians, working at court*
The cemetery is situated next to the Temple of the Five Pagodas (Wu ta si) in Beijing. The tombstone is that of Fr. Parennin, S.J. © JPC

24 A. *Cathedral of Guiyang, provincial capital of Guizhou Province*
The façade was damaged during the Cultural Revolution, leaving the building
in a bad state of repair. The church was fully renovated in 2005. © JPC

24 B. *Church of Dali, Yunnan Province, built in the style of the Bai ethnic group*
© J. A. Rollin, M.E.P.

25. *The Marian Basilica at Donglü*
In 1900 the Catholic village of Donglü in the Hebei plain was successfully defended for two months against a large force of Boxers. The Basilica was destroyed in the Cultural Revolution and rebuilt by local farmers in 1992.
© JPC

26. *Painting of the Holy Mother of China at Donglü*
The painting of the Blessed Virgin Mary and Child was blessed in 1924 and
venerated at Donglü, Hebei province, under the title of the Holy Mother of
China. The crowns, scepter and features are European in style. © JPC

27. Painting of the Madonna and Child by Lu Hong Nian
Archbishop Celso Costantini came to China in 1922 to represent Pope Pius XI
as Apostolic Delegate. He encouraged Catholics to develop higher studies and
inaugurated the Furen Catholic University at Beijing in 1927. Costantini was
a pioneer of "inculturation" before the word was used. He urged Catholics to
adopt Chinese styles of idiom, art and architecture. By chance he met Chen
Yuan De, a painter in the traditional manner, and asked him to use the text of
the New Testament, and not previous Christian iconography, as the basis for his
work. Archbishop Costantini baptized Chen in 1932 and gave him the name
Luke. Chen was influential in training a group of Christian artists and became
professor in the Art Department of Furen University. One of Chen's pupils was
Lu Hong Nian, whose painting of the Madonna and Child is characterized
by diaphanous tones and delicacy of line; he uses the depiction of a fairy in a
Chinese folktale to represent the Madonna.

28 A. *New cathedral at Zhouzhi, Shaanxi Province* © JPC

28 B. *Regional Seminary for the eastern provinces at Sheshan, 25 miles (40 kms) southwest of Shanghai* © JPC

29 A.*Major Seminary of the Hebei Province at Shijiazhuang, provincial capital of Hebei* © JPC

29 B. *Church at Shashi on the bank of the Yangzi River in Hubei Province, built with the help of Chinese Franciscans from America* © JPC

30 A. *The New Year ritual at the Holy Family Church, Taipei; Archbishop Stanislaus Lokuang, Archbishop of Taipei, celebrating the prayers for the ancestors in 1975* © JPC

30 B. *Chinese Bridge Church group meeting at Yangmingshan, Taiwan, with delegates from Hong Kong, Taiwan and Singapore, 1992* © JPC

31 A. *Shanghai, the east bank of the Huangpu (Pudong)* © JPC

31 B. *Catechesis for children; 1996 summer session at the shrine of Our Lady of Lourdes, Tangmuqiao, Shanghai* © JPC

32. *Saint Francis Assisi Cathedral in Xi'an, 17 Wuxing Street*
A candy factory, built during the Cultural Revolution to obstruct this facade, has lately been removed. © JPC

19

PRESSURE FROM THE WEST

The Western powers bear a heavy responsibility for having used force in 1840 so as to open China to foreign trade in order to promote the profitable sale of opium. In 1839 a conscientious civil servant called Lin Zexu had been sent to Guangzhou (Canton), and, since it was forbidden to import opium into China, he impounded 20,000 cases of opium in the port and expelled the British from the city. The latter retaliated by bombarding the forts along the Chinese coast. The government was forced to open negotiations, and in 1842 it signed the Treaty of Nanjing. Guangzhou and three other ports were opened to trade from abroad, and China ceded the small island of Hong Kong to Britain. A breach had been made, into which other European nations were not slow to penetrate.

A Forced Opening

In 1844 the French sent M. Théodore de Lagrené to Guangzhou, and on October 24, a treaty was signed at Whampoa on the corvette *Archimède* between France and China. The United States and other Western powers concluded similar agreements, which gave to foreigners the following advantages:

—Five ports were opened to exterior trade, and foreigners were allowed to reside in them: they were Guangzhou, Amoy (Xiamen), Fuzhou, Ningbo, and Shanghai.

—Foreigners were to benefit from a privileged extraterritorial status. They were to be judged in their own courts, and, if they lodged a complaint, their consuls could demand that they be given justice by the Chinese courts.

—Any foreigners arrested outside the boundaries of the designated open ports were to be made over to their own consul. Thus article 23 of the Treaty of Whampoa stipulated that "a French citizen thus arrested may not be injured or ill treated in any way by any person whatsoever".[1]

M. de Lagrené, a practicing Catholic, took it upon himself to negotiate with the governor, Qi Ying, an edict of toleration to the advantage of Christians. This initiative was in line with the policy of the French king, Louis-Philippe, and his prime minister, François Guizot, who considered that the moral influence of French missionaries could counterbalance the commercial lead of the British. Lagrené wrote confidentially to Guizot that

> he considered it worthy of France and of its government to intervene in its turn and, following on the commercial advantages obtained by the English, to draw attention to the action of France from the moral and civilizing point of view.[2]

Qi Ying agreed to draw up a memorandum for the emperor; in it he stated:

> When one examines the past, one can see that the religion of the Lord of heaven [Catholicism] is the one professed by the nations of the West; the purpose of this religion is to do good and to avoid evil. . . . This being the case, the request of the French ambassador, de Lagrené, seems a fair one, since he asks that Chinese of good standing, who practice this religion, should not be considered as guilty of any offense. I therefore beg for imperial approval of the following: that henceforth any person, whether Chinese or foreign, who studies or practices the religion of the Lord of heaven, who behaves well in other respects and who causes no trouble, should be considered innocent of any offense or guilt.[3]

Qi Ying's petition was approved by the Dao Guang emperor on December 28, 1844, and confirmed by a decree of February 20, 1846. In fact, it was never published and remained a dead letter, but it did mark the beginning of French intervention in the religious affairs of China.

---

[1] Text quoted in A. Thomas (*vere* J. M. Planchet, C.M.), *Histoire de la Mission de Pékin; Depuis l'arrivée des Lazaristes jusqu' à la révolte des Boxers* (Paris: Louis-Michaud, 1925), vol. 2, p. 272.

[2] Louis Wei Tsing-sing, *La politique missionnaire de la France en Chine 1842–1856* (Paris: Nouvelle éditions latines, 1960, 653 pp.), p. 252.

[3] A. Thomas, *Histoire de la Mission de Pékin*, p. 273.

In 1856 war broke out again as the result of an incident involving the lorcha[4] *Arrow*, a cargo ship belonging to a Chinese from Hong Kong and sailing under the British flag. Chinese police, searching for a pirate, boarded her, arrested twelve Chinese sailors, and hauled down the British flag. The British authorities were outraged and retaliated by bombarding the fortifications of Guangzhou. The French also entered the fray, but for another reason—Fr. Chapdelaine had been put to death in Guangxi Province, together with his catechist, a certain Agnes. Bishop Guillemin, prefect apostolic of Guangxi, denounced this murder to M. de Coucy, the *chargé d'affaires*, as a violation of article 23 of the 1844 Treaty of Whampoa between France and China. Hostilities ended in 1858. The French Treaty of Tianjin, negotiated by Baron Gros, included a clause guaranteeing the protection of Christians. Article 13 stipulated that Christians of all denominations could practice their religion in full security and that missionaries in possession of an authorized safe conduct could circulate freely in the Chinese hinterland.

Hostilities broke out yet again when the envoys, who were negotiating the ratification of this treaty in Beijing, were massacred. This time an Anglo-French expedition took Beijing on October 13, 1860, and sacked the summer palace. The Peking Convention guaranteed the official recognition of Christianity. Article 6 laid down that Church properties, confiscated during times of persecution, should be handed back through the mediation of the French ambassador. Permanent legations at Beijing were then created. For the first time in the history of the Chinese Empire, these legations did not represent vassal countries but the governments of independent sovereign states. For its part, the Chinese government created a special Ministry of Foreign Affairs, the *Zongli Yamen*, to treat with these legations.

The French legation thus created at Beijing exercised a quasi-monopoly as regards the protection of Christians. The French consul issued safe conducts or "passports" to missionaries of all nationalities. Even Chinese nationals who were Christians could appeal to the French legation against Chinese law; many criminals began to make use of such an opportunity. Foreign protection made it possible for Christians to build schools, churches, and orphanages. In the provinces, however, this often led to the resentment of local mandarins and

---

[4] A *lorcha* is a cargo ship with hull of European shape but with a Chinese rig.

ended in renewed persecution. The population could easily be roused by sinister rumors about the perverse behavior of Christians. Everywhere Christians were assaulted and their buildings destroyed; more often than not, such incidents went unpunished.[5]

The Manchu government tried to leave these things to the local authorities. Its religious policy was guided by two main preoccupations: it was concerned to prevent foreigners from penetrating into the interior of China and to prevent criminals from operating under a Christian label to evade the law of the land. The purchase of land and property on the part of Christian Churches often led to litigation. It seemed as if the principle of religious freedom was causing even greater foreign penetration into China. Another grievance was that the frequent intervention of missionaries into judicial matters involving Chinese Christians seemed to be undermining Chinese sovereignty.

From 1880, the Manchu government attempted to establish relations with the Holy See so as to have better control over religious affairs within its own country and to lessen the monopoly of France over missionary matters. There was actually armed conflict between China and France over Annam from 1882 to 1885. After this war was over, the Holy See tried to establish diplomatic relations directly with China. The great reforming politician Li Hongzhang proposed the nomination of a Chinese representative to the Holy See, so as to disassociate the missions from the colonial powers. Xu Jincheng was appointed Chinese envoy to the Vatican, and in 1886, Pope Leo XIII appointed Archbishop Antonio Agliardi as apostolic nuncio to the Chinese imperial court. However, the opposition of France blocked this move. The prime minister of the Third Republic, Charles de Freycinet, threatened to recall the French ambassador to the Holy See and informed the Pope that France would only tolerate the sending to China of an apostolic delegate, without diplomatic status. However, even this solution turned out to be impracticable; Bishop François Tagliabue, C.M., vicar apostolic in Beijing, argued strongly against it, and relations between the papacy and the French Republic were

---

[5] The penetration of missionaries into the interior provoked the xenophobia of mandarins and of the population. Cf. Paul A. Cohen, *China and Christianity: The Missionary Movement and the Growth of Chinese Antiforeignism 1860–1870* (Cambridge, Mass.: Harvard University Press, 1963).

at a critical stage at the time. The anticlerical education law of the previous prime minister, Jules Ferry (1885), had excluded the Catholic Church from any place in the state system of education. So as not to make things worse for the French Church, Leo XIII had no alternative but to back down; later he spoke of this setback as "the greatest sorrow of my pontificate".[6] France was thus able to maintain its virtual protectorate over the missions in China. However, some of the missions from other European countries later passed under the control of their own governments, the Germans in 1891 and the Italians in 1902.

The Society of the Divine Word, "the Steyl missionaries", were mostly Germans, and after 1879 they took over the Franciscan and Jesuit missions in the southern part of Shandong Province. Two Divine Word missionaries, the dynamic Bishop J. B. Anzer and Saint Joseph Freinademetz, an Austrian who was more moderate in his approach, repeatedly requested their consul to intervene so as to overcome rooted opposition to their establishment in the area of Yanzhou, twelve miles (twenty kilometers) from Qufu, the holy place associated with Confucius.

In 1858 Italian missionaries were sent by P.I.M.E., the Pontifical Institute for Foreign Missions of Milan, to be responsible for the Hong Kong missions and then, from 1865, to replace the Vincentians in Henan Province.

The Flourishing of the Vincentians

The protection given by foreign powers caused a greater influx of missionaries into China than ever before. Moreover, in Europe and in America, colonial expansion was accompanied by a greater missionary consciousness on the part of Christians. Europe was then experiencing the full tide of progress in the scientific, technical, and industrial fields; it had confidence in the values of its civilization and in the superiority of the white man. A certain romantic heroism combined with the prevalent enthusiasm to inspire men and women to

---

[6] Cf. Louis Wei Tsing-Sing, *Le Saint-Siège et la Chine de Pie XI à nos jours* (Paris: Éditions A. Allais, 1968), p. 83.

deeds of heroic generosity, so that zealous Christians were prepared to face martyrdom in order to bring salvation and the benefits of civilization to remote areas of the globe. In 1822, Pauline Jaricot in Lyons, France, formed the project of an Association for the Propagation of the Faith. In 1848, Charles de Forbin-Janson, bishop of Nancy in France, called a first meeting of churchmen in Paris to form the *Société de la Sainte Enfance*, the "Society of the Holy Childhood"; the children of France were to be asked to offer a few coins from their savings to save the lives and the souls of the little children of China.

The arrival in China of this new wave of missionary activity undoubtedly caused an increase in the numbers and activities of the missions, but the structures of the Catholic Church in China, which had been established as the result of so much effort over the previous two centuries, seem to have been somewhat overwhelmed by this impetuous onrush. What happened to the Vincentians is perhaps particularly significant. In the eighteenth century outstanding Vincentians, like Fathers Appiani and Müllener, worked hard to train Chinese priests, who later proved their worth. When Pope Clement XIV suppressed the Jesuits in 1773 by the brief *Dominus ac Redemptor*, the Vincentians took over many of their missions, thus greatly increasing their area of activity. They were responsible for the central provinces, Hunan, Hubei, and Henan; they were also responsible for the eastern provinces of Jiangxi and Zhejiang. Above all, they took charge of the Beijing mission, the Zhili (Hebei), and their activity spread to the northern provinces. Even to this day in the Church of the Savior in Beijing, the Beitang, there are memorials to the French Vincentians who were there in the nineteenth century. In the parish premises, there used to be a large painting of St. Gabriel Perboyre, who was tortured and killed by strangulation at Wuhan in 1840; and a large stone tablet, fixed to the wall in the chapel, which is beyond the apse to the north of the church, bears a carved inscription to the memory of Bishop Favier, who survived the siege of the Boxers in 1900.

Between 1840 and 1900, it was the foreign missionaries, who had been at first persecuted and then relatively protected, who gradually took control of Catholic Church life in China. Another famous Vincentian, Bishop Mouly, presided over this evolution. A. Thomas was to write of him: "for nearly thirty years, he seemed to personify the destinies of the Catholic Church in China."[7]

Joseph Martial Mouly, like St. Gabriel Perboyre, came from the diocese of Cahors in southwest France. He had been ordained in France in his twenty-fourth year and arrived at Macao in 1834. He then crossed China secretly, pretending to be a sick man and being carried in a palanquin; every day he washed his face in tea, hoping thus to acquire a yellow complexion. He arrived in Beijing in 1835 and was welcomed by the Chinese Vincentian, Joseph Han, who treated him with all the honor due to the new superior of the mission. From there, Mouly went to Xiwanzi (now Chongli), north of the Great Wall, a village that, since the persecution of 1829, had become the center of the French mission in the Beitang. There he found another Chinese Vincentian, Matthew Xue, who for fifteen years had acquitted himself well as superior. As Fr. Andrew Li in Sichuan Province had done previously on the arrival of Fr. Pottier, so Fr. Matthew Xue immediately submitted to the authority of this young French priest who did not have even one year's experience of China, and yet Matthew Xue and Joseph Han had given proof of outstanding zeal and efficiency in fostering Church life in the Zhili area and in founding new Christian communities in Mongolia. Most foreign missionaries would have been envious of their achievements. Later, when Joseph Mouly had become vicar apostolic, he paid tribute to the achievements of his two Chinese predecessors in the biographical reports, which he sent from Beijing to his Paris superiors. What he wrote about these two priests makes one regret, with hindsight, that Bishop Mouly had thought it necessary to overshadow them by becoming superior of the mission.

Joseph Han and Matthew Xue: Vincentians

Joseph Han was born in 1772, in Zhili (Hebei), and belonged to a noble family of army dignitaries. His parents were Christians, and he was baptized as a child and received the education of a mandarin. As the eldest child and a brilliant student he was destined for a public career, so that there were many objections when he announced that

---

[7] Thomas, *Histoire de la Mission de Pékin*, p. 151.

he wanted to become a "priest of the mission", that is, a member of the religious community founded by St. Vincent de Paul in the seventeenth century, whose members are called *Lazaristes* in France and Vincentians in English-speaking countries. Round about the year 1790, Joseph Han was admitted to the seminary of the Beitang, which had been founded by M. Raux, six or seven years previously. He studied Latin and theology under M. Ghislain and was ordained priest in 1798 by Bishop de Gouvea of Beijing. During the first years of his ministry, Fr. Han visited about ten Catholic missions a year, communities that had been neglected after the departure of the Jesuits, fifteen to twenty years previously. These missions had been harassed by successive persecutions, so that many Christians had fled the Beijing area and had found a refuge in Inner Mongolia. Without hesitation, Joseph Han went to these northern steppes, which few Chinese had as yet penetrated and, like a good shepherd, sought out the scattered sheep, thus gathering the first Christian communities in Mongolia. It was hard work; he lived on very little and spent the night either in small local temples or with Christian families. He was not always made welcome, and sometimes the very poor, ill instructed in the faith, complained that he was coming to eat their rice. Most Christians, however, appreciated his preaching in pure Mandarin and liked the beautiful stories that he told from the Old and the New Testaments. At the request of M. Ghislain and together with a scholarly catechist, he translated into Chinese the *Enchiridion piarum meditationum* of Johannes Busaeus, S.J. (1547–1611). This book of meditations, first published at Mainz in 1606 and subsequently often reedited and translated in Europe, soon came into current use in China for retreats given to the laity. Bishop Pires, bishop of Nanjing and administrator of the diocese of Beijing, showed how much he trusted Fr. Han by choosing him, about 1835, as his confessor; "much more than he trusted his own priests!" was Bishop Mouly's rather sour comment. Fr. Joseph Han died of old age in 1844 at the Christian center of Xuanhua, to the northwest of Beijing. His priestly ministry had lasted forty-seven years, and a great crowd came to his funeral, which was presided over by his colleague, Fr. Xue.

Fr. Matthew Xue rivaled Joseph Han in apostolic zeal. He was born in 1780, and his family were Catholics from Shanxi Province, which had been entrusted by Rome to Italian Franciscan missionaries. His parents were poor peasants, strong in their faith, who taught their son how to pray. In spite of their limited means, they sent him to school and then had him trained as a tailor; but Matthew had been impressed by the missionary, who came every year in secret to visit the Christians in his village, and he dreamed of becoming a priest. There was as yet no center for priestly formation in the province, and the few candidates had to go to Beijing, to the West Church (*Xitang*), Our Lady of the Seven Sorrows. Although he was devoid of resources, Matthew made his way to *Xitang*, where disappointment awaited him; the missionaries of his vicariate refused to accept this unimpressive young peasant. Then he tried the South Church (*Nantang*), but was turned away there too. Finally the Vincentian M. Raux accepted him for the French mission at the North Church (*Beitang*). Matthew Xue made his vows as a Vincentian in 1807 and was ordained priest soon afterward. He began his mission by traveling through the countryside, riding a little donkey.

A crisis occurred in 1820 when M. Lamiot, the Vincentian provincial in Beijing, was apprehended by the imperial courts. Hastily he appointed Fr. Matthew Xue to replace him as superior of the French mission in Beijing; as such, he was responsible for the Catholic missions in the provinces of Zhili (Hebei), Mongolia, Henan, Jiangxi, Zhejiang, and Jiangnan (Jiangsu). However, the Beijing government had no intention of maintaining for the benefit of a Chinese priest the privileges conceded to the French Mission at the time of the Jesuits. Matthew Xue and the few Church students he had gathered round him were threatened with expulsion from *Beitang*. It was the Portuguese who came to the rescue by sending as representative to the Chinese government Bishop Gaetan Pires-Pereira, C.M., who was a member of the mathematics tribunal. Bishop Pires also helped Fr. Xue by teaching theology to the seminarians at *Beitang*. Unfortunately Pires died in 1838, and there were no other Europeans who could justify the continuation of the mission; the Beitang foundation was immediately taken over by the Chinese government and the property sold to a private individual. Matthew Xue and his pupils worked night and day to save the furniture, the books, and the vestments and then moved to Xiwanzi in Inner Mongolia, where Christians and catechists welcomed them with delight. The Xiwanzi mission, strengthened by this unlooked-for contribution, became a center of evangelization for the region. The nominal superiors of the mission continued to be the French missionaries, who were still restricted to Macao. After the death of M. Lamiot, M. Torrete succeeded him. Fr. Matthew Xue did not forget the fathers in Macao; he would send them seminarians for the final years of their theological studies, and even financial contributions from the sale of properties and furniture in Beitang. Then it was that the young Fr. Mouly, newly arrived in Macao from France, made his way across China incognito and joined Fr. Matthew Xue at Xiwanzi. He wrote:

> I was very young, twenty-eight years old, without experience, especially of things Chinese, since I knew neither the language of the country nor its customs, but he saw me as his superior, the representative of God, and that was enough for his spirit of faith and his piety. . . . I was really embarrassed to see this venerable old man, so humble and so submissive, before this youngster, who had just arrived.[8]

There was perhaps a fundamental misunderstanding here, working to the advantage of the Westerner, who was unaware of what was happening. The traditional culture of China prevents anyone from coming forward without being invited to do so. Moreover, a Chinese person would be doubly submissive in the presence of someone who is more powerful, richer, or more learned, but this is combined with an objective assessment of the situation on the part of the Chinese, because their inferiority complex is accompanied by a sense of moral superiority. The brashness of European colonials could take unfair advantage of this in-built phenomenon of Chinese culture. There was another reason, albeit a more political one, for the inferior situation of Chinese priests in relation to the missionaries; they were bereft of support in relation to their own government and thus felt the full weight of laws, which were hostile to Christianity as such.

Expansion, Sharing, and Division

In 1841 Bishop Joseph Mouly was appointed vicar apostolic of Mongolia, and soon afterward he welcomed to Xiwanzi another French Vincentian, Fr. Évariste Huc, who started to learn Mongolian and Manchurian at the Mission of the Valley of Black Waters (*Heishui*). In 1844 Fr. Huc and his Vincentian superior, Fr. Joseph Gabet, were

---

[8] A. Milon, *Mémoires de la Congrégation de la Mission en Chine*, vol. 3 *Les Vicariats Apostoliques* (Paris: Rue de Sèvres, 1912), p. 575.

sent on a long journey of exploration which took them as far as Tibet, but unfortunately they were expelled from Lhasa after only six weeks at the request of the Chinese ambassador. By 1846, they were back in China at Kangding, in Sichuan Province, and then crossed the whole empire from west to east to reach Macao. Fr. Huc wrote an account in French of their journey and adventures, which was published in Paris in 1850 and fired many an imagination; it went through several editions and was translated into eight languages.[9] However Fr. Huc, in spite of the many hardships that he faced on this epic journey, did not directly help the expansion of the Church in China. In Mongolia and Tibet he had passed himself off as a lama, and in China he demanded to be treated as a high-ranking mandarin; it was the only way to avoid disaster. His contribution was mainly cultural. It was an achievement on the part of the two Vincentians to have set up a small chapel in Lhasa, in a dwelling lent to them by the regent of Tibet. Although this Christian presence on "the Roof of the World" lasted such a short time, the news when it reached Europe was enough to whet the appetite of future missionaries, both French and Swiss.

Of the earlier attempts at bringing Christianity to Tibet, nothing remained by 1846. The Franciscan Odoric of Friuli (Odoric da Pordenone) had passed that way in 1330. At the beginning of the eighteenth century the Jesuits and then the Capuchins had established themselves for a few decades, but it was not until the end of the nineteenth century that some Christian communities were to be created in the eastern part of Tibet, to the west of the Chinese province of Sichuan and to the north of Yunnan. More recently, since the late 1980s, Fr. Shi Guangrong, a sixty-year-old Chinese priest who spoke Tibetan, had undertaken to travel regularly between the many Christian villages of the valleys of the Salween and upper Mekong Rivers. Fr. Shi died in March 2000; since then, Fr. Lu Rendi, a young Tibetan priest ordained in Xi'an in 1996, lives in Yerkalo itself and

---

[9] Fr. Huc's account of his journey was written at Macao and remains an important source of information on Mongolia, Tibet, and China in the mid-nineteenth century. Régis-Évariste Huc, *Souvenirs d'un voyage dans la Tartarie et le Thibet pendant les années 1844, 1845 et 1846, nouvelle édition annotée et illustrée pat. J. M. Planchet, missionaire lazariste*, 2 vols. (Beijing: Imprimerie des Lazaristes, 1924). English ed. Régis-Évariste Huc, *Christianity in China Tartary and Thibet*, 3 vols. (London: Longmans Brown, 1857–1858). Régis-Évariste Huc, *L'Empire chinois* (Monaco: Éditions du Rocher, Collection Itinéraire, 1980) is a reprint of the 1854 edition.

looks after the Tibetans of the area. At Kangding (formerly called Ta Tsien lou) in Sichuan Province, which was the center of the former mission to Tibet, about 800 Catholics have remained faithful; Fr. Li Lun, ordained in 1994, looks after the area and has had a new church built.

Fr. Huc and Fr. Gabet had had a soft spot for the Mongolians and compared them favorably to the Chinese. They were not the only Vincentians who felt this way and who found it hard when their missions in Mongolia were transferred to other religious orders. This is partly what happened in 1840, when Bishop Mouly welcomed as a visitor to Xiwanzi Bishop Emmanuel Jean-François Verrolles, from the Paris Foreign Missions. He came from Sichuan Province and had been consecrated bishop at Taiyuan on his way north by Bishop Joachim Salvetti, O.F.M., vicar apostolic of Shanxi Province. He was on his way to take possession of the new vicariate apostolic of Liaodong and eastern Tartary, i.e., Manchuria, which *Propaganda Fide* in Rome had entrusted to the Paris Foreign Missions. This missionary society needed bases in Manchuria to ensure access to the missions in Korea which it had accepted a few years previously. The two French vicars apostolic, meeting in Xiwanzi, agreed on a boundary, going due north from Beijing, as the demarcation between their two vicariates, but they failed to agree over who should be responsible for some of the Catholic villages dear to the Vincentians. Twenty-five years later, in 1865, the Vincentians had to give up their remaining missions in Mongolia to the new Congregation of the Immaculate Heart of Mary, founded at Scheut, a suburb of Brussels, and known as "the Scheut Fathers".

These changes of jurisdiction caused tensions between local Christians as well as between missionaries, because the faithful found that they had to adapt to the varying pastoral and liturgical practices of the religious orders which took them over. For instance, some missionaries allowed men to wear hats in church, whereas others forbade it; both groups had equally convincing reasons. More seriously, some Chinese congregations felt that they were being asked to be disloyal to the priests who had formed them in the faith. Thus in Hebei Province, south of Beijing, a minor schism occurred in the Zhengding and Zhaozhou region between 1847 and 1853. Some of the priests and faithful continued their allegiance to the Portuguese mission and refused to accept the Vincentian administration. This attitude was not welcome to Bishop Mouly, a man used to being in sole charge. The Catholics involved refused to obey him, however, and threatened the priests he had sent them; they even sent catechists all the way to Jiangnan for the holy oils rather than accept the oils that had been blessed by Bishop Mouly. Financial factors made things worse, since the Portuguese *Padroado* was considered to be better off than the poor Vincentians. These conflicts of loyalty, combined with material motives, continued to embitter the life of the Church in this region until today; but nowadays the internal quarrels between the Catholics of south Hebei Province find their outlet in the mutual ex-communications between the patriotic Church and the underground Church. The tendency to form rival clans is no doubt embedded in Chinese society, but conflicts of jurisdiction between missionaries belonging to different religious orders have intensified such disastrous tendencies.

Missionary Successes and Chinese Reactions

Fr. Matthew Xue died peacefully in December 1860 "like a candle which has burnt itself out".[10] Bishop Mouly was then at the height of his power. Under the protection of the Peking Convention, the Vincentians soon returned to the Beitang district, which they restored. The Church of the Holy Redeemer was rebuilt, taller and bigger than the previous one; it became a cathedral, since Bishop Mouly was the first bishop in modern times to reside in Beijing. In 1887 the church had to be rebuilt on a different site in the Xishiku district, because the boundaries of the Forbidden City had been extended westward; the towers of the church had been a problem anyway, because they were higher than the roofs of the imperial palaces. The new church, built in the style of a French Gothic cathedral, survived the attacks of the Boxers in 1900. Under the Communist regime, the Church of the Beitang was considered to be the very symbol of imperialism and was left for a long time to decay, while all the buildings of the mission were used as a school. In 1985, however, Catholics were allowed to restore the church and the Beijing Seminary was housed in 1989 on

---

[10] The phrase is from Bishop Mouly's biographical note on Fr. Xue in Milon, *Mémoires de la Congrégation*, p. 577.

the north side of the apse. The former French mission now belongs unmistakably to the Church in China.

On October 29, 1860, Bishop Mouly had presided over a solemn service to honor the victims of the campaign by which the French and the British had conquered Beijing. The newly restored Church of the Holy Redeemer was festooned with French tricolor flags, and the building reechoed to the band of the 101st regiment of the line of the French army, the soldiers who had just sacked the summer palace. An eyewitness wrote:

> There was general emotion as Bishop Mouly intoned the *Te Deum* celebrating the reopening of the church, and then finally the *Domine salvum fac Imperatorem nostrum Napoleonem*, calling down the blessings of heaven upon our illustrious emperor. . . . The cross, raised up anew, testified to the power of France, whose army could henceforth depart.[11]

The following year devotions to Mary during the month of May were introduced to Beijing, then the procession in honor of the Blessed Sacrament on the feast of Corpus Christi; members of the French legation carried the canopy above the priest with the monstrance. Congregations began to learn Gregorian plainchant melodies, and they sang the Mass by Dumont, a nineteenth-century French composer. Bishop Mouly, yielding to the requests of local Catholics, also allowed women to take part in the same Church gatherings as men, although they had to come in by a different door and the nave was divided in two by a railing. This was still a departure from the Chinese practice of avoiding any open contact between men and women, so that Catholic mixed congregations caused accusations of immoral or perverted behavior.

Peace in religious matters having been established in the capital, the main works of a mission could be set up. In 1862 Bishop Mouly brought the Daughters of Charity to Beijing; they had already established houses at Macao, then in 1847 at Ningbo. The new arrivals divided themselves into two, one group in Beijing and the other in Tianjin. The French established a territorial concession for themselves in the town of Tianjin, including within it a church built in 1773, the Wanghailou, which was restored in 1869 and renamed Our Lady of Victories. However, this victory cry turned out to be rather

---

[11] Charles de Mutrecy, *Journal de la Campagne de Chine*, quoted in Thomas, *Histoire de la Mission de Pékin*, p. 399.

premature, as appeared by what happened in Tianjin the following year.

Anti-Western feeling had built up because of the foreign troops that had been stationed in Tianjin from 1858 to 1865, and because in 1860 the French seized the imperial villa there for a consulate. The Daughters of Charity opened an orphanage in Tianjin, but, unwisely, they offered a premium for each child deposited there, which gave criminals the opportunity of kidnapping children so as to collect the premium; they became known as "child brokers". It seems too that xenophobia among the mandarins and the people of the town was stirred up by the son of a Chinese general who had been killed at the Battle of Palikiao (*Baliqiao*) which had opened the way for the foreign troops to enter Beijing in 1860. It was known that the sisters baptized sick and dying children, so, when thirty-four orphans died in an epidemic, the wildest rumors circulated: that the nuns bewitched the children, mutilated their bodies, and cut out their hearts and eyes for medicine. On June 21, 1870, the convent was inspected by a local official, who found no truth in the allegations; nevertheless a mob gathered and threatened the sisters. When the local magistrate failed to disperse the crowd, the French consul drew a gun and fired a shot, which missed the magistrate but killed his servant. The infuriated mob fell on the consul and his chancellor and hacked them to pieces; it then went on to massacre ten nuns and two priests, Fr. Chevrier and Fr. Wu. Three Russian traders and some other civilians, both French and Chinese, were also killed. The church was set on fire, and the convent and the orphanage destroyed, as were four British and American Protestant churches, recently opened. After that bloody incident, heavy indemnities were demanded of the Chinese government, although the local authorities were spared; 250,000 taels were paid in compensation to the vicar apostolic, who used them to rebuild the church and the other buildings. Some twenty of the rioters were tried and executed.

Such measures ensured a temporary peace at Beijing and Tianjin, but they were far from ending trouble in the provinces, where riots, killings, and the destruction of property continued to occur sporadically in different regions. Consulates claimed compensation and used it to build churches and schools. Apart from such sanctions, imposed on the populations because of incidents involving religion, there were other causes of discontent. Foreigners were introducing modernization through various new buildings, and these antagonized the conservative and the ignorant; the construction of railways seemed particularly scandalous because they were seen as destroying the *feng-shui*, a term that expresses the Chinese concept of respect for the environment by not interfering with the natural functioning of wind (*feng*) and water (*shui*) and involves magic, using geomancy to ensure the harmony between humanity and nature. The railways also caused unemployment for those working on the land routes and canals of the country.

By the end of the nineteenth century there was widespread economic decline in China; the competition of foreign imports, which had been forced on the country by gunboat diplomacy, contributed to the ruin of many domestic trades and to the rising unemployment. It was natural to blame foreigners for the bankruptcy that threatened the country and to feel deep resentment at the humiliation of China through military defeat. The scholar-gentry were influential in the provinces and considered themselves as defenders of Confucian propriety; they were particularly riled by the inroads of Christianity and by its disruption of traditions like the kowtowing to images and taking part in local festivals. It was easy to blame such departure from the traditions of the past for the unhappy conditions of the present.

The resentment, which had thus gradually built up, burst out in 1900 in the Boxer Rebellion, which had the support of high Chinese dignitaries and of the dowager empress Cixi herself. The Boxers were teams of men practicing the martial arts, from which they took the name of *Yihe quan*, "the fist of just harmony". They did not only do this by cultivating fitness; an essential part of their appeal was the belief that magic arts made them immune to bullets after one hundred days of training, and that after four hundred days they acquired the power to fly. In battle they used rituals and incantations to call upon supernatural powers, burning for instance a small yellow paper with the picture of a footless man while murmuring a magic spell, in the belief that this would bring heavenly generals and warriors to their side. Also their hatred of foreign ways led them to avoid the use of guns and to prefer old-style swords and spears as weapons.

On June 13, 1900, with the approval of the court, large groups of Boxers overran Beijing with this rallying cry: *bao guo mie yang*, "Defend the country; destroy the foreigner." On the orders of the court, government troops joined with the Boxers, and the massacre of Catholic and Protestant missionaries began; churches were burned down, and Christian villages were sacked. Foreign troops reacted by seizing the forts of Dagu, which control the approach to Tianjin, whereupon the dowager empress declared war on the foreign powers on June 21 and issued a decree three days later, ordering the execution of foreigners throughout the whole of the empire. The German minister in Beijing, von Ketteler, was murdered by a Manchu soldier, whereupon all the foreigners in the city sought refuge in the quarter of the legations, where 425 soldiers of the Western powers held out for two months against thousands of Boxers. The survival of the Westerners, beleaguered by such a large number of Chinese, seemed miraculous, but in fact it had natural causes, as Immanuel C. Y. Hsü explains in *The Rise of Modern China*:

> This miracle was made possible by Jung-lu, the commander-in-chief of the Peiyang forces, who had no sympathy for the Boxers but lacked courage to oppose the dowager. He carried out the attack halfheartedly, firing noisy but empty guns and withholding the new and large-caliber cannon from use. As a result, the legation defense was not broken.[12]

Relief came on August 14, when an international force of 18,000 men from eight different nations forced their way into Beijing and began acts of repression and looting, which were on a par with those of the Boxers.

Although the Boxer Rebellion was directed against foreigners, tens of thousands of Chinese Christians were slaughtered without pity as traitors. For Protestants in China, this was the first experience of a major persecution. Catholics too suffered considerable damage. In Beijing, the Nantang was destroyed; the Church of the East with all the Christians who had sought refuge there was burned; the Church of the West was also burned down. In the Beitang Bishop Favier, the vicar apostolic, was defended by a handful of French marines, together with three thousand Chinese Christians, mostly women and children, who had sought refuge there. Losses of Catholics throughout the whole country were estimated at five bishops, 312 European priests, nine European sisters, and two Marist brothers. The total number of Chinese Catholics who lost their lives was probably over

---

[12] Immanuel C. Y. Hsü, *The Rise of Modern China* (New York: Oxford University Press, 2000), 6th ed., p. 398.

30,000.[13] The number of Protestants who were killed is estimated at 135 adult missionary personnel, including the wives of missionaries, and 1,900 Chinese Protestants.

For the Orthodox missions, which were beginning to take root in a Chinese milieu, the losses were fewer in number but more devastating. The first Chinese Orthodox priest, Mitrophan Tsi, had only been ordained in 1884; Innocent Figourovsky, an energetic missionary, had just established a printing press with 30,000 characters, engraved on wood. Everything was destroyed, and more than two hundred Orthodox Christians were killed, including one priest, one catechist and one teacher. All the Orthodox churches were burned, apart from one at Hankou. In spite of this terrible ordeal, the Orthodox found new strength in their suffering; henceforth, they held their own among the Christians of China. On the occasion of the centenary of their massacre by the Boxers, 222 Orthodox Christians, killed in Beijing in June 1900, were canonized in Moscow by the Patriach in August 2000.

---

[13] Cf. Kenneth Scott Latourette, *A History of Christian Missions in China* (Taipei: Ch'ong-Wen Publishing Co., 1970), p. 512, using a report of the Oeuvre de la Propagation de la Foi for figures concerning Catholics: *Dix années d'apostolat catholique des missions* (1898–1907), pp. 52–53.

[In the section "Missionary Successes and Chinese Reactions", paragraph 7 has been added to the French text.

Paragraphs 8, 9, 10 and 11 have been expanded by supplementary material.—TRANS.]

20

CATHOLIC VILLAGES

The extraordinary story that follows comes from the written notes of Fr. Jean-Marie Trémorin, a Vincentian who was parish priest of Donglü in Hebei Province in the 1920s and 1930s. Fr. Trémorin's handwritten report was communicated to Fr. J. Charbonnier by Br. Cui, a Marist teacher in Malaysia, after a visit to Donglü. The manuscript is now kept in the *Relais France-Chine* Documentation room, at the *Missions Étràngères* in Paris. Fr. Trémorin's notes were written down by him in 1966, and they are based on the oral traditions of his parishioners which he had collected. In June 1900, 40,000 Boxers attacked the village of Donglü, which is situated about ninety miles (150 kilometers) south of Beijing. They were armed with spears and cutlasses and thought themselves immune from harm; however, they came up against unexpected resistance. The 700 or so Christians, plus over 9,000 refugees, had organized their defense. Broad ditches had been dug around the village and the earth heaped up to form ramparts, defended by branches with long thorns. Two of the villagers had been bandits in Mongolia and had some experience of fighting; they each had a rifle and some ammunition. Four times the Boxers attacked and were repelled with losses. The Christians chased after them, shouting, "Death to the devil!" Any prisoners taken were briefly interrogated before a tribunal and then buried alive in the rampart, in a pit prepared in advance; the villagers were very short of food, and they feared that any prisoner who got away would reveal that the village was practically without defenses. Every day a priest took the Blessed Sacrament in procession around the ramparts, accompanied by the women and children reciting the Rosary and the Litany of Our Lady, which included the apposite invocation: *Salus Christianorum, ora pro nobis*, "Help of Christians, pray for us".

In July the Boxers appealed for help to the imperial army. Several thousand soldiers, armed with rifles and antiquated cannon, attacked the village, forty-four times it is said (this number, as spoken in Chinese, evokes certain death). Each time they were repelled, leaving cannon and rifles on the ground. Some time after August 15, news of the capture of Beijing by the Westerners reached Donglü; the soldiers retreated, shouting as they went, "Live in peace! We're off". Twenty-two Christians had been killed, mostly from accidents with the firearms, which they had never used before. The villagers found boxes of ammunition hidden in the ground; does this mean that some of the soldiers had been sympathizers? Several of the Boxers became Christians afterward; they reported that what had frightened them most was the "Lady in White", who often appeared above the place, a sure sign, they thought, that anyone who entered the village would not get out alive.

The Two Clans of Donglü

Even before the Boxer attacks, Donglü had had an unusual history. In 1862 there was not a single Christian among its 2,000 inhabitants. The population was divided into two family clans, the Yang, who were very poor and lived on the west side of the village, and the Cai, who lived on the east. Between them there were a pond and a small pagoda, built on a sepulchral mound in the middle of the pond. One winter the Yang went to consult a soothsayer as to why they were so desperately poor. He answered, "Because of the pagoda in the middle of the pond." One night the Yang set fire to the pagoda, then stole the bricks from the walls that remained. The pagoda belonged to the Cai, who caught the Yang redhanded, tied them up, and brought a case against them at the court of the prefecture of Baoding. Destroying a pagoda was a serious crime, which could deserve the death penalty. The Yang took fright and went to ask advice from a relative in a nearby village who was a Catholic. He said, "It's quite simple. Catholics don't like pagodas, and, if they have one, they will pull it down. If you become Catholics, your problem will be solved." Fr. Liu, a Chinese Vincentian, happened to be in a neighboring village. The Yang went to see him, as their relative had advised, knelt at his feet, and said, "We want to become Christians." "Why?" asked the priest, as they had expected. "Because we want to save our souls", they answered, without saying a word about the pagoda. Fr. Liu gave them catechisms, went to see them at Donglü, and said he would baptize them six months later.

It was the Cai's turn to get worried, because they knew that Christians were under the protection of foreign powers, so they also went to see Fr. Liu, and they also began to study the catechism, but without having any contact with the Yang. In the spring of 1863, Fr. Liu came to Donglü and baptized some fifty villagers, both Yang and Cai. Only then did he learn from the Cai how their pagoda had been destroyed by the Yang, who had gone unpunished. Fr. Liu gave them a reply based on reason. "It's quite simple", he said. "Now that you are Catholics, you would have had to destroy the pagoda if it were still there. The Yang have done it for you, so there is no problem." This might have been so in theory, but it was far from the truth in practice. The Yang and the Cai went to Mass separately; there was one church in the west (*Xitang*) and one church in the east (*Dongtang*). By 1870 Fr. Liu decided that it was time to bring the two clans together, so he built a chapel in the middle and refused to say Mass anywhere else. Gradually Christians from both sides came together, and after many years they actually began to talk to each other. As the years passed, the population of the village became mainly Catholic: 103 in 1874; 698 in 1896; 1,766 in 1905; 3,040 in 1928; and 3,500 in 1939. After the successful resistance against the Boxers, the fortifications were improved and four great gates were, built, facing north, south, east, and west. Above each gateway was an inscription: "Help of Christians", "Tower of David", "Saint Michael", and "Saint Louis King". The Vincentian fathers built a large church, schools, and a convent for Chinese nuns, the Josephines, who provided education for the girls. On August 15, 1915, Donglü became the center of a deanery of thirteen parishes which had nineteen priests and some 42,000 Catholics spread over 200 village communities.

This part of the country also became a great center of devotion to Mary, the Mother of Jesus. A painting of the Virgin Mary, holding the Child Jesus and surrounded by the faithful of Donglü, was placed above the altar of the church. It became "Our Lady of Donglü". In 1908 Fr. Flamant had another more majestic painting made in the workshop of the Jesuits in Shanghai. It was called *Zhonghua zhi Hou*, "Mary Queen of China"; it showed the Virgin in the robes of an empress of China, seated on the imperial throne, with the Child Jesus, standing to her left on the throne, dressed as a Chinese prince. The inscription at the top of the painting reads, "Mother of God, queen of Donglü, pray for us." In 1928 the apostolic delegate to China, Bishop

Costantini, and several other bishops asked Fr. Trémorin, the parish priest, to make Donglü a place of pilgrimage, and it was solemnly inaugurated as such in May 1929 in the presence of four bishops.

During the Second World War, Japanese troops and Communist guerrillas ravaged the region. All the church buildings were burned down on Holy Saturday 1941. Catholic Donglü rose again from its ruins when the basilica of Our Lady of China was rebuilt from March 1989 to May 1992. It is a huge brick building on the edge of the village with a metal roof, which glints in the sun. Twin spires rise heavenward and, like a Chinese gothic cathedral, dominate the immense plain with its ripening harvest of wheat and maize. All this is the work of poor peasants who have clung to their Catholic faith through thick and thin. Each year in May more than 20,000 pilgrims come here on foot, in spite of the roadblocks put up by the police. Unfortunately the old antagonism between east and west Donglü has surfaced again. Some Catholics see themselves as utterly faithful to the Church and to the Pope, whereas the rest are suspected of compromise with the patriotic association and of being in the pay of the Communist Party. The rebuilding of the basilica was delayed because of these divisions.

The story of Donglü illustrates the importance of the clan structure in China. Christianity permeates this family structure and derives unfailing strength from it, but it also receives with it certain limitations that are more pagan than Christian and are incompatible with the charity required by the Gospel. It is no doubt the same inherited responses that explain many of the conflicts between Catholic villages of south Hebei. Quarrels are waged in terms of fidelity to the Pope, canon law, clandestine episcopal directives, and excommunications, but the deep causes of conflict often seem to derive from age-old vendettas.

Mountain Refugees

It is unusual for clan tensions to divide the same village, as happened at Donglü. Generally Catholic villages are well bonded together. Sometimes they are made up of refugees who have, as a group, fled from persecution in other provinces. Thus, in the remote deserts of central Asia, there are villages composed of descendants of peasants exiled by former Chinese emperors, as in the Christian villages of the Ili Valley on the borders of Chinese Xinjiang and Russian Turkestan.

In the Gucheng district, to the northwest of Hubei Province, there is a group of fervent Catholics, who have taken refuge on a mountainous plateau difficult of access, called Chayuangou, "the Ravine of the Tea Garden". Their origins go back to 1702, when the first Christians of this community were baptized by a Jesuit at Xiangyang. During the 1724 persecution, some gave up the faith, but the more courageous emigrated to the mountains above Gucheng, two days' march to the west of Laohekou, where they found deserted and uncultivated land. Under the guidance of a catechist, the Christians from Xiangyang bought a whole valley and shared out the land among the poorest families.

Fr. Dominique Parrenin, S.J., who was at the time superior of the Beijing mission, heard about this foundation, and it gave him the idea of organizing a refuge for persecuted Christians and for priests threatened with arrest. He sent a Christian member of the scholar-gentry to purchase lands on the mountain of Moupan, "the Millstone", lands contiguous to the valley acquired by the Xiangyang Christians, but far more extensive. The contract of purchase was duly signed before the local magistrate, and catechists came from Beijing to help organize the local community. In 1731 Fr. Joseph Labbe, S.J. (1679–1745), came to say the first Mass; he divided the Christians into eight areas, each under the direction of a catechist. Pagans were only allowed to belong to it if they converted to Christianity. The community was dedicated to the Sacred Heart of Jesus, and by 1734 it had 600 residents.[1] Fr. Labbe had the help of a young Chinese Jesuit, Fr. John Stephen Gao (Gao Ruowang 1705–1766), who was a native of Xuanhua. Later on Fr. Sylvain de Neuville (1696–1764) took over from Fr. Labbe; during Fr. de Neuville's six-year ministry at the colony of the Sacred Heart, the numbers of Christians increased tenfold. Many were recent refugees; others were converts, baptized in the colony. The conditions for admission to baptism, however, and the instruc-

---

[1] Cf. Joseph Motte, S.J., *Chinese Lay Apostles* (Chinese text published Taipei: Guangqi, 1978), pp. 147–54; quoting the work of Théodore Chaney, *La Colonie du Sacré-Cœur dans les Cévennes de la Chine* (Paris: Lille, 1889) and Noël Gubbels, O.F.M., *Trois Siècles d'Apostolat: Histoire du Catholicisme au Hukwang depuis les origines 1587 jusqu' à 1870* (Paris: 36 Avenue Reille, and Wu-chang Hupeh: Franciscan Press, 1934), Collection "Missionaries" no. 4, pp. 129–39.

tion which preceded it were very strict, so that many catechumens and Christians left for other provinces.

The way of life in this mountain colony was regulated like that of a monastery. Every evening, after a hard day's work, families came together for prayer. The Jesuits had set up a confraternity, which was very structured and whose membership was demanding; it constituted the framework of the whole community and allowed it to survive if there were no priests. The members were divided into five sections, which were responsible for liturgy, catechesis, moral discipline, the intellectual apostolate, and the care of the sick with prayer for the dead. There was a similar organization for women, many of whom took the vow of virginity.

In some respects, this little Eden, remote from a hostile world, was like the Jesuit reductions in Paraguay. Unfortunately the Confucian emperor was no more tolerant than the Catholic conquerors of Latin America. Soon persecutors unearthed the refuge of the Catholics, confiscated the land, and gave them a choice between apostasy or exile. In 1779 an armed force was dispatched by the Qianlong emperor and occupied the area. The flock was scattered; those who remained worked as serfs of the new masters, who shamelessly reaped the fruits where they had not sown. Gradually, however, the community was reconstituted and became once again a place of refuge. From 1793 to 1819 the Vincentian Fr. François Clet made it the center of his mission, until he too was arrested and taken to Wuchang, where he died a martyr in February 1820. His colleague Gabriel Perboyre followed the same road in 1840; Fr. Perboyre took notes during his stay at the Colony of the Sacred Heart, which show that the community remained strong and faithful during those times of intense persecution. When he arrived at the foot of the mountains, there was not a sound to be heard or a person to be seen; then he climbed up to the heights and at evening reached the residence, hidden in bamboo thickets. From the various parts of the mountain, the tinkling of bells could be heard, and next morning four or five hundred people attended his Mass.

When peaceful conditions had returned for Christians, the community continued to develop. It became the nucleus of the diocese of Laohekou, which was entrusted to the Italian Franciscans in 1870. The seminary, which was founded at Chayuangou at that period, trained some thirty priests.

Those who had been expelled from the community by persecution had sometimes reconstituted Catholic villages in other parts of China. This is what happened in the province of Anhui; the population of this province had been decimated to such an extent during the Taiping Rebellion that the local authorities appealed for new settlers. Christians from the diocese of Laohekou therefore emigrated to Xuancheng and Shuidong and formed the solid nucleus of several Catholic villages. In 1868 two Jesuits, on a visit to the prefecture of Ningguo, found at Xucun near Shuidong "some fifty faithful, originally from Hubei Province, who were sorely affected by disease and poverty. Out of seventy immigrants, eleven had died since their arrival in Anhui Province."[2]

On May 15, 1931, Communist bands, led by He Long, who was called "the Robin Hood general" because he plundered the landlords to give to the peasants, overran the area.[3] They attacked the community at Chayuangou, killing four Chinese priests and taking Bishop Ricci and some Italian religious prisoners. From 1949 onward, the community was progressively deprived of its priests, first the foreigners and then the Chinese. Eventually, after an ordeal lasting thirty years, the Church of the Sacred Heart at Gucheng was reopened on May 16, 1985, the community being served by Fr. Nie Yifeng. When the bishop of Hankou, Joseph Dong Guanqing, came to Chayuangou for a pastoral visitation, he was greeted by thousands of jubilant Catholics.

Chinese Christians in Inner Mongolia

As well as villages that welcomed persecuted Christians, there were also villages that were created anew to promote conversions. This happened in Inner Mongolia under the direction of the Scheut Fathers from Belgium, who combined evangelization and development. They were assigned to the vast Mongolian plain, stretching for 746 miles (1,200 kilometers) from east to west where they came up against a migratory problem. Starving Chinese peasants were leaving their over-

---

[2] J. de la Servière, S.J., *Histoire de la Mission du Kiang-nan* (Shanghai: T'ou-Sewe, 1914), vol. 2, p. 165.

[3] Harrison E. Salisbury, *The New Emperors: China in the Era of Mao and Deng* (New York, 1992), pp. 59–60.

populated provinces to clear for cultivation the land of the Ordos, surrounded by the great loop of the Yellow River. Mongol chieftains resisted this process, which was depriving them of their best grazing land. The imperial government of the Manchus authorized the migration within certain limits, while trying to maintain peace with the Mongols. The cultivation of the new lands was in fact favoring the rich landowners who exploited the settlers without mercy, taking from 60 to 70 percent of their crops. The missionaries were faced with the following options, which are thus described by Bishop Carlo Van Melckebecke:

> The missionaries realized that, as things stood, there were only two choices for the Chinese immigrants: either to become virtually the slaves of the big landowners, or to try to survive as individuals bereft of any support, which would have given them a very precarious existence. The missionaries decided to offer them a third option, which would be humane, social, and Christian.[4]

At the outset of their work in Mongolia, the Belgian missionaries, like the Frenchman Fr. Huc mentioned in the previous chapter, had had a liking for Mongolians, but they had made few converts. They did however find some well-disposed Christians among the Chinese immigrants; they also found that many of the Chinese peasants, reduced to utter poverty, were willing to undergo instruction in the Christian faith, if they were offered a piece of land, some tools, and security. It was Fr. Steenackers (1848–1912) who had the idea of grouping such converts into a community where they could be formed to a Christian way of living. In 1879, he bought land from some Chinese settlers and founded the village of St. John the Baptist at Xiaoqiaopan, "little bridge strand", along the Great Wall and 125 miles (200 kilometers) southeast of Yinchuan (Ningxia). The beginnings were slow because land was short and not much could be found to offer to the newcomers. In 1900 there were only 472 inhabitants, of whom 392 had been baptized and 80 were catechumens.[5] Later Bishop A. Bermyn actively promoted this project and successfully ne-

---

[4] Carlo Van Melckebecke, C.I.C.M., *Service social de l'Église en Mongolie* (Brussels: Éditions de Scheut, 1968), p. 27.

[5] Cf. Joseph Van Hecken, C.I.C.M., *Les réductions catholiques du pays des Ordos: Une méthode d'apostolat des missionaires de Scheut* (Switzerland: Schoneck-Beckenried, 1957), Cahiers de la nouvelle Revue de Science Missionnaire, no. 15, p. 6.

gotiated the purchase of large stretches of land, so that Catholic Chinese settlements multiplied in the whole region of the "Three Bian" (San Bian; that is, the towns of Dingbian, Anbian, and Jingbian).

The sites for settlement were chosen with an eye for the necessary amenities; clay for building; access to drinking water through wells easy to dig; groves of tamarisk and willow trees for firewood. The low houses were built of mud bricks and grouped in rows of ten or fifteen. The principal street led from the main gate in the outer wall to the church. At Xiaoqiaopan the church had two aisles at right angles to each other, one for the men and one for the women. The men's aisle opened on to a courtyard and faced the priests' residence and the boys' school. The women's aisle opened on to another courtyard, with the sisters' residence, the girls' school, and the Holy Childhood Orphanage.

The population of these villages was built up round a nucleus of Catholic families; then immigrants were brought in by a caravan of camels and a guide. Often one of the missionaries would go to meet the new settlers, giving to each family an ox and cart, food and fodder for a journey of about twenty days. On arriving at the village, each family was given a house. Then they received a field, a pair of oxen, a plow, spades, straw, and seeds. All this was provided by the mission as a loan; in return the settlers were required to give annually 20 to 30 percent of their harvest. The missionary thus took on heavy administrative responsibilities, since he was both mayor, magistrate, and chief of police. It was his responsibility to record all property transactions on documents authenticated with the large crimson stamp seals of the Chinese authorities or the Mongol chieftains.

On the whole these Christian settlements prospered, though they were sometimes affected by famine and epidemics and were threatened by the bandits who roamed the surrounding deserts. There were also threats of Muslim uprisings, such as those that devastated the neighboring province of Gansu. At Xiaoqiaopan, a fortified wall was put around the mission buildings in 1895. The Boxers besieged it for fifty days and then withdrew, on the feast of St. Michael. In 1917 the rampart round the village was strengthened; it enclosed an area 275 yards (250 meters) long and 165 yards (150 meters) wide; the rampart itself was eighteen feet (six meters) high and fifteen to eighteen feet (five to six meters) wide at the base. It was flanked by seven large bastions and eight small ones; around the whole summit of the rampart ran a walkway, protected by a parapet with battlements and arrow slits. The villagers were, however, short of weapons, and those that they had were defective: shotguns, rifles, and pistols, and some culverins and arquebuses, made locally. However, this armament made it clear to local bandits that the Christian peasants were determined to defend themselves and acted as a deterrent. In October 1935 and in May 1936 Xiaoqiaopan was attacked by 1,500 Communist soldiers, who forced local inhabitants to precede them in the assault so as to draw the defenders' fire, but the eighty ill-armed peasants who defended the place warded off these attacks. In all, 236 fortified village enclosures were built during the first quarter of the twentieth century by the Catholic missions of Inner Mongolia.

As well as the *San Bian* region, other areas all over that vast territory were opened up. Thus in the Hetao area, "the loop of the river", to the northwest of the great loop of the Yellow River, Christian settlers carried out important irrigation projects. To the northeast, in the region of Toumet, a Chinese priest, James Liu Jianyin (1848–1900), founded the Mission of the Immaculate Heart of Mary in territories called *Ershisi qing di*, "The twenty-four qing", the qing being a measurement of fifteen acres (seven hectares). In 1895, this settlement comprised 800 Catholics. During the following years it founded several other settlements; already in 1896, one had been made at Balagai, near Baotou. An earth wall was built to prevent flooding from the Yellow River, and dikes were dug to direct the waters coming down from the torrents of the Daqing Mountains. Further east, in the Jining region, Catholic communities were founded that became flourishing. Thus Meiguiyingzi, "the village of the Rosary", founded in 1896 on a property of 8,900 acres (3,600 hectares), is still outstanding today for the number of fervent Catholics who converge on it for the big feasts. A Marian pilgrimage at Mozishan, "the Mount of the Millstone", attracts tens of thousands of pilgrims on August 2 every year.

One can question the quality of the faith of the Chinese settlers who were converted for material profit. To begin with, they submitted passively to the Christian framework that was imposed on them. In order to be admitted to the mission, candidates had to sign a written undertaking that their whole family would study the catechism and observe the commandments of God and of the Church and of the village. Catechism classes were compulsory for all the converts once the harvest had been brought in each September; men and women studied separately. Catechists and sisters taught the principal prayers by heart to begin with. Pupils all sat on the *kang*, the great brick bed, which was heated from underneath by a hypocaust, a channel of hot air. The teacher read out a phrase, and the group repeated it in a sing-song, swaying rhythmically from left to right. The text of these prayers was in a literary style, which was difficult to understand. Bishop Otto, C.I.C.M., who had been vicar apostolic in Gansu Province before retiring to Xiaoqiaopan in 1923, battled a long time before he could obtain an official simplification of the text of these prayers.[6] After the prayers, the catechism had to be learned by heart; its doctrinal content was scarcely understood. Christian initiation seems to have occurred mainly through liturgical practice and by observing the commandments under the attentive eye of the priest.

Sundays were mostly spent in church. Morning prayer, Mass, Stations of the Cross at 11:00 A.M.; the Rosary at 3:00 P.M.; then Benediction and evening prayer, following each other throughout the day. The rejection of pagan customs seems to have occurred as a matter of course in such a close-knit community, which was completely subjected to an earthly ruler, who was also the representative of the Lord of heaven. The cult of the ancestors was naturally replaced by the offering of Masses and the saying of prayers for the dead. All weddings took place in church; if the settlers were short of daughters to marry off, they could readily find brides among the orphans of the Holy Childhood.

Some of those who had been brought up in such a hothouse milieu gave up the faith when they were plunged into a hostile environment, but, on the whole, Christians supported each other and survived. Traditionally, Chinese family life is regulated by rites, with a great respect for ancestral tradition. When these rites become Christian and are transmitted to children and grandchildren, they become the religion of the ancestors, and no one can touch them.

There have been no foreign missionaries in Inner Mongolia since 1950, and the Catholic missions there have suffered thirty years of oppression. Since 1980, however, they have been able to come out into the open in their tens of thousands. Young priests, trained at Hoh-

---

[6] Cf. Carlo Van Melckebecke, C.I.C.M., *Notre bon Mgr Otto: 1850–1938* (Brussels: Éditions de Scheut, 1959), p. 255.

hot (*Suiyuan*, "the blue city") or at Beijing have come to the help of the old priests on their visitations across the steppes. They are always received with joy by the faithful, who want to go to confession and to Communion.

The backbone of the Catholic Church in Inner Mongolia was thus created by the settlements of Chinese converts, who cleared new lands for agriculture. Similar experiences occur elsewhere, but they are rarer. One example comes from Manchuria, where Fr. Henri Roubin, M.E.P., created the colony of St. Joseph, north of Harbin. This brought together 3,000 Catholics at Haibeizhen and caused problems at first, because their departure from other villages deprived them of their few Catholic residents, but the solid community thus founded at Haibeizhen survived many a storm and has an influence today on the chilly regions of northeast China.

Catholic villages, whatever their origins, are generally centers of fervent religious life and seedbeds of vocations. Special mention must be made in this respect of Xiaobajia, "the village of the eight families" in Jilin Province. In 1796, eight immigrant Chinese families settled among the nomadic Manchus, forty-five miles (seventy-five kilometers) north of Changchun. Five of these families were Catholic. For sixty years, no priest passed that way, but the Catholics were regular in saying their prayers. In 1840, Bishop Emmanuel Verrolles, M.E.P., came to the village and bought a piece of land to build a chapel and a priest's house, his idea being to create a stopover on the way to the Korean missions. Later a French priest and a Korean deacon, who were prevented from entering Korea, stayed at Xiaobajia, where they gave instruction to three young men and later to another ten. This was the nucleus of a seminary, which was transferred to Jilin in 1915. Over the last hundred years, Xiaobajia has produced twenty-nine priests, three of whom became bishops, and no less than eighty religious sisters.[7] Today the diocese of Jilin has many young priests and especially young sisters, and, as in the past, many of these come from Xiaobajia.

Since the establishment of the Communist People's Republic, Catholic villages have been either vilified or held up as an example. In the south of Guangdong Province, in the Leizhou peninsula facing the

---

[7] Figures contained in a private letter dated Sept. 24, 1990, from Li Zhixiang, a seminarian of the Jilin diocese.

island of Hainan, the village of the Trinity, which had been renamed ironically *Xianfeng*, "avant-garde", was allowed to fester for years in utter poverty, without even road access. Its thousand Catholics nevertheless kept smiling, and ten vocations to the novitiate of the sisters at Zhanjiang came from there.

Other villages earned the award-winning title *wenming*, "civilized", because of their contribution to moral development. Thus the model village of Weijiazhuang, ninety-five miles (150 kilometers) east of Jinan in Shandong Province, has 4,000 inhabitants of whom 3,750 are Catholics; a visitor describes it thus:

> The villagers are strict observers of the law whenever conscience permits; they are enthusiastic about achieving the goals of the Four Modernizations; they are hard workers, cooperating with one another and perfectly disciplined. Small wonder then that agricultural production in the village is usually far beyond the official quota. In fact, the director told me, it often was 20 percent higher than average.[8]

The visitor in question was a Chinese priest, who came to Weijiazhuang from abroad to see his dying mother. He described other things than the economic success of the village. Christians came from afar to pray with him, staying for hours on their knees.

> Wherever I went, Catholics gave their confidence. They even came from more than sixty miles (100 kilometers) on foot, on bicycle, or by bus. They never tired of hearing me; they prayed with me to the point that, every evening, I felt completely exhausted. But a mysterious force sustained me. I felt immersed in a sacred world, a world in which the three theological virtues, faith, hope, and charity, dictated every word and deed.[9]

This was one among hundreds of villages like it. Officially their survival is justified by the hard work that they do for the "modernization" of the country. What their real life is like can only be talked about confidentially. For many years, they suffered appalling humiliations, too painful to mention. The only language that can be used now for speaking about that period is the language of prayer.

---

[8] Joseph J. Spae, C.I.C.M., "Catholic Life in a Chinese Village", in *China Update* (The Chicago Institute of Theology and Culture: Sept. 1982), suppl. no. 1, p. 5.

[9] Ibid., p. 7.

21

THE UPSURGE OF PROTESTANTISM

In Macao, on a shady hilltop near the Camões Museum, there is a small graveyard that contains the tombs of the first Protestant missionaries to China. In a corner of the enclosure, a large white stone bears the following inscription, in black carved letters:

SACRED TO

THE MEMORY OF

ROBERT MORRISON, D.D.,

The first Protestant Missionary to

CHINA,

Where after a service of twenty-seven years,

Cheerfully spent in extending the kingdom of the blessed REDEEMER,

during which period he compiled and published

A DICTIONARY OF THE CHINESE LANGUAGE,

Founded the Anglo Chinese College of Malacca

And for several years labored alone on a Chinese version of

THE HOLY SCRIPTURES,

Which he was spared to see completed and widely circulated

Among those for whom it was destined

He sweetly slept in JESUS.

He was born at Morpeth in Northumberland

January 5th 1782

Was sent to China by the London Missionary Society in 1807,

Was for twenty-five years Chinese translator in the employ of

The East-India Company,

And died at Canton August 1st 1834

Blessed are the dead which die in the Lord from henceforth

Yea saith the Spirit

That they may rest from their labors

And their works do follow

Them.[1]

---

[1] Illustration on p. 230 in Lindsay Ride and May Ride, *An East India Company Cemetery: Protestant Burials in Macao: Abridged and Edited from Their Manuscripts with Additional Material by Bernard Mellor* (Hong Kong: Hong Kong University Press, 1996).

This epitaph gives the essential stages followed by Robert Morrison, stages also followed by the pioneers of the Protestant missions in China. They involved first of all a time of preparation, while waiting at the gateway to China; then an introduction to the Chinese language, using the Chinese text of the New Testament; finally a first direct contact with Guangzhou through trade relations.

The First Chinese Protestants

Protestants were newcomers to China, compared with Catholics, who had been there for two and a half centuries. Robert Morrison, for all his efforts, left ten converts when he died. In 1853 there were 350 Chinese Protestants, whereas Catholics were then estimated at 330,000. Protestants later grew rapidly in numbers. There were 37,289 in 1889, at which time Catholics approached 500,000.[2]

The slowness of these beginnings can be attributed to several factors: the novelty of missions in the Protestant world, the negative effect of the opium trade on the way in which Christians connected with England were considered, and the strangeness for the missionaries of their first experience of Chinese civilization. Generally speaking, Protestant missionaries stayed within the ports, which had been opened to foreign trade by the various treaties concluded between European nations and the Celestial Empire. However the Protestant missions quickly caught up, and this is readily explainable, firstly by the power of the spiritual witness given by the missionaries and by their social apostolate, and secondly by the modernity that they brought to a China hungry for progress. Whereas Catholics formed their converts by means of doctrine, the Commandments, and prayers learned by heart, Protestants appealed to an emotional experience that was more readily communicated—the consciousness of being a sinner, the fear of hell, the joy of experiencing forgiveness and a new life through faith in Jesus Christ. This missionary impetus was partly inspired by the apostolic spirit of John Wesley (1703–1791), the founder

---

[2] Kenneth Scott Latourette, *A History of Christian Missions in China* (Taipei: Ch'ong-Wen Publishing Co., 1970), p. 479, which refers for numbers of Catholics to Columba Cary-Elwes, *China and the Cross: Studies in Missionary History* (London: Longmans Green, 1957), p. 213.

of Methodism. Its message was addressed to all, without class distinction, but with a special concern for the victims of social injustice.

Protestant missions operated without taking any account of existing Catholic communities, apart from feeling an obligation to run down Catholic beliefs, since they considered that only they proclaimed the true faith in Jesus Christ as Savior—*Jidu jiao*, "the teaching of Jesus". Some Protestants claimed that Catholics worshipped Mary instead of Jesus, believed that the Pope was their savior, and, though they did believe in God, would call him *Tianzhu*, "the Lord of heaven". This appellation was also adopted by some Protestant theologians, but eventually all Protestants opted for the title *Shangdi*, "the Lord above", so as to mark the difference. They also called Catholicism *jiu jiao*, "the old religion", whereas Protestantism was presented as being ready to take its place as *xin jiao*, "the new religion", duly reformed and better adapted to the requirements of Chinese modernization. These arguments hardly affected the Catholics themselves, since they rejected Protestantism as a heresy responsible for the divisions between Christians, but they did have an effect on those Chinese who were interested in Christianity and who had to make a choice.

The Chinese had been humiliated by the Opium War and by the "unequal treaties"; they wanted to discover from Westerners the secret of their power. Missionaries for their part were shocked by the extreme poverty of the population, and they sought to transmit to the Chinese the benefits of civilization and progress. Protestants came as new arrivals with all the prestige of modern nations. They were mostly Americans to begin with, and this made them more acceptable, since the United States had banned the opium trade. In 1845, there were twenty American Protestant missionaries in China, as against ten English and one German. By 1855, there were forty-six Americans and twenty-four English.[3] These emissaries from the New World brought, together with the Christian faith, a message of democracy, science, and progress, ideals that were to be diffused among Chinese students and intellectuals by means of abundant Christian literature.

---

[3] Cary-Elwes, *China and the Cross*, p. 215.

During the first years of Protestant missionary effort in China, emphasis was laid on the diffusion of biblical texts. The American Bible Society began to spread the Scriptures among the Chinese. In 1833 and 1834 Liang Afa, a convert to Christianity, was employed by the American Press Bureau in Guangzhou; he had been trained by the London Missionary Society, in particular by the Scottish professor William Milne and by the printer, Henry Medhurst. Liang Afa began to distribute tracts and booklets to Chinese students in Guangzhou who were taking the provincial examinations for the civil service. The authorities reacted sharply and forbade the distribution of Christian literature; not entirely unreasonably, it may be said, since one of the booklets, entitled *Quan shi liang yan*, "exhortations for our time", was to have an unsettling effect on the mind of a Hakka, Hong Xiuquan, who later became the leader of the Taiping rebellion. The booklet was made up of biblical texts, which formed a summary of Protestant teaching. Hong Xiuquan had had a vision of an old man urging him to destroy demons. He thought he had found in the Bible a striking explanation of his dreams and a confirmation of his mission; God the Father and Jesus, big brother, were urging him to destroy the idols. He baptized himself and preached his version of the Bible to his parents and friends, whom he also baptized. Whereupon one of his first converts, Feng Yunshan, was instrumental in starting a new sect in Guangxi Province. It was tinged with Protestantism, and its members took the name *Bai Shangdi Hui*, "Society of the Worshippers of Shangdi". They destroyed idols and wrote out a confession of their sins on a piece of paper, which they burned before being baptized. They would recite prayers together and offer animal sacrifices. Some of them went into a trance, like Taoist *tang-ki*, and uttered oracles. Thus was formed a mixture of Chinese religious traditions, combined with ill-digested revelations from the Bible. The only Christian instruction that Hong Xiuquan had received, apart from reading the "exhortations for our times", were a few weeks when he was taught by a Baptist, J. Roberts, who subsequently refused to baptize him. In 1850 the Society of the Worshippers of Shangdi became a subversive group, possibly under the influence of a rebel chief from Hunan Province. Their aims were nothing less than the overthrow of Manchu power and the creation of a new order: *Taiping Tianguo*, "the heavenly kingdom of the great peace". In 1853 the rebels seized Changsha and then Wuhan. Proceeding down the Yangzi, they captured the cities on its banks and established their headquarters at Nanjing, which became for ten years *Tianjing*, "the heavenly capital". One of the Taiping leaders, Hong Rengan, who knew more about Christianity, established contact with the missionaries. Some foreigners too thought for a time that they could use the Taiping rebels to obtain a greater opening of China to trade and to the spread of Christianity. In many ways, the Taiping showed an impressive conformity to biblical teaching; they destroyed idols, suppressed the cult of the ancestors, obeyed the Ten Commandments of God, forbade the use of opium, respected women, and encouraged monogamy. They were, however, discredited by the fanaticism of their leaders and by the horrible massacres that are estimated to have cost China twenty million lives. They considered that they had founded a new dynasty, under direct mandate from heaven, and so they treated foreigners with the same arrogance as Manchu rulers; strangers were welcome as long as they were vassals. In 1861, the foreign powers opted for the Manchu government and subsequently helped it to crush the Taiping rebellion.

The Taiping were not recognized as Christians by Protestants, and even less by Catholics. The Taiping rebellion against the corrupt administration of the Manchus was inspired first of all by the Confucian tradition of the *geming*, the termination by the people of the emperor's *Tianming*, his "heavenly mandate"; in this respect, the Taiping could draw a parallel in European history with the Peasants' War of 1524–1525, which devastated Germany at the time of Martin Luther. The Taiping were also influenced by the Taoist ideal of an egalitarian society, as contained in the *Taiping jing*, "the book of the great peace". Some of these Taiping ideals were integrated into Chinese popular culture. Armed resistance against the oppressors of the people is also found in the biblical tradition, but the stories of the Old Testament were more influential with the Taiping than the spirit of the New. Only the good news of redemption by the Cross of Christ can bestow a spiritual dimension on such a struggle, i.e., freedom from sin for the establishment of the kingdom of God, a kingdom that is not of this world. The Taiping had not got that far; they wanted to establish an earthly kingdom. A hundred years later, Communism would also attempt to establish a classless society in the name of an eschatological view of history, i.e., Marxism, which is a reversal of Christian Messianism.

Far from helping Christianity, the Taiping Rebellion often resulted in renewed oppression for Christians, especially Catholics, who were the only ones present in the central provinces of the country. The Manchu authorities had already condemned Catholicism as a subversive religion, because they thought it was compromised with the rebels of the White Lotus Sect. It came as no surprise to the authorities therefore when the Taiping claimed to be Christian. They were seen as destroyers of idols, rejecting the cult of the ancestors, dangerous heretics who must be annihilated. Protestants, who were concentrated for the most part in the open ports of the country, were little affected by the repression that followed the Taiping Rebellion; it only delayed by some ten years their penetration of the interior.

Evangelists in the Interior

During these troubled times, an English evangelist from Yorkshire was getting ready to bring the message of salvation to the Chinese hinterland. James Hudson Taylor (1832–1905) had come to China in 1853, under the auspices of the Chinese Evangelization Society. He traveled around the provinces of the southeast, then settled for three years at Ningbo. That is where, in 1857, he was profoundly moved by the profession of faith of a Chinese man, which he describes as having confirmed his own vocation:

> On one occasion I was preaching the glad tidings of salvation through the finished work of Christ, when a middle-aged man stood up and testified before his assembled countrymen to his faith in the power of the Gospel:
> "I have long sought for the truth," said he earnestly, "as my fathers did before me; but I have never found it. I have traveled far and near, but without obtaining it. I have found no rest in Confucianism, Buddhism, or Taoism, but I do find rest in what I have heard here tonight. Henceforth I am a believer in Jesus. . . ."
> A few nights after his conversion he asked how long this Gospel had been known in England. He was told that we had known it for some hundreds of years. "What!" said he in amazement. "Is it possible that

for hundreds of years you have had knowledge of these glad tidings in your possession, and yet have only now come to preach it to us? My father sought after the truth for more than twenty years and died without finding it. Oh, why did you not come sooner?"

A whole generation has passed away since that mournful inquiry was made; but how many, alas, might repeat the same question today? More than two hundred million in the meanwhile have been swept into eternity, without an offer of salvation. How long shall this continue, and the Master's words, "to every creature", remain unheeded?[4]

Hudson Taylor was tortured by the thought of these millions of souls condemned to hell, whereas it would have been enough for them to hear the proclamation of salvation through Jesus Christ for them to be saved by a simple act of faith. In 1860 he had to return to England because of ill health; he and his wife prayed the Lord to raise up missionaries willing to shoulder the burden of evangelization to the Chinese multitudes. They knew of the Catholic presence in China, but considered that Catholics had received a false gospel, so that everything still had to be done; however, the presence of Catholics in the interior of the country proved that such a task was possible.

Once Hudson Taylor was back in China, he set to work, combining complete confidence in providence with an outstanding gift for administration. His undertaking did not aim to found congregations belonging to particular denominations—Anglican, Methodist, Baptist, Presbyterian, Lutheran, etc. He wanted only the proclamation of the Gospel, a simple appeal to faith. Therefore he concentrated on the eleven provinces of China where no denominations had so far taken root. Elsewhere he relied on the cooperation of pastors from the different churches and left to them the pastoral care of communities that had been converted by his method. He managed the financial side of his undertaking in a way that was both audacious and profitable. He was obsessed with the need to avoid debts. He prayed and got others to pray, with complete confidence that God would provide. His coworkers did not always have a guaranteed salary, but foreign aid poured in. His missionaries in fact lived abstemiously, sharing the lifestyle of the local population and dressing like the Chinese.

---

[4] J. Hudson Taylor, *To China with Love* (Minneapolis Minn.: Dimension Books, Bethany Fellowship Inc., n.d. [Taylor died in 1905]), pp. 126–27.

In 1865 his intention of prayer was to send twenty-two missionaries, two by two, into the eleven provinces that had not yet been touched by Christianity. He thus founded the China Inland Mission, which became by the end of the century the most important Protestant missionary enterprise in China. In 1895 the China Inland Mission had 641 missionaries, 462 Chinese helpers, and 260 stations and outstations with 5,211 communicants.[5] By the time of Taylor's death, at Changsha in 1905, the number of missionaries had increased to 828.

Although the dominant role in Taylor's undertaking was assumed by foreigners, his evangelical movement did arouse the apostolic zeal of the Chinese too. Taylor shows this in his story about Pastor Hsi (Xi). This Chinese scholar from Shanxi Province, who had taken the first of the three literary degrees, had been introduced to the Christian faith by a Wesleyan Methodist missionary, David Hill, who had come to the province to bring help to the victims of widespread famine. Hill was also concerned to make the Gospel known and had organized a literary competition on Christianity. Hsi won the first prize and then started giving Chinese lessons to David Hill. In 1879 Hsi became a Christian. His conversion involved a real change of lifestyle. He gave up opium; he was reconciled to his brothers and brought back his stepmother, whom he had driven away. His wife was laid low by a disease that was attributed to demonic possession; she was cured by the power of her husband's faith. Hsi opened some twenty rehabilitation centers for drug addicts, whom he tried to cure by prayer and medication. According to Latourette, "He was largely independent of the missionary, whom indeed, he tended somewhat to disdain, although he labored in connection with the China Inland Mission. He died, worn out, in 1896."[6]

Mission Stations as Centers of Influence

Although the China Inland Mission did not seek to be responsible for permanent communities, it did operate from well-equipped bases,

---

[5] Latourette, *A History of Christian Missions in China*, p. 393, quoting *China's Millions*, 1906, p. 124.

[6] Ibid., p. 481; quoting Mrs. Howard Taylor, *One of China's Scholars: Pastor Hsi* (London: China Inland Mission, 1903).

as did the missionary societies of all other denominations. Such mission stations comprised a church, a preaching hall, a school, a clinic, and a dwelling for the missionaries and for their Chinese colleagues and assistants. All these were not necessarily to be found in the same place. As well as the church, there was often a chapel, opening onto the street, a sort of information center for passersby. The church was entirely devoid of any statues and contained a prominent pulpit, a piano, and a large cross without a figure. The congregation practised hymns and chorales to tunes imported from England, America, or Germany. There were strict rules for the admission of new members to the community, since moral discipline was more important than doctrinal knowledge. The rule of life was generally strict and implied a break with the surrounding society; thus it was forbidden to take part in local religious customs, including the rites in honor of the ancestors; everything that smacked of superstition was rejected, particularly the distinction between propitious and unpropitious days. Sexual immorality, gaming, and opium were banned. An abyss was thus created between believers, "saved from this perverse generation", and unbelievers, condemned to hell. It was no doubt the concern for moral rectitude, that prevented Protestants from trying to protect Christians, who were in court under accusation of various offenses. Protestants criticized Catholics for appealing too readily to their foreign consulates; since Catholic France had the sole responsibility for the protection of the missions in China, it is understandable that British missionaries especially were not keen to turn to such a quarter for help.

Although the missionary societies had strong support from their churches of origin, both financially and morally, they were concerned to promote the growth of autonomous Chinese communities. They considered that missions would have a future if Chinese Christians became responsible for finances, self-government, and spreading the faith. Various measures were taken to ensure this. In Shandong Province for instance, T. P. Crawford, an American Southern Baptist, tried to promote complete financial independence for his community. All his assistants were unpaid volunteers. Circumstances had led him to this, since his food supplies had been cut off for several years as a result of the American Civil War (1861–1865). Not everyone followed this policy, though on the whole Chinese Protestants became accustomed to supporting their church, whereas most Catholics expected everything from their church.

Similar efforts were made to transfer pastoral direction to the Chinese. They were invited to sit on pastoral councils, where their number gradually increased. American Episcopalians in Hubei Province were in the forefront of this process. Church leaders capable of being fully responsible for the propagation of the faith also had to be trained. In 1866, English Presbyterians opened a theological college in Amoy (Xiamen); by 1876, there were twenty schools of theology with 231 students. In the same year, the General Conference of Protestant Missionaries was held at Shanghai and received the following statistics: there were seventy-three ordained Chinese ministers, 511 assistant preachers, seventy-six peddlers (who were referred to by the French word *colporteur*), and ninety Bible women.[7] The Bible women ensured the distribution of Bibles among women. The peddlers distributed Christian literature. The assistant preachers were often traveling evangelists. All these were receiving training that became more and more adapted as the years went by. In 1879 American Episcopalians founded St. John's College at Shanghai, an institution destined to have a brilliant future.

The Challenge of Protestant Presses

The 1877 General Conference of Protestant Missionaries also received statistics about Protestant publications in China: forty-three books or pamphlets of biblical commentaries, 521 books on theology, twenty-nine lives of saints, eighty-two catechisms, fifty-four prayer books and rituals, sixty-three collections of hymns, seven periodicals, and 101 tracts.[8] This rich crop of publications was not only due to the diversity of denominations and nationalities. Protestants were above all Christians of the Book. They preached the Word, but they did so with the Bible in hand. The Bible was at the heart of their publications, as they produced apologetic and devotional literature. Afterward

---

[7] Ibid., p. 427, quoting Baldwin, *Records of the General Conference of Protestant Missionaries of China*, 1877, p. 486.

[8] Ibid., p. 433, quoting Baldwin, *Records of the General Conference of Protestant Missionaries of China*, 1877, p. 206.

they tried to reach intellectuals and followed more or less the same path as the Jesuits in trying to reach the scholar-gentry. Aiming at reaching greater numbers, they imitated the Confucian tracts, which had popularized the moral norms of self-perfection. The German pioneer of missionary work in China, Karl Gutzlaff, had produced a booklet of thirty pages called *The Model of the Perfect Man*. He took up the Confucian ideal of *junzi*, "the gentleman", completing it in a Christian direction; Jesus in his relation to the Father and the eight Beatitudes indicate the way to perfection.

An American Presbyterian, William Martin (1827–1916), who landed at Ningbo in 1850, soon noticed the elements of natural theology contained in the Chinese conception of the universe, i.e., conscience and the moral ideal. Four years later he published in Chinese an introduction to Christianity entitled *Tiandao suyuan*, which can be rendered "tracing the origins of the way of heaven". He based his work on the natural theology that had been taught at the beginning of the nineteenth century by Scottish philosophers and widely used in American theological colleges. His book closely followed Dugald Stewart's treatise of moral philosophy—the capacity of human reason, the moral faculties, etc.—but he dwelled especially on the proofs for the existence of God and used biblical quotations to accompany his arguments. According to Ralph Covell, his method was to "investigate man in order to understand God".[9] His apologetic work resembled that of Matteo Ricci; in fact, William Martin expressly stated that he wanted to be a Protestant Matteo Ricci. His book was reedited several times and reprinted thirty to forty times over the next sixty years.

The Jesuit scholars and their scholar-gentry converts in the seventeenth century had published many works of purely scientific interest. In the same way, Protestant missionaries at the end of the nineteenth century made the scientific progress of the West known to China. They printed purely secular publications, sometimes inserting articles on Christianity. William Martin, who was known by then for his treatise on apologetics, founded with friends from Beijing a Society for the Propagation of Useful Knowledge. They published a periodical, *Zhongxi wenjian*, "Documents of China and the West",

---

[9] Ralph R. Covell, *Confucius, The Buddha, and Christ: A History of the Gospel in Chinese* (Maryknoll, N.Y.: Orbis Books, 1986), American Society of Missiology Series no. 11, p. 102.

known in English as *The Peking Magazine*, which contained articles on applied science, travel, adventures, and international news. Martin considered that modern science and liberal thought were the best weapons against the ancient superstitions that prevented the Chinese from acceding to the Gospel and to modern progress.

Timothy Richard (1845–1919), a Welsh Baptist, shared William Martin's concern for the transformation of Chinese society, but he was more attentive to the country's cultural values. He came to China in 1870 and founded a mission at Qingzhou in Shandong Province; he then moved to Shanxi Province to help the victims of famine. He witnessed the extreme poverty of the peasants and was moved to intervene with the ruling classes on their behalf. Without making any attempt at conversion, he tried to share Western methods of social progress. He wrote for the Society for the Diffusion of Christian and General Knowledge, which had been founded at Shanghai in 1887 by the Scotsman Alexander Williamson. Timothy Richard and his colleagues of the Baptist Missionary Society made some thirty converts at Shanghai over thirteen years, but they had considerable influence with Chinese intellectuals. Some of the great Chinese promoters of reform at the end of the nineteenth century were inspired by their writings. Thus Timothy Richard was a friend of Liang Qichao, who employed him for a time as his personal secretary; Kang Youwei also frequently consulted him. These two writers and politicians promoted the movement for constitutional reform and tried to open up Chinese culture to progress. Unfortunately their efforts were ruined by Empress Cixi when she abruptly terminated the *wuxu bianfa*, "the Hundred Days' Reform", in 1898.

Unlike most of the Protestants of his time, Timothy Richard was in favor of adapting Christianity to the traditional culture of China. Like the first Jesuits, he was tolerant toward Confucian rites; in addition, and unlike the Jesuits, he got on well with Buddhists and adopted the best of their traditions. He particularly admired the Sutra of the Lotus, venerated by the Tiantai School; he wrote:

> With regard to the doctrine of immortality taught in the New Testament to Western nations—we can find that in the Far East, there is what must be called a Fifth Gospel, or "Lotus Gospel", which for fifteen centuries has shone throughout the Buddhist world in China, Korea, and Japan with such brilliancy that countless millions trust to its light alone for their hope of immortal Life. It will be abundantly evident to Western

students that the wonderful truths taught therein have precisely the same ring as those in the Fourth Gospel, about *Life*, the *Light*, and the *Love*.[10]

Although such an attitude had little influence in the Protestant world at the time, this enthusiastic approach to the Buddhist tradition did have an influence some twenty years later. Karl Reichelt, a Norwegian missionary, established contact with Buddhist intellectuals, whom he called *Daoyou*, "friends of the Tao". In 1922 he founded at Nanjing a center for dialogue on *Jingfeng shan*, "the hill of the pure breath"; he called it the Hermitage of the Mount of the Holy Spirit, a name that recalls the first meeting between Christians and Buddhists at the time of the Syrian Church of the East.

Although Timothy Richard and Karl Reichelt were relatively isolated in their ecumenical endeavors, they never lost sight of their mission, and the heart of their teaching always remained salvation through Jesus Christ. Some Protestant missionaries, however, went further in their admiration for Chinese culture and were converted by it, so that they became its missionaries to the West. This was the case of the German Richard Wilhelm (1873–1930), a missionary in Shandong Province who boasted that he never baptized a single Chinese, in spite of the promptings of his missionary society. Wilhelm was a Christian Socialist; he concentrated on schools and hospitals, while acquiring a thorough knowledge of Chinese. He considered that those who wanted to become Christian would find their own way. His college at Qingdao was taken over by the German government, and Wilhelm thus became a state employee of the Third Reich and worked for the foundation of an Oriental institute. He was keen to share the life of the Chinese people, while living in a large Western-style villa, and he supported Chinese innovators, although his main interest was in traditional Chinese culture. He ended his days as professor of Sinology at the University of Frankfurt, where he used to invite Chinese lecturers.

The range of Protestant activities was thus considerable, and foreigners were preponderant until the first decades of the twentieth century. Although the methods used for Christian implantation were very varied, one can already see two main tendencies at work. One was represented by Hudson Taylor and could be called "pietist"; it was centered on the proclamation of salvation in Jesus Christ, al-

---

[10] Ralph R. Covell, ibid., p. 125.

though it did not neglect the works of mercy, especially medical care. The other, represented by Timothy Richard, was more "liberal" and emphasized service to Chinese society by the promotion of its economic, technical, and scientific development and by the renewal of its traditional culture, but it was also aware of the need for making a full knowledge of the Gospel accessible to the Chinese.

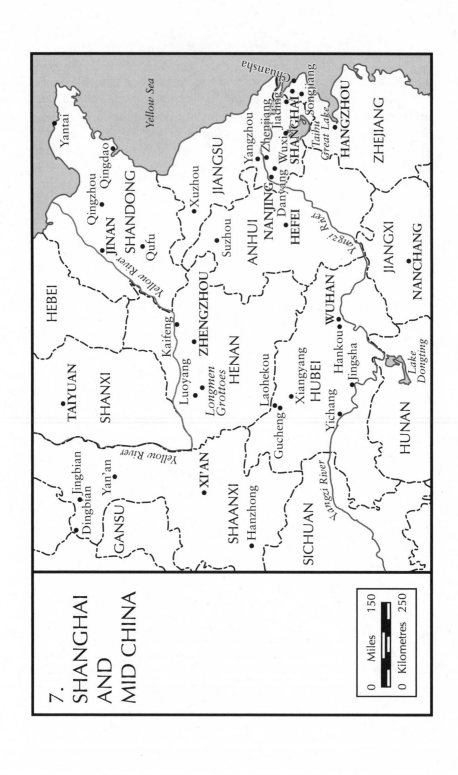

7.
SHANGHAI
AND
MID CHINA

CHRISTIANS FOR PROGRESS

Christians were accepted in China insofar as they served the interests of the country. The friends of missionaries were selective in what they learned from them, accepting what they considered useful to their own career and to China. During the colonial period, missionaries were considered more and more as representatives of the powerful and wealthy West and less and less as messengers of the Cross of Christ. Christian publications reflect this evolution. Immanuel Hsü, writing about the "new learning", describes the change of perspective:

> The influx of Western ideas began with the translation of the Bible and religious tracts in the pre-Opium War period. Of the 795 titles translated by Protestant missionaries between 1810 and 1867, 86 percent were in religion, and only 6 percent in the humanities and sciences. During the 1861–95 Self-Strengthening Movement, translations extended into diplomacy, military arts, science, and technology. Of 567 works translated between 1850 and 1899, 40 percent were in applied sciences, 30 percent in natural sciences, 10 percent in history and geography, 8 percent in social sciences, and about 3.5 percent in religion, philosophy, literature, and the fine arts.[1]

"Strength for China"

Lin Zexu, the hero of the struggle against opium who had cleared the British out of Guangzhou in 1839 after impounding their illicit imports, belonged, together with his friend Wei Yuan, to a reforming group. In 1844 Wei published a large compilation of material about Western countries "for the purpose of using barbarians to attack barbarians, using barbarians to negotiate with barbarians, and learning the superior techniques of barbarians to control the barbar-

---

[1] Immanuel Hsü, *The Rise of Modern China* (New York: Oxford University Press, 2000), 6th ed., p. 420.

ians".[2] This concern for reform was soon to be encouraged at the national level. After the death of the Xianfeng emperor, the reign of his successor, Tongzhi (1862–1874), saw an effort at restoring imperial power. The new emperor had acceded to the throne as a child, and the top civil servants around him worked for the modernization of the country, though it must be admitted that they did this far less effectively than the Japanese of the same period, the Meiji, that is, "the enlightened government" (*ming zhi* in Chinese). These efforts at renewal on the part of Chinese administrators were supported by the emperor's uncle, Prince Kung (1833–1898), president of the *Zongli yamen*, the Chinese foreign office, who opted for cooperation with Westerners. Zeng Guofan (1811–1872), the creator and leader of the Hunan army that had crushed the Taiping Rebellion, reassured conservatives by his reliance on Confucian principles. He was an upright and enlightened man who worked for the moral strengthening of the country. His friend Feng Guifen (1808–1874), a scholar from Suzhou, wrote a collection of forty essays on the different aspects of modernization. Although he was outraged by the aggression of foreigners, he nonetheless cooperated with them to obtain modern arms for China. He used to say, "The only thing to learn from foreigners is how to make strong ships and effective rifles." He also saw the importance of studying mathematics and the sciences, but he would tolerate no change in the sacred inheritance of Confucian ethics. Hence his famous saying, which was popularized by the reformer Zhang Zhidong: *Zhongxue wei ti, Xixue wei yong*, "Chinese learning for the essentials, Western learning for the practice."

This effort to modernize China through *ziqiang*, "self-strengthening", is referred to as the Self-Strengthening Movement, and it brought about the creation of the first modern arsenals in the country. Li Hongzhang (1823–1901), having also played an important part in the military defeat of the Taiping Rebellion, became one of the most powerful government officials and governor-general of northeastern China. He strongly supported the Self-Strengthening Movement and built the great Jiangnan arsenal at Shanghai, which became the center for the modernization of military techniques. Other important arsenals were created at Nanjing and Fuzhou. Such undertakings called for the scientific training of their personnel, and translation offices

---

[2] Quoted in ibid., p. 276.

were attached to the arsenals. The first office for translations, the *Tongwenguan*, founded at Beijing in 1862 for the training of interpreters, was complemented by a school for engineers; its president was the American William Martin. At Shanghai the Chinese scientist Li Shanlan worked with the missionary Alexander Wylie, a mathematician, to take up again the work that had been begun by Paul Xu and Matteo Ricci in the seventeenth century, continuing their translation of the *Elements* of Euclid from Book VII.

This attempt to modernize China by the adoption of Western techniques is also known as the *Yangwu* Movement (*Yangwu* meaning "things of the West"). It began with an attempt to strengthen China militarily, so as to pacify the country and prevent foreign encroachments. Afterward it evolved into a second phase, aimed at increasing the country's wealth. Foreigners, associated with Chinese partners, developed thriving industries, in contrast to the general poverty of the country. Once internal uprisings had been suppressed, it was urgent to create a civil industry as a source of wealth, and the aim of modernization became to make China *fu qiang*, "powerful and rich". The turning point came in 1872 with the founding of the *China Merchants' Steam Navigation Company*. Other commercial undertakings followed in the areas of mining and textiles. Chinese civil servants competed or cooperated in business, but they were often hampered by problems of management or by lack of expertise and outclassed by foreign competition.

The *Yangwu* Movement progressed steadily under Li Hongzhang's direction, and he also supported the first ventures in the field of communication. There was a lot of opposition to trains among the general population, but, in spite of it, a first railway line seven miles (eleven kilometers) long came into service for the coal mines of Tangshan in 1881. In the same year the first telegraph line linked Tianjin to Shanghai. A certain number of students from the language schools were then sent to America or Europe to complete their training. Some were organized in groups under government auspices; others went privately, mostly sponsored by the missions.

In 1876 some thirty students and apprentices from the Fuzhou arsenal were sent to France. With them went a former pupil of the Jesuits, Ma Jianzhong (1845–1900). He and his elder brother, Ma Xiangbo, played a leading role in promoting the modernization of China. They belonged to a Catholic family from Danyang, Jiangsu Province, and they both received a classical and scientific education at the Jesuit school in Shanghai. Although the Jesuits in China had been dispersed when the Society was suppressed in 1773 by Pope Clement XIV, they returned in 1842, twenty-eight years after their restoration by Pope Pius VII. However, by that time the Catholic missions in Beijing had been entrusted to the Vincentians, so the Jesuits went instead to Shanghai, to Jiangsu and Anhui Provinces, and to the vicariate apostolic of Zhili (Hebei Province) in the north.

When Ma Xiangbo was twelve years old, he went all alone to Shanghai without telling his parents. Friends found him a place at St. Ignatius College, the French Catholic School at Zikawei, where his younger brother, Ma Jianzhong, soon joined him. There they learned Latin, Greek, and French as well as studying mathematics and science. They studied Christian doctrine in Matteo Ricci's *Tianzhu shiyi* (*The True Meaning of the Lord of Heaven*), published in 1603, which had used natural theology as an introduction to basic Christian teaching. Their studies were somewhat disrupted when the Taiping rebels broke into Shanghai in 1860, but two years later Ma Xiangbo entered the Jesuit novitiate. His brother followed him but did not stay long, having been put off, it seems, by the disparity of treatment shown to the Chinese and to foreigners. Afterward each of the brothers went his own way.

In 1876 Ma Jianzhong was married at Nanchang, and it was then that Li Hongzhang invited him to accompany as interpreter the group of students from the Fuzhou arsenal that were being sent to France. Ma Jianzhong made friends with French civil servants and academics, and they encouraged him to start university studies while he was in Paris. He went to the *École Libre des Sciences Politiques* and obtained a B.A. in 1878, having studied international law, political institutions, and finance. He returned to China the following year and wrote a treatise on railways and on the raising of loans for building them. Li Hongzhang appreciated his qualities and his competence and entrusted him with various missions, first to the naval base at Tianjin, then to the authorities at Hong Kong, Saigon, Singapore, Calcutta, etc.

In 1882 the Manchu government made Li Hongzhang responsible for relations with Korea, a country that was technically a vassal of China and where there had been recent disturbances. The Japanese had forced entry into Korean ports in 1876, and it seemed to the Chinese that the only way to limit the ambitions of the Japanese was to make them compete with Western powers. Li Hongzhang sent Admiral Ding to Korea, and Ma Jianzhong went with him; he facilitated the signing of treaties with the United States, England, France, and Germany. However, a struggle for power took place within the Korean government, and Ma Jianzhong had to intervene again. There was more trouble when a Korean leader, who was opposed to the opening up of the country, had the Japanese legation burned down and some Japanese civil servants were killed. The person responsible was arrested and sent to China, and Japan received compensation, which included the right to quarter troops in their Korean legation, a concession that was to have dire consequences for the future.

Back in China once more, Ma Jianzhong devoted himself to the economic development of the country by promoting the creation of mines, the building of railways, the development of trade, and the increase of the revenues of the state; he also endeavored to see to the training of competent interpreters. When war broke out between the Chinese and the French (1884–1885), Ma Jianzhong tried to save the China Merchants Steam Navigation Company by having it registered under the American flag. Following the instructions of Li Hongzhang, he negotiated the sale of the company to Russell and Co.; a verbal agreement guaranteed the return of the ships to the Chinese, once the danger of capture by the French fleet was past. These agreements were seen in a very bad light by Chinese conservatives, who accused the negotiators of treason. In fact the Chinese merchant fleet was recovered after the end of the war, which turned out to be a theoretical victory, since the company had not made a profit for several years. Ma Jianzhong's career ended in August 1900 at Shanghai. He was struck down by illness and died in his house while the Boxers were ravaging the surrounding countryside.

His elder brother, Ma Xiangbo (1840–1939), was to outlive him by forty years. He had been baptized Joseph, and, unlike his younger brother, he completed his religious formation with the Jesuits. He was ordained priest in 1870 and was appointed two years later headmaster of the school at Zikawei, where he taught astronomy and mathematics. In 1876 he was transferred to Nanjing, where he was put to translating and editing books on mathematics. He hated this work and considered the European food provided by the Jesuits so disgusting that he left the Society and returned to Shanghai on his own. He found work as a civil servant in Shandong Province. Li Hongzhang appointed him inspector of mines, and in 1881 he was made attaché at the Chinese embassy in Japan. He then joined his brother in Korea to help with the development of trade, industry, and other modernizing projects. In 1886 Li Hongzhang sent him to the United States to obtain loans for the foundation of a national bank of China, but nothing came of this project. Xiangbo went to Europe, following his inquiries in England and France, and continued on to Rome, where he had an audience with Pope Leo XIII.

After the death of his brother in 1900, Ma Xiangbo returned to Zikawei, where he worked at a translation of the Bible. In 1903 he founded the Aurora University at the place where the Jesuits had set up a meteorological observatory. He wanted a new style university, capable of equaling the universities of Europe and America, but the foreign Jesuits modified the system that he had put in place, which provoked student protests, whereupon Xiangbo resigned, to avoid open conflict, it seems. In 1905 he opened the new school of Fudan, and his students followed him there. After the revolution of 1911, the republican government made use of his services in different capacities at the request of Cai Yuanpei, rector of the University of Beijing. By 1915 he was already preparing premises for the future Catholic University of Furen. Together with the Catholics of Beijing, he opposed the establishment of Confucianism as the state religion, a proposal made by *Dujun*, the warlords, to fill the ideological vacuum created by the disappearance of the imperial order and loyalty to the dynasty. At Tianjin he took part in the creation of a Society for Religious Freedom, which brought together Catholics, Protestants, Buddhists, Muslims, and Taoists in an effort to promote complete religious freedom. He was eighty-three when he wrote for *Shenbao* (The Shanghai Journal), the article "World Religions during the Last Fifty Years", in which he emphasized that there is no contradiction but harmony between religion and science. At eighty-eight he took part in the translation into Chinese of St. Thérèse de Lisieux' *Histoire d'une Âme* [*Story of a Soul*]. The Japanese invasion of 1938 forced him to flee to Guilin, Guangxi Province, then to Langson in Vietnam, where he died at the age of 100 on November 4, 1939. It was fitting that the first Catholic school to be opened in Beijing after the ravages of the Cultural Revolution was called the Xiangbo School, a name that enshrines ideals that are still relevant: the combination of patriotism and modernization by means of science and technology. The Xiangbo School is a school for foreign languages. Modernization requires international openings, as was the case one hundred years previously, and this is an area where Catholics have their contribution to make.

Father Lawrence Li and Catholic Publishing

When the Ma brothers entered Ignatius College in Zikawei, the Jesuit mission was flourishing. An orphanage had been opened at Tushanwan (Tousewe) to take in children who had been abandoned during the famine of 1848–1850. A printing press was later added to the orphanage, which made it possible for the orphans to learn a trade while providing useful service. When Aurora University was founded in 1903, the Tushanwan printers already had more than thirty years' experience. The pioneer of Chinese Catholic publishing was Lawrence Li.

Li Wenyu (1840–1911) was born at Chuansha; he was the same age as Joseph Ma Xiangbo, and they were at the same Catholic school in Shanghai. At sixteen Lawrence joined the Congregation of the Immaculate Conception, a pious association for pupils in Jesuit schools. After his secondary schooling, he entered the Jesuit novitiate at twenty-two and was ordained priest ten years later, in 1872. After six years of ministry, he was appointed superior of the junior seminary, situated at the church of Dongjiadu, to the southeast of old Shanghai, not far from the Huangpu River. Fr. Li taught Latin but had greater projects in mind. He had already founded a Catholic weekly, *Yiwen lu*, which could be translated "Useful News".

The American missionary Young John Allen, a Methodist from the deep south, had founded a Protestant weekly eleven years previously. It was called *Jiaohui xin bao* (*The New Journal of the Church*), its English name being *Review of the Times*. It covered scientific and educational topics, as did Fr. Li's weekly, which changed its name to *Xinwen he kexue huibao* (Collection of news and sciences) in 1907, and then became simply *Huibao*.

In 1887 Lawrence Li also started a Catholic monthly, entitled *Sheng Xin hao* (Bulletin of the Sacred Heart). He was still editing these two publications when he was appointed rector of Aurora University in 1906, after Ma Xiangbo's resignation. Fr. Li also lectured on philosophy at the university. When he died in 1911, the weekly *Huibao* ceased publication.

In addition to his contributions to these two reviews, Lawrence Li wrote or translated some sixty books. Over thirty-two years of literary activity, he wrote seventeen books, translated thirty-nine books into Chinese, and directed the edition of four collections.[3] He made a valuable contribution to the history of Catholicism in China and specialized in the origins of Christianity in Shanghai, working on the texts of Paul Xu and the poems of Wu Yushan, one of the first Chinese priests. He also translated into Chinese Fr. Colombel's *Histoire de la Mission du Jiangnan*. Fr. Lawrence Li thus helped the Church in China to become more aware of her roots and more conscious of her identity. Like the Ma brothers, he realized the need for modernization in China, but unlike them he had a passion for the Christian tradition itself. As a student of Christian origins in China, he was truly Chinese and truly Christian.

The Ma brothers and Fr. Li knew how to make use of Zikawei's publishing potential for the benefit of their fellow countrymen. Sometimes they suffered from foreign colleagues who ignored Chinese uses and conventions, but on the whole they adopted the general line of the Jesuit fathers at the service of science and local development.

In 1872 Zikawei became a center for scientific research, a museum of natural history having been created three years previously where Fr. Heude was to build up his collection of skulls of ruminants and *suidae* (members of the pig family). His observations on molluscs and mammals were published in his memoirs, printed at Tushanwan, and these studies were topical at a time when theories of evolution were arousing great interest among the Chinese. The observatory

---

[3] Fang Hao, *Zhongguo tianzhujiaoshi renwuzhuan* (*Biographies of the History of Catholicism in China*) (Hong Kong: Catholic Truth Society, 1967), vol. 3, p. 286; quoting a study by Chen Baixi. In Chinese.

was in touch with many meteorological stations throughout East Asia and published a daily bulletin that was much appreciated in this cyclonic region. The series of monographs entitled *Variétés sinologiques* began to appear in 1892. The Jesuits in the diocese of Xianxian (Zhili district in Hebei), especially Fathers Séraphin Couvreur and Léon Wieger, produced in-depth studies of Chinese language and civilization.

The printing press at Tushanwan was not the only one at the service of Catholic publications. At Beijing the Vincentians from Beitang published more than 500 titles between 1864 and 1930 in the following range of languages—Chinese, Mongolian, Tibetan, Latin, French, German, Flemish, Italian, and Spanish. In 1900, when defense against the Boxers was a priority, some of the machines were melted down to make ammunition, but afterward the work began again and included the publication of language studies, prayer books, theology, the writings of Fr. Huc, and also the printing of documents on the railways and law books in Chinese.

The Paris Foreign Missions also launched a printing press in 1884 on the island of Shangchuan, the place where St. Francis Xavier had died in 1552. As a location it was safe from bandits on the mainland, but pirate attacks forced a move to Macao; then the Portuguese proved troublesome, and the press moved again, to Hong Kong this time. The Nazareth Press there was built near the Bethany Home for retired priests, so that it was sometimes possible for them to help out with the work. Texts published by the Paris Foreign Missions in Hong Kong for a Chinese readership consisted mostly of prayer books, catechisms, apologetics, and lives of saints; there were also Latin textbooks for seminarians. As was the case with the Vincentians and the Jesuits, there were also many books in French, on linguistics, ethnography, botany, and natural history. The studies thus published had been made in distant provinces, Guizhou, Guangxi, Yunnan, and even Tibet. They constituted a new contribution to Chinese scientific studies, although it was an indirect contribution, since it was written in French and all the specimens that were the object of description and publication were shipped to museums in Paris.

As an example of this work, one can mention Fr. Jean Marie Delavay, from Savoy, who worked in Yunnan Province and became a distinguished botanist. He sent to Paris 3,200 specimens of plants, of which one thousand varieties had not yet been identified and described in China itself.[4] Fr. François Gore made the geography of Tibet known through his articles and through an overall study, *Trente ans aux portes du Tibet interdit 1908–1938*. Other priests of the Paris Foreign Missions, working in the northeastern provinces of China, were equally effective in making the culture of that region known; Fr. Henri Lamasse, from Alsace, published his *Nouveau Manuel de langue écrite chinoise* in 1920; in 1934 Fr. Lucien Gibert published the large *Dictionnaire historique et géographique de la Mandchourie*, which ran to 1,040 pages, with illustrations and maps.

Another scientific missionary worthy of special mention is Fr. Armand David (1826–1900), the first Westerner to describe the giant panda. Fr. David was a Vincentian who was born at Espelette in that part of the Basque homeland now within the French Republic. He undertook two extensive and dangerous expeditions in China (1862–1870; 1872–1874), often traveling alone; during these he collected a great number of specimens and made many observations that greatly increased the knowledge of Chinese flora and fauna. The butterfly bush that grows on wasteland all over the northern hemisphere bears his name, *Buddleja davidii*. In 1869 he was sheltering in the College of the Annunciation that had been founded by the Paris Foreign Missions for the training of Chinese priests at Muping in the remote Sichuan Province of southwestern China, an area surrounded by the high mountains that give it a subtropical climate. It was there that Fr. David identified the giant panda, the black-and-white bear that has become the symbol of friendship between China and the great nations of the world. In 1983 the civil authorities of the Baoxing district of Sichuan, near the Fengtongzhai Giant Panda Reserve, put up a memorial tablet to Fr. Armand David on the wall of the church that stands next to the former college of the Paris Foreign Missions, a fine wooden building that is still standing. In November 2000 a group of forty-five French visitors, twenty-six of them from *le pays basque*, unveiled another wall memorial to the memory of their great fellow countryman from Espelette, an inscription in Chinese, English,

---

[4] Andre Bareigts, *Travaux intellectuels des prêtres M.E.P. en Chine* (duplicated text of a lecture given at Hualien, Taiwan, July 4, 1989).

French, and Basque, engraved on a Basque cross (the fylfot or swastika counterclockwise, with rounded extremities to the arms).[5]

In October 2003, the French Basque cardinal, Etchegaray, a fellow countryman of the great scientist, was invited together with the mayor of Espelette by the mayor of Ya'an to attend the opening of the Armand David Museum in Baoxing.

Social Reform

Chinese Christians, who were suspected of having been bought by foreigners, sought to prove their loyalty by working for modernization. They accepted the ideal of a China both powerful and wealthy, but in fact the enrichment of merchants and business partners did nothing to lessen the dire poverty of a population that was rapidly expanding demographically. Old superstitions and irrational customs, many of them unhygienic, contributed to weakening the people even more.

Both Catholics and Protestants, responding to the demands of the same Gospel, multiplied their works of mercy. Their approach was, however, somewhat different, because of the differences in their religious traditions and their cultural background. Catholics were well known for their numerous orphanages. Their humanitarian concern for infants exposed to die was strengthened by their belief in the sacramental efficacy of baptism. They looked after the Christian education of these children and prepared the girls for Christian marriage, hoping to lay the foundation for Catholic families of the future. Unfortunately these orphanages had a bad press. The worst rumors circulated in the general population, which was both credulous and xenophobic. The sisters were accused of mixing the eyes of the children with lead to produce silver. When the girls grew up, their parents sometimes appeared and claimed them back, so as to make a profit by marrying them off. The sisters tried to protect the girls, and there were tensions, which reinforced popular hostility.

Protestants, aware of the orphanages' bad reputation, avoided such foundations, while trying to rescue the worst cases of exposure. They

---

[5] Cf. Emmanuel Boutan, *Le Nuage et la Vitrine: Une vie de Monsieur David* (Paris: Éditions Raymond Chabaud, 1993).

were not concerned to save the souls of babies by administering a sacrament that they understood differently; their primary concern was to bring about the moral conversion of adults. They were trying to save a sinful generation. They attacked the opium problem, and here they were concerned not only with the Chinese but also with British merchants. The General Conferences of Protestant Churches in 1877 and 1890 examined this problem and encouraged the formation of antiopium societies. As well as condemning drugs, Protestants vigorously condemned gambling, concubinage, and the prevalent habit of lying.

Foreign missionaries also discouraged the painful and unhygienic practice of binding the feet of little girls. Round about the year 1870 girls' schools, opened at Hangzhou, Wenzhou, Amoy, and Beijing, made it a condition of entry that the feet of pupils should be unbound. At first there was fierce opposition from the parents, who were afraid that they could not marry off daughters with large feet. It seems that small feet were an essential part of sex appeal. Later Chinese social reformers, inspired by the missionaries, took over the movement against the binding of feet.[6]

Unfortunately the humanitarian concerns of foreign missionaries were often discredited by the antisocial behavior of their fellow countrymen. Racial discrimination and the priority given to business interests belied the gospel of charity. In fact, the churches rarely intervened against the economic exploitation of Chinese manpower and the traffic in coolies, a word that comes from the Chinese *ku li*, "hard labor". Sin was only denounced in its individual and private manifestation; its social dimensions were overlooked.

Although Christians were ineffective in their attempts to control exploitation, they did better in the area of education. In fact their main contribution to social change came through the founding of schools. In the case of both Catholics and Protestants, the aim of the first schools was to provide religious instruction and to recruit catechists and preachers from the better pupils. At the General Conference of Protestant Missionaries in 1877, the American Presbyterian

---

[6] For a personal description of the experience of foot binding see Jung Chang, *Wild Swans: Three Daughters of China* (London: Harper Collins, 1991), paperback ed., 1993, pp. 31–32. In Yixian, Liaoning Province, a girl born in 1909 was subjected to foot binding, whereas "by the time her sister was born in 1917, the practice had virtually been abandoned"; ibid., p. 32.

Calvin W. Mateer maintained this priority but enlarged its purpose to include the formation of teachers through Christian schools and "through them to introduce to China to the superior education of the West", to prepare the Chinese "to take the lead in introducing to China the science and the arts of Western civilization" as "the best means of gaining access to the higher classes of China".[7] Up to the end of the twentieth century, most Christian schools were primary schools, and the aim of Christian formation remained paramount, but the Chinese classics were taught as well as Western subjects. However, few non-Christians sent their children to these schools, which were not good at preparing pupils for state examinations; the traditional preparation for these was only abolished in 1905. Christian schools did nevertheless offer some advantages. Their teaching was free, and they often offered free board as well. They also gave the possibility of a future career with foreign firms; this was a particularly attractive prospect for Christians, who had not for a long time been able to join the local civil service, since all official posts required the practice of Confucian rites.

At the beginning of the twentieth century, Protestant schools especially progressed to the secondary and tertiary levels of education. This was probably due to the influence of American missionaries, since in the United States at this time primary education became the responsibility of public authorities, whereas secondary schools often continued to be run by the churches. This was transposed to China; secondary colleges were opened at Nanjing and Beijing by "Northern Methodists", while American Presbyterians founded in Guangzhou a secondary college, which had 105 pupils in 1895.

Catholics too improved the level of their schools, thanks largely to the contribution of religious congregations, in both the girls' and the boys' sector. The French Marist brothers opened schools at Beijing and Tianjin in 1891; they were gradually replaced by Chinese brothers during the first decades of the twentieth century. By 1949 there were 242 Marist brothers teaching in forty schools. At Tianjin the boarding school for girls run by the Daughters of Charity was taken over by the Franciscan Missionaries of Mary sisters in 1914; there were seventy pupils at the time, and the numbers went up to 350

---

[7] Kenneth Scott Latourette, *A History of Christian Missions in China* (Taipei: Ch'ong-Wen Publishing Co., 1970), pp. 441–42.

in 1923; they were described as "belonging to the highest levels of Chinese society or to the European colony. Studies are carried out in either English or French."[8] In 1922 the Jesuits founded an industrial and commercial school at the tertiary level at Tianjin.

Although Protestants were fewer in numbers, they developed more rapidly than Catholics in the field of education. This can be explained in part by their use of English, their emphasis on secondary education, and by exchanges with America. The influence of the Y.M.C.A. on Chinese young people must also be taken into account. The Young Men's Christian Association originated in England but had been brought to China through the United States. The first groupings of young people were organized in 1885 at Fuzhou and in the Zhili district. The Y.W.C.A., Young Women's Christian Association, began in China in 1888. By 1900 the Y.M.C.A. had forty-eight associations in eight provinces. At the national convention of 1901, three-quarters of the delegates were Chinese. The Y.M.C.A. was active in Christian schools and also organized programs of religious, educational, social, and sporting activities. Eventually associations were formed in state schools with the aim of furthering the human, if not Christian, formation of new generations for China.

The contribution of Protestants was equally outstanding in the area of medicine. In 1905, out of 3,445 missionaries, 301 were doctors, (207 men and 94 women). They worked in 166 hospitals and 241 dispensaries. In the same year, 35,301 patients were admitted, and there were more than 1,044,000 outpatients.[9] In addition to the direct care of the sick, Protestants aimed at the formation of local medical personnel. In 1906 the Union Medical College was founded in Beijing, and other medical colleges opened in Shandong Province and at Hankou, Nanjing, and Changsha. Qualifications for medical doctors were given by the Department of Medicine at St. John's University in Shanghai, and the Catholic Aurora University, Shanghai, also had a medical faculty.

Catholics had opened a few hospitals, for instance, at Hankou, Shanghai, and in Shaanxi Province and Inner Mongolia, but they concentrated on medical care throughout the countryside, as was done

---

[8] Marie Bernard, F.M.M., *Volontiers: Marie Chrysanthe de Jésus 1894–1963* (Paris: Imprimerie Franciscaine Missionaire, 1966), p. 71.

[9] Latourette, *A History of Christian Missions in China*, p. 652.

later by Mao Zedong's "barefoot doctors". In Guangzhou a leper hospital was built by Fr. Conrady, a friend of Blessed Damian de Veuster, the Belgian priest who had given his life to care for the lepers on the island of Molokai, Hawaii. In Manchuria there was a hospital for plague victims. The sisters called the Franciscan Missionaries of Mary, who had come to China in 1886, combined medical care with education. They were to be found in the hospitals and community clinics of Hankou, Shanghai, Yantai, and Yichang; they went as far as the confines of Tibet to look after a leper hospital.

The influence of Christianity on the transformation of Chinese society at the end of the nineteenth and the beginning of the twentieth century is a fact of history. Whereas previously the Gospel had only reached the poor peasants, now intellectuals and the leaders of society were in touch with Christians. But the presentation of the Christian message had also changed. Christianity was seen as important because it represented a progressive Western civilization. Sun Yat-sen, "the father of the Chinese revolution", was perhaps the most representative figure of the period. When he was very young, he left Guangdong Province to join his elder brother, a wealthy businessman in Honolulu. Sun Yat-sen learned about Christianity at the Anglican mission school at Iolani in Hawaii. When he was seventeen he returned to Hong Kong and entered Queen's College, where he got to know Dr. Hager, a young American missionary who baptized him in 1884. Sun Yat-sen retained many moral principles from his Christian education. He used to say that Christians were more advanced than the Chinese when it came to practising charity, but he observed that the principle of universal love also belongs to the Chinese tradition, since it had been advocated by Mozi in the fourth century B.C.

Sun Yat-sen (1866–1925) with his wife
Soong Qingling (1893–1981)

Photograph taken in 1921. Sun Yat-sen came from a peasant family in Guangdong Province. He provided the revolutionary idealism and the organization of a group which was instrumental in overthrowing the Qing dynasty in 1912. Sun became provisional president of the Government of the Republic of China in 1912 but gave way to a fellow revolutionary, Yuan Shikai, who became President. Yuan developed into one of the warlords who ruined China, fighting each other until 1928, spurning democracy and seeking personal power. In 1919 Sun Yat-sen reestablished the Kuomintang which adopted the Three Principles of the People: nationalism, democracy, and the people's livelihood, but was unable to ensure stable government. He died of cancer in 1925.

THE CHURCH OUTDISTANCED

In the summer palace at Beijing, a marble boat on the edge of Lake Kunming evokes the banquets that were held there by Empress Cixi. It is said that a part of the budget of the Chinese admiralty was wasted on this luxurious folly. It was a symptom of the country's malady. Hardly were the new buildings of the summer palace completed than the Chinese navy was annihilated by the Japanese in 1894. Li Hongzhang, the man who had hoped to save China by building modern warships, was compelled to sign the cession of Formosa (Taiwan) to Japan.

The reformer, Yan Fu (1853–1921), drew the lessons of this bitter defeat in four essays, one of them entitled *Yuan qiang*, "The Origins of Power".[1] This enlightened scholar had been educated at the Fuzhou naval college and afterward in England, at Portsmouth and Greenwich naval colleges. He was not afraid of exposing the weakness of the Chinese cultural tradition. He argued that the fundamental obstacle to China's progress was not technical backwardness but mentality; it was a spiritual problem, and it manifested itself in the attitude of the Chinese. They are obsessed by the past; they dream of social harmony; they are paralyzed by the principle of submission to others. He had observed that Westerners, on the contrary, are turned toward the future; they have a spirit of struggle and conquest. In the West, the individual is free to start something new; competition allows the more enterprising members of society to make their mark. Yan Fu was very fond of horse racing because it was the best horse that won. He was also enthusiastic about the theory of evolution, and in 1896 he translated Thomas Huxley's *Evolution and Ethics* under the title *Tian yan lun*. It was a translation into particularly elegant classical Chinese and was much appreciated by Chinese intellectuals who were in favor of science and progress.

---

[1] Yan Fu's essays were translated into French and edited by Fr. François Houang with the title *Les Manifestes de Yen Fou* (Paris: Arthème Fayard, 1977).

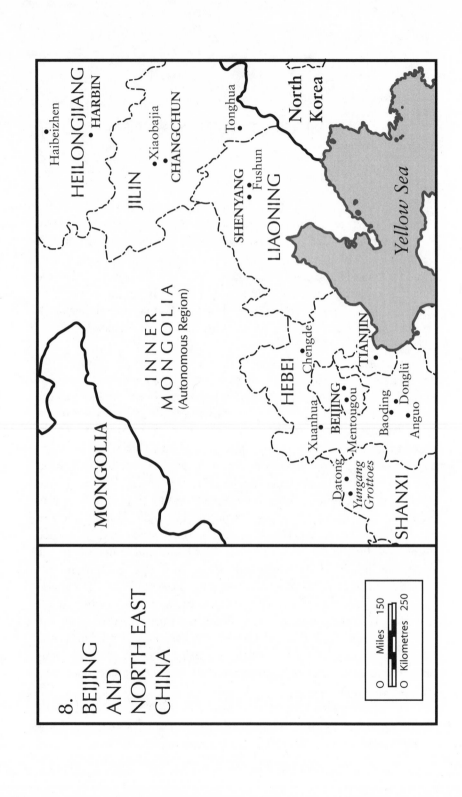

8.
BEIJING
AND
NORTH EAST
CHINA

MONGOLIA

INNER MONGOLIA
(Autonomous Region)

HEILONGJIANG
Haibeizhen
HARBIN

JILIN
Xiaobajia
CHANGCHUN

Tonghua

SHENYANG
Fushun

LIAONING

North Korea

Yellow Sea

HEBEI
Chengde

TIANJIN

Xuanhua
BEIJING
Mentougou

Baoding
Donglü
Anguo

Datong
Yungang Grottoes

SHANXI

O   Miles   150
O   Kilometres   250

Japan had modernized itself and had vindicated its strength by defeating China. The Japanese, although despised by the Chinese, had inherited from them the foundation of their culture; their written language derived partly from Chinese. In 1898 the Zhang Zhidong, a member of the scholar-gentry, wrote an *Exhortation to Study*, in which he recommended the sending of Chinese students abroad, to Japan for preference. He also pointed out that the writings of the West would be more accessible if they were read in Japanese translation. In the first decade of the twentieth century many Chinese students went to Japan to study, and, although they were closely monitored by emissaries of the Manchu government, many of them set up revolutionary groups. The most avant-garde were followers of Liang Qichao, who had had to flee to Japan after the failure of the "Hundred Day" Reform of 1898. Liang Qichao was the advocate of science, freedom, and nationalism; he called for the creation of a "new man", who would be courageous, well organized, and independent. Student groups, meeting in secret, sought for ways of creating that "new man" by reading Francis Bacon, Descartes, Montesquieu, Rousseau, Kant, Byron, Darwin, and the heroes of the struggle for a united Italy. The more activist students joined Sun Yat-sen, who favored a radical revolution. After the failure of several attempts in the region of Guangzhou, the Wuchang Uprising of October 1911 brought success to the struggle against the Manchu Dynasty, and on February 12, 1912, the six-year-old Xuantong emperor, whose personal name was Pu-yi, was made to abdicate, thus bringing to an end the last of China's twenty-five dynasties and over two thousand years of imperial rule. The Italian film director Bernardo Bertolucci produced in 1987 *The Last Emperor*, a film that evoked for Western audiences both the splendor of the ritual of the old imperial court and the sadness of the boy emperor's life. Pu-yi and his household were put on the civil list and continued to live in the seclusion of the Forbidden City until 1924, when Pu-yi was forced to leave Beijing. In the struggle for power between the revolutionary leaders, Sun Yat-sen was ousted by Yuan Shikai, who controlled the powerful army of the north and who was proclaimed on February 15, 1912, as the first president of the Chinese Republic.

The years that followed showed up the weakness of a republican government in a people without experience of democracy. Young intellectuals were to experience a whole series of bitter disappointments. Japan was on the side of the Allies during the First World War and occupied the German concessions in Shandong Province. The Japanese then imposed upon the Chinese government the recognition of their interests and of their privileged position in China by the infamous Twenty-One Demands, which were presented to Beijing in January 1915 and which Yuan Shikai accepted in May. This was seen by the Chinese as a *guochi*, a "national humiliation", and it provoked the indignation of intellectuals, who were even more disgusted when Yuan Shikai made moves to restore the empire, with himself as emperor. He attempted to reestablish the cult of Confucius, and he went annually to the Temple of Heaven in Beijing, as the emperors had done, to preside over the traditional rites. However, Yuan Shikai died in 1916 without having been able to realize his ambitions, and there followed a brief return to republican legality, but effective power was in the hands of the generals who governed the provinces. These *dujun*, the "warlords", were conservative, brutal, and corrupt; they exercised a kind of feudal power. For a time they managed the country as a group, and they thought they could maintain order by imposing Confucianism as the state religion, but they soon broke up into conflicting cliques, which looked for support to foreign powers, to the detriment of China's interests.

At that time a strong national feeling and a romantic enthusiasm inspired the young intellectuals of China. They wanted to free their country from feudalism and to defend it from foreign encroachments. The Chinese government was invited to Versailles for the Peace Conference of 1919, and the Chinese hoped that this would recognize their full autonomy and territorial integrity, but Chinese demands were ignored, and the former German territories in Shandong Province were entrusted to the Japanese. This political insult was the immediate cause of the May 4th Movement of 1919, when massive demonstrations of students and academics spread like wildfire from Beijing to the cities of the provinces.

What these young insurgents wanted above all were liberation from the bureaucratic yoke of a feudal government and the tearing down of the old-fashioned Confucianism of a traditional society, with its outdated moral norms and its debilitating superstitions. Their rallying cry was "democracy in politics; science in the realm of ideas", a formula taken from the manifesto of Chen Duxiu, "A Warning to Youth", which appeared in the first number of the review *Xin qingnian (New Youth)* published in 1915 in Chinese but with the French title *Jeunesse nouvelle*:

> Be independent and not submissive
> Be progressive and not conservative
> Be dynamic and not reserved
> Be international and not isolationist
> Be practical and not formal
> Be scientific and not imaginative

Chen Duxiu (1879–1942) had studied in Japan and then in France from 1907 to 1910. While in France he had been influenced by the ideas of the French thinkers of the previous century. He took his democratic ideals from Lafayette (1757–1834), the French aristocrat who led military support for the American colonists when they rebelled against the British crown in 1776; he adopted the evolutionism of Lamarck (1744–1829), the zoologist who was the first to formulate clearly a theory of the evolution of the species; his socialism derived from Babeuf (1760–1787), a French revolutionary advocating collectivization, and from Saint-Simon (1760–1825), the social philosopher who believed that the rational reorganization of society would remove most of the evils that afflict humanity. Chen Duxiu was also one of the first Chinese to adopt the ideas of Karl Marx (1818–1883), whose *Communist Manifesto* had appeared in 1848. Revolutionary enthusiasm as espoused by Chinese students expressed itself first of all in literary form. In 1917 Hu Shi, who was a student in America at Columbia University, New York, sent Chen Duxiu an article that spelled out eight conditions for the modernization of the Chinese language. These can be summed up as a straightforward and clear way of expressing oneself, having something to say, and being interested in the life of the people. Lu Xun (1881–1936) was one of the first to use this popular speech *baihua*. In 1918, he published a series of sarcastic little essays that appeared under the title *Diary of a Madman*. He denounced the hypocrisy of Confucian principles, saying that under the standard of the beautiful virtues of justice and benevolence, the Chinese eat each other alive, so that Confucianism can be described as *chi ren de lijiao*, "a ritual for cannibalism".

After the May 4th Movement, there were two possible ways ahead. One, the more pragmatic and rational way, was taken up by Hu Shi and derived its inspiration from the American John Dewey; if problems arose, they should be solved one by one. Hu Shi believed in science; he thought that science would ensure the happiness of the human race and that the scientific theory of evolution would ensure its progress. Hu Shi's name advertised his beliefs, since he had chosen to incorporate in it the word *shi*, which means "adaptation". The other way was more ideological and preferred "isms" to problems. It considered that the future of China lay with anarchism or populism or Bolshevism or Marxism. The writer Pa Kin (Ba Jin) favored anarchism, and he too used his name to show his convictions, since the first syllable stood for Bakunin and the last one for Kropotkin. By his novels he sought to take to pieces the oppressive structure of the traditional Confucian family.

The Russian Revolution of October 1917 fired the enthusiasm of Li Dazhao, a socialist intellectual who had been educated in Japan. He wrote:

> As for the recent coup d'état in Russia, the thing to do is to raise our head and welcome it as the dawn of the new civilization of the world. Let's listen for the message of the new Russia, based on freedom and humanism.[2]

Although Li Dazhao had been an anarchist and a populist to begin with, he rapidly evolved toward a Marxist view of history. He considered that the Western powers at the Treaty of Versailles in 1919 had backed the Japanese Pan-Asiatic policy through fear of the progress that Bolshevism was making in Asia. He also came to see the Bolshevik Revolution in a new light, as a revolt of oppressed peoples against the imperialism of international capitalism. He thus moved from an evolutionary view of China's renaissance to belief in the revolutionary struggle of the oppressed masses. From his study of Marxism, he concluded that such a struggle would inevitably lead to victory, since such a victory derives from a scientific law, the theory of history that

---

[2] Chinese text in Li Dazhao, "Comparative Views on the French and Russian Revolutions" in the review *Yanzhi jikan* (July 1, 1918); reproduced in Li Dazhao, *Selected Works*, p. 104.

Marx had expounded. He noted that the Marxist science of history eliminated any acceptance of supernatural forces outside human control. After having been a champion of liberty, he thus became a believer in historical determinism. In December 1920 he published an article entitled "The Value of the Marxist Conception of History". This proved to be a turning point; Chinese intellectuals turned to Marxism because they saw it as an ideology that was both scientific and moral. This new belief in "the scientific law of history" replaced their traditional belief in the necessity of *tian ming*, the law of destiny.

During the winter of 1918–1919, Li Dazhao, who was by then professor of political economy and librarian at the University of Beijing, met a young man, Mao Zedong from Hunan Province, who had revolutionary ideals. Li Dazhao offered him the post of assistant librarian for the meager salary of eight yuan a month. Mao, who was then twenty-five, must have subsisted mainly on reading, especially the articles of Li Dazhao and Chen Duxiu. Like Li Dazhao, Mao had originally been humanist and populist in tendency; he worked in Changsha at promoting popular education and mutual aid. The repressive measures of the military governor of Hunan Province later made him commit himself to the revolutionary struggle, inspired by the Marxist dialectic of class struggle. At that time his friends in the Society of the New Citizen left for France to follow a work and study program; among these young intellectuals were Deng Xiaoping, Zhou Enlai, and other future leaders of Chinese Communism. They were helped by French Communists and founded in Paris the first cells of the Chinese Communist Party. In China itself the first Party Congress took place in July 1921 under the protection of the French concession in Shanghai.

Isolated Catholic Patriots

The flood of revolutionary ideas that was overwhelming China came from sources that were humanist, antireligious, and which attributed to science a role that went beyond its proper boundaries; they were not strictly scientific but "scientistic". The French term *scientisme* means the use of science that goes beyond its proper sphere and encroaches on areas of thought and action that can only be adequately treated by philosophy and theology. In his encyclical letter of 1998, *Fides et*

Ratio, Pope John Paul II was to describe scientism as a philosophical approach which refuses to admit the validity of forms of knowledge, other than those of the positive sciences. Scientism dismisses values as mere products of emotions.[3]

The France of the Third Republic was itself anticlerical and only maintained its protectorate over the Chinese missions so as to promote French interests abroad. However, French missionaries came from strongly Catholic elements in French society and were proud of their homeland. On days of special celebrations they used to decorate their churches with French flags, and this at the very time when Chinese nationalism was asserting itself aggressively.

There was at that time a lone voice among the missionaries who proclaimed that Chinese Christians also had the right to love their own country: Fr. Frédéric Vincent Lebbe (1877–1940). He was the son of a Belgian Catholic father and a convert mother who had been born in Worcester, England. Lebbe had joined the Vincentians in 1895 and had been sent in 1901 to Beijing, where he was ordained priest. Already as a child living in Belgium but with multinational cultural influences from his family, he had affirmed his independent spirit. Once when he was in class with Flemish schoolchildren, who were actively promoting Flemish culture and the Flemish language in reaction to French cultural predominance in the Belgium of that time, young Lebbe had gone to the blackboard to write in large letters the slogan *Vive la France*; this was not well received. As a missionary in China, Fr. Lebbe found himself surrounded by French colleagues

---

[3] John Paul II, Encyclical Letter *Fides et Ratio* (1998), no. 88: "[s]cientism . . . is the philosophical notion which refuses to admit the validity of forms of knowledge other than those of the positive sciences; and it relegates religious, theological, ethical and aesthetic knowledge to the realm of mere fantasy. . . . Science would thus be poised to dominate all aspects of human life through technological progress. The undeniable triumphs of scientific research and contemporary technology have helped to propagate a scientistic outlook, which now seems boundless, given its inroads into different cultures and the radical changes it has brought.

Regrettably, it must be noted, scientism consigns all that has to do with the question of the meaning of life to the realm of the irrational or imaginary. No less disappointing is the way in which it approaches the other great problems of philosophy which, if they are not ignored, are subjected to analyses based on superficial analogies, lacking all rational foundation. This leads to the impoverishment of human thought, which no longer addresses the ultimate problems which the human being, as the *animal rationale*, has pondered constantly from the beginning of time. And since it leaves no space for the critique offered by ethical judgment, the scientistic mentality has succeeded in leading many to think that if something is technically possible it is therefore morally admissible."

with a colonialist mentality, and there his slogan became *Vive la Chine*. He took his inspiration from St. Paul, who had made himself a Jew with the Jews and a Greek with the Greeks, and so he tried to become Chinese with the Chinese. He learned to speak Chinese well, and he realized the importance of respecting the social conventions of the Chinese, although he avoided the practice of some of his colleagues, who insisted that their Chinese servants should serve them as they would a mandarin. He had a great admiration for St. Vincent de Paul, whose name he had taken at his confirmation, and like him he knew how to live as a poor man among the poor.

Many Chinese Catholics felt left behind by the rising nationalism in their country. They welcomed Fr. Lebbe's patriotic statements with enthusiasm, and they gave him the name *Lei Mingyuan*, "the thunder that sounds from afar".[4]

In 1906, Fr. Lebbe was put in charge of a Catholic church in the Tianjin district. Vincent Ying Lianzhi, an ardent convert, easily obtained the support of Fr. Lebbe for the development of welfare work in the city. Vincent Ying had experience of publishing, and so he and Fr. Lebbe launched a Catholic weekly, *Guang yi lu*, (*Light of justice*), which made known the apostolic work undertaken in Tianjin. In 1909 an association for the Propagation of the Faith was created, which replaced paid catechists with lay volunteers. The first congress of the association took place in 1911 in the Church of Our Lady of Victories and brought together sixty delegates, representing 300 active members. In October 1914 the first National Congress of Catholic Action took place in Tianjin, Fr. Lebbe presiding. The lay leaders present at the congress were sufficiently aware of the real interests of their country to protest against the government plans for imposing Confucianism as the state religion. In 1915, when China was being humiliated by the "twenty-one demands" imposed by the Japanese, the patriotic committee in Tianjin invited Fr. Lebbe to make a speech on the love of one's country. He electrified an audience of 6,000 by what he said. On October 10, 1916, the fourth anniversary of the proclamation of the Chinese Republic, a Catholic daily was launched in Tianjin, *Yishi bao* (*Social welfare*). It was objective, independent, and rapidly became the daily with the largest readership in north China.

---

[4] This translation of Fr. Lebbe's Chinese name is proposed by Jacques Leclercq in *Vie du père Lebbe* (Tournai and Paris: Casterman, 1964).

Fr. Vincent Lebbe, C.M. (1879–1940)

Born at Ghent in Belgium, he joined the Vincentians (Congregation of the Mission, known in French-speaking countries as Lazarists) in Paris when he was eighteen and was sent to China in 1901. He identified with Chinese patriots at a time when Church life was dominated by foreigners and played an active role in the nomination of the six Chinese bishops who were consecrated in Rome by Pope Pius XI in 1926. Fr. Lebbe had started a Chaplaincy for Catholic students in Paris in the 1920s. In China, among many other pastoral initiatives, he founded an order of brothers, which pioneered ambulance work for Chinese soldiers during the Sino-Japanese War which began in 1937. He was captured by Communist soldiers at the beginning of 1940 and released in a critical condition, dying at Chongqing on June 24, 1940. His tomb is in Gele Shan (Mountain of Gele in Congquing Municipality) has been restored and is a place where Christians go to pray.

Does this mean that Catholics were now in tune with national aspirations? Other events at the time seemed to indicate differently. In that same year, 1916, popular indignation was aroused over the Laoxikai affair. The French consul tried to annex the Church of St. Louis, which was in the Laoxikai district of Tianjin, to the French concession. The Catholic press protested, and Fr. Lebbe was on the side of the protesters. His religious superiors ordered him to be silent on the issue, and they moved him away from Tianjin. The following year he was sent to Shaoxing, 930 miles (1,500 kilometers) to the south, in the diocese of Ningbo. Shaoxing was the hometown of Zhou Enlai and of the writer Lu Xun. Fr. Lebbe was parish priest there for a few months and made his preferences clear when he draped the church on feast days with Chinese flags and papal flags.

In November 1919, Pope Benedict XV published a timely apostolic letter, *Maximum illud*, which proclaimed the necessity for native priests and bishops to be responsible for mission territories, without any colonial-type control. Immediately afterward, in December, an apostolic visitor was appointed in China with the task of visiting all the missions and reporting to Rome on the current situation. He was Jean-Baptiste Budes de Guébriant (1860–1935), a Breton priest of the Paris Foreign Missions, who had been in China since 1885 and had become a bishop in 1910. He met Fr. Lebbe and listened attentively to what he had to say. These two great missionaries had similar concerns: promoting local vocations and appointing Chinese bishops. They also agreed on the importance of looking after Chinese students in Europe, making sure that they were welcomed by local Christians and that there was a Catholic intellectual element in the education that they received. In February 1921, after the completion of his apostolic visitation, Bishop de Guébriant was elected superior general of the Paris Foreign Missions at their general assembly in

Hong Kong and returned to France through Siberia. He had persuaded Fr. Lebbe to come back to Europe to promote their ideas and to do something for Chinese students in France and Belgium.

In Rome, Fr. Lebbe saw Cardinal van Rossum, the prefect of the Vatican Congregation *de Propaganda Fide*, which oversaw the missions. He suggested to the cardinal some names of Chinese priests who were capable of taking charge of a diocese. By 1920 Fr. Lebbe was touring France and Belgium and beginning to organize an apostolate among Chinese students. Some 1,200 students had been sent to France in 1919 under the patronage of F.F.C., *Fédération franco-chinoise d'études*, an organization supported by the rector of the University of Beijing, Cai Yuanpei; the latter had himself been educated in Paris in a "scientistic" and anticlerical spirit. F.F.C. aimed at forming technologists, who could also provide leaders for the Chinese worker movement. Faced with this group of Socialist anticlericals, infiltrated by Communists, Fr. Lebbe tried to bring together students who were independent of the F.F.C. and had an openminded attitude to Christianity. He was helped by Bernard Liu, an enthusiastic young Catholic, and created *l'Amicale des étudiants libres*, "the club for independent students"; the word *libre* was intended to emphasize the difference from the sectarian F.F.C. At Easter 1922, Fr. Lebbe organized a retreat at Meudon, the country house of the Paris Foreign Missions, where seventy students, of which a dozen or so had been baptized, spent five days together. The closing ceremony of the retreat took place in the great Paris shrine of the Sacré Coeur on Montmartre. The Mass was celebrated by Bishop de Guébriant. Fr. Lebbe preached in Chinese, and the hymns were all in Chinese. Near the altar, proudly holding the Chinese flag, stood a Chinese student, who was under instruction to be baptized. In 1923 Fr. Lebbe founded in Paris an association for Catholic Chinese young people. It produced a weekly paper in Chinese and a monthly in French. Funds were obtained from the Congregation in Rome for the creation of a club for students from East Asia; it opened in 1925 with its own center at Bourg-la-Reine in the southern suburbs of Paris.

While Fr. Lebbe was working hard to help Chinese students in Europe, some Chinese Catholics in China were waging an *avant-garde* struggle. Vincent Ying Lianzhi (1867–1926) had been a friend of Fr. Lebbe at Tianjin, and he was close to him in his religious and political options. Ying Lianzhi was from a Beijing family and had come into contact with Christianity when he was nineteen through reading a book by Adam Schall. Ma Xiangbo was also a friend of his and encouraged him to study Catholic teaching; he traveled and learned more about the faith from the Chinese Jesuits in Shanghai. After the Boxer Rebellion, he worked at the launching of a publication called *Dagongbao*, (*Impartial*), which aimed at enlightening the people, especially on Christian teaching; the first number appeared in Tianjin on May 12, 1902.

In 1912 Vincent Ying and Ma Xiangbo wrote to Rome to inform Pope Pius X of the urgent need for developing Catholic university education in China. They pointed out the new challenges of the times; under the government of the new republic the rites in honor of Confucius were no longer compulsory in schools. Protestants—American, English, and German—were founding many institutions for higher studies; Catholics should be better prepared to take part in the political life of their country and to contribute to its modernization. They expressed their bitter disappointment at the way the Catholic Church was being left behind. Catholics had turned down an invitation from the Manchu government to found a modern university; it was Protestants who had taken it up. Moreover, Catholic schools taught in French and were thus training young people whose only future would be to work for the French.

In 1913 Vincent Ying Lianzhi founded a small academy for some forty young Catholics in *Xiangshan*, "the scented hills" to the west of Beijing. This modest foundation took the name *Furen xueshe*, which means "to foster the *ren*", the Confucian virtue par excellence that develops harmony in human relations and sees the virtue of humanity as the perfection of all the virtues. The study program was centered on history and Chinese literature; it included the study of Christian documents connected with China, such as the Xi'an Stele, Syrian Christians of the Mongol period, and the writing of the great Christian scholars.

In June 1918 Vincent Ying addressed a manifesto to the Catholic clergy of China entitled *Quan xue zui yan* (Guilty words exhorting to study):

> Could a fellow countryman who does not speak the language of our country communicate with the people? Could he respond to current events? Surely he would be cut off from educated society and would shrink away from those who are really qualified. . . . The Catholics of

China are the only ones to be thus hampered; they are stuck at the intersection of two worlds. They are neither Chinese nor Western, but constitute an absurd species that is neither horse nor donkey.[5]

Vincent Ying knew perfectly well that these "guilty words" would exasperate Church authorities and that he would be considered a Chinese Luther, but he rubbed salt in the wound and listed the opportunities that had been missed. For instance, he mentioned that he had once been asked to find teachers for the *Tongwenguan*, the state bureau for translation, but not one Catholic could he find; he had to recommend people whom he did not know and who were without any religion.

These bitter complaints did not go unheeded in Rome, and an American Benedictine, George Barry O'Toole, a doctor in philosophy and theology, came to talk things over with Vincent Ying. As a result, Vincent's small academy, *Furen xueshe* in Beijing, became in 1925 a Catholic institute of higher studies. Not long afterward it took the name Furen Catholic University and, on July 29, 1927, obtained official recognition from the Chinese government. Vincent Ying, who had become head of the Department of Chinese Studies, was unfortunately not there for the celebrations; he had died in January 1926, worn out by years of struggle and overwork. His friend Chen Yuan took over from him and later became vice-rector of the university.

These sharpshooters of the Catholic intelligentsia had fought for a good cause, but one has to ask whether it was not already too late. Catholic students missed the great university debate of 1922, when Protestant students took the initiative. In the spring of that year, a conference was organized in Beijing by the World Federation of Christian Students. This provoked an anti-Christian reaction that began in Shanghai and rapidly spread to nineteen provinces. When the congress opened at Qinghua University on April 2, 1922, the antireligious intellectuals met at the University of Beijing. Li Shizeng, who had been a student in France, declared that religion was an outdated concept. The rector, Cai Yuanpei, argued the case for the typically French concept of *laïcité*, the notion that religion is a matter of individual private choice and should have no public place or influence in society; he went on to defend the idea that aesthetic values

---

[5] Chinese text in Fang Hao, *Biographies of the History of Catholicism in China* (Hong Kong: Catholic Truth Society, 1967), vol. 3, p. 309. Translated from the Chinese.

should be substituted for religious beliefs, since these beliefs were but the dreams of a suffering humanity. Behind this salvo of anti-religious arguments, one can already see the outline of a growing anti-Christian nationalism, exploiting the resentment that had been caused by the power that the missions had wielded. Perhaps young converts to Marxism were also flexing their muscles, trying to inspire a mass movement aimed at the destruction of imperialism.

A Church on the Defensive

What was the Church's response to these new challenges? The initiative came from Rome. In 1922, Pius XI, who had been elected Pope in February of that year, sent an apostolic delegate to China. He was Celso Benigno Luigi Costantini, who was created titular archbishop of Theodosia.[6] It was an unofficial way of indicating the end of France's special protectorate over the missions, although the delegate was not accredited as nuncio to the Chinese government. Nevertheless the Chinese authorities were appreciative of this move; at the funeral of Sun Yat-sen in 1925, Archbishop Costantini received the same honors as the diplomatic corps.

The apostolic delegate was concerned to apply the Roman directives concerning the promotion of Chinese clergy, and he took as his secretary Fr. Philip Zhao, a friend of Fr. Lebbe. The delegate went to Tianjin to bless the press that printed the Chinese Catholic daily *Yishi bao*. In 1923 two Chinese priests were appointed to important posts; they became prefects apostolic and superiors of missions. In May 1924 Archbishop Costantini presided over the first council of the Catholic Church in China, a meeting of bishops that was partly inspired by the Protestant general conferences. The two Chinese prefects were on a completely equal footing with their European colleagues. Finally the Pope decided to mark the promotion of native clergy by consecrating six Chinese bishops in St. Peter's Basilica in Rome. The

---

[6] Archbishop Celso Costantini's Chinese experience was to have an effect on the missionary outlook of the whole Catholic Church. His personal notes were published as *Con i missionari in Cina: 1922–1933: Memorie di fatti e di idee* (Rome, 1958), 2 vols.; *Ultime foglie: Ricordi e pensieri* (Rome, 1958). Considerable extracts from these two works were translated into French by Jean Bruls and published as *Réforme des Missions au XXe siècle* (Tournai and Paris: Casterman, 1960).

ceremony took place on October 28, 1926, and lasted more than four hours. The six bishops elect were feted with enthusiasm on their way to Rome; in China at Beijing, Tianjin, Shanghai, and Hong Kong; and on their sea voyage at Manila, Singapore, and Colombo. When they landed at Naples they found that Mussolini had put a special train at the disposal of the new bishops and their entourage to take them to Rome. During the consecration Pius XI expressed his joy at welcoming them as brother bishops on the day when he himself was celebrating the seventh anniversary of his episcopal ordination. He said:

> You came here, Venerable Brethren, *to see Peter*, and from Peter you received the pastoral staff, of which you shall make use in your apostolic travels and to gather your sheep. And Peter very lovingly has embraced you, who make Us greatly hope you will spread the truth of the Gospel among your fellow countrymen.[7]

After the festivities in Rome, the new bishops visited various European countries and then went on to the United States. One of the six, Bishop Joseph Hu Ruoshan, appointed bishop of Taizhou in Zhejiang Province, spoke of the feelings of joy and consolation that he had experienced through the warm welcome of Christians in Europe:

> In Rome and Italy first of all, then in France, Belgium, and Holland, I felt everywhere a cordial and touching welcome and a sympathy that was truly *catholic*. Indeed, each time I realized with profound joy that the Catholic Church, according to the words of St. Paul, makes no distinction of races and tongues, and that she embraces in the same love of Christ all men in the whole world as brothers, whether they are from the East or from the West. Until I saw these countries, so distant from ours, receive us with so much brotherly kindness, I never really understood the majesty of Our Holy Mother the Church, which is her Catholicity. . . . *This is due to the Catholic faith*, I am sure of it.[8]

The other five new bishops were Philip Zhao Huaiyi, who had been Archbishop Costantini's secretary; he became bishop of Xuanhua to the northwest of Beijing; Melchior Sun Dezhen, the only Vincentian among them, who was appointed to Lixian, Zhili district in Hebei, and invited Fr. Lebbe to come to his new diocese; a Jesuit

---

[7] English translation in P. M. D'Elia, *Catholic Native Episcopacy in China: 1890–1963* (Shanghai: Zikawei, 1927), p. 87.

[8] Ibid., p. 88.

priest, Simon Zhu Kaimin, who was appointed to Haimen, Jiangsu Province; a Franciscan, Aloysius Chen Guodi, who became bishop of Fenyang, Shanxi Province; and Odoric Chen Hede, who became bishop of Puqi, Hubei Province.

The consecration of six Chinese bishops marked an important new stage in the life of the Church. It was a significant gesture on the part of the Pastor of the Universal Church. However, these Chinese pastors of the flock were very few compared with the number of foreign Catholic missionaries who poured into China. American Catholic missionaries started coming in 1917 when the Maryknoll fathers, who had been founded in 1911, took over from the Paris Foreign Missions in some districts of Guangdong Province, and later at Fushun in Manchuria. In 1921 American Passionists replaced Spanish Augustinian friars, who had been in north Hunan. Canadian missionaries also came to China: Jesuits to Xuzhou in north Jiangsu, Franciscans to north Shandong, Scarboro priests to south Zhejiang, priests of the Quebec Foreign Missions to Manchuria. In 1926 the number of foreign Catholic missionaries in China came to 3,059: 1,723 priests, 1,088 sisters, and 248 brothers.[9] However, the balance was beginning to alter; most of the missionary orders were conscious of the need for recruiting and training Chinese vocations, and whereas in 1918 there had been 834 Chinese priests, 35 percent of the clerical body, by 1926 the number came to 1,184 or 41 percent of the total. In 1916 Chinese sisters made up 66 percent of the total number of sisters, but ten years later they constituted 72 percent.[10]

Although the Catholic Church in China was clerically dominated, with a non-Chinese preponderance, the laity was trying to affirm itself, within the limits authorized by the hierarchy. The first council of the Catholic Church in China, which had been solemnly celebrated in Shanghai in 1924, considered lay associations and their status. Book II of the acts of the council, which were all in Latin, concerned itself with persons and had thirty-four sections on clerics, eight on sisters, and six on lay people. The lay people in question were first of all members of third orders, that is, lay men and women associated with religious orders, such as the Franciscans, the Dominicans, and the

---

[9] Cf. Kenneth Scott Latourette, *A History of Christian Missions in China* (Taipei: Ch'ong-Wen Publishing Co., 1970), p. 724.

[10] Ibid., p. 725.

Carmelites. Then came confraternities, pious unions, associations for the spreading of the faith, associations for social work, members of youth movements, and catechists. Section 45 on social action refers to the encyclical letter *Rerum Novarum*, which Pope Leo XIII had issued in 1891; article 201 of that section warned against subversive movements, which could destroy both the family and private property and which, far from promoting freedom, led in fact to the enslavement of citizens. The Fathers of the council supported order, condemned "social unrest", and forbade missionaries from becoming members of political factions (article 202). Article 208 defines the Christian view of the dignity of women and rejects movements for the "emancipation of women", which could be harmful to the family. These warnings are indicative of the clergy's nervousness in the face of new ideas, current in the younger generations. Section 46, specifically on young people, made it a condition for any association with the word "Catholic" in its name to have the approval of the local bishop. Associations of Catholic young people were reminded that they should not take part in politics. They were also required to oppose Protestant associations, the Y.M.C.A., and the Y.W.C.A., since these had been "condemned by the Holy Office on November 5, 1920".[11]

The Catholic Church was clearly on the defensive, both as regards political and social movements and in comparison with the Protestants, who were far more involved in the contemporary debate. Nevertheless, the Catholic laity gave of their best, at least in those areas where they could put into practice their faith and their charity, i.e., in the fields of education, medical care, and charitable relief. The president of Catholic Action, Lo Pahong (Lu Bohong), a businessman much given to good work, was heroic in his care for the poor and the marginalized. In 1950, Fr. J. Masson, S.J. wrote a little book that describes the dedication of this remarkable man.[12] Pahong was born into an old Shanghai Catholic family in 1875. His first aim in life had been to become rich and famous. He had to learn French so as to launch himself in the business life of Shanghai, and a cer-

---

[11] *Primum Concilium Sinense Anno 1924: Acta Decreta et Normae. Vota etc.* (Taiwan: Kuangchi Press, 1961), 3rd ed., p. 86.

[12] J. Masson, S.J., *Un millionaire chinois au service des gueux: Joseph Lo Pa Hong: Shanghai 1875–1937* (Tournai and Paris: Casterman, 1950). Collection Le Christ dans ses témoins.

tain Fr. Gong from the church of Dongjiadu agreed to give him French lessons, taking the opportunity, as he did so, of instructing him more fully in the Christian faith. Once Pahong had become proficient in French, he became secretary to a French lawyer. Fr. Gong got him to join the Congregation of Mary, a pious society of lay people, considering that the young man was becoming too worldly in outlook. Pahong managed to control his baser instincts and noted in his diary that he was becoming a "new man". At the age of twenty he married Mary Ai, who also came from an old Shanghai Catholic family. They had four children, and, in spite of his family commitments, Pahong joined the St. Vincent de Paul Society and began to work for the poor in his spare time. Before he reached the age of thirty, he suffered a series of personal tragedies: his eldest son died, Pahong himself caught a serious illness while he was teaching the catechism to the destitute, and his wife died in 1905. Pahong overcame these trials in a great spirit of faith. Once he had recovered, he started home visits with the St. Vincent de Paul Society again, and he also began to visit the sick in hospital and to baptize the dying. In 1909 he remarried; his second wife was Anne Zhu, a Catholic from Suzhou, by whom he had three sons and three daughters. Meanwhile his business career was prospering. At thirty-five he became manager of a large electricity firm and went on to be managing director of a water distribution company, a tramways company, and a steamship company. His management skills and his charitable work were appreciated in Shanghai, and he was elected to the city council. The city mayor asked him to take over a hospice founded in 1865 for orphans, the sick, and the aged, where about 500 inmates were languishing in appalling conditions; Pahong decided that the only thing to do was to pull the place down and rebuild it. The municipality gave him bricks from the city walls, which were being demolished at the time, but no funds were allocated to the project. Pahong turned in prayer to his special patron, St. Joseph, entrusted the project to him, and launched an appeal to the public. Thus it was that the infamous *Puji tang* (Public Assistance Home), infested with vermin, became the St. Joseph Hospice, clean and well managed, with separate buildings for different types of patients, including wards for mental cases. Many ladies from the city, as well as religious sisters, came to help with the work. Pahong himself would don an apron and help to wash the patients with the most repulsive diseases; he would bring his sons on these hospital visits, hoping thereby to make them love the poor.

The new hospice was hardly open before Pahong became deeply concerned by the living conditions in the working class district of Yangshupu. With the agreement of the bishop, he undertook the construction of a school, a community clinic, and a small church, since the main church was too far away for those who had to walk. This undertaking also flourished and later became the Hospital of the Sacred Heart. In 1917 he helped friends in Beijing to found the central hospital there. He then opened more dispensaries and hospitals in Shanghai, including a new residence for mental patients, since their wards at St. Joseph's Hospice had become too crowded.

As well as looking after the poor, Pahong was also concerned for education and saw to the opening of several new schools. Near St. Joseph's Hospice, he had a technical school built, which the Salesian fathers agreed to manage. Through the superior of the Jesuits, he obtained the help of American Jesuits for the creation of a secondary school called *Jinke*, "the Golden Law". He also cooperated in the foundation of a technical school for girls, which he entrusted to the Franciscan Missionaries of Mary, and he saw to the opening of schools for nurses, attached to the hospitals.

Pahong added his work for evangelization to all these medical and educational projects. Already in 1912 he had created a first missionary team of eighteen lay apostles. The statutes of their association were approved by the bishop and provided for daily spiritual exercises and weekly reunions, at which members reported on their activities: talks, catechisms, visits to prisoners, the sick, etc. Lo Pahong also became president of Catholic Action and had a center built, whence he sent out teams on mission work to rural areas without priests. These "weekend apostles", often businessmen like Pahong, would talk to local people while traveling third class on the train, or in shops and at market. They would tell them about the Catholic faith, group converts together, and then see to the building of a chapel and to the coming of a priest. Often a community clinic would be next to the chapel.

In 1926 Lo Pahong and his friend Zhu Zhiyao went to the Eucharistic Congress at Chicago. There he presented a magnificent piece of Chinese silk and gave an address that attracted considerable attention. Ten years later Pius XI himself invited him to attend the 1937

Eucharistic Congress at Manila, but that year was also to see Pahong's tragic death. In July 1937 Japan invaded China without declaring war and occupied Shanghai. Lo Pahong, who felt responsible for so many charitable projects, made a desperate appeal to the public for support, but as well as the relief of the poor in the city, there were now thousands of refugees to cope with. How were all of these people to be fed? Pahong could not accept inactivity in the face of this tide of human suffering. The city administration had disappeared, and General Chiang Kai-shek had moved the government from Nanjing to Chongqing in the remote Sichuan Province. For the sake of the poor, Lo Pahong accepted to join the committee for local reorganization of the Shanghai region created by the Japanese, but the Nationalist government in Chongqing had sent out urgent directives that contacts with the invading forces were to be avoided at all costs. On December 30, 1937, Lo Pahong received a call from St. Joseph's Hospice; as he left his home in response, two men posing as orange sellers gunned him down in the street.[13]

Once again Chinese society had entered a period of profound upheavals. From 1927 to 1937 the political options had become polarized, so that the only choice appeared to be between Chiang Kai-shek's Nationalist government and his sworn enemies, the Communists.

---

[13] Ibid., p. 155.

[The first paragraph of the English version in the section "Isolated Catholic Patriots" has received additional material.—Trans.]

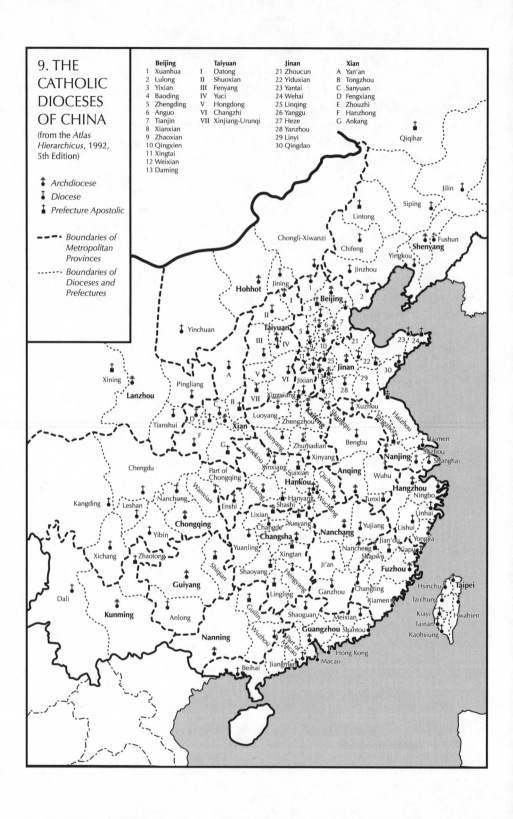

9. THE CATHOLIC DIOCESES OF CHINA

(from the *Atlas Hierarchicus*, 1992, 5th Edition)

✝ *Archdiocese*

✝ *Diocese*

✠ *Prefecture Apostolic*

━ ━ ━ *Boundaries of Metropolitan Provinces*

┈┈┈┈ *Boundaries of Dioceses and Prefectures*

Beijing	Taiyuan	Jinan	Xian
1 Xuanhua	I Datong	21 Zhoucun	A Yan'an
2 Lulong	II Shuoxian	22 Yiduxian	B Tongzhou
3 Yixian	III Fenyang	23 Yantai	C Sanyuan
4 Baoding	IV Yuci	24 Wehai	D Fengxiang
5 Zhengding	V Hongdong	25 Linqing	E Zhouzhi
6 Anguo	VI Changzhi	26 Yanggu	F Hanzhong
7 Tianjin	VII Xinjiang-Urunqi	27 Heze	G Ankang
8 Xianxian		28 Yanzhou	
9 Zhaoxian		29 Linyi	
10 Qingxien		30 Qingdao	
11 Xingtai			
12 Weixian			
13 Daming			

Qiqihar

Jilin

Siping

Lintong

Chongli-Xiwanzi

Chifeng

Fushun

Shenyang

Yingkou

Jinzhou

Jining

Hohhot

Beijing

Yinchuan

Taiyuan

Jinan

Xining

Pingliang

Lanzhou

Xingxiang

Jixian

Xuzhou

Haizhou

Tianshui

Luoyang

Xian

Zhengzhou

Kaifeng

Shangqiu

Bengbu

Haimen

Suzhou

Shanghai

Nanjing

Chengdu

Part of Chongqing

Wanxian

Nanyang

Zhumadian

Xinyang

Yichang

Suixian

Qichun

Anqing

Wuhu

Hangzhou

Ningbo

Kangding

Leshan

Nanchong

Enshi

Lixian

Shashi

Hanyang

Wuchang

Tunxi

Linhai

Lishui

Yibin

Changde

Yueyang

Yujiang

Yongjia

Xichang

Zhaotong

Yuanling

Xingtan

Nancheng

Jian'ou

Xiapu

Shaowu

Fuzhou

Hsinchu

Taipei

Guiyang

Shiqian

Shaoyang

Hengyang

Ji'an

Changsha

Nanchang

Changting

Taichung

Dali

Kunming

Anlong

Guilin

Shaoguan

Lingling

Ganzhou

Xiamen

Meixian

Kiayi

Hwahien

Tainan

Kaohsiung

Nanning

Wuzhou

Shaoguan

Shantou

Guangzhou

Part of Macao

Hong Kong

Beihai

Jiangmen

Macao

Laoekou

Xinxiang

Nanxiang

24

CHRISTIAN PATRIOTISM

After the First World War, progressive Chinese leaders had rallied to the ideals of national unification, full independence, and social transformation. The Soviet Union advised Chinese Communist leaders to form a united front with the Nationalist Party of the Guomindang under the leadership of Sun Yat-sen, whose power was growing in the south of the country. The Guomindang Manifesto of January 1923 gave a new and revolutionary meaning to the *San min zhuyi*, "the Three Principles of the People", which had already been formulated in 1905; they were *minzu*, national independence; *minquan*, democracy, and *minsheng*, socialism. In the context of 1923, this meant waging a struggle against the tyranny of the warlords and the encroachment of foreign powers.

The year 1925 was marked by the death of Sun Yat-sen in Beijing on March 12, and by a serious incident in Nanking Street, Shanghai, in May. Under the influence of the newly formed Communist Party, workers had organized a series of strikes from 1921 onward. These were crushed by military force in the north, but they broke out again in Guangzhou and in the factories of Shanghai. On May 15, 1925, a worker from a cotton factory in Shanghai, who was presenting the demands of his union, was shot dead by a Japanese foreman. On May 30, there was a massive uprising, and the police station in Nanking Street was attacked. The British police fired on the crowd, and there were ten dead and some fifty wounded. Workers, students, and Chinese industrialists united in a common front against foreign ascendancy and began a general strike that lasted for three months; at that time there were 170 trade unions in Shanghai with 217,000 members. The struggle against foreign imperialism had religious repercussions. Because of their connections with England, Protestants were particularly threatened, and many foreign missionaries left the country. Some Chinese Christians expressed their patriotism by rejecting adherence to Christianity.

The situation got worse in 1927 because of the break between the Communist Party and the Guomindang. The success of the worker movement and the peasant movement began to threaten the interests of the Chinese bourgeoisie so that a right wing emerged within the Guomindang, under the leadership of Chiang Kai-shek. This forty-year-old general had grown up at the side of Sun Yat-sen and had become commandant of the Military Academy of Whampoa, where he acquired the prestige of a modern military leader. He also had friends among the financiers of Shanghai. His education had been a Confucian one, and he dreamed of a social order founded on moral principles. Nor did he hide his dislike of Communist methods. His first aim was to recreate national unity by subjugating the generals of the north, but in order to launch the "northern expedition" he had to be sure of his rearguard and to obtain the financial support of Shanghai industrialists, both Chinese and Western. On April 27, 1927, Chiang Kai-shek disarmed the workers' militias of the city and had many militants of the Communist unions massacred.

Having defeated the warlord Zhang Zuolin in the north, Chiang Kai-shek moved his government to Nanjing. Beijing, "the capital of the north", was renamed Beiping, "the peace of the north". Communists, who were being pursued by the police and by Nationalist troops, attempted a series of armed uprisings. In December 1928, the Guangzhou commune was crushed by Guomindang troops. The Red Army fled eastward and mingled with the peasant unions that had been created five years previously by the Communist leader Peng Bai. A commune was established at Haifeng, and the Christian centers in the area were systematically put to fire and sword. In the church at Lufeng three Christians were killed, and four Catholic centers were burned down. The village of Pene (*Baileng*) suffered a fierce attack, and its thousand Catholics were dispersed, after five of them had been killed. The neighboring market town of Kuitan suffered the same fate; church, residence, and school were engulfed by the flames, and the six hundred parishioners had to flee to Jiexi and Shantou. Some 1,300 Catholic refugees left the country altogether and sailed for Singapore, Saigon, and Bangkok.

It was Peng Bai who thus gave China its first experience of a Communist peasant revolution. He had studied for three years at Waseda

University in Tokyo (1918–1921) and understood the possibilities of an agricultural socialism. He joined the Chinese Communist Party when it was founded in 1921 and began to attack the system of private property and the institutions that supported the dominant class. The peasant unions that he created led to the creation of the Peasant Soviet of Haifeng and pointed the way that Chinese Communism was to follow. Mao Zedong developed a similar peasant movement in Hunan in 1926–1927 and derived from his experience these important conclusions: the revolutionary struggle would be led by the poor peasants who formed the great majority of the Chinese population; it would comprise an agrarian reform, at the same time as the destruction of outdated feudal traditions, especially religious superstitions; the Christian religion would also be destroyed, not that it sanctioned feudal oppression but because it supported imperialist exploitation by foreigners. The Communists thus took on the characteristics of left-wing Nationalists.

On the opposite side, Chiang Kai-shek was trying to build up a right-wing Nationalism. He compelled the Red Army to retreat into the mountains of Jiangxi Province. From 1928 to 1934, he organized campaigns aiming at the encirclement and annihilation of the Communist forces, obliging them finally to undertake the "Long March" through the mountains of the west to their refuge base of Yan'an in north Shaanxi Province. However, the Nationalist victories on the ground were being threatened by the advance of Marxist propaganda in the big cities. Students, intellectuals, and writers were appalled at the miserable poverty of the people. In Shanghai a league of left-wing writers was formed in 1931; it was infiltrated by crypto-Communists who were in touch with the leaders of the underground.

Communists derived new arguments in their favor from the Japanese invasion of Manchuria in 1931, which led to the creation of the puppet state of Manchukuo; this included four provinces from northeastern China. Communists could argue that the Guomindang was proving incapable of repelling Japanese aggression and that Communists were the only real patriots capable of ensuring the freedom and integrity of China.

These were telling arguments. In order to answer them Chiang Kai-shek needed to create an even more patriotic ideology. Whereas Communists derived their ideology from Westerners—Russian, French, and German—Chiang put forward purely Chinese principles derived from the Confucian tradition. His model was Zeng Guofan, who, thanks to the moral force of Confucian ethics, had organized in Hunan the imperial troops that had crushed the Taiping Rebellion in 1864. Chiang recommended his officers to read the Four Books and the Five Classics, the core of the neo-Confucian curriculum.[1] In 1931 the birthday of Confucius became a national feast. Professors from Dongnan University, Nanjing, produced a renovated interpretation of the sages of the past. The writer Liang Shiqiu wrote that the basis of peace and order is to be found in the general requirements of universal human nature, to which left-wing writers retorted that there is no such thing as abstract human nature, only the concrete reality of classes in conflict.

Merely philosophical arguments, however, did not carry much conviction, and Confucian Nationalists realized that they had to organize their own propaganda movement. On February 19, 1934, *Xinshengyundong*, "the New Life Movement", was officially launched in Nanchang. Four norms of behavior were emphasized—the ancient virtues *li* (propriety), *yi* (uprightness), *lian* (integrity), and *chi* (modesty). Confident in this purely Chinese ideology, right-wing Nationalists lambasted the "Red Bandits" as lackeys of Soviet imperialism. Unfortunately their "New Life" ideology for moral strengthening lacked any analysis of modern industrial society. It ignored the economic mechanism for the exploitation of manpower, both local and international. Confucian thought had concentrated on attaining the perfection of the self and was thus naturally elitist, contrasting the good man to the vulgar. The educated man had the right to be treated with consideration "according to the rites", whereas the lower classes were subjected to repressive laws. The weakness of the Guomindang would lie in ignoring the corruption of generals and civil servants and in failing to put in place effective legislation to prevent the economic exploitation of peasants and workers.

The political Confucianism of the Guomindang also had the drawback of being dangerously close to a similar ideological movement among the Japanese. Order and peace were being established by the Japanese aggressor and to the detriment of the Chinese people. The situation became intolerable after 1937, when Japanese troops invaded

---

[1] Léon Wieger, *Chine Moderne* (Xianxian: Imprimerie de Hien-hien, 1927–1931), vol. 8, p. 143.

the north of China. The Nationalist generals in the north, weary of having to retreat before the Japanese, forced Chiang Kai-shek to stop the pursuit of the Communists in north Shaanxi Province and to negotiate with them. Chiang Kai-shek was obliged to reach an agreement with Zhou Enlai and to accept the creation of a common front against Japan.

Christians and the New Life Movement

At first the Nationalist government was hostile toward Christians and foreigners, but it moved rapidly toward a more favorable attitude. The Pope, Pius XI, issued a message on August 1, 1928, that welcomed the end of the civil war and the reunification of China. In 1929 the Jesuits published at Zikawei *Le Triple démisme de Sun Wen*, which was a translation by Pascal D'Elia of the *San min zhuyi* (Three people's principles), of Sun Yat-sen. Although the teaching of religion in schools was forbidden, religious freedom was on the whole respected; anyway, Chiang Kai-shek's anti-Communism was welcome to Catholics. In 1937 Pius XI's encyclical letter *Divini Redemptoris* condemned atheistic Communism as destructive of the human person and the family. Good relations between the Nationalist government and the Catholic Church thus developed. The American Maryknoll missionaries adopted this new attitude without any difficulty. They wrote:

> Maryknoll schools put up pictures of Sun Yat-sen, taught patriotism, and used the *San min zhuyi* (Three People's Principles) as a textbook. When the magistrates of Yeungkong (province of Guangdong) sponsored a speech and essay contest for lower schoolchildren in February 1937 to promulgate the Nationalists' New Life Movement, the sisters entered the schoolgirls in the competition. The next day, they accompanied the children to plant trees along the main road in celebration of Arbor Day. The sisters even participated in national cleanup campaigns such as "The Fly-Catching Program" of 1937.[2]

On the whole, the Catholic Church was encouraged to integrate more fully into Chinese society and culture. The official inauguration of Furen University in Beijing took place on September 26, 1927,

---

[2] J. P. Wiest, *Maryknoll in China: A History 1918–1955* (Armonk, N.Y.: M. E. Sharpe, 1988), p. 341.

and Archbishop Costantini presided. The university had three faculties, liberal arts, natural sciences, and education, which were divided into twelve departments. The administration of the university was entrusted to the Divine Word fathers in 1933, and they put particular emphasis on the thorough study of the Chinese cultural tradition. In 1935 the *Collegium Sinicum* was created, a university residence for priests who were following higher studies. These priests and the Catholic students made up 10 percent of the student body, which had access to what was best in the Chinese cultural heritage. The university published three reviews of Chinese studies: *Furen xuezhi,* (*Furen University Studies*), *Monumenta Serica,* and *Folklore.* A museum of ethnology was created, and the Department of Chinese Art produced some outstanding examples of religious art.

The influence of Archbishop Costantini also made itself felt in the area of Chinese Christian art. He cooperated with Chinese artists to produce a little book called *L'Art catholique en Chine.* The architecture of Furen University's building also reflected the concern to adapt to Chinese architectural forms: curved roofs and green semitubular tiles. The missionary orders too began to use a Chinese style for their fine new churches and residences, although local Christians were sometimes afraid that these might be taken for Buddhist temples and pagodas. One can still admire today the majestic cathedral of Guiyang, Guizhou Province, with its great façade rising in superimposed stories in the manner of local buildings, and its pagoda-like steeple above the sanctuary. In Hong Kong a major seminary was planned in 1930 for southern China, and imposing buildings in Chinese style were built on a promontory where they dominate the port of Aberdeen.

The apostolic delegate also saw to it that priority was given to the formation of a Chinese clergy who would be capable of taking over from foreign priests. At the council of Shanghai in 1924 it had been decided to build fourteen major seminaries, and by 1936 eleven of these had been opened. The bishops were encouraged to send to Rome their best candidates for the priesthood, but Archbishop Costantini was also concerned that Chinese priests should be convinced of the importance of their own culture, and, with this in mind, he founded the Society of the Disciples of the Lord in 1931.

Dom Lu Tseng-tsiang, O.S.B. (1871–1949)

Born in Shanghai and baptized by the Protestant *London Missionary Society*. Having studied French and English in Shanghai, Lu Tseng-tsiang became a member of *Tongwen guan*, the imperial school for interpreters in Beijing. He entered the diplomatic service in 1892 as interpreter to the Chinese legation in St. Petersburg and married Berthe Boxy, a Belgian Catholic who impressed him by her humble faith. After ten years of married life, he decided on his own initiative to become a Catholic. The Republic of China was created in 1912 and Lu Tseng-tsiang became Minister for Foreign Affairs but he refused to sign the shameful conditions imposed on China after 1919. In 1922 he withdrew to Switzerland to care for his sick wife, who died in 1926. Lu Tseng-tsiang then became a Benedictine monk at the Abbey of St. Andre-lez-Bruges in Belgium. He was looking for the source of the moral force that China needed, and that he had found in the contemplative life and the Catholic Church. His writings express the harmony between Confucian tradition and Christian faith.

By enhancing the merits of Chinese culture, Archbishop Costantini, Fr. Lebbe, and Catholic intellectuals were correcting in a very necessary way the vexations caused by Westerners during the colonial period. According to the mind of the Church, it was evidently right that such a culture should be Christianized in depth, but one has to ask whether this is what actually happened. There were certainly some unfortunate deviations. In some cases Chinese priests and nuns were confirmed in their feeling of cultural superiority, and this led them to adopt uncritical attitudes that increased their resentment toward foreigners; this was a chauvinistic and xenophobic deviation. There was also a political deviation that induced others to throw themselves completely into the Nationalist Confucian movement, supporting the Guomindang without any reservations and ignoring the corruption of its administration. Other Catholics fortunately were able to combine a deep commitment to the faith with enrichment derived from the sources of Chinese culture; such was the case of Lu Tseng-tsiang (Lu Zhengxiang), the politician who became a Benedictine monk.

A Christian Confucian

Dom Lu Tseng-tsiang published his spiritual autobiography a year before his death, which occurred in 1945 at the Abbey of Saint-André-lez-Bruges in Belgium.[3] He was born in Shanghai in 1871 in a well-to-do family. His father had been a catechist for the London Missionary Society and gave him a love for the Bible and for "improving literature". He learned French at a school for foreign languages in Shanghai and then acquired fluency in that language at *Tongwen*

---

[3] Dom Pierre-Celestin/Lu Tseng-tsiang, *Souvenirs et Pensées* (Paris: Cerf, 1948). English translation: *Ways of Confucius and of Christ* (London: Burns and Oates, 1948), translated by Michael Derrick.

guan, the Peking school of interpreters. In 1892 he was sent as interpreter at the Chinese legation at St. Petersburg, where he served for fourteen years under three departmental heads. The first of these, Shu Kingchen (Xu Wenxiao), became his intellectual guide. This remarkable diplomat wanted to see the renovation of Chinese society but in continuity with its deep-rooted traditions. In contrast to many contemporary Chinese, who were only interested in extracting from the West its scientific and technical expertise, Shu Kingchen tried to discover the secret of the moral strength of Westerners. What he taught Lu Tseng-tsiang during these years was to lead him one day to a Benedictine monastery. Lu wrote of his mentor's comments on Catholicism:

> I remember very clearly the first conversation in which he spoke to me of it, giving to the expression of his thought, as he often liked to do, the form of a fable. He had got me to call at his house, and he began thus: "One day the minister of commerce in England noticed the arrival and the entry into the country of a new commodity, previously unknown in Europe—tea; ten chests of tea, coming from China. The following year the number of these cases increased tenfold. Two years later it rose to a thousand. Surprised by the unexpected growth of this import, he called a tree planter and bade him set out for China and there study the cultivation of tea, instructing him to choose some of its finest seeds and then to betake himself to Ceylon, in order there to introduce this crop, so that England might no longer need to purchase her tea in China."
>
> Mr. Shu went on, "The strength of Europe is not to be found in her armaments; it is not to be found in her science; it is to be found in her religion. In the course of your diplomatic career you will have occasion to study the Christian religion. It comprehends various branches and societies. Take the most ancient branch of that religion, that which goes back most nearly to its origins. Enter into it. Study its doctrine, practice its commandments, closely follow all its works. And later on, when you have ended your career, perhaps you will have the opportunity to go still farther. In this most ancient branch, choose the most ancient society. If you can do so, enter into it also. Make yourself its follower, and study the interior life, which must be the secret of it. When you have understood and won the secret of that life, when you have grasped the heart and strength of the religion of Christ, bring them and give them to China."[4]

---

[4] Dom Pierre-Célestin/Lu Tseng-tsiang, *Ways of Confucius and of Christ*, pp. 11–12.

In 1899 at St. Petersburg Lu Tseng-tsiang met Berthe Bovy, who came from a family of Belgian army officers. They were married in St. Catherine's Catholic Church by Fr. Antonin Éveile-Lagrange, O.P. The same priest received Lu Tseng-tsiang into the Catholic Church in 1912; he had meanwhile lived for four years at The Hague as minister plenipotentiary. When the republic was proclaimed in China, Lu Tseng-tsiang undertook to modernize the department of foreign affairs while staying aloof from internal politics, but he was to be gravely disappointed. Yuan Shikai, the head of state, made him responsible for replying to the Japanese Twenty-One Demands on China of 1915. This negotiation was bound to fail and brought upon Lu Tseng-tsiang the contempt of his fellow countrymen. At the Versailles Peace Conference, Lu took it upon himself not to sign the clauses that handed over to Japan the Bay of Kiao-Chow, which Germany had seized in 1897 with most of Shandong Province. He was concerned to avoid another humiliation for his country. Although this won him popular acclamations when he returned to China in 1919, Lu had lost faith in the warlord government of Beijing and resigned from the department of foreign affairs. He took up work for the relief of famine victims, but his wife fell seriously ill, and in 1922 they went to Switzerland for her health. Lu Tseng-tsiang devoted all his time to the care of his sick wife and went on pilgrimage to Rome, where he was received in audience by Pope Pius XI. After his wife's death in 1926, Lu turned to the realization of a project that he had had in mind for a long time; remembering the advice of his departmental chief at St. Petersburg, he decided to become a Benedictine monk and joined the Abbey of St. André-lez-Bruges in Belgium. This came as a shock to his Chinese friends, who could not see the point of burying oneself in a monastery, so far from one's native land; later, however, they came to understand that what he had done promoted in a mysterious way his ultimate aim in life, which was to contribute to the spiritual strengthening of China.

In fact Dom Lu Tseng-tsiang's writings did have a liberating Gospel message for China; they showed how the Confucian virtue of filial piety finds its complete fulfillment in Jesus Christ, the Son of God, who is united to his Father by the bond of perfect love. In the midst of the world's disorder, Dom Lu discovered the true "encounter of humanities" (*rencontre des humanités*) by meditating on the Gospel of St. John, as translated into Chinese by his friend John Wu (Wu Jingxiong).

The Logos of the Greeks doubtless corresponds to the Far Eastern *Tao* of the Chinese. . . . In the beginning was the *Tao*, and the *Tao* was with God, and the *Tao* was God. Jesus Christ is the Tao made flesh, coming to reveal to us the life of God and to unveil his human heart and the filial piety that he shows to his father.[5]

Dom Lu found true happiness in Catholic worship, centered on the self-offering of the Son to the Father and celebrated with all the beauty of the Benedictine liturgy. There he discovered the fulfillment of the mystery of man's relation to God, a mystery that is foreshadowed in the Confucian ritual of sacrifice to heaven. Ceremonies that carry such a depth of meaning do not become merely formal ritualism. Liturgical prayer is essentially an opening to God and to humanity.

From War to Peace: a Mature Church

At the time when Lu Tseng-tsiang entered the Benedictine monastery of Saint-André-lez-Bruges in Belgium, the contemplative monastic life was beginning to flourish in China itself, the first Christian Chinese monastery in modern times having been founded in 1883. Fr. Alphonse Favier, a Vincentian missionary in China, had approached the abbot of the Trappist monastery of Sept-Fonts in the Bourbonnais region of France and persuaded him to make a foundation in the high valley of Yangjiaping, 112 miles (180 kilometers) to the northwest of Beijing. The Trappists were a reform of the Cistercian order, which had been founded by St. Bernard in the twelfth century. In the seventeenth century, the abbot of La Trappe in Normandy had instigated a reform of the Cistercians that placed renewed emphasis on community life, manual work, and silence. It was this tradition that was brought to China when the abbey of Our Lady of Consolation was established at Yangjiaping, and by 1926 there were some ninety monks (twenty-six priests, eight students in theology, six novices, and fifty lay brothers), most of whom were Chinese. The community was large enough to make a new foundation in 1928, Our Lady of Joy at Zhending, south Hebei Province. At Yangjiaping, the plantations of the monks had contributed to the agricultural development of the area. In 1939 they

---

[5] Translated from Dom Pierre-Celestin/Lu Tseng-tsiang, *La rencontre des humanités et la découverte de l'Evangile* (Paris: Desclée de Brouwer, 1949), pp. 58, 67.

were feeding daily one thousand victims of drought and local fighting. The peasants called the monastery *Cishan jiguan*, "the Welfare Institution". However, by 1947, the Communists controlled the mountains, and they turned the population against the monks. The community was spared no sufferings—trials by the people, the plundering of the monastery, theft of chalices and ciboria, beatings, and the imputation of imaginary crimes. On August 12, 1947, the monks were forced to leave their monastery, laden like pack animals with the equipment of the Red Army. During the ensuing weeks they were compelled to go on forced marches along the Great Wall; many of them died on the way. At the end of August they learned that their monastery had been burned down; the survivors were released in October, having signed a confession of their supposed crimes. One of these was cooperation with the Japanese; some of the monks had in fact gone out of their monastery during the Japanese occupation, but it had been to bring Communion to the sick.

During the war against the Japanese invaders (1937–1945), the Communists often accused Catholics of collaboration with the Japanese. This was partly because of the position taken by the Church in Manchukuo, the puppet state in Manchuria created by Japan in 1932. The emperor of this artificial creation was to be Pu-yi, the last emperor of China, who had abdicated in 1912 at the age of six; he had lived on in the Forbidden City until 1924, when he was forced to leave Beijing and had sought refuge in the Japanese concession in Tianjin. After that, he was under the control of the Japanese, who brought him to Manchukuo and enthroned him, aged twenty-four, as emperor of Manchukuo. His authority rested upon the Confucian principles of *Wang Tao*, the royal road of peace and harmony in submission to heaven and to the sovereign. In reality, it was the emperor of Japan to whom obedience had to be given.

Catholic schools in Manchuria were threatened with destruction if they did not accept the authority of the new regime. Schoolchildren were required to carry out the traditional rites in honor of Confucius and Sun Yat-sen's *Three Principles of the People* were replaced by the classical Confucian texts. In 1934 Bishop Gaspais of Jilin had to negotiate with the authorities of "the new capital", Changchun, which was renamed Xinjing. The prefect of the Congregation *de Propaganda Fide* in Rome had appointed him as representative of the Holy See, with the mission of defending the interests of the Catholic

Church in Manchukuo, but no diplomat was sent from the Vatican, as a sign of nonrecognition for the artificial new state. The Japanese then tried to win round the Catholic authorities, and a circular from the Manchukuo minister of education certified that the Confucian rites in schools were purely political and had no religious character. The matter was referred to Pope Pius XI by Bishop Gaspais, and Rome gave an official reply by a brief dated May 28, 1935, which authorized Catholics to pay homage to Confucius, to the ancestors, and to the great figures of the past, as long as all religious symbols were excluded. In 1939 this ruling was extended to the whole of China.

These official measures, devised so as to avoid the worst, did not mean that Chinese Catholics collaborated in fact with Japanese occupying forces; they shared the feelings of their fellow countrymen toward them. A few missionaries in Manchukuo had good relations with Japanese officers because they appreciated the advantages of the established order against the threats of "Red Bandits". However, missionaries living in the mountains controlled by guerrillas sometimes helped the latter. An American, Fr. Sylvio Gilbert, parish priest of Tonghua from 1930 to 1941, wrote, "These [so-called] bandits were my parishioners. They were my friends."[6] In fact, Fr. Gilbert sheltered some of the leaders of the Chinese Resistance in his house and looked after their wounded. He was one of the first to be arrested by the Japanese on the day of the attack on Pearl Harbor, December 7, 1941; the entry of the United States into the war against Japan certainly clarified the situation.

Throughout China, Christians displayed their patriotism by sheltering refugees in Church buildings and caring for the wounded in their hospitals. The Catholic press took up positions strongly opposed to the invaders. In Shanghai, *Shengjiao zazhi* (Catholic review, a new name for the former *Huibao*), had a Chinese Jesuit as editor. Fr. Xu Zongze was a historian and a theologian as well as a journalist, and he reacted sharply to every act of aggression on the part of the Japanese, urging Catholics on to patriotism. Fr. Lebbe, in the Hebei diocese, organized teams of stretcher-bearers who went out to help the wounded. Already in 1933, when the Japanese invaded Jehol, he had recruited 240 stretcher bearers, twenty of whom were Little Brothers of St. John the Baptist from the Monastery of the Beati-

---

[6] Wiest, *Maryknoll in China*, p. 352.

tudes, which he had founded in 1928 near Anguo. About the same time he had also founded a convent of Little Sisters of St. Teresa, which took its inspiration from the Carmelites.

When Japanese pressure increased in 1937, Fr. Lebbe took up the struggle again and organized his stretcher-bearers for work in the Shanxi Mountains. Chiang Kai-shek bestowed on him the rank of officer and gave him the task of promoting moral rearmament, in the spirit of the New Life Movement. At the beginning of 1940, Fr. Lebbe was arrested, together with his Little Brothers, by the Communist Eighth Army. He was accused of having links with the Guomindang and was subjected to a program of reeducation. Since this seemed to have no effect, he was released in April, by which time he was seriously ill. His eventful life came to an end on June 24, 1940, St. John the Baptist's day. He is remembered to this day, and groups of Christians go discreetly to pray at his tomb in the Gele Shan (Gele Mountain), near Chongqing.

Although the Communists condemned Fr. Lebbe and his young colleague Fr. De Jaegher because of their political collusion with the Guomindang, they did in some cases recognize the services of priests. Thus Fr. Zhao from the Mentougou region west of Beijing was commended in the following terms in a Beijing Catholic bulletin:

> In 1938 the Wanping district organized a democratic government to resist Japan. Fr. Zhao was elected as delegate by the Party and by the people. He was also made responsible for first aid. He had shared the struggle and the sufferings of the people before the war of resistance and welcomed to his church the civil and military executive to discuss with them how to save the country.[7]

In fact Communists often held their meetings in churches, with or without the agreement of the parish priest. Some turned out to be historic meetings, like the one at Zunyi in January 1935 that brought Mao Zedong to power, and the one at Yan'an in 1937 that decided on a common front with the Nationalists. However, it is not likely that they chose churches to ask for the blessings of heaven.

While the war was at its height in 1942, two events occurred that were to have important consequences for China. In October the Western powers retroceded all the territories that had been taken from

---

[7] Chinese text in *Beijing jiaoyou tongxun* (*Beijing Catholics Newsletter*), no. 9, 1988, p. 47. (Nantang Parish Bulletin, Beijing).

China by the "unequal treaties", the only exceptions being Macao and Hong Kong. A few months previously, in June, the Chinese government appointed Mr. Xie Shoukang as minister plenipotentiary and envoy extraordinary to the Vatican. Dom Lu Tseng-tsiang, who had been ordained a priest in 1935, had been at work personally during the previous three years to further the establishment of diplomatic relations between China and the Holy See. Mr. Xie Shoukang was replaced on February 16, 1947, by Mr. John Wu Jingxiong, a jurist with a Methodist background who had become a Catholic. Wu Jingxiong wrote an autobiography, *Beyond East and West*,[8] which reflected the development of his thought in a way that was deeply Christian but steeped in Chinese cultural traditions. Whereas Dom Lu considered himself a Confucian, John Wu was more qualified in his assessment; he saw in Buddhism a spiritual tradition closer to Christianity.

After the end of the Second World War in August 1945, the Catholic Church in China emerged spiritually strengthened in spite of great material losses; she had proved herself through the services that she had rendered to the country. In February 1946, Pope Pius XII created the first Chinese cardinal, Bishop Thomas Tian, S.V.D. Another first came on June 2, when Dom Lu became titular abbot of St. Peter's, Ghent; he received the mitre from Archbishop Celso Costantini on August 10.

In April 1946, Pius XII created a territorial hierarchy in China; no longer were bishops to be vicars apostolic with delegated jurisdiction as titular bishops of nominal sees. From now on they had their own territorial dioceses in China, bearing the name of Chinese cities. The Church was divided into twenty ecclesiastical provinces, each under the authority of an archbishop. Within these provinces, seventy-nine dioceses were created, each under a bishop, and there were still thirty-eight prefectures apostolic. Two years later, in July 1948, there were twenty archbishoprics, eighty-four bishoprics, and thirty-five prefectures apostolic, giving a total of 139 ecclesiastical circumscriptions; Chinese clergy were at the head of twenty-six of these. Out of 5,788 priests, 2,698 were Chinese. As regards religious sisters, 5,112 were Chinese out of a total of 7,463. There were 924 seminarians in major seminaries and 2,705 in minor seminaries. About 200 Chinese priests were following higher studies, either abroad or in China itself. Even

---

[8] Published by Sheed and Ward (London) in 1952.

Cardinal Thomas Tian, S.V.D. (1890–1967)

Born in Shandong Province, he had been brought up on the Confucian classics. He was ordained priest in 1918 and, after ten years of pastoral work, joined the missionary Society of the Divine Word. Tian became Vicar Apostolic of Yanggu in 1939 and was consecrated in Rome. In 1946 he was created first Chinese Cardinal, and moved, after the Communist takeover, to Hong Kong, Rome, and the United States. His knowledge of the United States enabled him to raise funds and to build up the Church in Taiwan, as a refuge for Christians from the mainland. He died at Chiayi in Taiwan on July 24, 1967.

if local Church leaders in the Chinese Catholic Church were still in a minority, a rapid increase in this respect was on the way in the years following, in Taiwan, Korea, Japan, and Southeast Asia.

The Orthodox Church also blossomed in China during the 1940s. The number of Chinese Orthodox baptisms rose from 636 in 1906 to 2,937 in 1912 and 5,035 in 1914. Some 80,000 Russian Orthodox had settled in Manchuria. The Russian Revolution of 1917 caused the migration into China of many White Russians. In 1934 the Orthodox University of St. Vladimir was founded in Harbin. It had four faculties: theology, Oriental studies, economics and politics, and electronics. By 1941 the Orthodox archdiocese of Harbin comprised three bishops, 217 priests, sixty churches, and three monasteries. The Orthodox faithful south of the Great Wall were under the jurisdiction of the Orthodox archbishop of Beijing; they numbered about 200,000.

The Protestant Movement for Independence

Whereas the Catholic bishops in China had remained very dependent on the authority of Rome, the Protestants of China had made great strides toward independence from the Western churches that had given them birth. This process went back a long way and had begun soon after the Boxer Rebellion. In 1903 the independent Baptist church *Hing Wah* was organized in Guangzhou. By 1922 there were about a hundred independent Protestant churches in China. A National Christian Council was created, and, from 1926, many missionary societies made Chinese leaders responsible for the administration of their churches. Christian sects that were entirely Chinese also made their appearance, such as the True Church of Jesus organized by Barnabas Dong. As with the Catholics, attempts were made at indigenization, so that Christianity could assume Chinese cultural forms. But there were still a great number of foreign missionaries, who were concerned to maintain the doctrinal purity of the faith and to provide financial support for churches that were often still very poor. Many of the foreign missionaries left the country hastily in 1927 after a serious incident in Nanjing on March 24. Nationalist troops took control of the city and looted the houses of foreigners; the vice-president of the university, Dr. J. E. Williams, was killed in front of his house. Only salvoes from foreign gunboats put an end to the massacre. The missionaries came back the following year, but the movement for independence had been greatly strengthened. On October 1, 1927, thirty-six denominations combined to form the Church of Christ in China, with the stated aim of promoting the "three autonomies" of government, finance, and propagation. Anglicans and Methodists, however, did not join, nor did the China Inland Mission and the Lutherans. This was for doctrinal reasons, because the new church had been created for reasons that were basically national ones, whereas the churches that stood aside were concerned that there was insufficient reference to the essential doctrines of Christianity.

However, there was an attempt at theological reflection, with a view to creating a Chinese theology. Zhao Zichen (T. C. Chao), a theologian who had studied in America from 1914 to 1917, later joined the Anglican Church in China and was ordained. While in the States he had absorbed the "social gospel", and he was concerned to harmonize Christianity and Chinese thought. He tried to show how God reveals himself at the heart of the cosmos in a flowering of the ego. This intuition, which was inspired by the poet Tao Yuanming (A.D. 365–427), did not turn him away from the task that had to be accomplished in this world. He remained deeply Confucian in his outlook and drew on the values of the Gospel as a way of reaching moral perfection. In 1930 he wrote an article, "Can Christianity Be the Basis for Social Reconstruction?" that showed how his concern for indigenization was linked to his desire for national reconstruction. In 1938 he went further with an article entitled "The Future of the Church in Social and Economic Thought and Action". Ten years later in 1948 he was writing:

> The Church in general lacks passion for Christ in the modern world. The most popular religious appeal in China today is contained in selfish preaching and selfish enthusiasm for individual salvation . . . there are numerous youths who do not value their heads and go over to the Communists. They see slight hope in the Church for the salvation of their nation.[9]

---

[9] T. C. Chao, "The Christian Spirit Tried by War", in *Christian Voices in China*, ed. Chester S. Mao (New York: Friendship Press, 1948), p. 17. Quoted in Bob Whyte, *Unfinished Encounter: China and Christianity* (London: Collins, Fount Paperback, 1988), p. 184.

Zhao Zichen understood the problem but was not able to draw out the theological link between faith and life, between the history of salvation and social transformation.

Some liberal Protestants were obsessed by the social question and did not hesitate to adopt Communist positions in the name of the Gospel itself. They identified Christian salvation with social improvement and formed a group round Wu Yaozong, who worked at the Y.M.C.A. Press Association. In February 1945 he launched the Protestant review *Tian Feng*, (*The Breath of Heaven*), in which he published an article on April 10, 1948, that provoked such a storm of protest that he had to resign as editor. Under the title "The Present Tragedy of Christianity" he denounced the collusion between Christianity, capitalism, and American policy in China. He wrote, "Christianity understands nothing about the present revolutionary movement" and went on:

> If our thinking had remained the same as Western Christian thinking, we should indeed have become unconscious tools of imperialism and cultural aggression. If the religion we preach should avoid reality and be concerned only with individualism and revivalism, then, in the eyes of the great masses who are demanding liberation, Christianity would be nothing but an opiate.[10]

Wu Yaozong considered that Christians were indifferent to the social struggle because they divided evangelization from social commitment. He considered that a believer should work within history, thus cooperating with God for a new creation. Whatever the value of these theological justifications, the thought of Wu Yaozong gave Communists a foothold within Chinese Christianity that they were to exploit to the full.

---

[10] Wu Yaozong, "The Present Tragedy of Christianity", in *Tian Feng, The Breath of Heaven*, Apr. 10, 1948. Quoted in Whyte, *Unfinished Encounter*, p. 188.

V

DEATH AND RESURRECTION

On October 1, 1949, in Tiananmen Square, Beijing, Mao Zedong proclaimed the People's Republic of China. The Chinese government affirmed Chinese independence of all foreign imperialism. Its religious policy was inspired by atheistic materialism and aimed at the gradual transformation of all religions into an instrument of Socialist reconstruction. The revolutionary activism that derived from Mao Zedong's thought reached its climax in 1966 with the launching of the Great Proletarian Cultural Revolution. All religions were buried, or rather they went underground.

However, among Catholic Chinese who had taken refuge in Taiwan and Hong Kong or who were settled in the Chinese diaspora throughout the world, a movement for conversions began to emerge, led by Chinese priests, sisters, and lay people and by the missionaries who had been expelled from mainland China. Inspired by the Second Vatican Council (1962–1965) they created communities that were truly renewed according to the changes going on in the Catholic Church and truly Chinese in thought and expression.

After 1978 the Chinese government adopted a new attitude of openness and modernization, and this entailed a certain liberalization of its religious policy. Many churches on the mainland were reopened, as well as seminaries and novitiates. These developments took place under the control of the Communist Party's United Front, whose aim was to bring about the progressive secularization of believers. Chinese Christians, however, have all suffered to maintain their faith and have given an extraordinary witness of fidelity. Chinese Christians throughout the world have taken advantage of the improved possibilities of communication with the mainland to express their support.

25

THE GREAT ORDEAL

In Europe, the end of the Second World War in May 1945 saw the defeat of Nazism and marked a new beginning. In the same year, Japanese occupying forces were defeated in China, thanks to the tenacity of the Chinese resistance and to the help of the Americans. China thus recovered its full political independence, but this is not celebrated today as the true liberation of the country. It is October 1, 1949, that marks the decisive victory, because on that day Mao Zedong, having defeated his Nationalist fellow citizens, proclaimed from a platform in Tiananmen Square the inauguration of the People's Republic of China. For Communists it was not enough to have freed the Chinese people from the foreign invader, because the people needed to be delivered from capitalist oppression. The jubilant crowd that applauded Mao Zedong's words believed that true freedom had been brought to them at last.

In fact the people of China were able to breathe again after a long period of war and appalling sufferings. The new regime brought discipline and stamped out corruption and vice. Those who had exploited the people in the past were eliminated, and those who were to exploit them in the future were not yet identifiable, surrounded as they were by a blaze of revolutionary glory.

Mao Zedong had come a long way since he was assistant librarian at Beijing University on a salary of eight yuan a month. Matured by the experience of the Long March and conscious of having produced a version of European Marxism that was adapted to the situation of his country, he had also become a charismatic leader, with a great capacity for moving crowds. He was a self-taught intellectual and had used a selection of Marxist texts to construct a version of Communism that was more accessible to Chinese minds; it was a moral Communism, full of imagery and at the same time practical and dialectic. The Marxist doctrine of class struggle was adapted to become a universal principle of contradiction; conflict was seen as the motive force of all social transformation. Mao in fact experienced contradiction in practice. The Long March witnessed his successful struggle for power. This crucial exodus led the Red Army from its threatened shelter in Jiangxi Province to the remote refuge of Yan'an in Shaanxi Province (1934 to 1935). It covered over four thousand miles. One hundred thousand men left Jiangxi; fewer than ten thousand reached Yan'an in Shaanxi. Mao attained his full leadership in January 1935 at the Zunyi Conference in Guizhou Province. There followed long years of leaders' training in Yan'an (1937–1945). The thoughts of Mao Zedong then became the catechism of Chinese Communist leaders. From it the Party drew inspiration in order to define its religious policy.

China's New Masters and Religion

One of the characteristics of the new regime was that it assumed the advantages of constitutional legality, while attributing to itself the right to go beyond the law in the name of the proletarian revolution. Although an administrative structure was put in place, the real source of power was the Communist Party. As regards religion, the first constitution of the People's Republic of China, promulgated on September 20, 1954, affirmed in article 88 the freedom to believe or not to believe, but religious freedom only existed insofar as believers did not promote counterrevolutionary activities; these were defined according to the stage reached in the Socialist transformation of society. A government body, the Office for Religious Affairs, was created to control religions, and this operated at the different levels of the administration: national, provincial, and local. The different offices regulated religious activities according to the directives of the United Front, the Communist Party's organ of propaganda. The Party could thus claim the support of law in working for the transformation of religions according to Marxist principles. Belief was not directly attacked, but it was gradually emptied of substance through a reorientation of active religious personnel toward purely social tasks.

Marxist doctrine is fundamentally atheist; religions are considered as the most evident expression of humanity's alienation when it is submitted to economic exploitation. Religions are the illusory dreams of suffering humanity and an instrument of domination for those who exploit their fellow human beings. Since they distract human beings from their real task in the world, they have a paralyzing and narcotic effect; they are "the opium of the people". However, Chinese Communist leaders had their own way of interpreting Marx's atheism. Marx followed the Hegelian dialectic of master and slave and conceived atheism as freeing mankind from the tyranny of God; he saw God as a tyrannical master on the model of the king of Prussia. The Chinese had never seen God that way. Atheism for them was a confirmation of their traditional humanism. Chinese Communists rejected religion as an outdated superstition, left over from the previous society. They were guided by one of the thoughts of Mao Zedong:

> The idols were set up by the peasants, and in time they will pull them down with their own hands; there is no need for anybody else prematurely to pull down the idols for them. The optimal line of the Communist Party in such matters should be: "Draw the bow to the full without letting go the arrow, and be on the alert."[1]

This did not mean that Communist leaders were prepared to wait passively for the disappearance of religion. Mao Zedong explained what he meant in his little treatise *On Correctly Handling Contradictions among the People* (February 27, 1957):

> We cannot abolish religion by administrative orders, nor can we force people not to believe in religions. We cannot coerce people into relinquishing idealism, nor can we coerce people into espousing Marxism. All questions of an ideological nature and all issues of debate among the people can be resolved only through a democratic method, the method of discussion, of criticism, of persuasion and education, and cannot be resolved by the method of coercion or repression.[2]

Believers were therefore invited to repeated study sessions where their faith was not directly attacked but where it was gradually replaced by faith in the people, in the results of science, in the construction of Socialism, and, finally, in the Party. Marxist thought was thus expected to make its way in the minds of believers according to the laws of Hegelian dialectic; it was necessary to introduce opposition and contradiction into believing communities. The aim was not

---

[1] "Report on an Investigation into the Peasant Movement in Hunan", Mar. 1927; *Selected Works of Mao Tse-Tung* (London: Laurence and Wishart, 1954), vol. 1, pp. 47–48. The archery metaphor is from Mozi.

[2] "On Correctly Handling Contradictions among the People", Feb. 27, 1957; *The Writings of Mao Tse-Tung: 1949–1976* (Armonk, New York: M. E. Sharpe, 1992), ed. John P. Leung and Michael Y. M. Kau; vol. 2, pp. 314–15.

so much that they should destroy themselves, although that was in itself an appreciable result, but that believers should be trained in the only valid way of thinking and behaving, i.e., dialectic materialism.

This general method was applied according to a policy that varied according to each religion. Thus Buddhists were criticized because of their escapist attitude toward the world. Therefore bonzes and nuns, in critical study sessions, were encouraged to marry and thus to take part in the reproduction of the human race. Temples and monasteries were confiscated and their lands reallocated under the Land Reform Law of 1951. In May 1953 the Chinese Buddhist Association was created, whose stated objectives were "to unite the Buddhists of China so that they might participate under the leadership of the people's government in the movement to love the fatherland and defend peace".[3]

Taoists were targeted for what were declared to be their superstitious practices, divination, exorcisms, healings, etc. Taoist priests were branded as parasites and were reeducated so as to become productive members of society. Many temples and sanctuaries were pulled down or transformed into meeting rooms, cooperatives, or barracks. Taoist monks were often dragged before the courts, suspected of connivance with secret societies. Finally, at the beginning of 1957 a Taoist Association was created with aims similar to those of the Chinese Buddhist Association.

In China Islam is a minority both ethnic and religious. Appropriate treatment was devised for it, in the form of autonomous regions in which government and Communist leaders were responsible for the Socialist transformation of society. In 1952 a new translation of the Koran was published by the Commercial Press of Shanghai, with a preface in which Ma Jian provided a Marxist interpretation of certain verses of the Sacred Book. In May 1953 the Islamic Association of China was organized in Beijing, its aim being to "assist the people's government in developing the Muslim people's cultural and educational enterprises and strengthening the patriotic ideological education among the Muslim people".[4]

As regards Christians, they had two special characteristics. On the

---

[3] Richard C. Bush, Jr., *Religion in Communist China* (New York: Abingdon Press, 1970), p. 304.

[4] Ibid., p. 273.

one hand they were better educated and more modern than the members of other religions; efforts at reeducation were therefore intensified so that their various qualifications could contribute to the creation of the Socialist society. On the other hand, they had been closely linked to Westerners and had been the instruments of imperialist aggression; all their links outside China were therefore severed.

Between 1951 and 1955 all foreign missionaries were expelled from China, about 5,000 Catholic priests and sisters and 1,000 Protestant ministers. Their departure was prepared and hastened by an oft-repeated process: they were subjected to heavy taxes, which compelled them to sell houses, land, and sometimes churches; to manual labor, so that they could be classified as producers and thus obtain the right to survive; to a ban on travel, followed by arrests, interrogations, signed confessions, sometimes to trial by the people; and to death sentences that were usually commuted to expulsion. This Communist strategy has been analyzed by Fr. François Dufay, M.E.P., in his book *En Chine, l'Étoile contre la Croix.*[5] Other missionaries have also described their ordeal in prison, like the Belgian, Fr. Dries Van Coillie in *J'ai subi le lavage de cerveau.*[6] Nuns were not spared; their care for orphans and the sick was viciously caricatured by the Communists, who revived the worst popular calumnies that had been current in the nineteenth century; for instance, they were accused of killing children so as to extract their bone marrow. Exhibitions were organized to support such allegations.

Christians were forced to demand the expulsion of the missionaries so as to give proof of their anti-imperialist convictions. Trials were enacted that were really theatrical performances, where the villain who had to be destroyed was the priest or sister whom Christians respected and loved. To be convincing in their play acting, they sometimes had to invent fictitious cases of cruelty and ill treatment. Those who did not speak out were suspected of complicity with the missionaries or of lacking in patriotism. Those who had been most involved with the mission were sometimes compelled to be the most extreme in their allegations, so as to avoid reprisals against themselves or their

---

[5] François Dufay, *En Chine, L'Étoile contre la Croix* (Tournai and Paris: Casterman, 1955).

[6] Dries van Coillie, *J'ai subi le lavage de cerveau*. Original version in Dutch, Anvers De Vlijt. French version by Fondation-Stichting C.C.L. (Groede, 1964), Preface by Gabriel Marcel.

families. After the agrarian reforms of the 1950s, painful sessions of *douzheng*, "struggle", were multiplied with accompanying denunciations and abuse. At a time when hundreds of thousands of landowners were being handed over to condemnation by the people and execution, the owners of mission lands were not spared.

The Triple Autonomy Movement

In order to carry out the Socialist transformation of the churches, the Communist government needed to do no more than respond favorably to the request of Chinese Protestants who defended the principle of the three autonomies in administration, finance, and apostolate. In 1950 the overall number of Protestants in China was nearing the million mark. The largest group was the Church of Christ in China (177,000). Then came the Methodists (147,000); the True Church of Christ (125,000); then the China Inland Mission, Baptists, Anglicans, Lutherans, Presbyterians, Seventh Day Adventists, and the Chinese Independent Church, making up 30,000. The clergy came to 2,024 Chinese and 939 foreigners.[7] These statistics for 1950 put at the head of all the Protestant denominations the Church of Christ in China, a group that had upheld the principle of triple autonomy for a long time.

In June 1949 Wu Yaozong, the liberal Protestant intellectual, and three other Christian leaders were invited to take part in a national meeting of the Political Consultative Conference of the Chinese People, organized by the United Front. This body represented the different groups that constituted Chinese society: youth, women, professionals, ethnic minorities, and religions. The Protestant delegation, together with representatives of Y.M.C.A. and Y.W.C.A. and the Christian National Council, were invited to draw up a religious policy. In May 1950 nineteen Protestant leaders met the prime minister, Zhou Enlai, in Beijing and discussed the content of a *Christian Manifesto*. The manifesto was signed by forty Christian leaders in July 1950. The New China News Agency published it on September 24,

---

[7] Statistics quoted by Bob Whyte, *Unfinished Encounter: China and Christianity* (London: Collins Fount Paperback, 1988), p. 200, from the *Revised Directory of the Protestant Christian Movement* (1950).

which marked the official beginning of the Patriotic Triple Autonomy Movement. The text affirmed the commitment of the signatories to supporting the "common program" of the government, to purging the Church of imperialist influences, to supporting the agrarian reform, to cultivating a patriotic spirit, and to promoting triple autonomy. In October the manifesto was ratified by the National Christian Council; it was signed by 180,000 people over the next two months. Half the Protestants in China expressed their adherence to it in two years.

This massive acceptance of the aims of the government was partly due to the fact that Protestant opinion was already favorable to independence. But Chinese Protestants, as well as Catholics, were also subjected to strong political pressure on the occasion of various government campaigns: the Land Reform in 1950; the law of February 21, 1951, on the suppression of counterrevolutionaries; the campaign of the three antis (*San fan*) against corruption, waste, and bureaucracy in August 1951; the campaign of the five antis (*Wu fan*) against private businesses in January 1952. Above all, the intervention of the United States in Korea was strongly felt in China as an immediate threat by imperialism. In October 1950 Chinese troops crossed the Yalu River, and China entered the war. Christians were more than ever required to give proof of their patriotism. In 1951 a preparatory committee of the Triple Autonomy Movement was formed to promote the critique of imperialism and to aid a fuller understanding of the three autonomies. These reunions and campaigns were the occasion for numberless denunciations between Christians, which poisoned Church life for many years to come.

Where Catholics were concerned, the Triple Autonomy Movement was officially launched on December 13, 1950, when the New China News Agency published the Guangyuan Manifesto. The thrust of this document is contained in the following declaration:

> We are determined to sever all relations with imperialism, to do all we can to reform ourselves, to establish a new Church that shall be independent in its administration, its resources, and its apostolate.[8]

The manifesto was signed by the parish priest of Guangyuan, Fr. Wang Liangzuo, and by 500 Catholics, which was surprising as the

---

[8] *Jiefang ribao* (Liberation Daily), Shanghai, Dec. 16, 1950.

number of Catholics in this north Sichuan Province town was known
to be less than 100. The faithful who took part in the meeting
of November 30, 1950, at which "the manifesto was spontaneously
adopted", numbered about thirty adults. Nonetheless the movement
grew in Sichuan Province. On January 23, 1951, twenty-six priests
signed the Declaration of Nanchong, which was published in the People's Daily on February 12; it spoke of "breaking off all relations with
imperialist countries, the chief of which is America", and "breaking
the bonds of economic aid and all correspondence with the Vatican".

Subsequently "reform committees" were organized under the direction of the Bureau for Religious Affairs. These committees were
designed to become the democratic organs of a national church. This
proved difficult to achieve in north Sichuan, but the new structure
was imposed on the dioceses, first in Tianjin, then in Shanghai and in
other big cities. The initiative was taken by the Beijing government,
which promoted a campaign for obtaining signatures that were generally forced, although the movement was described as "spontaneous".
However, a minority of Catholics did join the movement willingly
enough. Some priests and lay people saw it as a way of putting into
place a Chinese management structure for the Church; for some it
was a protest against the humiliations to which they had been subjected by foreign missionaries.

The response of most Catholics was, to say the least, very reti-
cent, which is why the government organized "an exchange of views
concerning the movement of Catholic reform". The meeting was
summoned by the Central Committee for Education and Cultural
Questions. The New China News Agency subsequently published the
contents of the debate on January 20, 1951. Lu Dingyi, assistant director of the committee, highlighted the success of the Triple Autonomy Movement among Protestants. The prime minister, Zhou Enlai, declared that it was necessary to promote the Triple Autonomy
Movement, which had originated in religious milieux. He was fully
aware of the Catholic objection that "all the Catholics of the world
are one family", to which he answered, "That is true for sincere
and virtuous Catholics, but it does not apply to the perverse race of
traitors, such as was Judas in former times and such as imperialists
today and their instruments, the gang of Yu Bin."[9] Zhou Enlai took a

---

[9] Quoted in French translation in Léon Trivière, "Le Mouvement des Trois autonomies"

diplomatic approach; in a long two-hour speech he expressed appreciation of the services of the Catholic Church in China and even of the self-sacrifice of missionaries. He admitted the necessity for Catholics of remaining united to Rome in spiritual matters. It is to be noted that these concessions on the part of the prime minister were not reported by the press; on the contrary, it denounced the Pope as imperialist. Nevertheless, Catholic leaders did try to take advantage of what Zhou Enlai had said to produce an acceptable version of the principle of the three autonomies.

The principle of triple autonomy is an ambiguous one. Its orthodox interpretation is in fact accepted by the churches, both Protestant and Catholic. It is indeed good that the Catholic Church of China should be fully responsible for her destiny, provided that ecclesial communion is not broken and the Catholic faith is transmitted in its entirety. But the Triple Autonomy Movement is in fact a political campaign, Communist in inspiration. Administrative autonomy means being directed by the Party and rejecting all imperialist influence; economic autonomy means financing oneself by productive activities and possibly grants from the state, while refusing all imperialist subsidies, especially American ones; autonomy in the apostolate means propagating the faith by Chinese people only, using a Chinese theology and rejecting all foreign missionaries who are "saboteurs, spies, secret agents, reactionaries, antirevolutionaries, etc."

The inter-nuncio, Archbishop Riberi, tried in vain to enter into relation with the new Communist government in China, which refused to recognize him as a diplomat. He then wrote to all the Catholic bishops in China, vigorously taking up a position against the Triple Autonomy Movement, whereupon the Committees for Catholic Reform began a campaign to demand his expulsion. The government pretended that he was a mere European national. Since he had been born in Monaco, although he spent his life in the diplomatic service of the Holy See, he was referred to as "the Monegasque citizen". On September 5, 1951, he was expelled from China.

Rome was not slow to react. On January 18, 1952, Pope Pius XII addressed a first encyclical letter to the bishops, priests, and faithful of

---

in *Mission Bulletin*, Jan. 1953, p. 22. Archbishop Yu Bin of Nanjing had played a patriotic role during the war against the Japanese, obtaining help from the United States, but this had been on behalf of the anti-Communist Guomindang.

China with the title *Cupimus in primis*: "We desire firstly to manifest our burning affection for the whole Chinese nation." Having spoken of the esteem in which he held China, the Pope deplored all the more that the Church was considered as an enemy of China. He recalled that the Church is at the service of God and not of any particular country. He exhorted the Catholics of China to remain strong and faithful under persecution. On October 7, 1954, a second encyclical letter, *Ad Sinarum gentem*, was addressed "to the Chinese people", emphasizing that Catholics are not less patriotic than others and that they are being falsely accused. As for their administrative autonomy, it is indeed desirable and will be realized as soon as possible, but it cannot exclude submission to the Sovereign Pontiff. The Pope declared that the Triple Autonomy Movement aimed at creating a national Church that, by denying its universality, would no longer be Catholic.

In China itself, government propaganda continued its work. The centers of Catholic resistance were isolated and destroyed. A National Assembly of Chinese Catholics was inaugurated on July 15, 1957, with 241 delegates from all parts of China, including some bishops and some priests. The assembly approved the creation of the Patriotic Association of Catholics, and Archbishop Pi Shushi of Shenyang was elected president.

The Orthodox Church in China had experienced a considerable loss in numbers by the departure of the Russians, but it had as a result become more Chinese in character. Responding to this new situation, the patriarch of Moscow consecrated Simeon Du (Du Runchen) bishop of Tianjin on July 30, 1950; he thus became the first Chinese Orthodox bishop. He later took charge of the diocese of Shanghai. In May 1957 the Chinese archimandrite of Beijing, Basil Yao Fu'an, visited Moscow with an Orthodox delegation, whereupon the Russian Church declared the Orthodox Chinese Church to be independent, and Basil, commonly named Shuan, was promoted to be archbishop of Beijing. He was consecrated on May 30, 1957, in the Church of the Transfiguration in Moscow. Henceforth the Chinese Orthodox Church had no political ties with Russia but remained under the spiritual care of the Moscow patriarchate.[10]

---

[10] A general history of the Orthodox Church has been published in Chinese in 1986 by

The Triple Autonomy Movement had been launched by Protestants and was finally imposed with much more difficulty on Catholics. It would, however, be a mistake to think that there was no opposition to it on the part of Protestants or that the problems which Catholics had with it were due solely to their relationship with the Pope.

In fact, many Protestant communities refused all compromise with politics when they were faced with the movement of collaboration proposed by Wu Yaozong. Evangelical students, who were organized as the China InterVarsity Fellowship, were accused of being idealists and replied by distributing a booklet entitled *Xinyang wenti* (*Questions of faith*), which began by showing that they were neither materialist nor idealist but realist.[11] During the first six months 60,000 copies were issued, before the book was banned and its author imprisoned.

The independent evangelist Wang Mingdao was a particularly influential personality among students. He could not be accused of imperialism since he had no connections outside China and had been a patriot in the struggle against Japan. He had built his own church in Beijing, from which he sent out his termly review Spiritual Food (*lingshi jikan*). One of his messages was that "in the Scriptures, there is nothing else but the pure truth of God without any 'imperialist poison' ". In September 1954 he was denounced by the Patriotic Triple Autonomies Movement following on his sermon "The Son of Man Betrayed by a Kiss". In June 1955 he published a theological critique of the Triple Autonomies Movement under the title *We, because of Our Faith*, in which he wrote that the positions taken up by the movement constituted a form of Christian modernism that compromised the faith. He was arrested in August 1955 and submitted to brainwashing sessions, being released a year later after having signed

Zhang Sui with the title *Dongzhengjiao he Dongzhengjiao zai Zhongguo* (*The Orthodox Religion and Orthodoxy in China*). The part "Orthodoxy in China" covers the period from the seventeenth century to 1956 with some detail on Simeon Du, who was ordained bishop of Tianjin in 1950 and later moved to Shanghai. The evolution of Orthodoxy in China since then has been analyzed by the priest Dionisy Pozdnyaev in an article published by the London bulletin *China Study Journal* 14, no. 1 (Apr. 1999):15–22.

[11] David H. Adeney, *China: Christian Students face the Revolution* (London: InterVarsity Press, 1973), p. 59.

a forced confession. Once he had recovered, he repudiated his confession and was again thrown into prison, where he remained until 1979.

Evangelicals thus gave witness to the transcendence of biblical revelation. Most of them were not narrowminded fundamentalists, unaware of the requirements for a practical application of their faith, as their opponents claimed. They did, however, believe that effective action in this world required a prior act of faith in Jesus Christ as Savior. They were well aware that new life in Jesus Christ demands the manifestation of the "fruits of the Spirit"—that is, a renewing of the world through love. The way they refused all compromise proved to be an effective weapon which prevented them from being drawn into Communist secularization. Many of them suffered for their faith. As persecution intensified, they gradually had to disappear from view. In fact, all Protestants felt the gradual tightening of the screw; in 1958 there were only twelve or so Protestant churches open in Shanghai, whereas previously there had been two hundred, and in Beijing only four remained out of sixty-five.[12]

The resistance put up by Catholics was also a question of faith. Fidelity to the Pope was considered by them as so important precisely because he is seen as the one who guarantees the integrity of the faith. From 1951 the Catholic bishops began to publish, through the Catholic Central Bureau, a series of warnings. The document *xuexi cankao* (Matters for study), explained that Triple Autonomy did not require a reform since the Church had been concerned about reform for many years. At Chongqing on June 3, 1951, Fr. John Dong (Dong Shizhi), a young Chinese priest who came from Shanghai, was present at a rally of Catholics who were being skillfully manipulated by progressives. Agitators were getting the crowd to chant, "Down with Riberi! Riberi Out! Out! Out!" With great courage John Dong went up to the platform, made the Sign of the Cross, said a prayer to the Immaculate Hearts of Jesus and Mary and to the apostles Peter and Paul, and addressed the crowd:

> Certain people who do not believe in the existence of God or in the soul, who do not acknowledge the Pope as the representative of Jesus Christ, or recognize the Catholic hierarchy, are presenting the Triple Autonomy Movement to us as a purely patriotic movement. . . . They

---

[12] Victor E. W. Hayward, *Christians in China* (Dublin: Cahill & Co., 1974), p. 63.

say that they recognize the freedom of the Catholic faith; they admit
that there can be purely spiritual relations between the faithful and the
Pope. But a movement that operates outside the hierarchy invites us
to attack the representative of the Pope, His Excellency Msgr. Riberi.
Perhaps tomorrow it will ask us to attack the Pope, the representative
of Jesus Christ; and perhaps the day after it will ask us to attack our
Lord and God, Jesus Christ himself.[13]

Fr. Dong was well aware of the danger he was running and added:

Gentlemen, I have only one soul that I cannot divide. But I have a body
that can be torn to pieces. I think it best to offer my soul to God and
the Church, and my body to my homeland.[14]

This courageous witness completely turned the crowd round. The
Catholics of Chongqing went to the cathedral for a service of expi-
ation, and priests, who had compromised themselves with Communism, retracted; but a month later, on July 2, 1951, Fr. John Dong
was arrested and thrown into prison.

In Shanghai it was the martyrdom of Fr. Beda Tsang (Zhang Boda)
that galvanized the Catholic community. He was a Jesuit, highly qualified, who had obtained a doctorate at the University of Paris with a
dissertation on "Chinese Writing and the Human Gesture". He became successively rector of St. Ignatius College, dean of the faculty of
letters of Aurora University, and director of the Sinological Bureau.
He was an outstanding Shanghai personality. In the spring of 1951,
when he was forty-six, he was invited to a congress of private schools
in eastern China, together with all the heads of Christian schools in
the city. The Communist chairman of the congress invited them to
give an example of patriotism by breaking all links with the Vatican,
"agent of American imperialism". If they agreed, all they needed to
do was sign a declaration that had been circulated. Fr. Beda Tsang
rose to his feet and declared, "No. I do not agree." He spoke for
a good half hour, mentioning all the evidence of patriotism that the
Catholic Church had given by resisting the injustices of the Japanese
occupation, by providing medical care at the front, by her work
for education and her creation of scientific institutes. He concluded
thus:

---

[13] Rémy, *Pourpre des Martyrs* (Paris: Arthème Fayard, 1953), p. 68.
[14] Jean Monsterleet, *Les Martyrs de Chine parlent* (Paris: Amiot Dumont, 1953), p. 70.

Is all of that to be considered as imperialism? I can state categorically that, in everything that the Catholic Church undertakes in China, there is nothing that is not in the interests of the Chinese people and consequently, nothing that is not for the good of the country. In a word the Catholic spirit is essentially love for human beings. This shows that the Catholic Church is in no way an instrument of imperialism. That is why as a Catholic, and especially as representing the Church, I cannot sign this declaration, which destroys the harmony between the state and religion. Our government in Beijing is prudent. I hope that it will accept this declaration from the people.[15]

Fr. Beda Tsang knew the danger to which he was exposed. On August 10, 1951, he was summoned by the security police. In prison he was harassed daily by sessions of reeducation, followed by interrogations at night. By the beginning of November he was a dying man, reduced to a skeleton. His death on November 11, 1951, was attributed to natural causes, a brain tumor.

The laity were as courageous as their priests, especially members of the Legion of Mary, an organization targeted by the Communists. The Legion, an association of lay men and women, had been founded in 1921 in Dublin by Frank Duff, an Irish layman. The Legion has a strong Marian spirituality and a tight organization based on weekly meetings and set prayers from a standard handbook. Its groups have names derived from the ancient military usage of the Roman Empire, the local cell being called the *praesidium*. Its strength resides to a large extent in its contacts with the Catholic homes of a locality. Its members are used to visiting from door to door, undertaking every kind of social help and keeping lapsed Catholics in touch with the Church. Archbishop Riberi had done a great deal to foster the Legion of Mary while he was *en poste* as nuncio in various African countries. In China, before his ignominious expulsion in 1951, he had asked a Columban missionary, Fr. Mac Grath (Mu Kexin), to launch the Legion whose groups became schools of faith and training for a courageous apostolate. Chinese legionaries became particularly active among the young, in schools and universities. The Legion was especially developed in Tianjin and Shanghai; by 1950 there were six

---

[15] Rémy, *Pourpre des Martyrs*, pp. 175–76. Beda Tsang had been born on May 27, 1905, and ordained priest on May 30, 1940, in Shanghai.

curias grouping fifty-eight *praesidia* in Tianjin, and five *curias* grouping fifty *praesidia* in Shanghai.[16]

Legionaries found an effective way of countering the Triple Autonomy Movement by advising young people, who were being misled by official propaganda, how to avoid the traps laid by the Communist Party. The legionaries reminded Christians of their overriding duty to observe the Commandments of God, and this at the height of the Land Reform Campaign, when denunciations and summary executions were becoming more and more frequent. They pressed home the message that God's Commandments forbid lying, calumny, taking part in the work of executioners, in the sordid conflicts between parents and children and between husband and wife—everything, in fact, that was then being required in the name of the "class struggle". They made it clear that it was because Christians wanted to be faithful to the Commandments that they were being persecuted.

On July 13, 1951, the government ordered the dissolution of the Legion of Mary in Tianjin. Then legionaries throughout China were ordered to register and to repudiate the Legion as being "a system of espionage at the service of the United States". A decree of October 7, 1951, demanded that legionaries should sign a declaration against the Legion. Searches by the police produced many acts of heroism, some on the part of young children. Fr. Monsterleet quotes the case of a young legionary called to the police station to sign the declaration against the legion:

— No, I will not sign, she said.
— *If you don't sign, you will go to prison.*
— O.K. Put me in prison.
— *You will have your head cut off.*
— O.K. Cut off my head; she stretched out her neck.
— *Silly girl! Think it over and ask your parents whether they want you to go to prison.*
— I have thought it over. I have asked, and I have got an answer.
— *Who did you ask?*
— I asked Jesus. He is in my heart, and he told me not to sign.[17]

---

[16] Figures from the Chinese text by Gu Yulu, *Catholicism in China: Past and Present* (Shanghai: Academy of Sciences, 1989), p. 110.

[17] Monsterleet, *Les Martyrs de Chine parlent*, p. 160.

Episcopus Opportet Judicare:
The Duty of the Bishop Is to Judge

Truth comes from the mouths of children; it can also come from the mouths of bishops who benefit from the assistance of the Holy Spirit. It seems that in 1951 the Communists had planned to create a Pope for China. Archbishop Joseph Zhou Jishi, a Vincentian, was approached.

— *You are so gifted. You are just the person to take the lead of the progressive Chinese. Wouldn't you like to become the Pope of China?*
— Do you think I have the necessary qualities?
— *Certainly.*
— In that case I would rather become Pope of the whole world.[18]

Archbishop Zhou Jishi had a proper sense of the universality of the Catholic Church, but in May 1951 he was arrested, subjected to three trials by the people, and sent to prison. His crimes were to have listened to the Voice of America, to be opposed to the reform of the Church, and to have recruited members for the Legion of Mary.

Bishop Dominic Tang (Deng Yimin), who had been consecrated bishop at Guangzhou on February 13, 1951, was a friend of Ignatius Gong, archbishop of Shanghai and Suzhou. Both were Jesuits, and they had the support of the strong Catholic community in Shanghai. Bishop Tang followed the directives of the archbishop of Shanghai and the Catholic Central Bureau: Catholics are forbidden to join the Communist Party or the League of Communist Youth; members of the Legion of Mary are forbidden to register with the state security; priests are forbidden to join the reform committees of the triple autonomy. Any Catholic who disobeys is not allowed to receive Holy Communion.

Bishop Tang invited all his priests at Guangzhou to come and live at the bishop's house so that they could give each other moral support and decide together what needed to be done. In 1955, during the campaign for the elimination of counterrevolutionaries, Bishop Gong was arrested in Shanghai, together with forty priests and one thousand Catholics. Many priests and legionaries were arrested in Guangzhou in December. In 1956 citizens were invited to express their views freely under the slogan "Let a hundred flowers bloom; let a hun-

---

[18] Ibid., p. 42.

dred schools contend!" Those who were foolish enough to speak out became the first victims of a new anti-right-wing campaign. Bishop Tang was exposed to popular obloquy; a public address system was set up outside his residence and ranted on all day: "Tang Yee-ming, you should repent quickly." Posters were stuck everywhere on walls and inside the house with the slogan "Tang Yee-ming, the most loyal running dog of the reactionary Vatican".[19] Eventually Bishop Tang was arrested, subjected to renewed interrogations, and condemned to many years in prison. He emerged twenty-two years later, physically weakened but spiritually strong, thanks to his constant prayer during this long period of suffering.

Between 1949 and 1955, eighteen Chinese bishops were appointed by Rome; about seventy bishops were expelled. According to the 1962 *Annuario Pontificio*, there were then thirty-four Chinese bishops who had been appointed by Rome,[20] of whom twelve were in prison or prevented from exercising their ministry. Those who could still operate as bishop were obliged to accept a more or less conciliatory attitude toward the civil authorities.

The year 1958 marked a critical juncture in the life of the Catholic Church in China because in that year Chinese bishops were elected and consecrated without the agreement of Rome. On March 18, two bishops were appointed in Wuhan: Bernardine Dong Guangqing for the diocese of Hankou and Mark Yuan Wenhua for the diocese of Wuchang. They were both Franciscans and immediately submitted their election to the Congregation *de Propaganda Fide* in Rome and to the Franciscan superior general. Since the two dioceses in question already had bishops who were in prison, Rome replied on March 25 by a refusal. The two candidates were, however, consecrated solemnly in the Cathedral of Hankou on April 13. Twenty-four other bishops were consecrated that year, and between 1959 and 1963 another twenty-six bishops were consecrated. A certain number of bishops who had been elected refused consecration. They not only feared the canonical sanctions incurred by those who are consecrated without the permission of the Pope; they were also afraid of being rejected

---

[19] Dominic Tang, S.J., archbishop of Guangzhou, *How Inscrutable His Ways! Memoirs 1951– 1981* (Hong Kong: Aidan Publicities and Printing, 1987), p. 85.

[20] Figures from Thadée Hang, *L'Église Catholique face au monde chinois* (Paris: Spes, 1965), p. 103. Translated by J. de la Forêt Divonne from the German. Thaddäus Hang, *Die Katholische Kirche in Chinesischen Raum: Geschichte und Gegenwart* (Munich: Verlag Anton Pustet, 1963).

by most of the faithful. In principle both consecrating bishops and candidates in such circumstances were liable to excommunication reserved to the Holy See. Some bishops systematically refused to take part in such consecrations; such was Bishop Han Tingbi, bishop of Hongdong, Shanxi Province. Others accepted, although they were basically faithful to Rome, such as Bishop Matthias Duan, bishop of Wanxian, Sichuan Province. Bishop Duan was able to explain his attitude later; he felt he had to make a practical decision for the good of priests and people in the dioceses bereft of pastors. It was impossible to refer beforehand to the Holy See; what he had done was in no way intended as a schism.

On June 29, 1958, Pope Pius XII addressed a third encyclical letter to the Catholics of China, *Apostolorum principis*, in which he clearly condemned the Patriotic Association:

> Under the misleading pretext of patriotism, the association seeks above all to lead Catholics gradually to accept and support the principles of atheistic materialism, which is a negation of God and of all spiritual values.[21]

The Pope went on to deplore the episcopal consecrations that had taken place without Rome's agreement as a very serious act of disobedience. He stated that such bishops could have no power of teaching or jurisdiction; their official acts, even if they are valid, are gravely unlawful. This call to order continues to weigh heavily to this day on the consciences of many bishops, many of whom applied secretly to Rome asking to be recognized. The new Pope, John XXIII, elected in October 1958, talked of "schism" at a secret consistory of December 15, 1958, but the word was not used again. The bishops of China for the most part had only acted under political pressure and out of a desire to maintain the pastoral care of Catholics; at heart they remained faithful to Rome.

Later events, however, made it clear that the Chinese Communist Party was following a policy aiming at the destruction of the Catholic Church. In January 1962 a second Plenary Assembly of Chinese Catholics took place with 256 delegates. Then the freedom of worship was progressively withdrawn, as numerous churches were closed. At the time when the universal Church was experiencing unprecedented re-

---

[21] Translation from the French, quoted by Louis Wei Tsing-sing, *Le Saint Siège et la Chine de Pie XI à nos jours* (Paris: Éditions A. Allais, 1968), p. 342.

newal thanks to the Second Vatican Council (1962–1965), the Church in China was entering into the night. Pope Paul VI sent another message of peace to President Mao Zedong on December 31, 1965, but a few months later the Cultural Revolution began, interrupting China's laborious progress toward development by what was later recognized as a "decade of catastrophe".

The Cultural Revolution was an extraordinary phenomenon, due primarily to Chairman Mao's conviction that his power as revolutionary leader was being eroded by the established cadres of the Communist Party and by those who were profiting from the new order. Mao decided that his theory of progress through contradiction required the creation of incessant upheaval, and he attempted to ensure this by calling into being, with the acquiescence of the PLA (the People's Liberation Army), groups of young revolutionaries who had the license to humiliate and sometimes kill representatives of the old order and to destroy all evidence of China's ancient culture. In the words of C. Y. Hsü, "This ushered in a decade of turmoil and civil strife which drove the country to utter chaos and the brink of bankruptcy."[22] A description of the sufferings that were then inflicted on many loyal Communists and their families is given by the account of these years in Jung Chang's *Wild Swans*.[23] As well as making such unexpected victims, the Cultural Revolution targeted Christians who were always suspected of counterrevolutionary activities. All the churches were closed and destroyed or turned into warehouses, prisons, workshops, or wood stores. All the bishops, the priests, and the members of religious orders, whether they were patriotic or not, were arrested, insulted, and sent to hard labor or to prison. Many suffered a miserable death as a result of ill treatment. Christian families were undermined by an odious system of mutual denunciation and lapsed into silence. Religious books were burned, although some of the Sacred Texts survived by being buried or walled up. In 1969 Pierre Darcourt published *Requiem for the Church in China*.[24] In fact, the outside world was without news of Christians in China for about ten years; the Church there was effectively buried, but with the hope of resurrection.

---

[22] C. Y. Hsü, *The Rise of Modern China* (New York and Oxford: Oxford University Press, 2000), sixth ed., p. 703.

[23] Jung Chang, *Wild Swans: Three Daughters of China* (London: Harper Collins Publishers, 1991), 696 pp.

[24] Pierre Darcourt, *Requiem pour l'Église de Chine*, Éditions de la Table Ronde, 1969, p. 285.

26

CHINESE MISSIONARIES

Those who were scattered went about preaching the word.

Acts 8:4

When the early Christians were expelled from Jerusalem, they went to the Jewish communities, dispersed throughout the world, and announced the Good News. The extent and the diversity of the Jewish diaspora were manifested on the day of Pentecost; Greeks, Romans, Persians, Arabs, and Africans received the message of the apostles in their mother tongue.

The only parallel to the Jewish diaspora throughout the world has been the Chinese diaspora. Today there are Chinese minorities in about a hundred different countries. There are about twenty-five million Chinese in Southeast Asia, two million on the American continent, 600,000 in Europe, 160,000 in Oceania, 125,000 in Australia, 70,000 in the islands of the Indian Ocean, and 11,000 in the Republic of South Africa.[1] According to the *Worldwide Overseas Chinese Catholic Directory 2000*, published by the Office for the Promotion of Overseas Chinese Apostolate, "The Catholic population is less than 5 percent of the estimated 30 million people of Chinese descent, scattered in the entire diaspora".[2]

From 1950, many priests and members of religious orders naturally found a place in the communities of the Chinese diaspora. Some were foreign missionaries who had been expelled from China; others were Chinese who could not go back home. Among them were more than two hundred Chinese priests and seminarians who had been sent abroad for study. They became apostles to the Chinese and to the residents of the five continents.

---

[1] These figures are approximate and are derived from statistics in the *Overseas Economy Year Book 1982–1983* (Taiwan, 1983).

[2] *Worldwide Overseas Chinese Catholic Directory 2000*, published by The Office for the Promotion of Overseas Chinese Apostolate, Via Urbano VIII, 16, Rome, p. 14. See also Jean Charbonnier, M.E.P., "Les Chinois de la Diaspora", in *Études* (July-Aug. 1987):15–16.

In fact, Chinese Christians began to have an influence outside their own country long before the twentieth century. Their contacts with Korea go back over two hundred years. Koreans are a homogeneous Mongolian people with their own language and traditions of family life and food preparation, which are different from the Chinese. They had also produced, as early as the fourteenth century A.D., an alphabet of twenty-six letters, which made it possible for their language to be written without having recourse to the several thousand ideograms (characters) needed to read and write Chinese. However, they had later been heavily influenced by Chinese literature, and they had received Confucianism from China.

At the time of the Manchu Dynasty, a Korean delegation went every year to Beijing to pay tribute to the emperor and to receive the imperial calendar. Korean scholars brought back from China scientific and literary works. They knew Fr. Matteo Ricci's *Tianzhu shiyi* (*The True Meaning of the Lord of Heaven*) (1603) and also *Qi ke* (*The Seven Disciplines*), by Fr. Diego de Pantoja, S.J. (1571–1618). A young Korean scholar, Yi Pyok, was influenced by them, and in 1777 he brought together a number of friends for group study of the Christian religion. This meeting was part retreat and part seminar, a practice that was popular at the time; it took place at a small Buddhist monastery south of the River Han near Seoul, with the auspicious name *Chonjinsa*, Hermitage of Heavenly Truth. The group decided to adopt the Christian books as guides for thought and action.[3]

In 1784 the great caravan that wound its way every winter from Korea to Beijing included the twenty-eight-year-old Yi Sunghun, whose father was an official envoy. Members of the annual embassy had plenty of time for sightseeing in Beijing, so that Yi Sunghun, who had been at the Hermitage meeting, was able to contact the French Vincentians and the Portuguese Bishop Alexander de Gouvea. Fr. Jean de Grammont, a Jesuit still in Beijing, although his Society had been suppressed in 1773, gave Yi Sunghun books, crucifixes, and other Christian objects and baptized him with the name Peter before he

---

[3] Missions Étrangères de Paris, *Lumière sur la Corée: Les 103 martyrs* (Paris: Fayard Le Sarment, 1984), p. 22. Richard Rutt, *Martyrs of Korea* (London: Catholic Truth Society, 2002), pp. 9–11.

returned to Korea with the embassy in 1785. While he was in Beijing, Yi Sunghun had carefully observed all the Christian ceremonies that he could attend, and, once he was back in Korea, he and his friends decided to create a secret Christian Church. They were fascinated by what they read in the books that Yi Sunghun had brought back, and, as good Confucians, they decided to celebrate the rites. In 1787 Peter Yi baptized the others, and they chose one to be a bishop and others to be priests. They began to celebrate Mass, confession, and confirmation. After a time, however, they wondered whether they were entitled to do this, and so in 1789 they sent one of their number, Paul Yun Yuil, on the convenient Beijing embassy to consult Bishop de Gouvea. He gave all the necessary explanations and promised to send them a priest; he also made it clear that they were not allowed to practice Confucian rites. The Korean authorities reacted immediately when they heard of this, and many recent converts were martyred before ever a priest had been able to come to Korea.

In 1794 a young Chinese priest, James Zhou Wenmu, at last managed to enter "the Hermit Kingdom"; it was impossible to do this officially and extremely difficult to do so unofficially as all the roads and passes were guarded, but in winter the rivers froze over, making it possible to cross, and this is what Fr. Zhou did. When he reached Seoul, his presence was known surprisingly quickly to the authorities; he managed to hide, but his host and two other Christians were discovered and executed. Fr. Zhou then exercised a clandestine apostolate for several years because of a remarkable Christian woman of independent means, Columba Kang, who sheltered the priest in the woodshed of her house in Seoul. "He made her a catechist. The Korean word for catechist literally means 'leader of the congregation', and catechists had a broad pastoral role in teaching, organizing, guiding, and encouraging the faithful. Columba became the most powerful member of the Church, because she controlled access to Fr. Zhou, and she alone always knew where he was."[4] For seven years the only priest in the country worked in this way, with the woodshed as his base for visiting Christians and giving the sacraments in Seoul and the surrounding countryside. When Fr. Zhou arrived the number of baptized was said to be 4,000, and it increased during his time, although it is impossible to know by how much. In 1801, however, persecution

---

[4] Rutt, *Martyrs of Korea*, p. 14.

broke out again, more violently than before; Columba Kang was tortured but gave nothing away. Then letters, books, and pious objects were discovered by the police; they arrested one of her slave girls, who confessed under torture. Columba herself was obliged to confess the whole truth. She did not, however, know where Fr. Zhou was at that point. The police circulated notices throughout the provinces offering a reward for his capture and used torture in a sustained attempt to find him. Eventually the priest, who thought that if he were caught persecution might cease, gave himself up at the Department of Justice. After having suffered much ill treatment, he was beheaded on May 31, 1801. Columba Kang was executed in the same year, and altogether some 300 Catholics were martyred.

The Christian community in Korea was then without a priest for thirty-five years, but during that time Church life was organized and sustained by catechists. In the 1830s some missionaries belonging to the Paris Foreign Missions were able to enter Korea and to work there secretly for a few years. Fr. Jacques Chastan, from the Alps region of France, and Fr. Pierre Maubant, from Normandy, both crossed the ice in 1836 and contacted the scattered groups of Catholics. The French priests had a roving mission, never staying long in one place, but they baptized over a thousand converts; by 1837 there were reckoned to be 6,000 Christians in the country. In that year a bishop joined the two missionaries; he was Laurent Imbert, from Provence, who was appointed vicar apostolic in Korea after twelve years of ministry in Sichuan Province, southwest China. He too crossed over a frozen river, but in 1839 the incredibly difficult apostolate of these men came to an end; they were betrayed to the authorities and executed together on September 21, 1839. The number of Christians in the country was then estimated at 10,000.

Once more Korean Christians were without a priest. However, Fr. Pierre Maubant had in 1836 sent a young Korean, Andrew Kim Taegon (Jin Dajian), to Macao; he went on to Shanghai to study and to be ordained. In 1845 he managed to get into Korea by sea, but the following year he was arrested and beheaded; he was twenty-five years old, the first Korean priest to be martyred. In 1925 Andrew Kim Taegon was beatified and on May 6, 1984, in Seoul he was declared a saint by Pope John Paul II, before a crowd estimated at more than half a million people. With him 102 other martyrs from Korea were canonized, ten of whom were French missionaries.

In 1990 Catholic leaders in China invited a Catholic delegation from Korea to visit China, where the leader of the delegation, Zhang Zaizhe, evoked what the Church in Korea owed to China: the baptism of Peter Yi Sunghun in Beijing in 1784 and the ordination of St. Andrew Kim in Shanghai.[5] As for the Chinese Fr. James Zhou Wenmu, the first priest to enter Korea who was martyred in Seoul in 1801, he could not be canonized because of the lack of documentation about the circumstance of his death, nor could Columba Kang for the same reason. However, the Suwon diocesan process for beatification is hard at work examining government archives of the period, which had not previously been available, to see whether further evidence exists which can shed light on their case.

Singapore a Crossroad

In the Good Shepherd Catholic Cathedral in Singapore a commemorative plaque honors Saint Laurent Imbert, the bishop who, as mentioned above, was martyred in Korea in 1839; he was also, it seems, the first priest to look after Catholics in the island of Singapore. He arrived there in 1820, one year after the foundation of the port by the Englishman Sir Stamford Raffles. From there, Fr. Imbert went on to stay for a few months at the seminary at Penang, Malaysia, before going on to his mission station in Sichuan Province, southwest China. In the nineteenth century, foreign missionaries as well as Chinese priests and Chinese Christians frequently traveled along the seaways of *Nanyang*, the Southern Ocean. Singapore, benefiting from the monsoon winds, had become a major port; this encouraged a large number of Chinese to settle there, especially from the overpopulated areas of southern China, where famine was endemic.

Another marble tablet on the wall of the cathedral commemorates Fr. John Zhu Dezhi who died on July 13, 1848, aged sixty-five. He spent the last five years of his life on the site of the cathedral, which was then being built, his whole life having been spent at the service of the Gospel among the Chinese of Southeast Asia.

---

[5] *Zhongguo Tianzhujiao, The Catholic Church in China* (Beijing, 1990), no. 4, p. 52. Translated from the Chinese.

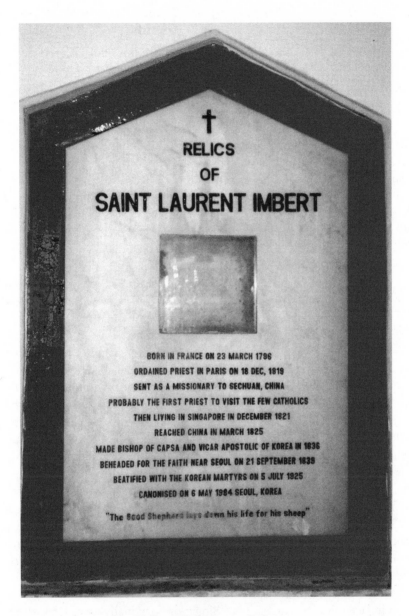

Shrine of St. Laurent Imbert

Good Shepherd Cathedral, Singapore. Laurent Imbert (1796–1839), a priest of the *Missions Étrangères de Paris*, came to Singapore in 1820. After twelve years' ministry in Sichuan, he was sent to Korea as Vicar Apostolic in 1837. Christians in Korea had suffered fierce persecution and had been without a priest since 1801, the life of the Church being effectively organized by catechists. After a few months in Korea, Bishop Imbert was arrested and beheaded on December 21, 1838. He was canonized in Seoul by Pope John Paul II on May 6, 1984.

John Zhu belonged to a family of Christian scholars from Huizhou in Guangdong Province and was sent to the Penang seminary. However, at the end of his studies, he was not ordained but became a catechist in Bangkok, where many Chinese had settled. He was eventually ordained at the age of fifty-five in 1838 by Bishop John-Paul Courvezy, the vicar apostolic whose responsibility extended to Thailand, the Malay Peninsula, and Singapore. According to the *Singapore Free Press* of 1848, from which these details are taken, Fr. John Zhu was sent to Singapore the following year.[6]

While Fr. Zhu was in Singapore, Chinese Catholics were so bold as to clear the jungle in the center of the island and establish new plantations, but this provoked the fury of the secret societies that were then flourishing. There were riots in 1851, and the sheds of the Catholic planters were destroyed. It seems that Catholics had refused to observe the rituals and rules imposed by these societies; by doing so, they had put themselves outside the protection system operated by the Chinese community and had, of course, avoided paying the required contributions. Moreover, by opening up the center of the island, they had disturbed the safest hideouts of these secret societies. Singapore, however, was not China; the British administration firmly imposed the rule of law, which was of benefit to most of the Chinese immigrants, who were able to start their business enterprises in security and without tearing each other to pieces.

Just as the different clans found a focal point in the temples and their *huiguan*, "association premises", so Catholics tended to gather round their churches. The community thus organized its work for education and its relief agencies, including societies to pray for the dead, funerals having a special importance for the Chinese.

Those Catholics who came to Singapore originally from Chaozhou, in the east of Guangdong Province, had formed a solid core of *teochew*-speaking people, a word, rendering the English transcription of Chaozhou, as pronounced in the dialect of the region. They had a

---

[6] Charles Burk Buckley, *An Anecdotal History of Old Times in Singapore: 1819–1867* (Kuala Lumpur: University of Malaya Press, 1965), pp. 246–47.

long history, which is fairly typical of the contacts between Southeast Asia and south China. Their Catholic ancestors in Chaozhou had been baptized by the first Portuguese missionaries, 300 years previously, but the expansion of the community had been due to seven Chinese laymen who had been sent from Bangkok by Fr. Albrand in 1844.[7] Fr. Étienne-Raymond Albrand, a priest of the Paris Foreign Missions and future vicar apostolic in Guiyang, Guizhou Province, had worked mainly among the Chinese who had emigrated to Bangkok; the catechists whom he sent back to mainland China were effective in forming leaders firmly attached to the Church and capable of taking responsibility for their communities. In 1931 the Catholics of Pene and Kuitan in east Guangdong Province were harassed by Communist troops, and many emigrated, some to Singapore, some to Melaka, and some to Bangkok. In China itself the port of Swatow (Shantou) then became the center of "teochew" country. The diocese of Swatow had been flourishing before the arrival of the Communists; it emerged from thirty years of persecution with renewed vigor and with numerous vocations among young people wanting to become priests or members of religious orders. Since 1980 contacts have begun again between Catholics on the mainland and those in Singapore, Melaka, and Bangkok, who have contributed to the rebuilding of churches in Pene and Kuitan.

The same thing happened among Catholics who came originally from Fujian Province and who settled in Singapore, Indonesia, and other countries in Southeast Asia. Since the reopening of China to international contacts, these Christians have renewed links with the villages of their ancestors and have contributed effectively to the rebuilding of churches in the dioceses of Fuzhou and Xiamen (Amoy).

The Chinese Catholic communities in Malaysia and Singapore experienced considerable development from 1950 onward through the arrival of some fifty foreign missionaries and Chinese priests who were prevented from continuing their ministry in continental China. They came at a time when the numerous Chinese schools in these countries started using Mandarin as a medium of teaching, whereas other schools taught in English. Since then older people have continued to speak the different dialects of southern China, whereas younger peo-

---

[7] Adrien Launay, *Histoire des Missions de Chine: Mission du Kouang-tong* (Paris: Téqui, 1917), p. 45.

ple have more and more been using Mandarin or English. Education
was increasingly continuing up to university level, with Mandarin as
the language of instruction. In 1956 the University of Nanyang was
founded in Singapore by private initiative and soon became a center
for Communist influence among ethnic Chinese students, who were
impressed by the new China, liberated by Mao Zedong. It was a time
of armed struggle against British colonialism, when Chinese Communist guerrillas were active in the Malaysian jungle, while strikes were
becoming more and more frequent in Singapore. After eleven years
of fighting, the armed insurrection in Malaya was finally defeated by
British Commonwealth forces, and the Federation of Malaysia became independent in 1963, a country with an ethnic Malay majority
in political control and an ethnic Chinese population contributing
primarily to the economic life of the country. In Singapore Mr. Lee
Kuan Yew and his People's Action Party came into power in 1959,
and two years afterward Marxist students and left-wing trades unions
were reduced to silence. Singapore left the Federation of Malaysia in
1965 and became an independent country.

The large Catholic Chinese schools which had been created in Singapore remained immune to Communist influences, their heads being members of religious orders who had experienced the true nature of Communism while they were in mainland China. Moreover,
since 1953 Singapore had become a center of support for a Catholic
apostolate among the Chinese throughout the world. The bishop of
Ningxia, Carlo Van Melckebecke, a Belgian Scheut father, who had
been expelled from China in 1952, gave himself totally to promoting
this work. In May 1953, the Congregation *de Propaganda Fide* in Rome
appointed him as apostolic visitor to all the Chinese overseas. His first
urgent task was to find appointments for some 200 young Chinese
priests who were studying abroad at the time when the Communists
came to power in China. Later he saw to the continuation of this
ministry in the future by founding two Chinese junior seminaries,
one at Phulam near Saigon and the other on the island of Cebu in
the Philippines. The greatest number of Chinese, after the mainland,
Taiwan, and Hong Kong, was to be found in Singapore, and it was
there that Bishop Van Melckebecke created the Catholic Central Bureau, which soon acquired a worldwide reputation. It consisted of a
news agency and a bookshop; it offered a correspondence course in
religious education and a catechetical service; it also created an asso-

ciation to pray for China. In 2000 the whole complex was renamed The Carlo Center.[8]

Both in Malaysia and in Singapore the priests who had been expelled from China were able to exercise an important pastoral ministry, especially by their work with young people through the Young Christian Workers, the Young Christian Students, and the Legion of Mary; they could use Mandarin to instruct catechumens. The renewal which was taking place in the Catholic Church throughout the world, thanks to the reforms of the Second Vatican Council, made it possible for these priests to lead Chinese-language communities to a fuller religious flowering through liturgical celebrations and Bible study groups.

Chinese-Filipino Relations

Another traditional exchange that remained very active linked the Philippines to the mainland provinces of Hebei in the north of China and Fujian in the southeast. Ever since the first Chinese bishop, Gregory Luo (1616–1691), had studied in Manila, Chinese Catholics living in the Philippines had maintained friendly contacts with mainland China. In 1966, at the time when the Cultural Revolution was sweeping away what was left of the Catholic Church in China, the number of ethnic Chinese living in the Philippines was 358,488, of whom 80,838 were Catholics. They were looked after by ninety priests, many of them from the mainland.[9]

Even before pressure from the Communists, missionary contacts had been encouraged by a Chinese bishop from Hebei Province, Francis Xavier Zhao (Zhao Zhensheng), a Jesuit educated in France and Belgium, who had been appointed vicar apostolic of Xianxian diocese by Pope Pius XI in 1937. He was very attentive to the formation given to his priests and also wanted to give them a missionary spirit. Fr. Stanislaus Zhang Yanqiu, from the same diocese, gave this appreciation of him:

---

[8] The information concerning the apostolic visitor to the overseas Chinese is taken from Jean Charbonnier, M.E.P., "Le Christianisme chinois hors de Chine", *Concilium* no. 146 (1979), p. 131.

[9] Carlo Van Melckebecke, *Diasporae Sinicae Statisticarum Tentamen* (Singapore, 1966), ninth ed.

Bishop Zhao is not only bishop of Xianxian, a bishop in China; he is a
bishop of the whole world, a bishop of the universal Church. His disciples are scattered over the five continents. They not only work with the
Chinese or the Chinese overseas, but they also work in the developed
countries—France, England, America. Their work is not limited to the
parish ministry. They can be found in schools, hospitals, farms.[10]

As for the Philippines, in 1976 thirteen priests from the diocese
of Xianxian were managing five secondary schools and one primary
school there; five priests from the same diocese were in charge of
parishes.

Priests from China carried out more far-reaching work for their
country by producing religious broadcasts from Manila on Radio *Veritas*. The broadcasts in Mandarin are put together by the Kuangchi Society of Taiwan and are clearly audible in the northern part of China,
where they produce interesting responses from panels of listeners.
The programs of Radio Vatican, produced in Rome by a group of
Chinese priests, are also being received in China. A Shanghai priest,
interned in a work camp, managed to get a letter through to his
brother, a Jesuit in Rome, saying, "I had the joy of hearing you saying Mass in Chinese over Radio Vatican. I felt I was concelebrating
with you in spirit."

After China began to open up in the 1980s, the Philippines became
a place where hundreds of priests and nuns from the mainland were
able to receive their religious formation. This had great advantages
for them, in comparison with what they could have expected in Europe or America. In the Philippines they could practice their English,
take part in the Catholic life of a people not all that different from
those they knew in China, and also benefit from university resources
for their theological and pastoral studies.

The Jesuits played a particularly important role in the Filipino
Church by maintaining its awareness of the situation of the Church
in China. In 1976 the East Asia Pastoral Institute, at the Ateneo in
Manila, put on a series of lectures on "Chinese Marxism and Christianity", which was followed by a hundred priests and members of
religious orders from eastern Asiatic countries, making them aware
of developments within contemporary Chinese society. The fact that

---

[10] *To the Memory of Bishop Zhao Zhensheng;* a tribute coedited in 1976 by the priests of the
diocese of Xianxian. Translated from the Chinese.

Catholics outside China were studying Chinese Marxism corresponded to the attempts of the post-conciliar Church to be more open to
the world and to Pope Paul VI's call for "dialogue" in his encyclical
letter of 1964, *Ecclesiam Suam*. However, it must be said that those
who had had experience of Communist prisons remained sceptical
about the relevance of all this to the situation in China.

While Catholics were thus experiencing deep self-questioning, Protestant evangelicals showed a boldness worthy of the Acts of the Apostles. They organized in Manila a congress with 420 representatives
from some twenty different countries on the theme *Love China 75*.
Most of the delegates came from the Philippines and from eastern
Asia, but a forty-strong delegation represented South Africa. Evangelical groups were strong in the Philippines and were also supported by
American sects, young Chinese Americans being particularly active.

As regards China itself, evangelicals did not allow the official block-
ade to make them lose heart. They launched a movement called
"Open Doors", inspired by a Dutchman, Brother Andrew, who pref-
aced a book written by Brother David under the title *God's Smuggler
to China* (London: Hodder and Stoughton, 1981). They practised an
underground evangelism in an attempt to help Christians who were
being persecuted but who were nevertheless willing to convert their
persecutors. Faced with a country torn apart by the conflicts of the
Cultural Revolution, evangelists proclaimed the love of Christ the
Savior. They said that the Holy Spirit had laid on them the burden
of announcing this good news to 800 million Chinese; one of them
said, "If God has created so many Chinese, it must be because he
loves them very specially." In March 1975 they organized a week
of continuous prayer for the people of China; this was observed by
2,000 Chinese churches throughout the world, and a further 13,000
churches were associated with the week of prayer.

How could one bring the Gospel to China? Evangelicals set about
it first of all by trying to make the faith of Christians throughout the
world more lively and by witnessing to God all round the Great Wall,
like the Jews of old who walked round the walls of Jericho. Since it
was difficult to reach people in China itself, they tried to contact the
Chinese working abroad on development projects or as diplomats or
athletes. At the Manila Congress of 1975 a Chinese girl from Hong
Kong described how she had gone to Zambia as a midwife so as to be
able to meet Chinese workers building the railway; on October 1, the

Feast of the Liberation, she met a lady working as an attaché at the Chinese embassy. "We talked for two hours", she said "For the first hour she talked to me about Mao and Communism. For the second hour I talked to her about God."

Evangelicals were proud to report such bold witness from outside, but they were even more pleased to be able to draw attention to the fervor of Christians within the country. They announced loud and clear the good news: "God still lives in China." This was the title of a book published by the China Bible Fund, which contains some twenty stories about life in China, true stories, sometimes somewhat improved, perhaps, so as to be more edifying. This was the style of Chinese Communist tales, which had been widely diffused at the time of the Cultural Revolution, such as the story of Lei Feng, a young hero of the People's Liberation Army, who was inspired by *The Little Red Book* of quotations from Chairman Mao to sacrifice himself in the service of the people. Lei Feng multiplied good actions as a worker, as a soldier of the Red Army, and as a Party member until he died in an accident, aged twenty-two. Catholics in China were also collecting a long martyrology about heroes of the faith who had suffered for the salvation of the people, inspired by "the little book of the Gospels".[11]

Chinese Sages in America and Europe

The Chinese evangelical missionary movement was supported by communities in North America. These communities had come a long way since the first Chinese immigrants who, in the nineteenth century, had been either expelled or exploited. They had been attracted originally by *Jin shan*, the "Golden Mountain" of San Francisco, which they discovered meant in fact working on the construction of the Transcontinental Railway. Many specialized in laundries; they opened small businesses or restaurants. Thanks to their hard work and endurance, they saved enough to pay for the education of their children, who thus acquired university degrees and acceded to a respected status in society. The Chinese are by tradition concerned to observe

---

[11] Cf. Jean Charbonnier, M.E.P., *Les 120 Martyrs de Chine Canonisés le 1er Octobre 2000* (Paris: Missions Étrangères de Paris, 2000), Archives des Missions Étrangères: Études et Documents 12.

social conventions and willingly adopt the rituals of the society they have entered. Conversions to Christianity among the Chinese abroad were thus proportionally more numerous than in China. In the United States by the middle of the twentieth century, there were 15,000 Catholics out of an estimated total of 200,000 Chinese. These 15,000 were concentrated mainly in San Francisco and Los Angeles, followed by New York, Philadelphia, and Chicago. In Canada the Chinese were mostly in Montreal, Toronto, and Vancouver; in 1983 the Catholics among them numbered 2,500 out of 90,000. These Catholic communities were to develop as the result of a combination of favorable circumstances; many Chinese priests and seminarians who were unable to return to China came to work in the States or Canada; many Chinese Christians from Taiwan and elsewhere came to North America for their studies; the pastoral and liturgical renewal set in motion by the Second Vatican Council influenced the quality of development of these communities just at the time when the number of Chinese in America was growing steadily. By 1983 there were 1.4 million ethnic Chinese in the United States and 350,000 in Canada.

During the same period the numbers of Chinese in Europe increased tenfold, compared to what they were at the time of the Cultural Revolution. In 1966 they had been 55,038.[12] The number went up to 583,000 in 1983.[13] France and Great Britain were the main host countries. Young Chinese had started coming to France during the First World War; they found work in factories, replacing workers who went into the army. Many later returned to China, but some 3,000 remained in France, where many opened small businesses. They were joined in the 1930s by Chinese immigrants, coming mostly from Zhejiang Province. After the Second World War more came, mainly refugees from the Communist regime in 1950, followed after 1975 by Chinese from Vietnam, Cambodia, and Laos.

The pastoral care of the Chinese in France after the Second World War began in Paris in 1954, thanks to Fr. Joseph Li from Hebei Province. He was a student in international law at the University of Paris and gathered a group of Catholic Chinese at the parish church of St. Étienne du Mont in the university quarter on the left bank of the Seine. In 1988 the number of Catholic Chinese in France was

---

[12] *Statistics from the Catholic Central Bureau of Singapore* (1966), p. 11.
[13] Figures derived from the *Overseas Chinese Economy Yearbook 1982–1983* (Taiwan).

between 2,500 and 3,000, of whom two-thirds were in Paris.[14] The total number of Chinese living in France in 1988 had probably topped 200,000.

During the last decades of the twentieth century, many immigrants came to Paris from the Wenzhou region, south Zhejiang Province; a certain number were Catholics from the underground Church, wanted by the police. Most of them, however, had been recruited by "snake heads", that is, gang leaders with mafia connections in the black market and the clothing industry. Many of these young Chinese, often rather bewildered, were made welcome by Christian missions in France, French Protestants being especially active in this work. In general, however, the proportion of Christians was small, which may have reflected the de-Christianization of French society.

Things are very different in Mauritius, an island in the Indian Ocean with strong French traditions, both social and linguistic. The total number of ethnic Chinese in Mauritius was estimated in 2000 at 30,000. The Chinese Catholic Mission in Mauritius celebrated its fiftieth anniversary in December 2000, and it was noted then that 85 percent of the Chinese population had become Christian.[15] Most of them were Hakka, whose ancestors came from the Meizhou (Meixian) region in Guangdong. During the last fifty years a Chinese catechist from that part of China, Philip Kwok, has been very effective in working with Chinese priests to reach immigrants in Mauritius. In the large island of Madagascar, between Mauritius and the African continent, many Chinese immigrants have had contacts with Christianity, especially through the Franco-Chinese school in Tamatave (Toamasina) and the Chinese Catholic Centre in Antananarivo. However, because of the economic difficulties that beset Madagascar, many of them later moved to Canada.

In North America, as in Europe, the most significant contribution of Chinese Christians was perhaps to be found in universities. Chinese Christian lecturers, both lay and clerical, gave witness to their spiritual journey, thus enabling Westerners to understand Chinese culture better, while also deepening their own faith.

---

[14] According to Thomas Elhorga, M.E.P., "La Diaspora chinoise en France", *Les Échos de la rue du Bac*, no. 227 (Apr. 1988), p. 111.

[15] Cf. the bimonthly magazine of the Chinese Catholic Mission in Mauritius, *L'Aurore*, no. 85 (Feb. 2001).

Paul Sih (Xue Guangqian), a former diplomat who had become professor at Seton Hall University in South Orange, New Jersey, wrote in 1952 an account of his spiritual odyssey called *From Confucius to Christ*.[16] He had spent his childhood in Shanghai and remembered what he was later to recognize as signs of the presence of God in his life: his devotion to Guanyin, the goddess of mercy in the Buddhist religion, which would lead him later to the Virgin Mary; the extraordinary charity of the Shanghai businessman Lo Pahong (see pp. 398–401); the Confucian virtue of filial piety; the teaching of the philosopher Mozi on heaven "which has done everything for the good of man". His initiation into Christianity was the result of a slow process of growth, involving meeting with friends and personal reflection, as well as three violent episodes. When he was at secondary school in Shanghai, an English lady made him read the Bible, but this did not convince him of the existence of God. He then studied law at the University of Suzhou in Anhui Province and followed a course of religious teaching with Methodists but fiercely kept his independence. During his time as a diplomat, he visited Rome several times but remained at the level of aesthetic appreciation when visiting its great churches. However, it was in Rome that his friend John Wu led him toward Christ by his prayer life and by his devotion to St. Thérèse of the Child Jesus. Paul Sih read her *Story of a Soul* and discovered the way of spiritual childhood. He was intellectually convinced but remained full of his own importance. Three serious accidents were needed before he could understand that his existence was entirely in the hands of God. Three times he was literally thrown to the ground as St. Paul had been, which is why he took the name Paul when he was baptized: first during a false landing in Greece; then in Salonika, where the Chinese delegation was bombed; finally in a car accident in Milan. After that, he gave up his self-importance and committed himself to the grace of God. He already knew the United States, where he had been at the head of a delegation to the United Nations, and he settled there in 1950, putting his experience at the service of Chinese studies. In 1974, during the violent anti-Confucius campaign in China, Paul was requested to supply two copies of his book, one for Pope Paul VI and one for Cardinal Pignedoli, secretary

---

[16] Paul Sih, *De Confucius au Christ* (Paris: Casterman, 1959).

for non-Christian affairs. Bishop Fulton Sheen, then auxiliary bishop in New York, wrote in 1952 in the preface to Paul Sih's book:

> The story of Dr. Paul Sih's book is much more than the story of an Oriental who has found Christ. It is the symbol of the yeast which is already at work in the soul of China.[17]

The soul of China was also what Fr. François Houang, a priest of the French Oratory, was trying to reveal to French readers by his book *Âme chinoise et christianisme*, which was published in 1958. He dedicated it "To the memory of my mother, who brought me up in the faith and piety of Buddhism and prepared me to know the light of Christ".[18] In that text "my mother" also refers to China, which he deeply loved. François Houang was born on the banks of the *Taihu*, the great lake to the west of Shanghai, in 1911, the year of the republican uprising. His father died when he was only six so that he was brought up by his mother. As a student he shared in the revolutionary enthusiasm of the times. He had just started his studies in biology and medicine at Nanjing when he was awarded a scholarship and arrived in France in 1932. Once he had learned French, he became resident at the Hostel of the Franco-Chinese Institute, which had been founded at Lyons on the initiative of Édouard Herriot, the mayor of Lyons, who was several times premier of France during the Third Republic. Here François Houang met Jean Wahl, professor in metaphysics, a meeting that changed the direction of his life. He gave up science and began to study philosophy in search for the metaphysical foundation of personal existence. Much later, in 1954, he was to defend a thesis on *Neo-Hegelianism in England*. He also began to study Christianity, with the intention of understanding the root causes of imperialism, so as to destroy it more effectively. He was put in touch with two remarkable priests, the Jesuit Fr. Henri de Lubac, who was professor of fundamental theology at the Catholic University in Lyons (*Facultés catholiques de Lyon*), and Fr. Jules Monchanin, a diocesan priest who later founded an ashram in India and became an expert in Hinduism. At the Franco-Chinese Hostel he also met Fr. Édouard Duperray, who was to publish in 1956 a study in Chinese missiology under the title *Ambassadeurs de Dieu à la Chine* (Casterman, 1956). He also got

---

[17] Ibid., preface, p. 12.

[18] François Houang, *Âme chinoise et christianisme* (Paris: Casterman, 1958), p. 148.

in touch with some active Chinese members of the Catholic Action group, which had been started by Fr. Lebbe (cf. pp. 388–92).

Shortly before the Second World War, François Houang also met in Lyons an unusual Chinese Catholic, Louis Wei, who was thirty years old and had just walked all the way from China to Rome. Louis came from an old Shanghai Catholic family and had participated when he was nineteen years old in the preparation of the Council of Shanghai. He was deeply patriotic and eager to claim for the Chinese Church the right to full independence in union with Rome, which he found fascinating too. In 1953 Louis Wei went off to the Abbey of St. André-lez-Bruges, where he worked on a doctoral dissertation on *France's Missionary Policy in China 1842–1856*. He obtained his doctorate at the arts faculty of the University of Paris and then started to prepare for the priesthood. He studied at the Séminaire des Carmes of the Institut Catholique de Paris and was ordained in Rome in 1965 by Cardinal Tisserant. Louis was delighted to read the friendly greeting of Pope Paul the VI in January 1967 to China, which was then undergoing the horrors of the Cultural Revolution, but he was aghast soon afterward when he learned that the same Pope had promoted to the rank of pro-nuncio the representative of the Holy See in Taiwan. His disapproval led him to write a large book, *Le Saint-Siège et la Chine de Pie XI à nos jours*, published in 1968.[19]

When the two young intellectuals, François Houang and Louis Wei, met in Lyons in the 1930s, they shared the same deep resentment at the way foreigners were exploiting China; however, they did make a distinction between the Christian faith itself and the way in which the Catholic Church had compromised with French colonial policy. François Houang, who was not yet a Christian, found the faith during the Second World War, at a time when the Germans had overrun France and he had to seek refuge in a peasant family of the Haute Loire area of the Auvergne province. The mother of the family he was with said to him once, "You have certain practices and ideas; but, as for us, we have life" (*Vous avez des pratiques et des idées; nous, nous avons la vie*). Somehow that lit up the way ahead for him. He seemed to find in that peasant woman his own mother, who had died in 1942.

---

[19] Fr. Louis Wei was appointed to the parish of St. Michel des Batignolles in Paris and was also chaplain to a children's hospital. He was very happy to visit China in 1978, when things were beginning to open up for the churches. He became very deaf toward the end of his long life and died on May 4, 2001, age 101.

He was baptized in 1945 by Fr. Yves Raguin, a young Jesuit who was destined to go to Shanghai and would later spend forty years of his life on the production of the great Ricci Chinese-French Dictionary published in 2001. François Houang had a friend, Ou Chen-yang, who was baptized a year after him, taking the name Vincent; both of them entered the French Congregation of the Oratory, and both were ordained priests in 1952. Fr. François Houang could not return home, and so he became a missionary for China in France. He gave lectures to the Cercle Saint Jean Baptiste, a study center on non-Christian religions founded in 1944 by Fr. Jean Daniélou, S.J., later cardinal. He also took part in the summer camps run by the lay missionaries of *Ad Lucem*. Above all, he made people in France aware of the riches of Chinese wisdom by his books on the history of Buddhism in China[20] and by his translation of the *Daode Jing* of Laozi,[21] the basic text of Taoism, one of the two major Chinese philosophical traditions.

In the early 1970s Fr. François Houang gave a course of lectures on Chinese philosophy at the *Institut Catholique*, the Catholic University in Paris; in them he considered what the renewal of Chinese civilization would be like if it developed in a way that was faithful to its own tradition. He turned his attention to the protagonists of the Hundred Days Reform in 1898, especially Tan Sitong and Yan Fu. He particularly admired the young Buddhist Tan Sitong, who wrote *Ren xue*, "Science of Love", before being killed by the conservative repression. Fr. Huang translated into French the difficult writings of Yan Fu, who had been an ardent follower of evolution, and published a translation of his *Manifestos* of 1895, which had criticized the disadvantages of the Confucian tradition. Houang felt closer to Taoism than to Confucianism, and, as a Christian, he felt particularly close to the philosopher Mozi (c. 470–391 B.C.), a thinker who listened to the people, preached universal love, and venerated heaven. Fr. Houang himself had the popular touch; he was close to the people in the Oratorian parish of St. Eustache where he worked, near *Les Halles*, the great covered market of Paris, which was removed in 1970 to make way for stores and gardens next to the Centre Pompidou. He knew

---

[20] François Houang, *Le Bouddhisme de l'Inde à la Chine* (Paris: Arthème Fayard, 1963), Collection Je Sais-Je Crois, no. 145.

[21] Lao Tzeu, *La voie et sa vertu: Tao-tê-king* (Paris: Le Seuil, 1979), texte chinois présenté et traduit par François Houang et Pierre Leyris. Point Sagesse 16, 2nd ed.

how to foster friendship through the hospitality of a good table and a glass of brandy; in this, he was following the way recommended in the past by Fr. Matteo Ricci in his *Treatise of Friendship*. Fr. Houang died in 1991 but had composed his epitaph some years previously:

Here lies François Xavier Houang
He loved Jesus Christ
He loved his friends
He loved Western civilization without disowning Chinese culture
And
He loved French cuisine as much as Chinese food
While awaiting
The Eternal Banquet.[22]

---

[22] "Ci-gît François Xavier Houang / Il a aimé Jésus-Christ / Il a aimé ses amis. / Il a aimé la civilisation occidentale / sans renier la culture chinoise / et il a aimé la cuisine française / à l'égal de la chinoise / en attendant le banquet eternel."

27

HONG KONG: REFUGE AND SPRINGBOARD

In 1991, when Hong Kong still had six years to go under the British flag, it celebrated its 150-year anniversary. It was retroceded to China on July 1, 1997, and Macao followed in December 1998; the last vestige of the Western venture into eastern Asia thus disappeared. There was uncertainty about the entry of the former colony under the red, five-starred flag, but the economic liberalism and political organization of Hong Kong have been maintained with the slogan "one country; two systems". Hong Kong remains a center for international exchange, and 40 percent of China's external trade passes through it. It is in China's interests to maintain the prosperity of the "Scented Harbor", but there was the danger that too many fat cats would scare away the goose with the golden eggs. Since 1990 a good many highly competent and skilled businessmen, as well as companies, have left for Vancouver or elsewhere; some have returned while often retaining a base abroad.

Christians have not been the last to leave, concerned as they were with their children's future. Most of them, however, have stayed on, because of their attachment to the local Church and their feeling of solidarity with the population of Hong Kong. The role that they could play in relation to the mainland no doubt influenced some of them as well. The major Hong Kong daily, *South China Morning Post*, carried an article on June 3, 1991, which said:

> When the first Catholics arrived in Hong Kong in 1841, their eyes did not only rest on the few farmers and fishermen who lived on the island; they also saw the thousands of potential converts on the mainland. Now, 150 years later, China is more than ever the essential concern of the Church of Hong Kong.

There was, however, a difference. In 1841 it was missionaries from abroad who had been thinking about a strategic base for the missions in China and who saw Hong Kong as taking over from Macao in that respect. In 1991 it was mainly Chinese priests, sisters, and lay people who were assuming that mission. They were also mindful of their own people in Hong Kong, no longer a few farmers and fisherfolk, but six and a half million inhabitants, of whom 263,000 are Catholics and many more are Protestants.

Springboard for Mission: Land of Refuge

The Catholic Church in Hong Kong has developed through the following stages. Soon after the occupation of the island by the British in 1841, Rome detached Hong Kong from the diocese of Macao and appointed a Swiss priest as prefect apostolic. In 1846 the first seminary was opened for the formation of future Chinese priests. In 1847 the prefecture was entrusted to the Paris Foreign Missions, who set up there the ecclesiastical equivalent of a ship chandler for all the requirements of the missions in China. Then in 1850 the Hong Kong prefecture was entrusted to P.I.M.E., the Pontifical Institute for Foreign Missions of Milan. When the first Italian priests arrived in 1858, the colony numbered about 73,000 inhabitants, of whom 70,000 were Chinese. Fewer than 3,000 were Catholics; they were made up of 1,500 Portuguese, 600 Chinese, and 300 soldiers from Europe.[1] Religious sisters soon began their educational and social work in the colony. The Sisters of St. Paul de Chartres came in 1848 and opened a community clinic; the Canossian Sisters arrived in 1860 and founded schools.

In 1874 the prefecture was upgraded to being a vicariate apostolic, with territory extending beyond the colony to include a part of Guangdong Province, on the mainland north of Hong Kong. The colony also increased in size, the Kowloon Peninsula facing Victoria Island was added to it in 1860, and in 1898 the New Territories were leased to Great Britain on a ninety-nine year lease. These rural areas increased the population by 100,000, bringing the total population of the colony up to 250,000.

A seminary for Hong Kong having been opened in 1846, the first

---

[1] According to Sylvain Rabiller, M.E.P., in "De quoi demain sera-t-il fait? L'Église de Hong Kong devant l'échéance 1997" in *Églises d'Asie*, suppl. 97, Oct. 1990, p. 3. The social and political situation in Hong Kong on the eve of retrocession has been analyzed by two journalists, Maryna Dyja and Dorian Malovic, in *Hong Kong, un destin chinois* (Paris: Bayard, 1997).

Chinese priest ordained from it was Mark Liang in 1861.[2] In 1931 this became the major seminary for south China, administered by the Jesuits. There was development too as regards the sisters; a purely Chinese congregation was created in 1922 when the Sisters of the Precious Blood became an independent offshoot of the Canossian community.

The first decades of the twentieth century saw the beginnings of Catholic publications. Fr. Granelli, working with Fr. Philip Lu (Lu Luzhong), started a *Catholic Newspaper* (*Kung Kao Po, Gongjiao bao*) in 1928. The Hong Kong *Catholic Truth Society* was founded in 1934 and produced pamphlets and books of apologetics, catechesis, and spirituality.

The Japanese occupation of Hong Kong lasted from Christmas 1941 to August 15, 1945, and was a terrible ordeal. The Japanese army pillaged the missionary properties, and all public religious ceremonies were forbidden.

When on April 11, 1946, territorial dioceses were created all over China, Hong Kong became a diocese whose limits extended far beyond the frontiers of the colony. Catholics in the Huizhou and Haifeng regions were thus cut off from their bishop when the Communists came to power at the end of 1949.

In the early 1950s refugees from the mainland poured into Hong Kong. The population went up from 600,000 to 2,360,000 between 1945 and 1951. The British authorities coped with this in a practical and disciplined way; mass-produced housing was put up, the so-called chicken coops. The Churches built schools and churches and provided help of all kinds for the new arrivals, who were often bereft of everything. The refugees, rootless and distraught as they were, often wanted to become Christians, having found through them a new community to belong to and new hope. Many baptisms of adults took place, and some of the refugees were Christians already, so that the numbers of Catholics rose to 131,698 in 1958 and 241,986 in 1968. The well-organized aid services no doubt accounted for a great deal of this movement of conversions. In 1953 a Catholic Conference for Social Aid was created; it was affiliated to *Caritas Internationalis* in 1955 and later became *Caritas Hong Kong*. Among the refugees were

---

[2] *Xianggang Tianzhujiao — Hong Kong Catholic Annals* (Hong Kong: Holy Spirit Study Centre, 1983), p. 94.

many missionaries and Chinese priests, some of whom remained at the service of the diocese. The community of Trappist monks, Our Lady of Joy from Zhending, south Hebei Province, settled in the island of Lantau.

Chinese Catholic Bishops of Hong Kong

At the end of 1968, Rome accepted the resignation of Bishop Lorenzo Bianchi, P.I.M.E., the last Italian missionary bishop. His auxiliary, Francis Hsu Chen-ping (Xu Chenbing), who had been consecrated in October 1967, assumed the direction of the diocese.

Francis Hsu was born in 1920 at Ningbo, Zhejiang Province, in a Protestant family; his father, who worked at the Shanghai Chamber of Commerce, was one of the directors of the Y.M.C.A. Francis was a precocious child who had learned to speak English and to use the telephone by the age of five. He went to the secondary school attached to St. John's University, where the education was thought to resemble that of an English gentleman and included tennis and playing the piano. He went to the university itself in 1936 and spent four years studying journalism. Having obtained his degree at the age of twenty-five, he worked with an English press agency and was sent to Chengdu with responsibility for "China" coverage. In 1944 he took up a post as lecturer in English at Fudan University, Shanghai, and while there shared lodgings with a Catholic colleague, Fr. Fang Hao, who explained to him something about Catholic doctrine. He then obtained a grant from the British Council and went for three years to the University of Oxford, as a member of Merton College. He was admitted to the college in March 1945 and obtained a B. Litt. in English language and literature. By 1948 he was back in China with a teaching post at the Central University of Beijing. Just before the Communists occupied the city, he was baptized conditionally as a Catholic, taking the name Francis. He was allowed to join his parents in Hong Kong, where he remained, becoming associated as a researcher with the British Institute for Southeast Asia. It was then that he began to think of the priesthood and attended Latin courses at the university. In 1955 he went to Rome and studied theology at the Beda College, the English-speaking seminary for late vocations. After his ordination in 1959, Bishop Bianchi accepted him for the diocese of Hong Kong and made him chief editor of *Kung Kao Po* until 1964. From 1961 to 1964 he was also responsible in the diocese for Catholic Action and for the *Catholic Truth Society*.

When Bishop Francis Hsu took over the diocese of Hong Kong, he was perhaps the first Chinese bishop to be in charge of a group of priests more than half of whom were still non-Chinese. His English education no doubt helped. He was also fully qualified to promote activities in Chinese. In 1969 a Chinese translation of the Bible, the result of twenty years of work, was published by the Duns Scotus Society for Biblical Studies, which the Franciscans had created. From 1975 the *Studium Biblicum* published *Shengjing shuang-yue kan* (*The Bible Fortnightly*) from its premises in Henderson Road. The Franciscans also encouraged the creation of biblical study groups. In March 1970, Bishop Hsu called a diocesan synod to take stock of the situation of the local Church after twenty years of rapid growth and to see how the directives of the Second Vatican Council were being put into practice. More than 400 representatives of the clergy, the religious orders, and the laity took part in this undertaking, which lasted until August 1971. They were divided into eleven working groups, and the suggestions that surfaced were to guide the life of the diocese during the years to come. While the Catholics of Hong Kong were thus deeply involved in a process of *aggiornamento*, the presidents of the bishops' conferences of thirteen countries of Asia met in March 1971 and established in Hong Kong the secretariat of the Federation of Asian Bishops' Conferences (F.A.B.C.). Bishop Hsu, however, was unable to reap the benefits of all this work, as he fell gravely ill and died prematurely, aged fifty-three, in 1973.

Another Chinese bishop succeeded as bishop of Hong Kong in April 1974. He was Li Hongji from Guangzhou, who had been a student at the Seminary of South China, of which he had become rector in 1971. Unfortunately the new bishop was struck down by a heart attack after only three months. He was succeeded by John Baptist Wu Cheng-chung (Hu Zhenzhong), who was born in 1925 at Wuhua, a district of Guangdong Province belonging to the diocese of Kaying (Jiaying), which was looked after by the Maryknoll fathers. He had been ordained priest in 1952 in Hong Kong Cathedral and went for higher studies to the Urbanian University in Rome, where he obtained a doctorate in canon law. He resided in the United States for a time, in New York, Boston, and Chicago, where he worked in the diocesan secretariat. He then gained valuable pastoral experience as parish priest of St. Anne's, Miaoli, Taiwan, in the diocese of Sinchu. In April 1975 Pope Paul VI appointed him bishop of Hong Kong; he was consecrated on July 25, in Hong Kong Cathedral by Cardinal Rossi, prefect of the *Congregatio de Propaganda Fide*, which in 1982 was renamed the Congregation for the Evangelization of Peoples. In 1988 Pope John Paul II made him a member of the Sacred College; in 1996, Cardinal Wu's health began to fail, and he was given the help of a coadjutor bishop, Joseph Zen (Chen Rijun), and an auxiliary bishop, John Tong (Tang Han), both consecrated on the ninth of December. Cardinal Wu died on September 23, 2002, after six years of grave illness and was automatically succeeded by his coadjutor, according to the provision of canon law.

Listening Post for the Mainland

The years that saw Chinese bishops taking charge of the diocese of Hong Kong also witnessed increased contacts between the local population and mainland China. In December 1974 the population of Hong Kong was reckoned to be 4,388,200; during that year the Immigration Bureau counted 900,000 visitors from Hong Kong to Guangdong Province. The most popular festivals for visiting the mainland were Chinese New Year and the two commemorations of the dead, *Qingming* and *Chongyang*. Visitors from Hong Kong would bring gifts of food, although they themselves were not well off and often lived in huts, clinging to rocky outcrops; but the conditions of life were much worse in China, where the results of the Cultural Revolution were still being felt. There had been some material improvements in the villages, such as electricity, radio, regular postal services, and bicycles, but young people suffered greatly from the lack of freedom. In 1974 the *Manifesto of Li Yizhe* was posted up on the walls of Peking Street, Guangzhou. "Li Yizhe" was a pseudonym, composed from the names of the three authors of the manifesto: Li Zhengtian, Chen Yiyang, and Wang Xizhe. They denounced political manipulations that were keeping in power neo-Fascist cliques, and they put forward a program for a more democratic society in China, subject to the rule of law. Young people in the Guangzhou region had an idealized view of Hong Kong society and did everything possible to cross the "Bamboo

Curtain" so as to reach Hong Kong. In 1974, 7,000 of them swam across, but 207 bodies, mauled by sharks, were found on the shore by the Hong Kong police.[3] Many would-be refugees were unable to get past the barbed wire fences and were arrested by the Chinese police and sent to hard labor camps. The Hong Kong government, unable to cope with the flood of refugees, also tried to bring this illegal immigration to an end; thus the *South China Morning Post* of June 4, 1975, reported that, since December 1974, 591 illegal immigrants had been arrested, of whom 581 were repatriated. There were also many legal immigrants to Hong Kong, about 30,000 a year, many of them Chinese from abroad who had returned to China and had found the conditions of life on the mainland too hard to bear.

These new arrivals often had dramatic stories to tell about conditions in mainland China, which raised a lot of questions for Christians in Hong Kong. Chinese government propaganda had succeeded in spreading throughout the world an ideal picture of the Cultural Revolution. Chinese society was presented as abstemious and self-disciplined, a society where inequalities had been abolished between soldiers, workers, and peasants; between city dwellers and country dwellers. In this Socialist society a "new man" was said to be emerging, closer to the Gospel than the middle-class Christians of Hong Kong. In 1975, from June 16 to 19, some fifty Christian students held a meeting in the Chinese University of Hong Kong, in Chungchi College, the faculty of Protestant theology. They expressed their anti-colonialism and their solidarity with the revolution in China. Dr. Raymond Whitehead, a researcher with the National Council of Churches of the United States, sought to draw out the spiritual lessons emerging from the Chinese experience.[4] He pointed to the self-discipline required by Mao in the struggle for a new society as containing the positive values of an ethical system of revolution. However, a young Chinese woman, who had escaped from the mainland two years previously, rejected this vision as too optimistic. She reported that the present regime involved the leveling of all values and the elimination of the human personality. In fact, she said that people in China had lost faith in Mao. Nor was it possible to see all this as a passing

---

[3] *Asian Report*, no. 61 (June 1975), p. 3.

[4] Raymond Whitehead's views are expressed in his book *Love and Struggle in Mao's Thought* (Maryknoll, N.Y.: Orbis Books, 1977).

phase, because the bureaucratic regime that was in place was set to perpetuate itself indefinitely. There was only one possible critique: to work through Marx's writings again and to bring out their original humanist inspiration.[5] Those Protestants who had inherited a liberal theology tried to emphasize the positive aspects of the Marxist contribution to Chinese society.[6] Evangelical Protestants, in contrast, made use of the to-ing and fro-ing between Hong Kong and the mainland to promote mutual encouragement in the faith. They collected evidence of the fervor shown by underground Christians, and they crossed the border on missionary journeys. *Asian Outreach* published an edition of the Gospel in the simplified form of Chinese characters that had been introduced on the mainland after 1949. The Gospel of St. John had a Chinese boat on the cover with the title *Good News for Our Time: The Memoirs of a Fisherman*. It was the message of God's love, proclaimed to men and women who dared not talk to each other any more, after years of mutual denunciation. Pastor Jonathan Chao (Zhao Tian'en) started a high school of theology in Hong Kong with the intention of forming young apostles for the mainland. He and his team recorded a great number of interviews with young people who had come out of China; in fact, he created an information center during the 1980s with a staff of thirty.[7] During the 1970s Catholics in Hong Kong did not as yet have a center specialized in the affairs of mainland China. The Nazareth Press, operated by the Paris Foreign Missions, closed in 1953, and Fr. Léon Trivière, who had followed events in China closely, was recalled to Paris in 1960. The *Bulletin des Missions Étrangères* then ceased publication. Fortunately the Jesuits provided an extremely valuable information service through

---

[5] Cf. Jean Charbonnier, "Hongkong-Canton 1975: va-et-vient révélateur?" *Échanges France-Asie* (Paris: 26 rue de Babylone, 75007), dossier no. 9, Sept. 1975.

[6] In the 1980s the *Christian Study Center on Chinese Religion and Culture*, which had been located on Taofengshan Hill in Shatin, moved to 566 Nathan Road, Kowloon. The center published the review *Ching Feng* to promote dialogue between Christianity and Chinese culture. From 1983 onward a review called *Qiao* in Chinese and *Bridge* in English appeared fortnightly, covering current events on the continent. After 1994 the Taofengshan Center expanded its activities with the publication of the twice yearly review *Logos and Pneuma* and the translation of Western theological works. A termly bulletin, in Chinese and English, reports on the activities of the *Institute of Sino Christian Studies*: E-mail: info@iscs.org.hk; Web: http://www.iscs.org.hk.

[7] The Evangelical Centre at Shatin published a Chinese monthly called *Zhongguo yu jiao-hui* (*China and the Church*). It moved to Taiwan about 1995.

their fortnightly bulletin in English, *China News Analysis*, the first number of which appeared on August 15, 1953. A Hungarian Jesuit, Fr. Laszlo Ladany, was editor for thirty years, during which 1,250 issues were published. He was helped by a Chinese team of five, who systematically monitored the newspapers and radio programs of the mainland. In 1983 four young Jesuits took over the editorial work from Fr. Ladany. *China News Analysis* provided a topical analysis of the current state of affairs in China from the economic, political, social, and sometimes religious points of view, without being a Church newspaper, and was widely read in the diplomatic missions of many countries throughout the world. It moved to Taiwan in July 1994 and ceased publication at the end of 1998.

Other researchers from various missionary institutes also tried to collect the news that filtered through from the mainland. Frequent meetings for this purpose took place between priests from the Paris Foreign Missions, the Pontifical Institute for Foreign Missions of Milan, the Maryknoll fathers, the Scheut Fathers, the Society of the Divine Word, the Jesuits, and the Franciscans. They expressed their common concerns by calling themselves the Matteo Ricci Group.

From 1970 onward, a few encouraging signs concerning China were noticed by Catholics all over the world. That year the members of SEDOS (a liaison group consisting of some fifty superiors of missionary institutes) expressed a desire for more information on the religious situation within the Chinese People's Republic. With this aim in view they tried to obtain the cooperation of the congregations working in Hong Kong.[8] Pope Paul VI, on a journey through eastern Asia, stopped off at Hong Kong in October 1970 and spoke of his love for the Chinese people. The previous May the Catholic Bishops' Conference of the United States had issued a statement encouraging the American government to develop its relations with China. In August China had made a small gesture in response by freeing Bishop James Walsh, the superior of Maryknoll; he had been bishop of Kongmoon (Jiangmen) from 1927 to 1937, then director of the Catholic Central Bureau in Shanghai, after which he spent twelve years in prison. In October 1971 the Chinese People's Republic was admitted to the United Nations, and the Vatican expressed its approval. The

---

[8] Cf. Angelo Lazzarroto, P.I.M.E., "Holy Spirit Study Center: Breakthrough and Response", *Tripod*, no. 60 (1990): 6.

following month, the Italian senator Vittorino Colombo, on a visit to China, brought up the question of religion with the prime minister, Zhou Enlai. *Nantang* in Beijing, the South Church, was reopened for the celebration of a Sunday Mass, and the first public Mass in China since 1966 was celebrated there on November 21, 1971. The Mass in *Nantang*, the only official one in China, was celebrated regularly afterward, although until 1978 the congregation was restricted to foreigners, who usually numbered about thirty.

The Catholic Study Centre *Pro Mundi Vita* in Brussels then undertook, in the spirit of the Second Vatican Council, a more profound study of the Chinese experience. It received an offer of help from the Department of Marxist Studies of the World Federation of Lutheran Churches based in Geneva. These two centers organized a first meeting at Båstad in Sweden (February 1974), which was followed by a larger colloquium in Louvain in September 1974.[9] The Catholic and Protestant delegations from Hong Kong were particularly dynamic and managed, through their practical experience of the situation in China, to moderate some of the overidealistic resolutions that had been put forward. Three Hong Kong personalities represented the main tendencies of the colloquium: Dr. Peter Lee (Li Jingxiong), of the Christian Study Centre, was close to the group of ecumenical Protestant denominations, who were favorable to dialogue with Christians in a Socialist context; Pastor Jonathan Chao expressed the views of those who felt an evangelical urge to proclaim salvation to the Chinese masses. Fr. John Tong (Tang Han), lecturer in theology at the Catholic Seminary, was attentive to the various options while expressing solidarity with his Catholic colleagues.

Rome took note of these new ripples in the Christian world, and prominent theologians were invited to study closely the contributions to the Louvain Colloquium.[10] At the behest of the Congregation for the Evangelization of Peoples, a center for the study of contemporary China was opened, in connection with the Urbanian University

---

[9] The papers from these two conferences were published under the title *Christianity and the New China* (California: Ecclesia Publications, William Carey Library, 1976). Fr. René Laurentin was present at the 1974 Louvain Colloquium and brought together the content of the various talks in a book published three years later: *Chine et Christianisme: après les occasions manquées* (Paris: Desclée de Brouwer, 1977).

[10] The comments of the Roman theologians were edited by Fr. Michael Chu, S.J., under the title *The New China: A Catholic Response* (New York: Paulist Press, 1977).

in Rome. Msgr. Peter Tchao (Zhao Yunkun), who originated from Manchuria, was put in charge; after his death, Fr. Paul Pang, a Franciscan, continued this work, which he combined with the coordination of the pastoral care of the Chinese in the diaspora.[11] In October 1976 the Congregation for the Evangelization of Peoples invited experts on China from different countries to come to Rome on the occasion of the fiftieth anniversary of the consecration of the first six Chinese bishops. The interest of the congregation tended thereafter to be concentrated on Hong Kong, where it supported various information and contact services. After May 1989, an unofficial representative of the Holy See was stationed in Hong Kong with the task of studying the possibilities of relations with the Church on the mainland.

Hong Kong's privileged position continued to be of interest to all the Christian denominations. His Holiness Bartholomew I, ecumenical patriarch of Constantinople, created an Orthodox metropolitan of Hong Kong and Southeast Asia during a brief visit to the territory on November 5–7, 1996. He drew attention at the time to the fact that the creation of the new archdiocese showed that the Church had confidence in the future of Hong Kong: "There are more and more democratic openings, and we are therefore optimistic about the future of the Orthodox Church in China." On the mainland, the Orthodox community remained very small; during the 1950s there were about 20,000 Chinese members of the Orthodox Church. The Orthodox Church in China had become independent of the Moscow patriarchate in 1957, and there were two Chinese Orthodox bishops, one in Beijing and one in Shanghai. Many of the faithful had fled to Hong Kong, Japan, and other places in Asia and Australia. Only in 1986 was the first Orthodox parish, St. Luke's, founded in Hong Kong.

Chinese Theologians Reflect

An ecumenical colloquium of some fifty Chinese theologians took place in Hong Kong from February 2 to 10, 1979. Dr. Peter Lee, di-

---

[11] From 1979 to 1986 the center for Chinese studies in Rome published a *Bulletin*, which appeared, to begin with, in three editions: Italian, French, English; this was later reduced to one edition with texts in English and Italian. Later still the development of the Catholic Information Agency of Hong Kong made the publication of the Roman bulletin superfluous.

rector of the Christian Study Centre, prepared the program in conjunction with Fathers John Tong and J. B. Tsang (Zeng Qingwen) from the Catholic Seminary. The general theme was "Chinese Theology at the Crossroads", and participants reviewed critically Chinese Christian thought over the previous decades.

The question raised by Protestant liberals in the years between 1920 and 1950 had been: Can Christianity save Chinese society? Dr. Ng Lee Ming, professor of theology at Chung Chi College, the faculty of Protestant theology, responded: Christianity has something specific to say to men and women who are committed to the development process but does not solve social problems as such. An evangelical, taking up the thought of Wang Mingdao, defined more closely the "something specific"; it is the gift of salvation which is new life according to the law of the spirit and not of the flesh. The interior adherence to faith must be proved by outward behavior.

The main Catholic contributions came from two Jesuits at the faculty of theology of Fujen University, Taipei. Aloysius Chang (Zhang Chunshen) presented firstly the massive output of Fr. Wang Changzhi, a Jesuit from Shanghai who had received his theological formation at the Jesuit Theologate at Fourvières in Lyons, France, and at the Institut Catholique in Paris. His doctoral research before the Second World War had prepared him for taking from Chinese culture the best that it had to give. His dissertation had been on the pagan virtues according to St. Augustine, with a secondary thesis on Wang Yangming and the moral conscience. He had produced a veritable Chinese *Summa Theologica* in three parts: apologetic, dogmatic, and practical. It was written in modern Chinese and benefited from the pastoral experience of the author so that it was a useful book for priests and committed lay people; however, the political and social implications of the faith were not dwelled on. Such a theology provided a basis for further work; it was up to believers to adapt their witness to their milieu. Wang Changzhi tried to help them to do this by producing little guidebooks showing how a Christian should decide and behave in concrete situations, especially where the demands of the Movement for Three Autonomies were concerned.

Fr. Aloysius Chang described a second stage of Chinese Catholic theology in the texts published between 1955 and 1962 in *Xin Duosheng, The New Voice of the Clergy*, a review published in Rome by Msgr. Lokuang and priest students at the Urbanian University. This was a more academic approach, which lacked contact with the world of believers. Its grasp of Chinese thought and culture remained abstract, and its approach was one of apologetics. This was also true of the theological synthesis elaborated by Tian Liang upon the traditional Chinese norm of *xiao*, filial piety.

The Second Vatican Council had opened up new vistas in the areas of ecumenism, the values of non-Christian religions, and the service of mankind in the modern world. Theology became more concrete insofar as it was called to serve the believing community. Each year theological conferences which went in this direction were organized in Taiwan.

This is illustrated by the work of the Scripture scholar Mark Fang (Fang Zhirong), who advocated that Scripture studies should be "Sinicized", i.e., should take on a properly Chinese form. He thought that a gradual transformation of the Scriptures was needed that would be like the translation of Buddhist sutras in the sixth and seventh centuries A.D. The traditional exegesis of the Chinese classics could provide the technique of interpretation for this change, since the meaning of a text was always sought within the context of the time when it was composed. Once the original meaning of the text had been clearly established, one had to show what its scope would be today, bearing in mind the cultural context of Chinese history. Whereas Western Scripture scholars dwell on the analysis of the text and defend their interpretation of it in opposition to what their predecessors had put forward, a Chinese approach would seek to bring out the way in which different interpretations complement each other; nor would they neglect an allegorical exegesis, which fits in with their traditional awareness of the symbolic. The study of God's word would thus make a new existence possible in a new world.

These basic positions did not directly reflect life as it was being lived in mainland China. This is understandable at a time when the island of Taiwan was separated from the continent by a watertight barrier. The Catholic theology of those days tended to float serenely at the level of principles; although it had become more open to the realities of the contemporary world, its approach was still academic and technical.

Evangelicals, however, had a much more direct approach. One of them, Wan Wai-yu (Wen Weiyao), produced the best analysis of the Communist ideal, its limitations, and the questions it raises for believers. He asked a crucial question: "How true is the Marxist conception of the new man?"[12]

He pointed out to begin with that Mao Zedong's idea of the new man is a humanist one because, for Mao, the new man is not the product of a new society but its creator. How does such a humanist approach survive the test of history? The Campaign of the Hundred Flowers had aimed at being a critique of bureaucracy within the Communist Party; it had ended up with the expression of general dissatisfaction with the government and Socialism. The Great Leap Forward was intended to liberate the creativity of the masses by involving everyone in industrial production and thus making everyone a proletarian; in fact, it led to a serious economic crisis.

So what could be considered as the real content of the Maoist concept of the new man? According to Mao's own expression, it involves "serving the people with all one's strength and all one's heart". It is a doctrine of political altruism. The collective will was supposed to replace individual wills. However, for simple workers and peasants this abnegation of self for the benefit of a collective interest remained a somewhat abstract notion. That is why Mao Zedong, from the 1960s, redefined the gift of self as "loyalty toward the leaders of the Party". In order to provide an example of such loyalty a national hero was created, Lei Feng, an admirable young man from a peasant background who joined the army and died aged twenty-two in 1962 as the result of an accident. Fortunately he had kept a diary, which was published and which gives, on nearly every page, examples of his dedication: how he went out of his way to help the elderly, the sick, and the needy; how he donated his savings to disaster relief funds and gave up his food rations to comrades in hospital. Although he had a rather weedy physique to begin with, he trained day and night and became a muscular and skilled grenade thrower, hurling hand grenades a long way with unerring accuracy.[13] His ideal, often expressed in the diary, was "to walk all my life in the way indicated by the Party". In fact, Lei Feng went further and centered all his affection on the person of Mao Zedong. Almost every page of the

---

[12] In Dec. 1978 Wan Wai-yu published a book in Chinese, *Gongchanzhuyi yu jidujiao*, English title *A Christian Introduction to Communism* (Hong Kong: Tiandao Publishing, 1978).

[13] Jung Chang, *Wild Swans: Three Daughters of China* (London: Harper Collins Flamingo, 1993), pp. 339, 357. 1st ed. 1991.

diary contained self-exhortations like: I must study Chairman Mao's works, heed Chairman Mao's words, follow Chairman Mao's instructions, and be a good soldier of Chairman Mao.[14] After his untimely death, Lei Feng was held up as the ideal for Chinese youth, who were required to submit themselves unquestioningly, as he had done, to the control of the Great Leader. Jung Chang, who was a teenager at that time, comments on her experience of the period: "The cult of Mao and the cult of Lei Feng were two sides of the same coin: one was the cult of personality; the other, its essential corollary, was the cult of impersonality."[15]

It was still possible in the years 1966 to 1968 to present love of Mao as a positive gift of oneself. Afterward the known power struggles among Party leaders eventually raised doubts about the Party itself. The sending of Red Guards into the countryside also struck a blow at the cult of Mao, while the "struggle within the ideological superstructure" became more and more abstract and less related to production. After Mao's death in September 1976 the weakening of Communist ideology lessened the affirmation of the Socialist identity of Chinese society.

Dazibao, "big-character posters" written by hand, are a feature of Chinese life. They are hung on walls in public places to provide information. Government officials use them to communicate ideas and to stimulate public discussion on issues that they consider timely, but the posters are often anonymous and can also express the concerns and the complaints of the general population. In Beijing, the Xidan wall is the place for displaying *dazibao*, and toward the end of 1978 and at the beginning of 1979, it was the posters on the Xidan that proclaimed the rebirth of individual hopes in the name of democracy. The democratic Socialism that the government advocated seemed to have run out of steam.

Would the Chinese discover an alternative vision of the new man through the Christian faith? The new man that Christians proclaim is rooted in the redemptive work of Christ crucified. The new birth of man in Jesus Christ is a radical experience. It is not man creating himself anew by relying on his own strength; it is the result of the gift of the Holy Spirit. The real presence of the Holy Spirit in the

---

[14] Ibid., p. 340.
[15] Ibid.

heart of man is the driving force of man's renewal. What the Gospel emphasizes are faith and love; Christian asceticism is thus completely different from that of Mao Zedong because it does not proclaim the difference between individualism and collectivism. It is the Holy Spirit in the heart of man who ensures that truth and honesty prevail in the relations between human beings (Eph 4:17, 22–32). It is thus that the Holy Spirit can renew the whole of life, both the life of the family and the life of society (Eph 6:1–9). He can create a "new man", as the Epistle to the Colossians says (Col 3:9–11), a new nature for human beings which can make social barriers and class distinctions irrelevant.[16]

When China, by its new policy of openness, authorized in 1979 a renewal of contacts with the outside world, many hopes for the future seemed justified. In September 1980 the ecumenical liaison group, which had been constituted in the followup to the Louvain Colloquium of 1974, met in Hong Kong and reviewed the new possibilities for communication with Christians in China.

It was then that Bishop John Baptist Wu of Hong Kong, in an attempt to encourage these new openings in a prudent and practical way, invited Fr. John Tong to become the director of a new specialized study center, the Holy Spirit Study Center, founded in October 1980. It aimed at promoting the exchange of information and thought through its review *Tripod*, which was published in English and Chinese. The center would also play an important part through its communications with Christians in China.

Similar efforts on the part of Protestants and Chinese intellectuals open to Christianity took place at the Christian study center of Taofengshan, located on the heights overlooking Shatin in the Hong Kong New Territories. During the 1990s university teachers and Chinese researchers worked together to study and translate the writings of Western theologians and to make them known in the East. Their work was regularly published in the Chinese theological review *Logos and Pneuma*. Among the researchers of Taofengshan the most outstanding personality was no doubt that of Liu Xiaofeng.

Liu Xiaofeng, professor in comparative cultures at Shenzhen, in Guangdong Province near Hong Kong, had undergone a conversion

---

[16] From notes edited in 1979 by J. Charbonnier, M.E.P., "Le Colloque de Hong Kong (2–10 février 1979)", *Dossiers Échanges France-Asie*, no. 48, 1979.

of the heart to Christianity after having been a Red Guard during the Cultural Revolution. He had been sickened by the violence and the executions carried out by his group. He was to say, "My sin and my weakness were too great; I needed someone who could forgive me." Once he had rejected Marxism, he returned to China's traditional religion, but, as he said, Confucianism "has no place for the suffering, the weakness, the temptations or for the misery of man". As for Buddhists and Taoists, he was to say that they believe that "man can give salvation to himself." Through reading Dostoyevsky and through his contacts with some Christians, he was drawn to the overwhelming discovery of the Christian God and of the Cross of Jesus Christ as the sign of love and forgiveness. He then cooperated with other intellectuals to found the review *Jidujiao wenhua pinglun*, *Christian Culture Review* (Guizhou Popular Press, April 1990), which compared Chinese culture and Christian culture and later brought to China for the first time translations of Von Balthasar, Rahner, Moltmann, Barth, Simone Weil, etc.

Liu Xiaofeng and certain other Chinese philosophers and historians defined themselves as "Christians without church", or "cultural Christians". They gave two reasons for this; first, they wanted to introduce the cultural influence of Christianity into Chinese culture; second, they did not belong to any particular church. This can appear surprising. Does it mean that these intellectuals want to adhere to Christian values rather than to Jesus the Savior, as proclaimed by the tradition of the Church? Or else are they put off by certain aspects of the Church that make them prefer to go their own way? Whatever the reasons, it is certainly the case that their translations and other writings have been undertaken from a positive point of view and have brought very useful complements to the studies of Christianity, which have also developed in the universities and the institutes of social sciences of China.

28

TAIWAN: TREASURE ISLAND

When Portuguese seafarers first saw Taiwan in 1590, they called it *Formosa Insula*, the beautiful island. Taiwan is in the tropics, a hundred miles (160 kilometers) off the coast of Fujian Province, and has an area of 13,970 square miles (36,000 square kilometers). On the west side of the island, a coastal plain rises by a series of wooded plateaus to the central chain of mountains, whose peaks reach over 12,000 feet (4,000 meters). To the east, steep slopes, scarred by the ravines of rushing torrents, overlook the Pacific Ocean. The population numbers over 22 million, of whom 600,000 are of aborigine stock and constitute the original population of the island. About half of these indigenous people have adopted Chinese ways and the Chinese language during the last hundred years; the other ten or so tribes still retain their original language and their customs, even though the younger generation has been learning Chinese at school. The first Chinese immigrants came to Taiwan between the tenth and the thirteenth centuries A.D. and belonged to the Hakka (*kejia*) group. Other Chinese have joined them since, of whom the Minnan belonged to the coastal province of Fujian. These Chinese inhabitants are deeply rooted in Taiwan and are often called "Taiwanese" to distinguish them from the "mainlanders" who poured into Taiwan in 1949 to escape from the Communist regime on the mainland.

At the beginning of the seventeenth century Japanese, Spanish, and Dutch traders settled on the island. In 1642 the Dutch imposed their rule on Taiwan, but they were expelled twenty years later by a Chinese corsair from Amoy, Koxinga (Zheng Chenggong), who was faithful to the Ming Dynasty. In 1683 the Manchu Dynasty imposed its sovereignty on Taiwan for more than two hundred years, but in 1895 the island was ceded to the Japanese by the Treaty of Shimonoseki, which ended the Sino-Japanese War. The new rulers crushed a local independence movement, which aimed at creating a republic of Taiwan, and made the island into a province of the Japanese Empire. The 1943 Cairo Agreement between the Allies planned to return Taiwan to China after the war and allowed the Chinese Nationalists to assume control. The Nationalist government was initially welcomed by the local Taiwanese, but its policies sparked resentment, and the police and army reacted violently. In 1947, the infamous "February 28 incident" was a bloody repression resulting in the death of at least 20,000 Taiwanese. Ongoing martial law, imposed 1949–1987, may have been a factor encouraging opposition forces to advocate complete Taiwan independence.

Since 1949 Taiwan has become a bastion of resistance to Communism. The Kuomintang government and the remains of its army entrenched itself there, and the country is administered according to Sun Yat-sen's doctrine of the Three Principles of the People. A combination of favorable factors brought about rapid economic expansion in Taiwan: these factors were capital brought from the mainland; American aid; the infrastructure that the Japanese had put in place; disciplined habits based on Confucian principles; the success of agrarian reform during the first years of the new regime; large development projects that mobilized the energy of the population; and a network of international relations, both political and commercial, which have been well maintained in spite of the diplomatic victories of Beijing since 1971. The government of the Republic of China in Taipei claims to be the legitimate government of the whole of China, although plans for an armed reconquest of the mainland have been gradually given up since the death of Chiang Kai-shek on April 5, 1975.

Conversions

The first Catholic priest known to have set foot on Taiwan was a Spanish Dominican, Fr. Juan Cobo, who had evangelized the Chinese community in Manila and was on his way back from a mission to Japan. He reached the shore of Taiwan, only to die there in 1592. In 1626 the Spaniards established a mission at the port of Keelung, in the north of Taiwan, as a counterweight to the Dutch, who had just settled in the south of the island. A first church was built, but the mission failed to develop for various reasons: twenty-five priests were massacred by aborigines in 1633; the Dominicans were expelled by the Protestant Dutch in 1642; and, as on the continent, Chinese xenophobia took its toll.

In 1859 the imperial Chinese government opened the ports of Anping (Tainan), Keelung, and Takao (Kaohsiung) to foreign trade and to foreign missionaries. The Spanish Dominicans took up evangelization in the island again, but they faced many difficulties, whereas Presbyterians had greater success with the local population. The English Presbyterian mission began in 1860, and a Canadian Presbyterian, Dr. George Leslie Mackay (1844–1901), arrived in Tamshui in 1872. He worked indefatigably in the service of the Gospel; by the time of his death, he had created a network of sixty churches, as well as clinics and schools, and had established a community of 2,400 Christians.[1]

The Japanese administration tolerated relative religious freedom within its boundaries, so that in 1913 a prefecture apostolic, separate from Fujian Province, was created in Taiwan for Catholics, at Kaohsiung. A major seminary was founded there in 1920, and the first priest from Taiwan was ordained in 1936 in Amoy Cathedral. At the time of the Japanese surrender in 1945 there were only twelve priests in the whole island and hardly 10,000 Catholics in all. Father Tu was the administrator of the prefecture from 1946 to 1948. In 1948 Bishop Arregui, a Dominican, was appointed prefect apostolic and fostered the evangelization of the indigenous people.

The year 1949 marked a watershed in the Christian history of Taiwan as more than 400 Catholic priests, both Chinese and foreign, arrived on the island during the 1950s. Conversions began on a considerable scale, among both aborigines and Chinese refugees from the mainland. In 1952 Taiwan became the twenty-first Catholic ecclesiastical province of China, with an archbishopric at Taipei. Fr. Joseph Kuo, C.D.D., was appointed as the first archbishop, and Archbishop Riberi, the erstwhile pro-nuncio who had been expelled from China in 1952, came from Hong Kong to preside at the consecration of the new archbishop. By a mysterious dispensation of Vatican diplomacy, Riberi then stayed in Taiwan as a representative of the Holy See. The Taipei government, flattered by the creation of the new archbishopric, accepted the creation of an inter-nunciature at Taipei and sent Mr. Xie Shoukang to Rome as minister plenipotentiary of the Republic of China to the Holy See. The Vatican thus recognized the progress

---

[1] Mark Chang, S.J., A *History of Christianity in Taiwan* (Taiwan: Window Press, 1984), p. 16.

made in the evangelization of Taiwan, but it was also committing itself politically to a Chinese government hostile to the Beijing government. These diplomatic links, still maintained as of 2006, have
given the Communist government of China an additional argument
for forbidding the Catholics of the mainland from owing allegiance
to the Pope.

By 1959 the number of Catholics in Taiwan had gone up to 170,000,
and there were seven dioceses. Four years later, in 1963, the number of Catholics had increased to more than 240,000, most of whom
were recent converts, both aborigines and mainland Chinese. How
can one explain this flood of conversions? As regards the indigenous
people, who had been reduced to extreme poverty after the Japanese
occupation, there is no doubt that they were affected by the material
help that they received from the Church. Having received medical
care or distributions of rice, they came in large numbers, sometimes
whole villages at a time, to be instructed in the faith.

Their motivations, however, were spiritual too. Their traditional
norms having been overturned by the Japanese, they were looking
for new cultural norms, and they found these in Christianity. They
were most numerous in the Hualien region, and the priests of the
Paris Foreign Missions counted baptisms in the thousands and called
it "the Taiwan miracle".

Why were refugees from mainland China more receptive to the
Gospel than local Chinese? Fr. Thaddaeus Hang gives the following
reasons:

> The continentals had had to leave their native land; they had endured
> many sufferings; they felt isolated and they were conscious of a spiritual
> void in their lives, whereas the Chinese in Taiwan province remained
> attached to the customs of their ancestral religion.[2]

Another factor was that the Chinese from the mainland had had
a taste of Communism and appreciated the condemnation of atheistic materialism by the Catholic Church. As for the Taiwanese Chinese, they were in fact much attached to popular cults derived from
Taoism and concerned primarily to ensure their good luck and their
prosperity.

---

[2] Thäddaeus Hang (Xiang Tuijie), *Liming qian de Zhongguo Tianzhujiao* (*Catholics in China before Dawn*) (Taipei: Kuangchi, 1963), p. 109

Evangelization on the part of the Protestant churches was equally successful. Whereas in 1954 there had been 82,613 baptized Protestants, belonging to twelve denominations, by 1959 there were 230,000, of whom 150,000 were Presbyterians. Their growth among the aborigines was approximately the same as for Catholics, but they were more active among the Taiwanese Chinese. Presbyterians were especially successful in creating communities among the Hakkas and the Minnan. Wolfgang Grichtig carried out a survey in 1970 which showed that Catholic Chinese in Taiwan were divided into the following categories:

Continentals	73.6%
Minnan	18%
Hakka	7.5%

whereas Protestants were divided into the following:

Continentals	39.4%
Minnan	57.8%
Hakka	1.4%[3]

Some Catholic missionaries, especially the American Maryknoll fathers, did concentrate on the Taiwanese Chinese, but on the whole the Catholic Church in Taiwan, administered as it was by Chinese bishops from the continent, concentrated its efforts on refugees from the mainland.

Champions of Chinese Catholic Thought

In Taiwan bishops and priests of high intellectual caliber concentrated on trying to create an expression of the faith using the Confucian cultural tradition. In this they were close to the Nationalist government, which was concerned to find its own ideology. The rulers of Taiwan, reacting against the destructiveness, real or imagined, of "Communist bandits", presented themselves as the defenders of "5,000 years of Chinese culture"; in fact they were able to display many of the treasures of that culture, artifacts from the Forbidden City of the emperors in Beijing (called Peiping in Taiwan), which had been brought to Taiwan in 1949 and are now in the National Palace Museum at Taipei. This houses the largest collection of Chinese art in the world: paintings,

---

[3] Wolfgang L. Grichtig, *The Value System in Taiwan* (Taipei, 1970), p. 87.

calligraphy, porcelain, jade, imperial robes, bronzes, and rare books.

Several outstanding personalities contributed to the transfer of the elite of Chinese Catholicism to Taiwan. Cardinal Thomas Tian only arrived in 1960, and his few remaining years were interrupted by the sessions of the Second Vatican Council, but he brought his support to the development of higher studies. As a child in Shandong Province, he had been initiated very early to the great texts of China's official culture: the *Three Character Classic*, the *Four Books*, and the *Five Classics*. Later he benefited from the rigorous formation given by the Fathers of the Divine Word. After becoming archbishop of Beijing in 1946 he founded *Shang zhi*, "The Publishing House of Wisdom", and he also opened the St. Thomas Institute of Philosophy at Fujen University. When in December 1959 he was appointed archbishop of Taipei, replacing Archbishop Joseph Kuo, who had resigned as a result of ill health, he first of all undertook an extensive tour of the United States, which he knew well. There he collected funds for building churches in Taiwan and also for the upkeep of the many priests who had sought refuge from the mainland. He then founded St. Joseph's Seminary and St. Thomas' Major Seminary in Taiwan. Cardinal Tian fostered the intellectual formation of future priests, but he put spiritual fervor first. His former student in Shandong, Ti-Kang, who later became archbishop of Taipei in 1988, quoted Cardinal Tian as saying often, "Holiness comes first; intellectual brilliance comes second."[4]

Soon after the appointment of Cardinal Tian as apostolic administrator of Taipei, the Holy See, as the supreme authority for Catholic universities, resited Fujen (*Furen*) University in the southwest suburb of Taipei and appointed as vice-chancellor Archbishop Yu Bin, bishop of Nanjing in exile. Paul Yu Bin came from St. Joseph's Mission, Haibeizhen, north Manchuria, and had studied in Rome at the Seminary of Propaganda. He was ordained priest in 1929 and stayed on in Rome for another four years as librarian and lecturer. In 1933 he returned to China, where he became spiritual director to Catholic Action, and later inspector to Catholic schools throughout the country. It was a time when teachers hardly dared to admit that they were Catholics. Somehow Paul Yu Bin got them to join Catholic Action and to help with catechetical instruction, urging them to create Christian formation teams in schools. In 1936 he was appointed

---

[4] *Heng Yi (Costantinian)*, no. 442, (Dec. 1990):3.

archbishop of Nanjing at the age of thirty-five. He played an active role in support of the Chiang Kai-shek government during the war against the Japanese and was called "the political bonze".[5] According to Raymond de Jaegher, Paul Yu Bin had been for a long time on the Japanese black list because he had used his influence while in Rome in an attempt to prevent Japanese aggression in Manchuria and north China. Later, as mentioned above, he and his "gang" were publicly denounced by Zhou Enlai as instruments of imperialism (chapter 25, p. 432–33). He left China in December 1948 and went to America in a final attempt to obtain support for the Nationalist government from President Truman. Condemned by the Communist leaders as a "war criminal", he could not return to Nanjing. The Holy See advised him to stay in the States in the service of the overseas Chinese Catholics rather than accompanying the Kuomintang government in exile to Taiwan. After ten years of apostolate in the Chinese diaspora, he settled in Taiwan to work for the development of Catholic schools. When he became rector of Fujen University, he was well placed for promoting the cultural improvement of the Catholic community, and he also encouraged conversions among the students. The diocesan priests and the numerous members of religious orders who were teaching in the university formed Christian Life teams and helped with catechetical work. In March 1969 Archbishop Yu Bin was created a cardinal. This was seen by Kuomintang supporters as papal approval for Yu Bin's anti-Communist crusade. Others, such as Madame Su Xuelin, interpreted it differently. She was a writer who had become a Catholic while studying at Lyons, France, and she saw Paul Yu Bin's elevation to the Sacred College as the crowning of a career at the service of intellectual promotion among Chinese Catholics. Like many Chinese intellectuals, she considered it absolutely essential to have a Catholic presence among the leaders of the country's thought. She wrote:

> As we all know the intellectual class constitutes the soul of a people. No ideology or religion, however many members it may have, can claim serious consideration if it is not rooted in the intellectual class and remains confined to an inferior social level. Its influence would then remain superficial and uncertain.[6]

---

[5] Raymond de Jaegher, *Life of Archbishop Paul Yu Bin* (Cholon, Vietnam: Free Pacific Editions, 1959), p. 20.

[6] *Vox cleri* (*Duo sheng*, no. 79, (April 1969):7.

Cardinal Paul Yu Bin (1901–1978)
with Ma Xiangbo (1840–1939)

Born in Lanxi, near the St. Joseph Mission in Haibeizhen, Heilongjiang
Province, Yu Bin studied at Jilin Seminary, then at the College of Propaganda in Rome, where he taught after his priestly ordination in 1928.
He returned to China in 1933 and became secretary of the representative
of the Holy See in China; he was also put in charge of Catholic Action,
and worked especially with Catholic teachers in his capacity as inspector
for all Catholic schools, seeking to involve them in catechetics and group
formation. He was consecrated Vicar Apostolic of Nanjing in 1936 and
Archbishop of Nanjing in 1946. Yu Bin gave strong support to the Nationalist government of Chiang Kai-shek and left China after 1949, becoming
Rector of the Catholic University of Fujen that had been relocated from
Beijing to Taipei. He was created Cardinal in 1969.

Ma Xiangbo joined the Society of Jesus and, in 1870, was ordained
priest. He taught science at the renowned Jesuit Zikawei College, but left
the Jesuits because he disapproved of French teaching methods and found
French cuisine unpalatable. After some years in the Chinese civil service,
he had a distinguished career as a Catholic academic, founding the Aurora

University in Shanghai in 1903 and the Fudan University in September 1905. The first Catholic school opened in Beijing after the Cultural Revolution bears his name.

Many of the Catholic bishops in Taiwan were scholars whose work was well known in the Chinese Catholic world. Such was Archbishop Lo Kuang (Luo Guang), who succeeded Cardinal Tian as archbishop of Taipei and then succeeded Cardinal Yu Bin as rector of Fujen University. He had been a priest in Hunan Province and studied for many years in Rome, writing extensively on philosophy and the history of the Church. He analyzed especially the contribution of each missionary society to the growth of the Church in China.[7] The complete works of Cardinal Lo Kuang were published in Taiwan in 1996 by the Students Bookshop; they came to forty-two volumes, of which thirty-eight were in Chinese and the last four in English.

Another bishop influential through his writing was Paul Ch'eng (Cheng Shiguang), originally from Shanxi Province, who had a degree in literature from Furen University in Beijing. He was bishop of Tainan from 1966 until his retirement in 1990 and published in 1974 a work of pastoral theology, *Tian ren zhi ji* (*The Meeting of Heaven and Man*). In it he said that Confucian thought implies being conscious of the command of heaven. For a Christian the command of heaven is the will of God. Salvation is a free gift from God which is made available in Jesus Christ. Chinese ethics demand that faith be sincere, and this is achieved by putting salvation into practice in a concrete way.

The priests in Taiwan who taught or wrote books had often studied at the universities of Rome, Hong Kong, or America. They carried out a work of critical evaluation on the traditional material transmitted to them by the theological sciences of the West and themselves translated or composed what suited the mentality and the needs of Chinese Catholics. The contribution made by historians was particularly significant in shifting the perspectives that had been those of Western missionary historians. Chinese historiography brought out of the shadows persons or events that had previously been little known or whose importance had been underestimated. Fr. Fang Hao, a priest

---

[7] Luo Guang, *Tianzhujiao zai Hua chuanjiao shi ji* (*History of the Catholic Missions in China*) (Hong Kong: Catholic Truth Society, Taiwan: Kuangchi Publishers, 1967), 368 pp.

who came originally from Hangzhou, the capital city of Zhejiang Province, contributed significantly to this process by establishing a comprehensive list of all those Christians, both Chinese and foreign, who had contributed in any way to the development of the Church in China.[8]

There was one missionary order, the Congregation of the Disciples of the Lord, *Congregatio Discipulorum Domini* (C.D.D.), which devoted itself especially to emphasizing the importance of China's cultural heritage. It had been founded in 1930 by Archbishop Costantini when he was apostolic delegate. Fr. Andrew Chih (Chi Fengtong), who died in Taiwan in 1990, belonged to that congregation; he wrote in French a doctoral dissertation, *L'Occident chrétien vu par les Chinois. 1870–1900*, which he defended at the Pontifical Gregorian University in Rome in 1960. He too came from St. Joseph's Mission, Haibeizhen, in north Manchuria, and learned Latin and French at school; after his secondary education he joined the Congregation of the Disciples of the Lord at Xuanhua. He began his studies for the priesthood at Beijing in 1945 and finished them in Manila in 1950. He was ordained priest at the same time as Fr. John Liu (Liu Hongkai), and they began their apostolic work among the Chinese in the Philippines, where they built a church, Our Lady of the Apostles, in the south, at Cotabato. Andrew Chih then went on for further studies in Rome from 1953 to 1958 and taught at tertiary level in the United States from 1960 to 1986. He wrote a book in English under the title *Chinese Humanism*[9] which aimed at introducing the American reading public to a knowledge of Chinese culture. He was also concerned to prove the historicity of Christ and produced a large book on the origins of Christianity. After his retirement in Taiwan, he wrote various articles on the apocryphal Gospels.

Fr. John Liu, C.D.D., also stayed in America for a time, studying sociology, but was back in Taiwan by 1963 and spent twenty-five years on a fruitful ministry to young intellectuals. He had grown up in Tianjin, in a milieu that had been strongly influenced by Fr. Lebbe, and he tried to promote Catholic thought in a way that showed that

---

[8] Fang Hao, *Zhongguo Tianzhujiao shi renwu zhuan* (Biographies of Personalities in Chinese Catholic History), 3 vols. (Hong Kong: Catholic Truth Society, 1973).

[9] Andrew Chih, C.D.D., *Chinese Humanism: A Religion beyond Religion* (Taipei: Fujen Cath. Univ. Press, 1981), 548 pp.

it could absorb Chinese culture. He offered courses of lectures at several centers of higher studies: Taipei University, Fujen University, the Chinese Cultural University; also at some Church institutions such as the Huaming Pastoral Centre, founded by the Scheut Fathers, and the *Fons Vitae* Catechetical Institute. Fr. Liu was also concerned with social problems; in 1970 he involved female university students in organizing summer camps for primary and secondary school children. This was a very Chinese way of doing things, since it involved older children in the training of younger ones. Many Chinese priests readily adopt a teaching role; they introduce their pupils to the faith and offer them spiritual direction in a master-to-disciple relationship. In Chinese tradition *laoshi*, the teacher, is also *shifu*, the master of life; one can point to a resemblance to the Semitic tradition of the rabbi as seen in the Gospels.

From 1973 to 1986, Fr. John Liu edited the review *Jianzheng*, (*Witness*). Then he became editor of a review called *Hengyi* (*Costantinian*), incorporating the Chinese name for Archbishop Costantini: Kang Hengyi. He continued as editor until his death in 1989 and produced for these publications a steady output of articles promoting Catholic education and analyzing Church news. A large two-volume work, *Jiaohui yu Zhongguo* (*Church and China*), was published by Fujen University a year after his death; this was a summary of his life's thought and experience.

The Congregation of the Disciples of the Lord, whose creation had been inspired by Archbishop Costantini and Fr. Lebbe, continues to be a community of Chinese priests that spearheads the Chinese cultural apostolate. Fr. Matthias Chao (Zhao Binshi), C.D.D., editor of *Hengyi* (*Costantinian*), has written two books that represent this tendency: *Tian ren yi jia* (*Heaven and Man: One Family*, 1977) and *Lingxiuxue zai Zhongguo* (*Spirituality in China*, 1979).[10]

The Work of the Religious Orders for Education

In Taiwan about 200 Jesuits and some fifty Franciscans played a key role in Christian education. The Franciscans ran a *Studium Sociale*,

---

[10] Two major works by Zhao Binshi: *Zhongguohua shenxue, Tian ren yijia* (*Essay in Chinese Theology: Heaven and Man, One Family*) (Taipei: Hengyi, 1977), 257 pp. *Lingxiu zai Zhongguo* (*Spirituality in China*) (Taipei: Hengyi Monthly, 1979).

which had been begun in Singapore and later transferred to Taiwan. They translated and published in Chinese the main texts on the social teaching of the Church. They also worked on promoting the reading of the Bible, in conjunction with the *Studium Biblicum* in Hong Kong.

The Jesuits were active in both universities and parishes. In Fujen University they provided lecturers in the theology and the law faculties. The faculty of science was entrusted to the Divine Word fathers and the arts faculty to Chinese diocesan priests. The Jesuits were particularly successful in the sphere of the mass media, thanks to the various operations of their Kuangchi Society. Kuangchi Publications covered a range of subjects concerning Christian life and thought, so that the faithful were provided with useful tools for learning more about the faith. Kuangchi Radio and Television scored impressively high ratings. Some of their radio programs were fed regularly into Radio *Veritas* Manila. Kuangchi TV programs, which were broadcast on the Taiwan channels, were not necessarily religious but often consisted of serials or plays with a Christian point of view, which tried to get across a positive message in support of family and social life.

The Jesuits also had a large parish near National Taiwan University, the Holy Family, which brought together many intellectuals, artists, and actors, as well as Christian families, eager to absorb Christian values. Some of the fathers were particularly influential among lay people looking for truth, such as Fr. Luke Yuan (Yuan Guowei), who ran the Kuangchi Society until his death in 1990, and Fr. Joseph Lee (Li Zhexiu), who chaired an association of "communicators" in the media. In the same part of Taipei there was a Christian cultural center, *Tian Educational Center*, which was attended by crowds of students, who found there a spirituality open to contemporary civilization and culture. Many foreigners, members of religious orders, were associated with this work, bringing to it their expertise as spiritual directors, well versed in Chinese lore and language.

Outstanding among these Catholic Sinologists were a number of Jesuit fathers. Fr. Yves Raguin researched Buddhist and Taoist writings, finding in them a way of enriching Christian spirituality. Fr. Jean Lefeuvre is the equal of the Chinese scholars who studied the earliest examples of Chinese writing, incised on bone or tortoise plastrons, and going back to the eighteenth century B.C. The Ricci Institute had been created fifty years previously to work on a massive Chinese-French dictionary, and Fr. Raguin, aided by Fr. Jean Camus, also worked on this task for thirty years. The first edition appeared in 2000, one year after Fr. Raguin's death. It bears the title *Dictionnaire Ricci des caractères singuliers chinois* and comprises 3,600 pages in two folio volumes. Some 13,500 Chinese characters are presented historically; the various ways in which each character has been depicted, from the most ancient forms to the present ones, are described and analyzed pictorially, so that the dictionary is an inventory of Chinese ideograms, explained and translated into French. This colossal task was but the prelude to an even more ambitious project, to be called *Le Grand Ricci*, a Chinese-French dictionary of the Chinese words or expressions. It comprises 300,000 entries of signs or ideographic combinations in six volumes of 1,216 pages each, plus a volume of appendices. The words that they represent are studied morphologically and semantically, and once again this is done historically, so that changes in the form and meaning of words are explained over four thousand years of Chinese history. This colossal work was published in February 2002. It is a veritable encyclopedia of the Chinese language in French, covering 200 branches of human knowledge, such as science, technology, finance, law, philosophy, literature, art, etc.

Although there was one priest for every 300 Catholics in Taiwan, there was a shortage of priests for parish ministry. This shortage was partly made up by the devoted work of sisters from the many religious congregations. The sisters, unlike the priests, had been joined by many local recruits, both Taiwanese and aborigines. In 1974 there were 720 nuns with Chinese citizenship, of whom about 460 were from the mainland, 200 were Minnan and Hakka, and 60 were aborigines; 369 were foreigners. During the same period, the figures for the priests were 364 with Chinese citizenship, of whom 353 were from the mainland, ten Minnan and Hakka, and one from an indigenous tribe.

Foreign missionaries numbered 412. By 1990 the number of local priests had increased; there were about sixty Minnan, Hakka, and aborigine priests. The sisters, who were closer to the local population, contributed very valuable work in the fields of education, medical care, and relief work.

The flourishing of many educational projects within the Catholic Church was a result of the directives given by the Second Vatican Council. These were integration into local culture through the use of local languages in the celebration of the liturgy and the sacraments, ecumenism, dialogue with non-Christian religions, and the service of mankind in the modern world. The Constitution on the Liturgy was adopted by the council on December 4, 1963, and found an immediate response in "Free China". On January 1, 1965, the bishops of Taiwan, Hong Kong, and Macao authorized the use of Chinese for the celebration of Mass and the sacraments. The first Chinese-Latin ritual was published and, over the ensuing years, a complete missal in Chinese for both Sunday and weekday Masses was composed. The traditional Chinese rites in honor of heaven and the ancestors, which had been banned for Catholics until 1939, were celebrated officially within the setting of the liturgy for the lunar New Year. In Taipei, the archbishop, surrounded by dignitaries in long black robes, presided over the offering of fruit and incense before the great red tablet of wood, on which the following inscription had been inscribed in gold characters. "Honor to Heaven; Honor to the Ancestors". In some Catholic churches, a small altar of the ancestors was permanently placed in a side chapel.

The Chinese Bishops' Conference, later renamed Regional (Taiwan) Bishops' Conference, presided over this evolution and created specialized commissions for different areas of Church life. In 1974 the General Assembly of the Federation of Episcopal Conferences for the Bishops of Asia took place in Taipei. The Taiwanese bishops launched a program with the title "Building the Local Church", which adopted the three autonomies of government, finance, and apostolate, but this was not directed against Rome and foreign missionaries, as it had been on the Chinese mainland; it was now a question of encouraging a local Church to take responsibility for its administrative functioning in a Chinese context. Foreign missionaries were welcomed to take part in this program, especially where "autofinance" was concerned. In fact, the Catholic Church in Taiwan was still to a large extent dependent on financial help from Rome, the United States, and Germany. The contributions were substantial and helped to put up a large number of buildings, which corresponded no doubt to the increasing number of the faithful but whose cost was far above what could be raised locally. In the 1980s demands for such expensive building programs continued, although by then the flow of conversions had dried up, the local population had become much more wealthy, and Mass attendances were declining.

In fact, the effectiveness of the bishops in Taiwan was limited. For practical reasons, they asked the missionary congregations to fund their own undertakings and to be responsible for their personnel. The bishops thus only had to find resources for the upkeep of diocesan priests. Emphasis was laid on trying to persuade the faithful to be responsible for the costs of their church, but most of the recent converts had been used to receiving help from the Church, not to sharing its expenses. It was not until the 1980s that the faithful began to assume a larger share in financial responsibility. Many Chinese priests, with shrinking parishes to look after, found it hard to see to their own upkeep, harder than their colleagues in religious orders who had nevertheless taken a vow of poverty. This was one of the reasons why diocesan priests tended to look for teaching posts, at the risk of neglecting pastoral responsibilities.

At the very time when the Second Vatican Council's call for renewal was opening up new possibilities of evangelization and growth, the life of the Catholic Church in Taiwan was losing its impetus. Parents who were converts and who had not inherited a Christian tradition did not necessarily see to the Catholic education of their children; they were much more interested in evidence of academic success. Taiwan's economic growth led to a general improvement of the standard of living, and in the 1980s it became a consumer society. Christians, who had often a rather sketchy religious instruction, found all the attractions of the material improvements of life very appealing and could not always make their choices in response to spiritual values. There also occurred a rapid industrialization in Taipei, Kaohsiung, and other large towns, which attracted young people in large numbers, with the result that Catholic communities, which had only recently been formed in the villages, especially in aborigine areas, suddenly found themselves bereft of their most active members. There were problems in the cities too, where religious practice often flagged. In some cases, parishes composed of mainland Chinese were not ready to welcome "mountain people", i.e., aborigines, who had little Chinese language or culture.

Many pastoral problems were caused by these rapid changes in Taiwanese society and in the life of the Catholic Church, so that annual pastoral sessions were organized to examine these. In September 1974, the fifth such session was organized at Kaohsiung to study "Industrialization and the Proclamation of the Gospel". This studied the impact of the transformation of Taiwanese society on moral values and religious beliefs. A religious sister declared:

> The industrialization of society has brought up many thorny questions, such as the transformation of village life, urbanization, education in the family and in the school, divorce, contraception, abortion, changes in moral values, etc. The Chinese Church needs to pay more attention to these things, to study practical methods and to seek out solutions. In other words, the Church cannot go on keeping its eyes shut. Otherwise the more we carry on as we are, the more we shall diverge from modern society, which will make the proclamation of the gospel even more difficult.[11]

She ended by an appeal to theologians and philosophers to set out the basic principles that can guide the lives of the believers of today.

Can one say that the theological sessions organized every year since 1971 answered the questions put by the religious sister and many others? The subjects chosen for these meetings did indeed concern essential aspects of the Church: penance, the Eucharist, the historicity of the Gospels, salvation, the local Church, evangelization, Jesus Christ.

The pastoral implications were discussed in groups, so that one cannot say that theology was without links with pastoral concerns; and yet the lecturers, distinguished academics, hardly mentioned the situations that people were experiencing in Taiwan itself. The fourth theological session, held in Fujen University from January 28 to 31, 1975, examined "salvation in the context of Taiwan". This lacked any reference to the fifth Kaohsiung pastoral session, whose results had been published by the review *Vox Cleri* in November 1974. The thought of the theologians assembled at Fujen University had three sources, all of them remote from Taiwan; either classical Catholic

---

[11] Catharina Chang, "Moral and Social Problems of Industrial Society", *Duo sheng* (Vox Cleri) 79 (Apr. 1969):7.

theology, renewed, it is true, by the Council, but still distant from real human situations; or an intellectual tradition that was more concrete but which derived from foreign authors, like French Existentialists; or else Confucian thought, which was certainly more Chinese but still very far from the realities of life for the people of Taiwan.

In 1976 the program launched by the Catholic bishops of Taiwan, "Build the Local Church", was in full swing; it was then that Fr. Paul Lee (Li Shanxiu) published at the Kuangchi Press a book called *Tianzhujiao zhongguohua de tantao* (*The Sinaization of Catholicism*). In it he tried to integrate the Confucian norms, which had been put forward by the New Life Movement since 1934, into a Christian perspective. The last chapter considered "Chinese culture today", and this did contain some comments that pointed out the limitations of Confucian tradition in modern society. However, the whole approach of the book consisted in combining the Christian message with a very idealized form of Confucian culture. It failed adequately to consider the conditions of modern life. The whole approach was an ethical one. The local Church was considered in relation to a "great China", with its age-old values contemplated from a somewhat timeless point of view. Where in this idealized vision of the Church were the actual Christians of Taiwan, the aborigines, the Minnan, and the Hakka? The approach was rather like a revival of the cultural perspectives of the old Han Empire, with its sense of superiority over ethnic minorities and the immoral West. It could be branded as "culturalism", and it ran the danger of exaggerating still more the abstract character of classical Catholic theology and detaching it from its true vocation at the service of a real community of believers.

Presbyterian theologians in Taiwan did not, however, make the mistake of promoting an official theology, permeated by Confucian ideology. They were closer to the life of the Taiwanese people and shared their lifestyle. Their standpoint was not official Confucian culture but popular culture. In 1978 the Presbyterian theologian Song Choan Seng (Song Quansheng), formerly director of the Tainan School of Theology, published *Rentong* (*Belonging*). His inspiration came from the biblical notion of the People of God, a people whose history has been one of progressive liberation from every form of slavery. He claimed that theology must be a prophetic witness; theology is part of a very worldly struggle, an echo of God's anger and of his love. A neutral theology would not belong to a real people. He claimed that theology begins when it identifies its dwelling and its color. It must reject all compromise and declare the truth. The cries of a people for truth and justice are the cries of God. Each country has its own history, which is part of the redemptive work of God. China too has such a history; Christian belonging is thus the same as Chinese belonging.

This close identification of the work of redemption with culture and politics had an explosive potential. During the course of Chinese history, popular religions, Taoism in particular, had produced subversive movements against an oppressive and corrupt central administration. If Christianity were to take up such movements, was there not a risk that it would adopt their fanatical sectarianism? If belief in the People of God were equated with an earthly messianism, would it not be in danger of adopting unjustified political violence or partisan movements? There had been zealots among the Jewish people too, but Jesus kept his distance from them.

There can be conflict between popular culture and official culture if they both eliminate the transcendent dimension brought by Christian salvation, but it is also possible for both of these cultural expressions to remain open to the saving grace that is the love of God as revealed in Jesus Christ; in which case there need not be a conflict between cultures but a productive dialogue between popular culture and the culture of the sages.

Taiwan from the 1950s to the 1980s became a crucible for the fusion of Christian thought and Chinese thought. The various Christian groups produced a large library of books, videos, and tapes. They diffused a great number of educational programs, ranging from theology lectures to children's stories, via Bible classes, the history of Christianity, and family and sexual ethics. Collections of color slides were gradually replaced by videos, since most families owned a video recorder. This range of audiovisual material and the considerable Christian literature produced in Taiwan did not only benefit the local population. The Chinese of the diaspora benefited greatly, and during the whole of the 1980s it was they who introduced such material into mainland China. The watertight division between Taiwan and the continent was gradually disappearing, and, as it did so, Taiwanese Christians were becoming aware of their calling to become a "bridge Church".

From 1987 onward, Chinese from Taiwan were able to travel more easily to the continent. Thus priests and sisters were able to contact their home dioceses again and to bring them substantial help, both financial and religious. Some of the professors from Fujen University went to give courses of lectures in the major seminaries of the mainland. A Catholic group from China was even welcomed to Taiwan for a stay of fifteen days, though this did not happen without some difficulty. Since the state's control of all religious activities on the continent remained very strict, Taiwanese Catholics learned to bear witness to the existence of a Chinese patriotism distinct from Communist ideology. Thus, they set up an ad hoc commission to collect the necessary documents for the canonization of the 120 beatified martyrs of China. Archbishop Paul Shan Kuohsi, S.J. (Shan Guoxi), of Kaohsiung, who had been made a cardinal in 1998, played a particularly active role in Rome over this project. It was his personal intervention with the Pope that overcame certain diplomatic difficulties, so that the canonizations were able to take place on October 1, during the Year of Jubilee 2000. (See Appendix D.)

RESURRECTION IN MAINLAND CHINA

On Whitsunday 1978 the Sunday Mass in *Nantang* Church, Beijing, was still open to foreigners only, as it had been since 1971. There were about thirty of them, from Africa, the Philippines, and a few from Europe. After Mass was over, three Chinese priests were talking in the nave to two priests from abroad, an Italian and a Frenchman. People were allowed to talk again, and there was a great deal to talk about. One of the Chinese priests said that he was teaching Latin to some young people, so there was a seminary in embryo somewhere. Another revealed that he was a Vincentian, so the past was not entirely forgotten.

A few months later, on August 15, the Feast of the Assumption of Mary, Chinese Catholics flooded into that church. They had at last been authorized to practice their religion openly and to receive the sacraments. After more than twelve years of total silence, they took up again the singsong prayers in Chinese that they had been used to reciting during Mass. The priest wore an old-style Roman chasuble, which had been hidden somewhere all that time, and he said the Tridentine Mass in Latin. Lots of candles were burning, and faces were marked by intense joy, eyes filled with tears. It was as if God's children, who had been dead, had come to life again.

Open but under Control

What exactly had happened? Did this mean that the Communist Party had changed its views on religion? Since the death of Mao Zedong on September 9, 1976, many things had changed in China. Revolutionary activists rallied round Jiang Qing, Mao's widow, and tried to seize power. They were stopped in time by the leaders of the Party, who had decided to put in place a realistic policy for economic development. After so many interior upheavals, China had fallen behind badly in the international sphere. It was high time to redress the situation within the country so as to follow up the exterior diplomatic successes that had begun with China's entry into the United Nations in 1971. For many years Zhou Enlai and Deng Xiaoping had been trying to launch a big campaign for modernization. The death of Chairman Mao and the elimination of the "Gang of Four" opened the way to putting into place a practical program for "Four Modernizations": agriculture, industry, armed forces, and science and technology. In December 1978 the Third Plenum of the XIth Congress of the Party resolutely adopted the new policy of reform and openness. A realistic slogan was produced for the occasion: "Seek the truth in the facts."

The modernization of China could only be envisaged with the cooperation of intellectuals and their friends from abroad. It was also necessary to banish the fear and suspicion that had been produced by the constant vexations to which people had been submitted. The "class war" had to be put on hold, in favor of a "united front" policy. It seemed as if a fresh breeze of freedom were blowing through the land. Intellectuals were not slow in taking the lead and advocated a "Fifth Modernization". Had not Deng Xiaoping himself spoken of an "emancipation of minds"? From the end of 1978 to March 1979 *dazibao*, big-character posters, covered the walls of the Xidan quarter in Beijing, each more daring than the last. It looked as if a movement for democracy were gathering strength.

Was this not going too fast in a society that had had no preparation for exercising democracy in a responsible way? Deng Xiaoping thought so. He was determined that order and discipline should accompany economic reform. Stability had to come first. Limits were drawn beyond which it was not allowed to go, and freedom of expression was soon suppressed. The Four Basic Principles, written into the Constitution of March 5, 1978, were strongly reaffirmed: a Socialist system, rule by the Party, dictatorship of the proletariat, the Marxist-Leninist thought of Mao Zedong. The brake had to be put on repeatedly during the following years: in 1983 there was a campaign against delinquency; at the end of 1986 it was against bourgeois liberalization; in 1988 "spiritual pollution" (i.e., foreign influence) was eradicated; and finally in Tiananmen Square on June 4, 1989, the student movement was brutally crushed. The young had asked for more justice and more freedom in the face of the enormous bureaucratic system, which was both oppressive and corrupt. They were reduced to silence in the interest of stability. It must be said that the vast majority of Chinese have only had experience of passive submission to the bureaucratic machine, so that a relaxation of controls tends to breed anarchy and even more corruption. There is no effective legal system in mainland China to provide the framework for civil society, and there are no intermediate bodies with a tradition of responsible action. Previously, a certain cohesion was maintained in China by the moral imperatives of Confucianism, but these had lost their effectiveness through constant undermining by revolutionary criticism and had been swept away by the Cultural Revolution. In 1982 the Communist government had tried to give new life to moral rules by launching the slogan *wu jiang si mei*, "Five Concerns Four Beautiful Things". The concerns were courtesy, good manners, hygiene, order, and morality; beauty resided in mind, language, behavior, and environment.[1]

A Directed Religious Freedom

The various religions of China benefited from the general policy of openness and from the government's attempts at unifying all the energies of the country in a program of modernization. They also suffered from the way the government put the brakes on periodically. In fact, the degree of religious freedom that was permitted at any one time was a useful indication of the democratic climate in the country.

The Political Consultative Conference of the Chinese People, which had not met since 1959, was summoned again in February 1978. Some two thousand representatives of all community organizations gathered, among whom were sixteen delegates from the main religions, including two Catholic bishops, Pi Shushi of Shenyang, president of the Patriotic Association; and Zhang Jiashu, S.J., patriotic bishop of Shanghai. Nearly all the priests, members of religious orders, and committed lay people, who had been in prison or condemned to hard labor during the previous twenty years, were released and rehabilitated. When they returned to their villages, they found the church demolished or turned into a factory or a goods depot. Soon they were taking up the practice of visiting local Christians and saying Mass in

---

[1] See J. Charbonnier, *La Chine sans muraille: héritage culturel et modernité* (Paris: Fayard Le Sarment, 1988), parts 3 and 4, for an analysis of the moral crisis and the return to Confucian ethics.

their homes, but the joy of meeting again was often short lived. Because religion had to be subordinated to the Socialist ordering of society, it was made clear to them that their duty was to ensure that believers were docile to the directives of the Party.

As for the Catholic Church, patriotic bishops were reinstated in 1978; the appointment of bishops without any reference to Rome also began again. In December 1979 Fu Tieshan was consecrated bishop of Beijing. A comment from Rome on the illicit character of such an ordination provoked a storm of abuse. Criticisms of the Pope became sharper and quite vicious in 1981, when he announced the promotion of Dominic Tang as archbishop of the diocese of Guangzhou. The principle of the complete independence of the Catholic Church in China was upheld by the government's separatist line, which plunged many priests into an acute crisis of conscience.[2] They were hoping to use the new freedom of worship to serve the faithful who had been for so long deprived of the sacraments, but they could not bring themselves to compromise on a matter of faith for which they had suffered for so many years. Some of them adopted a minimum of exterior submission, while remaining faithful at heart. Others considered any compromise as a snare and went to join the underground Church.

The Patriotic Association had such a bad reputation that it was unable to stem such losses on its own. It met in 1980, its third session since those of 1957 and 1962, and convened a meeting of the Assembly of Representatives of the Catholics of China for May 31. Two hundred and seven bishops, priests, sisters, and lay persons came together, many of whom were already involved in the Patriotic Association. They decided to create an Administrative Commission for Religious Affairs.[3] Once the constitution of the new association had been adopted, Bishop Zhang Jiashu became its president on June 2.

---

[2] Cf. Angelo Lazzarrotto, *The Catholic Church in Post-Mao China* (Hong Kong: Holy Spirit Study Center, 1982), p. 133. It is possible that it was this incident that provoked the "official" Church into abandoning the title of archbishop, since it was considered as an unwarranted interference in Chinese internal affairs to group the dioceses of China into twenty ecclesiastical regions, each presided over by an archbishop. In fact the official Church has continued to regroup dioceses and redraw their boundaries, whereas the Holy See continues to operate on the list of dioceses as published in the *Annuario Pontificio*.

[3] These new structures were described in the text published by the French Bishops' Conference: "L'Église de Chine, convalescente en quarantaine—le point des cinq dernières années (1978–1983)", *Documents de l'Épiscopat*, no. 5 (Mar. 1984).

He also became president of the "Episcopal Conference of China", composed of thirty-three bishops. This Bishops' Conference was responsible in theory for doctrinal questions and international relations, but it had no real power. The official life of the Church was governed in fact by two *hui* (associations), the Chinese Catholic Patriotic Association (CCPA) and the Administrative Commission for Religious Affairs (ACRA), which were really two sides of the same organism, one being more political and the other more pastoral.

In 1989 an attempt was made to give to this organization a more ecclesiastical appearance. The Assembly of Catholic Representatives was put first; then the Episcopal Conference, as head of the Church; then came CCPA, the Chinese Catholic Patriotic Association; and finally ACRA, the Administrative Commission for Religious Affairs. This was a purely cosmetic operation. The bishops, placed at the front, were mere figureheads, while CCPA, at the end, continued to give effective directions. Nothing has indicated up to now that the bishops have any effective power as Church leaders. CCPA keeps them subjected to the directives of the state's Bureau of Religious Affairs on the one hand and to the general line adopted by the United Front of the Chinese Communist Party on the other. In return for which honor, the bishops represent the "independent" Catholic Church of China, with its three autonomies: administration, finance, and apostolate.

Protestants in China have been organized in the same way into two complementary associations. The Patriotic Movement of the Three Autonomies conveys to the churches the party line, while the China Christian Council has a more direct concern for religious matters. Ding Guangxun, Anglican bishop of Nanjing, presided over both bodies.

The religious policy of the Communist Party in China has been clearly set out in Document 19 of the Central Committee, dated March 31, 1982. It begins with a statement of fact that turns out to be a nonverified Marxist dogma: "With the advent of Socialism, the exploitation that produced religious belief has basically been removed; however, during the period of Socialist construction, which can be a very long one, the people still have to endure many sufferings and therefore still seek refuge in outdated ideas and customs." Document 19 then proceeds to self-criticism for the mistakes committed: in the 1950s many religious activists were won over to the patriotic cause, but this satisfactory result was ruined by the excesses of the Cultural Revolution. The Central Committee of the Communist Party therefore proposed a plan of action; since the United Front policy required the united support of all the active elements in the country, ideological differences must be relegated to a secondary position. The support of active believers must be won back, and they must be given a scientific and Socialist education. Religious practice must be officially recognized by the reopening of places of worship in cities and towns. The education of young believers must be the object of special attention. The last point was clarified as follows:

> Seminaries are responsible for creating a group of young professionals in religion who will be fervent patriots in politics, supporting the direction of the Party and the Socialist system, and who will be adequately competent in religious matters.

There were certain practical concomitants to this declaration of religious policy on the part of the Communist Party. Paragraph 11 of the same document stated that members of the Communist Party, who are atheists by definition, are not entitled to be believers. The international contacts of the major religions may be considered as an asset in the program of modernization; but it is also necessary to prevent the return of the hostile forces of reaction, especially the imperialist religious forces represented by the Roman curia and Protestant missions.

Party managers received precise instructions about the application of these directives in an article published in the July 1982 issue of *Red Flag*. These directives from the Party provided the operational background to article 36 of the Constitution, which had been revised by the Popular National Assembly and adopted in December 1982. This was the article guaranteeing religious freedom:

> The citizens of the People's Republic of China enjoy freedom of religious belief. Neither the institutions of the state, nor public organizations, nor individuals may compel citizens either to believe or not to believe. The state protects normal religious activities. No one may use religion to promote activities causing a breach of public order or harming the health of citizens or opposing the state system of education. Religious associations and religious matters may not be subjected to foreign control.

The last stipulation in the text is aimed at the Catholic Church; it must remain independent of the Pope. The phrase "normal religious activities" refers to a distinction, which is often made in the Chinese press, between religion and superstition. The great religions are the ones that have scriptures, a moral code, and an official structure, approved by the state, whereas superstitions appeal to occult forces, such as divination, magic, and the recourse to healers. Superstitions are considered as particularly virulent in the case of subversive sects, which constitute a danger for public order. As for the phrase about the freedom "to believe or not to believe", it is obvious that the Communist Party jealously defends the second to the detriment of the first. For instance, it stipulates that young people may not be baptized before they reach the age of eighteen.[4]

Churches Everywhere

The Communist Party must have been surprised at the response to the change in the official attitude to religion. It half opened a window and admitted a whirlwind. Catholics, who for so long had been deprived of the sacraments, flocked in large numbers to the reopened churches. When the major festivals came round, many were prepared to travel for a week to get to Mass. Thus some of them from the area bordering on Tibet climbed a pass over 12,000 feet (4,000 meters) high to celebrate Christmas and Easter at Chengdu. At Taiyuan, Shanxi Province, more than 2,000 faithful packed the cathedral for the paschal vigil and spent hours kneeling on the floor; there was a choir and a complete orchestra to ring out the alleluias again. Above the high altar a large painting of the Virgin Mary, surrounded by electric lights, illuminated the huge nave. At Tianjin a congregation of more than 500 sang the requiem Mass in Latin every morning; perhaps it was the only one that they knew well; they certainly had many dead people to pray for. At Harbin on Palm Sunday Catholics, holding little branches of fir trees in their hand, filled the vast cruciform sanctuary that they had inherited from the Orthodox; the latter, who had been established at Harbin at the time of trade with

---

[4] For a fuller account of the whole situation see J. Charbonnier, "L'Église et l'État en Chine aujourd'hui", *Dossier Échange France-Asie*, no. 9 (1985).

Russia, were soon to have another church of their own. At Shanghai the large Catholic Church, Zikawei, had had its steeples removed; the parishioners obtained help from the city council to have them replaced above the twin towers. At Zhaoqing, Guangdong Province, twenty blind people traveled more than sixty miles (100 kilometers) on the West River by boat to attend Sunday Mass. As for Beijing, Catholics restored the large white crosses on the three towers of St. Joseph's Church (*Dongtang*). The Holy Redeemer Church (*Beitang*) had been turned into a school. This famous former French mission had for long been identified as the very symbol of imperialism, but now a surprising development occurred. The church was returned to the Catholics in May 1985, and, through unremitting hard work, it was restored and ready for the Christmas midnight Mass that same year.

In many other towns, Catholic and Protestant churches were re-opened. Sometimes there were many difficulties in obtaining the restitution of the buildings, as the work units that occupied them had to be moved out and relocated. Such questions were discussed at the meetings of the local section of the Political Consultative Conference of the Chinese People. Representatives of the various religions came to these monthly meetings: the Catholic priest, the Protestant pastor, the Muslim imam, the Buddhist bonze, and sometimes a Taoist monk. This was an unexpected exercise in ecumenism, resulting from the government's United Front program, whereby the great religions of China came together in pursuit of a common goal: recovering the use of their sanctuaries so as to provide "normal religious activities" according to the stipulations of the Constitution.

Believers were, however, not satisfied by having churches open only in towns, because Christian villages wanted to have their churches too. If a patriotic association was needed in order to obtain official permission, then one was created without hesitation. Sometimes the initiative came from the parish priest, who thus had a way of keeping an eye on his parishioners. In cases where no one wanted a patriotic association, a "house" where Christians could hold their prayer meetings was built instead of a church. The authorities finally accepted that a place of worship could be opened if there were at least one hundred worshippers and if they could obtain the services of a priest. The frequency of the priest's visits was not laid down. In the Pinghai district, a peninsula in Fujian Province, the villages rebuilt twenty churches, although the priest could come only once a year. Throughout the whole country thousands of places of worship were thus opened by both Catholics and Protestants. Worshippers undertook the task, providing the work force and somehow finding the necessary building materials. Since the villagers were often very poor, financing these projects was obviously a problem. Usually part of the cost would be provided by the Office for Religious Affairs; this constituted a very modest restitution, considering the number of Church properties that had been confiscated by the state in the past. In some cases, the Catholic community, once it had recovered its houses and land, ceded a part to the local authority in return for the funds needed to build the church. This happened, for instance, at Yinchuan in the Autonomous Region of Ningxia. In addition, appeals for help from abroad were not only tolerated but encouraged by the state, which was short of foreign currency. In fact, new buildings went up at such a rate that they tended to monopolize the attention of bishops and priests, at the cost of the training of church personnel. Many wanted to put up large and fine buildings as a form of prestige, and in fact some converts were attracted in this way. During 2000, more than 5,000 Catholic churches were opened throughout the country.

Churches in China are often hidden behind large modern high-rise constructions, even when the architecture of the church would have been an adornment to the locality, as is the case in Xichang in west Sichuan. Sometimes miserable tenements had been built, right up against the façades of cathedrals; this is what happened at Guiyang, Guizhou Province, where the faithful could not use the main portals, but had to go round by a side door, which was watched by the patriotic association's guardian; the compulsory detour is an apt symbol of the situation of the Church in China, which can be described as limited freedom under supervision. Only in 2000 were the façades of the churches in the main towns cleared at last of various accretions, as happened in Xi'an, where the sweet factory that hid the Cathedral of St. Francis of Assisi was pulled down.

Every church officially registered as operative is in fact controlled by one member of its patriotic association who has the confidence of the Party and reports back to it. It can be one of the priests, or a religious sister, or a lay person, who is more or less practicing. This is hardly surprising, as it is the system by which the whole of China is controlled. What do the other members of the association think about this? In some cases the Party member may be said to be *jing er yuan zhi*, "revered but kept at a distance", according to the expressions that Confucius used to express his attitude to deities (*guishen*). Elsewhere positive cooperation may exist between the community and the members of the association; they may well be good Christians who are doing their best for the welfare of their church, in which case the parish patriotic association becomes like a parish council that manages the finances, sees to the upkeep of the buildings, and guarantees a salary for the priest and pensions for the old retired sisters. Lay people in that case are much more involved than in many neighboring countries.

Following the principle of self-financing, dioceses and parishes try to ensure that they have some sources of income. In many places, rents come in from church properties occupied by work units or by families. Some parishes have built hostels to house lodgers or travelers. Patriotic associations sometimes run small businesses that produce some profit for the parish, while stimulating local development; however, this can be a temptation to make use of church personnel while neglecting spiritual activities.

When the Young Take Over

In 1978 some white-haired bishops and priests had already grouped young men together, taught them the rudiments of Latin, got them to read the Gospels, and tried to improve their knowledge of the catechism. The first major seminary was opened in October 1982 in Shanghai on the Hill of Sheshan, a place of pilgrimage to Mary Help of Christians. Another major seminary opened in March 1983 in Shenyang, Liaoning Province, for the northeastern provinces. In September of the same year a national seminary of philosophy and theology was created in Beijing. The rector, Bishop Tu Shihua of Hanyang, together with a committee of seminary lecturers, drew up the curriculum. Following the sacrosanct principle of independence, the lecturers composed textbooks of theology and Church history; in fact they drew on the classic Latin textbooks that were in use in China when they were students, that is, during the "semicolonial" period. The more recent books in Chinese, produced in Taiwan or Hong Kong since the Second Vatican Council, were kept in a special library to which the students did not have access. It must be said that the level of education was not high to begin with. In order to improve the general culture of the seminarians, the first years were spent on nonreligious subjects: history, geography, literature, and English. Political studies were obligatory, especially the study of the constitution of the Chinese People's Republic. In some seminaries, at Hohhot for instance, the capital city of Inner Mongolia Autonomous Region, students also learned a trade, in case they ever needed to earn their living.

A certain number of religious books were published in China from 1981 onward: the *Book of Daily Prayers*; the *Question and Answer Catechism*, which had been approved after the Council of Shanghai of 1924, but with all the references to the Pope omitted; the *New Testament*; the *Imitation of Jesus Christ*; an introduction to Bible history; some hymn books; and the *Liber Usualis* of Gregorian plainchant.

Other regional major seminaries were created, at Chengdu for the provinces of the southwest, at Wuhan for the central and southern provinces, at Xi'an for the northwest. Some former seminarians, who had studied theology thirty years previously, came forward to start their studies again and were ordained fairly quickly, after only one or two years of preparation. They had remained faithful to their vocation and to celibacy. These new priests of mature years provided an intermediary generation between the very old and the very young priests. Between 1988 and 1991, more than two hundred priests were ordained throughout the country, and by the year 2000, there were more than 1,500 young priests. The gradual diminution in numbers of the older men meant that they now constituted hardly a quarter of the total number of priests. In the nineteen official major seminaries and the five junior seminaries, there were 1,000 seminarians in training.

It was not always easy to ensure within these seminaries an intellectual and spiritual formation of the required quality. Lecturers had to be found, and, until the last years of the twentieth century, only old priests had the necessary qualifications. Some of these refused to teach in seminaries run according to "patriotic" principles; others did accept for the good of the students. Most of the candidates came from solidly Catholic families and were put forward by holy priests who were taking a risk in sending them to such seminaries, knowing their political slant, but who also knew that there were no other means of theological formation. In some provinces like Hebei, the underground Church was more numerous and better organized; there some possibilities for clandestine training did exist, but in circumstances that made it very difficult for the students to lead a community life. They lodged with Catholic families, and their studies could be interrupted at any time by police raids. However, these students were able to use books printed in Taiwan and Hong Kong and were thus introduced to the post-Vatican II liturgy of the Catholic Church. Sometimes two or three years of study were all that they could manage. These young priests from the underground Church are full of zeal, but they are also very harsh in their attitude toward priests and faithful who go to the official churches. Everything that has to do with the patriotic association seems to them to reek of the devil.

Students in patriotic seminaries also faced considerable difficulties. Some of their fellow students had no real vocation and were only there as a way of doing further studies or because the Party had sent them to report on the political orientation of the place. In some cases the spirit of the community deteriorated to such an extent that discipline became impossible. At Chengdu the whole student body had to be sent back to their dioceses so as to make it possible to make a new start on a better basis. At Wuhan more than half the seminarians gave up in the course of the year "for health reasons". Seminarians had to put up with constant denunciations of the Pope and of the imperialism of the missionaries who had brought them the Gospel. Even if they could do that without flinching, they still had to face the difficulties caused by ordination at the hands of a patriotic bishop. They knew that it would be a valid ordination, but would it be accepted by the Catholics of their village? They would certainly need a lot of courage to face other trials awaiting them in their diocese. As young priests they were pulled two ways; on one side were the staunch Catholics, mistrustful of a man trained under the auspices of CCPA (the Chinese Catholic Patriotic Association); on the other were seasoned "patriotics", who would supervise the activities and movements of the young priest and try to steer his ministry in a particular direction. It sometimes happened that a newly ordained priest was confined to a provincial capital with nothing to do, when he would have liked to go and look after Catholics in distant villages. Those young priests who were given more freedom and could begin an active ministry were conscious of their limitations and of the gaps in their training, They lacked basic books on liturgy, catechetics, and preaching; often they did not have a breviary. The more gifted ones were sometimes obliged to stay in the major seminary to teach, because the older lecturers were few in number and failing in strength. This was the situation from 1982 to 1992.

Between 1992 and 2002, however, the conditions of priestly training have noticeably improved, thanks in particular to the pioneering role of the Shanghai Major Seminary, under the direction of Bishop Jin Luxian. When it was opened in September 1982, it was the first major seminary in China to make the documents of the Second Vatican Council known. In 1985 new buildings were put up at the foot of the Hill of Sheshan, which accommodate 150 students from the eastern provinces and others from fifteen different provinces. The new library contains 20,000 volumes, collected by Fr. Edward Malatesta, S.J., professor at Fujen University, Taipei. Most important of all was the fact that, from 1993 onward, Bishop Jin was able to make up for the lack of qualified personnel by inviting lecturers from Taiwan and Hong Kong to teach at Shanghai Major Seminary. He was also able to send a certain number of priests to study in Europe and in America, an example that has been followed by five regional seminaries. Some of those sent to study have not returned to China, but since 1998 there has been a regular influx of young lecturers into the more important seminaries of the country.

What does the future hold in store? The rigorous government policy for the limitation of births has reduced families to having only one child, who may or may not be male. If the child is a boy, he is thoroughly spoiled by parents and grandparents and becomes a "little emperor". Although the standard of living is still very low, many young people are fascinated by the material improvements that money can buy. How many young men will be willing in the future to offer up their lives to the higher service demanded by the priesthood?

From about 1982, it became possible to form convents of religious sisters again. The first ones consisted of aged sisters from Chinese diocesan congregations, who also took in sisters from various other orders. Soon they were joined by younger women who wanted to consecrate their lives to God. In Jilin Province, for instance, four young postulants joined a small community of ten aged nuns in 1984. Four years later, there were some forty young sisters, ten of whom had made their private vows. They were all packed into a stuffy dormitory and lived very poorly but cheerfully. Their old bishop, aged eighty, was the spiritual director of the community 1,200 miles (2,000 kilometers) from there. In Guangxi Province in the south of the country, an old priest of eighty, Fr. Meng Ziwen, recruited twenty postulants from the Catholic families of the surrounding villages. With the help of two or three old sisters, he set up a foundation course for religious sisters, spread over two years; this consisted of evening classes in catechesis, Bible study, liturgy, and spirituality, since the novices had to go out to work during the day to earn their bread. They also learned singing, sewing, and medical care. Afterward they went out in twos and threes into the Catholic villages, where they worked wonders through their catechism classes and prayer groups. Some of them have gone to other regions of the province, where they have created more communities for formation in the religious life.

In the cities too it has been possible to create communities of sisters with novitiates. In Wuhan, the capital of Hubei Province, the Franciscan Missionaries of Mary used to be firmly established. Since 1985 a new convent has been flourishing in Hankou (a part of Wuhan city), where some fifteen old sisters are supported by forty young ones. The initial classes of the novices are wide ranging: English, piano, and sewing. After four or five years of study and practical courses, the sisters can make private vows. Solemn vows were envisaged as taking place after some fifteen years. In 1988 a medical school was opened near the convent.

By 1990 there were about forty such novitiates in the whole country. Twelve religious congregations with communities in Taiwan and Hong Kong began to send sisters on visits to continental China. Retreats and study sessions took place discreetly, making it possible to improve the formation of the sisters in China; some of them were also sent to study abroad, in the United States, Europe, and the Philippines. By the year 2000, a relatively important number of young sisters, with ten to fifteen years of religious life behind them, were able to make their solemn vows. They were also becoming aware that they needed better organization so as to administer their communities more effectively. They are very dependent on the bishops and priests for whom they work; but these sometimes find it difficult to train their sisters adequately and to find for them ministries corresponding to their religious vocation.

Far from being weakened by thirty years of suffering and isolation, the Christians of China have come out of their ordeal with a faith that is vibrant and without fear. In the other countries of the world, the Second Vatican Council put in hand an attempt to remove outmoded aspects of the life of the Church and to renew its vitality, but the life of faith has not always become more vigorous as a result. In China the opposite has happened. The prayers and devotional practices of the people seem out of date, but the people themselves are real witnesses to the faith.

Among Protestants, too, Christian vitality is everywhere in evidence. "Domestic churches", that is, prayer meetings in private homes, have greatly increased.[5] Evangelicals especially have made a great leap forward, and nobody can say how many millions of Chinese have heard the message of Jesus Christ the Savior. According to official statistics, the number of Protestants had gone up from one million in 1949 to five million in 1990. Catholics were perhaps as numerous, but, since nearly half of them are clandestine, official statistics only accounted for three and a half million.

In fact, the process of evangelization has never stopped, even at the height of the Cultural Revolution. In prisons and forced labor camps, priests, sisters, members of the Legion of Mary, and other fervent Christians did not remain inactive. They converted many of their fellow sufferers to Christianity, and sometimes their guards as well. They wrote out by heart long expositions of the faith on exercise books of rough paper. A group of priests from Shanghai, who were in a camp for re-education through work, carved on wood a defense of Christianity, remarkable for its conciseness and power, answering the challenge of atheistic materialism point by point. To the Marxist axiom "Religion is opposed to science", they responded, "What about Pasteur, Teilhard de Chardin, and all the other scientists who are Christians?" When told, "Religion is an outdated superstition", they answered, "The history of the Bible shows that faith in the one true God has fought a long struggle against superstition." When taunted that "Christians are said to be individualistic", they pointed out that

---

[5] Cf. Raymund Fung, *Households of God on China's Soil* (Geneva: World Council of Churches, 1982).

the great commandment of Christ is to love God and one's neighbor.

Profiting from the new freedom of worship, groups of catechumens come together in each diocesan center. They are normally between forty and fifty years old, seekers after truth, peace, and charity. They have often been touched by the perseverance of Christian communities and by their fervent prayer. Many young people also put their name down for catechism classes; they are often the children of Christian families who could not receive any religious instruction during the Cultural Revolution. Elderly bishops traveled for hundreds of miles to confirm thousands of young adults. Catholics were still using the old question-and-answer catechism, whose expressions sounded odd in a collectivist society, e.g., *Question*: "Why were you born into this world?" *Answer*: "To honor God and to save my soul." In cities like Beijing or new towns like Yangling near Xi'an, many university students requested Christian instruction with a view to baptism. Catechesis had to be adapted to their level of instruction so that they too would be able to give a good account of their faith.

Protestants put together an interdenominational catechism composed by a hundred pastors. It was made up of one hundred questions, called *Yaodao wenda* (*Basic Teachings: Question-Answer*) and was published in September 1983 by the Christian Council of China.[6] The Nanjing Common Theological Seminary also produced a catechetical correspondence course.

For the celebration of the liturgy, Catholics were hampered, even more than for catechesis, by having only old books that had been saved from destruction with the greatest difficulty. The Latin altar missal was reprinted, but again all mention of the Pope was left out. This was a real taboo with retroactive effect; for instance, Pope St. Marcellus I, who died in 309, was no longer referred to as Pope, the word "Pope" being obliterated in the reprint with a thick black line. In fact, since priests said Mass in Latin and in a low voice, nothing prevented them from celebrating the Pope as before, which was generally done. Many church choirs were formed; they sang the Latin kyriale and Chinese hymns. The choir of the Holy Redeemer Church in Beijing even managed Gounod's polyphonic Mass. A commission

---

[6] The Protestant review *Tian Feng*, no. 2 (1974), published an article on the way in which this catechism was composed. It was a significant effort of transdenominational cooperation.

was created to introduce Chinese in the liturgy gradually; meanwhile the liturgy of the Mass was explained section by section in the Beijing magazine *Zhongguo Tianzhujiao* (*The Catholic Church in China*). In fact, many priests had gone ahead with using Chinese, thanks to missals and hymn books imported from Hong Kong, Singapore, and Taiwan. Around 1985 at Ürümqi, the capital of Xinjiang-Uighur Autonomous Region in northwest China, Catholics printed their own altar missal in Chinese; their choir was able to sing Chinese texts to Gregorian plainchant melodies. The priest said Mass out loud in Chinese, and his voice was loud enough to be heard at the back of the church, as he commemorated the Pope by name. At Fuzhou, capital of Fujian Province, another step in liturgical reform was taken from 1989 onward and the priest said Mass facing the people. As the churches of the region were restored, altars were positioned so that Mass could be said facing the people. Similar changes were made in Shanghai Major Seminary, where Fr. Thomas Law (Luo Guohui), a liturgist from Hong Kong, had been invited to lecture.

In 1992 there was a major change throughout the country when the General Assembly of the Catholic Representatives of China decided officially to apply in China the liturgical reforms of the Second Vatican Council, which had been received by the rest of the Church nearly thirty years previously. The faithful learned with surprising efficiency to take an active part in celebrating Mass in Chinese. A few Masses in Latin were maintained for older people who were used to saying Chinese prayers during Mass; some older priests too found it difficult, because of failing eyesight, to read the new Chinese missal. One of the important results of the use of Chinese for Mass and the sacraments was that the faithful had direct access to the public reading of the Bible. Many of them had thought that the Bible was made up of moral teaching. In fact they were struck by the impressive account of man's sin and of the history of salvation. Bible study groups began to proliferate, and young priests were much better trained than formerly in explaining the sacred text. Bible study groups and catechism classes were allowed by the Communist authorities as being linked to worship, and the same applied to choirs and groups of altar servers.

From the Communist point of view, religion is a private matter that should not go further than places of worship. There was therefore no question of authorizing the Legion of Mary or any movement aiming at making the faith effective within society. In fact, Catholic Action had hardly existed in China in 1949, when the laity was only represented by the Legion of Mary, the St. Vincent de Paul Society, and various confraternities. Protestants, however, were able to start the Y.M.C.A. again. In Shanghai, where there was a centuries-old tradition of Catholic lay activity, an Association of Catholic Intelluctuals could be organized in 1986. It had more than 400 members, mostly doctors, lawyers, writers, and teachers. They provided free medical treatment for the destitute, put on lectures on technical and social topics, and organized outings, pilgrimages, and various meetings.

In several dioceses training sessions for lay people began toward the end of the 1990s. In Taiyuan, Shanxi Province, an association of Catholics was formed in 2000 with the aim of contacting lapsed Catholics so as to bring them back to church, which showed that it was felt necessary to react against a trend, which was perhaps on the increase. The civil authorities could not forbid such activity, since they knew that Catholics had a rule about attending Mass on Sunday.

Catholic work for education and the relief of sickness and poverty, which had been traditional before the Communists came to power, had all been taken over by the state, because the churches were not supposed to interfere in social maters, still less in education. However, here and there, such activities did reappear, either to promote the self-financing of the church, or as part of modernization and the service of society. In Beijing, the Ma Xiangbo Catholic School opened in 1985 and offered foreign-language courses to several hundred adult students. In Shanghai the Catholic Centre, which included the Church of Christ the King, opened a school of information technology for children and teenagers; the school has been authorized under the category "evening lectures", but the evening seems to have begun at midday. In different places, the Church has been able to open medical centers, courses of professional formation, schools for the deaf and dumb, reeducation courses for the handicapped, nursery schools, and old people's homes. All this church work takes place under the auspices of the patriotic association and is symptomatic of a wider contribution to society on the part of Christians. In fact, the local press regularly draws attention to the contribution made by doctors, engineers, technicians, nurses, teachers, and priests. Sometimes they are decorated with the title "model worker". The review *Zhongguo Tianzhujiao* (*The Catholic Church in China*) has a feature entitled *duo zuo shan gong*, *"Yet More Good Deeds"*. In north Hebei, a priest was often mentioned for his contribution to reforestation and for his initiatives in the area of rural development.

Considerable publicity has also been given to certain professionals in Nanjing who have been decorated for their professional contribution. In fact, the interpretation given to their achievement reflects the prevailing Communist mentality: Catholics are not as bad as all that; they can on occasion do as well as nonbelievers; they should not be discriminated against. In other words, in spite of their beliefs and their quest for individual salvation, they can still be good citizens. Some bishops express it more positively; Christians are called to be the salt of the earth. Some Catholic villages also merit congratulations for their discipline and their productivity. They are awarded the title of *wenming cun (civilized village)*. Thus the government encourages Christians to become more aware of their social task, offering them a more honorable social status as incentive.

This change of attitude should lead to a theological reflection based on the document concerning the Church in the modern world, *Gaudium et Spes*, promulgated by the Second Vatican Council in 1965. Previously, Christian spirituality tended to put the emphasis on reaching personal perfection, which included, of course, fulfilling one's family and professional duties. The social and educational work of the Church, too, was often undertaken with a view to promoting conversions and aimed therefore at the good of the Church as well as the common good. The achievements of the past have kept their value, but the Council and later documents have shown a change of emphasis, whereby the service of mankind has come to be seen as an integral part of the proclamation of salvation. Christians in China were isolated from the developments that occurred in the Catholic Church in the aftermath of the Council. It was the Chinese government, following its Marxist materialism, which urged Catholics to correct their perspective of individual salvation and to put themselves more at the service of the people. The difference between believer and nonbeliever was considered as of secondary importance in comparison with the common effort required for modernization.[7] From the Christian point of view, the salvation of the community can never

---

[7] The Presbyterian researcher Philip L. Wickeri, in his extensive work *Seeking the Common Good: Protestant Christianity, The Three-Self Movement, and China's United Front* (New York: Maryknoll Orbis Books, 1988), p. 356, analyzes the question of how far the Socialist context in China has promoted the positive development of Chinese Christianity. The cover

be a purely material one. This is where Marxist propaganda has led to an unexpected result. Compelling Christians to be more social in their concerns was an invitation to them to introduce into society as a whole the values of justice, truth, charity, and respect for persons. How could these then be denounced as "spiritual pollution" and evil influences coming from the West?

Some Catholic theologians, especially those in the Guangqi Association in Shanghai, endeavored to make the teaching of the Second Vatican Council on service to humanity better known. The theology of liberation thus became for them an effort at inculturation and sharing in the modernization of the country. Since 1985 the Guangqi Society has published a series called *Catholic Documentation* that has made postconciliar developments known in the area of social studies, liturgy, ecclesiology, biblical studies, Church history, etc.[8] These publications have provided a useful supplement to the few books available to seminarians, novices, and young Catholic intellectuals.

A crucial question was constantly being raised in ecclesiology. Was the experience of independence on the part of the Catholic Church in China a significant indicator of the way a local Church would develop once it was freed from Roman centralization? The question was the subject of an in-depth study undertaken at the University of Ottawa by a Chinese evangelical from Hong Kong.[9] Unfortunately his reliance on the notion of contextualization to make the necessary distinction between true and inauthentic development in this area lacked a theological foundation. A closer analysis was needed to distinguish between adaptation, conformism, opportunism, and a truly redemptive incarnation.

On this same question, the Shanghai theologians tended to prefer the approach of Fr. Aloysius Chang, S.J., professor at the faculty of theology of the University of Fujen in Taipei. Postconciliar theology emphasizes the importance of the local church and highlights the role

---

of the book bears as its epigraph a slogan suggested by the United Front policy: *qiu tong cunyi*, "Seek unity, preserve differences".

[8] For an account of theological publications in Communist China, see J. Charbonnier, "La sinisation de l'Église chinoise", *Dossier Échange France-Asie*, no. 1 (1988).

[9] Kim-Kwong Chan, *Towards a Contextual Ecclesiology: The Catholic Church in the People's Republic of China 1979–1983: Its Life and Theological Implications* (Hong Kong: Phototech Systems Ltd., Eleventh Floor, Breakthrough Center, 191–197 Woosung Street, Kowloon, 1987), p. 465.

of bishops as successors of the apostles. In Taiwan, where the Episcopal Conference is in communion with Rome, such developments do not constitute a problem. However, the patriotic theologians of China have a different interpretation. They emphasize the apostolic succession of all the bishops, without giving a special position to the Bishop of Rome. They use historical criticism to describe the directive role that the papacy gradually assumed during the course of history, and they condemn such an evolution as an abuse of religious authority. They consider the universal Church as an aggregate of local Churches, maintaining fraternal relations on a basis of equality and mutual respect. In terms of ecclesiology, this has a strong resemblance to the worldwide Anglican communion. How then can such theologians explain papal primacy? They would allow Catholics to pray for the Pope, if needs be, but they would refuse to allow the Pope any say in the religious affairs of the Church in China. One has to ask whether, in that case, the Pope would be capable of fulfilling his mission as one who guarantees the integrity of the faith and the unity of the whole Church.

In actual fact, the Catholics of China, taken as a whole, continue to consider the Pope as the head of the whole Church. That is why the pretensions of the Patriotic Association are experienced as an unjustifiable imposition and why they cause constant unease. In spite of the progress brought about by the policy of religious freedom, the rejection of the Pope's authority in China has caused a revival of the underground Church, so that the Catholic Church in China is still deeply divided.

Jubilee Year—2000—was marked by two events that emphasized the sharp tension that still exists between Beijing and Rome. During the course of the previous year, rumors of a coming *rapprochement* had circulated both on the mainland and in Hong Kong. During the same period, however, the Communist Party had ordered that the Patriotic Associations should come under greater control and that they should be set up in areas where they did not yet exist. On January 6, 2000, the Feast of the Epiphany, while the Pope was consecrating twelve bishops from different countries in Rome, the Chinese government asked the "patriotic" Chinese bishops to consecrate twelve bishops too. Only five of the bishops-designate agreed, under strong pressure, to being consecrated. The political interference was so blatant that the lecturers and students of the National Catholic Seminary in Beijing refused to attend the ceremony.

On October 1, 2000, Rome affirmed its authority. On that day, Chinese National Day, the Pope canonized 120 martyrs from China, who had previously been beatified. (See Appendix D.) In the calendar of the Roman Church, October 1 is the feast of St. Thérèse of Lisieux, patron of the missions. Beijing reacted extremely sharply, in the name of the struggle against foreign imperialism and for Chinese independence. From its point of view, some of the martyrs were blameworthy because they were associated with the colonial undertaking of the Western powers. Although most of the martyrs were Chinese, it was stated that they could not be considered as a glory to their country, since they did not fit into the conception of strictly Communist patriotism. The vengeful abuse that was poured out on that occasion gave the impression that nothing had changed in the religious policy of the Party over the last fifty years, and yet the general improvement in the country, due to economic reforms, was bringing about the emergence of a new society, a society in which Christians and the adherents of other religions were seeking to find their place.

30

ONE BIG FAMILY
UNDER HEAVEN

Eighty historians from sixteen different countries met at Louvain in Belgium in September 1990 to take stock of contemporary studies on the history of Christianity in China. Bishop Jin Luxian, the patriotic bishop of Shanghai, spoke on Catholicism in China:

> I want to share with you my joys and my sorrows. My joys stem from the renewal of the Catholic Church in China, with the 140 seminarians at Sheshan, the thirty or so churches open in the municipality of Shanghai, the publications of the Guangqi Catholic Research Centre, and the brand new printing works. . . .
>
> My sorrows are due to the internal divisions between patriotic and underground Catholics and to the separation of the Church of China from the Holy See.
>
> Let us pray for the unity of the Church in China and for the unity between the Church of China and the Holy See; then will I be able to sing my *Nunc dimittis*—"Lord, now lettest thou thy servant depart in peace."

Ten years later, in 2000, the bishop of Shanghai could congratulate himself on having opened eighty-five churches in his diocese, but his prayer for unity had not yet been answered.

To create unity in the great family of the children of God had been the prayer of Christ himself. Unfortunately, there is disagreement as to how this unity can be brought about. For the Chinese government it is a question of uniting all the Christians in the country under the control of the state because of the political requirements of the united front for modernization. For the Holy See and for the faithful in China, it is a question of creating a religious unity by gathering together the whole flock under the crook of the one shepherd, the successor of St. Peter.

Internal Wounds

The existence and development of an underground Church are due to the excessive and brutal interference of the Chinese government in religious affairs and also to its use of methods contrary to the commandments of God in campaigns employing denunciations, lies, and the systematic elimination of those declared to be undesirable for political reasons. No faithful Christian, Catholic or Protestant, could accept unconditionally the use of such methods, which destroy the family and the human person. For both Catholics and Protestants, especially evangelicals in the case of the latter, going underground was the only way to survive. When government policy changed in 1978 and a policy of religious freedom was adopted, the underground phenomenon should have disappeared, but in fact it got worse.

In the case of the evangelicals the multiplication of house churches and conversions had become so great that they could not be controlled. Their message was so firmly religious that it refused any compromise with "the powers of this world". The state reacted violently: many wandering preachers were arrested; illegal meetings were broken up; Bibles and hymn books were confiscated. To justify these actions, the government invoked various reasons connected with public order: permissions had not been obtained; heretical behavior had breached public order; subversive views, inspired by the so-called defense of human rights, had been expressed; there had been secret understanding with foreign imperialism or bourgeois liberalism.

Underground Catholics had not increased in number as quickly as the evangelicals, but they formed indestructible small groups, held together by unbreakable loyalty to the Pope. Why did underground Catholics eventually attract attention? In August 1988 Bishop Ma Ji of Pingliang, Gansu Province, attributed the growth of the underground movement to the blunders of the Patriotic Association. He blamed the actions of a small number of patriotic bishops: some had got married; they had rejected the authority of the successor of St. Peter; they had destroyed the bridge that the Patriotic Association was supposed to be between the government and the Church. Bishop Ma Ji also accused it of continuing obstinately with its outdated anti-imperialist abuse, at the very time when the government was trying to obtain cooperation from abroad and to unite the forces within the country to create a form of Socialism with an authentic Chinese character.

Finally he laid the blame for the failure to obtain the restitution of Church properties at the door of the association.

These criticisms were publicized throughout the country and must therefore have been at least tacitly approved by the Communist authorities; they corresponded no doubt to a government move to improve working relations in the religious sector. Communists know how to take one step forward and two steps back, the better to reach their goal. A typical example concerned the marriage of priests. In the 1950s and 1960s the official line was to encourage priests and nuns to marry, but in the 1980s celibacy was recognized as a requisite. The authorities had realized that the faithful lost all confidence in married priests. Things were more difficult where the return of church property was concerned. Local authorities did not want to upset work units, and the citizens who were occupying former church buildings. Local people with influence were not slow either in getting hold of most of the property involved, by planning imaginary schemes for restitution, whereby the church only received a derisory compensation.

Anyway, the real issue was elsewhere. It was not so much the way the association was operating that was at stake, but the fact that it was interfering in matters concerning the faith. For evangelical Protestants, the refusal to accept control by the Patriotic Movement of the Three Autonomies derived from the basic principle that one must obey God rather than the powers of this world. Catholics for their part maintained their unity in faith, that is, their unity in what they believe, by means of their allegiance to the Pope, the visible head of the Church. Bishop Ma Ji's public intervention had been useful, but it ran the risk of distracting attention from the real issue. The sticking point for the underground Church was not that the Patriotic Association was behaving badly but that its very existence was not authorized by the Pope and was a challenge to his authority. Clandestine Catholics never weakened on the issue, and, toward the end of the 1980s, they affirmed their position even more forcefully. In September 1988 a document began to circulate in Hebei Province and beyond. It was called *The Thirteen Articles* and was signed by Bishop Fan Xueyan of Baoding.[1] What it said substantially was that

---

[1] Bishop Fan Xueyan was kept under close supervision and died on April 13, 1992, of

Catholics who go to Mass in a patriotic Church are committing a grave sin. Bishop Fan was a man who had suffered for the faith and was universally respected; his directives did not fail to have an effect, and Mass attendances noticeably diminished. Well-intentioned parish priests, wrongly accused of being patriotic, saw their flock disappear. Local leaders of the Patriotic Associations and executives of the Communist Party were angry at this sabotage of their policy of religious freedom. An abyss opened between patriotic and underground Catholics. The latter called their opponents "Judases" or "henchmen of Satan"; they retaliated by calling the clandestines "integrists" without any charity, who were leading the Church to her ruin.

Clandestine Catholics began to make the reasons for their opposition publicly known. A duplicated typescript entitled *My Views on the Patriotic Association* was passed from hand to hand; it had been composed by a bishop from south Hebei. According to the author, priests who cooperate with the Patriotic Association are deceiving themselves when they say that their conscience is at peace. They imagine that a purely exterior and formal adherence does not commit their faith; but from the moment when they accept a compromise on the primacy of the Pope, they are committed in spite of themselves to a process that will lead them inevitably to abandoning one by one the central articles of the Creed. The bishop argues that it is wrong to accept any cooperation whatsoever with the Patriotic Association, and this for twenty-two reasons, which he sets out, more or less objectively. Among other things he condemns the oath that must be taken at episcopal and priestly ordinations, by which a candidate promises to reject the authority of the Pope and to follow the directives of the Party.

Some other bishops avoided denouncing anybody and limited themselves to affirming their faith openly. Thus Bishop Xiao Liren of Xintai, south Hebei, did not hesitate to say in his Christmas message for 1988:

> Our efforts must concentrate on the two following points: we are firmly resolved, with the supreme leader of our Catholic Church, the Pope, and under his direction, to nourish and develop our religious life, to

---

ill treatment, as indicated by the photographs of his dead body, with telltale bruises on the face.

Bishop Fan Xueyan of Baoding (1907–1992)

Fan Xueyan was ordained a priest in 1934 and consecrated Bishop of Baoding in 1951. He was in prison from 1957 to 1979, and in 1984 he was condemned to an additional ten years' imprisonment. Fan Xueyan was released on parole in November 1987, but in 1988 he circulated a document condemning Catholics who attended Mass in the official Patriotic Church. For that, and because he was charged with unofficially consecrating bishops for the underground Church, he was committed to strict surveillance in Baoding and died of ill treatment on April 13, 1992.

increase progressively our doctrinal knowledge, to develop the Church and to save souls for the glory of God.

Secondly, we naturally do not want to lag behind in relation to our country. We are firmly resolved, under the rightful direction of the government, to build a prosperous and powerful country, to contribute with our whole strength in the service of a happy life in unity and mutual love with all the people of the country.

Unfortunately, as a result of this declaration, the civil authorities forbade Bishop Xiao Liren from exercising his episcopal ministry.

The underground Church felt that it must assert itself publicly for two reasons. Firstly, more and more Catholics were playing the game of government propaganda and taking advantage of the conditions on which religious freedom was being offered to them; secondly, those who were collaborating with the regime were making a favorable impression on foreign visitors. It was a fact that tourists and Chinese from abroad were impressed by the renewal of the Church that they could see in China. They were bringing their moral and financial support to the patriotic Church. Such resources were not reaching the underground Church, which was finding it difficult to make ends meet. But the spiritual anguish of the clandestines was perhaps more acute than their material poverty, since they were beginning to feel that the universal Church would perhaps abandon them, although they were the very ones who had borne the full brunt of Communist persecution.

On November 21, 1989, some thirty bishops, priests, and lay people of the underground Church decided to strike a blow. They met in a village of Shaanxi Province and constituted themselves into an Episcopal Conference, according to canon 447 of the new Code of Canon Law, which had been promulgated for the Latin Church in 1983.[2] The aim of this group was to work for greater unity in the pastoral direction of the Church, and they saw this initiative as continuing the tradition of the first council of the Catholic Church in

---

[2] Canon 447 of the 1983 Code of Canon Law reads: The conference of bishops, a permanent institution, is a grouping of bishops of a given nation or territory whereby, according to the norm of law, they jointly exercise certain pastoral functions on behalf of the Christian faithful of their territory in view of promoting that greater good which the Church offers human kind, especially through forms and programs of the apostolate, which are fittingly adapted to the circumstances of the time and place. (Translation by the Canon Law Society of America, 1983.)

China, which had taken place in Shanghai in 1924. They were thus affirming their right to exist in complete and open fidelity to the Holy See.

Repression of the Underground Church

In the months that followed the Shaanxi Conference every one of those who had taken part in it was arrested. Even before the unofficial conference, the Communist Party had begun to respond harshly to the activities of clandestine Catholics. News of the more notorious police raids reached the outside world through Hong Kong:

Youtong, Hebei Province, April 18, 1989:

> The church of this village of 1,700 Catholics has been demolished, and the parish premises that surrounded it have been turned into a school. On Palm Sunday 1989, Christians put up a tent on their former land, which had become the school playground. They celebrated the Holy Week ceremonies in the tent. On April 18, 5,000 armed policemen invaded the village and began to take down the tent-chapel. Women who tried to stop them were brutally beaten with sticks. A young sister was struck on the head and lost an eye as a result. Some Christians gathered in the presbytery and blocked the entrance. The police climbed on the roof, tore off the tiles, and hurled them onto the crowd inside the building. About 300 wounded were left behind.

Qiaozhai, Hebei Province, May 1989:

> Important police units have blocked all access to the village of Qiaozhai. Some forty clandestine seminarians and some twenty novices have been arrested, insulted, and ill treated. Books and equipment have been confiscated. Two priests aged seventy-five have been arrested, as well as two sisters, aged seventy-eight and eighty-eight, respectively. It seems that a Catholic priest played the sorry role of informer.

In February 1989, Document 3, issued by the Central Committee of the Communist Party, tightened up official policy concerning dissidents. The policy of the Party became to rally as many clandestines as possible by granting more freedom for the worship that was officially authorized. For instance, the great pilgrimage center of Our Lady of Joy at Guiyang, the capital of Guizhou Province,

Cardinal Gong Pinmei, S.J. (1901–2000)

Born in Shanghai, Gong was ordained priest in 1930 and became Bishop of Shanghai in 1950, to which was added in 1951 the responsibility of administrator of the dioceses of Nanjing and Suzhou. He was arrested in 1951 and sentenced to life imprisonment in 1960. Bishop Gong was released on parole in 1985 after more than thirty years in prison. His civil rights were restored in 1988 and in that year he was able to go to the United States for medical treatment. Pope John Paul II announced in 1991 that he had created Gong Pinmei a Cardinal in 1979, but that the appointment had been kept secret for fear of provoking the reaction of the Chinese government. Cardinal Gong Pinmei died in Connecticut in 2000.

which had been banned for a long time, finally received official authorization in the mid-1980s. But new and severe directives were issued that aimed at the destruction of those who would not conform: their leaders were to be isolated, any illegal activities were to be exposed, and those who took part in them were to be punished. Numerous arrests followed, and they recurred frequently from 1989 to 1991, to the point that Catholic world opinion was alerted. China already had a very bad press because of the crushing of the democratic movement in Beijing's Tiananmen Square on June 3–4, 1989. Could China still be considered a civilized country, respecting the rights of human beings to live and to express themselves? The country's image was not improved by news of what was happening to Christians who had been declared "illegals", although they had not committed any crimes. Amnesty International published the names of many of the victims. The good impression made by China during the previous years tended to evaporate completely. Christians throughout the world showed their sympathy toward the sufferings of underground Catholics, whom they heard about often for the first time. Pope John Paul II added his support by revealing on May 29, 1991, that he had created the faithful archbishop of Shanghai, Gong Pinmei, a cardinal. This nomination had been made in 1979 when the archbishop was still in prison, but had not been published at the time to avoid provoking the Chinese government. After thirty years in prison, Cardinal Gong had been freed in 1985 and had been authorized to go to the United States to recover his health. He and Archbishop Dominic Tang of Guangzhou were the prominent standard bearers of those Chinese Christians who had remained unshakable in their faith, despite all the ill treatment to which they had been subjected.

International Exchanges

The Chinese government did, however, make an attempt to create abroad a more favorable attitude toward its religious policy. Some Chinese Church leaders were allowed to travel outside China. They were carefully vetted and never alone; the team had to be sufficiently representative and to follow the line of government propaganda. An international conference at Montreal in October 1981 began a series of such exchanges.[3] It was arranged by the Canada-China Program of the Canadian Council of Churches and brought together 150 Christians from the five continents, who were glad to welcome ten Church leaders from Beijing, Nanjing, and Shanghai—seven Protestants and three Catholics. The theme of the conference was "God's call for a new start". The Montreal meeting crowned ecumenical efforts that had been launched in 1974 at Båstad and Louvain; these two meetings had been held as the result of European initiatives and had included Chinese from Hong Kong, Taiwan, and Rome but had had no representative from within the Chinese People's Republic. The Canada meeting was the result of prudent contacts made by Chinese delegates at the Third World Conference of Religion and Peace, held in the United States at Princeton in November 1979. Four of the Protestant delegates at Montreal had been present at Princeton, one of the four being Bishop Ding Guangxun, Anglican bishop of Nanjing. As a result the general lines of the Montreal Conference had been agreed. This first contact in friendship and prayer had served to defrost relations.

The political and theological implications of the papers given at Montreal deserve careful study.[4] The speakers from America and the Third World were, for the most part, committed theologians, deep into contextualization and liberation theology. They denounced all social exploitation (except in China) and criticized the way in which ecclesiastical institutions have been compromised with oppressive regimes. Some of the Catholic speakers were hostile to Roman centralization; knowing little about the situation in China, they expressed unreserved acceptance for the position of the delegates from the People's Republic and fully supported an independent Church of China. However, Doug Roch, a Catholic member of the Canadian Parliament, intervened and expounded unequivocally the requirements for real communion within the Catholic Church under the direction of the Holy Father.

---

[3] For the contents and the dynamics of the Montreal Conference, see J. Charbonnier, "Une voie chinoise pour les Chrétiens—La conférence de Montréal (2–9 octobre 1981)", *Dossiers Échange France-Asie*, no. 70 (Déc. 1981).

[4] The documents of the Montreal Conference have been published by the Canada-China Program of the Canadian Council of Churches: *A New Beginning, An International Dialogue with the China Church*, ed. Theresa Chu and Christopher Lind (1983).

From the theological point of view, the most substantial contributions to the Montreal Conference came from the Protestant theologians from China. Their reflection on grace presented it as capable of transforming a human nature that has been wounded by sin but not annihilated by it, and this brought them closer to the Catholic position. Throughout the conference, Bishop Ding Guangxun guided the Chinese participation; he insisted on being involved in the preparation of all future international meetings. A conference was planned in New York for January 1986, but this had to be canceled as it did not satisfy the demands of the Chinese. A certain number of those who had taken part in previous meetings, both Catholics and evangelicals, were excluded by the organizers because their theological positions were considered undesirable. It was felt that Christians under political pressure must be able to distinguish between those who are friends of China and those who are enemies of China.

The aborted New York Conference was replaced by an international meeting at Nanjing in May 1986.[5] This concentrated on how to provide financial support for the Christians in China and also for the churches in the Third World that were engaged in the process of Socialist transformation. The discussions were stormy, since the institutions that were supposed to provide the funding belonged naturally to the establishment, especially in America.

Since 1985, contacts with Christians in China have taken the practical form of economic aid projects, which included the transfer of capital and the sending of specialized personnel. The International Bible Society funded the setting up of a modern printing press in Nanjing. More than a million Bibles were printed there in three years, and by 2000 over twenty million Bibles had been printed in Nanjing, including several thousand for the blind in Braille. In 1985 a Protestant charity called Amity had been founded in Nanjing, with Chinese directors, liaising with an American coordinator in Hong Kong; this soon produced appreciable results. Already in the first year of Amity's existence some fifty language teachers and specialized lecturers had taken up posts in the Chinese universities of Jiangsu Province and the neighboring regions; most of them were missionaries, who established

---

[5] For the papers given at this conference, see *Nanjing '86. Ecumenical Sharing: A New Agenda. An Ecumenical Conference. May 14–20 1986.* The papers were prepared for publication by Susan Perry, research assistant, China Research Program, Maryknoll Fathers and Brothers.

K. H. Ting (Ding Guangxun) Anglican Bishop of Zhejiang

Born in Shanghai in 1915, studied at St. John's University, Shanghai, and was ordained to the Anglican priesthood in 1942. He married Siu-may Kuo in 1942 and was in Canada and Geneva 1946–1948, working with the Student Christian Movement. Returning to China in 1951, he identified with the program of the government of the People's Republic of China and the Three-Self Patriotic Movement. In 1953 he became principal of the Nanjing Union Theological Seminary and in 1955 Bishop of the Anglican Diocese of Zhejiang. Bishop Ting's theology stresses the continuity of creation and redemption, and this brought it nearer to the Catholic view of grace as transforming a human nature wounded by sin but not totally corrupted by it. Ting disappeared from view during the Cultural Revolution (1966–1976) but emerged afterward as leader of Protestant Christians, traveling widely and meeting Christian leaders worldwide. Ting's international contacts have been controlled by the official China Christian Council, but they have made possible an increasing number of aid programs and personal exchanges between Christians in China and the outside world. Ting's approach was recognized in 1991 at Canberra, when the China Christian Council was admitted as member of the World Council of Churches.

excellent relations with students and colleagues. Two or three years later, Catholics followed the same path, spurred on by Dr. Audrey Donnithorne, an Australian lady born in Sichuan Province, who was an expert on the Chinese economy. With the help of Columban missionaries and other friends from Hong Kong, she founded the International Association for Technical Economic and Cultural Exchanges with China. Priests, sisters, and lay people, who volunteered through the association to work in China, had to be dedicated and ready to put up with a simple lifestyle and various administrative frustrations in order to witness to the human and Christian values that they had at heart. Such experts were welcomed in China as long as they limited themselves to their secular work and did not proselytize. Their presence also witnessed to the friendly dispositions toward China that the countries they came from entertained.

The new open policy toward the foreign governments and international exchanges had anyway permitted more traveling time abroad for study, trade relations, and tourism. Within that context, religious exchanges also took place: Chinese delegations, Catholic or Protestant, went to different countries, and foreign religious personalities or groups visited China. Thus, among well-known Catholics who visited China in those years were Cardinal König from Austria, Cardinal Etchegaray from France, Cardinal Sin of Manila, and Mother Teresa from Calcutta. On the Chinese side, patriotic Bishop Jin Luxian of Shanghai was the most traveled; he went to Europe, America, Hong Kong, and the Philippines. His personal diplomacy was successful and led, as mentioned above, to the building of a new major seminary at Sheshan and the creation of new printing works at Zikawei. Protestants obtained even more significant results at the seventh Assembly of the World Council of Churches held at Canberra from February 7 to 20, 1991. This voted unanimously for the admission of the Christian Council of China as the 317th member of the World Council.

Could one interpret this ecumenical achievement as forecasting similar developments for the Catholic Church? At the highest official level, relations between Rome and Beijing in 1991 remained blocked. Relations were still being maintained between the Vatican and the government of Taipei. The status of the nuncio at Taipei had been reduced somewhat, and his mission was limited to the island of Taiwan, but his presence was important to the Nationalist government, which would have been practically totally isolated without it. In 1991, in replacement of an aged diplomat, a new ambassador from the Republic of China was appointed to the Holy See; he was the only official representative from Taiwan in Europe. Rome, however, sent friendly messages in Beijing's direction by means of the Pope's speeches or through the visits to China of personalities close to the Holy See. Beijing also seemed to indicate a certain easing in its attitude by abandoning, for instance, the aggressive tone of the early 1980s and by allowing Chinese Catholics to pray publicly for the Pope. However, the Communist government firmly maintained the principle of the Church of China's independence and refused all interference from Rome in Chinese religious affairs. Thus in public there was total exclusion, but both the Italians and the Chinese are good actors; a lot was happening behind the scenes. Was it possible to look forward to a new act in the play?

The "independent" Catholic Church in China continued its "democratic" way of nominating and consecrating bishops, but a number of these bishops secretly contacted Rome to obtain its approval, which it received. Beijing closed its eyes to this. It even happened that Catholics from Rome on a visit to China urged good priests, who had been appointed to bishoprics by democratic election, to accept their nomination. In the year 2000, there were seventy patriotic Catholic bishops in China, of whom some sixty had been secretly recognized by Rome. At the same time there were about fifty "underground" bishops, who had been consecrated by their fellow bishops using their canonical faculties. Rome approved them, of course, but sought to limit their proliferation, either because it wanted to ensure their pastoral qualifications or because it wanted to avoid conflict with the patriotic bishop, when there was one in the same diocese, especially if he had been secretly recognized by Rome.

Catholic Chinese Abroad

Although official relations still seemed nonexistent at the highest level, at the grassroots expressions of Christian fraternity were becoming more frequent, especially from Catholics in Hong Kong, Taiwan, Singapore, and the Chinese diaspora. Often visitors from abroad traveling in China visited the village they or their family came from; they reestablished contact with their relatives and saw for themselves how much mainland China had developed. They brought generous presents and financial support. Visiting Christians were thus able to discover the conditions of Church life in the remotest countryside, a thing that foreign tourists could hardly ever do.

In this movement for renewed contacts with the mainland, Hong Kong had the first place. During the 1980s there were a great many meetings and aid projects. The Catholic relief agency Caritas Hong Kong maintained some twenty projects on the mainland in the area of training for teaching, hotel management, and the care of the handicapped. There was also help in more specifically religious areas, such as the formation of seminarians and religious sisters. The Holy Spirit Study Centre in Hong Kong and various other institutes provided a great number of books in Chinese; about thirty titles had been reprinted using the many abbreviated characters and the simplified forms that had been introduced on the mainland since 1949. Lecturers in theology came from outside to give courses at the Shanghai Seminary. A small group of Chinese Catholic theologians, led by Fr. Anthony Chang (Zheng Shenglai) and Fr. Luke Tsui (Xu Jinyao), were often invited to give talks in the seminaries of the mainland. This was a privilege that the government authorities reserved for those who were fully appreciative of the way the patriotic Church was developing in China. The Catholic review *Yi-China Message* published by Fr. Anthony Chang in Hong Kong favored this tendency; it reported with enthusiasm the good news of churches opened, vocations among the young, and the numerous signs of vitality in the Chinese Church.

However, Catholics in Hong Kong were also well informed about the inherent difficulties of the Communist regime's religious policy. Having no illusions about the value of the legal guarantees obtained by the agreement between Beijing and the British government, they concentrated on renewing the life of the Church. They tried to develop a more personal religious life among the faithful, to group them in fervent small communities, and to develop their social conscience. They felt that the Church could thus hold out, even if it lost its schools and other institutions. Hong Kong Catholics were greatly encouraged when their archbishop, John Baptist Wu, was elevated to the rank of cardinal in 1988. On June 30, Pope John Paul II received in private audience the new cardinal and the Catholic delegation from Hong Kong, and he said to them:

The Church now has a Cardinal from the great Chinese family, and I am happy to see so many friends of Cardinal Wu gathered here in the Vatican to share with him these moments of joy. I am sure that your Chinese brothers and sisters throughout the world are rejoicing at the honor that has been given to him. It is above all a new responsibility for him, a more evident sharing in that care for the universal Church that the Lord has entrusted to Peter and to his successors.

The Pope was also concerned to open a more substantial dialogue with the Chinese authorities and sent to Hong Kong a representative of the Holy See in the person of Msgr. Jean-Paul Gobel, whose mission was to study the situation of the Church in China and the possibility of establishing relations in the future. Msgr. Gobel was succeeded in 1992 by Msgr. Fernando Filoni, who was succeeded in 2001 by Msgr. Eugene Martin Nugent.

One must never forget that Chinese throughout the world feel concerned by the developments happening in the land of their ancestors. Priests, religious sisters, and lay people, who had for thirty years been cut off from their families and their former dioceses, plucked up courage to visit China after it had opened up again. These visits became more and more frequent and progressed from being discreet family reunions to having a pastoral dimension. Many visitors found ways of contributing to the rebuilding of what they considered as their Church and providing books and equipment, although this was officially forbidden. In areas with no priests, priests from abroad on visit would baptize catechumens, bless marriages, and arrange for candidates to be admitted to the seminary. Chinese priests in the Philippines helped to build some forty churches in China and to open a hospital in Hebei Province.

In Singapore a team of young lay apostles came together in 1981 and made more than ten journeys to China, starting in 1985. Their center in Singapore, *Zhonglian (China Catholic Communication Centre)* published a *Guide to the Catholic Church in China*, in Chinese and English, which made it possible for thousands of tourists to meet personally many of their coreligionists in China. Four hundred subscribers on the mainland received a bimonthly review that gave them news of the Church throughout the world and also contained catechism lessons for young people.

From the end of 1987 onward, Catholics in Taiwan were also able to take part in this renewed contact with the continent. In fact, bish-

ops and priests in Taiwan had not waited for the green light to be
concerned about the Church in China. There had been a study group
called "Bridge Church", later renamed "Sister Churches", which met
with colleagues from Hong Kong, Singapore, and other countries for
a yearly update on the situation in China. Once travel was authorized, there was a great surge of visits to the mainland. Out of the
two million continental Chinese who had settled in Taiwan over the
previous forty years, hundreds of thousands went to all the provinces
of China to see relatives and friends. Ten percent of them must have
been Christians, if one counts Catholics and Protestants, but very few
of the Catholics seem to have considered the visit as an opportunity
for witnessing to their faith. Many of them had been baptized in the
1950s after a few months of instruction and no longer practiced. If
their family on the continent knew nothing of Christianity, the question of religion would not have come up. A few committed and active
Catholics had created groups in Taiwan with the express purpose of
bringing the Gospel to the continent, but, apart from these, it was
mostly priests and nuns who made a point of visiting their home
parishes and trying to help them.

The bishops of Taiwan had encouraged the creation of a center
for the study of the situation on the continent; this was part of the
philosophy faculty of Fujen University, and Fr. Gabriel Ly (Li Zhen)
was the director. Later one of the bishops was put in charge of a
Commission for the "Bridge Church", to which five or six specialized groups were linked. A service for documentation and supplies
was set up in Taipei's *Central Building*, which housed many Catholic activities. Effective contacts, however, were created by the priests
and sisters who visited China privately. To begin with, they were very
suspicious of the official Church, controlled as it was by the patriotic
association, but their attitude often changed completely. They were
pleasantly surprised by the warm welcome that they received, and they
could see for themselves the progress that the Church was making.
They appreciated that it had been able to survive and flourish under
wholly Chinese leadership, although one can be surprised by the fact
that forty years of anti-Communist propaganda in Taiwan had not
alerted them to the strategy of the United Front.

However, on both sides of the Taiwan Strait, Communists and anti-
Communists were becoming less virulent as ideologies were becoming less attractive. It was the standard of living that brought prestige,

and what mattered most was the land of China itself, the Motherland. Communism was coming to be seen not as an end in itself but as an instrument for the modernization of the country. The real progress achieved made it possible for everyone to become more aware of the deficiencies of the system. During the whole of the 1980s Chinese intellectuals had been trying to identify where exactly the so-called scientific ideology was going wrong. They denounced the inhuman cruelty of the Cultural Revolution, the new forms of alienation in the Socialist regime, the reappearance of the flaws of feudalism under the cloak of Marxism. It was only the need for stability and order that was maintaining the Party in power, but the bureaucratic structure of power was now being called into question in the name of a more democratic political ideal. Young Chinese intellectuals, in China itself but especially in America and Europe, were trying to imagine the kind of democracy that could be viable in their country. This was bringing them up against an even more fundamental question: What mentality and cultural traditions are proper to the world of China? Some writers, following the tradition of Lu Xun, produced a biting critique of certain paralyzing aspects of their culture. The film *Heshang* (*The Agony of the River*) followed that tradition and provoked a conservative reaction on the part ·of the establishment.[6] Other researchers undertook a closer study of non-Chinese cultural traditions and tried in particular to assess the part played by Christianity in Western culture. In April 1990 the first number of *Jidujiao wenhua pinglun* (*Christian Culture Review*) was printed in Guiyang, the capital city of Guizhou Province, a poor mountainous province of southwestern China, which was an unexpected venue for such an initiative. This undertaking has later developed into the broad program of translations and publications that is run by the Institute of Sino-Christian Studies in Taofengshan, Hong Kong. The editors have promoted the line that Christianity can occupy a modest place among the principal currents of Chinese culture. They reject all identification between culture, ideology, and political power. These distinctions are full of wisdom. If accepted, they could open the way to fruitful exchanges between different cultures, exchanges that would be immensely advantageous to the future of the great human family.

---

[6] The different aspects of this Chinese self-criticism were analyzed in J. Charbonnier, "Les Chinois interrogent leur culture", *Dossier Échange France-Asie*, no. 2 (1989).

CONCLUSION

There is no need to conclude, because the history of Christians in China is ongoing. However, the memory of centuries past does allow the identification of certain constants, six of which can be summarized as follows:

• The history of China depends to a considerable extent on a cultural context that is very different from that of Western civilization. The world of China is a huge entity. Its ideographic writing and the innate respect for a ritual ordering of human beings within their universe guarantee its unity and its amazing continuity. The prophetic message of the Gospel comes as a shock to such a world and can easily appear as aggression, although some Chinese have recognized it as the Way of Wisdom.

• Confucianism is an ambivalent doctrine. An open and critical form of Confucianism can respond to the transcendent call of the God of the Bible. A formal and closed form of Confucianism can be the greatest enemy of the Gospel and oppose it with xenophobic and pedantic conservatism. The currents within traditional Chinese culture that are critical of Confucianism, such as the philosophy of the sages of Taoism and Mohism, have a greater affinity with Christian teaching. It is significant that some outstanding modern converts to Christianity have been attracted by the way of spiritual childhood promoted by St. Thérèse of Lisieux.

• Christianity first came into China in the footsteps of Buddhism. However, the Jesuits and the great convert scholars of the seventeenth century took as their starting point an archaic Confucianism, stripped of its Buddhist and Taoist elements. The present ecumenical openness should encourage Christians to take up again the dialogue with Buddhist spiritual masters. Certain Protestant groups have already begun to do this.

• The last decades of the twentieth century have been marked by the spectacular growth of Protestantism. Their traditional churches have been renewed through the influence of strongly motivated and dynamic evangelical groups. The enthusiastic witness of young Christians is catching and has brought over great numbers, eager for truth and brotherly relationships. Catholics have grown more slowly, perhaps because of their ecclesial framework. The strong hierarchical structure of Catholicism and the traditional emphasis on the observance of the commandments seem to induce a certain passivity. The fact that traditionally Catholics were implanted in the impoverished countryside has limited their present influence, whereas Protestants, since the middle of the nineteenth century, have taken root in large cities. Protestants have taken a more active part in the movements that have led to the modernization of China, and they have also benefited from the special relations that exist between the United States and present-day China. However, since the beginning of the twenty-first century a stronger Catholic influence is emerging in urban areas. The most lively Catholic communities are to be found in large cities, where they draw on the active support of believers from the emerging middle classes. In their relations with Protestants, Catholics are beginning to hold their own through dynamic Bible study groups, the liturgy in Chinese as reformed by the Second Vatican Council, and the outreach of a renewed catechumenate.

• Christians in China are a small minority, but, like the salt of the earth, they can provide inspiration for others. To use another New Testament image, the grain of wheat falls into the earth and dies, and for centuries Christians have suffered from repeated persecutions. Through their witness, the redemptive sacrifice of Christ is now inscribed in letters of blood upon the tablets of Chinese history. Today Christians are fully integrated in their civilization and their society, and they can work for the transformation of civilization and society. They can help to build the "civilization of the spirit" that their fellow citizens dream of.

• For centuries Catholics in China were rejected by the wise and the powerful of the Celestial Empire, and their faith took root among poverty-stricken peasants. The controversy over traditional rites led to converts being forbidden from celebrating them in honor of the ancestors, but this was disconcerting mainly for conservative scholar-gentry; they were rather like the sages and scribes of ancient Israel, who looked for salvation to the observance of the law and its ritual. From the point of view of the Gospel, the poverty of Christians is not necessarily a source of weakness. Christians should maintain their solidarity with the poorest, while hoping to gain the respect of the elite of their country. They would thus contribute to raising the level of the whole people.

China is gaining in importance as part of the international community of the nascent Third Millennium. Its contribution to world trade is growing more and more, and Beijing has been chosen as the site for the 2008 Olympic Games. Chinese society as a whole is evolving, as a middle class emerges; gradually a social security system is being created to cope with the uncertainties of the market economy. As the increase in population slows down, the number of old people is increasing. In this new context, the various religions are also being called upon to reinterpret their traditions.

Christians too have to divest themselves of their old self, their ritualistic and closed communities, and to project themselves as modern in outlook. This means constituting urban communities open to society and nourished by the reading of the Bible and by a more accessible sacramental life, thanks to the use of Chinese and the art forms of the country. During the twenty-first century, the Christians of China are thus called to contribute effectively to the spiritual welfare of their country and to bring new energy to the Church throughout the whole world.

APPENDIX A

CHRONOLOGICAL TABLE
年代表

TANG DYNASTY (A.D. 618–907) 唐朝

636   Bishop Abraham of the East Syrian Church arrives at Chang'an (Xi'an), capital of the Tang. Decree of the TANG TAIZONG emperor, authorizing Christianity in China.

景教士阿罗本载经典抵长安　唐太宗予以尊崇　立景教。

781   The inscription on the Xi'an Stele gives evidence of the presence of Christianity in China for the previous 150 years.

立"大秦景教流行中国碑"于长安。

845   Imperial decree banning foreign religions; Buddhist temples are destroyed and monks secularized; Christian missionaries are secularized or expelled.

皇帝御旨扫　外来宗教　拆毁佛寺　还俗和尚　基督教传教士遭到　逐。

SONG DYNASTY (960–1278) 宋朝
YUAN DYNASTY (1279–1368) 元朝

1279   KHUBLAI KHAN establishes the Mongol Yuan Dynasty in China.

忽必烈建元朝。

1289   Pope Nicholas I sends Giovanni da Montecorvino on a diplomatic mission to China.

教宗尼各老四世派遣若望孟　维

1307   Pope Clement V creates the archbishopric of Beijing and makes Giovanni da Montecorvino archbishop.

教宗格来孟五世建立北京总教区

MING DYNASTY (1368–1644) 明朝

1368   ZHU YUANZHANG expels the Mongols and founds the Chinese dynasty of the Ming.
朱元璋击败蒙古人　建立明朝。

1552   St. Francis Xavier dies on the island of Shangchuan near Macao.
圣方济各沙勿略抵广东上川岛　卒于斯。

1583   The Italian Jesuits Matteo Ricci and Michele Ruggieri move from Macao to Zhaoqing, capital of the two provinces of Guangdong and Guangxi.
意大利人耶稣会会士利玛窦与罗明坚从澳门抵肇庆。

1622   Creation in Rome of the Congregation *de Propaganda Fide*, which later sent the vicars apostolic to China.
罗　圣座创立传信部。

QING DYNASTY (1644–1912) 清朝

1644   The rebel Li Zicheng occupies Beijing; the Manchu Qing Dynasty establishes its rule in the capital.
李自成攻入北京　引清兵入关　占北京。

1662–1722   Reign of the KANGXI emperor.
康熙皇帝

1684   Louis XIV, king of France, sends Jesuit mathematicians to Beijing.
法国国王路易十四派遣耶稣会数学家去北京。

1685   Gregory Luo Wenzao, first Latin Catholic Chinese bishop, is consecrated in Guangzhou (Canton).
第一位华人主教罗文藻在广州晋牧。

1704   Pope Clement XI forbids Catholic converts from practicing the traditional rites in honor of Confucius and the ancestors.
教宗格来孟十一世令禁敬孔祭祖。

1736–1795   Reign of the QIAN LONG emperor.
乾　皇帝

1803   The first Catholic synod in China is held in Sichuan province by Bishop Jean-Gabriel Dufresse.
四川教会第一次大会

1807   Robert Morrison, Presbyterian Minister, sent to China by the London Missionary Society, is the first Protestant missionary in China.
礼逊牧师被伦敦传教团派往中国
是第一个去中国的新教传教士。

1840   The Opium War. Colonial powers intervene in China.
片战争

1842   The Treaty of Nanjing. Five ports are opened to foreign trade. Beginning of the "protectorate" by the French consular authorities over the Catholic missions in China.
南京条约开五口通商　并有保护传教士一条。

1900   The Boxer Rebellion. Murder of five Catholic bishops, forty-eight Catholic priests, and nearly 30,000 Catholic faithful.
义和拳运动。5 位天主教主教　48 位神父和近 30,000 教徒被杀。

1911   Uprising against the imperial government in Wuchang. Sun Yat-sen proclaims the REPUBLIC OF CHINA.
武昌起义。孙中山推翻满清建立民国。

1919   May 4th Movement with the slogan "science and democracy."
五四运动

1921   July: First Communist Party Congress in Shanghai.
中国共产党第一次全国代表大会在上海举行。

1922   Pope Pius XI appoints Archbishop Celso Costantini as first apostolic delegate to China.
教宗庇护十一世委派刚恒毅大主教为第
一位教廷　华专使。

1924   First National Council of the Catholic Church in China held in Shanghai.
中国　届天主教主教会议在上海举行。

1926　October 28: Consecration of six Chinese Catholic bishops in Rome.

10月28日　6位中国主教在罗　晋牧。

1939　Pope Pius XII lifts the ban on the participation by Catholics in the traditional rites in honor of Confucius and the ancestors.

教宗庇护十二世解禁中国天主教徒的尊孔祭祖。

1945　Surrender of the Japanese occupying forces in China. Bishop Tian Gengxin is made the first Chinese cardinal.

日本投　。田耕辛主教升为中国第一位枢机。

1946　The Chinese government appoints John Wu Jingxiong as ambassador to the Holy See. Pope Pius XII establishes a Catholic hierarchy in China with twenty ecclesiastical provinces, seventy-nine dioceses, thirty-eight vicariates apostolic. Archbishop Antonio Riberi is appointed first nuncio to China.

国民政府任命吴经熊为　罗　教廷公使。
教宗建立中国教会圣统体制。

The People's Republic of China

1949　October 1: In Tiananmen Square, Beijing, Mao Zedong proclaims the liberation of the Chinese people and the creation of the People's Republic of China.

10月1日　中华人民共和国诞生。

1950–1953　The Korean War.

朝　战争

1951　May: *The People's Weekly* accuses Archbishop Riberi, papal nuncio, of sabotaging the movement for independence. He is expelled. Foreign missionaries are condemned as agents of foreign imperialism and are expelled from China.

五月　"人民日报"猛烈抨击教廷公使　培理大主教
控其迫害教会独立运动　不久　逐出境。

1955　September, in Shanghai: Archbishop Gong Pinmei and some forty priests and 1,000 Catholics are accused of obstructing the patriotic movement for independence and are condemned and sent to prison. Violent campaign against the Legion of Mary.

九月　上海　　品梅大主教和40多位神父以及1000位教徒被捕入狱　"圣母军"成员受迫害。

1957　July 15: The Catholic Patriotic Association is officially created in Beijing.

七月十五日　北京　中国天主教爱国会正式成立。

1958　April at Wuhan the first consecration of Catholic bishops without the approval of the Holy See.

Pope Pius XII issues his third encyclical letter to the Catholics of China *Apostolorum Principis*, condemning the Catholic Patriotic Association and the illegal appointment of Catholic bishops in China.

四月　武汉　第一位未经教宗批准的中国主教晋牧。教宗庇护十二世在第三封致中国天主教徒通谕中谴责爱国会的　法任命主教。

1959　May 20: Archbishop Caprio is appointed as second apostolic pro-nuncio to the government of the Republic of China at Taipei.

五月二十日　台北　教庭命　理耀蒙席为第二任　华公使。

1962–1965　The Second Vatican Council is held in Rome.

梵蒂冈第二次大公会议

1966　The Cultural Proletarian Revolution. The Red Guards devastate what is left of the Catholic Church. All the Catholic churches in China are closed. Priests and religious sisters are sent to prison or to labor camps for reeducation.

文化大　命爆发。红卫兵摧毁教堂所有的天主教教堂关闭神父修女入狱或接受劳动改造。

1971　October 25: The People's Republic of China is admitted to the United Nations. From November 20 one Sunday

Mass can be celebrated in the Nantang Church in Beijing.

10月25日　中国加入联合国。11月20日起
北京南堂可以举行主日弥撒。

1976　September 9: Death of Mao Zedong. Hua Guofeng succeeds in 1977. Revolutionary activism ceases with the elimination of the Gang of Four.

9月9日　毛泽东去世。1977 年　华国锋继位
粉碎四人帮。

1978　December: Third Plenum of the Eleventh Party Congress. DENG XIAOPING launches a policy of economic reform and modernization.

12月　十一届三中全会。
邓小平提出经济改　政策和现代化目标。

1980　May–June: Third General Assembly of the Catholic Patriotic Association. Creation of the Administrative Commission of Religious Affairs and of the Catholic Bishops' Conference of China.

五月至六月　天主教爱国会第三次全体会议
成立中国天主教教务委员会及中国主教团。

1982　October 11: Opening of the Catholic Major Seminary in Shanghai.

10月11日　上海佘山天主教大修　开幕。

1983　Opening of Catholic regional seminaries and of the National Seminary of Beijing.

天主教地区修　和北京国家修　开幕。

1985　March: Opening in Nanjing by Chinese Protestants of the *Amity Foundation* to promote contacts with Christian international institutions throughout the world.

三月　南京　中国基督教爱德基金会成立
帮助中国教徒与世界联系。

1987　September: Taiwan authorizes its residents to visit mainland China.

九月　台湾允许民众赴中国大陆。

1989   June 4: Student demonstrations in Tiananmen Square, Beijing, are dispersed with considerable loss of life.
六月四日　北京　天安门　学生运动　丧生众多。

1992   End of January: DENG XIAOPING visits the special economic zones in the south of the country and relaunches the program for economic reform.
一月底　邓小平南巡推动经济改　。

1992   September 15–20: The Fifth National Assembly of Catholic Delegates held in Beijing decides to apply in China the reforms of the Catholic liturgy put in place elsewhere by the Second Vatican Council (1962–1965).
9月15　20日　第五届中国天主教全体代表大会在北京举行。按照梵二精神进行天主教礼仪改　。

1993   March 15: The Eighth National People's Congress held at Beijing. JIANG ZEMIN becomes secretary general of the Communist Party and president of the People's Republic of China.
3月15日　第八届全国人民代表大会在北京召开。
中国共产党总书记江泽民兼任国家主席　李　连任总理李瑞环任政协主席。

1996   Consecration in HONG KONG of two bishops, Joseph Zen, coadjutor to Cardinal John Baptist Wu, and John Tong, auxiliary bishop.
港新任命两位主教
日君助理主教和汤汉辅理主教晋牧。

1997   July 1: Great Britain retrocedes Hong Kong to Chinese sovereignty.
7月1日　港回归。

2000   October 1: Pope John Paul II canonizes 120 Blessed Martyrs of China.
10月1日　教宗若望保禄二世封圣120位中国殉道士。

APPENDIX B

LEXICON OF THE CHINESE EXPRESSIONS

552

CHAPTER 9
juren, 举人
jinshi, 进士
Xujiahui, 徐家汇
Bianxue zhangshu, 辩学章疏
Fuguo qiangbing, 富国强兵
Qi ren shi pian, 畸人十篇
Tianxue chuhan, 天学初函
Ren hui, 仁会
Fuli shuyuan, 复礼书院
xiao, 孝
ren hou, 仁侯
qiankun, 乾坤
qi ke, 七克
Dao, 道
mingwu, 明悟
aiyu, 爱育

CHAPTER 10
yang, yin,   ,

CHAPTER 11
Chongyi tang, 崇一堂
Xiru er mu zi, 西儒耳目资
Wei tian ai ren ji lun, 畏天爱人极论
Chongyi tang riji
suibi, 崇一堂日记随笔

CHAPTER 12
qufo buru,   佛补儒
xie jiao, 邪教
Qingzhen daxue, 清真大学
Qingzhen zhinan, 清真指南
cheng, 乘
chang dao, 常道
zhong dao, 中道
zhi dao, 至道
zhen cheng, 真乘

CHAPTER 13
Po xie ji, 破邪集
tongji, 童乩
Kong Meng zai nali, 孔孟在那里
jijin, 祭巾
Shengjiao rike, 圣教日课
Ge co (rike), 日课
Tianzhu shengjiao, 天主圣教
nianjing congshu, 念经丛书
tang nei tangwai, 堂内, 堂外

CHAPTER 14
Bu de yi, 不得已
Pi xie lun, 辟邪论

CHAPTER 15
Bei tang, 北堂
Dong tang, 东堂
Ming shi, 明史
Kangxi zidian, 康熙字典
Ruyi guan, 如意
Zhi tong, 治统
Dao tong, 道统
Jiaohuang, 教皇

CHAPTER 16
Bai lian jiao, 白莲教
tongxiang, 同乡

CHAPTER 17
fan Qing fu Ming, 反清复明
huizhang, 会长

CHAPTER 18
Qingshui jiao, 清水教

CHAPTER 19
Zongli yamen, 总理衙门
Xi tang, 西堂

Hei shui, 黑水
Baliqiao, 八里桥
Yihe quan, 义和拳
bao guo mie yang, 保国灭洋
Zhonghua zhi hou, 中华之后

CHAPTER 20
San bian, 三边
ershisi qing di, 二十四　地

CHAPTER 21
jidujiao, 基督教
Tianzhu, 天主
Shangdi, 上帝
jiu jiao, 旧教
xin jiao, 新教
Quan shi liang yan, 劝世良言
Bai Shangdi hui, 拜上帝会
Taiping Tianguo, 太平天国
geming, 革命
tian ming, 天命
Taiping jing, 太平经
junzi, 君子
Tiandao suyuan, 天道溯源
Zhongxi wenjian, 中西闻见
wuxu bianfa, 戊戌变法
Daoyou, 道友
Jingfeng shan, 净　山

CHAPTER 22
ming zhi, 明治
zongli yamen, 总理衙门
zi qiang, 自强
zhongxue wei ti,, 中学为体
xixue weiyong, 西学为用
tongwen guan, 同文
Yangwu, 洋务
fu qiang, 富强
dujun, 督军

Tushanwan, 土山湾
Yiwen lu, 益闻录
Shen bao, 申报
Jiaohui xinbao, 教会新报
Xinwen he, 新闻和
kexue huibao, 科学汇报
Hui bao, 汇报
Shengxin bao, 圣心报

CHAPTER 23
Yuan qiang, 原强
Tianyan lun, 天演论
guo chi, 国耻
chi ren de lijiao, 吃人的礼教
Lei Mingyuan, 雷　远
Guangyilu, 光义录
Yishibao, 益世报
Dagong bao, 大公报
Xiangshan, 香山
Furen xueshe, 辅仁学社
Quan xue zui yan, 劝学罪言
Puji tang, 普济堂
Jinke zhongxue, 金科中学

CHAPTER 24
San min zhuyi, 三民主义
minzhu, 民主
minquan, 民权
minsheng, 民生
Baileng, 白冷
Kuitan, 葵潭
Shantou, 汕头
Xinsheng yundong, 新生运动
li, yi, lian, chi, 礼义廉耻
Furen xuezhi, 辅仁学志
Cishan jiguan, 慈善机关
Shengjiao zazhi, 圣教杂志
Tian feng, 天

CHAPTER 25
douzheng, 斗争
san fan, wu fan, 三反，五反
Xinyang wenti, 信仰问
Lingshi jikan, 灵食季刊
Xuexi cankao, 学习参考

CHAPTER 26
huiguan, 会
Chaozhou, 潮州
Shouli zhongxin, 守礼中心
Jin shan, 金山
Ren xue, 仁学失

CHAPTER 27
Gongjiaobao, 公教报
Shengjing, 圣经
shuangyuekan, 双月刊
Qingming, 清明
Chongyang, 重
Liyizhe, 李一哲

CHAPTER 28
Shang zhi, 上智

Zhongguo yu Jiaohui, 中国与教会
Xin duosheng, 新铎声
Tian ren zhi ji, 天人之
Laoshi, shifu, 老师，师傅
Jianzheng, Hengyi, 见证，恒毅
Jiaohui yu Zhongguo, 教会与中国
Tian ren yi jia, 天人一家
Lingxiuxue, 灵修学
zai Zhongguo, 在中国
Shenxue congshu, 神学丛书
Tianzhujiao, 天主教
zhongguohua de, 中国化的
tantao, 探讨
Rentong, 认同

CHAPTER 29
da zi bao, 大字报
wujiang simei, 五讲四美
jing er yuan zhi, 敬而远之
Yaodao wenda, 要道问答
Duo zuo shangong, 多作善工
wenming cun, 文明村
qiutong cunyi, 求同存异
Heshang, 河殇

APPENDIX C

PERSONAL NAMES

In Alphabetical Order
with their Chinese Equivalents
References are to chapter numbers only

APPENDIX D

MARTYROLOGY

Saints and Blessed from China
As Listed in the Roman Martyrology
2001 and 2004

Abbreviations

Bd	Blessed
Bp	Bishop
Br	Brother
Catec	Catechist
CDD	Congregatio Discipuli Domini
CM	Congregation of the Mission (Vincentian/Lazarist)
FMM	Franciscan Missionaries of Mary
Laym	Layman
Layw	Laywoman
M	Martyr
MEP	Missions Étrangères de Paris
Nom	Nominated
OFM	Order of Friars Minor (Franciscan)
OP	Order of Preachers (Dominican)
PIME	Pontificio Istituto per le Missioni Estere
Prov	Province
SDB	Salesian of Don Bosco
Sem	Seminarian
SJ	Society of Jesus (Jesuit)
Soc	Society
Sr	Sister
St	Saint
SVD	Society of the Divine Word
V	Virgin

	Name	Status	Dates	Prov	Place of Death
January					
15	St. Francis Fernandez de Capillas, OP	PrM	1607–1648	Fj	Fu'an
28	St. Agatha Lin Zhao	VCatecM	1817–1858	Gz	Maokou
28	St. Jerome Lu Tingmei	CatecM	1811–1858	Gz	Maokou
28	St. Lawrence Wang Bing	CatecM	1802–1858	Gz	Maokou
28	St. Joseph Freinademetz, SVD	Pr	1852–1908	Sd	Daijiazhuang
February					
7	St. John Lantrua Da Triora, OFM	PrM	1760–1816	Hn	Changsha
13	St. Paul Liu Hanzuo	PrM	1778–1818	Sc	Chengdu Dongjiaochang
18	St. Francis Regis Clet, CM	PrM	1748–1820	Hb	Wuchang
18	St. John Peter Néel, MEP	PrM	1832–1862	Gz	Kaizhou
18	St. Martin Wu Xuesheng	CatecM	1815–1862	Gz	Kaizhou
18	St. John Zhang Tianshen	CatecM	1805–1862	Gz	Kaizhou
18	St. John Chen Xianheng	CatecM	1820–1862	Gz	Kaizhou
19	St. Lucy Yi Zhenmei	VCatecM	1815–1862	Gz	Kaizhou
25	St. Lawrence Bai Xiaoman	LaymM	1821–1856	Gx	Xilinxian
25	St. Aloysius Versiglia, SDB	BpM	1873–1930	Gd	Shaozhou Litouzui
25	St. Callistus Caravario, SDB	PrM	1903–1930	Gd	Shaozhou Litouzui
29	St. Augustus Chapdelaine, MEP	PrM	1814–1856	Gx	Xilinxian
March					
1	St. Agnes Cao Guiying Widow	CatecM	1821–1856	Gx	Xilinxian
12	St. Joseph Zhang Dapeng	CatecM	1754–1815	Gz	Guiyang
21	St. Augustine Zhao Rong	PrM	1746–1815	Sc	Chengdu

April

7 Bl. Maria Assunta Pallotta, FMM	VM	1878–1905	Sx	Donggergou

May

17 St. Peter Liu Wenyuan	CatecM	1760–1834	Gz	Guizhu
26 St. Peter Sans I Jorda, OP	BpM	1680–1747	Fj	Fuzhou

June

15 St. Barbara Cui Lian	LaywM	1849–1900	Heb	Qianshengzhuang Liushuitao
19 St. Remy Isore, SJ	PrM	1852–1900	Heb	Wuyi
19 St. Modestus Andlauer, SJ	PrM	1847–1900	Heb	Wuyi
24 St. Joseph Yuan Zaide	PrM	1766–1817	Sc	Chengdu
26 St. Joseph Ma Taishun	CatecM	1840–1900	Heb	Qianshengzhuang Liushuitao
28 St. Mary Du Zhao	LaywM	1849–1900	Heb	Hengshui Wangjiadian
28 St. Mary Fan Kun	LaywM	1884–1900	Heb	Dongguangxian Wanglajia
28 St. Mary Qi Yu	LaywM	1885–1900	Heb	Dongguangxian Wanglajia
28 St. Lucy Wang Cheng	LaywM	1882–1900	Heb	Dongguangxian Wanglajia
28 St. Mary Zheng Xu	LaywM	1889–1900	Heb	Dongguangxian Wanglajia
29 St. Paul Wu Ju'an	LaymM	1838–1900	Heb	Shenxian Xiaoluyi
29 St. John Baptist Wu Mantang	LaymM	1883–1900	Heb	Shenxian Xiaoluyi
29 St. Paul Wu Wanshu	LaymM	1884–1900	Heb	Shenxian Xiaoluyi
29 St. Mary Du Tian	LaywM	1858–1900	Heb	Shenxian Dujiatun
29 St. Magdalen Du Fengju	LaywM	1881–1900	Heb	Shenxian Dujiatun
30 St. Peter Li Quanhui	LaymM	1837–1900	Heb	Jiaohexian Chentun
30 St. Raymund Li Quanzhen	LaymM	1841–1900	Heb	Jiaohexian Chentun

Name	Status	Dates	Prov	Place of Death
July				
3 St. John Baptist Zhao Mingzhen	LaymM	1839–1900	Heb	Shenxian Dongyangtai
3 St. Peter Zhao Mingxi	LaymM	1844–1900	Heb	Shenxian Dongyangtai
4 St. Caesidius Giacomantonio, OFM	PrM	1873–1900	Hn	Hengzhou
5 St. Teresa Chen Jinjie	VM	1875–1900	Heb	Ningjinxian Huangerying
5 St. Rosa Chen Aijie	VM	1878–1900	Heb	Ningjinxian Huangerying
6 St. Peter Wang Zuolong	LaymM	1842–1900	Heb	Jixian Shuangzhong
7 St. Antoninus Fantosati, OFM	BpM	1842–1900	Hn	Hengzhou
7 St. Joseph Gambaro, OFM	PrM	1869–1900	Hn	Hengzhou
7 St. Mark Ji Tianxiang	LaymM	1834–1900	Heb	Jizhou
7 St. Mary Guo Li	LaywM	1835–1900	Heb	Shenxian Hujiachi
8 St. John Wu Wenyin	CatecM	1850–1900	Heb	Yongnian
9 St. Joachim Hao Kaizhi	CatecM	1774–1839	Gz	Guiyang
9 St. Theoderic Balat, OFM	PrM	1858–1900	Sx	Taiyuan
9 St. Andrew Bauer, OFM	BrM	1866–1900	Sx	Taiyuan
9 St. Simon Chen Ximan	LaymM	1854–1900	Sx	Taiyuan
9 St. Anne Dierk, FMM	SrM	1866–1900	Sx	Taiyuan
9 St. Patrick Dong Bodi	SemM	1882–1900	Sx	Taiyuan
9 St. Elias Facchini, OFM	PrM	1839–1900	Sx	Taiyuan
9 St. Matthias Feng De	LaymM	1855–1900	Sx	Taiyuan
9 St. Francis Fogolla, OFM	BpM	1839–1900	Sx	Taiyuan
9 St. Mary Anne Giuliani, FMM	SrM	1875–1900	Sx	Taiyuan
9 St. Gregory Grassi, OFM	BpM	1833–1900	Sx	Taiyuan

	Name	Status	Dates		Location
9	St. Irma Grivot, FMM	SrM	1866–1900	Sx	Taiyuan
9	St. Pauline Jeuris, FMM	SrM	1872–1900	Sx	Taiyuan
9	St. Joan Kerguin, FMM	SrM	1864–1900	Sx	Taiyuan
9	St. Ann Francoise Moreau, FMM	SrM	1866–1900	Sx	Taiyuan
9	St. Clelia Nanetti, FMM	SrM	1872–1900	Sx	Taiyuan
9	St. Thomas Shen Jihe	LaymM	1851–1900	Sx	Taiyuan
9	St. Peter Wang Erman	LaymM	1864–1900	Sx	Taiyuan
9	St. John Wang Rui	SemM	1885–1900	Sx	Taiyuan
9	St. Peter Wu Anbang	LaymM	1860–1900	Sx	Taiyuan
9	St. James Yan Guodong	LaymM	1853–1900	Sx	Taiyuan
9	St. Peter Zhang Banniu	LaymM	1849–1900	Sx	Taiyuan
9	St. John Zhang Huan	SemM	1882–1900	Sx	Taiyuan
9	St. John Zhang Jingguang	SemM	1878–1900	Sx	Taiyuan
9	St. Francis Zhang Rong	LaymM	1838–1900	Sx	Taiyuan
9	St. Philip Zhang Zhihe	SemM	1880–1900	Sx	Taiyuan
9	St. James Zhao Quanxin	LaymM	1856–1900	Sx	Taiyuan
11	St. Zhang Huailu (*Baptism by blood*)	LaymM	1843–1900	Heb	Zhuhedian
11	St. Ann An Xin	LaywM	1828–1900	Heb	Anping Liuguanying
11	St. Mary An Guo	LaywM	1836–1900	Heb	Anping Liuguanying
11	St. Ann An Jiao	LaywM	1874–1900	Heb	Anping Liuguanying
11	St. Mary An Linghua	LaywCatecM	1871–1900	Heb	Anping Liuguanying
13	St. Paul Liu Jinde	LaywM	1821–1900	Heb	Hengshui Langziqiao
13	St. Joseph Wang Kuiju	LaymM	1863–1900	Heb	Nangong
14	St. John Wang Kuixin	LaymM	1875–1900	Heb	Nangong

Name	Status	Dates	Prov	Place of Death
July, continued				
16 St. Paul Lang Fu	LaymM	1893–1900	Heb	Qinhe
16 St. Lang Yang	LaywM	1878–1900	Heb	Qinhe
16 St. Teresa Zhang He	LaywM	1864–1900	Heb	Ningjinxian Zhanggjiaji
17 St. Peter Liu Ziyu	LaymM	1843–1900	Heb	Shenxian Zhujiaxiezhuang
19 St. John Baptist Zhu Wurui	LaymM	1883–1900	Heb	Jingxian Lujiazhuang
19 St. Simon Qin Chunfu	LaymM	1886–1900	Heb	Renqiushi Liucun
19 St. Elizabeth Qin Bian	LaywM	1846–1900	Heb	Renqiushi Beiluo
20 St. Paul Denn, SJ	PrM	1847–1900	Heb	Jingxian Zhujiahe
20 St. Mary Fu Guilin	LaymM	1863–1900	Heb	Wuyixian Daliucun
20 St. Leo Mangin, SJ	PrM	1857–1900	Heb	Jingxian Zhujiahe
20 St. Qi Zhuzi (*Baptism by blood*)	LaymM	1882–1900	Heb	Dechaocun
20 St. Peter Zhu Rixin	LaymM	1881–1900	Heb	Lujiazhuang
20 St. Mary Zhu Wu	LaywM	1850–1900	Heb	Jingxian Zhujiahe
20 St. Mary Zhao Guo	LaywM	1840–1900	Heb	Wuqiao Zhaojia
20 St. Rosa Zhao Luosha	LaywM	1878–1900	Heb	Wuqiao Zhaojia
20 St. Mary Zhao Mali	LaywM	1883–1900	Heb	Wuqiao Zhaojia
21 St. Alberic Crescitelli, PIME	PrM	1863–1900	Sn	Yanzibian
21 St. Joseph Wang Yumei	LaymM	1831–1900	Heb	Yongnian
22 St. Anne Wang	VM	1886–1900	Heb	Yongnian Daning
22 St. Mary Wang Li	LaywM	1851–1900	Heb	Weixian
22 St. Andrew Wang Tianqing	LaywM	1891–1900	Heb	Yongnian Daning
22 St. Lucy Wang Wang	LaywM	1869–1900	Heb	Yongnian Daning

29	St. Paul Cheng Changpin	SemM	1838–1861	Gz	Qingyan
29	St. John Baptist Luo Tingyin	CatecM	1825–1861	Gz	Qingyan
29	St. Martha Wang Luo Mande	WidowM	1802–1861	Gz	Qingyan
29	St. Joseph Zhang Wenlan	SemM	1831–1861	Gz	Qingyan
30	St. Joseph Yuan Gengyin	LaymM	1853–1900	Heb	Zaoqiang Dayingzhen

August

8	St. Paul Ge Tingzhu	LaymM	1839–1900	Heb	Xinhexian
16	St. Rosa Fan Hui	LaywM	1855–1900	Heb	Wuqiao Fanjiazhuang

September

11	St. Gabriel Perboyre, CM	PrM	1802–1840	Hb	Wuchang
14	St. Gabriel Taurin Dufresse, MEP	BpM	1750–1815	Sc	Chengdu

October

28	St. Francis Diaz del Rincon, OP	PrM	1713–1748	Fj	Fuzhou
28	St. John Alcober, OP	PrM	1694–1748	Fj	Fuzhou
28	St. Joachim Royo, OP	PrM	1691–1748	Fj	Fuzhou
28	St. Francis Serrano, OP	BpNomM	1695–1748	Fj	Fuzhou

November

7	St. Peter Wu Guosheng	CatecM	1768–1814	Gz	Zunyi
30	St. Thaddeus Liu Ruiting	PrM	1773–1823	Sc	Quxian

BIBLIOGRAPHY

BOOKS AND ARTICLES IN ENGLISH

Adeney, David H. *China: Christian Students Face the Revolution*. London: InterVarsity Press, 1973.

Allsen, Thomas T. *Culture and Conquest in Mongol Eurasia*. Cambridge: Cambridge University Press, 2001.

Bays, Daniel H., ed., *Christianity in China, from the 18th C. to the Present*. Stanford, Calif.: Stanford University Press, 1996, 483 pp.

Birrell, Anne. *Chinese Mythology: An Introduction*. Baltimore: Johns Hopkins University Press, 1993.

———. (Transl. and introduction.) *The Classic of Mountains and Seas* Harmondsworth: Penguin Classics, 1999.

———. "Women in Literature" in *The Columbia History of Chinese Literature*, ed. Victor H. Mair. New York: Columbia University Press, 2001.

Bold Bat-Ochir. *Mongolian Nomadic Society: A Reconstruction of the "Medieval" History of Mongolia*. New York: St. Martin's Press, 2001.

Bolz, William G. "The Invention of Writing in China". *Oriens Extremus* 42 (2000/01).

Brock, Sebastian. "Christians in the Sasanian Empire: A Case of Divided Loyalties" in *Studies in Church History* 18 (Oxford, 1982).

———. *Syriac Perspectives in Late Antiquity*. London: Variorum Reprints, 1984.

———. *Studies in Syriac Christianity*. Aldershot: Ashgate Variorum, 1992.

———. "The 'Nestorian' Church: A Lamentable Misnomer". *Bulletin of the John Rylands University Library of Manchester*, 3, no. 78 (autumn 1996).

Broomhall, Marshall. *Islam in China: A Neglected Problem*. London: Morgan Scott, 1910.

Buckley, Charles Burk. *An Anecdotal History of Old Times Singapore, 1819–1867*. Kuala Lumpur: University of Malaya Press, 1965.

Budge, Ernest. *The Monks of Kublai Khan Emperor of China or The History and the Life and Travels of Rabban Sawma, Envoy and Plenipotentiary of the Mongol Khans to the Kings of Europe, and Markos Who as Mar Yahballaha III Became Patriarch of the Nestorian Church in Asia*. London: Religious Tract Society, 1928.

Bush, Richard C. *Religion in Communist China*. New York: Abingdon Press, 1970.

Camps, Arnulf, O.F.M. and Pat McCloskey, O.F.M. *The Friars Minor in China, 1294–1955. Especially the years 1925–1955*. Rome: General Curia of Friars Minor, 1995.

Cary-Elwes, Columba. *China and the Cross*. Longmans, 1957.

Charbonnier, Jean. *Guide to the Catholic Church in China 2004*. Singapore: China Catholic Communication, 2004, 745 pp.

Chu, Michael, S.J., ed. *The New China: A Catholic Response*. New York: Paulist Press, 1977.

Chu, Theresa, and Christopher Lind, ed. *A New Beginning, An International Dialogue with the China Church*. Canada-China Program of the Canadian Council of Churches, 1983.

Cohen, A. *China and Christianity. The Missionary Movement and the Growth of Antiforeignism 1860–1870*. Cambridge, Mass.: Harvard University Press, 1967.

Covell, Ralph R. *Confucius, The Buddha, and Christ: A History of the Gospel in Chinese*. Maryknoll, N.Y.: Orbis Books, 1986. American Society of Missiology Series no. 11.

Criveller, Gianni. *Preaching Christ in Late Ming China, Jesuits' Presentation of Christ from Ricci to G. Aleni*. Variétés sinologiques n. 86, (1997), 483 pp.

Dawson, Christopher. *The Making of Europe: An Introduction to the History of European Unity*. London: Sheed and Ward, 1946.

de Bary, W. Theodore, and Irene Bloom. *Sources of Chinese Tradition*. New York: Columbia University Press, 1999.

D'Elia, Pasquale, S.J. *Catholic Native Episcopacy in China*. Shanghai: Zikawei, 1927.

Fogel, Joshua A. *Chinese Women in a Century of Revolution 1850–1950*. Stanford, Calif.: Stanford University Press, 1989.

Foster, John. "Crosses from the Walls of Zaitun". *J.R.A.S.* (1954).

Fung, Raymund. *Households of God on China's Soil*. Geneva: World Council of Churches, 1982.

Gernet, Jacques. *China and the Christian Impact: A Conflict of Cultures*. Cambridge, U.K.: Cambridge University Press, 1985.

———. *A History of Chinese Civilization*. Cambridge, U.K.: Cambridge University Press, 2nd ed., 1996.

Giles, Lionel. *Six Centuries at Tunhuang: A Short Account of the Chinese Manuscripts in the British Museum*. London: The China Society, 1944.

Godinho, Jno. *The Padroado of Portugal in the Orient: 1454–1860*. Bombay: 1924.

Grichtig, Wolfgang L. *The Value System in Taiwan*. Taipei, 1970.

Hayward, Victor E. W. *Christians in China*. Dublin: Cahill, 1974.

Heyndrickx, Jeroom, C.I.C.M., ed. *Historiography of the Chinese Catholic Church, Nineteenth and Twentieth Centuries*. Ferdinand Verbiest Foundation, K. U. Leuven, 1994.

Hickley, Dennis. *The First Christians in China: An Outline History and Some Considerations Concerning the Nestorians in China During the Tang Dynasty*. London: China Study Project, 1980.

Hiu, Peter C. H. "An Historical Study of Nestorian Christianity in the T'ang Dynasty between A.D. 635–845". (Unpublished Ph.D.

dissertation, School of Theology, Southwestern Baptist Theological Seminary, Ft. Worth Tex., 1987).

Hopkirk, Peter. *Foreign Devils on the Silk Road: The Search for the Lost Cities and Treasures of Chinese Central Asia*. Oxford: Oxford University Press, 1984.

Hsü, C. Y. Immanuel. *The Rise of Modern China*. Santa Barbara, Calif., Oxford University Press, 2nd ed., 1975, 1002 pp.

Huc, Évariste Régis. *Christianity in China Tartary and Thibet*. London: Longmans Brown, 1857–1858.

Hummel, Arthur W. *Eminent Chinese of the Ching Period, A Biographical Dictionary*. Washington: Library of Congress, 1943.

Hunter, Alan, and Kim-Kwong Chan. *Protestantism in Contemporary China*. Cambridge University Press, 1993, 291 pp.

Hunter, Erica C. D., "The Church of the East in Central Asia". *Bulletin of the John Rylands University Library of Manchester* 78 (1996).

Israeli, Raphael. *Muslims in China, A Study in Cultural Confrontation*. Curzon: Humanities Press, 1978, 272 pp.

Jackson, Peter, "Marco Polo and His Travels". *B.S.O.A.S.* 61 (1998).

Jaegher, Raymond de. *Life of Archbishop Yu Bin*. Vietnam, Cholon: Free Pacific Editions, 1959.

Jennes, Jos, C.I.C.M. *Four Centuries of Catechetics in China*. Taipei: Huaming, 1976.

Jung Chang. *Wild Swans: Three Daughters of China*. London: Harper Collins, 1991, paperback 1993.

Kim-Kwong, Chan. *Towards a Contextual Ecclesiology: The Catholic Church in The People's Republic of China 1979–1983: Its Life and Theological Implications*. Hong Kong: Phototech Systems Ltd., 11th Floor, Breakthrough Center, 191–197 Woosung Street, Kowloon, 1987.

Lam, Anthony S. K. *The Catholic Church in Present Day China: Through Darkness and Light*. Hong Kong: Holy Spirit Study Center. Chinese ed. 1994, English ed. 1997.

Latham, R. E., tr. *The Travels of Marco Polo*. London: Penguin Books, 1958.

Latourette, Kenneth Scott. *A History of Christian Missions in China*. London: Society for Promoting Christian Knowledge, 1929. 2nd ed. Taipei: Ch'engwen, 1973.

Lazzarroto, Angelo, P.I.M.E. *The Catholic Church in Post-Mao China*. Hong Kong: Holy Spirit Study Center, 1982.

———. "Holy Spirit Study Center: Breakthrough and Response", Hong Kong: *Tripod*, no. 60 (1990):6.

Leung, Beatrice. *Sino-Vatican Relations: Problems of Conflicting Authority (1976–1986)*. Cambridge, Mass.: Cambridge University Press, 1992.

Lieu, S. N. C. *Manichaeism in Central Asia and China*. Leiden: Brill, 1998. Nag Hammadi and Manichaean Studies 45.

Lippiello, Tiziana, and Roman Malek. *Scholar from the West: Giulio Aleni SJ (1582–1649) and the Dialogue Between Christianity and China*. MSMS XLII. Sankt Augustin, Nettetal: Monumenta Serica, Steyler Verlag, 1997.

Madsen, Richard. *China's Catholics. Tragedy and Hope in an Emerging Civil Society*. University of California Press, 1998, 183 pp.

Malatesta, Edward J., ed. Introduction and notes by Douglas Lancashire and Peter Hu Kuo-chen, S.J. *The True Meaning of the Lord of Heaven (T'ien-chu Shih-i)*, a Chinese-English ed., S.J. Variétés Sinologiques: New Series 72 Taipei-Paris-Hong Kong: Ricci Institute, 1985.

Malek, Roman, S.V.D., ed. *The Chinese Face of Jesus-Christ*, MSMS L/1–2, jointly published by Institut Monumenta Serica and China-Zentrum, Sankt Augustin Nettetal: Steyler Verlag 1 (2002); 2 (2003), 844 pp.

Mao Tse-Tung "Report on an Investigation into the Peasant Movement in Hunan". Mar 1927. *Selected Works of Mao Tse-Tung*. London: Laurence and Wishart, 1954.

———. "On Correctly Handling Contradictions among the People", Feb. 27, 1957; *The Writings of Mao Tse-Tung: 1949–1976* (New York: M. E. Sharpe, Armonk, N.Y., 1992), ed. John P. Leung and Michael Y. M. Kau; vol. 2.

Mayers, W. F. *The Chinese Government.* Shanghai: 1897.

McManners, John. *Church and Society in Eighteenth-Century France.* Oxford: Oxford University Press, 1998, 2 vol.

Minamiki, S.J. *The Chinese Rites Controversy, from Its Beginning to Modern Times.* Chicago: Loyola University Press, 1985.

Morgan, David O. "Aspects of Mongol Rule in Persia". Unpublished doctoral dissertation, School of Oriental and African Studies, University of London, 1977.

———. "Marco Polo in China—or Not". *J.R.A.S.* 6 (1996),.

———. *The Mongols.* Oxford: Blackwell, 1990.

Moule, A. C. *Christians in China Before the Year 1550.* London Society for Promoting Christian Knowledge, 1930.

Mullarky, Peter. "An Analytical Account of the Muslim Rebellions in North-West China (1862–1878): The Causes, Course, Suppression and Subsequent Pacification, with an Examination of the Significance of this Period for Contemporaneous and Subsequent Developments in China". Unpublished M.A. dissertation, School of Oriental and African Studies, University of London, 1998.

Mungello, D. E. ed. *The Chinese Rites Controversy Its History and Meaning.* Proceedings of the International Symposium held in San Francisco, Oct. 16–18, 1992, jointly published by Monumenta Serica and the Ricci Institute, San Francisco, Steyler Verlag, Nettetal, 1994.

———. *The Forgotten Christians of Hangzhou.* University of Hawaii Press, 1994, 248 pp.

Myers, James T. *Enemies without Guns. The Catholic Church in China.* New York: Paragon House, 1991, 333 pp.

Newman, J. H. *The Arians of the Fourth Century.* London, 1876.

Noll, Ray R., ed. *100 Roman Documents concerning the Chinese Rites Controversy (1645–1941)*. University of San Francisco, Ricci Institute for Chinese-Western Cultural History, 1992.

Pan, Lynn, gen. ed. *The Encyclopedia of Chinese Overseas*. Singapore: Chinese Heritage Centre, Archipelago Press, Landmarks Books, 1998.

Pelliot, Oeuvres Posthumes de Paul Pelliot. *Recherches sur les Chrétiens d'Asie Centrale et d'Extrême Orient*. Paris: Imprimerie Nationale, 1973.

Perry, Susan, ed. *Nanjing '86. Ecumenical Sharing. A New Agenda. An Ecumenical Conference. May 14–20 1986*. China Research Program, Maryknoll.

Pulleybank, Edwin G. "The Roman Empire as Known to Han China". *J.A.O.S.* 119, 1 (1999).

Quattrochi, Paolino Beltrame. *Monaci nella Tormenta, Moines dans la tourmente, Monks in the Blizzard*. Citeaux, 1991.

Ricci, Matteo, S.J., *Tianzhu shiyi, The True Meaning of the Lord of Heaven*. Taiwan: Institute of Jesuit Sources, 1985.

Ride, Lindsay and May Ride. *An East India Company Cemetery. Protestant Burials in Macao*. Hongkong University Press, 1996.

Rossabi, Morris. *The Jurchens in the Yuan and the Ming*. Ithaca, N.Y.: Cornell University China-Japan Project, 1982.

Rouleau, Francis A., S.J. "The Yangzhou Latin Tombstone as a Landmark of Medieval Christianity in China". *Harvard Journal of Asiatic Studies* 17 (1954).

Rudolph, Richard C. "A Second Fourteenth-Century Italian Tombstone in Yangchou". *J.O.S.* 13 (1975).

Rutt, Richard. *Martyrs of Korea*. London: Catholic Truth Society, 2002.

Ryan, James D. "Christian Wives of Mongol Khans: Tartar Queens and Missionary Expectations in Asia". *J.R.A.S.* 8 (1998).

Saeki, P. Y. *The Nestorian Documents and Relics in China.* Tokyo: Maruzen, 1951, 525 pp.

Salisbury, Harrison E. *The New Emperors: China in the Era of Mao and Deng.* New York, 1992.

Spae, Joseph J., C.I.C.M. "Catholic Life in a Chinese Village" in *China Update* (The Chicago Institute of Theology and Culture; Sept. 1982), suppl. no. 1.

Standaert, Nicolas. *Yang Tingyun Confucian and Christian in Late Ming China: His Life and Thought.* Leiden: Brill, 1988.

————, ed. *Handbook of Christianity in China*, vol. 1, 635–1800. Leiden: Brill, 2001, 964 pp.

Stein, Aurel. *Ruins of Desert Cathay: Personal Narrative of the Three Expeditions in Central Asia and Westernmost China.* London: Macmillan, 1912, 2 vols.

————. *Serindia: Detailed Report of Explorations in Central Asia and Westernmost* China (Delhi: Motilal Banansidas, 1980), 5 vols., a reprint of the 1st ed., Oxford, 1921.

Stirnemann, Alfred, and Gerhard Wilflinger. Edited on behalf of Pro Oriente. *Third Non-official Consultation on Dialogue within the Syriac Tradition.* Vienna: Pro Oriente, 1998.

Tang, Dominic, S.J. Archbishop of Guangzhou. *How Inscrutable His Ways! Memoirs 1951–1981.* Hong Kong: Aidan Publicities and Printing, 1987.

Tang, Edmond, and J. P. Wiest. *The Catholic Church in Modern China.* Maryknoll, N.Y.: Orbis Books, 1993, 260 pp.

Taylor, James Hudson. *To China with Love. A Retrospect.* U.S.A. Bethany Fellowship, 159 pp.

White, William Charles. *Chinese Jews: A Compilation of Matters Relating to the Jews of K'ai-feng Fu.* New York: Paragon Books Reprint, 1966, 2nd ed. The 1st ed. was published in 1942 by the University of Toronto Press and the Department of Chinese Studies, Royal Ontario Museum, Toronto.

Whitehead, Raymond L. *Love and Struggle in Mao's Thought.* New York: Orbis Books, 1977, 166 pp.

Whitfield, Roderick. *The Art of Central Asia: The Stein Collection in the British Museum.* Tokyo: Kodansha International, 1982–1985, 3 vols.

Whyte, Bob. *Unfinished Encounter, China and Christianity.* Collins, Fount Paperbacks, 1988, 537 pp.

Wickeri, Philip L. *Seeking the Common Good. Protestant Christianity, The Three-Self Movement, and China's United Front.* New York: Maryknoll Orbis Books, 1988.

Wiest, Jean-Paul. *Maryknoll in China.* M. E. Sharpe, 1988, 591 pp.

Wilkinson, Endymion. *Chinese History: A Manual.* Cambridge, Mass.: Harvard University Asia Center, 2000.

Wood, Frances. *Did Marco Polo Go to China?* London: Secker and Warburg, 1995.

———. *The Silk Road* London: Folio Society, 2002.

BOOKS AND ARTICLES IN FRENCH

Aubin, Françoise. *En Islam chinois: A quels Naqshbandis?* A dans Varia Turcica XVIII, Naqshbandis, Actes de la Table Ronde de Sèvres, 2–4 mai 1973.

Bareigts, André. *Travaux intellectuels des prêtres M.E.P. en Chine* (duplicated text of a lecture given at Hualien, Taïwan, July 4, 1989).

Bernard-Maître, Henri, S.J. *Aux Portes de la Chine. Les Missions du XVIᵉ siècle, 1514–1588.* Tientsin, Hautes Études, 1933.

Bontinck, François. *La Lutte autour de la liturgie chinoise aux XVIIᵉ et XVIIIᵉ siècles* Edit. Nauwelaerts, 1962, 547 pp.

Boutan, Emmanuel. *Le Nuage et la Vitrine: Une vie de Monsieur David.* Paris: Éditions Raymond Chabaud, 1993.

Bruls, Jean. *Réforme des Missions au XXᵉ siècle.* Casterman, 1960.

Brunner, Paul, S.J. *L'Euchologie de la mission de Chine.* Ed. Princeps 1628 et développements. Münster, Aschendorff, 1964, 367 pp.

Chaney, Théodore. *La Colonie du Sacré-Cœur dans les Cévennes de la Chine*. Paris: Lille, 1889.

Charbonnier, Jean "Hongkong-Canton 1975: va-et-vient révélateur?". *Dossiers Échanges France-Asie*, no. 9, Sept. 1975.

——. "Le Colloque de Hong Kong (2–10 février 1979)". *Dossiers Échanges France-Asie*, no. 48 (1979).

——. "Une voie chinoise pour les Chrétiens—La conférence de Montréal (2–9 octobre 1981)". *Dossiers Échange France-Asie*, no. 70 (Dec. 1981).

——. "L'Église et l'État en Chine aujourd'hui". *Dossier Échange France-Asie*, no. 9, 1985.

——. "Les Chinois de la Diaspora", in *Études* (July–Aug. 1987): 15–16.

——. *La Chine sans muraille: héritage culturel et modernité*. Paris: Fayard Le Sarment, 1988.

——. "La sinisation de l'Église chinoise" in *Dossier Échange France-Asie*, no. 1 (1988).

——. "Les Chinois interrogent leur culture". *Dossier Échange France-Asie*, no. 2 (1989).

——. *Les 120 martyrs de Chine canonisés le 1er octobre 2000*. Paris: Églises d'Asie. Études et Documents 12.

Civezza, Marcelin de, M. O. *Histoire universelle des Missions franciscaines*, traduit de l'italien par le P. Bernardin de Rouen, O.F.M. Paris: Tobra, 1898, tome 2 Chine.

Colombel, Auguste M., S.J. *Histoire de la Mission du Kiangnan*. Shanghai, 1898.

Couplet, Philippe, S.J., Historia Nobilis Feminae Candidae Hsiu Christianae Sinensis, traduit en français par le P. d'Orléans, Paris, 1688: *Histoire d'une Dame chrétienne de la Chine, Candida Hiu*.

Daniel-Rops, Henri. *L'Église de la Renaissance et de la Réforme. Une ère de renouveau: la Réforme Catholique*. Paris: Librairie Arthème Fayard, 1955, 558 pp.

Darcourt, Pierre. *Requiem pour l'Église de Chine*. Éditions de la Table Ronde, 1969, 285 pp.

Dehergne, Joseph, and Donald Daniel Leslie. *Juifs de Chine, a travers la correspondance inédite des jésuites du XVIIIᵉ siècle*. (Rome: 1980), published by Les Belles Lettres, Paris.

Delacroix, S., ed. *Histoire universelle des missions catholiques*. Paris: 1957.

Destombes, Paul, M.E.P. *Le Collège général de la Société des Missions Étrangères de Paris 1665–1932*. Hongkong, Soc des M.E.P., 1934.

Dries van Coillie. *J'ai subi le lavage de cerveau*. Original version in Dutch, Anvers De Vlijt. French version by Fondation-Stitching C.C.L., Groede, 1964. Preface by Gabriel Marcel.

Dufay, François. *En Chine, L'Étoile contre la Croix*. Tournai-Paris: Casterman, 1955.

Duperray, Edouard. *Ambassadeurs de Dieu à La Chine*. Casterman, 1956.

Dupeyrat, Elizabeth. *De Genghis Khan à la Chine populaire. 700 ans d'histoire franciscaine XIIIᵉ–XXᵉ siècle*. Paris: Éditions franciscaines, 1961.

École Française d'Extrême Orient. *Catalogue des Manuscrits Chinois de Touen-Houang*. Fonds Pelliot Chinois de la Bibliothèque Nationale, vol. 4; nos. 3501–4000. Publications hors serie de l'École Française d'Extrême Orient, 1991.

Egami Namio. "Olon-Sume et la découverte de l'Église Catholique Romaine de Jean de Montecorvino". *Journal Asiatique* 240 (1952).

Elhorga, Thomas, M.E.P. "La Diaspora chinoise en France". *Les Échos de la rue du Bac:* no. 227 (April 1988).

Fiey, J. M. *Histoire de l'Église en Iraq*. Louvain: C.S.C.O., 1970.

———. "Adarbaygan Chrétien". *Le Museon* 86. Louvain, 1973.

———. *Chrétiens Syriaques sous les Mongols*. Louvain: C.S.C.O., 1975.

———. *Pour un Oriens Christianus Novus: Répertoire des Diocèses Syriaques Orientaux et Occidentaux*. Beirut: Franz Steiner Verlag Stuttgart, 1993, Beiruter Texte 49.

Gernet, Jacques. *Chine et Christianisme, Action et Réaction.* Paris: Gallimard, 1982.

Gies, Jacques. *La collection Paul Pelliot du musée national des arts asiatiques—Guimet.* Tokyo: Kodansha International, 1994, 2 vols.

Goyau, Georges. *Jean-Martin Moye, missionaire en Chine 1772–1783* Paris: Alsatia, 1937.

Gubbels, Msgr Noël. *A Trois siècles d'apostolat. Histoire du catholicisme au Hu-Kwang depuis les origines, 1587 jusqu'à 1870.* Collecta Missionaria, Édit. 36 avenue Reille, Paris, 1934.

Guennou, Jean, M.E.P. *Missions Étrangères de Paris.* Col. des Chrétiens. Paris: le Sarment-Fayard, 1986.

———. *Le Bienheureux Jean-Martin Moye (1730–1793) Une spiritualité missionnaire.* Paris: Apostolat des Éd., 1970.

Guignard, Marie-Roberte: preface to *Catalogue des Manuscrits Chinois de Touen-Houang* (Fonds Pelliot Chinois). Paris: Bibliothèque Nationale, 1970.

Hang, Thaddée. *L'Église Catholique face au monde chinois.* Paris: Spes, 1965. Translated by J. de la Forêt Divonne from the German Thaddäus Hang *Die Katholische Kirche in Chinesischen Raum: Geschichte und Gegenwart.* Munich: Verlag Anton Pustet, 1963.

Havret, Henri, S.J. *La Stèle chrétienne de Si-Ngan-fu.* Shanghai: Variétés sinologiques, no. 12 (1897).

Hecken, Joseph Van, C.I.C.M. *Les réductions catholiques du pays des Ordos. Nouvelle Revue des Sciences Missionnaires.* Suisse, Schöneck/Berkenried, 1957.

Hopkirk, Peter, *Bouddhas et rôdeurs sur la route de la soie.* Arthaud, traduction française, 1981, 283 pp.

Houang, François. *Âme chinoise et Christianisme.* Casterman, 1958, 148 pp.

———. *Le Bouddhisme de l'Inde à la Chine.* Paris: Arthème Fayard 1963, 126 pp.

———. *Les Manifestes de Yen Fou.* Paris: Fayard, 1977, 151 pp.

Houang-Kia-Tcheng, P. Leyris. *Lao-Tzeu. La voie et sa vertu*. Textes chinois présentés et traduits par . . . Paris: Seuil, 1949, 133 pp.

Huc, Régis-Évariste. *L'Empire chinois, suite à Voyage dans la Tartarie et le Tibet*. Monaco: Éditions du Rocher, 1980, 526 pp.

———. *Souvenirs d'un voyage dans la Tartarie et le Tibet*. Pékin: Lazaristes, 1924; Paris: Domaine tibétain, l'Astrolabe-Peuples du Monde, 1987.

Kappler, Claude et René, traducteurs. *Guillaume de Rubrouck, Envoyé de Saint Louis Voyage dans l'Empire mongol*. Paris: Payot, 1985, 318 pp.

Kwong Lai Kuen Madeleine. *Qi chinois et Anthropologie chrétienne*. Essai théologique d'inculturation, L'Harmattan, 2000, 429 pp.

Launay, Adrien, M.E.P. *Les Trente-cinq vénérables serviteurs de Dieu*. Paris: Lethielleux, 1909.

———. *Mémorial de la Société des Missions Étrangères*. Deuxième partie 1658–1913. Paris: Séminaire des ME, 1916.

———. *Histoire des Missions de Chine*. Paris: Téqui. *Mission du Kouang-tong* (1917). *Mission du Se-tchouan* (1920).

———. *Journal d'André Ly, Prêtre chinois, missionnaire et notaire apostolique* 1746–1763. Hong Kong: Imprimerie de Nazareth, 1924, 707 pp.

———. *Lys de Chine (Agathe Lin, Lucie Y) Vierges du Guizhou*. Paris: MEP, 1924, 83 pp.

Laurentin, René. *Chine et Christianisme, Après les occasions manquées*. Paris: Desclée de Brouwer, 1977.

Leclercq, Jacques. *Vie du Père Lebbe. Le Tonnerre qui chante au loin*. Casterman, 1955, 347 pp.

Lecomte, Louis, S.J. *Un Jésuite à Pékin. Nouveaux Mémoires sur l'état présent de la Chine* (1687–1692). Paris: Éditions Phébus, 1990.

Lou Tseng-Tsiang. *Souvenirs et pensées. Suivi d'une lettre à mes amis de Grande Bretagne et d'Amérique*. Paris: Cerf, 1948, 171 pp.

———. *La Rencontre des humanités et la découverte de l'Évangile*. Paris: Desclée de Brouwer, 1949, 152 pp.

Malovic, Maryna Dyja, and Dorian Malovic. *Hong Kong, un destin Chinois*. Paris: Bayard, 1997.

Marie, A., O.P. *Missions dominicaines dans l'Extrême-Orient*. 1865.

Marie-Bernard, F.M.M. *Volontiers. Marie-Chrysanthe de Jésus, 1894–1963*. Paris: Imprimerie FMM, 1966.

Masson, J., S.J. *Un Millionnaire chinois au service des gueux, Joseph Lo Pahong, Shanghai 1875–1937*. Collection le Christ dans ses témoins, Casterman, 1950.

Missions Étrangères de Paris. *Lumière sur la Corée—Les 103 martyrs*. Paris: Le Sarment-Fayard, 1984.

Melkebecke, Carlo Van. *Notre bon Mgr Otto 1850–1938*. Bruxelles: Éditions de Scheut, 1959.

———. *Diasporae Sinicae Statisticarum Tentamen*. Singapore: Éditions Nona, 1966.

———. *Service social de l'Église en Mongolie*. Bruxelles: Scheut, 1968.

Milon, A., *Mémoires de la Congrégation de la Mission*. Paris, rue de Sèvres, 1912.

Monsterleet, Jean, S.J. *Les Martyrs de Chine parlent*. Paris: Amiot Dumont, 1953.

Nahal, Tajadod. *Les Porteurs de Lumière. Église chrétienne de Perse, IIIe-VIIe siècle*. Paris: Plon, 1993, 369 pp.

———. *A l'est du Christ. Vie et mort des chrétiens de la Chine des Tang*. Paris: Plon, 2000, 295 pp.

Namio Egami. "Olon-Sume et la découverte de l'Église Catholique Romaine de Jean de Montecorvino". *Journal Asiatique* 240 (1952).

Olichon, Msgr. Armand. *Les Missions*. Paris: Bloud et Gay, 1930.

———. *Le Prêtre André Ly, Missionnaire au Se-tchoan. Aux origines du clergé chinois*. Paris: Bloud et Gay, 1933.

Pages, Léon, (trans.) *Lettres de Saint François Xavier*. Paris: Poussielgue-Rusand, 1855.

Pelliot, Paul, "Une bibliothèque mediévale retrouvée au Kan-sou". *Bulletin de l'École Française d'Extrême Orient* 8 (1908).

———. Oeuvres Posthumes. *Recherches sur les Chrétiens d'Asie Centrale et d'Extrême-Orient II,1: La Stèle de Si-Ngan-Fou*. Paris: Éditions de la Fondation Singer-Polignac, 1984.

Pfister, Louis. *Notices biographiques et bibliographiques sur les Jésuites de l'ancienne mission de Chine 1583–1773*. Shanghai, 1932.

Rabiller, Sylvain M.E.P., in "De quoi demain sera-t-il fait? L'Église de Hong Kong devant l'échéance 1997" in *Églises d'Asie*, suppl. 97 (Oct. 1990).

Raguin, Yves, S.J. "Le Jésus-Messie de Xi'an" in *Le Christ Chinois: Héritages et Espérance*. Paris: Desclée de Brouwer, 1998, Collection Christus no. 87.

Rémy, *Pourpre des Martyrs*. Paris: Librairie Arthème Fayard, 1953.

Ricci, Matteo and Nicolas Trigault. *Histoire de l'expédition chrétienne au Royaume de la Chine 1582–1610*. Paris: Desclée de Brouwer, 1978, 740 pp.

Schmitt, Clement, O.F.M. *Histoire des Mongols*. Paris: Éditions Franciscaines, 1961.

Sedes, Jean Marie. *Une grande âme sacerdotale le prêtre chinois André Ly 1692–1775*. Paris: Desclée de Brouwer, 1944.

Servière, Jean de la. *Les anciennes missions de la Compagnie de Jésus en Chine (1552–1814)*. Shanghai, 1924.

Shih, Joseph, S.J. *Le père Ruggieri et le problème de l'Évangelisation en Chine*. Rome: Pontificia Universitas Gregoriana, 1964.

Sih, Paul. *De Confucius au Christ*. Casterman, 1958.

Thomas, A. *Histoire de la Mission de Pékin depuis les origines jusqu'à l'arrivée des Lazaristes*. Paris: Louis Michaud, 1923, 463 pp.

Trivière, Léon. "Le Mouvement des Trois autonomies" in *Mission Bulletin*. (Jan. 1953).

Wei Tsing-sing, Louis. *La Politique missionnaire de la France en Chine 1842–1856*. Paris: Nouvelles Éditions Latines, 1960, 653 pp.

———. *Le St Siège, la France et la Chine sous Léon XIII Projet d'une nonciature à Pékin . . . 1880–1886*. Nouvelle Revue de Science Mission, 1966, 95 pp.

Wieger, Léon. *Chine Moderne*. Xianxian: Imprimerie de Hien-hien, 1927–1931.

BOOKS AND ARTICLES IN OTHER WESTERN LANGUAGES

Bartoli, Danielle. *Dell' Historia della Compania de Giesu: La Cina. Terza parte dell' Asia*. Rome, 1663.

Borbone, Pier Giorgio. *Storia di Mar Yahballaha e di Rabban Sauma*. Turin: Silvio Zamorani, 2000.

Bortone, Fernando, S.J., A. and P. Matteo Ricci, S.J. *Il "Saggio d'Occidente" 1552–1610*. Rome: Desclée et C. éditeurs pontificaux, 1965, 479 pp.

Costantini, Archbishop Celso. *Con i missionari in Cina: 1922–1933: Memorie di fatti e di idee*. Rome, 1958, 2 vols.; *Ultime foglie: Ricordi e pensieri*. (Rome, 1958).

D'Elia, Pasquale, S.J. *Il Trattato Sull'Amicizia*. Rome: Studia Missionalia, VII (1952).

Gonzalez, José Maria, O.P. *Historia de la Misiones dominicanas de China*, t. 1, 1632–1700. Madrid, 1964.

Klein, Wassilios, and Jurgen Tubach. "Ein syrisch-christliches Fragment aus Dunhuang/China". *Z.D.M.G.* 144 (1994).

Politi, Giancarlo. *Martiri in China. Noi non possiamo tacere*. Editrice Missionaria Italiana, Via di Corticella 181—40128 Bologna, 1998.

Quattrochi, Paolino Beltrame. *Monaci nella Tormenta, Moines dans la tourmente, Monks in the Blizzard*. Citeaux, 1991, 393 pp.

Rodríguez, Isacio Rodríguez, O.S.A., and Jesús Álvarez Fernández, O.S.A. *Diccionario Biográfico Agustiniano: Provincia de Filipinas*. Valladolid: Estudio Agustiniano, 1992.

Vâth, Alfons, S.J. *Johann Adam Schall von Bell, S.J., Missonar in China . . . 1592–1666*. Mon. Ser. Steyler Verlag, 1991, 421 pp.

Vela, Gregorio de Santiago, O.S.A. *Ensayo de una Biblioteca Ibero-Americana de la Orden de San Agustín*. Madrid: Provincia de Filipinas, 1922.

CHINESE BIBLIOGRAPHY

Bai Shouyi 白寿彝. Zhongguo Yisilanshi cungao 中国伊斯兰教存稿, *Essays on the History of Islam in China*. Ningxia: Popular Press, 1983, 421 pp.

Beijing Chin. Ac. of Soc. Sciences. *Wei Kuangguo* 卫匡国 *Martino Martini*. Italia: Universita Degli Studi di Trento, 1996, 362 pp.

Bouvet, Joachim 白晋. Qing Kang Qian liang di yu Tianzhujiao chuanjiaoshi 清康乾两帝与天主教传教史, *The Two Qing Emperors Kang Xi, Qianlong and Catholic Missionaries*. Taipei: Kuang ch'i, 1966, 218 pp.

Charbonnier, Jean 沙百里. Zhongguo jidutushi 中国基督徒史, *History of Christians in China*. Beijing: 中国社会科学出版社, 1998, 414 pp. Taipei, new edition, 2005, 479 pp.

———. Zhongguo tianzhujiao zhinan 中国天主教主教团指南, *Guide to the Catholic Church in China 2004*. Singapore: Zhonglian, 5th ed., 2004, 745 pp.

Chen Dongfeng 陈东风. Yesuhuishi mubei renwuzhi kao 耶稣会士墓碑人物志考, *Studies of the Inscriptions on the Jesuit Tombstones in Beijing*. 中国文联出版社 1999, 230 pp.

Chen Fangzhong 陈方中. *Minzhu chunian Zhongguo tianzhujiao de bendihua yundong*, 中国天主教的本地化运动, *The Movement for Catholic Inculturation in Early Republican China*. Taipei: Zhengda History Dept. 1991, 260 pp.

Chen Yuan, etc. 陈垣等. *Minyuan yilai tianzhujiaoshi lunji* 民元以来天主教史论 , *Studies on the History of Catholicism in China since 1911*. Taiwan: Fujen, 1985, 216 pp.

Chih, Andrew, CDD. *Chinese Humanism: A Religion beyond Religion*. Taipei: Fujen University Press, 1981, 548 pp.

China Cultural Renaissance Movement. *Zhonghua jindai xiandai shi lunji* 中国近代现代史论 , *Chinese Modern History, The Anti-Christian Persecutions*. Taiwan: Commercial Press, 1985, 553 pp.

China Three-Self Patriotic Movement. *Huiyi Wu Yaozong xiansheng* 回忆吴耀综先生, *In Memory of Wu Yaozong*. Zhonghua Printing Press, 1982.

Dehergne, Joseph 荣振华, Geng Sheng transl. 耿升译. *Zai Hua Yesuhuishi liezhuan ji shumu bubian* 在华耶稣会士列传及书目补编 *Biographies of the Jesuits in China and Complementary Bibliography*. Paris 1973, Beijing translation by Geng Sheng, Zhonghua Shuju, 1995 (上下).

De Marchi F., and R. Scartezzini, eds., Wei Kuangguo 卫匡国 *Martino Martini* 国际研讨会论文 , Beijing, April 5–7, 1994. Italy: Trento, 1996, 369 pp.

Discipuli Domini, C.D.D. 主徒会. *Gang Hengyi shuji huiyilu* 刚恒毅枢机 回忆录, *Memories of Cardinal Costantini*. Taipei: Franciscans, 1992, 369 pp.

Ethnographic Institute of Gansu. *Yisilanjiao zai Zhongguo* 伊斯兰教在 中国 *Islam in China*. Ningxia: RMCBS, 1982, 490 pp.

Fang Hao 方豪. *Zhongguo tianzhujiaoshi renwuzhuan* 中国天主教史 人物传 *Biographies of Personalities in Chinese Catholic History*. Hong Kong: Catholic Truth Society, 1967–1973, 3t.

Ferreux, Octave, C.M. Qianshihui zai Hua chuanjiaoshi 遣使会在华 传教史, *History of the Vincentian Missions in China*, transl. from French by Fr. Wu Zongwen 吴宗文. Taipei: Huaming, 1977, 740 pp.

Geng Sheng, transl. 耿升 译 *Ming Qing jian ruhua Yesuhuishi he Zhong Xi wenhua jiaoliu* 明清间入华耶稣会士和中西文化交流, *The Coming of the Jesuits to China under the Ming and Qing Dynasties and East-West Intercultural Relations*. Sichuan: Popular Press 巴蜀书社出版社, 1993, 311 pp.

Gu Weimin 顾卫民, etc. *Shitu zhi ji* 使徒之跻 *Traces of Discipleship in China*. Taipei: Fujen University, 1995, 349 pp.

Gu Yulu 顾裕禄. *Zhongguo tianzhujiaoshi guoqu he xianzai* 中国 天主教史 过去和现在, *History of Catholicism in China, Past and Present*. Shanghai: Academy of Social Sciences, 1989.

Hang, Thaddaeus 项退结. *Limingqian de Zhongguo tianzhujiao* 明前的中国天主教, *Catholics in China before Dawn*. Taipei: Kuangchi, 1963.

Huang, Vincent, ed. *Quanqiu haiwai huaren Tianzhujiao shouce* 海外华人天主教手册, *Worldwide Overseas Chinese Catholic Directory*. Office for the Promotion of Overseas Chinese Apostolate, Nov. 28, 1999.

Jennes, Jos, C.I.C.M. *Zhongguo jiaoli jiangshou shi* 中国教理讲授史, *Four Centuries of Catechetics in China*. Taipei: Huaming, 1976.

Jin Yijiu 金宜久. *Sufeipai yu hanwen yisilanjiao zhushu* 苏　派与汉文 伊斯兰教著述, *The Sufi Sect and Muslim Books in Chinese*, in *Zhongguo Yisilanjiao yanjiu, Studies in Chinese Islam*. Qinghai: Popular Press, 1987.

Leung, Beatrice 梁结芬. *Zhonggong yu Fandigang guanxi* 中国 与樊蒂冈 关系, *Chinese Communists and the Vatican 1976–1994*. Taiwan: Fujen University Press, 1995, 610 pp.

Liu Yusheng 刘宇声. *Taibei zongjiaoqu 25 nian shi* 台北总教区二十五 年史, *25 Years History of the Archdiocese of Taipei*. Taipei: Wisdom Publication, 1974, 376 pp.

———. *Zhonghua xundao xianliezhuan* 中华殉道先烈传, *The Blessed Martyrs of China*. Taiwan: CCBC, 中国主教团秘书处.

Lo-Kuang 罗光. *Lu Zhengxiang zhuan* 陆徵祥传, *The Life of Dom Lu Tseng-tsiang*. Hong Kong: Catholic Truth Society, 1949, 301 pp.

———. *Xu Guangqi zhuan* 徐光启传, *Life of Paul Xu*. Hong Kong: Catholic Truth Society, 1953, 138 pp.

———. *Limadou zhuan* 利玛窦传 *The Life of Matteo Ricci*. Taipei: Kuangchi, 1960, 235 pp.

———. *Tianzhujiao zai Hua chuanjaoshiji* 天主教在华传教史　, *The History of Catholic Missions in China*. Taiwan: Kuangchi, Hong Kong: Catholic Truth Society, 1967.

Ma Qicheng 马启成. *Lueshu yisilanjiao zai zhongguo de zaoqi quanbo* 略述伊斯兰教 在中国的早期传播, A Brief Account of the Early Spreading of Islam in China, p. 176, in book *Yisilanjiao zai Zhongguo*, 伊斯兰教在中国. Ningxia: Popular Press, 1982.

Motte, Joseph, S.J. 穆启蒙. *Zhongguo tianzhujiaoshi* 中国天主教史, *History of Catholicism in China*. Taipei: Kuangchi, 1970, 178 pp.

———. *Zhongguo jiaoyou yu shitu gongzuo* 中国教友与使徒工作, *Chinese Catholics and the Lay Apostolate*. Taipei: Kuangchi, 1978, 261 pp.

Ng Lee-ming 吴利明. *Jidujiao yu Zhongguo shehui bianqian* 基督教与中国社会变迁, *Christianity and Social Change in China*. Hong Kong: Chinese Christian Literature Council, 1981, 280 pp.

Pfister, Louis, S.J. 费赖之. *Ming Qing jian Yesuhuishi liezhuan* 明清间耶稣会士列传, *Biographies of the Jesuits in China under the Ming and Qing Dynasties*. Shanghai: Guangqishe, 1997, 1,237 pp.

Ricci, Matteo, S.J. 利玛窦. *Tianzhu shiyi* 天主实义, *The True Meaning of the Lord of Heaven*. Taiwan: Institute of Jesuit Sources, 1985, 485 pp.

Taiwan Bishops College. *Zhonghua xundao shengren liezhuan* 中华殉道圣人列传, *Short Biographies of the Martyr Saints of China*: Taipei: Kuangchi, 2000, 220 pp.

Ticozzi, Sergio 田英杰 *Xianggang Tianzhujiao zhanggu* 港天主教掌故, *Catholic Annals of Hongkong*. Hong Kong: Holy Spirit Study Center, 1983.

Wang Shouli 王守礼. *Bianjiang gongjiao shehuishiye*

边疆公教社会事业, *Catholic Social Service along the Great Wall*.
Taipei: Huaming shuju, 1965, 157 pp.

Wang Zhixin 王治心. *Zhongguo jidujiao shigang* 中国基督教史纲,
General History of Christianity in China, Hong Kong: C.C.L.C.,
1977, 372 pp.

Wan Wai-Yiu 温伟耀. *Gongchanzhuyi yu jidujiao* 共产主义与基督教,
Communism and Christianity. Hong Kong: Tiandao, 1979, 316 pp.

Weng Shaojun 翁绍军. *Hanyu jingjiao wendian quanshi*
汉语景教文典诠释, *Chinese Nestorian Documents Annotated*.
Beijing: 生活, 读书, 新知 三联书店, 1996, 215 pp.

Xu Zongze 徐宗泽. *Ming Qingjian yesuhuishi yizhu tiyao*
明清间耶稣会士译著提要, *Translations by the Jesuits under the
Ming and Qing*. Beijing: Zhonghua shuju, 1989, 482 pp.

Zhang Kai 张铠. *Pang Diwo yu Zhongguo* 庞迪我与中国, *Diego de
Pantoja and China (1597–1618)*. Beijing: Tushuguan, 1997, 466 pp.

Zhang Li 张力 and Liu Jiantang 刘鉴唐. *Zhongguo jiao'anshi* 中国教
案史, *History of Religious Persecutions in China*. Sichuan: Academy
of Social Sciences, 1987, 890 pp.

Zhang Sui 张绥. *Dongzhengjiao he dongzhengjiao zai Zhongguo*, 东政教
和东政教在中国, *The Orthodox Religion and its Presence in China*.
Shanghai: ed. Xuelin.

Zhang Ze 张泽. *Qingdai jinjiaoqi de tianzhujiao* 清代禁教期的天主教,
Catholicism under the Ban during the Manchu Period. Taipei:
Kuangchi, 1992, 260 pp.

Zhao Binshi 赵宾实. *Zhongguohua shenxue, Tian ren yijia* 中国化神学,
天人一家, *Chinese Theology*. Taipei: Hengyi, 1977, 257 pp. *Lingxiu
zai Zhongguo* 灵修在中国 *Spirituality in China*. Taiwan: Hengyi
Monthly 恒毅月刊, 1979.

Zhao Qingyuan 赵庆源. *Zhongguo tianzhujiao jiaoqu huafen ji qi
shouzhang jieti nianbiao* 中国天主教 教区划分及其　长接替年表,
Brief History of the Hierarchy in China. Taiwan: Windows, 1976.

Zheng Tianxiang 郑天祥. *Luo Wenzao shiji* 罗文藻史 , *Historical Accounts of Bishop Luo Wenzao*. Kaohsiung: 教区主教公署, 1973, 234 pp.

Zhu Qianzhi 朱谦之. *Zhongguo jingjiao* 中国景教. 中国古代基督教研究, *The Nestorianism of China*. Beijing: Xinhua shudian, 1993, 256 pp.

MAPS

Cartography by David Notley
The national and regional boundaries shown on the maps are modern.

ILLUSTRATIONS

INDEX